PRIVATE PILOT MANUAL

GUIDED FLIGHT discovery

JEPPESEN
Sanderson Training Products

© Jeppesen Sanderson, Inc., 1997, 1998, 1999, 2000
All Rights Reserved
55 Inverness Drive East, Englewood, CO 80112-5498
International Standard Book Number 0-88487-238-6
Printed in Canada

JS314500—004

ACKNOWLEDGMENTS

This manual could not have been produced without the tireless commitment of the Guided Flight Discovery (GFD) team members listed below. Special thanks also is extended to the other personnel in Jeppesen's Aviation Courseware Development department who, although not directly involved in the creation of this text, assumed responsibility for other projects so that the GFD team members could fully devote their energies to the project.

Managing Editor
Pat Willits

Associate Editors/Primary Writers
Mike Abbott
Liz Kailey

Technical Support
Jerry Farrell
Michelle Gable
Judi Glenn
Jon Hiles
Tanya Letts
George McCray
Dick Snyder
Chuck Stout
Anthony Werner

Media Productions Manager
Rich Hahn

Lead Artists
Pat Brogan
Dean McBournie

Graphic Artists
Amy Aguirre
Mark Bebernes
Cliff Carrillo
Jennifer Crowe
Paul Gallaway
Andy Juarez
Larry Montano
Rick Patterson
Scott Saunders
Jay Weets

Photographers
Dave Chance
Gary Kennedy
Virgil Poleschook

Welcome to Guided Flight Discovery

Jeppesen Sanderson has developed the Guided Flight Discovery Pilot Training System to provide the finest pilot training available. Through extensive use of colorful graphics, state-of-the-art computer-based training, and broadcast quality video, Guided Flight Discovery ensures that your training will be enjoyable and exciting. Guided Flight Discovery is totally different than other systems because its entire philosophy of pilot training is a departure from the conventional methods of the past. Rather than just teaching facts, Guided Flight Discovery concentrates on an application-oriented approach to pilot training. The comprehensive and complete system emphasizes the why and how of aeronautical concepts when they are presented. As you progress through your training, you will find that the revolutionary Guided Flight Discovery system leads you through essential aeronautical knowledge and exposes you to a variety of interesting and useful information which will enhance and expand your understanding of the world of aviation.

Although each element of the Guided Flight Discovery Pilot Training System may be used separately, the effectiveness of the materials can be maximized by using all of the individual components in a systems approach. To help you efficiently organize your studies and get the most out of your training, Guided Flight Discovery incorporates cross-references which are used to direct you to related Guided Flight Discovery study materials. The main components of the Private Pilot Program are described below.

Core Study Materials
Private Pilot Manual

The Private Pilot Manual is your primary source for initial study and review. The text contains complete and concise explanations of the fundamental concepts and ideas that every private pilot needs to know. The subjects are organized in a logical manner to build upon previously introduced topics. Subjects are often expanded upon through the use of Discovery Insets which are strategically placed throughout the chapters. Periodically, human factors principles are presented in Human Element Insets to help you understand how your mind and body function while you fly. Throughout the manual, concepts which directly relate to FAA test questions are highlighted by FAA Question Insets. Additionally, you can evaluate your understanding of material introduced in a particular section by completing the associated review questions. A more detailed explanation of this manual's unique features is contained in the section entitled "How the Manual Works" starting on page x.

The Private Pilot Manual also contains a FAR/AIM CD-ROM. Federal Aviation Regulations (FARs) covered on the CD-ROM include Parts 1, 43, 61, 67, 71, 73, 91, 97, 119, 125, 133, 135, 141, 142, HMR 175, and NTSB 830. FAR Study lists, along with FAR Exercises (and answers) are included. The Aeronautical Information Manual (AIM) segments consist of the complete AIM with color graphics and the entire Pilot/Controller Glossary.

Private Pilot Maneuvers Manual

This manual uses colorful graphics and step-by-step procedure descriptions to help you visualize and understand each maneuver which you will perform in the aircraft. Additional guidance is provided through highlighted text which contains helpful hints, and FAA practical test standards.

Private Pilot Syllabus

The syllabus provides a basic framework for your training in a logical sequence. Ground and flight lessons are coordinated to ensure that your training progresses smoothly and that you are consistently introduced to topics on the ground prior to being required to apply that knowledge in the airplane.

Private Pilot Maneuvers CD-ROMs

These revolutionary CD-ROMs combine art, video, animation, and interactivity to create a dynamic learning experience. From preflight inspection to takeoffs and landings, you will learn how to perform each maneuver step-by-step with an instructor as your guide. The Maneuvers CD-ROMs also examine safety and human factors issues, as well as provide you with a unique opportunity to explore the world of aviation in a fun and exciting new format.

Support Materials

In addition to the core study materials described above, a variety of support materials are available to further enhance your understanding of pilot training subject matter. A brief description of these resources is provided below.

Private Pilot Airmen Knowledge Study Guide

This valuable study tool provides you with all the FAA questions which may be included on the Private Pilot computerized test. Answers and explanations for each question are provided to allow you to instantly check your understanding of required material.

Private Pilot Test Preparation Software

The test preparation software contains information similar to the *Private Pilot Airmen Knowledge Study Guide* with the added features of question search, simulated test taking, and performance tracking. Cross-references to Jeppesen Sanderson and FAA material are also included for every question.

Private Pilot Home-Study Videos

The *Private Pilot Test Prep Video Course* provides you with a take-home video review of aeronautical knowledge needed to pass your Private Pilot computerized test. Convenient cross-references direct you to the related questions contained in the *Private Pilot Airmen Knowledge Study Guide* and *Private Pilot Test Preparation Software.*

Private Pilot Practical Test Study Guide

This study aid combines the requirements of the FAA's Practical Test Standards with background information on each required task for the FAA practical test, including illustrations which show proper performance of maneuvers. Appropriate background information from Jeppesen Sanderson and FAA material is cross-referenced throughout this study guide.

Flight School Support Materials

Flight schools which use the Guided Flight Discovery Pilot Training System may provide a variety of additional resources and instructional support materials. Designed specifically to provide you with a well administered, quality training program, Guided

Flight Discovery flight school support materials help foster an environment which maximizes your potential for understanding and comprehension on your way to becoming a fully competent pilot. Some of these resources are described below.

Private Pilot Videos

The *Private Pilot Videos* are divided between basic aeronautical material and maneuvers analysis. The dynamic videos use state-of-the-art graphics and animation, as well as dramatic aerial photography to help easily explain complex ideas.

PC-Based Aviation Training Device (PCATD)

Flight schools may also provide access to Jeppesen Sanderson's PC-based aviation training device. The PCATD is designed specifically for pilot training and skill enhancement, and can be a great tool for giving you a head start on certain flight maneuvers.

Instructor's Guide

The *Instructor's Guide* is available for use by flight instructors and flight school operators. The *Instructor's Guide* helps flight training professionals effectively implement the Guided Flight Discovery Pilot Training System.

Feeling comfortable with your grasp of aviation concepts and your ability to apply them is fundamental to conducting safe and enjoyable flight operations. Historically, the majority of problems which occur during flight can be traced to a pilot's judgment and decision making. Aeronautical judgment is based primarily on the pilot's ability to apply the knowledge which was learned during training and gained through experience. The information presented in this textbook and the related Guided Flight Discovery materials is designed to provide you with the foundation of knowledge and experience needed to exercise good judgment and make sound decisions throughout your flying experience.

Preface

The purpose of the *Private Pilot Manual* is to provide you with the most complete explanations of aeronautical concepts in the most effective and easy-to-use manner possible. Through the use of colorful illustrations, full-color photos, and a variety of innovative design techniques, the *Private Pilot Manual* and other Guided Flight Discovery materials are closely coordinated to make learning fun and easy. To help you organize your study, the *Private Pilot Manual* is divided into five parts:

Part I — Fundamentals of Flight

The information needed to begin your aviation journey is introduced in this part. The first chapter, Discovering Aviation, answers many of your questions about the training process. Chapter two introduces you to the basics of airplane systems. In Chapter three you will gain an understanding of aerodynamic principles.

Part II — Flight Operations

Part II contains information you need to know about the environment in which you will fly. You will study subjects such as airport facilities, air traffic control services, communication procedures, and sources of flight information.

Part III — Aviation Weather

In Part III, you will be introduced to the variable atmosphere and its effect on aircraft operations. A thorough understanding of the information contained in this Part will help you maximize safety by minimizing your exposure to weather-related aviation hazards.

Part IV — Performance and Navigation

Aircraft capabilities and limitations in terms of performance parameters are covered in Part IV. You also will learn the basics of navigation using charts and radio aids.

Part V — Integrating Pilot Knowledge and Skills

The application of aeronautical decision-making principles and flight-related physiological factors is discussed in Chapter 10. A scenario in Chapter 11 provides insight into how previously learned knowledge and skills can be applied during a cross-country flight.

Table of Contents

How the Manual Works

The *Private Pilot Manual* is structured to highlight important topics and concepts and promote an effective and efficient study/review method of learning. To get the most out of your manual, as well as the entire Guided Flight Discovery Pilot Training System, you may find it beneficial to review the major design elements incorporated in this text.

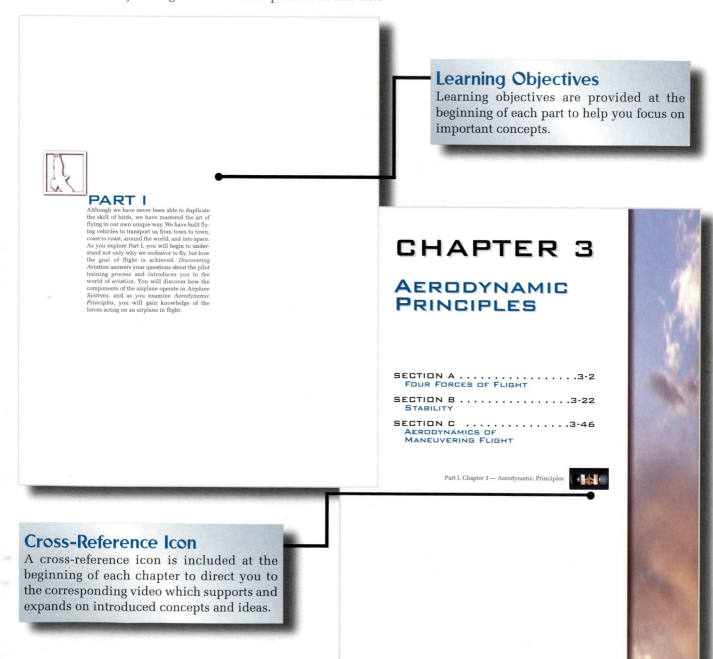

Learning Objectives
Learning objectives are provided at the beginning of each part to help you focus on important concepts.

PART I

Although we have never been able to duplicate the skill of birds, we have mastered the art of flying in our own unique way. We have built flying vehicles to transport us from town to town, coast to coast, around the world, and into space. As you explore Part I, you will begin to understand not only why we endeavor to fly, but how the goal of flight is achieved. *Discovering Aviation* answers your questions about the pilot training process and introduces you to the world of aviation. You will discover how the components of the airplane operate in *Airplane Systems*, and as you examine *Aerodynamic Principles*, you will gain knowledge of the forces acting on an airplane in flight.

CHAPTER 3

AERODYNAMIC PRINCIPLES

SECTION A 3-2
FOUR FORCES OF FLIGHT

SECTION B 3-22
STABILITY

SECTION C 3-46
AERODYNAMICS OF
MANEUVERING FLIGHT

Part I, Chapter 3 — Aerodynamic Principles

Cross-Reference Icon
A cross-reference icon is included at the beginning of each chapter to direct you to the corresponding video which supports and expands on introduced concepts and ideas.

SECTION C
AERODYNAMICS OF MANEUVERING FLIGHT

The extent to which an airplane can perform a variety of maneuvers is primarily a matter of design and a measure of its overall performance. Although aircraft design and performance may differ, the aerodynamic forces acting on any maneuvering aircraft are essentially the same. Understanding the aerodynamics of maneuvering flight can help you perform precise maneuvers while maintaining your airplane within its design limitations.

CLIMBING FLIGHT

The aerodynamic forces acting on an airplane established in a stabilized climb are in equilibrium; however, since the flight path is inclined, the relationship between these forces is altered. For example, the total force of weight no longer acts perpendicular to the flight path, but is comprised of two components. Although one component still acts 90° to the flight path, a rearward component of weight acts in the same direction as drag, opposing thrust. [Figure 3-48]

A transition from level flight into a climb normally combines a change in pitch attitude with an increase in power. If you attempt to climb just by pulling back on the control wheel to raise the nose of the airplane, momentum will cause a brief increase in altitude, but airspeed will soon decrease. The amount of thrust generated by the propeller for cruising flight at a given airspeed is not enough to maintain the same airspeed in a climb. Excess thrust, not excess lift, is necessary for a sustained climb. In fact, as the angle of climb steepens, thrust will not only oppose drag, but also will increasingly

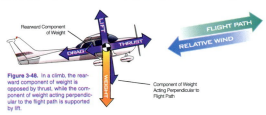

Figure 3-48. In a climb, the rearward component of weight is opposed by thrust, while the component of weight acting perpendicular to the flight path is supported by lift.

Rearward Component of Weight
LIFT
THRUST
DRAG
WEIGHT
FLIGHT PATH
RELATIVE WIND
Component of Weight Acting Perpendicular to Flight Path

LOAD FACTOR AND STALL SPEED

The additional load factor incurred during constant altitude turns will also increase stall speed. [Figure 3-69] In fact, stall speed increases in proportion to the square root of the load factor. For example, if you are flying an airplane with a one-G stalling speed of 55 knots, the airplane will stall at twice that speed (110 knots) with a load factor of four G's. Stalls that occur with G-forces on an airplane are called **accelerated stalls**. An accelerated stall occurs at a speed higher than the normal one-G stall speed. These stalls demonstrate that the critical angle of attack, rather than airspeed, is the reason for a stall.

Figure 3-69. If you attempt to maintain altitude during a turn by increasing the angle of attack, the stall speed increases as the angle of bank increases. The percent of increase in stall speed is fairly moderate with shallow bank angles — less than 45°. However, once you increase the bank angle beyond 45°, the percent of increase in the stall speed rises rapidly. For example, in a 60°, constant-altitude bank, the stall speed increases by approximately 41%; a 75° bank increases stall speed by about 100%.

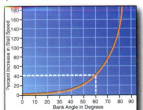

Percent Increase in Stall Speed
Bank Angle in Degrees

Increasing the load factor will cause an airplane to stall at a higher speed.

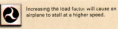

HOW MANY G'S ARE TOO MANY?
From the files of the NTSB...
Aircraft: Pitts S-2A — destroyed
Crew: One — seriously injured
Narrative: The witness stated the pilot was performing aerobatic maneuvers. At the top of the loop (approx. 3,000 ft AGL), the aircraft remained inverted, power was reduced, and an inverted spin was entered. The aircraft remained in the inverted spin to water impact. The pilot does not recall the accident flight, but stated he had been having problems with G-loads and low blood pressure.

It is possible, even likely, that some aerobatic aircraft may be able to withstand more G's than the pilot. A particular pilot's G-tolerance is a function of many factors, including the intensity, duration, and direction of the G-forces. The main physical problems associated with G-forces are caused by basic changes within the cardiovascular system. Positive G's create a pooling of blood in the lower extremities of the body, impairing circulation and reducing blood pressure at head level. Continued or increased G-loading will result in a decrease of visual acuity, ultimately followed by unconsciousness, or blackout.

The human body is less tolerant of negative G's, which force blood into the head. Large amounts of sustained negative G's can result in uncomfortable symptoms such as facial pain and redout. Although some experienced aerobatic pilots may be able to withstand 7 or 8 positive G's before blackout occurs, most will be incapacitated by only -3G's. You can improve your G-tolerance by maintaining good physical conditioning and avoiding smoking, hyperventilation, and hypoxia. Most civil pilots, however, will not encounter G-forces of sufficient strength during normal flight to cause any major problems.

Maximum Acceleration in G's
Time in Seconds at Maximum
7 G's / sec
1 G / sec
0.4 G / sec
Unconsciousness
Blackout
Loss of Peripheral Vision

Discovery Insets

Discovery Insets are included throughout the text beginning with Chapter 2 to expand on ideas and concepts presented in the accompanying material. The information presented in each Discovery Inset varies, but is designed to enhance your understanding of the world of aviation. Examples include references to National Transportation Safety Board investigations, aviation history, and thought-provoking questions and answers.

Color Photographs

Color photographs are included to enhance learning and improve understanding.

Key Terms

For ease of recognition and quick review, key terms are highlighted in red type when they are first introduced and defined. A list of key terms is included at the end of each section.

The following is a reproduction of a sample manual page:

CHAPTER 3   AERODYNAMIC PRINCIPLES

D The Canard Design

Although the tail-down force created by the horizontal stabilizer is excellent for longitudinal stability and balance, it is aerodynamically inefficient. The wings must support the negative lift created by the tail, and the negative angle of attack on the stabilizer increases drag. If an airplane design permitted two lifting surfaces, aerodynamic efficiency would be much greater.

A canard is a stabilizer that is located in front of the main wings. Canards are something like miniature forward wings. They were used in the pioneering days of aviation, most notably on the Wright Flyer, and are now reappearing on several original designs. The Beechcraft Starship (see photo) employs a variable sweep canard design. The canard provides longitudinal stability about the lateral axis by lifting the nose of the airplane.

Courtesy of Raytheon Aircraft

Since both the main wings and the canard produce positive lift, the design is aerodynamically efficient. A properly designed canard is also stall/spin resistant. The canard stalls at a lower angle of attack than the main wings. In doing so, the canard's angle of attack immediately decreases after it stalls. This breaks the stall and effectively returns the canard to a normal lift-producing angle of attack before the main wings have a chance to stall. Ailerons remain effective throughout the stall because they are attached to the main wings. In spite of its advantages, the canard design has limitations in total lift capability. Critical design conditions also must be met to maintain adequate longitudinal stability throughout the flight envelope.

POWER EFFECTS

If you reduce power during flight, a definite nose-down pitching tendency occurs due to the reduction of downwash from the wings and the propeller which reduces elevator effectiveness. Although this is a destabilizing factor, it is a desirable characteristic because it tends to result in a nose-down attitude during power reductions. The nose-down attitude helps you maintain, or regain, airspeed. Increasing power has the opposite effect. It causes increased downwash on the horizontal stabilizer which decreases its contribution to longitudinal stability and causes the nose of the airplane to rise.

A power reduction in airplanes, other than T-tails, will decrease the downwash on the horizontal stabilizer from the wings and propeller slipstream. This is what causes the nose to pitch down after a power reduction.

The influence of power on longitudinal stability also depends on the overall design of the airplane. Since power provides thrust, the alignment of thrust in relation to the longitudinal axis, the CG, the wings, and the stabilizer are all factors. The **thrustline** is determined by where the propeller is mounted and by the general direction in which thrust acts. In most light general aviation airplanes, the thrustline is parallel to the longitudinal axis and above the CG. This creates a slight pitching moment around the CG. If thrust is decreased, the pitching moment is reduced and the nose heaviness tends to decrease. An increase in thrust increases the pitching moment and increases nose heaviness. [Figure 3-37] Notice that these pitching tendencies are exactly the reverse of the pitching tendencies resulting from an increase or decrease in downwash. This thrustline design arrangement minimizes the destabilizing effects of power changes and improves longitudinal stability.

3-30

V_A normally is not marked on the airspeed indicator, since it may vary with total weight. V_A decreases as weight decreases since an aircraft operating at lighter weights is subject to more rapid acceleration from gusts and turbulence. The POH and/or a placard in the airplane are the best sources for determining V_A.

The amount of excess load that can be imposed on an airframe depends on the aircraft's speed.

SUMMARY CHECKLIST

✓ In climbing flight, one component of weight acts perpendicular to the flight path, and another component of weight acts rearward, in the same direction as drag.

✓ Four left-turning tendencies associated with propeller-driven airplanes are torque, gyroscopic precession, asymmetrical thrust, and spiraling slipstream.

✓ During descending flight, one component of weight acts forward along the flight path, while another component acts perpendicular to the flight path.

✓ The least drag, best glide angle, and maximum gliding distance can be obtained by maintaining the angle of attack that corresponds to L/D_{max}.

✓ Changes in aircraft weight will not affect glide ratio, but a higher airspeed will have to be maintained in a heavier aircraft in order to cover the same distance over the ground.

✓ Centripetal force, which is created by the horizontal component of lift, is the center-seeking force that acts on a turning airplane.

✓ The effects of adverse yaw can be countered by maintaining a coordinated turn using rudder.

✓ Rate of turn increases and radius of turn decreases as angle of bank is increased in a constant airspeed turn. If angle of bank is held constant and airspeed is increased, turn rate will decrease and turn radius will increase.

✓ The ratio of the weight that the wings must support to the actual weight of the aircraft is termed load factor.

✓ Accelerated stalls occur when the critical angle of attack is exceeded at an airspeed higher than the one-G stall speed.

✓ The V-g diagram defines the airplane's envelope, which is bounded by the stall region, limit load factor, and V_{NE}.

KEY TERMS

Torque	Spiraling Slipstream
Gyroscopic Precession	Maximum Lift-to-Drag Ratio
Asymmetrical Thrust	Best Glide Speed
P-Factor	Glide Ratio

Summary Checklists

Summary Checklists are included at the end of each section to help you identify and review the major points introduced in the section.

Glide Angle	Radius of Turn
Centripetal Force	Load Factor
Centrifugal Force	Accelerated Stalls
Adverse Yaw	Limit Load Factor
Overbanking Tendency	V-g Diagram
Rate of Turn	Design Maneuvering Speed (V_A)

QUESTIONS

1. Identify the aerodynamic force that opposes the rearward component of weight in a climb.

2. What relative airspeed, power, and angle of attack conditions produce the most noticeable left-turning tendencies common to single-engine, propeller-driven aircraft?

3. Name at least three design elements that can be used to help offset left-turning tendencies.

4. All else being equal, will two aerodynamically identical aircraft with different weights be able to glide the same distance over the ground? If so, how can this be accomplished and why?

5. What causes an airplane to turn?

6. If angle of bank and altitude are held constant, what can be done to increase the rate of turn?

Given a wings-level, 1G stall speed of 55 knots, use the chart provided to determine the stall speed under the following conditions:

7. Bank angle, 30°

8. Bank angle, 45°

9. Bank angle, 75°

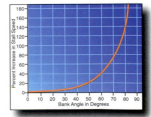

10. True/False. Maneuvering speed increases with an increase in weight.

Questions

Questions are provided at the end of each section beginning with Chapter 2 to help you evaluate your understanding of the concepts which were presented in the accompanying section. Several question formats are provided including completion, matching, true/false, and essay. Perforated answer sheets, which are organized by chapter, are included at the back of the text.

PART I
FUNDAMENTALS OF FLIGHT

The bird has learned [his] art . . . so thoroughly that its skill is not apparent to our sight. We only learn to appreciate it when we try to imitate it.

— Wilbur Wright

PART I

Although we have never been able to duplicate the skill of birds, we have mastered the art of flying in our own unique way. We have built flying vehicles to transport us from town to town, coast to coast, around the world, and into space. As you explore Part I, you will begin to understand not only why we endeavor to fly, but how the goal of flight is achieved. *Discovering Aviation* answers your questions about the pilot training process and introduces you to the world of aviation. You will discover how the components of the airplane operate in *Airplane Systems*, and as you examine *Aerodynamic Principles*, you will gain knowledge of the forces acting on an airplane in flight.

CHAPTER 1

DISCOVERING AVIATION

SECTION A
PILOT TRAINING

WHAT IS FLYING ALL ABOUT?

Science, freedom, beauty, adventure — aviation offers it all.
— Charles Lindbergh

Welcome to the world of aviation. You are about to embark on a journey of adventure, exploration, and discovery. Throughout history, we have dreamed about achieving the freedom and power of flight. We have looked to the sky, marveled at the birds, and wondered what it must be like to escape the bonds of earth to join them.

For once you have tasted flight,
You will walk the earth with your eyes turned skyward;
For there you have been,
And there you long to return.
— Leonardo da Vinci, *On Flight of Birds*

One of history's creative geniuses was Leonardo da Vinci; an artist, scientist, and dreamer who was fascinated with flight. He spent countless hours studying the flight of birds and his 15th century manuscripts contained approximately 160 pages of descriptions and sketches of flying machines. One such machine was the ornithopter which was designed to imitate the wing structure of birds and bats. [Figure 1-1] A human-powered

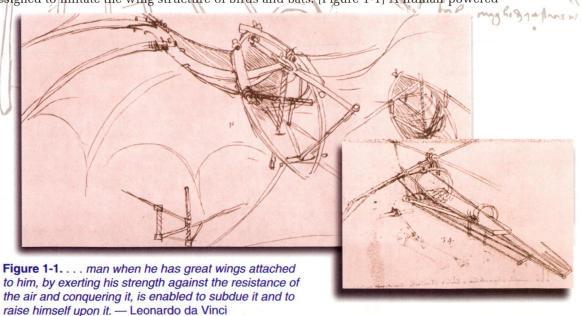

Figure 1-1. . . . *man when he has great wings attached to him, by exerting his strength against the resistance of the air and conquering it, is enabled to subdue it and to raise himself upon it.* — Leonardo da Vinci

ornithopter is virtually incapable of flight due to the dramatic difference in the strength-to-weight ratio of birds compared to humans. Da Vinci's manuscripts also contained well-developed descriptions of finned projectiles, parachutes, and the helicopter. These ideas could have advanced the course of aviation history and flight may have been achieved centuries sooner, but unfortunately, the manuscripts were not made public until 300 years after da Vinci's death.

While the story of aviation has its share of missed opportunities, unrealized dreams, and failures, it is nonetheless a story of unparalleled success. When you learn to fly you become a part of this success story. You may never break a record or have your flying feats recorded in the history books, but as a pilot, you make your mark as one of the unique individuals who has dared to do what others only dream about. At the controls of an airplane, you can experience some of the same magic that the pioneers of aviation realized.

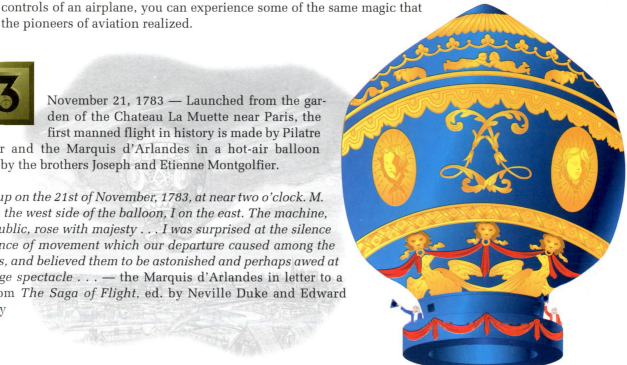

1783

November 21, 1783 — Launched from the garden of the Chateau La Muette near Paris, the first manned flight in history is made by Pilatre de Rozier and the Marquis d'Arlandes in a hot-air balloon designed by the brothers Joseph and Etienne Montgolfier.

We went up on the 21st of November, 1783, at near two o'clock. M. Rozier on the west side of the balloon, I on the east. The machine, say the public, rose with majesty . . . I was surprised at the silence and absence of movement which our departure caused among the spectators, and believed them to be astonished and perhaps awed at the strange spectacle . . . — the Marquis d'Arlandes in letter to a friend from *The Saga of Flight*, ed. by Neville Duke and Edward Lanchbery

1881

1881 through 1896 — German engineer and inventor, Otto Lilienthal with the help of his brother Gustav proved to the western world that flight in a heavier-than-air machine was achievable. The Lilienthal brothers used their mechanical training to translate conclusions made about the flight of birds into practical air vehicles. From an artificial hill constructed for launching his gliders, Otto Lilienthal made over 2,000 successful glides.

There can be no doubt, in my opinion, that by perfecting our present apparatus, and by acquiring greater skill in using it, we shall achieve still more favorable results with it, and finally succeed in taking long sails even in strong winds . . . Of course it will be a matter of practice to learn how to guide such a flying machine . . . Actual trial alone can decide this question, as we must let the air and the wind have their say in the matter. — Otto Lilienthal

December 17, 1903 — Near Kitty Hawk, North Carolina, Orville and Wilbur Wright achieved the first powered, sustained, and controlled airplane flights in history. Four flights were made; the first for 12 seconds, the last for 59 seconds.

Flight was generally looked upon as an impossibility, and scarcely anyone believed it until he actually saw it with his own eyes. — Orville Wright

The flight lasted only twelve seconds, but it was nevertheless the first in the history of the world in which a machine carrying a man had raised itself by its own power into the air in full flight, had sailed forward without reduction of speed, and had finally landed at a point as high as that from which it started. — Orville Wright

1927 May 21, 1927 — Charles Lindbergh lands his airplane, the *Spirit of St. Louis*, at Le Bourget field in Paris after completing the first solo nonstop transatlantic flight. His total flight time from New York to Paris was 33 hours, 30 minutes and 29.8 seconds.

The Spirit of St. Louis *swings around and stops rolling, resting on the solidness of the earth, in the center of Le Bourget. I start to taxi back toward the floodlights and hangars—But the entire field ahead is covered with running figures!* — Charles Lindbergh, *The Spirit of St. Louis*

What Lindbergh was the first to do, by an act of superb intelligence and will, millions of us accomplish regularly with the expenditure of no more intelligence and will than is required to purchase a ticket and pack a bag . . . That first New York — to — Paris flight, with its awesome risk coolly faced and outwitted by a single valorous young man had led to an ever-increasing traffic in the sky above the Atlantic and an ever-decreasing awareness of awe and risk on the part of the army of non-flyers who have followed him. His valor is hard to keep fresh in our minds when the most we are asked to face and outwit above the Atlantic is boredom. — Brendan Gill, *Lindbergh Alone*

Courtesy of The Ninety-Nines Inc. International Organization of Women Pilots Archive Collection, Oklahoma City, Oklahoma

1932

May 21, 1932 — Amelia Earhart became the first woman to pilot an airplane solo across the Atlantic. Gaining fame for being the first woman passenger in a flight across the Atlantic four years earlier, Earhart was disappointed that pilot Wilmer Stultz did all the flying while she just rode along like "a sack of potatoes" as she phrased it. She was determined to prove that she could accomplish the flight herself, and she did when she landed in Northern Ireland after taking off from Newfoundland 14 hours and 52 minutes earlier. On August 25 of the same year, Earhart completed the first woman's solo nonstop transcontinental flight which covered 2,448 miles from Los Angeles to Newark.

If Amelia wanted to do something, she was going to do it, and there really wasn't much point in saying, "You can't do this." — Mrs. Muriel Morrissey, sister of Amelia Earhart as quoted in *The American Heritage History of Flight*

1942

October 1, 1942 — Piloted by Robert M. Stanley, the Bell XP-59A Airacomet, the United States' first turbojet aircraft made its inaugural flight at Muroc Dry Lake, California. The Bell XP-59A is the direct ancestor of all American jet-propelled airplanes.

One day in 1945, I landed to refuel at a California base, and I heard a noise, a sound totally new to me, insistent, demanding, permeating the whole revetment area. I tumbled out of my cockpit and joined a group of pilots and crew chiefs beside the strip. And we watched a Bell P-59, the first American jet, begin its takeoff. Engines howling, it lumbered forward, then strode, then raced and finally was aloft. We watched it quietly, staying close together as people do when they meet the future. — pilot Edwards Park as quoted in *The Smithsonian Book of Flight*

1947

Courtesy of NASA Dryden Research Center

October 14, 1947 — Captain Charles E. "Chuck" Yeager becomes the first man to fly an aircraft beyond the speed of sound. He pilots the air-launched experimental Bell X-1 rocket-propelled research airplane named *Glamorous Glennis* (after Yeager's wife) at a speed of 700 mph at 42,000 feet over Muroc Dry Lake, California.

Leveling off at 42,000 feet, I had thirty percent of my fuel, so I turned on rocket chamber three and immediately reached .96 Mach. I noticed that the faster I got, the smoother the ride. Suddenly the Mach needle began to fluctuate. It went up to .965 Mach—then tipped right off the scale. I thought I was seeing things! We were flying supersonic! . . . I was thunderstruck. After all the anxiety, breaking the sound barrier turned out to be a perfectly paved speedway. — Yeager: An Autobiography by General Chuck Yeager and Leo Janos

In those few moments, the supersonic age was born.

May 25, 1961 — I believe that this nation should commit itself to achieving the goal, before this decade is out, of landing a man on the moon and returning him safely to earth. No single space project in this period will be more impressive to mankind or more important for the long-range exploration of space. And none will be so difficult or expensive to accomplish. — President John F. Kennedy

1969

July 20, 1969 — As astronaut Michael Collins maintained orbit in the Apollo 11 Command Module *Columbia*, astronauts Neil Armstrong and Edwin Aldrin landed the Lunar Module *Eagle* on the moon and become the first humans to step on another celestial body.

HOUSTON: *Okay, Neil, we can see you coming down the ladder now.* NEIL ARMSTRONG: *Okay, I just checked — getting back up to that first step. Buzz, it's not even collapsed too far, but it's adequate to get back up . . . It takes a pretty good little jump . . . I'm at the foot of the ladder. The LM footpads are only depressed in the surface about one or two inches. Although the surface appears to be very, very fine-grained, as you get close to it. It's almost like a powder. Now and then, it's very fine . . . I'm going to step off the LM now . . . THAT'S ONE SMALL STEP FOR A MAN, ONE GIANT LEAP FOR MANKIND.*

Courtesy of NASA

1981

April 12, 1981 — The United States launches the space shuttle *Columbia*, the world's first reusable manned space vehicle and the most complex flying machine ever built. Pilot Robert L. Crippen describes *Columbia's* landing by space shuttle commander John W. Young.

We made a gliding circle over our landing site, runway 23 on Rogers Dry Lake at Edwards Air Force Base. On final approach I was reading out the airspeeds to John so he wouldn't have to scan the instruments as closely. Columbia *almost floated in. John only had to make minor adjustments in pitch. We were targeted to touch down at 185 knots, and the very moment I called out 185, I felt us touch down. I have never been in any flying vehicle that landed more smoothly. If you can imagine the smoothest landing you've ever had in an airliner, ours was at least that good. John really greased it in. "Welcome home,* Columbia,*" said Houston. "Beautiful, beautiful." "Do you want us to take it up to the hangar?" John asked.* — "Our Phenomenal First Flight," by John Young and Robert Crippen in *National Geographic*

Courtesy of NASA

1986

December 23, 1986 — Piloted by Jeana Yeager and Dick Rutan, the aircraft *Voyager* completes the first nonstop-without-refueling flight around the world. The flight took 9 days, 3 minutes, and 44 seconds. *Voyager* was designed by pilot Dick Rutan's brother Burt Rutan.

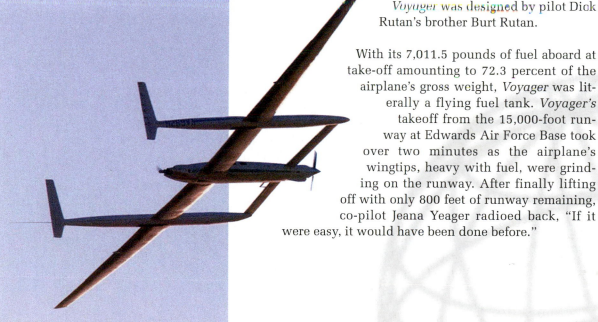

Courtesy of NASA Dryden Research Center

With its 7,011.5 pounds of fuel aboard at take-off amounting to 72.3 percent of the airplane's gross weight, *Voyager* was literally a flying fuel tank. *Voyager's* takeoff from the 15,000-foot runway at Edwards Air Force Base took over two minutes as the airplane's wingtips, heavy with fuel, were grinding on the runway. After finally lifting off with only 800 feet of runway remaining, co-pilot Jeana Yeager radioed back, "If it were easy, it would have been done before."

Breaking new ground is never easy. It may be difficult to understand what an incredible achievement Lindbergh's flight from New York to Paris was when thousands of airliners cross the Atlantic nonstop every week and space shuttle flights seem routine. In our quest for flight, we have suffered many defeats but our successes outweigh our failures, for today, what once seemed impossible is commonplace.

THE TRAINING PROCESS

In the early days of aviation, there were no certificates and no government regulations to control pilot training or aircraft construction. Little guidance was provided for individuals who desired to fly airplanes and, for most would-be aviators, learning to fly was accomplished by trial and error. As a result, flight training was a risky business which required a tremendous amount of courage and commitment. Although you may never encounter the same obstacles and hazards faced by the early aviators, becoming a pilot still presents a challenge which requires hard work and dedication. However, the time and energy which you invest in flying will yield countless rewards.

These rewards are unique to each pilot since individuals learn to fly for different reasons. Some relish the challenge of achieving an extraordinary goal, some yearn to travel and experience the world from a new perspective, some are looking for an exciting career, and still others simply desire the satisfaction and sense of accomplishment which come from mastering a skill. You may be thinking about learning to fly for one or more of these reasons, or you may have an entirely different motivation. Whatever the reason, if you yearn to spread your wings and expand your horizons, this is your chance.

HOW DO I GET STARTED?

The first step is to have your questions answered. The more information you have about the training process, the easier it will be for you to make effective decisions about pilot training, and the more positive your flying experience will be.

WHAT IS THE FAA?

Pilot training today is regulated by an agency called the **Federal Aviation Administration (FAA)** which governs commercial and general aviation. The **Federal Aviation Regulations (FARs)**, which are issued by the FAA, provide rules which apply to all areas of aviation, including flight operations, the construction of aircraft, and the training requirements which must be met to obtain pilot certificates and ratings. The FARs are identified by a specific title number (Aeronautics and Space Title 14) within the larger group of rules contained in the Code of Federal Regulations (CFR).

The FARs are divided into numbered parts (FAR Part 61, FAR Part 91, etc.) and regulations are typically identified by the part number, followed by the specific regulation number, for example; FAR 91.106. During your training, you will become familiar with the regulations which apply to you.

As outlined in the FARs, you must meet specific training requirements to obtain a private pilot certificate. During your course of training you will take a knowledge test and at the completion of your pilot training, you are required to take a practical test to obtain your pilot certificate. Although certain requirements must be met to prepare you for these exams, pilot training is generally very flexible, and to a large degree you have the ability to choose your instructor, the type of training, and the lesson schedule which will best suit your needs.

WHERE CAN I OBTAIN PILOT TRAINING?

You usually don't have to travel any further than your local airport to launch your aviation journey. Many pilot training schools are located at airport facilities called **fixed base operators (FBOs)**. In addition to pilot training, FBOs provide a variety of services to pilots, including aircraft rental, fueling, maintenance, parking, and the sale of pilot supplies. There are two types of pilot training schools; FAA-approved schools governed by FAR Part 141 and schools governed by FAR Part 61. Both schools employ **FAA certificated flight instructors (CFIs)** who can provide dual instruction in the airplane. A Part 141 approved school must meet prescribed standards for equipment, facilities, personnel, and curricula.

You can make a more-informed decision about a pilot training school by conducting some research. For example: Does the school's instructional program and lesson schedule fit your needs? How long has the school been operating? What is the school's reputation and safety record? How many, and what type of aircraft are available for flight training? How are aircraft maintenance issues resolved?

Most schools offer an introductory flight lesson during which you will be able to operate the controls of the airplane. This flight provides an opportunity for you to become familiar with the flight training process, evaluate the flight school, and get acquainted with a flight instructor. Probably the most important decision you will make regarding your pilot training is the selection of a flight instructor. You may want to speak with several CFIs and ask other pilots for instructor recommendations. If you are uncomfortable or have trouble communicating with a CFI, don't be afraid to select a different instructor. Students learn differently and another CFI may have a teaching style which you find more effective.

If you plan to pursue aviation as a career, you may want to consider a large flight school, college, or university which provides highly structured professional pilot training. Pilot instruction also can be obtained from a freelance CFI who is not employed by a school or FBO.

WHAT ABOUT GROUND INSTRUCTION?

Ground instruction is an essential part of pilot training. To operate an aircraft safely as a private pilot, you must be knowledgeable in a wide variety of subject areas, such as weather, aerodynamics, aircraft systems, flight planning, and regulations. You can obtain the required ground instruction individually from your flight instructor or through formal ground school classes offered by a school or FBO. In addition, there are home-study courses and self-study material available which include videotapes and computer-based training. However, your instructor still will need to cover certain subject areas with you to determine that you have gained the necessary knowledge to pass your exams and operate safely as a private pilot. Some organizations offer concentrated weekend test preparation courses which focus on passing the knowledge test. Although these courses may help you prepare for the knowledge test, they do not provide the comprehensive ground instruction necessary for you to become a competent and safe pilot.

HOW IS A SYLLABUS USED IN PILOT TRAINING?

Typically, both flight and ground lessons are organized by a **syllabus** which provides structure to your training and helps ensure that no procedures are overlooked. A syllabus is normally based upon the building-block theory of learning, which recognizes that each item taught must be presented on the basis of previously learned knowledge and skills. Academic support materials are coordinated with the flight lessons so that the material pertinent to a flight lesson is taught prior to the flight. [Figure 1-2]

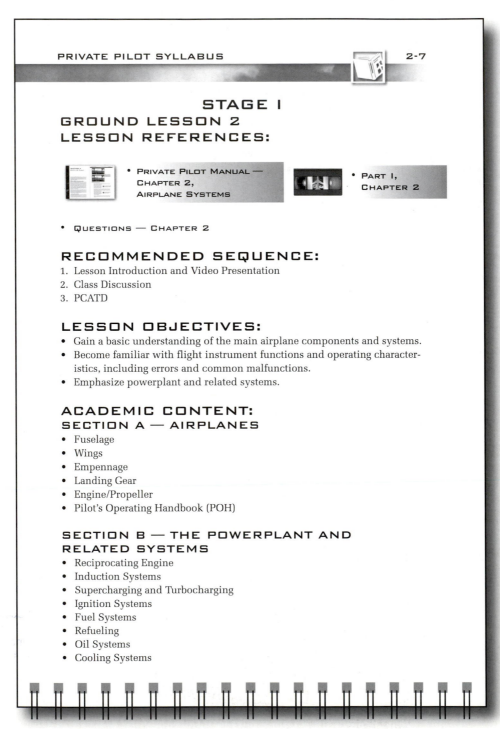

Figure 1-2. The items which are to be performed during each lesson are outlined in a training syllabus.

PRIVATE PILOT SYLLABUS   2-7

STAGE I
GROUND LESSON 2
LESSON REFERENCES:

- PRIVATE PILOT MANUAL — CHAPTER 2, AIRPLANE SYSTEMS
- PART I, CHAPTER 2

- QUESTIONS — CHAPTER 2

RECOMMENDED SEQUENCE:
1. Lesson Introduction and Video Presentation
2. Class Discussion
3. PCATD

LESSON OBJECTIVES:
- Gain a basic understanding of the main airplane components and systems.
- Become familiar with flight instrument functions and operating characteristics, including errors and common malfunctions.
- Emphasize powerplant and related systems.

ACADEMIC CONTENT:
SECTION A — AIRPLANES
- Fuselage
- Wings
- Empennage
- Landing Gear
- Engine/Propeller
- Pilot's Operating Handbook (POH)

SECTION B — THE POWERPLANT AND RELATED SYSTEMS
- Reciprocating Engine
- Induction Systems
- Supercharging and Turbocharging
- Ignition Systems
- Fuel Systems
- Refueling
- Oil Systems
- Cooling Systems

- Exhaust Systems
- Propellers
- Propeller Hazards
- Electrical Systems

SECTION C — FLIGHT INSTRUMENTS
- Pitot-Static Instruments
- Airspeed Indicator
- Altimeter
- Vertical Speed Indicator
- Gyroscopic Instruments
- Magnetic Compass

STUDY ASSIGNMENT:

- PRIVATE PILOT MANUAL — CHAPTER 3, AERODYNAMIC PRINCIPLES

COMPLETION STANDARDS:

- Demonstrate understanding during oral quizzing by instructor at completion of lesson.

- Student completes Chapter 2 questions for Sections A, B, and C with a minimum passing score of 80%. Instructor reviews incorrect responses to ensure complete student understanding prior to progression to Ground Lesson 3.

WHEN CAN I START TAKING LESSONS?

You can begin taking lessons at any time, but you must hold a **student pilot certificate** to solo (fly alone) in the airplane. As required in the FARs, to be eligible for a student pilot certificate you must be at least 16 years of age, be able to read, speak, write, and understand the English language, and hold at least a third-class medical certificate.

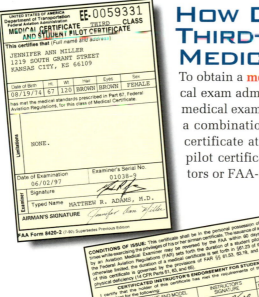

HOW DO I GET A THIRD-CLASS MEDICAL CERTIFICATE?

To obtain a **medical certificate**, you must pass a physical exam administered by an FAA-authorized aviation medical examiner (AME). You can request to be issued a combination medical certificate and student pilot certificate at the time of your examination. Student pilot certificates also may be issued by FAA inspectors or FAA-designated pilot examiners. [Figure 1-3]

Figure 1-3. The student pilot certificate is actually printed on the same form as the medical certificate. Your instructor will sign the appropriate spaces on the form when you are qualified to fly an airplane solo and to conduct solo cross-countries.

There are three classes of medical certificates: first-class which is designated for the airline transport pilot, second-class which is required for the commercial pilot, and third-class for student, recreational, and private pilots. [Figure 1-4] The third-class medical certificate is valid for 36 calendar months if you are less than 40 years of age, and valid for 24 calendar months if you are 40 years of age or older. For example, if you are 25 years old, your third-class medical certificate will expire in 3 years on the last day of the month in which it was issued.

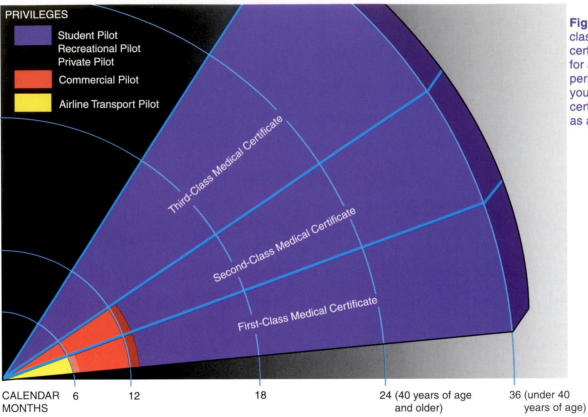

PRIVILEGES

- Student Pilot / Recreational Pilot / Private Pilot
- Commercial Pilot
- Airline Transport Pilot

Third-Class Medical Certificate

Second-Class Medical Certificate

First-Class Medical Certificate

CALENDAR MONTHS   6   12   18   24 (40 years of age   36 (under 40
                                                             and older)   years of age)

Figure 1-4. Each class of medical certificate is valid for a specific time period and allows you to exercise certain privileges as a pilot.

The medical standards for each class of certificate are described by FAR Part 67. First-class medical certificates require the highest physical standards, followed by second-class, and then third-class. Once you have made the decision to begin pilot training, you should obtain a medical certificate as soon as possible to ensure that you meet the required standards. If your future plans include a career as a commercial pilot or your goal is to fly for the airlines, you should consider applying for a second- or first-class medical early in your course of training to confirm your physical suitability for a flying career. There are several serious medical conditions which would require an AME to deny you a medical certificate. However, under certain circumstances such as your current health situation or medical history, the FAA may still grant the certificate.

Many FBOs and flight schools furnish information about facilities which provide FAA medical exams. You may want to obtain a recommendation for a medical examiner from your flight instructor or another pilot. Directories which list all FAA-authorized aviation medical examiners by name and address are available at local FAA offices called Flight Standards District Offices (FSDOs). In addition, air traffic control facilities and flight service stations may provide this information.

WHAT ARE THE REQUIREMENTS TO BECOME A PRIVATE PILOT?

In addition to the student pilot requirements, to be eligible for a private pilot certificate, you must be at least 17 years of age, complete specific training and flight time requirements described in the FARs, pass a knowledge test, and successfully complete a practical test which consists of oral quizzing, performing pilot operations, and executing maneuvers in the airplane.

Normally, you will take the knowledge test after you have progressed through a substantial portion of your ground and flight training so that you have gained a sufficient understanding of the subject material. The knowledge test is administered in a computer-based testing format. The questions are presented on the computer screen and your answers are entered using the keyboard. Your test is graded by the computer and the results are available immediately. You must score 70 percent or better to pass. The test results are valid for 24 calendar months.

The FARs require that you have received instruction in specific flight operations and maneuvers, as well as ground instruction in certain knowledge areas. In addition, there are minimum flight hour requirements which must be completed to apply for a private pilot certificate. According to FAR Part 61, you must have at least 40 hours of flight time consisting of at least 20 hours of dual instruction and at least 10 hours of solo flight. If you are enrolled at an approved school governed by FAR Part 141, you are required to have at least 35 hours of flight time including 20 hours of dual instruction and at least 5 hours of solo flight. You should remember that these are *minimum* hour requirements. The average student with no prior flying experience requires approximately 65 to 75 flight hours to meet the proficiency standards necessary to pass the practical test and operate safely as a private pilot.

HOW MUCH DOES PILOT TRAINING COST?

The cost of each flight lesson is based on the price of aircraft rental and your instructor's fee. The aircraft rental charge is normally based on the time spent in the airplane from engine start to engine shutdown. This period is determined by a digital recording clock in the airplane called the hours meter. Your instructor usually charges you for the time recorded by the hours meter, as well as additional time spent conducting preflight and postflight discussion.

Your pilot training environment determines the method of payment for instruction. You may be charged separately for each lesson or the school may offer a set number of lessons for a fee paid in advance. The total cost of your flight training largely depends on the number of flight hours which are necessary for you to complete your training program.

The number of hours required for you to become proficient depends on several factors, such as your initial comfort level with the airplane, whether you have any previous flying experience, and the frequency of your flight lessons. For example, the longer the time period between lessons, the less information you retain, and the more time you spend reviewing during each lesson. If you are able to fly at least several times a week, your training may be more cost-effective.

In addition to the expense of flight lessons, you will have to consider the cost of ground instruction. This cost will depend on which method of ground instruction you have selected; ground school classes, individual lessons with your instructor, home study, or a combination of several methods.

The total expense of pilot training also includes the cost of study materials, a logbook, a copy of the pilot's operating handbook for the training airplane, aeronautical charts, a flight computer, and navigational plotter. In addition, fees are charged for the knowledge test, the services of the aviation medical examiner, and the designated examiner who administers your practical test. While the cost of pilot training is significant, you'll find most pilots agree that the benefits of learning to fly are well worth the expense.

WHAT ARE FLYING LESSONS LIKE?

A typical flight lesson (excluding cross-country flights) lasts approximately two hours. An hour to an hour and a half is spent in the airplane and the remainder of the period consists of pre- and postflight discussion. Although each flight lesson is unique, a general sequence normally is followed.

 The lesson begins with a weather check. Your instructor will teach you how to obtain weather information to determine if the conditions are good for flying.

2 During a discussion with your instructor, the maneuvers to be performed during the flight lesson are covered and the material which you have studied in preparation for the lesson is reviewed.

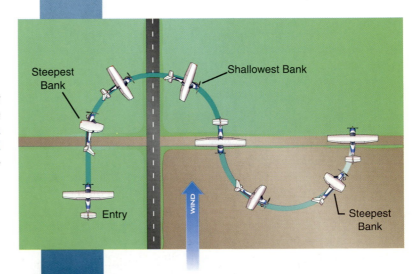

Steepest Bank

Shallowest Bank

Entry

WIND

Steepest Bank

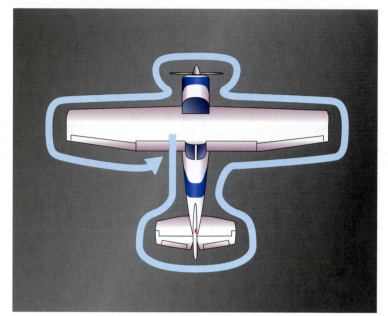

3 Using a checklist, you perform a visual inspection of the airplane to ensure that it is in a safe condition for flight.

4 During the flight, you will review previously learned procedures, and new maneuvers will be demonstrated by your instructor. As you practice these pilot operations, your instructor will critique your performance and provide guidance to help you execute each maneuver correctly.

5 After the flight, the lesson is evaluated and your logbook is endorsed. Your instructor points out the procedures which you performed well and also offers constructive criticism and suggestions to improve your future performance. You can discuss how you felt about the lesson and ask any pertinent questions. Finally, you are briefed on the next lesson and assigned study material.

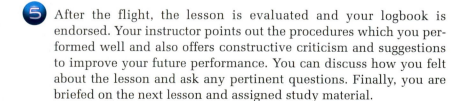

| DATE 19**97** | AIRCRAFT TYPE | AIRCRAFT IDENT | ROUTE OF FLIGHT | | NR INST. APP. | REMARKS AND ENDORSEMENTS | NR LDG | AIRCRAFT CAT |
			FROM	TO				SINGLE-ENGINE LAND	
9/12	C-172	8963K	APA	LOCAL		STALLS, SLOW FLIGHT Jane Kaley CFIS23940887 Ex7-98	1	1	2
9/14	C-172	8963K	APA	LOCAL		S-TURNS, TURNS AROUND A POINT	1	1	1

WHAT IS THE TRAINING COURSE SEQUENCE?

A private pilot training program can generally be divided into three phases: presolo, cross-country, and practical test preparation. Each phase includes both flight and ground training.

PRESOLO

During the presolo phase, your training progresses from the initial flight lesson with your instructor to your first solo flight. Your flight training includes such operations as preflight inspection of the airplane, operation of airplane systems, taxiing, emergency procedures, takeoffs and landings, as well as maneuvers away from the airport area such as climbs, descents, and turns. During ground lessons you learn how to obtain weather information, examine characteristics of the make and model of aircraft in which you will solo, and review pertinent regulations.

CROSS-COUNTRY

1ST SOLO

The FARs state specific knowledge and flight proficiency standards which must be met prior to your first solo flight. Before endorsing your student pilot certificate and logbook for solo flight, your flight instructor will ensure that you are competent to perform the required pilot operations safely. In addition, prior to your solo flight, you must pass a written test administered by your instructor to verify that you understand the necessary ground material. Typically during your first solo, you complete several takeoffs and landings at your local airport while your instructor supervises from the ground. On subsequent solo flights, your instructor assigns specific maneuvers for practice in the local area.

An introduction to night flying normally is included in the cross-country phase. Although you can obtain a private pilot certificate without meeting all night flying experience requirements, a restriction will be placed on your certificate limiting you to flights during daylight hours.

During the cross-country phase, you learn how to plan flights to airports outside of the local area. You will gain skill in using aeronautical charts, procuring and interpreting weather information, calculating airplane performance, and determining the weight and balance condition of your airplane.

At least one cross-country flight to several airports is completed with your instructor and after you have gained the necessary skill and knowledge, you will conduct several solo cross-country flights. In addition to endorsing your student pilot certificate, your instructor will review your preflight planning and preparation for each cross-country to determine if the flight can be made safely under the known circumstances and conditions.

The final phase of your training includes a review of all the flight maneuvers and ground study material which has been covered throughout the training program. Prior to your practical test, which pilots generally refer to as the checkride, your instructor endorses your logbook to indicate that you have completed the required training and are competent to perform each pilot operation safely as a private pilot.

PRACTICAL TEST PREPARATION

The checkride is administered by an FAA-designated pilot examiner or FAA inspector pilot. To assess your aeronautical knowledge, the checkride typically begins with oral quizzing. You are asked to prepare a cross-country flight which includes calculating aircraft performance and determining the weight and balance condition of your airplane. During the flight portion of the checkride, you are evaluated on tasks which are listed in the *Private Pilot Practical Test Standards (Private Pilot PTS)*. Your instructor should have a copy of the current *Private Pilot PTS* and this publication is also available for you to purchase. After you have passed the checkride, the examiner issues you a temporary private pilot certificate which is valid for a specific time period. You will receive your permanent certificate in the mail.

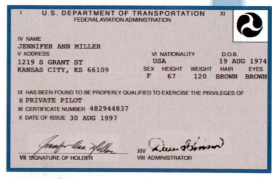

WHAT ARE MY PRIVILEGES AS A PRIVATE PILOT?

You can exercise the privileges of your pilot certificate immediately after passing the practical test. As stated in the FARs, the **pilot in command (PIC)** of an aircraft is directly responsible for, and is the final authority as to, the operation of that aircraft. As a private pilot, you can act as pilot in command of an aircraft carrying passengers and share operating expenses, such as the cost of fuel. You may not carry passengers or property for compensation or hire. Under certain circumstances specified in the regulations you may operate an aircraft in connection with a business, as an aircraft salesperson, and during flights sponsored by charitable organizations.

WHAT KIND OF AIRCRAFT CAN I FLY?

For pilot certification, aircraft are organized into category, class, and type. Category is the broadest grouping of aircraft and contains only five entries; airplane, rotorcraft, glider, lighter-than-air, and powered-lift. With the exception of gliders and powered-lift, each category is further broken down into classes. Finally, the type designates the make and model. (Figure 1-5) Your private pilot certificate will state the category (airplane), class (single-engine land), and type (if appropriate) of aircraft which you are authorized to fly. The type normally is not listed for small airplanes.

AIRPLANE

Single-Engine Land

Multi-Engine Sea

Multi-Engine Land

Single-Engine Sea

Figure 1-5. For pilot certification, aircraft categories are airplane, rotorcraft, glider, powered-lift, and lighter-than-air. Classes include single-engine land, single-engine sea, multi-engine land, multi-engine sea, helicopter, gyroplane, airship, and free balloon. Type refers to the make and model such as Cessna 172, Hughes 500, or Boeing 747.

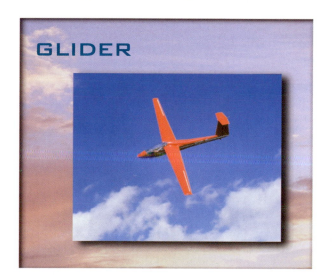

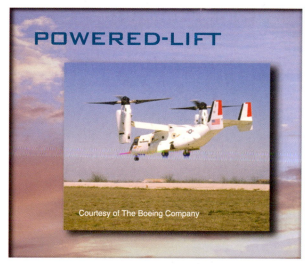

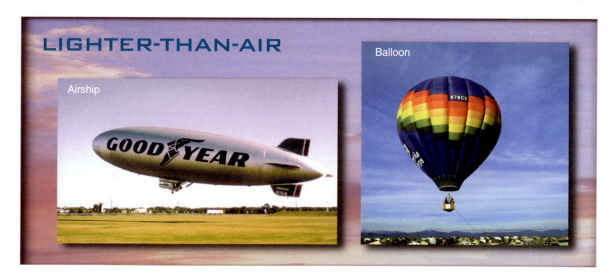

Aircraft are organized into different categories during the certification process. For aircraft certification, category relates to the intended use of an aircraft and sets strict limits on its operation. The normal and utility categories are common to most small airplanes. Depending on how they are loaded, many airplanes used in flight training are certificated in both of these categories. When loaded for the utility category, the airplane can withstand heavier stresses than it can in the normal category. Acrobatic aircraft have the fewest operating limitations because their design requirements demand more strength than those of the normal or utility category. Commuter aircraft are designed to carry passengers, but are limited to 19 seats and 19,000 pounds or less. Transport usually refers to airliners and other large aircraft which exceed certain weight limits or passenger-carrying capacity.

Normal

Experimental

Utility

Figure 1-6. Aircraft are organized into categories during the certification process. Examples include normal, utility, transport, acrobatic, restricted, and experimental categories.

Restricted

Courtesy of The Boeing Company

Transport

Acrobatic

The restricted category is for special-purpose aircraft such as agricultural spray planes or slurry bombers used to fight forest fires. Limited refers to military aircraft which are now allowed to be used only for limited purposes in civil aviation. The provisional category is really an interim measure for newly designed aircraft which have not met all the requirements for initial certification, but still can be operated for certain purposes. Experimental refers to a wide range of aircraft such as amateur-homebuilt and racing planes, as well as research and development aircraft used to test new design concepts. Some small aircraft which are intended exclusively for pleasure and personal use are certificated in the primary category. [Figure 1-6]

DOES MY PRIVATE PILOT CERTIFICATE EXPIRE?

The private pilot certificate does not expire, although to continue acting as pilot in command, you must meet specific currency requirements which are described in the FARs. You must satisfactorily complete a **flight review** every 24 calendar months to act as pilot in command. The flight review, which can be administered by a CFI, consists of at least one hour of ground instruction and one hour of flight instruction. During the review, your knowledge of current regulations and procedures is evaluated, as well as your proficiency in performing pilot operations and maneuvers. The CFI will endorse your logbook to indicate that you have completed the review satisfactorily and that you can safely exercise the privileges of your pilot certificate.

In addition to the flight review, to act as pilot in command of an aircraft carrying passengers, you must have performed at least three takeoffs and landings in an aircraft of the same category and class within the preceding 90 days. Keep in mind that these currency requirements are *minimums*. To truly maintain your proficiency, you must fly regularly and accomplish frequent refresher training with an instructor. In addition to maintaining sharp flying skills, it is necessary to review pilot knowledge areas on a regular basis and keep up-to-date on current pilot information and regulation changes.

There are many options available which will allow you to maintain flight proficiency, and increase your piloting skills and knowledge, as well as provide new and exciting challenges. You may want to pursue additional certificates and ratings or learn how to operate a different make and model of airplane. Section B of this chapter introduces you to additional training opportunities, avocational flying options, and the many aviation careers which you can pursue.

I cannot answer except to assure you that it will be spectacular. – Orville Wright, when asked to forecast the future of aviation.

The story of aviation continues. Your future awaits you.

SUMMARY CHECKLIST

✓ The Federal Aviation Administration (FAA) is the agency which governs commercial and general aviation.

✓ The Federal Aviation Regulations (FARs) provide rules which apply to all areas of aviation, including flight operations, the construction of aircraft, and the training requirements which must be met to obtain pilot certificates and ratings.

✓ Many pilot training schools are located at airport facilities called fixed base operators (FBOs). These facilities provide a variety of services to pilots, including aircraft rental, fueling, maintenance, parking, and the sale of pilot supplies.

✓ There are two types of pilot training schools; FAA-approved schools governed by FAR Part 141 and schools governed by FAR Part 61.

✓ A syllabus provides structure to pilot training by organizing flight and ground lessons.

✓ To be eligible for a student pilot certificate you must be at least 16 years of age, be able to read, speak, and understand the English language, and hold at least a third-class medical certificate.

✓ There are three classes of medical certificates: first-class which is designated for the airline transport pilot, second-class which is required for the commercial pilot, and third-class for student, recreational, and private pilots.

✓ In addition to the student pilot requirements, to be eligible for a private pilot certificate you must be at least 17 years of age, complete specific training and flight time requirements described in the FARs, pass a knowledge test, and successfully complete a practical test which consists of oral quizzing, performing pilot operations, and executing maneuvers in the airplane.

✓ A private pilot training program can generally be divided into three phases: presolo, cross-country, and practical test preparation. Each phase includes both flight and ground training.

✓ The pilot in command of an aircraft is directly responsible for, and is the final authority as to, the operation of that aircraft.

✓ For pilot certification, aircraft are organized into category, class, and type. Your private pilot certificate will state the category, class, and type (if appropriate) of aircraft which you are authorized to fly.

✓ For aircraft certification, category relates to the intended use of an aircraft and sets strict limits on its operation.

✓ To act as pilot in command of an aircraft, you must satisfactorily complete a flight review every twenty-four calendar months.

✓ To act as pilot in command of an aircraft carrying passengers, you must have performed at least three takeoffs and landings in an aircraft of the same category and class within the preceding 90 days.

KEY TERMS

Federal Aviation Administration (FAA)

Federal Aviation Regulations (FARs)

Fixed Base Operator (FBO)

FAA Certificated Flight Instructor (CFI)

Syllabus

Student Pilot Certificate

Medical Certificate

Pilot In Command (PIC)

Flight Review

SECTION B
AVIATION OPPORTUNITIES

Courtesy of Lockheed Martin

At age 72, Orville Wright took the controls of a Lockheed Constellation during his last flight. The Constellation, nicknamed "Connie" had four 2,200-hp Wright Duplex Cyclone engines, was fully pressurized, had a range of 2,400 miles, a cruise speed of over 300 mph, and could carry 65 to 90 passengers.

In 1937, Jackie Cochran set a new speed record for women pilots by flying a Beech D-17 "Staggerwing" biplane at 203.89 mph. In 1964 Cochran set a new woman's speed record by flying in a Lockheed F-104G Starfighter at 1,429.2 mph.

Courtesy of The Ninety-Nines Inc. International Organization of Women Pilots Archive Collection, Oklahoma City, Oklahoma

On July 16, 1969, Charles Lindbergh and Claude Ryan, the builder of the *Spirit of St. Louis,* were at Cape Kennedy to watch the launch of Apollo 11.

Courtesy of NASA

Welcome to your future. One of the unique joys of aviation is that there is always a challenge to be met; a new adventure on which to embark; one more goal to be achieved. A private pilot certificate opens a door to a future of exciting opportunities and endless possibilities. Completion of private pilot training does not signify an ending, but a beginning to an aviation journey filled with new experiences. Whether you are flying for personal pleasure or have career aspirations, there are many different courses that you can navigate on this voyage.

This section introduces you to a wide variety of avocational options and careers that you can pursue as a pilot. As you explore these aviation opportunities, symbols will provide a guideline to the type of training and experience necessary to meet each goal. The requirements described are based on the assumption that you will obtain a private pilot certificate with an airplane category rating and single-engine land class rating.

Ground instruction and flight training are necessary to become competent in this skill but no specific requirements are described by the FARs.

Training in specific pilot operations and a logbook endorsement from a qualified flight instructor are required by the FARs.

You must pass a computerized knowledge test.

Specific ground instruction and flight training are required by the FARs and you must pass a practical test.

Prior to beginning any additional instruction, you should refer to the FARs for specific experience requirements and discuss the training course thoroughly with your flight instructor to ensure that all your questions are answered.

NEW AVIATION EXPERIENCES

As soon as you are granted your private pilot certificate, new experiences await you; new scenery, new airports, and new responsibilities. You will be able to carry passengers for the first time, and you can fly cross-country to airports which you have not yet explored. As you gain flying experience and confidence, you may feel the need to expand your aviation horizons. The best way to sharpen your abilities, master new skills, and reenergize your enthusiasm for flight is to pursue additional training.

REFRESHER TRAINING

While your objectives may not include exploring a new area of aviation, frequent **refresher training** is essential to keep your skills sharp and to keep you informed on current pilot information. In addition, you may want to seek instruction in pilot operations that you do not perform frequently. For example,

You are planning a trip to an unfamiliar airport, but have not ventured out of the local area very often.

You are accustomed to operating at a small airport with very little traffic and would like to gain experience operating at a larger, busier airport.

You plan to fly frequently at night and do not have extensive night flying experience.

A substantial period of time has passed since you have practiced a series of takeoffs and landings, attitude instrument flying, or emergency procedures.

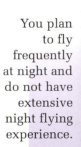

MOUNTAIN FLYING

If all of your flight training was accomplished at low-elevation airports, learning to fly in the mountains can be a fresh, rewarding experience. **Mountain flying** is challenging and requires proficiency in all of your piloting skills. While flying in the mountains is beautiful, it can be hazardous if you have not received proper training. Special considerations have to be made for weather, airport operations, course selection, and aircraft performance.

Before you fly at high elevations or in mountainous terrain, it is essential that you obtain ground and flight training from a qualified instructor. You may have the opportunity to attend a mountain flying course which can consist of both ground and flight instruction. In addition, to prepare for your training, there are many publications that can provide information about mountain operations.

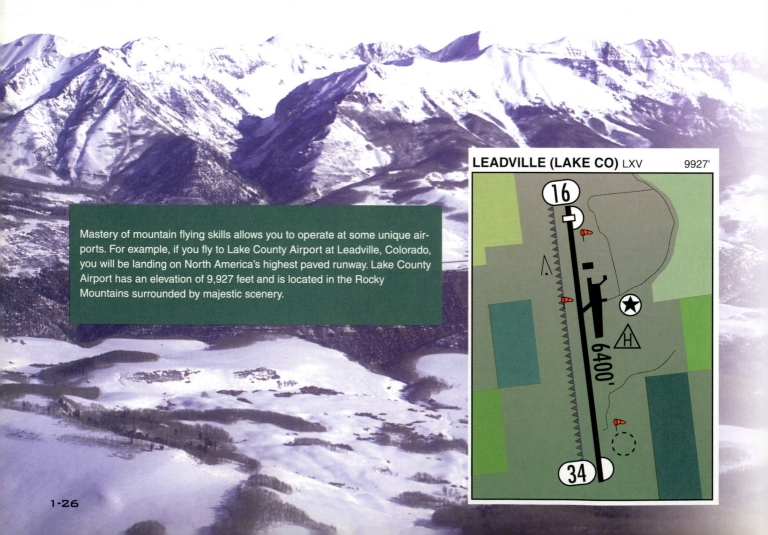

Mastery of mountain flying skills allows you to operate at some unique airports. For example, if you fly to Lake County Airport at Leadville, Colorado, you will be landing on North America's highest paved runway. Lake County Airport has an elevation of 9,927 feet and is located in the Rocky Mountains surrounded by majestic scenery.

LEADVILLE (LAKE CO) LXV   9927'

16

6400'

34

Aerobatic competition is full of thrills and excitement, and pilots must perform at the best of their abilities. Competitors are required to execute a series of predetermined maneuvers in a box of air above the competition field. In addition to horizontal parameters, the box contains a floor and ceiling. Judges evaluate the pilots on how smoothly and precisely maneuvers are performed within the prescribed course.

The aileron roll, snap roll, barrel roll, Cuban eight, loop, and Immelmann turn are all maneuvers which you may perform during **aerobatic flight training**. In addition to being just plain fun, aerobatics instruction increases your proficiency as a pilot. As you master each aerobatic maneuver, your timing, coordination, and reactions will improve, your confidence level as a pilot will increase, and you will gain a better understanding of the capabilities and limitations of the airplane. Aerobatic training also presents aerodynamics in a unique way which can not be duplicated in a classroom.

AEROBATIC FLIGHT

While there are no specific flight hour training requirements to operate an aircraft in aerobatic flight, the FARs do place certain restrictions on aerobatic maneuvers. For example, the aircraft must be certificated in the acrobatic category and parachutes are required when carrying passengers.

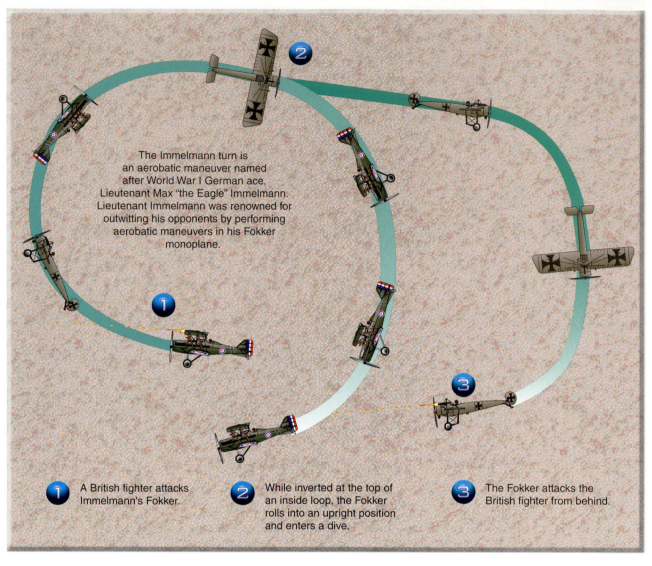

The Immelmann turn is an aerobatic maneuver named after World War I German ace, Lieutenant Max "the Eagle" Immelmann. Lieutenant Immelmann was renowned for outwitting his opponents by performing aerobatic maneuvers in his Fokker monoplane.

1 A British fighter attacks Immelmann's Fokker.

2 While inverted at the top of an inside loop, the Fokker rolls into an upright position and enters a dive.

3 The Fokker attacks the British fighter from behind.

AVIATION ORGANIZATIONS

One way to become involved as a pilot is through membership in an aviation organization or club. Numerous associations furnish pilots with information, sponsor flying activities, and promote safety. You may want to ask other pilots in your area about local flying clubs. There also are many national and international groups which have local chapters. Several examples of unique aviation organizations are described here.

AIRCRAFT OWNERS AND PILOTS ASSOCIATION

Aircraft Owners and Pilots Association (AOPA) is a nonprofit organization dedicated to general aviation. AOPA provides a wide variety of benefits to their members including pilot information, legal services, and loan programs, as well as pilot and aircraft insurance. In addition, the AOPA Air Safety Foundation sponsors safety seminars and clinics.

EXPERIMENTAL AIRCRAFT ASSOCIATION

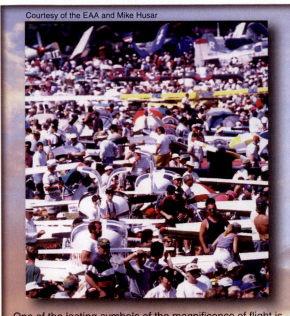

Courtesy of the EAA and Mike Husar

One of the lasting symbols of the magnificence of flight is the airshow and the EAA sponsors one of the world's greatest. Each year, hundreds of thousands of aviation enthusiasts converge on the town of Oshkosh, Wisconsin to experience the best aviation has to offer.

The **Experimental Aircraft Association (EAA)**, which was founded in 1953 by a dozen aircraft homebuilders, has grown to be one of the most significant forces in general aviation. In addition to homebuilt aircraft, the EAA has divisions which include antique aircraft, warbirds, aerobatic airplanes, and ultralights. The EAA is a leader in aviation education, and provides inspiration for innovative ideas in aircraft design, construction, and flight technique.

Burt Rutan who designed the *Voyager* aircraft also is the designer of one of the most popular homebuilts, the VariEze. As quoted in the EAA publication *Sport Aviation*, Rutan expressed the following thoughts on aviation, Oshkosh, and the EAA:

I hope in the not too distant future . . . that my Oshkosh trip will be about a half an hour, and half of that time will be spent outside the atmosphere, just coasting along . . . getting ready for re-entry over Oshkosh. That sounds a little crazy, but it's not. It's much sooner than you think. We're at a period when the barnstormer, entrepreneur and businessman are gonna get into space . . . So I'm looking forward to it and I can see an EAA moving forever upward doing more and more exciting things . . . we are no where near our limits.

THE NINETY-NINES, INC.

The Ninety-Nines, Inc. is an international organization of women pilots with members from 35 countries. The mission of The Ninety-Nines is to promote fellowship through flight, to provide networking and scholarship opportunities for women, sponsor aviation education in the community, and to preserve the unique history of women in aviation.

Courtesy of The Ninety-Nines Inc. International Organization of Women Pilots Archive Collection, Oklahoma City, Oklahoma

On November 2, 1929, twenty-six women gathered in a hangar at Curtiss Airport in New York to form an organization for women pilots. Membership would be open to any woman holding a pilot's certificate. The club's goals included promoting fellowship, locating aviation jobs, and maintaining a central office with files on women in aviation. Some suggestions for a club name included The Climbing Vines, Noisy Birdwomen, Homing Pigeons, and Gadflies. Amelia Earhart and Jean Davis Hoyt proposed that the name be taken from the sum total of the charter members. The group was briefly called the Eighty-Sixes, then The Ninety-Sevens and finally the Ninety-Nines. In 1931, Amelia Earhart became the organization's first elected president.

Women must try to do things as men have tried. When they fail their failure must be but a challenge to others.

— Amelia Earhart

Courtesy of Civil Air Patrol

CIVIL AIR PATROL

In 1946, President Truman declared the **Civil Air Patrol (CAP)** a benevolent, nonprofit organization with three primary missions: Aerospace Education, Cadet Programs, and Emergency Services. In 1948, the CAP became an all-volunteer auxiliary of the U.S. Air Force. The Civil Air Patrol operates one of the world's largest fleets of civil aircraft and one-third of all CAP members are FAA-certificated pilots. Approximately 90 percent of all search and rescue missions issued by the Air Force Rescue Coordination Center are performed by CAP volunteers. The CAP also plays a vital role in national disaster relief and CAP pilots fly drug interdiction reconnaissance missions on behalf of several government agencies.

The CAP Cadet Program provides young people the opportunity to develop leadership skills through their interest in flight and many CAP cadets pursue aviation careers. For example, each year approximately 10 percent of the U.S. Air Force Academy appointees are former CAP cadets. In addition, CAP provides aerospace education materials and workshops to thousands of teachers at universities throughout the nation.

The Civil Air Patrol was organized on December 1, 1941, as part of the U.S. Office of Civil Defense. During World War II, CAP pilots flew more than 24 million miles on coastal patrol and summoned assistance for 91 ships in distress. These CAP missions helped save the lives of 363 survivors of submarine attacks.

Courtesy of Civil Air Patrol

AIRPLANE TRANSITIONS

There is an enormous variety of airplanes to explore, and a transition to another make and model of airplane can be one of the most fascinating aspects of flying. To safely pilot an unfamiliar airplane, it is essential that you receive training in the new make and model. This transition training is often referred to as an **aircraft checkout**.

By studying the pilot's operating handbook, and during discussions with your instructor, you will become familiar with the airplane's systems, performance, and limitations. During flight training, you will practice normal and emergency procedures and learn how to safely control the airplane in all phases of flight. Whether you own or rent an airplane, insurance companies normally require that you have a specific number of hours of instruction in the make and model of airplane before you can fly it as pilot in command.

HIGH PERFORMANCE AIRPLANES

If you desire faster cruising speeds and increased performance, or you want to master more complex systems, a checkout in a high performance or complex airplane is the solution. A **high performance airplane**, as defined by the FARs, has an engine with more than 200 horsepower. A **complex airplane** has retractable landing gear, flaps, and a controllable-pitch propeller. To act as pilot in command of an airplane which meets either of these specifications or both, you must receive instruction and a logbook endorsement stating that you are competent to pilot a high performance or complex airplane as the case may be. In addition to areas covered in any aircraft checkout, training in high performance or complex airplanes will focus on the operation of systems which are new to you, such as the retractable landing gear.

Now, there are two ways of learning to ride a fractious horse: one is to get on him and learn by actual practice how each motion and trick may be best met; the other is to sit on a fence and watch the beast a while, and then retire to the house and at leisure figure out the best way of overcoming his jumps and kicks. The latter system is the safest; but the former, on the whole, turns out the larger proportion of good riders. It is very much the same in learning to ride a flying machine; if you are looking for perfect safety, you will do well to sit on a fence and watch the birds; but if you really wish to learn, you must mount a machine and become acquainted with its tricks by actual ritual.

— Wilbur Wright

September 28, 1920 — Aviators met in France to compete for the annual Gorden Bennett Cup. The Dayton-Wright R.B. Racer, flown by American pilot Howard Rinehart caused a sensation as spectators watched the wheels disappear into the airplane's belly. It was the first time an airplane had been constructed with retractable landing gear to decrease drag and increase its performance. Unfortunately, a rudder cable broke after Rinehart's first lap and he had to land and concede the race.

TAILWHEEL AIRPLANES

Learning to fly a tailwheel, or conventional gear, airplane presents a new challenge to many pilots trained in tricycle gear aircraft. To act as pilot in command of a tailwheel airplane, you are required to obtain training in specific pilot operations outlined in the FARs. A logbook endorsement from a qualified flight instructor must state that you have achieved competency in normal and crosswind takeoffs and landings, wheel landings (unless the manufacturer has recommended against such landings), and go-around procedures.

A vast array of conventional gear airplanes exist in the world of aviation. A tailwheel checkout is a perfect way for you to expand your airplane options, and can be the first step toward aerobatic training.

HOMEBUILT AIRCRAFT

While building your own aircraft can be an extremely satisfying experience, it also requires hard work and a substantial commitment of time and resources. You can con-

Courtesy of Van's Aircraft, Inc.

struct a **homebuilt aircraft** from scratch using wood, fabric, metal, and composite material, or you can purchase a kit which requires assembly of larger components. Although there may be hundreds of completed aircraft of a particular design, no two homebuilts are ever the same. Builders add an individual touch to their aircraft which makes each one unique. The spectrum of homebuilt aircraft range from very light airplanes which cruise at 50 mph to composite airplanes which reach speeds of 350 mph.

You can request FAA certification of your homebuilt airplane as an experimental, amateur-built aircraft. The FAA certification process requires documentation of the construction process, aircraft inspections, and specific test flights. Since flying characteristics of homebuilt aircraft can vary widely, effective training requires an instructor which has considerable flight experience in the same type of aircraft. To obtain information on building and flying home-built aircraft, you can contact the local chapter of the Experimental Aircraft Association or your local FAA Flight Standards District Office.

> You may want to ask yourself these questions before committing to the construction of your own airplane.
>
> • Do I have the experience to do the work?
>
> • Do I have the money and time to complete the project?
>
> • Where am I going to construct the aircraft?
>
> • Do I have my family's support for the project?

ADDITIONAL PILOT RATINGS

The FARs describe several ratings which may be added to your private pilot certificate; the instrument rating which will introduce you to new procedures and flight operations, and class ratings which will allow you to expand your airplane options. Type ratings are required for turbojet aircraft, aircraft which weigh more than 12,500 pounds, certain helicopter operations, and other aircraft which are specified by the FAA during certification procedures.

INSTRUMENT RATING

The addition of an **instrument rating** is an option that allows you to fly in a wider range of weather conditions, and increases your skill at precisely controlling the aircraft. As a private pilot without an instrument rating, you must fly under visual flight rules (VFR) conditions. To remain in VFR conditions, the FARs require that you maintain a specific flight visibility and that your aircraft is operated a certain distance from clouds. Operating under instrument flight rules (IFR) allows you to fly in the clouds with no reference to the ground or horizon.

Among other requirements, you must have at least 40 hours of instrument flight time to obtain an instrument rating. To accumulate the required flight time, you will train with a view limiting device. This device restricts your view outside the aircraft so that you maintain reference only to the cockpit instruments. Since instrument procedures are much different than VFR operations, you are required to pass a knowledge test and practical test to add the instrument rating to your certificate.

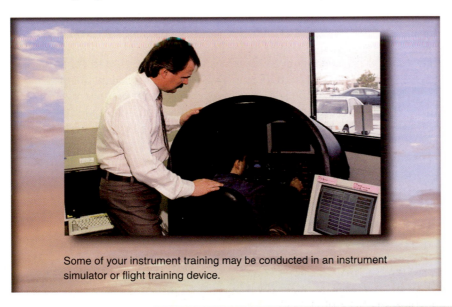

Some of your instrument training may be conducted in an instrument simulator or flight training device.

On September 24, 1929, Jimmy Doolittle made the world's first blind flight in a Consolidated NY-2. Army Lt. Benjamin Kelsey rode in the front cockpit as Doolittle piloted the airplane from the closed back cockpit. Doolittle was guided only by his gauges which included three new aviation instruments: a Kollsman precision altimeter, a Sperry Gyrocompass, and a Sperry artificial horizon. Doolittle also used special radio receivers to guide him from takeoff to landing at Mitchell Field, Long Island. Lt. Kelsey never had to touch the controls.

AIRPLANE CLASS RATINGS

Adding a multi-engine rating or a seaplane rating to your certificate can be an exciting way to explore new airplanes without requiring a substantial amount of training time.

MULTI-ENGINE RATING

If you are pursuing a career in aviation, the **multi-engine rating** is an essential requirement for most flying jobs. There are no specific ground or flight instruction hours required for the addition of the multi-engine rating, but you will have to pass a practical

test. Typically, the training can be completed in a short period of time, but most aircraft insurance policies require that you obtain a substantial amount of multi-engine flight time before operating the airplane as pilot in command. To accumulate the necessary experience, you may be able to share flight time and expenses with a qualified pilot who meets the insurance requirements.

SEAPLANE RATING

Seaplanes conjure up images of flying to exotic and distant locations that other humans haven't yet encountered. Although you may never be the first individual to set foot on the shores of a remote jungle lagoon, as a seaplane pilot, you may rediscover some of the romance of flight when you touch down on the glassy surface of a clear mountain lake.

> The first man in history to devise an aircraft capable of lifting off and landing on water was a French marine engineer named Henry Fabre. Fabre's flight on March 28, 1910, marked the first successful water takeoff and landing.

Seaplanes can have twin floats or can be designed with a single main float plus small wing floats or similar lateral supports. The single-main-float seaplane is frequently referred to as a flying boat. A twin float seaplane is known as a floatplane. In addition, when a seaplane is equipped with wheels, it becomes an amphibian, which is capable of operating from land or water. Learning to fly a seaplane is an easy transition for most pilots. Your pilot training will focus on the characteristics of water and its effect on the seaplane. There is no minimum number of flight hours required to add a **single-engine sea rating** or **multi-engine sea rating** to your private pilot certificate, but you must pass a practical test. To determine what lakes or other water surfaces are legal for seaplane operations, the Seaplane Pilot's Association (SPA) publishes an all-inclusive listing in the *Water Landing Directory*.

CATEGORY AND CLASS RATINGS

Once you have experienced the thrill of flight behind the controls of an airplane, you may want to spread your wings and explore a new category and class of aircraft.

ROTORCRAFT — HELICOPTER RATING

The principal difference between an airplane and a **helicopter** is how each aircraft develops lift. The airplane's source of lift is derived from the wing which is a fixed surface, while the helicopter derives lift from a rotating surface called the rotor. Aircraft are classified as either fixed-wing or rotating-wing. Lift generation by a rotating wing enables the helicopter to accomplish its unique mission of hovering.

Helicopters are one of the most maneuverable types of aircraft, and while hovering, the helicopter can be moved in every possible direction or combination of directions. Flying a helicopter requires precise control inputs and coordination from the pilot. To add a rotorcraft category rating with a helicopter class rating to your private pilot certificate,

you must have a minimum of 40 hours of flight time which includes at least 20 hours of dual instruction in helicopters and at least 10 hours of solo flight in helicopters and you must pass a practical test.

An advantage to the helicopter is its ability to take off and land in a confined or restricted area. Helicopters are used in a variety of commercial operations such as corporate transport, pipeline laying and patrolling, news and traffic reporting, aerial photography, sightseeing tours, and general police work. In addition, helicopters play an important role in the oil, timber, and agriculture industries.

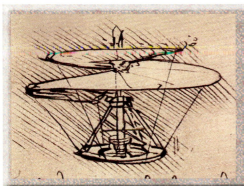

In the 15th century, Leonardo da Vinci made sketches of a helicopter design which was to be composed of wood, reeds, and tafetta. The vehicle had a screw-type thread on a vertical shaft, which if properly shaped and powered, would be able to takeoff vertically, hover, and land. Nearly 500 years later, on November 13, 1907, a two-rotor helicopter built by Paul Cornu lifted a man off the ground during a flight test in France, but it would be another 30 years until practical helicopters were actually in use.

Courtesy of The Boeing Company

The role of rotor equipment in the aviation industry may be considerably expanded with the use of the tilt-rotor aircraft. This powered-lift category aircraft combines the hovering capability and vertical takeoffs and landings of helicopters with the horizontal flight of airplanes. Some tilt-rotor aircraft can reach cruise speeds of close to 300 mph.

WHAT IS A GYROPLANE?

Gyroplanes are rotating-wing aircraft which generate lift as the aircraft's forward movement drives air up through the rotor blades. Most gyroplanes are home-built from kits, have only one or two seats, and few have radios or lights. To add a gyroplane class rating to your private pilot certificate you must pass a practical test after obtaining a minimum of 20 hours of dual instruction in gyroplanes and at least 10 hours of solo flight in gyroplanes.

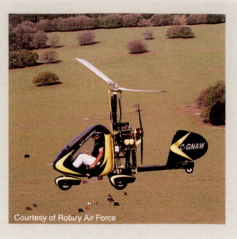

Courtesy of Rotary Air Force

GLIDER RATING

If you are seeking a new challenge, yet want to remain with a fixed-wing air-craft, a **glider rating** is an excellent transition. A glider allows you to soar with the hawks, and share thermals with the eagles. Gliders are unpowered and typically are towed by an airplane to a source of good thermal activity or they also can be launched using an auto or winch tow.

To add a glider rating to your private pilot certificate, the FARs require a total of 40 hours of flight time as a pilot in a heaver-than-air aircraft with at least 3 hours of flight training in a glider and 10 solo flights. The glider rating does not require a knowledge test, provided you hold a powered category rating.

LIGHTER-THAN-AIR — BALLOON RATING

From the first manned flight in 1783 to the present, pilots have relished the quiet, tranquil sensation of floating aloft in a balloon. The **hot air balloon** is the most common of the three types of balloons; gas, hot air, and Rozier (combination gas/hot air). The hot air balloon rises due to the fact that as the air inside the balloon is heated, it becomes less dense than the outside air. Balloons usually fly within two to three hours of sunrise or sunset when the air is cool, the winds are calm, and conditions are most stable.

To obtain a lighter-than-air certificate with a balloon rating, you must accumulate a total of ten hours of flight training that includes at least six training flights. There is no knowledge test requirement for a fixed-wing pilot, but you must pass a practical test. To find a qualified balloon instructor, you can contact the Balloon Federation of America (BFA), the world's largest organization of balloonists. The BFA can provide you with a list of balloonists who participate in the Master Instruction program.

To share the experience with the passengers, crew, and spectators, balloonists traditionally end each flight with a toast of champagne, a practice dating back to the 1700s.

Many balloon students get their start by being part of the balloon crew. A two or three person crew helps the pilot rig the balloon, holds open the envelope as it fills with air, and applies weight to the outside of the basket before the launch. The crew then follows by car, and after the balloon lands, helps the pilot pack up.

Courtesy of Kolb Aircraft, Inc.

WHAT IS AN ULTRALIGHT?

An ultralight is a flying vehicle which is intended for recreation or sport only. It must have an empty weight of less than 155 pounds if unpowered, and less than 254 pounds if powered. It can not be capable of holding more than 5 gallons of fuel or attaining a speed of more than 55 knots at full power. Ultralights are not certificated by the FAA and do not require an FAA certificated pilot. Students and operators are responsible for their own training and safety.

ADDITIONAL PILOT CERTIFICATES

COMMERCIAL PILOT

Obtaining the **commercial pilot certificate** is the first step toward a professional pilot career. As stated in the FARs, the privileges of a commercial pilot certificate include the ability to "act as pilot in command of an aircraft carrying persons or property for hire." However, the types of commercial operations which you can perform are limited unless you receive additional training beyond the commercial certificate.

To apply for a commercial pilot certificate, you must meet fairly substantial flight time requirements. Depending on the type of pilot school you attend, a total of 190 to 250 hours of flight time is required, which normally includes a minimum of 100 hours of pilot-in-command time and 50 hours of cross-country time. In addition, you must have 10 hours of flight training in an airplane that has retractable landing gear, flaps, and a controllable pitch propeller. To become a commercial pilot, you must pass a knowledge test and complete a practical test on precision flight maneuvers.

During commercial training, you will perform several maneuvers which require a high level of proficiency in advanced planning, accuracy, coordination, and smoothness. For example, the chandelle, a climbing 180° turn, involves changes in pitch, airspeed, and control surface pressures.

CERTIFICATED FLIGHT INSTRUCTOR

To become a certificated flight instructor (CFI), you must continue training beyond the commercial certificate. Your instruction will focus on aspects of teaching which include the learning process, student evaluation, and lesson planning. There is no specific number of flight hours specified for CFI training, but you are required to pass two knowledge exams and a practical test.

AIRLINE TRANSPORT PILOT

You must hold an **airline transport pilot certificate (ATP)** to operate as an airline captain. To apply for an ATP certificate, you must be at least 23 years of age. The flight time requirements to obtain an ATP certificate are demanding: a total of 1,500 hours of flight time including 250 hours of pilot-in-command time, 500 hours of cross-country time, 100 hours of night flight, and 75 hours of instrument experience. The ATP knowledge test emphasizes subjects such as navigation, meteorology, aircraft performance, and air carrier flight procedures. During the practical test, your instrument skills will be evaluated, as well as your ability to correctly perform emergency procedures.

Courtesy of The Boeing Company

WHAT IS A RECREATIONAL PILOT CERTIFICATE?

For some pilots, the **recreational pilot certificate** is a good choice as a stepping stone toward a private pilot certificate. Recreational pilot training is not as extensive as that required for the private pilot certificate, but the recreational pilot has fewer privileges and more restrictions. For example, recreational pilots are restricted to small single-engine aircraft and only can operate within a 50 nautical mile radius from their local airport unless they receive a logbook endorsement from an instructor. In addition, recreational pilots cannot carry more than one passenger nor operate at night.

> *It is my belief that flight is possible and, while I am taking up the investigation for pleasure rather than profit, I think there is a slight possibility of achieving fame and fortune from it.*
>
> — Wilbur Wright

AVIATION CAREERS

Some pilots transform flying as a hobby into flying as a career. To choose between sitting behind the controls of an airplane and sitting behind a desk may not be as easy as it sounds. The pursuit of an aviation career requires a solid commitment of time, energy, and financial resources. However, as most professional pilots will tell you, the rewards of a flying career are worth the hard work and dedication.

In the early days of aviation, finding employment as a pilot was not a simple task. In 1919, European commercial airlines provided jobs for many World War I fliers, but the airline system had not yet developed in the United States. American pilots often had to choose between the unstable life of a barnstormer and the dangerous career of flying the mail.

> *A career in flying was like climbing one of those ancient Babylonian pyramids made up of a dizzy progression of steps and ledges, a ziggurat, a pyramid extraordinarily high and steep; and the idea was to prove at every foot of the way up that pyramid that you were one of the elected and anointed ones who had the right stuff and could move higher and higher and even — ultimately, God willing, one day — that you might be able to join that special few at the very top . . .*
>
> — *The Right Stuff* by Tom Wolfe

The United States Airmail Service was founded in 1918 and was operated by the government for nine years. An airmail pilot's life expectancy was four years, and thirty-one of the first forty pilots were killed before the service was turned over to private industry. While the Airmail Service was in operation, one in every six pilots was killed in a flying accident while delivering the mail.

It was the spring of 1920. There has not been a great deal of airmail flying, and the pilots were getting killed almost as fast as the Post Office Department could employ them . . . So the airmail was considered pretty much a suicide club, and only pilots desperate to fly would join it. But the pay was excellent. We were soon making from $800 to $1,000 a month, and in the early twenties this was really a tremendous amount of money.

— Dean Smith, United States airmail pilot in 1920, as quoted in *The American Heritage History of Flight*

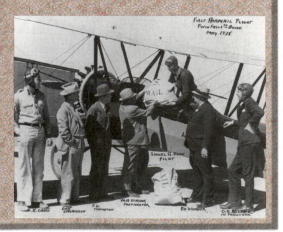

Today, a primary concern of the aviation industry is flight safety, and highly trained professional pilots utilize their skills in a wide variety of fields.

- Air taxi and charter operations fly passengers or cargo during scheduled flights or provide on-call services.
- Aircraft sales representatives deliver aircraft from the factory to the dealer or from the dealer to the customer, as well as demonstrate aircraft.
- Land survey and photography services provide businesses and government agencies with information about commercial property, highways, mining operations, and drilling sites.
- In addition to providing a unique view of metropolitan areas and natural wonders, sightseeing services fly tourists over scenic areas which may be hard to reach by other means.

- Powerline and pipeline patrol flight operations consist of checking powerlines, towers, and pipelines for damage, as well as transporting repair crews.
- Air ambulance operations transport patients to health care facilities for specialized treatment. Helicopter pilots with trained paramedics on board carry critically ill or injured persons from accident scenes to hospitals.
- Specialized agencies fly food, supplies, and medical workers to areas affected by disasters.
- Environmental services employ trained pilots to perform such operations as fire fighting and wildlife surveying.
- Test flying involves checking aircraft systems at various stages of design and production to make sure equipment meets safety and performance specifications.

Law enforcement agencies use aircraft for traffic surveys, and search and rescue missions, as well as border and coastline patrol.

News agencies often use aircraft to transport reporters to sites of accidents or crimes, and for reporting traffic or special events.

- Various companies employ pilots to perform such services as banner towing, glider towing, and transporting parachute jumpers.
- The FAA employs pilots as safety inspectors, test pilots, and airspace inspection pilots.

Courtesy of Eagle Jet Charter, Las Vegas, Nevada

Courtesy of J.J. Johnson

FLIGHT INSTRUCTING

Many career-oriented pilots use flight instruction as a stepping stone to enhance their professional qualifications. For example, a substantial amount of flight experience must be gained to apply for most flying jobs, and as a flight instructor, you can accumulate flight time as you earn money. This does not mean that flight instructors are not dedicated professionals who take the job of teaching very seriously. Some instructors focus on instruction for beginning students, while others expand their instructing privileges to include teaching instrument or multi-engine students. Many pilots have established careers in other fields, but find part-time flight instructing an extremely satisfying part of their lives.

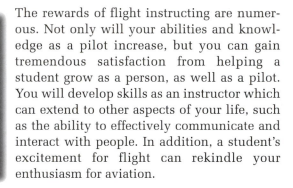

As a flight instructor you can be self-employed or apply for a position at a pilot training school. While many flight instructors are paid per flight hour, you may earn a salary and receive benefits if employed at a larger pilot training facility. One advantage to many flight instructor positions is your ability to determine your own lesson schedule.

The rewards of flight instructing are numerous. Not only will your abilities and knowledge as a pilot increase, but you can gain tremendous satisfaction from helping a student grow as a person, as well as a pilot. You will develop skills as an instructor which can extend to other aspects of your life, such as the ability to effectively communicate and interact with people. In addition, a student's excitement for flight can rekindle your enthusiasm for aviation.

REGIONAL AIRLINES

Many pilots view flying for a regional, or commuter, airline as a way to enhance their qualifications while working toward an airline position. As a pilot for a **regional airline** you will be flying advanced turboprop or small jet aircraft during scheduled passenger-carrying flights. This type of flying can prove to be an excellent training ground for the airlines.

Regional airlines hire pilots with a variety of backgrounds and flight experience. While some companies will hire pilots with fairly low flight time and allow them to upgrade as they build experience, others prefer co-pilots with sufficient skills to upgrade to captain in a short period of time.

To qualify for a position as a pilot at a regional airline, you should accumulate as much total flight time, pilot-in-command time, and multi-engine time as possible. In addition, the ATP certificate will strengthen your credentials.

MAJOR AIRLINES

Flying for a **major airline** is a rewarding career which requires a serious commitment and hard work. Hiring qualifications for major airlines vary as the job market shifts. While each airline has specific minimum requirements, you must achieve competitive qualifications for the market at the time. The qualifications for an airline pilot position can be divided into four categories:

Courtesy of The Boeing Company

1. Flight experience — Most pilots hired by major airlines have regional airline, corporate, or military flight experience. As the number of qualified pilots grows, the average total flight time expected by the airlines increases. Multi-engine, turboprop, or jet time accumulated by flying in the military or in commercial operations is more impressive to an airline employer than recreational flight time.

2. Certificates and ratings — You must hold at least a commercial pilot certificate with instrument and multi-engine ratings. Most airlines also prefer that you hold an ATP certificate since this is a requirement to become an airline captain. In addition, you must hold a first-class medical and have a passing score on the flight engineer knowledge test.

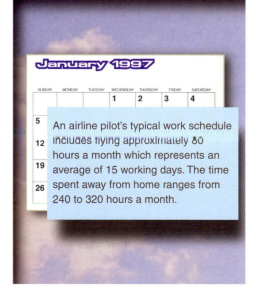

An airline pilot's typical work schedule includes flying approximately 80 hours a month which represents an average of 15 working days. The time spent away from home ranges from 240 to 320 hours a month.

3. Education — At a minimum, your credentials should include a four-year college degree. The airlines do not require a particular degree or major area of study.

4. Interview skills — During an airline interview you will be evaluated on how well you communicate, your leadership skills, and your ability to perform as a crewmember. Typically, you also will have to pass a stringent medical exam and your flying skills will be assessed during a simulator flight.

One of the first commercial passenger services in the U.S. used a combination of airline and railroad transportation. Passengers left New York City's Pennsylvania Station by train and traveled to Columbus, Ohio where they boarded a Ford Trimotor transport for a flight to Waynoka, Oklahoma. Upon arrival in Waynoka, the passengers boarded a train which took them to Clovis, New Mexico. A Ford Trimotor delivered them to their final destination on the west coast. This service reduced travel time from the east coast to the west coast from 72 hours to 48 hours. Today, a Boeing 767 makes the journey nonstop in 6 hours.

CORPORATE FLYING

Corporate flying offers some unique benefits. Typically there are few layovers, and flying on holidays is rare. A benefit offered by some corporations is the opportunity to bring a spouse along for any extended layovers. While some corporate flight departments operate regularly scheduled flights, most have very few prescheduled trips and pilots are on-call most of each month.

Corporate airplanes can range from a single-engine Cessna 172 to jet aircraft such as a Gulfstream IV. Most corporate jobs are not advertised and pilots are hired upon referral by another pilot. Although most corporations prefer that you have experience in the type of aircraft operated by the company, your lack of experience may not be a factor if you have been recommended by a pilot within the corporation. Typically, the minimum pilot qualifications for corporate flying include a commercial pilot certificate with an instrument rating and a multi-engine rating. An ATP certificate and type rating in a jet or turboprop airplane are preferred by many corporations.

Courtesy of Cessna Aircraft

Courtesy of Falcon Dassault

AERIAL APPLICATION

In the United States, there are over 2,000 agricultural aircraft operators flying over 6,000 aircraft. **Aerial application**, or crop dusting, provides farmers with seeding, pollinating, and control over damaging insects and weeds. Pilots working as aerial applicators should have a knowledge of chemistry, agriculture, and aviation. Many aerial applicators have a degree in agriculture or chemical engineering. To become employed as an aerial applicator you must hold a commercial pilot certificate and receive additional training in agricultural aircraft operations.

Huff-Daland Dusters, Inc., formed in 1923, was the first commercial agricultural flying operation in the United States. With a 50-foot wingspan and a 400-hp Liberty engine, Huff-Daland's biplane, the Petrel, could carry up to 1,000 pounds of insecticide. In 1928, Huff-Daland was sold and renamed Delta Air Service. The company expanded its operations to include transporting passengers and parcels and eventually gave up agricultural operations. To reflect its new air transportation business, the company again changed its name to Delta Air Lines.

Courtesy of Air Tractor

Courtesy of Air Tractor

MILITARY AVIATION

The United States military offers a wide variety of aviation career opportunities. The Army, Navy, Air Force, and Marines provide extensive and demanding pilot training in some of the most technologically advanced aircraft in the world.

As a candidate for military pilot training, you must meet specific academic qualifications, demonstrate certain physical abilities, and possess strong leadership skills. In addition, you must be willing to commit to a specified service obligation at the completion of your training. While many pilots choose a career in the military, others find that the flight training and experience gained during military service are excellent preparation for similar jobs in civilian life.

The Harrier aircraft is the most successful V/STOL (vertical/short takeoff and landing) aircraft currently in service. The McDonnell Douglas AV-8 Harrier is operated by the U.S. Marine Corps and its primary function is to attack and destroy surface targets. The AV-8 is propelled by one Rolls-Royce turbofan engine which incorporates four exhaust nozzles. The nozzles are rotatable 98° from the full-aft position. Vertical takeoff is accomplished by vectoring the thrust of the engine downward. To transition to horizontal flight, the exhaust nozzles are rotated slowly rearward and once sufficient forward speed is obtained for wing lift to support the airplane, the nozzles are rotated fully aft.

Courtesy of McDonnell Douglas

Courtesy of U.S. Coast Guard

Vessels traveling the great circle shipping lanes in the North Atlantic pass through an area near the Grand Banks of Newfoundland which has a high potential for iceberg collisions. This area is particularly dangerous due to the combination of shipping traffic, fishing vessels, icebergs, fog, and severe storms. In 1912, 1,517 persons perished when the R.M.S. Titanic sunk after striking an iceberg in this vicinity.

Flying Hercules HC-130s, the Coast Guard's International Ice Patrol provides a service to monitor the extent of iceberg danger in the North Atlantic. Patrol time for the HC-130 is between 5 to 7 hours with each flight covering an expanse of water 30,000 square miles or more.

THE COAST GUARD

The U.S Coast Guard also conducts extensive flight operations as the principal federal agency with maritime authority for the United States. In peacetime, the Coast Guard is part of the Department of Transportation, but during wartime, it operates under the Department of Defense. The four primary missions of the Coast Guard are maritime law enforcement, maritime safety, marine environmental protection, and national security.

All experiences of your life are training and developing for your next level of expertise.

— Jeana Yeager, co-pilot of *Voyager*, the first aircraft to fly nonstop around the world without refueling.

MORE AVIATION CAREERS

Your interest in flight may lead to a career in the aviation industry which does not require you to pilot an aircraft. For example, airlines employ flight dispatchers, flight attendants, ticket agents, and ramp service personnel. Airport managers, linepersons, and fixed base operators are just some of the jobs which can be explored at an airport. Aircraft manufacturing provides jobs for scientists, engineers and technicians who specialize in aircraft design and construction. You may be interested in pursuing a career as an aircraft maintenance or avionics technician. In addition, the government employs air traffic controllers, meteorologists, and flight service station control specialists. These are just a few of the occupations which you can pursue in the field of aviation, and obtaining a pilot certificate greatly enhances your job qualifications. So what are you waiting for?

SUMMARY CHECKLIST

✓ Frequent refresher training is essential to keep your flying skills sharp and to keep you informed on current pilot information.

✓ Mountain flying requires proper training since special considerations have to be made for weather, airport operations, course selection, and aircraft performance.

✓ Aerobatics instruction increases your proficiency as a pilot. While there are no specific flight hour training requirements to operate an aircraft in aerobatic flight, the FARs do place certain restrictions on aerobatic maneuvers.

✓ Aviation organizations such as AOPA, the EAA, The Ninety-Nines Inc., and the CAP sponsor flying activities, promote safety, and furnish pilot information.

✓ The FARs require that you receive training and a logbook endorsement stating competency before you can operate as pilot in command of either a high performance airplane or tailwheel airplane.

✓ To obtain an instrument rating, you are required to have a least 40 hours of instrument flight time as well as pass a knowledge test and practical test.

✓ There are no specific ground or flight instruction hours required for the addition of a multi-engine rating to your certificate, but you will have to pass a practical test.

✓ To obtain a seaplane rating, your pilot training will focus on the characteristics of water and its effect on the seaplane.

✓ To pilot aircraft such as helicopters, gliders, or hot air balloons, you will need to obtain an appropriate category and class rating.

✓ To apply for a commercial pilot certificate, you must accumulate a total of 190 to 250 hours of flight time (depending on the type of pilot school that you attend) which typically include a minimum of 100 hours of pilot-in-command time and 50 hours of cross-country time.

✓ There is no specific number of flight hours specified for CFI training, but you are required to pass two knowledge exams and a practical test.

✓ The flight time requirements to obtain an ATP certificate are a total of 1,500 hours of flight time including 250 hours of pilot-in-command time, 500 hours of cross-country time, 100 hours of night flight, and 75 hours of instrument experience.

✓ If you are seeking a position with a regional airline, you should accumulate as much total flight time, pilot-in-command time, and multi-engine time as possible.

✓ To obtain a position as an airline pilot, you must meet specific minimum requirements, and competitive qualifications which vary as the job market shifts.

✓ Typically, the minimum pilot qualifications to fly as a corporate pilot include a commercial pilot certificate with an instrument rating and a multi-engine rating.

✓ To become employed as an aerial applicator you must hold a commercial pilot certificate and receive additional training in agricultural aircraft operations.

✓ The Army, Navy, Air Force and Marines provide extensive and demanding pilot training in some of the most technologically advanced aircraft in the world.

KEY TERMS

Refresher Training

Mountain Flying

Aerobatic Flight Training

Aircraft Owners and Pilots
Association (AOPA)

Experimental Aircraft Association
(EAA)

The Ninety-Nines, Inc.

Civil Air Patrol (CAP)

Aircraft Checkout

High Performance Airplane

Complex Airplane

Homebuilt Aircraft

Instrument Rating

Multi-Engine Rating

Single-Engine Sea Rating

Multi-Engine Sea Rating

Helicopter

Glider Rating

Hot Air Balloon

Commercial Pilot Certificate

Airline Transport Pilot Certificate
(ATP)

Recreational Pilot Certificate

Regional Airline

Major Airline

Corporate Flying

Aerial Application

SECTION C
INTRODUCTION TO HUMAN FACTORS

There is more to pilot training than acquiring technical knowledge and gaining proficiency in aircraft control. Understanding how your mind and body function when you fly is as important as knowing the operation of your airplane's systems and equipment. The goal of human factors training for pilots is to increase aviation safety by optimizing human performance and reducing human error. Instruction in human factors principles focuses on explaining how performance is affected by elements such as the interaction between individuals within the aviation environment, emotions, and human physiology. Learning human factors concepts is essential to becoming a safe and effective pilot and is an important part of comprehensive pilot training.

This section provides a foundation for further exploration of human factors in aviation. The Human Element Insets located throughout this manual help you to correlate human factors concepts to specific pilot operations and expand upon the fundamental principles introduced in this section. Chapter 10 provides a more extensive examination of the application of human factors concepts and their impact on you as a pilot and the aviation community.

AERONAUTICAL DECISION MAKING

In the early years of aviation, there was little else to rely on but perseverance and luck to get a pilot safely to his or her destination. Compared with the advanced systems of today, aircraft equipment was extremely primitive, less redundant, and more prone to failure. There were no services such as air traffic control, or facilities which provided comprehensive weather briefings. The majority of accidents were the result of mechanical difficulties or weather conditions which were so severe that the pilot's skills were not sufficient to cope with the situation.

Aviation's safety record steadily improved as technology progressed. Today, aircraft are equipped with sophisticated equipment and systems, a multitude of aviation services exist, and pilot skills have increased through advanced training methods. Yet accidents still occur. Why? Despite all the changes in aviation, one factor has remained the same; the human factor. It is now estimated that approximately 75 percent of all aviation accidents are human factors related.

Historically, the term *pilot error* has been used to describe the causes of these accidents. Pilot error means that an action or decision made by the pilot was the cause of, or contributing factor which lead to, the accident. This definition also includes failure of the pilot to make a decision or take action. From a broader perspective, the phrase *human factors related* more aptly describes these accidents since it usually is not a single decision made by the pilot which leads to an accident, but a chain of events which is triggered by a number of factors.

CREW RESOURCE MANAGEMENT TRAINING

These four accidents were the prime motivators which led the airline industry to implement human factors training called **crew resource management (CRM)**. The focus of CRM programs is the effective use of all available resources; human resources, hardware,

> We had to find our way from one place to another mostly by sight and contact flying, and, of course, in those days we had a great deal of engine trouble, which caused the forced landing to be a fairly common occurrence.
>
> — Alan Campbell Orde, British air transport pilot who served in 1919, as quoted in *The American Heritage History of Flight*

1972, Eastern, L-1011, Miami — The aircraft descended into the Everglades while the crew was distracted trying to resolve a landing gear problem which turned out to be a burned-out bulb.

1977, Pan American and KLM, both B-747s, Tenerife, Canary Islands — During the takeoff roll, the KLM airplane collided with the Pan American 747 due to a mix-up in communications.

1978, United, DC-8, Portland — The aircraft ran out of fuel and crashed short of the runway due to confusion among the crew about the status of the landing gear, and a breakdown in cockpit communications about the fuel state.

1982, Air Florida, B-737, Washington National — The aircraft crashed shortly after takeoff due to airframe and engine icing. The co-pilot expressed concern about the flight situation prior to, and during, the takeoff roll.

and information. Human resources include all groups routinely working with the cockpit crew (or pilot) who are involved in decisions which are required to operate a flight safely. These groups include, but are not limited to: dispatchers, cabin crewmembers, maintenance personnel, and air traffic controllers.

In addition to the effective use of resources, CRM training encompasses human factors principles such as workload management, situational awareness, communication, the leadership role of the captain, and crewmember coordination. Many of these concepts apply to the general aviation community as well. The goal of human factors training is increased safety, and this objective can be met by teaching accurate, effective decision making.

THE DECISION-MAKING PROCESS

Problem definition is the first step in the decision-making process. Defining the problem begins with recognizing that a change has occurred or that an expected change did not occur. You perceive a problem by using your senses, insight, and experience. You then use these same abilities, as well as objective analysis of all available information, to determine the exact nature and severity of the problem.

After you have identified the problem, you evaluate the need to react to it and determine the actions which may be taken to resolve the situation in the time available. The expected outcome of each possible action is considered and the risks assessed before deciding on a response to the situation. After you have implemented your decision, its outcome is evaluated to determine if additional steps need to be taken.

When the decision-making process is applied to flight operations it is termed **aeronautical decision making (ADM)**. Your ability to make effective decisions as a pilot depends on a number of factors. Some circumstances, such as the time available to make a decision, may be beyond your control. However, you can learn to recognize those factors which you can manage, and learn skills to improve your decision-making ability and judgment.

The factors which influence aeronautical decision making can be organized into five elements: pilot-in-command responsibility, communication, workload management, resource use, and situational awareness. In this section, these elements are defined, and concepts which apply to each element are introduced. In subsequent chapters, the Human Element Insets provide examples of these concepts and their relationship to pilot operations. In Chapter 10, you will learn how to apply decision-making principles to increase your effectiveness as a pilot.

PILOT-IN-COMMAND RESPONSIBILITY

As pilot in command, you are the ultimate decision maker and your choices determine the outcome of the flight. You are directly responsible for your own safety, as well as the safety of your passengers. An important **pilot-in-command responsibility** is to understand your own personal limitations. Your general health, level of stress or fatigue, attitude, knowledge, skill level, and recency of experience are several factors which affect your performance as pilot in command. Whether you are fit to fly depends on more than your physical condition. For example, your attitude will affect the quality of your decisions. Studies have identified five attitudes among pilots which are considered to be particularly hazardous.

I could not honestly claim to be the best pilot, because as good as you think you are, there is always somebody that probably is better . . . As much as I flew, I was always learning something new, whether it was a switch on the instrument panel I hadn't noticed, or handling characteristics of the aircraft in weather conditions I hadn't experienced . . . All pilots take chances from time to time, but knowing — not guessing — about what you can risk is often the critical difference between getting away with it or drilling a fifty-foot hole in mother earth.

— Yeager: An Autobiography by General Chuck Yeager and Leo Janos

Anti-authority — People with this attitude resent having someone tell them what to do, or they regard rules and procedures as unnecessary.

Impulsivity — This is the attitude of people who feel the need to do something — anything — immediately. They do not stop to consider the best alternative, but do the first thing which comes to mind.

Invulnerability — Many people believe that accidents happen to others, but never to them. Pilots with this attitude are more likely to take chances and increase risk.

Macho — By taking risks, these people attempt to prove that they are better than anyone else. While this pattern is thought to be a male characteristic, women are equally susceptible.

Resignation — People with this attitude do not see themselves as making a great deal of difference in what happens to them. When things go well, they think, "That's good luck." When things go badly, they attribute it to bad luck or feel that someone else is responsible. They leave the action to others — for better or worse.

These hazardous attitudes can lead to poor decision making and actions which involve unnecessary risk. As pilot in command, you must examine your decisions carefully to ensure that your choices have not been influenced by a hazardous attitude.

The type and recency of your pilot experience is a key factor in your ability to be an effective pilot in command. Prior to a proposed flight, you may want to ask yourself the following questions. How long has it been since I have flown this airplane, studied the pilot's operating handbook, or reviewed emergency procedures? Has my training prepared me for the circumstances of this flight? How recently have I received training? Developing a personal limitations checklist to review will help you determine if you are prepared to perform the tasks which are expected on a particular flight.

PILOT-IN-COMMAND RESPONSIBILITY CONCEPTS

1. **Self-Assessment** — Evaluating your condition to fly includes an awareness of your personal limitations.

2. **Hazardous Attitudes** — By learning to recognize hazardous attitudes, you can help prevent poor decision making and actions which involve unnecessary risk.

3. **Interpersonal Relationships** — As pilot in command, you are responsible for establishing the proper relationship with other persons on board the aircraft.

COMMUNICATION

Communication is the exchange of ideas, information, or instruction. The process of communication is comprised of three elements; the source (a sender, speaker, writer, instructor); the symbols used in composing and transmitting the message (words, illustrations, music); and the receiver (reader, listener, student). The relationship between these components is dynamic and each element influences the other.

Effective communication requires that ideas are not only expressed but that they are conveyed in a clear and timely manner so that the message is received and understood with a minimum of confusion and misunderstanding. To communicate effectively, you must possess skills in verbal and nonverbal communication, and have an awareness of potential barriers to communication. Your ability to listen is as important as your ability to convey information. As a pilot, you will be using these skills while communicating with your instructor, air traffic controllers, passengers, weather briefers, and other pilots.

Exchanging information and ideas with your instructor is the first step in developing effective communication skills. If you are uncomfortable or are having difficulty understanding something, don't hesitate to ask questions. Your instructor may not realize that you are having trouble unless you speak up. By conveying this information to your instructor, you can increase the effectiveness of your pilot training.

COMMUNICATION CONCEPTS

1. **Effective Listening** — This skill involves proper interpretation and evaluation of the message before responding.

2. **Barriers to Communication** — Barriers can include a lack of a common core of experience between the communicator and receiver, overuse of abstractions, and misuse of terminology.

3. **Verbal and Nonverbal Communication** — It is essential to learn how to interpret both verbal and nonverbal cues during the communication process.

RESOURCE USE

Resources sometimes can be found in unusual places. Since useful tools and sources of information may not always be readily apparent, it is important that you learn to recognize and utilize the resources available to you. **Resource use** is an essential part of human factors training. Resources may exist both inside and outside the airplane. For example, internal resources may include the pilot's operating handbook, checklists, aircraft equipment, aeronautical charts, your instructor, another pilot, and passengers, as well as your own ingenuity, knowledge, and skills. Air traffic controllers, maintenance technicians, and flight service personnel are examples of external resources.

RESOURCE USE CONCEPTS

1. **Resource Recognition** — Before you can effectively use resources, you must learn to identify potential sources of assistance and information.

2. **Internal Resources** — During pilot operations, these are sources of information found within the airplane, such as the pilot's operating handbook, checklists, aircraft equipment, aeronautical charts, your instructor, another pilot, and passengers, as well as your own ingenuity, knowledge, and skills.

3. **External Resources** — Many potential resources exist outside the cockpit, such as air traffic controllers, maintenance technicians, and flight service personnel.

Flying on from Greenland to Labrador, we got halfway across when two of our gas pumps failed — we had to pump the gas by hand. It got tiresome and my arm began to get numb. So I thought the only way to do it was to use a combination of my belt and handkerchief around my neck like a sling and to pull it with my other hand. I did that for close to four hours. It was tiresome, but it beat the hell out of swimming!

— incident which occurred during the first flight around the world from April to September, 1924, recalled by pilot Leslie P. Arnold as quoted in *The American Heritage History of Flight*

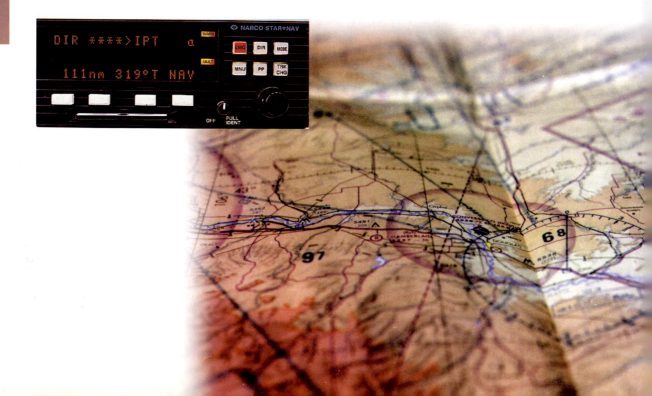

WORKLOAD MANAGEMENT

Effective **workload management** ensures that essential operations are accomplished by planning, prioritizing, and sequencing tasks to avoid work overload. If you are flying with another pilot, sharing the responsibility for completing specified tasks also may be an element in managing workload. Effective workload management begins with preparation and planning before the flight so that pilot operations can be performed more efficiently. As you gain piloting experience, you will learn to recognize future workload requirements and you can prepare for high workload periods during times of low workload. Recognizing when you are overloaded is another important part of managing workload.

WORKLOAD MANAGEMENT CONCEPTS

1. **Planning and Preparation** — Work overload can be prevented by thorough planning and preparation, including delegation of workload to others, if necessary.

2. **Prioritizing** — As pilot in command, you are responsible for determining the order in which tasks should be accomplished so that items which are essential for safe operation of the aircraft are performed first.

3. **Work Overload** — Recognizing when you have become task saturated and how to prevent overload from occurring is necessary to effectively manage workload.

SITUATIONAL AWARENESS

Situational awareness is the accurate perception of the operational and environmental factors which affect the aircraft, pilot, and passengers during a specific period of time. Maintaining situational awareness requires an understanding of the relative significance of these factors and their future impact on the flight. When you are situationally aware, you have an overview of the total operation and are not fixated on one perceived significant factor. Some of the elements inside the airplane which must be considered are the status of aircraft systems, pilot, and passengers. In addition, an awareness of the spatial orientation of the airplane, and its relationship to terrain, traffic, weather, and air traffic control must be maintained.

SITUATIONAL AWARENESS CONCEPTS

1. **Operational Conditions** — These include elements such as the status of aircraft systems, and your own ability to function properly.

2. **Environmental Conditions** — These are elements which affect the flight such as the airplane's relationship to terrain, traffic, and weather conditions.

3. **Obstacles to Maintaining Situational Awareness** — Stress, fatigue, distractions, and emergencies can cause you to fixate on a single item and can impair situational awareness.

We had no instruments to speak of, and we learned to fly by feel . . . There were no official weather reports at that time, and so we would try to locate some farmer to tell us what the weather was like. A farmer's idea of a weather report was whether it was hot or cold, raining or not . . . The planes were drafty, and the first ones had poor windshields and holes in the bottom around the base of the stick where the air would come billowing up, and the temperatures would get below zero. Pretty soon, you'd sit there and you couldn't move much. I'm sure this resulted in some accidents because pilots got so bitterly cold and so numb, and so obsessed with the misery that their judgment was poor.

— Dean Smith, United States airmail pilot in 1920, as quoted in The American Heritage History of Flight

AVIATION PHYSIOLOGY

An essential component of human factors training is aviation physiology, which is the study of the performance and limitations of the body in the flight environment. Most healthy people do not experience any physical difficulties as a result of flying. However, there are some physiological factors which you should be aware of as you begin flight training. An expanded description of how your body functions in flight is contained in Chapter 10.

PRESSURE EFFECTS

As the airplane climbs and descends, variations in atmospheric pressure affect many parts of your body. As outside air pressure changes, air trapped in the ears, teeth, sinus cavities, and gastrointestinal tract can cause pain and discomfort.

EAR AND SINUS BLOCK

Ear pain is normally the result of a difference between air pressure in the middle ear and outside air pressure. When the air pressure in the middle ear is equal to the pressure in the ear canal, there is no blocked feeling or pain. [Figure 1-7]

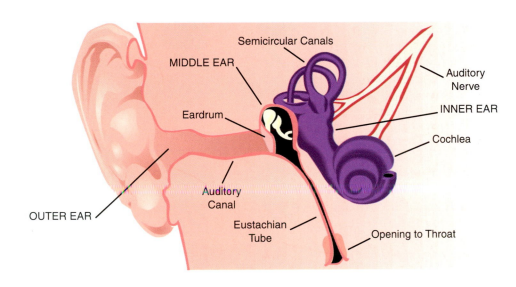

Figure 1-7. The ear is composed of three sections: the outer ear, the middle ear, and the inner ear. The outer ear includes the auditory canal which extends to the eardrum. The eardrum separates the outer ear from the middle ear which is located within the temporal bone of the skull. A short slit-like tube called the eustachian tube connects the middle ear cavity to the back wall of the throat. The inner ear, which contains the semicircular canals and cochlea, is used for both hearing and maintaining a sense of equilibrium.

As you ascend during flight, the pressure in the auditory canal decreases and usually the higher pressure in the middle ear will open the eustachian tube to equalize the pressure. If the tube does not open, you may feel a fullness in the ear, notice a slight hearing loss and experience discomfort because the eardrum is distended and cannot vibrate as freely. During a descent, the outside air pressure in the auditory canal will become higher than the pressure in the middle ear. This situation is harder to correct, since the eustachian opens more easily to let positive pressure out than it does to allow air back into the middle ear. Slow descent rates can help prevent or reduce the severity of ear problems and the eustachian tube can sometimes be opened by yawning, swallowing, or chewing.

In addition, pressure can be equalized by holding the nose and mouth shut and forcibly exhaling. This procedure, which is called the Valsalva maneuver, forces air up the eustachian tube into the middle ear. If you have a cold, an ear infection, or sore throat, you may not be able to equalize the pressure in your ears. A flight in this condition can be extremely painful, as well as damaging to your eardrums. If you are experiencing minor congestion, nose drops or nasal sprays may reduce the chance of a painful ear blockage. Before you use any medication, though, check with an aviation medical examiner to ensure that it will not affect your ability to fly.

If you have an inflammation of the sinuses from an allergy or a cold, you may experience pain from trapped air in your sinus cavities. As with the ears, slow descent rates, use of nasal sprays, or employing the Valsalva maneuver can help equalize the pressure.

TOOTHACHE

Expansion of trapped air in the cavities caused by imperfect fillings, damaged root canals, and dental abscesses can produce pain at altitude. If you experience a toothache while flying, a descent to a lower altitude may bring relief, but it is recommended that you visit a dentist for examination and treatment.

GASTROINTESTINAL PAIN

At any given time, your gastrointestinal tract contains about one quart of gas. Most of this is swallowed air, and the rest is gas caused by the digestion process. As altitude increases, this gas expands and can cause abdominal pain. You are less likely to have this problem if you maintain good eating habits and avoid foods which produce excess gas prior to flying.

SCUBA DIVING

The reduction of atmospheric pressure which accompanies flying can produce physical problems for scuba divers. Decompression sickness, more commonly referred to as "the bends," occurs when nitrogen absorbed during a scuba dive comes out of solution and forms bubbles in the tissues and bloodstream, much like uncapping a bottle of soda. This condition is very serious and can produce extreme pain, paralysis, and, if severe enough, death.

Even though you may finish a dive well within the no-decompression limits, the reduced atmospheric pressure of flying can cause the onset of decompression sickness. If you or a passenger plan to fly after scuba diving, it is important that enough time is allowed for the body to rid itself of excess nitrogen absorbed during diving. The recommended waiting time before ascending to 8,000 feet MSL is at least 12 hours after a dive which has not required a controlled ascent (nondecompression stop diving), and at least 24 hours after a dive which has required a controlled ascent (decompression stop diving). The waiting time before going to flight altitudes above 8,000 feet MSL should be at least 24 hours after any scuba dive.

MOTION SICKNESS

Motion sickness, or airsickness, is caused by the brain receiving conflicting messages about the state of the body. You may experience motion sickness during initial flights, but it generally goes away within the first 10 lessons. Anxiety and stress, which you may feel as you begin flight training, can contribute to motion sickness. Symptoms of motion sickness include general discomfort, nausea, dizziness, paleness, sweating, and vomiting.

It is important to remember that experiencing airsickness is no reflection on your ability as a pilot. Let your flight instructor know if you are prone to motion sickness since there are techniques which can be used to overcome this problem. For example, you may want to avoid lessons in turbulent conditions until you are more comfortable in the airplane or start with shorter flights and graduate to longer instruction periods. If you experience symptoms of motion sickness during a lesson, you can alleviate some of the discomfort by opening fresh air vents or by focusing on objects outside the airplane. Although medication like Dramamine can prevent airsickness in passengers, it is not recommended while you are flying since it can cause drowsiness.

STRESS

Stress can be defined as the body's response to physical and psychological demands placed upon it. Reactions of your body to stress include the release of chemical hormones (such as adrenaline) into the blood and the speeding of the metabolism to provide energy to the muscles. In addition, blood sugar, heart rate, respiration, blood pressure, and perspiration all increase. The term stressor is used to describe an element which causes you to experience stress.

Stressors include conditions associated with the environment, such as temperature and humidity extremes, noise, vibration, and lack of oxygen. Your physical condition can contribute to stress. For example, lack of physical fitness, fatigue, sleep loss, missed meals (leading to low blood sugar levels), and illness are sources of stress. Psychological stressors include social or emotional factors, such as a death in the family, a divorce, a sick child, a demotion at work, or the mental workload of in-flight conditions.

A certain amount of stress is good for you since it keeps you alert and prevents complacency. However, stress effects are cumulative and if not coped with adequately, they eventually add up to an intolerable burden. Performance generally increases with the onset of stress, peaks, and then begins to fall off rapidly as stress levels exceed your ability to cope.

There are several techniques which can be applied to manage the accumulation of life stresses and help prevent stress overload. Including relaxation time in your schedule and maintaining a program of physical fitness can help reduce stress levels. Learning to manage your time more efficiently can help you avoid the heavy pressures imposed by getting behind schedule and not meeting deadlines. By taking an assessment of yourself, you can determine your capabilities and limitations which will enable you to set realistic goals. Whenever possible, avoid stressful situations and encounters, and finally, be aware of specialized techniques, such as meditation, which can help you cope with stress.

FATIGUE

Fatigue is frequently associated with pilot error. Some of the effects of fatigue include degradation of attention and concentration, impaired coordination, and decreased ability to communicate. These factors can seriously influence your ability to make effective decisions. Physical fatigue can result from sleep loss, exercise, or physical work. Factors such as stress and prolonged performance of cognitive work can result in mental fatigue.

If you become fatigued in the cockpit, no amount of training or experience can overcome the detrimental effects. Getting adequate rest is the only way to prevent fatigue from occurring. You should avoid flying when you have not had a full night's rest, when you have been working excessive hours, or have had an especially exhausting or stressful day.

NOISE

Cockpit noise can contribute to fatigue, stress, and even airsickness. The understanding of speech also can be severely impeded by cockpit noise which can impair communication between persons on board the aircraft and radio exchanges with air traffic controllers. Tests have shown that in certain airplanes under full takeoff power conditions, the intelligibility of a communication from an air traffic controller can sometimes drop from 100 percent to zero.

The long-term effects of cockpit noise can be serious. Although some hearing loss will be experienced by every person during an average lifetime, the problem may occur sooner for pilots who fly frequently without ear protection. Hearing loss generally occurs very slowly over an extended period of time so you may not be aware of the problem until a permanent hearing loss has occurred. For example, if you fly more than five hours a week without ear protection in a light single-engine airplane, you can expect to have trouble understanding speech after ten years.

Almost all of the problems associated with noise in the cockpit can be eliminated with the use of earplugs. Earplugs are devices which are inserted in, or pressed against, the external ear canal to reduce the effect of ambient sound on the auditory system. Wearing noise-attenuating headsets or earphones also can reduce the impact of aircraft noise, but you should verify that the specific device provides the necessary noise reduction. Both headsets and earplugs must fit snugly to work properly.

ALCOHOL, DRUGS, AND PERFORMANCE

Illness and disease also can affect the functioning and performance of your body, as can the drugs which are meant to fight these illnesses. There are two things you should consider before flying while using a drug. First, what is the condition you are treating, and second, what are the side effects of the drug used to treat the condition? Some conditions are serious enough to prohibit flying, even if the illness is being treated successfully with drugs. Always let your physician know you are a pilot and ask about the side effects of prescription medication. You should consult an aviation medical examiner about any medication, including over-the-counter drugs which you suspect will adversely affect your ability to pilot an aircraft.

DEPRESSANTS

Depressants are drugs which reduce the body's functioning in many areas. These drugs lower blood pressure, reduce mental processing, and slow motor and reaction responses. There are several types of drugs which can cause a depressing effect on the body, including tranquilizers, motion sickness medication, some types of stomach medication, decongestants, and antihistamines. The most common depressant is alcohol.

ALCOHOL

Ethyl **alcohol** is the most widely used and abused drug. Although some alcohol is used for medicinal purposes, the majority of it is consumed as a beverage. Alcohol requires no digestion and can be absorbed into the bloodstream unchanged from the stomach and small intestine. It then passes almost immediately through the liver. This produces a depressing effect on the nervous system and a dulling of the senses is experienced. The rate at which alcohol is absorbed into your body varies with the percentage of alcohol in the drink, the rate at which it is consumed, the amount and type of foods you have eaten, and the length of time you have been drinking.

Intoxication is determined by the amount of alcohol in the bloodstream. This is usually measured as a percentage by weight in the blood. [Figure 1-8] The FARs require that your blood alcohol level be less than .04 percent and that 8 hours pass between drinking alcohol and piloting an aircraft. If you have a blood alcohol level of .04 percent or greater after 8 hours, you cannot fly until your blood alcohol falls below that amount. Even though your blood alcohol may be well below .04 percent, you cannot fly sooner than 8 hours after drinking alcohol. Although the regulations are quite specific, it is a good idea to be more conservative than the FARs. Most pilots allow a minimum of 12 hours to pass after the last drink before flying; commercial airlines generally require their pilots to wait 24 hours.

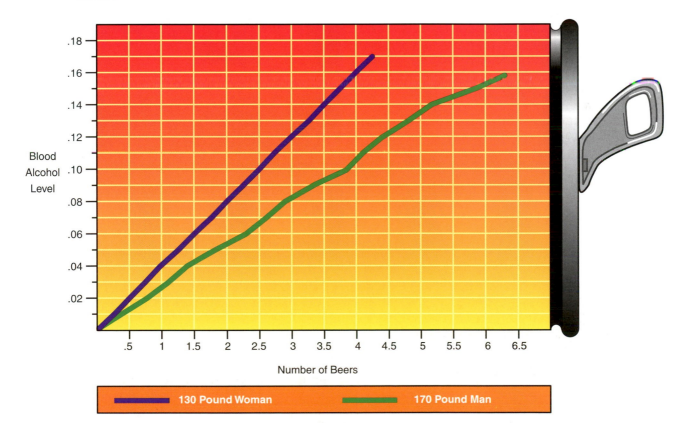

Figure 1-8. This chart depicts the number of 12 ounce, 5% alcohol beers consumed and the corresponding blood alcohol level for a 130 pound woman and a 170 pound man.

Hundreds of decisions, some of them time-critical, must be made during the course of a flight. The safe outcome of any flight depends on your ability to make the correct decisions and take the appropriate actions during routine occurrences, as well as abnormal situations. The influence of alcohol drastically reduces the chances of completing your flight without incident. Even in small amounts, alcohol can impair your judgment, decrease your sense of responsibility, affect your coordination, constrict your visual field, diminish your memory, reduce your reasoning power, and lower your attention span. As little as one ounce of alcohol can decrease the speed and strength of your muscular reflexes, lessen the efficiency of your eye movements while reading, and increase the frequency at which you commit errors. Impairments in vision and hearing occur at alcohol blood levels as low as .01 percent.

There are several regulations in FAR Parts 61 and 91 which apply to drug and alcohol violations and testing requirements, including motor vehicle offenses involving alcohol. Any violation or refusal to submit to an alcohol test may result in the denial of an application for a pilot certificate. If you already hold a pilot certificate, it can be suspended or revoked. If you have any questions about how a violation may affect your pilot training, you should discuss these regulations with your instructor.

HANGOVER

When you have a hangover, you are still under the influence of alcohol. Although you may think that you are functioning normally, the impairment of motor and mental responses still remains. Considerable amounts of alcohol can remain in the body for over 16 hours, so you should be cautious about flying too soon after drinking.

PAIN KILLERS

Pain killers can be grouped into two broad classes: analgesics and anesthetics. Analgesics, such as aspirin and codeine, are drugs which decrease pain. The majority of the drugs which contain acetylsalicylic acid (Aspirin), acetaminophen (Tylenol), and ibuprofen (Advil) have few side effects when taken in the correct dosage. Although some people are allergic to certain analgesics or may suffer from stomach irritation, flying usually is not restricted 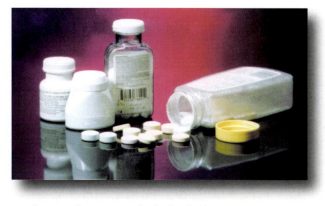 when taking these drugs. However, flying is almost always precluded while using prescription analgesics, such as Darvon, Percodan, Demerol, and codeine since these drugs may cause side effects such as mental confusion, dizziness, headaches, nausea, and vision problems.

Anesthetics are drugs which deaden pain or cause a loss of consciousness. These drugs are commonly used for dental and surgical procedures. Most local anesthetics used for minor dental and outpatient procedures wear off within a relatively short period of time. The anesthetic itself may not limit flying so much as the actual procedure and subsequent pain.

STIMULANTS

Stimulants are drugs which excite the central nervous system and produce an increase in alertness and activity. Amphetamines, caffeine, and nicotine are all forms of stimulants. Common uses of these drugs include appetite suppression, fatigue reduction, and mood elevation. Some of these drugs may cause a stimulant reaction, even though this reaction is not their primary function. In some cases, stimulants can produce anxiety and drastic mood swings, both of which are dangerous when you fly.

OTHER PROBLEM DRUGS

Some drugs which can neither be classified as stimulants nor depressants, have adverse effects on flying. For example, some forms of antibiotics can produce dangerous side effects, such as balance disorders, hearing loss, nausea, and vomiting. While many antibiotics are safe for use while flying, the infection requiring the antibiotic may prohibit flight. In addition, unless specifically prescribed by a physician, you should not take more than one drug at a time nor mix drugs with alcohol. The effects are often unpredictable.

The dangers of illegal drugs are well documented. Certain illegal drugs can have hallucinatory effects which occur days or weeks after the drug is taken. Obviously, these drugs have no place in the aviation community.

FITNESS FOR FLIGHT

Prior to operating an aircraft, you should ask yourself several key questions to determine your physical suitability for flight. If I have an illness, does the condition present a hazard to safe flight? If I am taking a drug for an illness and it wears off during a flight, will it cause an unsafe condition? Can the drug which I am taking produce any side effect which would influence my motor, perceptual, or psychological condition? Am I fatigued? Am I experiencing excessive stress from work or home? If the answer to any of these questions is "Yes" or "I don't know," you may not be fit to operate an aircraft. In addition, if you have a known medical deficiency which would make you unable to meet the qualifications of your current medical certificate, the FARs prohibit you from acting as pilot in command. If you are not sure of your physical suitability for flight, consult an aviation medical examiner.

Your ability to assess your mental and physical fitness for flight, and your skill at making effective decisions are essential to flight safety. As you explore the Human Element insets in this manual, your human factors training will continue and your knowledge in this subject area will grow. Now that you have been introduced to how your mind and body operate in flight, you are ready to learn about the operation of the airplane in Chapter 2.

SUMMARY CHECKLIST

✓ When the decision-making process is applied to flight operations it is termed aeronautical decision making (ADM).

✓ Your general health, level of stress or fatigue, attitude, knowledge, skill level, and recency of experience are several factors which affect your performance as pilot in command.

✓ Communication is the exchange of ideas, information, or instruction.

✓ Since useful tools and sources of information may not always be readily apparent, learning to recognize and utilize the resources available to you is an essential part of human factors training.

✓ Effective workload management ensures that essential operations are accomplished by planning, prioritizing, and sequencing tasks to avoid work overload.

✓ Situational awareness is the accurate perception of the operational and environmental factors which affect the aircraft, pilot, and passengers during a specific period of time.

✓ Ear pain is normally the result of a difference between air pressure in the middle ear and outside air pressure.

✓ Slow descent rates can help prevent or reduce the severity of ear problems and to equalize pressure, the eustachian tube can sometimes be opened by yawning, swallowing, chewing, or employing the Valsalva maneuver.

✓ The reduction of atmospheric pressure during flight can cause scuba divers to experience decompression sickness. Recommended waiting periods are specified before ascending to 8,000 feet MSL or above after scuba diving.

✓ Motion sickness is caused by the brain receiving conflicting messages about the state of the body.

✓ Stress can be defined as the body's response to physical and psychological demands placed upon it.

✓ Some of the effects of fatigue include degradation of attention and concentration, impaired coordination, and decreased ability to communicate.

✓ Cockpit noise can contribute to excessive fatigue, stress, and airsickness, as well as severely impede the understanding of speech.

✓ Pilots who fly frequently may experience serious hearing loss over a period of time unless ear protection is used.

✓ Depressants are drugs which reduce the body's functioning in many areas. The most common depressant is alcohol.

✓ Intoxication is determined by the amount of alcohol in the bloodstream which is usually measured as a percentage by weight in the blood. The FARs require that your blood alcohol level be less than .04 percent and that 8 hours pass between drinking alcohol and piloting an aircraft.

✓ Stimulants are drugs which excite the central nervous system and produce an increase in alertness and activity. Amphetamines, caffeine, and nicotine are all forms of stimulants.

✓ Your ability to assess your mental and physical fitness for flight, and your skill at making effective decisions are essential to flight safety.

KEY TERMS

Crew Resource Management (CRM)

Aeronautical Decision Making (ADM)

Pilot-In-Command Responsibility

Communication

Resource Use

Workload Management

Situational Awareness

Motion Sickness

Stress

Fatigue

Depressants

Alcohol

Stimulants

CHAPTER 2

AIRPLANE SYSTEMS

Part I, Chapter 2 — Airplane Systems

Discovery Workshop — Airplane Systems

SECTION A
AIRPLANES

Although airplanes are designed for a variety of purposes, the basic components of most airplanes are essentially the same. Once the practical aspects of building an airworthy craft are resolved, what ultimately becomes the final model is largely a matter of the original design objectives and aesthetics. In a sense then, airplane design is a combination of art and science. Although the artistic possibilities are virtually limitless, the relatively inflexible scientific requirements for manned flight dictate that most airplane structures include, at a minimum, a fuselage, wings, an empennage, landing gear, and a powerplant. [Figure 2-1]

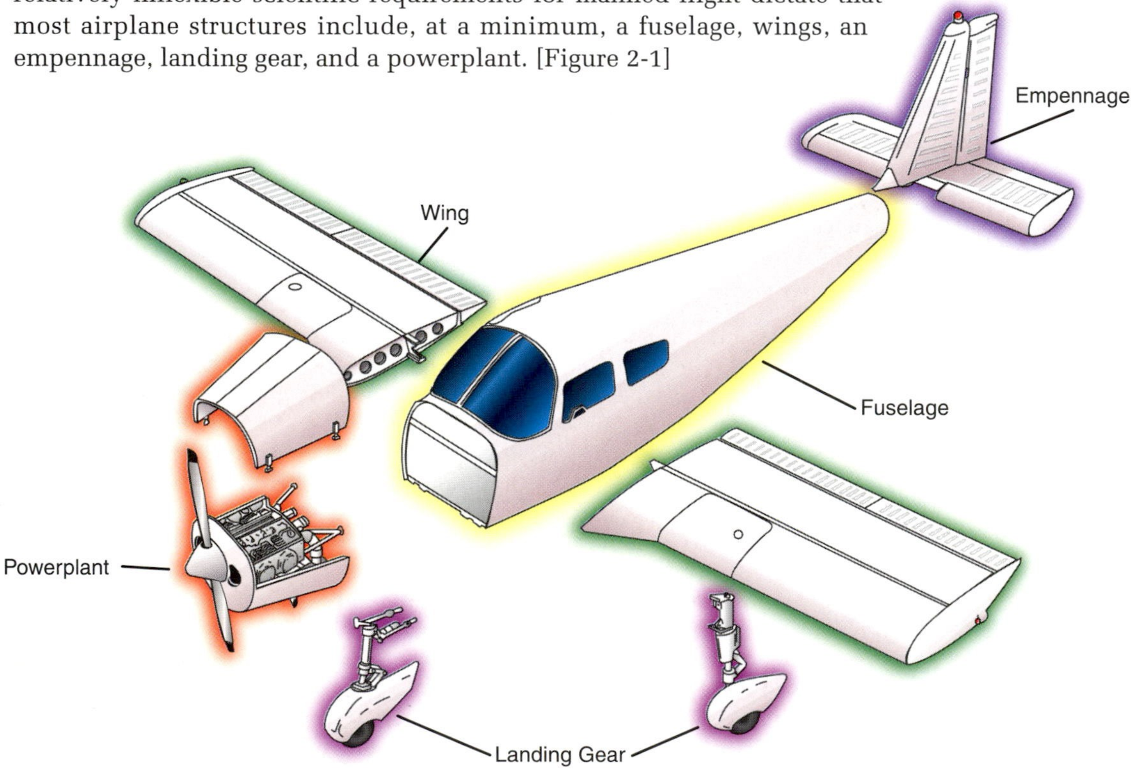

Figure 2-1. Typically, an airplane is made up of five major parts. The fuselage is considered to be the central component, since the powerplant, wings, empennage, and landing gear are attached to it.

The First Airplane

Although several attempts at powered flight were made during the late 19th and early 20th centuries, the Wright brothers were the first to accomplish the feat when their airplane flew for a distance of 120 feet over the sands of Kill Devil Hill, North Carolina on December 17, 1903. The famous airplane was constructed by Orville and Wilbur Wright in a shop not far from the site of the fateful flight. Several of the principles of aircraft design and construction employed by the Wrights are used in today's aircraft. For example, the aircraft used wings that could be slightly warped to operate in conjunction with the rudder to make coordinated turns. In addition to the wings and rudder, the Wright Flyer was composed of an open truss fuselage, an empennage, skid-type landing gear, as well as a small powerplant and propeller.

THE FUSELAGE

The **fuselage** houses the cabin and/or cockpit which contains seats for the occupants and the controls for the airplane. In addition, the fuselage may also provide room for cargo and attachment points for the other major airplane components. Although somewhat uncommon today, most early aircraft utilized an **open truss** structure. Aircraft employing open truss construction can be identified by the clearly visible struts and wire-braced wings. [Figure 2-2]

As technology progressed, aircraft designers began to enclose the truss members to streamline the airplane and improve performance. This was originally accomplished with cloth fabric, which eventually gave way to lightweight metals, such as aluminum. In some cases, the outside skin can support all, or a portion, of the flight loads. Most modern aircraft use a form of this **stressed skin** structure known as monocoque or semi-monocoque construction.

Figure 2-2. Open truss construction was common to many early aircraft.

Figure 2-3. Semi-monocoque construction incorporates a substructure for added strength.

The **monocoque** design uses the skin to support almost all imposed loads. This structure can be very strong, but cannot tolerate any dents or deformation of the surface. This characteristic is easily demonstrated by a thin aluminum beverage can. You can exert a large force to the ends of the can without causing any damage, however, if the side of the can is dented only slightly, the can will collapse easily. Due to the limitations of the monocoque design, a semi-monocoque structure is used on many of today's aircraft. The **semi-monocoque** system uses a substructure riveted to the airplane's skin to maintain the shape of the airframe and increase its strength. [Figure 2-3]

THE WING

When air flows around the wings of an airplane, it generates a force called lift that helps the airplane fly. **Wings** are contoured to take maximum advantage of this force, and may be attached at the top, middle, or lower portion of the fuselage. These designs are referred to as high-, mid-, and low-wing, respectively. The number of wings can also vary. Airplanes with a single set of wings are referred to as **monoplanes**, while those with two sets are called **biplanes**. [Figure 2-4]

Attached to the rear, or trailing, edges of the wings are two types of control surfaces referred to as ailerons and flaps. **Ailerons** extend from about the midpoint of each wing outward to the tip and move in opposite directions to create aerodynamic forces that cause the airplane to turn. **Flaps** extend outward from the fuselage to the midpoint of each wing. The flaps are normally flush with the wing's surface during cruising flight. When extended, the flaps move simultaneously downward to increase the lifting force of the wing for takeoffs and landings. [Figure 2-5]

Figure 2-4. Monoplanes incorporate a single set of wings while biplanes use two sets of wings stacked vertically.

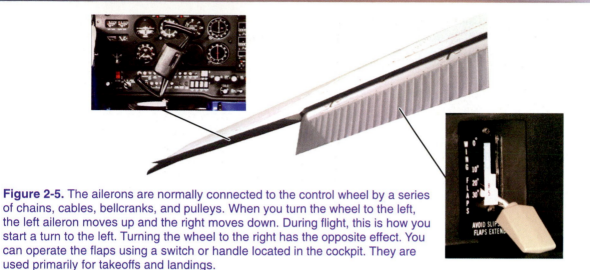

Figure 2-5. The ailerons are normally connected to the control wheel by a series of chains, cables, bellcranks, and pulleys. When you turn the wheel to the left, the left aileron moves up and the right moves down. During flight, this is how you start a turn to the left. Turning the wheel to the right has the opposite effect. You can operate the flaps using a switch or handle located in the cockpit. They are used primarily for takeoffs and landings.

THE EMPENNAGE

The **empennage** consists of the **vertical stabilizer**, or fin, and the **horizontal stabilizer**. These two surfaces act like the feathers on an arrow to steady the airplane and help you maintain a straight path through the air. [Figure 2-6]

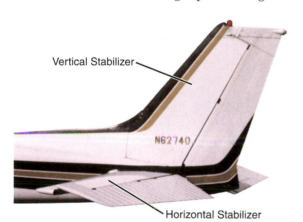

Vertical Stabilizer

N62740

Horizontal Stabilizer

Figure 2-6. The vertical and horizontal stabilizers are located on the empennage.

The **rudder** is attached to the back of the vertical stabilizer and can be used to move the nose of the airplane left or right, much like a rudder is used to turn a ship. However, the airplane differs in that you will normally need to use the rudder in combination with the ailerons to turn an airplane correctly. [Figure 2-7]

Figure 2-7. You operate the rudder with your feet, using pedals located in the cockpit. When you press the left rudder pedal, connecting cables move the rudder to the left which causes the airplane's nose to move to the left. Pressing the right pedal moves the rudder and nose to the right.

N62740

Rudder

The **elevator** is attached to the back of the horizontal stabilizer. During flight, you can use it to move the nose up and down, directing the airplane to the desired altitude, or height. [Figure 2-8]

Figure 2-8. The elevator is controlled by the control wheel through a system of cables, pulleys, and other connecting devices. When you pull back on the wheel, the elevator and nose move up; when you push forward, the elevator and nose move down.

Elevator

Some empennage designs use a one-piece horizontal stabilizer called a **stabilator**. Used in lieu of an elevator, the stabilator pivots up and down on a central hinge point. When you pull back on the control wheel, the nose moves up; when you push forward, the nose moves down. [Figure 2-9]

Figure 2-9. Some airplanes use a stabilator which performs the same function as the horizontal stabilizer/elevator combination.

Stabilator

TRIM DEVICES

Some airplanes may include small hinged trim devices attached to the trailing edge of one or more of the control surfaces. These mechanisms are used to help minimize your workload by aerodynamically helping you move a control surface, or maintain the surface in a desired position. One such device commonly used on many training airplanes is called a **trim tab**. If an airplane uses only one trim tab, it is usually located on the elevator. [Figure 2-10]

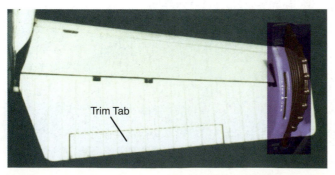

Trim Tab

Figure 2-10. The trim tab lessens the resistance you feel on the flight controls due to airflow over the associated control surface. This trim tab, located on the elevator, is controlled by a wheel in the cockpit (inset).

A stabilator normally uses an **anti-servo** tab to provide you with a control "feel" similar to what you experience with an elevator. Without the anti-servo tab, control forces from the stabilator would be so light that you might "over control" the airplane or move the control wheel too far to obtain the desired result. The anti-servo tab also functions as a trim tab to maintain the stabilator in the desired position.

LANDING GEAR

The landing gear absorbs landing loads and supports the airplane on the ground. Typically, the landing gear consists of three wheels — two **main wheels** which are located on either side of the fuselage and a third wheel positioned either at the front or rear of the airplane. Landing gear employing a rear-mounted wheel is called **conventional landing gear**. Airplanes equipped with conventional landing gear are sometimes referred to as **tailwheel** airplanes. [Figure 2-11]

Figure 2-11. Because of the added clearance between the propeller and the ground, conventional gear airplanes are desirable for operations on unimproved fields.

When the third wheel is located on the nose, it is called a **nosewheel**, and the design is referred to as **tricycle gear**. Nosewheels are normally either steerable or castering. Steerable nosewheels are linked to the rudders by cables or rods while castering nosewheels are not. In both cases, you steer the airplane using the rudder pedals, however, airplanes with a castering nosewheel may require you to combine the use of the rudder pedals with independent use of the brakes, particularly in tight turns. [Figure 2-12]

Figure 2-12. Tricycle landing gear is used on many of today's aircraft, including almost all modern transport category airplanes.

Landing gear can also be classified as either fixed or retractable. **Fixed gear** always remains extended and has the advantage of simplicity combined with low cost. **Retractable gear** is designed to streamline the airplane by allowing the landing gear to be stowed inside the structure during cruising flight. The increased weight and cost of retractable gear systems normally limits their use to high performance aircraft. [Figure 2-13]

Figure 2-13. Most small training airplanes use fixed landing gear while higher performance airplanes are generally equipped with retractable landing gear.

Water, Water Everywhere...

Many years ago when hard surfaced runways were more of a luxury than a common occurrence, the Navy and several airlines used large flying boats to ferry passengers around the world. [Figure A] The excessive size and weight of these aircraft eventually made the use of flying boats unprofitable and they disappeared from the military and airline fleets, particularly with the proliferation of hard surfaced runways and advanced long range airplane designs.

Martin Mars

The desire to operate from water has not faded, however. In fact, water-capable airplanes can be extremely practical for flights to remote areas where even dirt or grass landing strips are not available. Many of today's landplanes can be fitted with twin floats that support them on water. Normally, these types of airplanes are referred to as seaplanes. [Figure B] A plane that has the capability to operate from both land and water is known as an amphibian. A true amphibian airplane uses a hull much like that of a boat and outrigger floats on the wings for support during water operations. Retractable wheels are used for land-based takeoffs and landings. [Figure C]

Luscombe 8

Grumman Widgeon

LANDING GEAR STRUTS

The wheels of an airplane are attached to the airplane structure by struts that usually have some ability to absorb the shock of landing and taxiing over rough ground. The spring steel and bungee cord struts do not actually absorb any shock, but accept the shock and transmit it to the airplane structure at an acceptable rate that reduces stress as well as the tendency for the airplane to bounce. [Figure 2-14]

Figure 2-14. Spring steel (left) and bungee cord struts (right) accept and transmit shocks to the airplane at an acceptable rate.

Figure 2-15. The oleo strut consists of an enclosed cylinder which houses a piston, oil, and air. It absorbs pressure rapidly and then slowly releases it.

The most widely used type of strut is the air-oil shock absorber which is usually included as an integral part of the wheel attachment assembly. Normally referred to as an **oleo strut**, this type of shock uses a piston enclosed in a cylinder with oil and compressed air to absorb the bumps and jolts encountered during landing and taxi operations. [Figure 2-15]

BRAKES

The typical training airplane uses **disc brakes** located on the main wheels. [Figure 2-16] Equal pressure may be applied to each brake simultaneously by pressing on the top of each rudder pedal to stop or slow the airplane in a straight line. The brakes may also be applied to varying degrees independent of each other. This technique, known as **differential braking**, is normally used to help steer the airplane during ground operations. Most airplanes also provide a hand-operated parking brake that holds pressure on both brakes to keep the airplane from rolling when your feet are off the pedals.

Figure 2-16. Most light general aviation airplanes use a hydraulically actuated disc brake on each main wheel.

THE POWERPLANT

In small airplanes, the **powerplant** includes both the engine and the propeller. The primary function of the **engine** is to provide the power to turn the propeller. Accessories mounted on, or connected to the engine generate electrical power, create a vacuum source for some flight instruments, and, in most single-engine airplanes, provide a source of heat for the pilot and passengers. A **firewall**, which is located between the engine compartment and the cockpit, not only protects the occupants, but also serves as a mounting point for the engine. The engine compartment is enclosed by a cowling. Aside from streamlining the nose of the airplane, the cowling helps cool the engine by ducting air around the cylinders. [Figure 2-17]

Figure 2-17. The engine generates power and transmits it to the propeller.

The **propeller**, mounted on the front of the engine, translates the rotating force of the engine into a forward-acting force called thrust that helps to move the airplane through air. Although the number of blades on a propeller can vary, most general aviation training airplanes use a two-bladed propeller. [Figure 2-18]

Figure 2-18. The propeller receives power from the engine and provides thrust to help move the airplane through the air.

CHAPTER 2

AIRPLANE SYSTEMS

PILOT'S OPERATING HANDBOOK

Most of the pertinent information about a particular make and model of airplane can be found in the **pilot's operating handbook (POH)**. In 1975 the format and content of the POH was standardized to make it easier for pilots to use and to allow for easier transitions between different makes and models of airplanes. A few years later, the FAA required all airplanes built after March 1, 1979, to be equipped with an **FAA approved**

Figure 2-19. The FAA approved airplane flight manual can contain as many as ten sections as well as an optional alphabetical index.

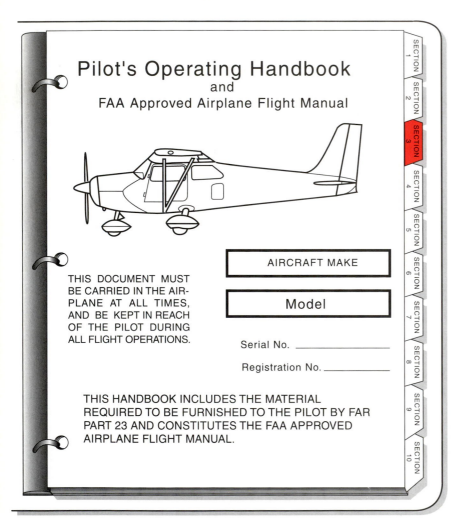

Pilot's Operating Handbook
and
FAA Approved Airplane Flight Manual

THIS DOCUMENT MUST BE CARRIED IN THE AIRPLANE AT ALL TIMES, AND BE KEPT IN REACH OF THE PILOT DURING ALL FLIGHT OPERATIONS.

AIRCRAFT MAKE

Model

Serial No. _____

Registration No. _____

THIS HANDBOOK INCLUDES THE MATERIAL REQUIRED TO BE FURNISHED TO THE PILOT BY FAR PART 23 AND CONSTITUTES THE FAA APPROVED AIRPLANE FLIGHT MANUAL.

1. **GENERAL** – Presents basic information such as loading, handling, and preflight of the aircraft. Also includes definitions, abbreviations, symbology, and terminology explanations.

2. **LIMITATIONS** – Includes operating limitations, instrument markings, color coding, and basic placards necessary for the safe operation of the airplane.

3. **EMERGENCY PROCEDURES** – Provides checklists followed by amplified procedures for coping with various types of emergencies or critical situations. Related recommended airspeeds are also included. At the manufacturer's option, a section on abnormal procedures may be included to describe recommendations for handling equipment malfunctions or other abnormalities that are not of an emergency nature.

4. **NORMAL PROCEDURES** – Includes checklists followed by amplified procedures for conducting normal operations. Related recommended airspeeds are also provided.

5. **PERFORMANCE** – Gives performance information appropriate to the airplane, plus optional information presented in the most likely order for use in flight.

6. **WEIGHT AND BALANCE** – Includes weighing procedures, weight and balance records, computation instructions, and the equipment list.

7. **AIRPLANE AND SYSTEMS DESCRIPTION** – Describes the airplane and its systems in a format considered by the manufacturer to be most informative.

8. **HANDLING, SERVICE, AND MAINTENANCE** – Includes information on airplane inspection periods, preventative maintenance that can be performed by the pilot, ground handling procedures, servicing, cleaning, and care instructions.

9. **SUPPLEMENTS** – Contains information necessary to safely and efficiently operate the airplane's various optional systems and equipment.

10. **SAFETY AND OPERATIONAL TIPS** – Includes optional information from the manufacturer of a general nature addressing safety practices and procedures.

 Aircraft operating limitations may be found in the approved flight manual, markings, placards, or a combination of these.

airplane flight manual (AFM) which is specifically assigned to the individual airplane and can be accessed by the pilot during all flight operations. To satisfy the regulatory requirement, the POH for most of these aircraft is also designated as the AFM. [Figure 2-19] Since the POH/AFM normally stays with the airplane and, therefore, is not usually available for you to review for extended periods of time, many manufacturers also publish a pilot's information manual (PIM). The PIM contains the same information as the POH/AFM except for precise weight and balance data and optional equipment specific to a particular airplane. Although the PIM is not updated, it is organized in the same manner as the POH/AFM and provides a useful study tool.

SUMMARY CHECKLIST

✓ The fuselage houses the cabin, or cockpit, and serves as the attachment point for the other major airplane components.

✓ Wings may be attached at the top, middle, or lower portion of the fuselage and are contoured to take maximum advantage of the lifting force created by the passing airflow.

✓ The empennage consists of the vertical stabilizer and the horizontal stabilizer which act to steady the airplane and maintain a straight path through the air.

✓ Trim devices are used to help minimize your workload by aerodynamically helping you move a control surface, or maintain the surface in a desired position.

✓ Landing gear employing a rear-mounted wheel is called conventional landing gear.

✓ When the third wheel is located on the nose, the design is referred to as tricycle gear.

✓ Brake pressure may be applied equally or to varying degrees by pressing on the top of each rudder pedal.

✓ The engine works to turn the propeller, generate electrical energy, create a vacuum source for some flight instruments, and, in most single-engine airplanes, provide a source of heat for the pilot and passengers.

✓ The propeller translates the rotating force of the engine into a forward-acting force called thrust that helps to move the airplane through the air.

✓ Most of the pertinent information about a particular make and model of airplane, including operating limits, can be found in the pilot's operating handbook (POH) and FAA approved airplane flight manual (AFM).

KEY TERMS

Fuselage   Wings

Open Truss   Monoplanes

Stressed Skin   Biplanes

Monocoque   Ailerons

Semi-Monocoque   Flaps

Empennage

Vertical Stabilizer

Horizontal Stabilizer

Rudder

Elevator

Stabilator

Trim Tab

Anti-Servo Tab

Main Wheels

Conventional Landing Gear

Tailwheel

Nosewheel

Tricycle Gear

Fixed Gear

Retractable Gear

Oleo Strut

Disc Brakes

Differential Braking

Powerplant

Engine

Firewall

Propeller

Pilot's Operating Handbook (POH)

FAA Approved Airplane Flight Manual (AFM)

Pilot's Information Manual (PIM)

QUESTIONS

1. Identify the major components of the airplane depicted in the accompanying illustration.

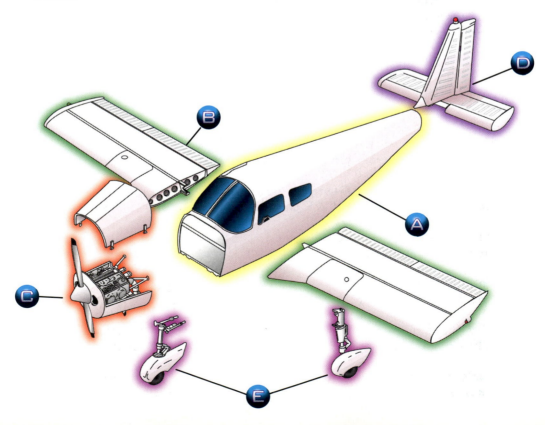

2. What is the primary difference between monocoque and semi-monocoque construction?

3. When you move the control wheel to the left, will the left aileron move up or down?

4. True/False. The rudder is located on the horizontal stabilizer.

5. What is the purpose of trim devices?

6. An airplane with a wheel mounted on the tail is equipped with what type of landing gear?

7. In addition to providing power to turn the propeller, what other functions does the engine in a typical training airplane perform?

Match the following publications with the most appropriate descriptor.

8. FAA Approved Airplane Flight Manual (AFM)

9. Pilot's Information Manual (PIM)

10. Pilot's Operating Handbook (POH)

A. This publication can serve as a useful study tool even though it may not contain information about optional equipment.

B. Federal regulations require that this publication be carried in the aircraft during all flight operations.

C. The format for this publication was standardized in 1975.

SECTION B
THE POWERPLANT AND RELATED SYSTEMS

As early as 1483, an aerial craft propelled by a screw-type device was conceived by Leonardo da Vinci. However, without a practical means of sustained power to drive the screw, the concept remained unachievable for centuries. It wasn't until 1860 that the first practical piston engine was developed. Although adequate for some land-based functions, further development was necessary before the engine could be used in airborne applications. By 1903, the Wright brothers and their mechanic, Charles Taylor, were able to refine previous designs and build a powerplant that was lightweight, yet powerful enough to meet the requirements of sustained flight. Although woefully inefficient by today's standards, it provided a starting point for continued development. The resulting modern aircraft powerplant still maintains several similarities with its predecessor, including the requirement for precise interaction of the engine, propeller, and other related systems.

ENGINES

Engines in widespread use today can be divided into two categories — reciprocating and turbine. Most large passenger carrying airplanes use a form of the **turbine engine**, which is relatively costly but extremely powerful. Since the large power output of the turbine engine is not required in most general aviation training airplanes, a form of the more economical, but still very reliable, **reciprocating engine** is used. [Figure 2-20]

RECIPROCATING ENGINE OPERATION

Although engine design may differ slightly between manufacturers, the principles of reciprocating engine operation are essentially the same. The basic process of converting the chemical energy in fuel into mechanical energy occurs within the cylinders of the reciprocating engine. Essentially, a fuel/air mixture within the cylinder is compressed by a piston, then ignited. The ensuing combustion creates energy which is converted into work and transferred through a crankshaft to the propeller. [Figure 2-21]

RECIPROCATING ENGINES

Radial

Courtesy of Gary Daniels

Horizontally Opposed

TURBINE ENGINES

Turboprop

Turbojet

Figure 2-20. A variety of reciprocating and turbine engines are in use today.

Figure 2-21. Movable pistons are attached to a crankshaft by connecting rods. The crankshaft and the connecting rods change the back-and-forth motion of the pistons to rotary, or turning, motion which drives the propeller.

THE FOUR-STROKE OPERATING CYCLE

In almost all reciprocating airplane engines, the continuous energy-creating process is referred to as the **four-stroke operating cycle**. The steps in this cycle are: the intake of the fuel/air mixture, the compression by the piston, the ignition and expansion of the gases, and the venting of the burned gases. [Figure 2-22]

Figure 2-22. Most reciprocating engines use a four-stroke operating cycle.

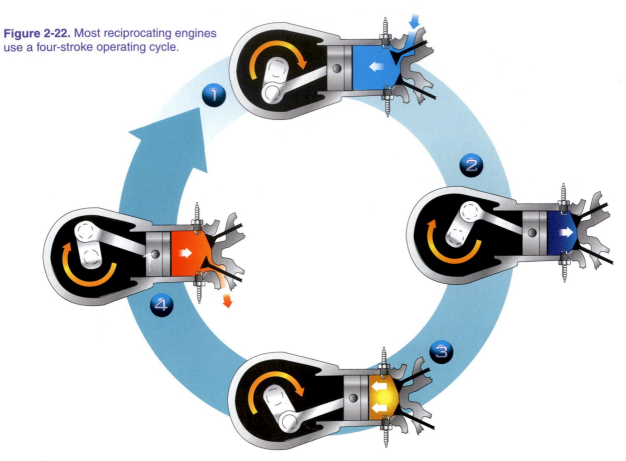

 INTAKE
When the piston moves away from the cylinder head on the intake stroke, the intake valve opens and the fuel/air mixture is drawn into the combustion chamber.

 COMPRESSION
As the piston moves back toward the cylinder head, the intake valve closes and the fuel/air mixture is compressed.

 POWER
When compression is nearly complete, the spark plugs fire and the compressed mixture is ignited to begin the power stroke. The rapidly expanding gases from the controlled burning of the fuel/air mixture drive the piston, providing the power that rotates the crankshaft.

 EXHAUST
The exhaust stroke expels the burned gases from the chamber through the opened exhaust valve.

Even when the engine is operated at a fairly slow speed, the four-stroke cycle takes place several hundred times each minute. In a four-cylinder engine, each cylinder operates on a different stroke. Continuous rotation of the crankshaft is maintained by the precise timing of the power strokes in each cylinder. Continuous operation of the engine as a whole is dependent on the simultaneous function of ancillary systems including the induction, ignition, fuel, oil, cooling, and exhaust systems.

An Engine Is An Engine Is An Engine...

At first glance, the turbine engine and reciprocating engine look decidedly different. The surprising fact is however, that the events that take place in converting fuel to thrust-producing energy are essentially the same — intake, compression, combustion, and exhaust. While the steps occur sequentially within the cylinder of the reciprocating engine, the turbine engine differs in that all four events occur simultaneously in sections of the engine specifically designed for each function. Thrust from a turbojet engine is obtained from the reaction to the rapidly expanding gases as they leave the engine.

INTAKE   COMPRESSION   COMBUSTION   EXHAUST

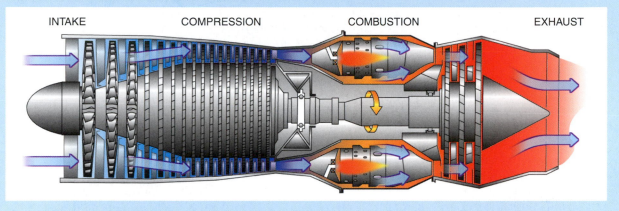

INDUCTION SYSTEMS

The purpose of the induction system is to bring outside air into the engine, mix it with fuel in the proper proportion, and deliver it to the cylinders where combustion occurs. Your control over the amount of fuel and air that is introduced into the engine cylinders is maintained by two controls in the cockpit — the **throttle** and the **mixture**. The throttle controls engine speed by regulating the amount of fuel and air mixture that flows into the cylinders, while the mixture controls the fuel/air ratio. [Figure 2-23]

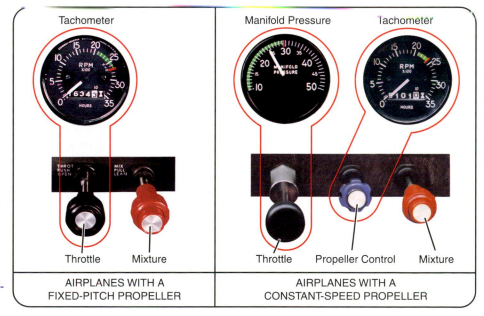

Figure 2-23. Many training airplanes are equipped with a fixed-pitch propeller. A typical powerplant control arrangement for these type of aircraft is shown on the left. Engine speed is controlled by the throttle and displayed on a tachometer in revolutions per minute (r.p.m.). Other airplanes may use a more efficient constant-speed propeller that is adjustable from the cockpit. As shown on the right, this type of airplane employs three powerplant controls. Movement of the propeller control sets the engine r.p.m. The throttle controls engine output as reflected on a manifold pressure gauge. The gauge displays the pressure of the fuel/air mixture inside the intake manifold in inches of mercury (in. Hg.). Both types of systems have a mixture control which is used to maintain the proper blend of fuel and air.

Figure 2-24. Engine intake air normally enters an intake port through an air filter.

Outside air enters the induction system through an **intake port** at the front of the engine compartment. This port normally contains an air filter that inhibits the entry of dust and other foreign objects. [Figure 2-24] Since the filter may occasionally become clogged, an alternate source of air must be available. Usually, the alternate air comes from inside the engine cowling where it bypasses a clogged air filter. Some alternate air sources function automatically, while others operate manually.

THE CARBURETOR

Once the air enters the induction system, it moves through a system of ducts and is introduced into the carburetor. The **carburetor** mixes the incoming air with fuel and delivers it to the combustion chamber. A float-type carburetor system is used on many light aircraft. When the air enters the

 The operating principle of float-type carburetors is based on the difference in pressure at the venturi throat and the air inlet.

carburetor it passes through a venturi. This increases its velocity and decreases its pressure. Fuel enters the carburetor from a float chamber where it is maintained at a nearly constant level by a float device. The float chamber is vented to the outside so that pressure inside remains equal to the atmospheric pressure, even during climbs and descents. Since the discharge nozzle is located in an area of low pressure created by the venturi, the fuel is forced through the discharge nozzle by the higher atmospheric pressure in the float chamber. [Figure 2-25]

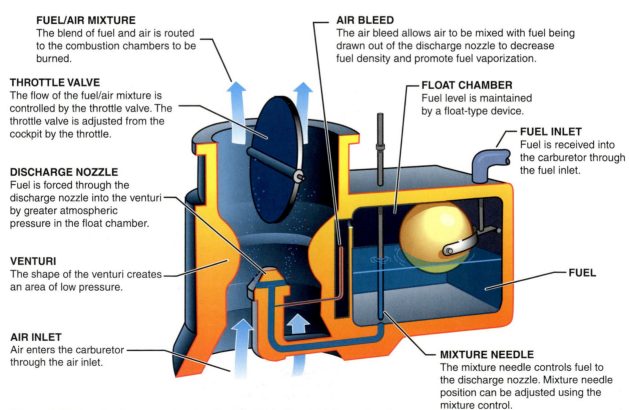

FUEL/AIR MIXTURE
The blend of fuel and air is routed to the combustion chambers to be burned.

THROTTLE VALVE
The flow of the fuel/air mixture is controlled by the throttle valve. The throttle valve is adjusted from the cockpit by the throttle.

DISCHARGE NOZZLE
Fuel is forced through the discharge nozzle into the venturi by greater atmospheric pressure in the float chamber.

VENTURI
The shape of the venturi creates an area of low pressure.

AIR INLET
Air enters the carburetor through the air inlet.

AIR BLEED
The air bleed allows air to be mixed with fuel being drawn out of the discharge nozzle to decrease fuel density and promote fuel vaporization.

FLOAT CHAMBER
Fuel level is maintained by a float-type device.

FUEL INLET
Fuel is received into the carburetor through the fuel inlet.

FUEL

MIXTURE NEEDLE
The mixture needle controls fuel to the discharge nozzle. Mixture needle position can be adjusted using the mixture control.

Figure 2-25. In a float-type carburetor, fuel is drawn from the float chamber past a mixture needle and into the venturi where it mixes with the incoming air.

Carburetors are calibrated at sea level, and the correct fuel-to-air mixture ratio is established at that altitude with the mixture control set in the FULL RICH position. However, as altitude increases, the density of air entering the carburetor decreases while the density of the fuel remains the same. This creates a progressively richer mixture which can result in engine roughness. The roughness normally is due to spark plug fouling from excessive carbon buildup on the plugs. This occurs because the excessively rich mixture lowers the temperature inside the cylinder, inhibiting complete combustion of the fuel. This condition may occur during the pretakeoff runup at high-elevation airports and during climbs or cruise flight at high altitudes. To maintain the correct fuel/air mixture, you must lean the mixture using the mixture control.

 When you lean the mixture, you decrease the fuel flow to compensate for decreased air density. Leaning the mixture may eliminate engine roughness during runup at high-elevation airports.

During a descent from high altitude, you must remember to enrich the mixture or it may become too lean. An overly lean mixture may result in high engine temperatures which can cause excessive engine wear or even failure over a period of time. The best way to maintain the proper mixture is to monitor the engine temperature and enrichen the mixture as needed. Since the process of adjusting the mixture can vary from one airplane to another, it's important that you refer to the pilot's operating handbook (POH) to determine the specific procedures for your airplane.

 If you do not adjust the mixture control during descents from high to low altitudes, the fuel/air mixture will be too lean.

One disadvantage of the float-type carburetor is its icing tendency. **Carburetor ice** occurs due to the effect of fuel vaporization and decreasing air pressure in the venturi which causes a sharp temperature drop in the carburetor. If water vapor in the air condenses when the carburetor temperature is at or below freezing, ice may form on internal surfaces of the carburetor, including the throttle valve. [Figure 2-26]

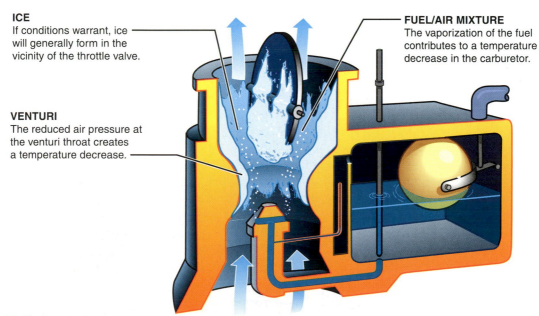

ICE
If conditions warrant, ice will generally form in the vicinity of the throttle valve.

VENTURI
The reduced air pressure at the venturi throat creates a temperature decrease.

FUEL/AIR MIXTURE
The vaporization of the fuel contributes to a temperature decrease in the carburetor.

INTAKE AIR
Carburetor ice is most likely to occur when intake air temperature is below 21°C (70°F) and the relative humidity is above 80%.

Figure 2-26. Carburetor ice reduces the size of the air passage to the engine. This restricts the flow of the fuel/air mixture and reduces power. If enough ice builds up, the engine can cease to operate.

Carburetor ice is more likely to occur when temperatures are below 21°C (70°F) and relative humidity is above 80%. However, due to the sudden cooling that takes place in the carburetor, icing can occur even with temperatures as high as 38°C (100°F) and humidity as low as 50%. [Figure 2-27]

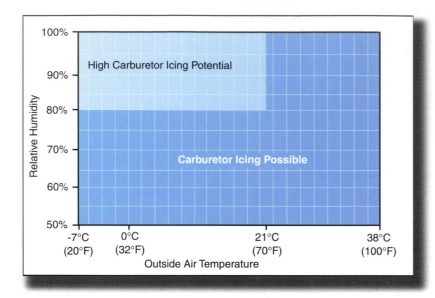

Figure 2-27. Carburetor ice can form when the temperature and humidity are in the ranges shown. However, since not all carburetors are designed exactly the same, carburetor ice is possible under conditions not depicted on this chart.

 You should expect carburetor ice when temperatures are at or below 21°C (70°F) and the relative humidity is high.

Your first indication of carburetor icing in an airplane with a fixed-pitch propeller will be a decrease in engine r.p.m., followed by engine roughness and possible fuel starvation. In an airplane with a constant-speed propeller, the power changes are reflected by shifts in manifold pressure. Although carburetor ice can occur during any phase of flight, it is particularly dangerous when you are using reduced power, such as in a descent. Under the right conditions, carburetor ice could build unnoticed until you try to add power. To combat the effects of carburetor ice, engines with float-type carburetors employ a **carburetor heat** system which is designed to eliminate ice by routing air across a heat source before it enters the carburetor. [Figure 2-28]

The use of carburetor heat causes a slight decrease in engine power, because the heated air is less dense than the outside air that had been entering the engine. This enriches the mixture. When ice is present in an airplane with a fixed-pitch propeller and you use carburetor heat, there is a slight decrease in r.p.m., followed by a gradual increase in r.p.m. as the ice melts. If ice is not present, the r.p.m. will decrease slightly, then remain constant. Remember, in an airplane with a constant-speed propeller these power changes are reflected by manifold pressure.

CARBURETOR HEAT ON

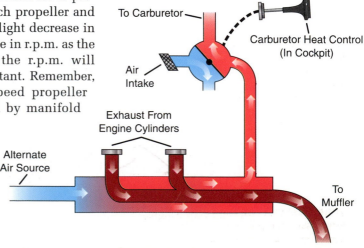

Figure 2-28. When you turn the carburetor heat ON, a valve cuts off air flow from the normal air intake and allows heated air from an alternate source to enter the carburetor.

The first indication of carburetor ice in an airplane equipped with a fixed-pitch propeller is a loss of r.p.m. The decrease in r.p.m. caused by the enriched mixture will be followed by an increase in r.p.m. as the ice melts.

The use of carburetor heat generally decreases engine performance.

Generally, you should use full carburetor heat whenever you reduce engine r.p.m. below the normal operating range for your airplane, or when you suspect the presence of carburetor ice. Normally, you do not use carburetor heat continuously when full power is required, such as during a takeoff, due to the decrease in engine output caused by the increased operating temperature of the engine. Be sure to check the POH for specific recommendations.

FUEL INJECTION

One way to eliminate the threat of carburetor ice is to remove the carburetor altogether. Recently, some manufacturers have done so by equipping new aircraft with fuel injection systems. These engines are more precise in metering fuel and distributing the fuel/air mixture than engines equipped with a float-type carburetor. **Fuel injection** offers lower fuel consumption, increased horsepower, lower operating temperatures, and longer engine life. From a safety standpoint, the most significant advantage is the relative freedom from the formation of induction icing.

A fuel injected engine uses a system that incorporates four basic components — a fuel pump, fuel control unit, fuel manifold valve, and fuel discharge nozzles. The fuel pump moves fuel from the tank to the fuel control unit which essentially replaces the carburetor. The fuel control unit meters fuel based upon the mixture control setting and sends it to the fuel manifold valve at the rate set by the throttle. Upon reaching the fuel manifold valve, the fuel is distributed to individual fuel discharge nozzles. The discharge nozzles, which are located in each cylinder head, introduce air into the fuel and inject the mixture into each intake port where it is drawn into the cylinders for combustion upon opening of each intake valve. [Figure 2-29]

Fuel injection systems are generally less susceptible to icing than float-type carburetors.

Figure 2-29. Fuel injection systems introduce the fuel/air mixture directly into the intake port of each cylinder. Although in many ways superior to engines equipped with a float-type carburetor, fuel injected engines have some disadvantages, including increased sensitivity to fuel contaminants and more complex starting procedures, particularly when the engine is hot.

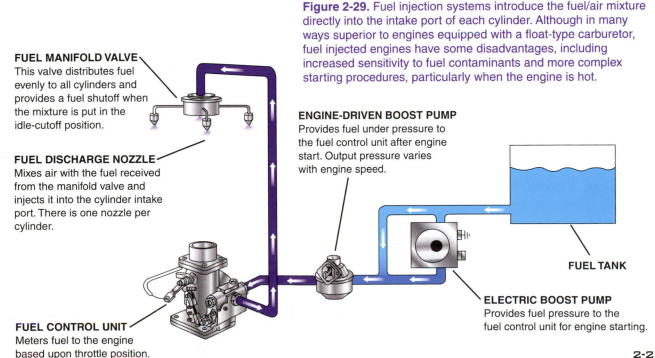

FUEL MANIFOLD VALVE
This valve distributes fuel evenly to all cylinders and provides a fuel shutoff when the mixture is put in the idle-cutoff position.

FUEL DISCHARGE NOZZLE
Mixes air with the fuel received from the manifold valve and injects it into the cylinder intake port. There is one nozzle per cylinder.

ENGINE-DRIVEN BOOST PUMP
Provides fuel under pressure to the fuel control unit after engine start. Output pressure varies with engine speed.

FUEL TANK

ELECTRIC BOOST PUMP
Provides fuel pressure to the fuel control unit for engine starting.

FUEL CONTROL UNIT
Meters fuel to the engine based upon throttle position.

SUPERCHARGING AND TURBOCHARGING

When you operate a reciprocating engine at high altitudes, efficiency of the engine diminishes as a result of lower air density, even though the volume of airflow into the engine remains the same. This is a characteristic of any normally aspirated engine, where the fuel/air mixture is not compressed. If intake air could be compressed, more fuel could be added to the mixture, producing an increase in overall engine power output.

Sea-level performance can be obtained even at high altitudes using either a supercharging or a turbocharging system. A **supercharger** compresses the incoming air using a pump driven by the engine. Although effective, some engine power must be used to drive the supercharger which decreases the net power increase. On the other hand, a **turbocharger** is more efficient because it pressurizes the air using a mechanism driven by engine exhaust gases, which would otherwise be vented overboard. [Figure 2-30] Both supercharged and turbocharged engines usually are fuel injected and have tight operating parameters which require that you make careful mixture adjustments and monitor engine operation closely.

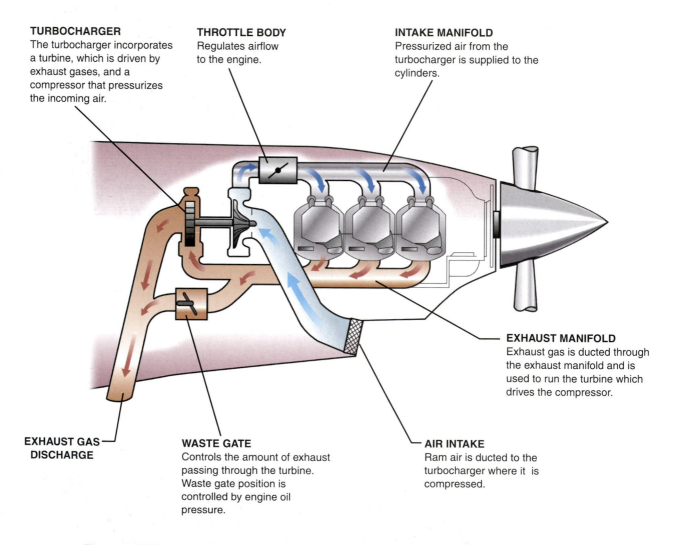

TURBOCHARGER
The turbocharger incorporates a turbine, which is driven by exhaust gases, and a compressor that pressurizes the incoming air.

THROTTLE BODY
Regulates airflow to the engine.

INTAKE MANIFOLD
Pressurized air from the turbocharger is supplied to the cylinders.

EXHAUST MANIFOLD
Exhaust gas is ducted through the exhaust manifold and is used to run the turbine which drives the compressor.

EXHAUST GAS DISCHARGE

WASTE GATE
Controls the amount of exhaust passing through the turbine. Waste gate position is controlled by engine oil pressure.

AIR INTAKE
Ram air is ducted to the turbocharger where it is compressed.

Figure 2-30. The typical general aviation turbocharging system can increase the power output of an engine. In some airplanes, the turbocharger supplies air for cabin pressurization in addition to compressed air for the engine induction system.

Power Hungry

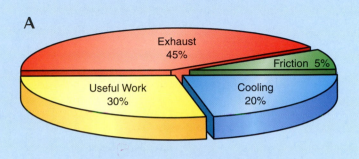

For all the improvements made over the years to the typical reciprocating engine, it is still, by many standards, underpowered. Consider the fact that only about 30% of all the heat energy released by a typical reciprocating engine translates to useful work. [Figure A] Add to that, the fact that only 90% of the torque received by the propeller is converted to actual thrust and you can see why reciprocating engines are rarely used on aircraft that require large amounts of power. Although reciprocating engine output can be improved through the use of superchargers or turbochargers [Figure B], it still may not be enough to satisfy design requirements.

It's not the fault of engine designers; it's simply that the intermittent action of the reciprocating engine makes it impractical to produce the huge amounts of power needed by some of today's aircraft. Although not necessarily as fuel efficient, the power output of the turbine engine more than outweighs this shortcoming for many applications. In some cases, power can be boosted even further for short periods of time through the use of a technique referred to as afterburning. Used by some high-performance airplanes, such as military fighters and supersonic transports, afterburning entails the introduction of raw fuel into the exhaust gases where it is ignited. The increased temperature and velocity of the gases exiting the tailpipe can increase thrust 10% to 120%. In figure C, you can see afterburners being used by a Grumman F-14 Tomcat as it prepares to takeoff from an aircraft carrier.

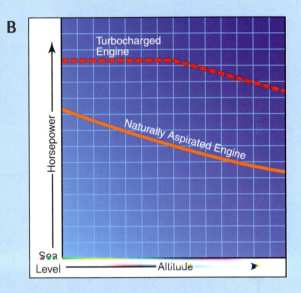

THE IGNITION SYSTEM

The ignition system provides the spark that ignites the fuel/air mixture in the cylinders. It is made up of magnetos, spark plugs, interconnecting wires, and the ignition switch. [Figure 2-31]

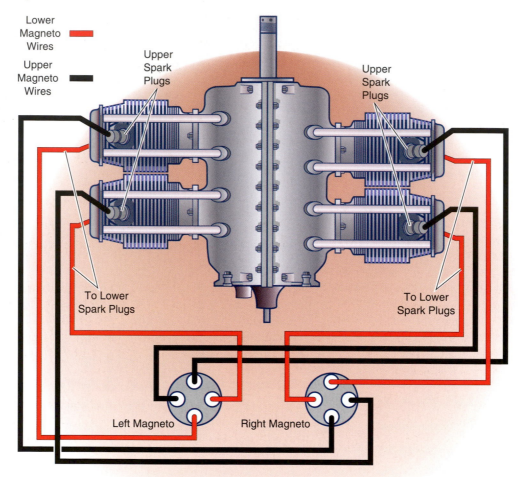

Figure 2-31. Each magneto is connected to one of the two spark plugs in each cylinder.

A **magneto** is a self-contained, engine-driven unit that supplies electrical current to the spark plugs. It uses a permanent magnet to generate an electrical current completely independent of the aircraft's electrical system. The magneto generates sufficiently high voltage to jump a spark across the spark plug gap in each cylinder. The system begins to fire when you engage the starter and the crankshaft begins to turn. It continues to operate whenever the crankshaft is rotating.

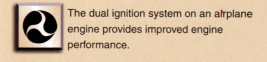

The dual ignition system on an airplane engine provides improved engine performance.

Most airplanes incorporate a dual ignition system with two individual magnetos, separate sets of wires, spark plugs, and other components to enhance safety and increase reliability of the ignition system. Each magneto operates independently to fire one of the two spark plugs in each cylinder. The firing of two spark plugs improves combustion of the fuel/air mixture and results in a slightly higher power output. If one of the magnetos fails, the other is unaffected. The engine will continue to operate normally, although you can expect a slight decrease in engine power. The same is true if one of the two spark plugs in a cylinder fails.

You control the operation of the magnetos from the cockpit with the **ignition switch**, which is normally labeled: OFF, RIGHT, LEFT, BOTH, and START. When you select the LEFT or RIGHT position, only the associated magneto is activated. When you select BOTH, the system operates on both magnetos. [Figure 2-32]

Figure 2-32. The magnetos are controlled by the ignition switch in the cockpit.

You can identify a malfunctioning ignition system during the pretakeoff check by observing the decrease in r.p.m. that occurs when you first move the ignition switch from BOTH to RIGHT, and then from BOTH to LEFT. A small decrease in engine r.p.m. is normal during this check, however, you should consult your POH for the permissible decrease. An excessive decrease could signal the presence of fouled plugs, broken or shorted wires between the magneto and the plugs, or improperly timed firing of the plugs.

Following engine shutdown, be certain that you turn the ignition switch to the OFF position. Even with the battery and master switches OFF, the engine can fire and turn over if you leave the ignition switch ON and the propeller is moved because the magneto requires no outside source of electrical power. The potential for serious injury in this situation is obvious.

Loose or broken wires in the ignition system also can cause problems. For example, if the ignition switch is OFF, the magneto may continue to fire if the ignition switch ground wire is disconnected. If this occurs, the only way to stop the engine is to move the mixture lever to the idle cutoff position, then have the system checked by a qualified mechanic.

ABNORMAL COMBUSTION

During normal combustion, the fuel/air mixture burns in a very controlled and predictable manner. Although the process occurs in a fraction of a second, the mixture actually begins to burn at the point where it is ignited by the spark plugs, then burns away from the plugs until it's all consumed. This type of combustion causes a smooth buildup of temperature and pressure and ensures that the expanding gases deliver the maximum force to the piston at exactly the right time in the power stroke. **Detonation**, on the other hand, is an uncontrolled, explosive ignition of the fuel/air mixture within the cylinder's combustion chamber. It causes excessive temperatures and pressures which, if not corrected, can quickly lead to failure of the piston, cylinder, or valves. In less severe cases, detonation causes engine overheating, roughness, or loss of power.

Detonation occurs when fuel in the cylinders explodes instead of burning smoothly.

Detonation can happen anytime you allow the engine to overheat or if you use a lower than recommended fuel grade. The potential for engine overheating is greatest under the following conditions: takeoff with an engine that is very near the maximum allowable temperature, operation at high r.p.m. and low airspeed, and extended operations above 75% power with an extremely lean mixture. If detonation is suspected on climbout, you can help cool the engine by retarding the throttle and by climbing at a slower rate.

 Detonation may result if you allow the engine to overheat or if you use an improper grade of fuel. If you suspect the engine is detonating on climbout, you can lower the nose to increase airspeed and the cooling airflow around the engine.

Detonation can often lead to another problem, known as **preignition**. As the name implies, preignition occurs when the fuel/air mixture is ignited in advance of the normal timed ignition. Preignition is caused by a residual hot spot in the cylinder such as a small carbon deposit on a spark plug, a cracked ceramic spark plug insulator, or almost any damage around the combustion chamber. [Figure 2-33]

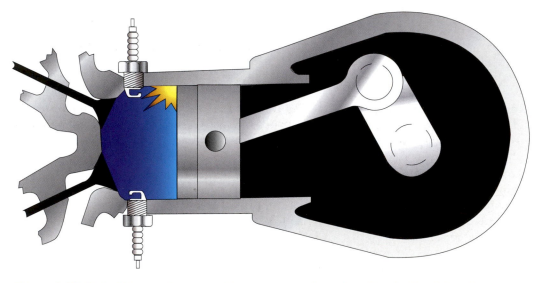

Figure 2-33. Preignition may be caused by an area roughened and heated by detonation.

Preignition and detonation may occur simultaneously. Since both are likely to cause engine roughness and high engine temperatures, you may find it difficult to distinguish between the two. If problems occur, you should attempt to lower cylinder temperature by retarding the throttle, enriching the fuel mixture, and/or lowering the nose attitude.

 Preignition is the uncontrolled combustion of fuel in advance of normal ignition.

FUEL SYSTEMS

Fuel systems may be quite complex and include a number of individual components such as tanks, lines, vents, valves, drains, and gauges. There are two general types of fuel systems found in light airplanes — those that require a fuel pump and those that operate on gravity feed. Regardless of the system on the airplane you use for training, you will eventually encounter both systems. [Figure 2-34]

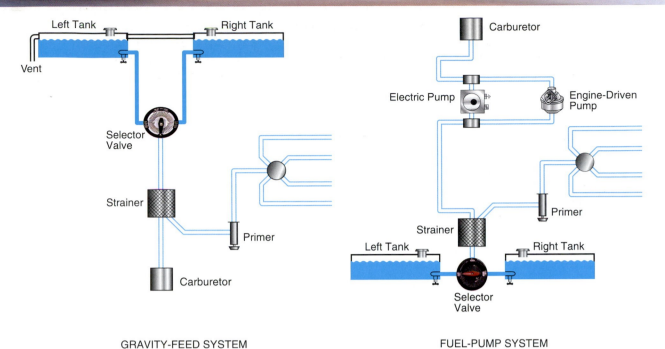

GRAVITY-FEED SYSTEM   FUEL-PUMP SYSTEM

Figure 2-34. Gravity-feed and fuel-pump systems are similar, except the gravity system normally does not include engine-driven or electric boost pumps and fuel pressure gauges.

A **fuel-pump system** is usually found in low-wing airplanes, where the fuel tanks may be located below the engine. It is also used in most high-performance airplanes with fuel-injected engines. In this type of system an engine-driven pump provides fuel under pressure from the fuel tanks to the engine. Because the engine-driven pump operates only when the engine is running, an electric boost pump, which is controlled by a switch in the cockpit, provides fuel under pressure for engine starting and as a backup, should the engine-driven pump malfunction.

 On aircraft equipped with fuel pumps, the auxiliary electric driven pump is used in the event the engine-driven fuel pump fails.

The fuel pump system usually includes a **fuel pressure gauge** which can be helpful in detecting fuel pump malfunctions. If fuel pressure drops below the normal operating range, turning on the fuel boost pump will ensure a steady flow of fuel to the engine. Any interruption of fuel flow in fuel pump system can cause problems. In a fuel pump equipped airplane, running a tank completely dry may allow air to enter the fuel system and cause a condition known as **vapor lock**. When this situation develops, it may be difficult, or impossible, to restart the engine.

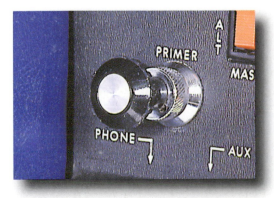

In a **gravity-feed system**, fuel flows by gravity from the fuel tanks to the engine. It works well in high-wing airplanes where the difference in height between the wing-mounted fuel tanks and the engine allows the fuel to flow under sufficient pressure to meet the requirements of the engine. Most gravity-feed, and some fuel-pump systems incorporate a manually operated pump called a primer. It is used to pump fuel directly into the intake system prior to engine start. The primer is useful in cold weather when fuel in the carburetor is difficult to vaporize. [Figure 2-35]

Figure 2-35. This manual pump-type primer can be used to help start a cold engine.

FUEL SYSTEM COMPONENTS

The **fuel tanks**, which are usually located in the wings, contain a vent which allows air pressure inside the tank to remain the same as that outside the tank. This prevents the formation of a vacuum which would restrict fuel from flowing out of the tank. The vents

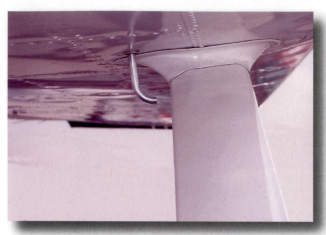

may be located in the filler caps, or the tank may be vented through a small tube extending through the wing surface. The tanks also contain an overflow drain that prevents the rupture of the tank due to fuel expansion. The overflow drain may be combined with the fuel tank vent, or it may have a separate opening. On hot days, it is not unusual to see a small amount of fuel coming from the overflow drain. [Figure 2-36]

Figure 2-36. On this Cessna 172, the left tank is vented through a tube (shown) while the right tank is vented through the filler cap.

The **fuel quantity gauges** are located on the instrument panel, where they are usually grouped with engine monitoring gauges. The amount of fuel is measured by a sensing unit in each fuel tank and is usually displayed on the gauge in gallons. Some newer gauges, however, may show the tank capacity in both gallons and pounds. [Figure 2-37]

Figure 2-37. Do not depend solely on the accuracy of your fuel quantity gauges. Always visually check the fuel level in each tank during the preflight inspection and then compare it with the corresponding fuel quantity indication.

The **fuel selector valve** allows you to select fuel from various tanks. A common type of selector valve contains four positions: LEFT, RIGHT, BOTH, and OFF. Selecting the LEFT or RIGHT position allows fuel to feed only from that tank, while selecting the BOTH position feeds fuel from both tanks. Normally, this type of selector is placed in the BOTH position. The LEFT or RIGHT position may be used to balance the amount of fuel remaining in each wing tank. [Figure 2-38]

Figure 2-38. Placards near the fuel selector may show the tank capacity in gallons of usable fuel. There also may be limitations on single tank operations, such as level flight only. Usually, you will find that the BOTH position is required for takeoffs and landings or maneuvering.

Another common type of fuel selector switch has three positions: LEFT, RIGHT, and OFF. With this type of system, you must monitor fuel consumption closely to ensure that you don't run a tank completely out of fuel or create an excessively unbalanced fuel load between tanks. [Figure 2-39]

Figure 2-39. The three position fuel selector demands that you pay close attention to fuel tank quantities.

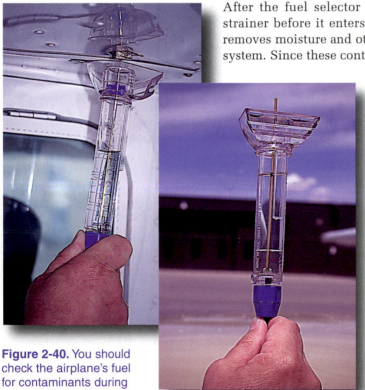

After the fuel selector valve, the fuel passes through a strainer before it enters the carburetor. The **fuel strainer** removes moisture and other sediments that might be in the system. Since these contaminants are heavier than aviation fuel, they settle in a sump at the bottom of the strainer assembly. It is generally recommended that you drain the fuel strainer before each flight. If the system design will allow it, you should also check the fuel visually to ensure that no moisture is present. [Figure 2-40]

If moisture is present in the sump, it probably means there is more water in the fuel tanks, and you should continue to drain them until there is no evidence of contamination. If you are in doubt, have the system inspected by a qualified mechanic. In any event, never take off until you are certain that all moisture has been removed from the engine fuel system. Moisture is hazardous because in cold weather it can freeze and block fuel lines. In warm weather, it can flow into the carburetor and stop the engine. To help prevent moisture buildup it is a good practice to ensure that an airplane's tanks are refueled following the last flight of the day since moisture can condense in partially filled fuel tanks.

Figure 2-40. You should check the airplane's fuel for contaminants during your preflight inspection. The sample on the right contains water. Since water is heavier than fuel, it, and other contaminants, will sink to the bottom of the tester.

Filling fuel tanks after the last flight of the day prevents moisture from condensing by eliminating air from the tanks.

REFUELING

The fuel tanks are replenished with fuel through a filler cap on top of the wing using a fuel nozzle and hose. There may be occasions when you will refuel your airplane yourself. While airplane fuel is a hazardous substance, refueling can be safely accomplished if you follow a few simple procedures.

Figure 2-41. A ground wire should be attached to the airplane during all refueling operations.

The major refueling hazard is the possible combustion of the fuel by a spark that causes fumes to ignite. The most probable cause of a spark is from static electricity that discharges between refueling equipment and the airplane. The possibility of sparking can be greatly reduced if you make sure that a ground wire from the fuel truck is attached to the airplane before the fuel cap is removed from the tank. The airplane should be grounded throughout the refueling procedure and the fuel truck should be grounded to the airport surface. [Figure 2-41] While refueling, be especially careful not to allow the fuel nozzle spout to project very far into the filler opening, since it can damage the tank. Once you finish, make sure you securely replace all fuel caps.

In addition to using the proper refueling technique, you must also ensure that you are using the proper grade of fuel. Airplane engines are designed to operate with a fuel that meets certain specifications. The recommended fuel grade and authorized substitutes for your airplane are listed in the POH. Fuel grades are identified according to octane, or performance number, and all fuel of the same grade is dyed a standard color to assist in identification. [Figure 2-42] Using an incorrect grade may seriously affect engine performance and may result in engine damage or failure.

Using a fuel grade lower than specified can cause cylinder head and engine temperatures to exceed normal operating limits. If the recommended fuel grade is not available, you may substitute the next higher grade, if approved by the manufacturer.

Figure 2-42. Color coding of fuel and placement of decals near fuel tank filler caps helps ensure that you use the proper grade of fuel.

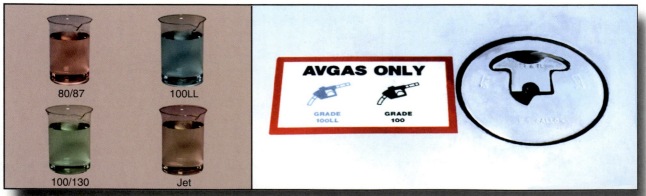

In an emergency, using the next higher grade of fuel for a short period of time is not considered harmful, provided it's authorized by the manufacturer. On the other hand, using a lower rated fuel may be extremely harmful. In addition, aviation fuel may lose its characteristic color and become clear if various fuel grades are mixed together. This can be particularly dangerous because turbine fuel, which reciprocating engines cannot tolerate, is nearly colorless.

The Airborne Gas Station

Fuel, although necessary for powered flight, is in many ways a burden. For every pound of fuel carried into the air, one less pound of passengers or cargo can be hauled aloft, reducing the utility of the aircraft. In most cases, the maximum fuel load determined by aircraft designers is a compromise between range and payload. For many military aircraft, however, limiting payload to increase range proved to be an unacceptable compromise. Therefore, a method was developed to conduct airborne refueling. The viability of the concept was realized on March 2, 1949, when a Boeing B-50A bomber nicknamed the *Lucky Lady II* completed the first nonstop flight around the world in 94 hours 1 minute. During the journey, the airplane refueled in the air four times from KB-29 tankers.

U.S. Air Force Photo by Senior Airman Jeffrey Allen

Over the years, many aircraft have fulfilled the role of airborne gas stations. One of today's most capable is the McDonnell Douglas KC-10 Extender, which can itself be refueled in flight. Even without refueling on its own, the KC-10 is capable of flying 2,200 miles round trip, while transferring one hundred tons of fuel to other aircraft enroute. A KC-10 is shown refueling a McDonnell Douglas C-17 in figure A.

The extraordinary capabilities of the KC-10 can be put into perspective if you consider the following example. On December 23, 1986, an aircraft designed by Burt Rutan landed at Edwards Air Force Base, California completing a record-setting nonstop, unrefueled flight around the world. The Voyager [Figure B], piloted by Burt's brother Dick Rutan, and Jeanna Yeager completed the feat in 9 days 3 hours 44 seconds. If the Voyager had in-flight refueling capability, one load of fuel from a KC-10 would have allowed it to continue around the world an amazing 27 additional times.

Courtesy of NASA Dryden Research Center

OIL SYSTEMS

The engine oil system performs several important functions including lubrication of the engine's moving parts and cooling of the engine by reducing friction and removing some of the heat from the cylinders. Additionally, engine oil improves engine efficiency by providing a seal between the cylinder walls and pistons. During circulation, engine oil also carries away contaminants which are removed as the oil passes through a filter. Reciprocating engines generally use either a wet-sump or dry-sump oil system. In a **dry-sump system**, the oil is contained in a separate tank and circulated through the engine by pumps. Many light airplanes use a **wet-sump system** in which all of the oil is carried in a sump which is an integral part of the engine. It is simple, reliable, and suitable for most small reciprocating engines. [Figure 2-43]

 Airplane engines depend on circulation of oil for lubrication of internal parts and cooling.

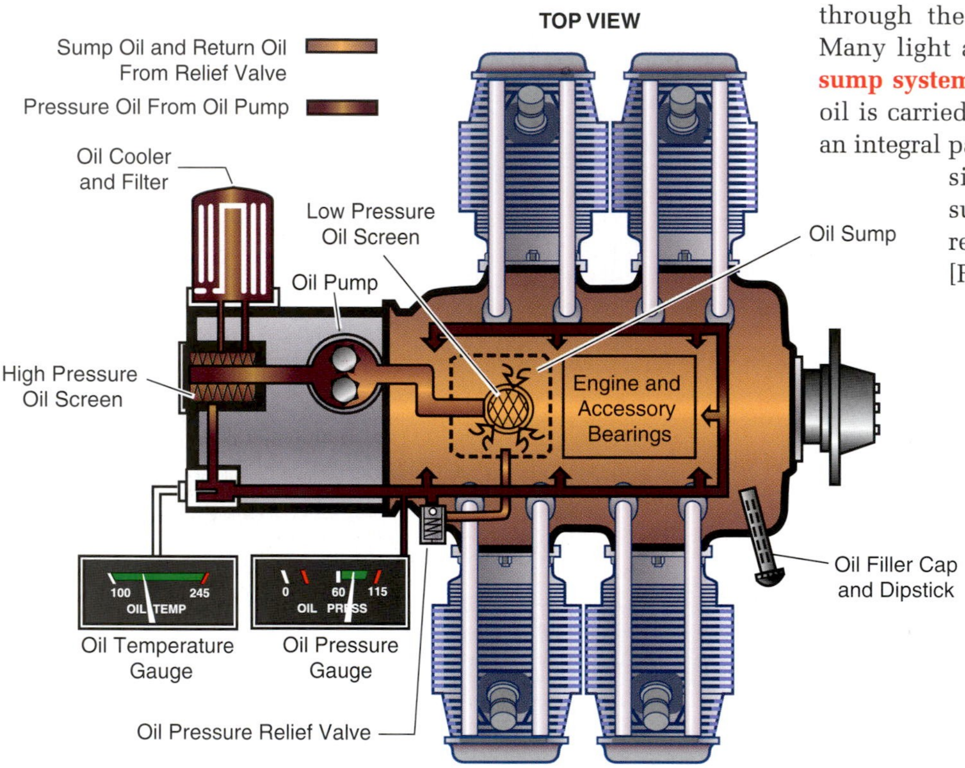

TOP VIEW

Sump Oil and Return Oil From Relief Valve

Pressure Oil From Oil Pump

Oil Cooler and Filter

Low Pressure Oil Screen

Oil Pump

Oil Sump

High Pressure Oil Screen

Engine and Accessory Bearings

Oil Filler Cap and Dipstick

100 OIL TEMP 245

0 60 115 OIL PRESS

Oil Temperature Gauge

Oil Pressure Gauge

Oil Pressure Relief Valve

Figure 2-43. The heart of a wet-sump system is the oil pump, which draws oil from the sump and routes it to the engine. After the oil passes through the engine, it returns to the sump. In some airplanes, additional lubrication is supplied by the rotating crankshaft, which splashes oil onto portions of the engine.

The oil filler cap and dipstick for measuring the oil quantity are accessible through a panel in the engine cowling. You should check the oil quantity before each flight. See your pilot's operating handbook or placards near the access panel for the minimum operating quantity, as well as the recommended oil type and weight for your airplane. [Figure 2-44]

Figure 2-44. Engine oil level should be checked during your pre-flight inspection. Note the placard on the inside of the access panel.

After engine start, you should use the oil pressure and oil temperature gauges to monitor the system. The **oil pressure gauge** provides a direct indication of the oil system operation. A below-normal pressure may mean that the oil pump is not putting out enough pressure to circulate oil throughout the engine, while an above-normal pressure may indicate a clogged oil line. You should consider any abnormal indication to mean that vital engine parts are not receiving the necessary lubrication. Under these circumstances, your best course of action is to follow the appropriate instructions in your POH. Most manufacturers recommend that you shut down the engine if the oil pressure does not begin to rise within 30 seconds after an engine start in warm weather, or 60 seconds in cold conditions. [Figure 2-45]

Figure 2-45. The oil pressure gauge measures the pressure in pounds per square inch (p.s.i.) of the oil supplied to the engine. Green typically indicates the normal operating range, while red indicates the minimum and maximum pressures.

The **oil temperature gauge** is usually located near the oil pressure gauge. This allows you to check both at the same time. Unlike oil pressure, changes in oil temperature occur more slowly. This is particularly noticeable after starting a cold engine, when it may take several minutes or longer for the gauge to show any increase in oil temperature. [Figure 2-46]

 Immediately after starting the engine, adjust r.p.m. and check engine instruments for the proper indications.

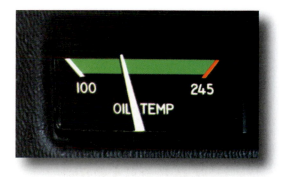

Figure 2-46. The oil temperature gauge measures the temperature of oil as it enters the engine. Normally, the green area shows the normal operating range and the red line indicates the maximum allowable temperature.

You should check the oil temperature periodically to see if it remains within the normal operating range. This is particularly important when you are using a high power setting, since this tends to increase oil temperatures. Abnormally high indications may also indicate a plugged oil line, a low oil quantity, or a defective temperature gauge.

 High engine oil temperature may be caused by an oil level that is too low.

COOLING SYSTEMS

The combustion process that takes place within the engine's cylinders produces intense heat. Excessively high engine temperatures can result in a loss of power, high oil consumption, and engine damage. While the engine oil system is essential to internal cooling of the engine, additional cooling is required to maintain normal temperatures. Much of the remaining heat is dissipated in the exhaust gases and through outside air flowing around the engine. [Figure 2-47]

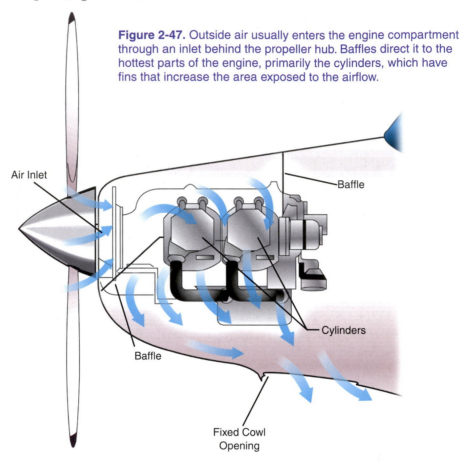

Figure 2-47. Outside air usually enters the engine compartment through an inlet behind the propeller hub. Baffles direct it to the hottest parts of the engine, primarily the cylinders, which have fins that increase the area exposed to the airflow.

Air cooling becomes less effective during takeoffs, go-arounds, or any other flight maneuver that combines low airspeed with high power. Conversely, during high-speed descents, the cooling effect of the airflow may be excessive. In order to give you more control over engine cooling, some airplanes are equipped with cowl flaps. Opening the **cowl flaps** creates a larger path for air to escape from the engine compartment, increasing the cooling airflow. [Figure 2-48]

 Excessive engine temperatures can result in loss of power, high oil consumption, and possible engine damage.

Figure 2-48. Cowl flaps, which are normally placed on the underside of the engine cowling, are likely to be installed on aircraft with high-performance engines that generate large amounts of heat. The proper use of cowl flaps can reduce extreme temperature fluctuations and prolong engine life.

Airplanes equipped with cowl flaps may have a **cylinder head temperature gauge** that provides a direct temperature reading from one of the cylinders. [Figure 2-49] By monitoring the cylinder head temperature, you can regulate the flow of cooling air by adjusting the position of the cowl flaps using a control in the cockpit. Other methods for reducing engine temperatures include enriching the mixture, reducing the rate of climb, increasing airspeed and, when conditions permit, decreasing the power setting.

 Engine temperature may be reduced by enriching the mixture, reducing the rate of climb, increasing airspeed, or reducing power.

 If oil and cylinder head temperatures are above normal, you may be using too much power with an overly lean mixture.

Figure 2-49. Like the other engine gauges, the normal range for the cylinder head temperature gauge is marked in green. You should compare the readings from the cylinder head temperature and oil temperature gauges. A disparity between the two may indicate a malfunction in one of the instruments. Oil and cylinder head temperatures above the normal operating range may indicate that you are using too much power with the mixture set too lean.

THE EXHAUST SYSTEM

In many airplanes, the exhaust system is used not only to vent burned gases overboard, but also to provide heat for the cabin and for defrosting the windscreen. A typical exhaust system for a light airplane directs exhaust out below the engine compartment through a muffler and tailpipe. As the hot exhaust gases heat the muffler, metal shrouds around the muffler capture the heat and duct it to the cabin. The amount of heated air entering the cabin can be controlled by a knob in the cockpit. [Figure 2-50]

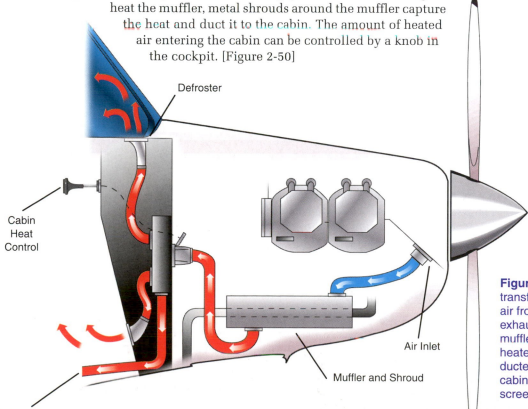

Figure 2-50. Heat is transferred to incoming air from the hot engine exhaust gases via the muffler and shroud. The heated air is then ducted to the cockpit for cabin heating and windscreen defrosting.

"EXHAUSTED"

From the Files of the NTSB...

Aircraft: *Cessna 150*
Crew: *One*
Narrative: *The student solo pilot returned from a cross country flight complaining of headache, nausea, and difficulty walking. The pilot stated that she had smelled exhaust fumes, was not taught of a potential connection between exhaust smells and carbon monoxide poisoning, and continued flight. Medical tests revealed elevated carbon monoxide, which required 5 1/2 hours of 100% oxygen to reduce to normal levels. Post-flight inspection revealed a crack in the repaired muffler which had been installed 18 hours earlier. The private pilot practical test standards require that an applicant exhibit knowledge of symptoms, effects, and corrective actions for carbon monoxide poisoning.*

The symptoms experienced by the student pilot described in the above narrative are common among people afflicted with carbon monoxide poisoning. In severe cases, carbon monoxide poisoning can result in death. Although carbon monoxide itself is colorless and odorless, if you detect a strong odor of exhaust gases, you can assume that carbon monoxide also is present. Anytime you smell engine exhaust or experience a headache, dizziness, drowsiness, and/or a loss of muscle power, you should take immediate corrective action. Procedures include turning off the heater, opening the fresh air vents, and using supplemental oxygen, if available.

PROPELLERS

Although the engine produces the power, the propeller provides the thrust to propel the airplane through the air. The propeller consists of a central hub with two or more blades attached. Each blade is an airfoil that acts like a rotating wing, producing thrust. [Figure 2-51]

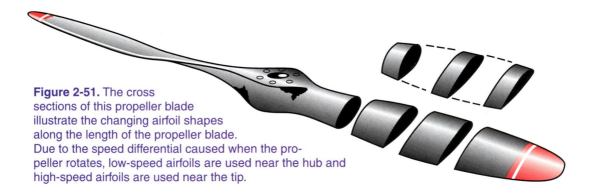

Figure 2-51. The cross sections of this propeller blade illustrate the changing airfoil shapes along the length of the propeller blade. Due to the speed differential caused when the propeller rotates, low-speed airfoils are used near the hub and high-speed airfoils are used near the tip.

The amount of thrust produced by each section of the propeller is not only a function of its shape, but is also dependent upon its rotational speed and position relative to the oncoming air. Since this varies along the propeller blade span, each small section of the propeller blade is set at a different angle to the plane of rotation. The gradual decrease in blade angle resulting from this gives the propeller blade its twisted appearance. Blade twist allows the propeller to provide more nearly uniform thrust throughout most of the length of the blade. [Figure 2-52]

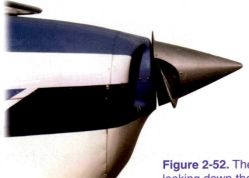

Figure 2-52. The twist of a propeller blade can be most readily seen by looking down the blade from the tip to the hub.

If the angle of each section of a propeller were averaged, you could determine an overall blade angle. A propeller with a low blade angle, known as a **climb propeller**, provides the best performance for takeoff and climb, while one with a high blade angle, known as a **cruise propeller**, is more adapted to high speed cruise and high altitude flight.

Multi-Bladed Propellers

As engine power is increased, greater propeller blade area is needed to efficiently convert the power to thrust. However, an increase in propeller size comes at a price. If the blades of the propeller are made broader, a reduction in overall efficiency may result. Increasing blade length can be a viable solution, but, at some point, increases in length become limited by ground clearance and blade tip speed. Blade tip speed becomes an issue because, as tip speed approaches the speed of sound, drag increases, and efficiency decreases. An alternative solution can be to increase the number of blades which allows engine power to be more easily absorbed. In addition, the propeller can turn more slowly which helps to reduce noise. You may notice that many higher-performance general aviation airplanes use three-bladed propellers. [Figure A]

The Lockheed C-130 Hercules military transport shown in figure B uses four-bladed propellers. Some modern commuter airplanes use propellers with five or six blades.

Another method to increase blade count is to employ two propellers per engine. The propellers contra-rotate, or turn in opposite directions. The four engines on the Tupolev Tu-95 Bear shown in figure C each drive eight-blade contra-rotating propellers.

FIXED-PITCH PROPELLER

Light airplanes may have either a fixed-pitch or a constant-speed propeller. With a **fixed-pitch propeller**, blade angle is selected on the basis of what is best for the primary function of the airplane, and cannot be changed by the pilot. The only power control for a fixed-pitch propeller is the throttle, and the only power indicator is the tachometer. [Figure 2-53]

Figure 2-53. A fixed-pitch propeller is connected directly to the engine's crankshaft. Engine power rotates the crankshaft as well as the propeller, and the propeller converts the rotary power into thrust.

CONSTANT-SPEED PROPELLER

Compared to a fixed-pitch propeller, the **constant-speed propeller** is much more efficient. It is often referred to as a variable-pitch or controllable-pitch propeller, since you can adjust the blade angle for the most efficient operation. The main advantage of a constant-speed propeller is that it converts a high percentage of the engine's power into thrust over a wide range of r.p.m. and airspeed combinations. The engine of airplanes equipped with a constant-speed propeller is controlled directly by the throttle and indirectly by the propeller control. The power output of the engine is indicated on the manifold pressure gauge and adjusted using the throttle. The **propeller control** is used to change the pitch of the propeller blades. The resulting engine r.p.m. is indicated on the tachometer. [Figure 2-54]

With a constant-speed propeller, the throttle controls engine power output, as indicated on the manifold pressure gauge, while the propeller control regulates engine r.p.m.

Figure 2-54. The propeller control changes the pitch of the propeller blades, thus controlling engine r.p.m., which is indicated on the tachometer.

The propeller control permits you to select a low blade angle and high r.p.m. setting for maximum thrust on takeoff. After you reach cruising flight conditions, you can use a higher pitch and a lower r.p.m. setting to maintain adequate thrust for the desired airspeed. This is comparable to using a low gear in your car to accelerate, then using a high gear for cruising speed. Most hydraulic pitch-change mechanisms found on single-engine airplanes use high-pressure oil to oppose the aerodynamic twisting forces acting on the blades. [Figure 2-55]

A constant-speed propeller allows you to select the blade angle that provides the most efficient performance.

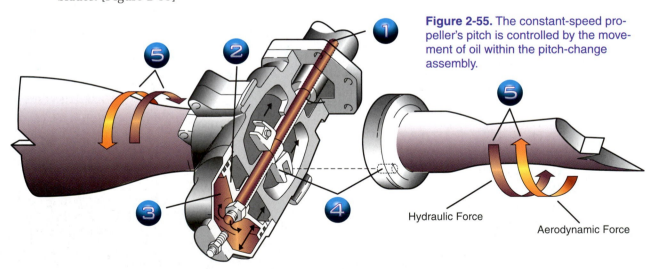

Figure 2-55. The constant-speed propeller's pitch is controlled by the movement of oil within the pitch-change assembly.

Hydraulic Force

Aerodynamic Force

 High-pressure oil enters the cylinder through the center of the propeller shaft and piston rod. The propeller control regulates the flow of high-pressure oil through a governor.

 A hydraulic piston in the hub of the propeller is connected to each blade by a piston rod. This rod is attached to forks that slide over the pitch-change pin mounted in the root of each blade.

 The oil pressure moves the piston toward the rear of the cylinder, moving the piston rod and forks aft.

 The forks push the pitch-change pin of each blade toward the rear of the hub, causing the blades to twist toward the high-pitch position.

 The governor regulates the oil pressure sent to the pitch-change mechanism to maintain an equilibrium between aerodynamic and hydraulic pitch-changing forces at the selected r.p.m.

For a given r.p.m. setting, there is always a maximum allowable manifold pressure. Operating above this level may cause internal engine stress. Specific operating instructions are contained in your POH. As a general rule, you should avoid high manifold pressures with low r.p.m. settings.

 With a constant-speed propeller, you should avoid low r.p.m. settings with high manifold pressure to prevent internal engine stress.

PROPELLER HAZARDS

The propeller can be the most dangerous part of the airplane, and should be treated with caution. You should routinely provide your passengers a thorough briefing on how to avoid propeller hazards, stressing the need to stay well clear of the propeller area at all times.

Occasionally, you may find it necessary to turn the propeller by hand to start the engine. Be sure you have seen a demonstration and received instruction on the correct procedure before attempting this yourself, since it can be extremely dangerous if done improperly. Always ensure that a qualified pilot is at the controls, and remember that the person hand-propping the airplane is in charge of the starting procedure.

 When hand-starting an airplane, a competent pilot must be at the controls.

 POWERPLANT NOISE

Aircraft noise is not only a problem as it relates to its effect on people and animals on the ground, but also as it affects pilots themselves. As you might expect, high cockpit noise levels can have both temporary and permanent effects on a pilot's hearing. In addition, noise can affect pilot performance by contributing to fatigue and communication difficulties.

Since powerplant noise is produced by many components, a variety of techniques may be used to improve the safety and comfort of aviation. For example, engine noise in small reciprocating engines can be decreased through the use of exhaust mufflers. Propeller noise can be diminished by increasing the number of blades, allowing the propeller to turn at a slower, more quiet, speed. In some cases, a reduction in cabin noise levels may be achieved by moving the entire powerplant aft of the pilot and passengers, as demonstrated by the Beechcraft Starship shown in the accompanying photo. Some problems associated with aft mounted pusher-type propellers include damage from debris thrown up by the landing gear and, in some instances, decreased performance due to the loss of airflow over the wings. Ultimately, the driving factors of efficiency, weight, simplicity, and cost determine the noise level associated with a particular aircraft and powerplant.

Courtesy of Raytheon Aircraft

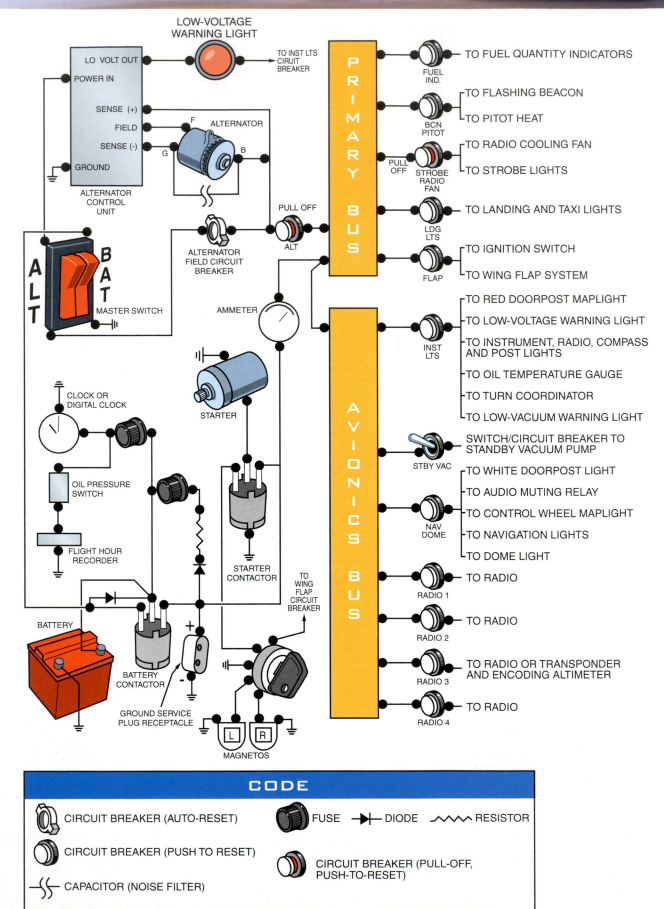

Figure 2-56. An electrical system schematic like this sample is included in most POHs.

ELECTRICAL SYSTEMS

The electrical systems found in light airplanes reflect the increased use of sophisticated avionics and other electrical accessories. Since most operations in today's flight environment are highly dependent on the airplane's electrical system, you should have an understanding of the system and its basic components. [Figure 2-56]

ALTERNATOR

On light airplanes, electrical energy is supplied by a 14- or 28-volt direct-current system, which usually is powered by an engine-driven **alternator**. Some older airplanes may be equipped with generators, but alternators have many advantages for airplanes, such as light weight, lower maintenance, and uniform output, even at low engine r.p.m. [Figure 2-57]

Alternators produce **alternating current (AC)** first, and then convert it to **direct current (DC)** for use in the system. Direct current is delivered to a bus bar which serves to distribute the current to the various electrical components on the aircraft. Although the various bus bar accessories are protected by circuit breakers, you should make sure all electrical equipment is turned off before you start the engine. This protects sensitive components, particularly the radios, from damage which may be caused by random voltages generated during the starting process.

Figure 2-57. Alternators are mounted to, and driven by the engine.

BATTERY

Another essential part of the electrical system is the storage battery. Its main purpose is to provide a means of starting the engine, but it also permits limited operation of electrical components, such as the radios, without starting the engine. In addition, the battery is a valuable source of standby or emergency electrical power in case of alternator malfunction.

AMMETER

An **ammeter** is used to monitor the electrical current in amperes within the system. Actually, there are two types of ammeters. One reflects current flowing to or from the battery. The other type simply displays the load placed on the alternator and is often referred to as a loadmeter. [Figure 2-58]

Figure 2-58. When the pointer of the ammeter on the left is on the plus side, it shows the charging rate of the battery. A minus indication means more current is being drawn from the battery than is being replaced. The loadmeter type on the right reflects the total load placed on the alternator by the system's electrical accessories. When all electrical components are turned off, it reflects the amount of charging current demanded by the battery.

A charging ammeter (needle on the plus side) is normal following an engine start, since the battery power lost in starting is being replaced. After the battery is charged, the ammeter should stabilize near zero and the alternator will supply the electrical needs of the system. A discharging ammeter means the electrical load is exceeding the output of the alternator, and the battery is helping to supply system power. This may mean the alternator is malfunctioning, or the electrical load is excessive. In any event, you should reduce your electrical load to conserve battery power and land as soon as practicable.

With a loadmeter, you can tell immediately if the alternator is operating normally, because it should reflect the amount of current being drawn by the electrical equipment. The POH will tell you the normal load to expect. Loss of the alternator will cause the loadmeter to indicate zero.

MASTER SWITCH

The **master switch** controls the entire electrical system. The airplane's ignition system is independent of the electrical system, since magnetos supply current to the spark plugs. However, the engine's starter won't operate unless the master switch is ON because power for the starter comes from the electrical system, not the magnetos. [Figure 2-59]

During normal operations, both sides of the master switch are on. In case of alternator malfunction, it can be turned OFF to isolate it from the system. If you want to check equipment on the ground before you start the engine, you can select only the battery side.

CIRCUIT BREAKERS AND FUSES

As the electrical system schematic shows, circuit breakers or fuses are used to protect various components from overloads. With circuit breakers, resetting the breaker usually will reactivate the circuit, unless an overload or short exists. If this is the case, the circuit breaker will continue to pop, indicating an electrical problem. [Figure 2-60] Manufacturers usually provide a holder for spare fuses in the event you need to replace one in flight. In fact, FARs require you to carry extra fuses for night flight.

Figure 2-59. Most airplanes use a split-rocker type master switch. The right half is labeled BAT and controls all power to the electrical system. The left half is labeled ALT and controls the alternator.

In some airplanes, certain electrical system problems may be signaled by the illumination of a low-voltage warning light. You should refer to the POH for a thorough description of normal and emergency operations for the electrical system.

Figure 2-60. As a pilot, you should know the location of the circuit protection device for each electrical component. Normally, the component's name is printed on the circuit breaker panel near its associated fuse.

SUMMARY CHECKLIST

✓ The continuous energy-creating process in almost all reciprocating airplane engines is referred to as the four-stroke operating cycle. The steps in this cycle are: the intake of the fuel/air mixture, the compression by the piston, the ignition and expansion of the gases, and the venting of the burned gases.

✓ Engine speed for aircraft equipped with a fixed-pitch propeller is displayed on a tachometer in revolutions per minute (r.p.m.).

✓ A constant-speed propeller is adjustable from the cockpit. A manifold pressure gauge is used on these types of airplanes to monitor engine output by displaying the pressure inside the engine in inches of mercury (in. Hg.).

✓ The carburetor mixes incoming air with fuel and delivers it to the combustion chamber.

✓ The operating principle of float-type carburetors is based on the difference in pressure at the venturi throat and the air inlet.

✓ The fuel/air mixture can be adjusted from the cockpit with the mixture control.

✓ Carburetor ice may be caused by fuel vaporization and decreasing air pressure in the venturi which causes a sharp temperature drop in the carburetor.

✓ Carburetor ice is more likely to occur when temperatures are below 21°C (70°F) and relative humidity is above 80%. To combat the effects of carburetor ice, engines with float-type carburetors employ a carburetor heat system which is designed to eliminate ice by routing air across a heat source before it enters the carburetor.

✓ One of the most significant advantages of the fuel injection system is the relative freedom from the formation of induction icing.

✓ Sea-level performance can be obtained even at high altitudes using either a supercharging or a turbocharging system.

✓ The ignition system is made up of magnetos, spark plugs, interconnecting wires, and the ignition switch.

✓ Detonation occurs when fuel in the cylinders explodes instead of burning smoothly.

✓ Preignition is a result of the fuel/air mixture being ignited in advance of the normal timed ignition.

✓ Fuel-pump and gravity-feed systems are similar, except the gravity system does not include engine-driven or electric boost pumps or fuel pressure gauges.

✓ To help prevent moisture buildup it is a good practice to ensure that an airplane's tanks are refueled following the last flight of the day.

✓ A wet-sump system uses an oil pump to draw oil from the sump and route it to the engine. Oil system operation can be monitored by referring to the oil pressure and temperature gauges.

✓ Cooling air enters the engine compartment through an inlet behind the propeller hub where it is further directed to the hottest part of the engine by baffles.

✓ Exhaust is normally directed out below the engine compartment through a muffler and tailpipe. Metal shrouds around the muffler capture heat which is used to defrost the windscreen and heat the cabin.

✓ A fixed-pitch propeller uses a single blade angle which is selected on the basis of what is best for the primary function of the airplane.

✓ A constant-speed propeller control permits you to select a blade angle that is the most appropriate for the flight operation being conducted. The propeller control regulates engine r.p.m. as shown on the tachometer, while the throttle controls engine power output, as indicated on the manifold pressure gauge.

✓ With a constant-speed propeller, you should avoid low r.p.m. settings with high manifold pressure.

✓ When hand-propping an airplane, always ensure that you have received instruction in the correct procedure, and a qualified pilot is at the controls.

✓ Alternators produce alternating current (AC) first, and then convert it to direct current (DC) for use in the airplane electrical system.

✓ One type of ammeter reflects current flowing to or from the battery while the other type, called a loadmeter, simply displays the load placed on the alternator.

KEY TERMS

Turbine Engine	Detonation
Reciprocating Engine	Preignition
Four-Stroke Operating Cycle	Fuel-Pump System
Throttle	Fuel Pressure Gauge
Mixture	Vapor Lock
Intake Port	Gravity-Feed System
Carburetor	Fuel Tanks
Carburetor Ice	Fuel Quantity Gauges
Carburetor Heat	Fuel Selector Valve
Fuel Injection	Fuel Strainer
Supercharger	Dry-Sump System
Turbocharger	Wet-Sump System
Magneto	Oil Pressure Gauge
Ignition Switch	Oil Temperature Gauge

Cowl Flaps   Propeller Control

Cylinder Head Temperature Gauge   Alternator

Climb Propeller   Alternating Current (AC)

Cruise Propeller   Direct Current (DC)

Fixed-Pitch Propeller   Ammeter

Constant-Speed Propeller   Master Switch

QUESTIONS

1. Identify the four-stroke operating cycle step shown in each of the following illustrations.

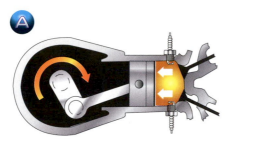
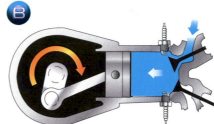

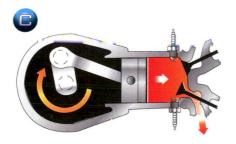
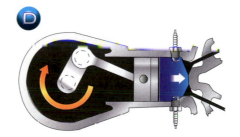

2. As an airplane climbs, do you enrichen or lean the mixture to maintain an optimum fuel/air ratio?

3. What is your first indication of carburetor ice in an airplane equipped with a fixed-pitch propeller?

4. Explain why an engine equipped with a fuel injection system is less susceptible to induction icing than one equipped with a float-type carburetor.

5. The uncontrolled, explosive ignition of the fuel/air mixture within the cylinder's combustion chamber describes which type of abnormal combustion? What actions can you take while airborne to help correct for this problem?

6. If the fuel grade specified for your airplane is not available, can you use a lower grade of fuel? A higher grade?

7. Describe at least two functions performed by the engine oil system.

8. If a constant-speed propeller is set to a high r.p.m., will the blade pitch (angle) be high or low?

9. True/False. To prevent internal engine damage in an airplane equipped with a constant-speed propeller, you should avoid low r.p.m. settings with a high manifold pressure.

10. Immediately after engine start you notice that the ammeter shows a discharge. Is this normal?

SECTION C
FLIGHT INSTRUMENTS

Of all the instruments located in the airplane cockpit, the indicators which provide you information regarding the airplane's attitude, direction, altitude, and speed are collectively referred to as the flight instruments. Traditionally, the flight instruments are sub-divided into categories according to their method of operation. The instruments that reflect your speed, rate of climb or descent, and altitude operate on air pressure differentials and are called pitot-static instruments. A pictorial view of the airplane's attitude and rate of turn is provided by the attitude indicator and turn coordinator, which operate on gyroscopic principles. The airplane's heading indicator, which also operates using a gyroscope, is usually set by using information from another flight instrument, the magnetic compass. [Figure 2-61]

MAGNETIC

Magnetic Compass

THE FLIGHT INSTRUMENTS

PITOT-STATIC

Airspeed Indicator

Altimeter

Vertical Speed Indicator

GYROSCOPIC

Attitude Indicator

Turn Coordinator

Heading Indicator

Figure 2-61. The flight instruments can be grouped according to method of operation — gyroscopic, magnetic, and pitot-static.

Welcome To The Electronic Age

Modern aircraft, particularly airliners and corporate jets, are increasingly rolling off the assembly line equipped with advanced electronic instrumentation. The push toward colorful displays has generally been in response to airline and flight crew preferences. A prime example of the current trend in airline flight deck instrument displays is exhibited by Boeing's 777, pictured below.

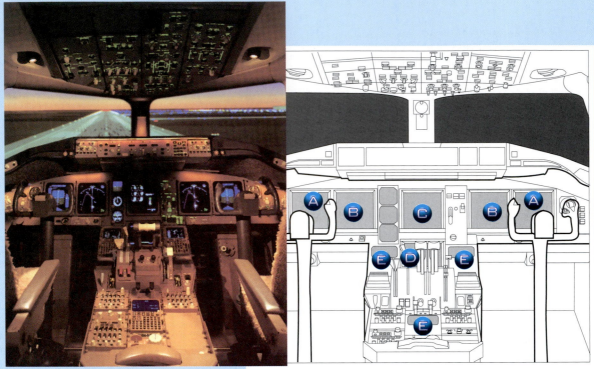

Primary flight, navigation, and engine information is presented on six large display screens laid out horizontally in front of the 777's flight crew. Three other color screens, called flight management control display units (CDUs) are located on the center console. The CDUs provide data display and entry capabilities for flight management functions. The

A Primary Flight Displays (PFD)   **B** Navigation Displays (ND)

C Engine Indicating and Crew Alerting System (EICAS)   **D** Multifunction Display (MFD)

E Flight Management Control Display Units (CDU)

Photo and graphic courtesy of Boeing Commercial Airplane Group

flat-panel displays are about half the size of the cathode-ray tube (CRT) screens used on earlier generation aircraft. The new display units generate less heat, save space, weigh less, and require less power. From a pilot's point of view, the 777 information display system is not only more reliable than previous systems, but it also uses advanced liquid-crystal technology that allows displayed information to remain clearly visible in all conditions, including direct sunlight.

PITOT-STATIC INSTRUMENTS

Pitot-static instruments rely on air pressure differences to measure speed and altitude. The airspeed indicator, altimeter, and vertical speed indicator all use surrounding, or static, air pressure. Pitot pressure, which is only used by the airspeed indicator, is the combination of the static pressure plus the pressure generated as the aircraft moves through the air.

EFFECTS OF ATMOSPHERIC CONDITIONS

Since changes in static pressure can affect pitot-static instrument operation, it is necessary to understand some basic principles of the atmosphere. Typically, air exerts about 14.7 pounds per square inch (lb/in²) at sea level. [Figure 2-62] As altitude increases, pressure steadily decreases. For example, at 18,000 feet, atmospheric pressure decreases to approximately one-half of sea level pressure.

In addition to changes in altitude, atmospheric pressure can be affected by changes in temperature. For instance, assuming that all other variables remain constant, a decrease in temperature will result in a lower atmospheric pressure. This occurs because a cooler temperature slows the movement of the air molecules, thereby lowering the pressure they exert on the surrounding atmosphere. On the other hand, a warmer temperature increases atmospheric pressure, all else being equal.

To provide a common reference for temperature and pressure, the **International Standard Atmosphere (ISA)** has been established. These

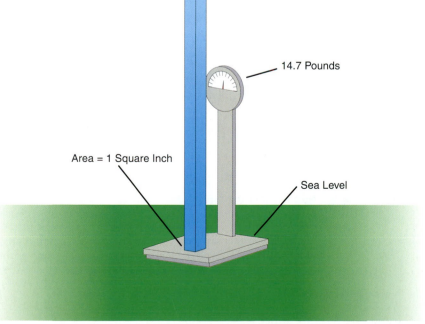

Top of the Atmosphere

14.7 Pounds

Area = 1 Square Inch

Sea Level

Figure 2-62. Atmospheric pressure may also be defined as the weight of a single column of air. The pressure decreases from the point of measurement at sea level to the top of the atmosphere.

CAN COCKPIT AUTOMATION MAKE A PILOT'S JOB EASIER?

The drive to automate the modern airplane cockpit is fueled by many desirable objectives: decrease pilot workload, improved airplane and pilot efficiency, reduced pilot error, and improved overall safety. To some, however, the increasingly computerized flight deck has as many disadvantages as advantages. These critics claim that the digital systems have channeled human error away from the relatively obvious minor occurrence to major blunders that remain hidden by technology until the end result is nothing short of disaster. Further, some analysts assert that, while manual tasks are reduced, the mental workload involved in monitoring the automated systems has increased. Regardless of the controversy, most concede that cockpit automation is here to stay. The question remains, however, how can pilots deal with increasing technology while maintaining a firm grip on command of the airplane? In the long run, the solution may lie in improved human-machine interface designs. For the present, a harmonious relationship between pilot and computer rests with complete and continuous training.

Although it may seem that these issues apply only to airline flight decks, technology has already reached the cockpits of many light general aviation (GA) aircraft. Small, hand-held Global Positioning System (GPS) satellite navigation units [Figure A] and moving map displays [Figure B] are already widely used by GA pilots. Even though these products may not be as complex as some of the systems used on large transport airplanes, they are considerably more complicated than most other equipment installed in the average light airplane cockpit.

Most experts agree that the technological advances in aviation can be beneficial. However, whether cockpit automation makes a pilot's job easier, or more complex, remains to be seen. Arguably, one the most critical problems with the use of most cockpit electronics is the increased "head down" time. As more time is devoted to operating the units and interpreting the displayed data, less time is spent looking outside the cockpit, compromising safety. The important thing to remember is that regardless of how many modern gadgets are on board, the pilot is still responsible for the safe conduct of the flight.

standard conditions are the basis for certain flight instruments and most airplane performance data. At sea level, the standard atmosphere consists of a barometric pressure of 29.92 in. Hg. (1013.2 millibars) and a temperature of 15°C (59°F). This means that, under these standard conditions, the weight of a column of air at sea level will weigh 14.7 lb/in². [Figure 2-63]

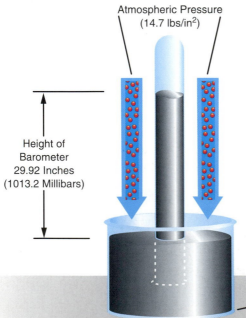

Atmospheric Pressure
(14.7 lbs/in²)

Height of
Barometer
29.92 Inches
(1013.2 Millibars)

Sea
Level

Figure 2-63. Atmospheric pressure can be measured with mercury in an inverted tube which is closed on one end. The weight of mercury in the column is balanced by the pressure (weight) of the atmosphere over the mercury reservoir. At sea level in a standard atmosphere, the weight of the atmosphere supports a column of mercury 29.92 inches high.

Since both pressure and temperature normally decrease with altitude, **standard lapse rates** can help you calculate the temperatures and pressures you can anticipate at various altitudes. In the lower atmosphere, the standard pressure lapse rate for each 1,000 feet of altitude is approximately 1.00 in. Hg., and the standard temperature lapse rate is 2°C (3.5°F). [Figure 2-64]

 ISA at sea level equals 29.92 in. Hg., or 1013.2 millibars, and has a temperature of 15°C. Temperature decreases approximately 2°C for each 1,000-foot increase in altitude.

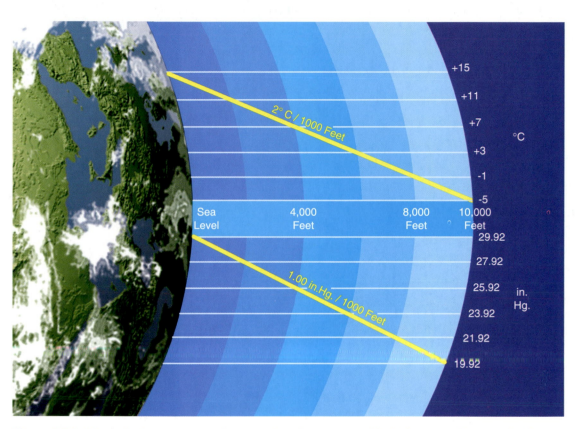

Figure 2-64. Atmospheric pressure and temperature decrease as altitude increases in a standard atmosphere. Although ISA is useful for planning purposes, it is important to remember that there can be large variations from standard conditions in the real atmosphere.

PITOT-STATIC SYSTEM

Pitot-static instruments use pressure-sensitive devices to convert pressure supplied by the pitot-static system to instrument indications in the cockpit. Pitot pressure, also called impact or ram air pressure, is supplied by the pitot tube or head. The **pitot tube** is usually mounted on the wing or on the nose section, so the opening is exposed to the relative wind. This arrangement allows ram air pressure to enter the pitot tube before it is affected by the airplane's structure. Since the pitot tube opening faces forward, an increase in speed increases ram air pressure. Static pressure

 The pitot-static system provides impact, or ram, air pressure to the airspeed indicator.

enters the pitot-static system through a **static port**, which is normally flush-mounted on the side of the fuselage in an area of relatively undisturbed air. [Figure 2-65]

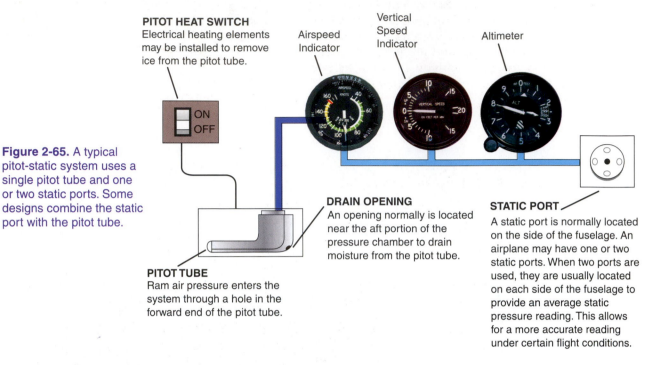

PITOT HEAT SWITCH
Electrical heating elements may be installed to remove ice from the pitot tube.

Airspeed Indicator

Vertical Speed Indicator

Altimeter

Figure 2-65. A typical pitot-static system uses a single pitot tube and one or two static ports. Some designs combine the static port with the pitot tube.

DRAIN OPENING
An opening normally is located near the aft portion of the pressure chamber to drain moisture from the pitot tube.

STATIC PORT
A static port is normally located on the side of the fuselage. An airplane may have one or two static ports. When two ports are used, they are usually located on each side of the fuselage to provide an average static pressure reading. This allows for a more accurate reading under certain flight conditions.

PITOT TUBE
Ram air pressure enters the system through a hole in the forward end of the pitot tube.

AIRSPEED INDICATOR

The airspeed indicator is the only instrument to operate using both pitot and static pressure. The speed of your airplane through the air is determined by comparing ram air pressure with static air pressure — the greater the differential, the greater the speed. The airspeed indicator is divided into color-coded arcs that define speed ranges for different phases of flight. The upper and lower limits of the colored arcs correspond to some airspeed limitations, called **V-speeds**. [Figure 2-66]

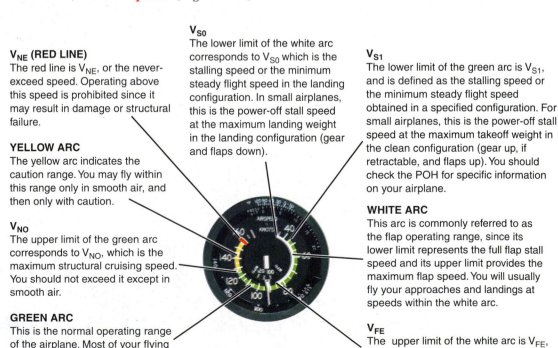

V_{NE} (RED LINE)
The red line is V_{NE}, or the never-exceed speed. Operating above this speed is prohibited since it may result in damage or structural failure.

YELLOW ARC
The yellow arc indicates the caution range. You may fly within this range only in smooth air, and then only with caution.

V_{S0}
The lower limit of the white arc corresponds to V_{S0} which is the stalling speed or the minimum steady flight speed in the landing configuration. In small airplanes, this is the power-off stall speed at the maximum landing weight in the landing configuration (gear and flaps down).

V_{S1}
The lower limit of the green arc is V_{S1}, and is defined as the stalling speed or the minimum steady flight speed obtained in a specified configuration. For small airplanes, this is the power-off stall speed at the maximum takeoff weight in the clean configuration (gear up, if retractable, and flaps up). You should check the POH for specific information on your airplane.

WHITE ARC
This arc is commonly referred to as the flap operating range, since its lower limit represents the full flap stall speed and its upper limit provides the maximum flap speed. You will usually fly your approaches and landings at speeds within the white arc.

Figure 2-66. In addition to delineating various speed ranges, the boundaries of the color-coded arcs also identify airspeed limitations.

V_{NO}
The upper limit of the green arc corresponds to V_{NO}, which is the maximum structural cruising speed. You should not exceed it except in smooth air.

GREEN ARC
This is the normal operating range of the airplane. Most of your flying will occur within this range.

V_{FE}
The upper limit of the white arc is V_{FE}, which indicates the maximum speed with the flaps extended.

Although the airspeed indicator presents important airspeed limitations, not all V-speeds are shown. For example, one very important speed not displayed is V_A, or maneuvering speed. This represents the maximum speed at which you may apply full and abrupt control movement without the possibility of causing structural damage. It also represents the maximum speed that you can safely use

 Airspeed ranges are shown by color-coded arcs on the airspeed indicator. The white arc is the flap operating range, the green arc is for normal operations, the yellow arc is the caution range, and the red line marks the never exceed speed. Important airspeeds are also marked by the boundaries of the color-coded arcs as shown in figure 2-66.

Faster Than A Speeding Bullet

Most airspeed indicators are calibrated in knots or miles per hour. Airplanes that fly at, or near, the speed of sound also are equipped with a device which measures the airplane's speed in relationship to the speed of sound, or Mach. The Machmeter indicates Mach 1.0 when the airplane is traveling at the speed of sound. Below the speed of sound, the indication is given as a decimal fraction. For example, flight at 75% of the speed of sound is displayed as Mach 0.75.

On October 3, 1967, U.S. Air Force test pilot Major William J. "Pete" Knight attained the fastest speed ever recorded in a manned airplane. After launching from a specially equipped Boeing B-52 Stratofortress over Edwards Air Force Base, California, Major Knight piloted the North American X-15A-2 rocket-powered research airplane to a top speed of 4,534 m.p.h., or Mach 6.72.

In comparison, the velocity of a .357 Magnum bullet is approximately 1,400 feet per second. This translates to a speed of 955 m.p.h., or about Mach 1.26. As you can see from the graph, the extraordinary X-15A-2 is considerably faster than a speeding bullet. In fact, at their respective top speeds, the X-15A-2 would be about 5 miles ahead of the .357 Magnum bullet in only 10 seconds.

Courtesy of NASA Dryden Research Center

Figure 2-67. You should be familiar with four types of airspeed, including indicated, calibrated, and true airspeed, as well as groundspeed.

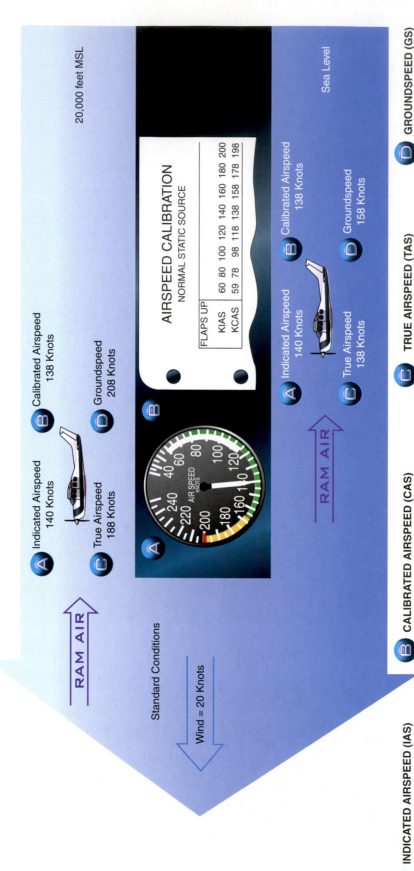

20,000 feet MSL

A Indicated Airspeed 140 Knots

B Calibrated Airspeed 138 Knots

C True Airspeed 188 Knots

D Groundspeed 208 Knots

RAM AIR

Standard Conditions

Wind = 20 Knots

AIRSPEED CALIBRATION
NORMAL STATIC SOURCE

FLAPS UP								
KIAS	60	80	100	120	140	160	180	200
KCAS	59	78	98	118	138	158	178	198

Sea Level

A Indicated Airspeed 140 Knots

B Calibrated Airspeed 138 Knots

C True Airspeed 138 Knots

D Groundspeed 158 Knots

RAM AIR

A INDICATED AIRSPEED (IAS)
Indicated airspeed is the reading you get from the airspeed indicator. Since the airspeed indicator is designed to indicate true airspeed under standard sea level conditions, IAS does not reflect variations in air density as you climb to higher altitudes. IAS is also uncorrected for installation (position) and instrument errors.

B CALIBRATED AIRSPEED (CAS)
Calibrated airspeed is indicated airspeed corrected for installation and instrument errors. Although attempts are made to minimize these errors, it is not possible to eliminate them entirely throughout the full range of operating speeds, weights, and flap settings. To determine calibrated airspeed, read indicated airspeed and then correct it by using the chart or table in the POH.

C TRUE AIRSPEED (TAS)
True airspeed represents the true speed of your airplane through the air. It is calibrated airspeed corrected for altitude and nonstandard temperature. As altitude or air temperature increases, the density of the air decreases. For a given IAS, TAS increases with altitude.

D GROUNDSPEED (GS)
Groundspeed represents the actual speed of your airplane over the ground. It is true airspeed adjusted for wind. Groundspeed decreases with a headwind and increases with a tailwind.

during turbulent flight conditions. V_A is listed in the POH and also may be found on a placard in the cockpit. It's important to check the corresponding aircraft weight when referencing these speeds since V_A changes with weight. For instance, V_A may be 100 knots when an airplane is heavily loaded and 90 knots when the load is light.

Since V_A changes with aircraft weight, it is not marked on the airspeed indicator.

When you are flying a retractable-gear airplane, two other important speeds, which are not specifically depicted on the airspeed indicator, should be taken into consideration. One speed, known as V_{LE}, should not be exceeded when the gear is extended. The other speed, called V_{LO}, is the maximum speed at which you can raise or lower the landing gear. You should reference the airplane's POH for the corresponding airspeeds.

TYPES OF AIRSPEED

The airspeed you are likely to become most familiar with is that read directly from the airspeed indicator, aptly referred to as indicated airspeed. Important performance airspeeds such as takeoff, landing, and stall speeds are always the same indicated airspeed, regardless of altitude. Other important airspeeds include calibrated airspeed, true airspeed, and groundspeed. [Figure 2-67]

As altitude increases, the indicated airspeed at which a given airplane stalls in a specific configuration remains the same.

ALTIMETER

The altimeter senses pressure changes and displays altitude in feet. It usually has three pointers, or hands, to indicate the altitude. The longest pointer shows hundreds of feet, the middle-sized pointer indicates thousands of feet, and the shortest pointer shows tens of thousands of feet. Since changes in air pressure directly affect the accuracy of the altitude readout, the altimeter is equipped with an adjustable barometric scale. [Figure 2-68]

The longest pointer of the altimeter shows hundreds of feet, the middle-sized pointer indicates thousands of feet, and the shortest pointer shows tens of thousands of feet.

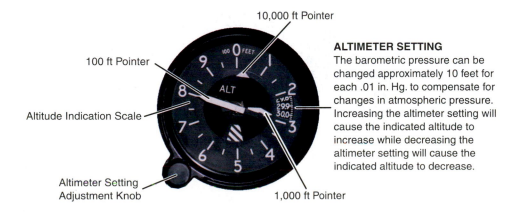

10,000 ft Pointer

100 ft Pointer

Altitude Indication Scale

Altimeter Setting Adjustment Knob

1,000 ft Pointer

ALTIMETER SETTING
The barometric pressure can be changed approximately 10 feet for each .01 in. Hg. to compensate for changes in atmospheric pressure. Increasing the altimeter setting will cause the indicated altitude to increase while decreasing the altimeter setting will cause the indicated altitude to decrease.

Figure 2-68. This altimeter shows an altitude of 2,800 feet. The barometric scale in the window on the right is set at 29.92 inches of mercury (in. Hg.).

TYPES OF ALTITUDE

The altimeter measures the vertical elevation of an object above a given reference point. The reference may be the surface of the earth, mean sea level (MSL), or some other point. There are several different types of altitude, depending on the reference point used. The six most common types are: indicated, pressure, density, true, calibrated, and absolute. **Indicated altitude** is the altitude measured by your altimeter, and the one you will use most often during flight. If you set your altimeter to the standard sea level atmospheric pressure of 29.92 in. Hg., your indicated altitude will be equivalent to **pressure altitude**. This is the vertical distance above the theoretical plane where atmospheric pressure is equal to 29.92 in. Hg. The theoretical pressure line is referred to as the standard datum plane. [Figure 2-69]

Pressure altitude is the height above the standard datum plane when 29.92 is set in the altimeter scale.

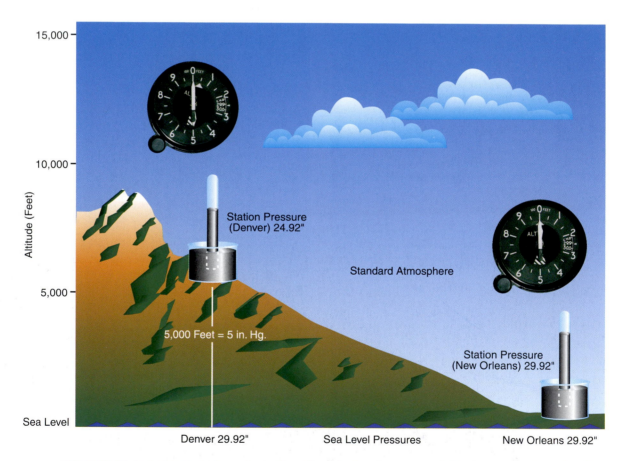

Figure 2-69. In a standard atmosphere, the atmospheric pressure, or station pressure, at sea level is 29.92 in. Hg., and the station pressure 5,000 feet above sea level is 24.92 in. Hg. That is, if you could set your altimeter to 24.92 at Denver, it would read 0 feet. Setting your altimeter to 29.92 in Denver would cause the altimeter to display your altitude as 5,000 feet above the standard datum plane (sea level in a standard atmosphere).

Pressure altitude can be combined with the existing temperature to compute a theoretical value called **density altitude**, which is an important factor in determining airplane performance. On a standard day, density altitude is equal to pressure altitude. When the outside (ambient) air tem-

Density altitude is the pressure altitude corrected for nonstandard temperature. Density altitude increases as ambient temperature increases.

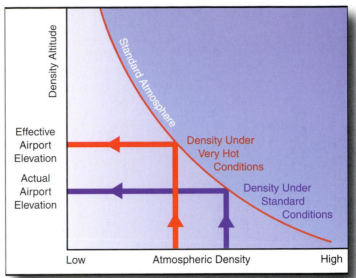

Figure 2-70. The standard atmosphere curve shows how density decreases with altitude in the standard atmosphere. Under standard conditions, the surface density altitude is equal to the elevation of the airport. Under very warm conditions, the air density is lower and the density altitude increases.

perature is above standard, density altitude is higher than pressure altitude, and aircraft performance is reduced. [Figure 2-70]

Calibrated altitude is indicated altitude corrected to compensate for instrument error.

True altitude is the actual height of an object above mean sea level (MSL). On aeronautical charts, the elevation figures for fixed objects, such as airports, towers, and TV antennas, are true altitudes. During flight, true, pressure, and indicated altitude are all equal, but only with the correct altimeter setting in a standard atmosphere. On the ground, true altitude will match indicated altitude (field elevation) when you set the altimeter to the local pressure setting. [Figure 2-71]

 True altitude is the actual vertical distance above mean sea level, and is equal to pressure altitude and indicated altitude when standard atmospheric conditions exist. True altitude is equal to field elevation when the altimeter is set to the local pressure setting.

Figure 2-71. The actual vertical distance of the airplane above mean sea level is called true altitude. The height of fixed objects is usually given in terms of true altitude.

The actual height of the airplane above the earth's surface over which it is flying is referred to as **absolute altitude**. This altitude varies with the height of the airplane, as well as the height of the surface. Absolute altitude is commonly referred to as height above ground level (AGL). [Figure 2-72]

 Absolute altitude is the height, or vertical distance, above the surface.

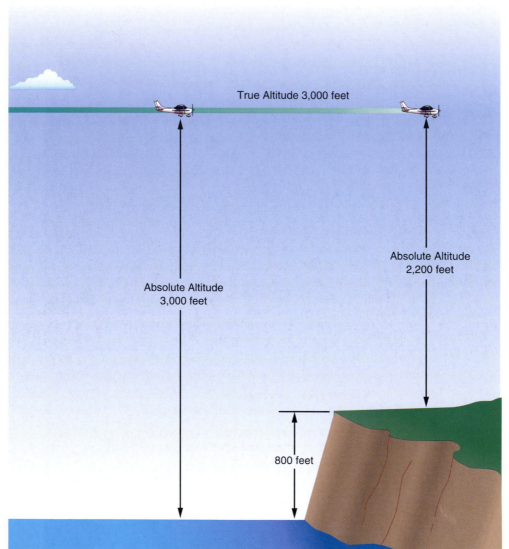

True Altitude 3,000 feet

Absolute Altitude
2,200 feet

Absolute Altitude
3,000 feet

800 feet

Figure 2-72. Your absolute altitude can change rapidly as you pass over varying terrain elevations.

ALTIMETER ERRORS

Although the altimeter is calibrated based on the International Standard Atmosphere, actual atmospheric conditions seldom match standard values. In addition, local pressure readings within a given area normally change over a period of time, and pressure frequently changes as you fly from one airport to another. As a result, altimeter indications are subject to errors. The extent of the errors depends on how much the pressure, temperature, and lapse rates deviate from standard, as well as how recently you have reset your altimeter.

The most common altimeter error is also the easiest to correct. It occurs when you fail to keep the altimeter set to the local altimeter setting. For example, assume your altimeter is set to 30.00 in. Hg. and you are flying at a constant altitude of 3,500 feet MSL. If you fly into an area where atmospheric pressure is 29.50 in. Hg., the altimeter will sense this decrease in pressure as an increase in altitude and will display a higher reading. To maintain your "desired" altitude, you will be inclined to lower the nose of the airplane and descend. [Figure 2-73]

 If you fly from an area of high pressure to an area of lower pressure without resetting your altimeter, the altimeter will indicate higher than the actual (true) altitude. If you do not reset your altimeter when flying from a low pressure area to an area of high pressure, your altimeter will indicate lower than actual (true) altitude.

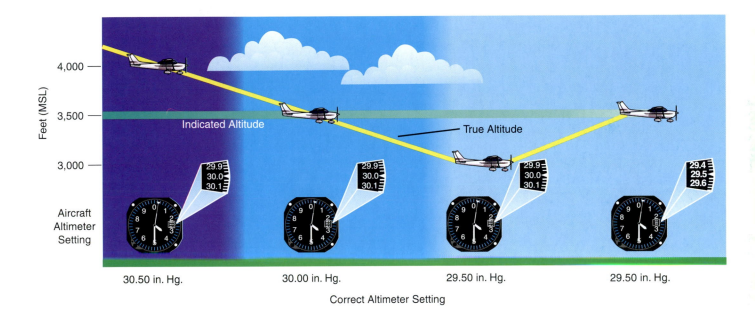

Figure 2-73. If you fly from an area of higher pressure to an area of lower pressure without resetting your altimeter, you may fly at a lower altitude than you had intended. If you reset the altimeter to the correct setting, you can maintain the desired altitude.

 A one inch change in the altimeter setting equals 1,000 feet of indicated altitude change in the same direction.

Since atmospheric pressure decreases approximately one inch of mercury for each 1,000-foot increase in altitude, you can compute potential altimeter errors. For example, if the altimeter setting decreased from 30.00 to 29.50, it would result in a change of 0.50 in. Hg. Since one inch equals 1,000 feet, 0.50 inches equals 500 feet (1,000 × .50 = 500). Maintaining your indicated altitude will result in a true altitude 500 feet lower than you intended. A good memory aid is, "When flying from high to low, look out below."

Atmospheric pressure decreases with altitude more rapidly in cold air than warm air. This means that if the atmosphere is warmer than standard, the indicated altitude will be lower than true altitude. In colder-than-standard air, the altimeter will indicate an altitude higher than true altitude. [Figure 2-74]

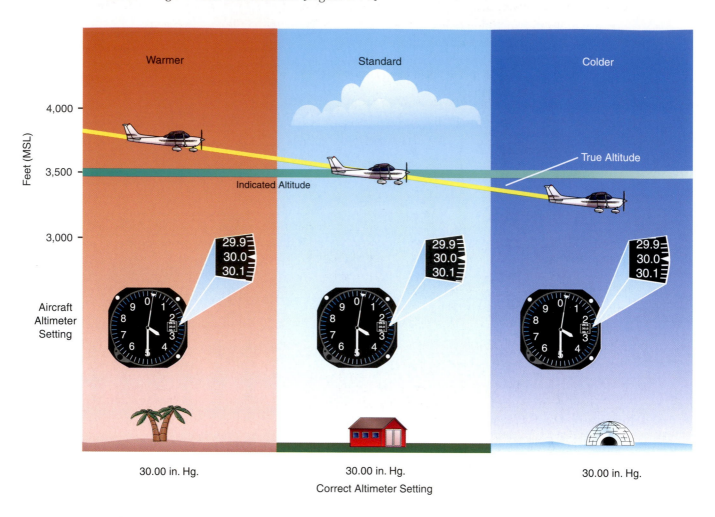

Figure 2-74. On warm days, true altitude is higher than indicated altitude. Aircraft true altitude is lower than indicated in colder air.

Temperature errors are generally smaller than those associated with sea level pressure variations. For example, if the actual temperature is 10°C warmer than standard, true altitude is about 4% higher. This is only 40 feet at 1,000 feet, but the error increases with increased altitude. At 12,000 feet MSL, a 500-foot error would exist. This discrepancy could be critical while flying over mountainous terrain.

 When atmospheric temperature is higher than standard, pressure levels are raised, and your true altitude is higher than your indicated altitude. When temperature is colder than standard, pressure levels are lowered, and your true altitude is lower than your indicated altitude.

The best way to minimize altimeter errors resulting from pressure changes is to update your altimeter setting frequently. In most cases, you use the current altimeter setting of the nearest reporting station along your route of flight. If you encounter areas of extremely low pressure (below 28.00 in. Hg.) or unusually high pressure (above 31.00 in. Hg.), you should exercise caution since large variations from standard atmospheric pressure conditions can have an increasingly detrimental effect on altimeter accuracy.

VERTICAL SPEED INDICATOR

The vertical speed indicator (VSI), which sometimes is called a vertical velocity indicator (VVI), uses static pressure to display a rate of climb or descent in feet per minute. As the airplane climbs or descends, the VSI determines the vertical speed by measuring how fast the ambient air pressure is increasing or decreasing. [Figure 2-75]

Figure 2-75. The vertical speed indicator tells you how fast you are climbing or descending. The VSI on the left shows a 300 f.p.m. descent, while the VSI on the right reflects a 300 f.p.m. climb.

The VSI is capable of displaying two different types of information. One is called trend, and the other is called rate. **Trend information** shows you an immediate indication of an increase or decrease in the airplane's rate of climb or descent. **Rate information** shows you a stabilized rate of change. For example, if you are maintaining a steady 500 f.p.m. climb, and you lower the nose slightly, the VSI will immediately sense this change and display a decrease in the rate of climb. This first indication is called the trend. After a short period of time, the VSI will stabilize and display the new rate of climb, which, in this example, would be something less than 500 f.p.m.

BLOCKAGE OF THE PITOT-STATIC SYSTEM

Although pitot-static instruments have some limitations, usually they are very reliable. Gross errors almost always indicate blockage of the pitot tube, the static port(s), or both. Blockage may be caused by moisture (including ice), dirt, or even insects. During preflight, you should make sure the pitot tube cover is removed. Then, check the pitot and static port openings. If they are clogged, the openings should be cleaned by a certificated mechanic. A clogged pitot tube only affects the accuracy of the airspeed indicator. However, a blockage of the static system not only affects the airspeed indicator, but can also cause errors in the altimeter and vertical speed indicator.

 Blockage of the pitot tube affects only the airspeed indicator, but a clogged static system affects all three pitot-static instruments, the airspeed indicator, altimeter, and VSI.

BLOCKED PITOT SYSTEM

The pitot system can become blocked completely, or only partially if the pitot tube drain hole remains open. If the pitot tube becomes clogged and its associated drain hole remains clear, ram air will no longer be able to enter the pitot system. Air already in the system will vent through the drain hole, and the remaining pressure will drop to ambient (outside) air pressure. Under these circumstances, the airspeed indicator reading decreases to zero, because the airspeed indicator senses no difference between ram and static air pressure. In other words, the airspeed indicator acts as if the airplane is stationary on the ramp. The apparent loss of airspeed is not usually instantaneous. Instead, the airspeed generally drops slowly to zero. [Figure 2-76]

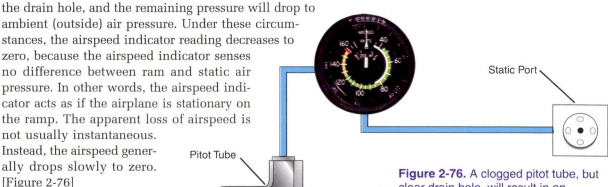

Figure 2-76. A clogged pitot tube, but clear drain hole, will result in an airspeed indication of zero.

If the pitot tube, drain hole, and static system all become clogged in flight, changes in airspeed will not be indicated due to the trapped pressures. However, if the static system remains clear, airspeed will change with altitude. An apparent increase in the ram air pressure relative to static pressure will occur as altitude increases above the level where the pitot tube and drain hole became clogged. This pressure differential causes the airspeed indicator to show an increase in speed. A decrease of indicated airspeed will occur as the airplane descends below the altitude at which the pitot system became obstructed. [Figure 2-77]

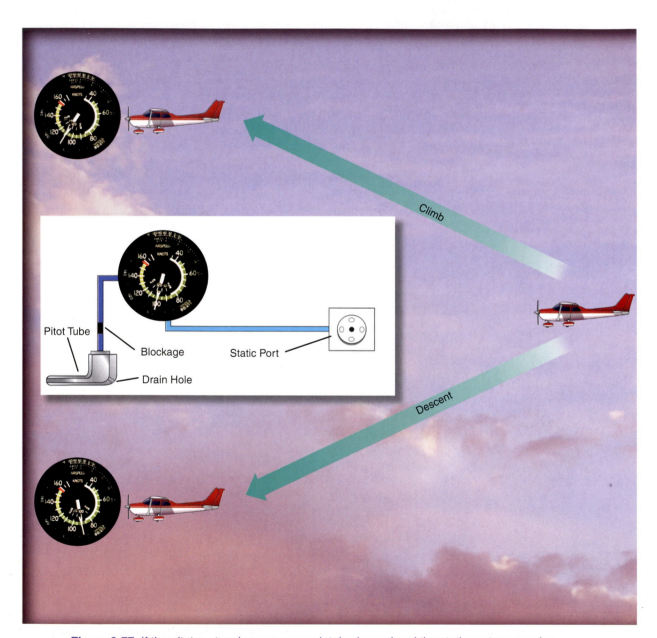

Figure 2-77. If the pitot system becomes completely clogged and the static system remains clear, indicated airspeed will vary as altitude is changed even though the speed through the air remains the same.

It is possible for the pitot tube to become obstructed during flight through visible moisture when temperatures are near the freezing level. If your airplane is equipped with pitot heat, you should turn it on to prevent the pitot tube from becoming clogged with ice. Consult your POH for specific procedures regarding the use of pitot heat.

BLOCKED STATIC SYSTEM

If the static system becomes blocked but the pitot tube remains clear, the airspeed indicator will continue to operate, however it is inaccurate. Airspeed indications will be slower than the actual speed when the airplane is operated above the altitude where the static ports became clogged because the trapped static pressure is higher than normal for that altitude. Conversely, when you operate at a lower altitude, a faster than actual airspeed will be displayed due to the relatively low static pressure trapped in the system.

A blockage of the static system also affects the altimeter and VSI. Trapped static pressure will cause the altimeter to freeze at the altitude at which the blockage occurred. In the case of the VSI, a blocked static system will produce a continuous zero indication. [Figure 2-78]

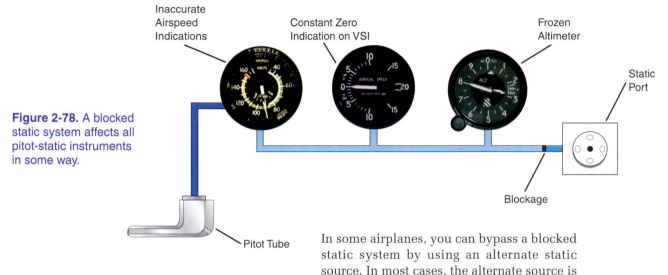

Inaccurate Airspeed Indications

Constant Zero Indication on VSI

Frozen Altimeter

Static Port

Blockage

Pitot Tube

Figure 2-78. A blocked static system affects all pitot-static instruments in some way.

In some airplanes, you can bypass a blocked static system by using an alternate static source. In most cases, the alternate source is vented inside the cockpit where ambient air pressure is lower than outside static pressure. As a result, minor pitot-static instrument errors may occur, such as slightly higher than normal airspeed and altimeter indications. In addition, the VSI may display a momentary climb immediately after the alternate static source is opened. You should check your POH for information on the use of alternate air.

GYROSCOPIC INSTRUMENTS

The primary gyroscopic instruments used on most training airplanes include the turn coordinator, attitude indicator, and heading indicator. [Figure 2-79] Gyroscopic instrument operation is based on two fundamental concepts that apply to gyroscopes — rigidity in space and precession.

Attitude indicator shows a right turn

Turn coordinator indicates a right turn

Heading moves from northerly to easterly direction indicating a right turn

Figure 2-79. As you climb, descend, or turn, you can cross-check the gyroscopic instruments to confirm your attitude and direction.

RIGIDITY IN SPACE

Rigidity in space refers to the principle that a wheel with a heavily weighted rim spun rapidly will remain in a fixed position in the plane in which it is spinning. By mounting this wheel, or gyroscope, on a set of gimbal rings, the gyro is able to rotate freely in any direction. Thus, if the gimbal rings are tilted, twisted, or otherwise moved, the gyro remains in the plane in which it was originally spinning. [Figure 2-80]

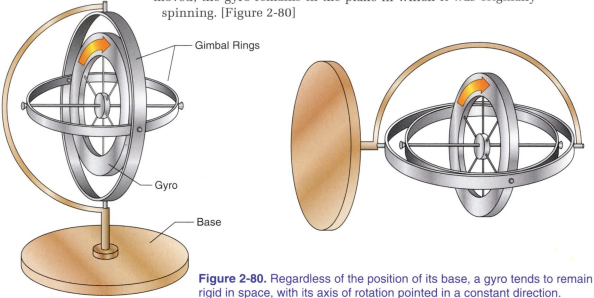

Gimbal Rings

Gyro

Base

Figure 2-80. Regardless of the position of its base, a gyro tends to remain rigid in space, with its axis of rotation pointed in a constant direction.

PRECESSION

Precession is the tilting or turning of a gyro in response to pressure. Unfortunately, it is not possible to mount a gyro in a frictionless environment. A small force is applied to the gyro whenever the airplane changes direction. The reaction to this force occurs in the direction of rotation, approximately 90° ahead of the point where the force was applied. This causes slow drifting and minor erroneous indications in the gyroscopic instruments.

SOURCES OF POWER

In order to provide accurate instrument indications, a source of power is required to keep the gyros spinning. Most small airplanes use two different sources of power to ensure that you have at least one reliable indication of aircraft bank attitude in the event of a power failure. The turn coordinator is typically an electrically powered instrument while the attitude and heading indicators normally receive power from a **vacuum (suction) system**. [Figure 2-81].

Figure 2-81. Air is first drawn into the vacuum system through a filter assembly. It then moves through the attitude and heading indicators where it causes the gyros to spin. After that, it continues to the engine-driven vacuum pump where it is expelled. A relief valve prevents the vacuum pressure or suction from exceeding prescribed limits.

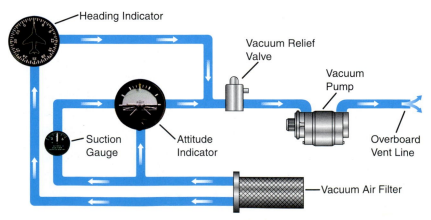

Heading Indicator

Vacuum Relief Valve

Vacuum Pump

Suction Gauge

Attitude Indicator

Overboard Vent Line

Vacuum Air Filter

Figure 2-82. During flight, the suction gauge should indicate in the proper range. If not, your attitude and heading indicators may not be reliable.

It is important for you to monitor vacuum pressure during flight, because the attitude and heading indicators may not provide reliable information when suction pressure is low. The vacuum or suction gauge generally is marked to indicate the normal range. [Figure 2-82]

Some airplanes are equipped with a warning light which illuminates when the vacuum pressure drops below the acceptable level. In addition, some airplanes also may be equipped with an electrically driven, standby vacuum pump.

TURN COORDINATOR

The turn coordinator is the relatively modern version of the early turn-and-slip indicator, many of which are still in use today. Both types of indicators provide an indication of turn direction and quality as well as a backup source of bank information in the event of attitude indicator failure. The primary difference between the two is the display of turn, or roll, information. The turn-and-slip indicator uses a pointer, called a turn needle, and the turn coordinator employs a miniature airplane. Both indicators use a ball in a tube, called an inclinometer, to provide information relating to the quality of the turn. [Figure 2-83]

Figure 2-83. During your training, you may encounter either a turn-and-slip indicator or a turn coordinator; both provide essentially the same information.

This discussion will concentrate on the turn coordinator since they are more prevalent in training aircraft. When you are rolling into or out of a turn, the miniature airplane banks in the direction the airplane is rolled. A rapid roll rate causes the miniature airplane to bank more steeply than a slow roll rate. You can use the turn coordinator to establish and maintain a **standard-rate turn** by aligning the wing of the miniature airplane with the turn index. At this rate, you will turn 3° per second and complete a 360° turn in two minutes. The turn coordinator only indicates the rate of turn and does not display a specific angle of bank. [Figure 2-84]

Figure 2-84. When the miniature airplane is level, as shown on the left, the airplane is neither turning nor rolling. When you establish a bank, the miniature airplane also banks. The indicator on the right shows a standard rate turn to the right.

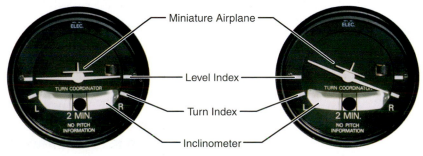

Level Flight   Standard-Rate Right Turn

The inclinometer is used to depict airplane yaw, which is the side-to-side movement of the airplane's nose. It consists of a liquid-filled, curved tube with a ball inside. During coordinated, straight-and-level flight, the force of gravity causes the ball to rest in the lowest part of the tube, centered between the reference lines. You maintain coordinated flight by keeping the ball centered. If the ball is not centered, you can center it using the rudder. To do this, you apply rudder pressure on the side where the ball is deflected. The simple rule, "Step on the ball," may help you remember which rudder pedal to depress.

The turn coordinator shows aircraft yaw and roll movement.

If aileron and rudder are coordinated during a turn, the ball will remain centered in the tube. If aerodynamic forces are unbalanced, the ball moves away from the center of the tube. In a **slip**, the rate of turn is too slow for the angle of bank, and the ball moves to the inside of the turn. In a **skid**, the rate of turn is too great for the angle of bank, and the ball moves to the outside of the turn. To correct for these conditions, and improve the quality of the turn, you should "Step on the ball." [Figure 2-85] You also may vary the angle of bank to help restore coordinated flight from a slip or skid. To correct for a slip, you should decrease bank and/or increase the rate of turn. To correct for a skid, increase the bank and/or decrease the rate of turn.

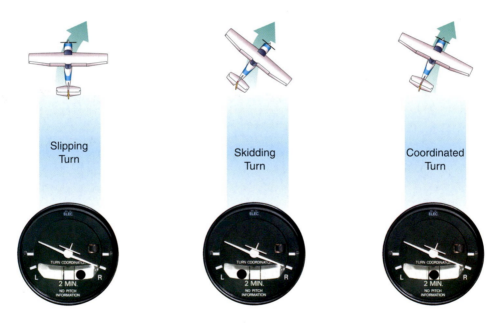

Figure 2-85. If inadequate right rudder is applied in a right turn, a slip will result. Too much right rudder will cause the airplane to skid through the turn. Centering the ball will result in a coordinated turn.

ATTITUDE INDICATOR

The attitude indicator senses roll as well as pitch, which is the up and down movement of the airplane's nose. The attitude indicator uses an artificial horizon and miniature airplane to depict the position of your airplane in relation to the true horizon. This is especially useful when the natural horizon is obscured by clouds, reduced visibility, or darkness. [Figure 2-86]

As the airplane banks, the relationship between the miniature airplane and the horizon bar depicts the direction of turn.

Figure 2-86. The attitude indicator presents you with a view of the airplane as it would appear from behind. The angle of bank is shown both pictorially by the relationship of the miniature aircraft to the deflected horizon bar and by the alignment of the pointer with the bank scale at the top of the instrument. Pitch is indicated by the position of the "nose," or center, of the miniature airplane with respect to the horizon bar.

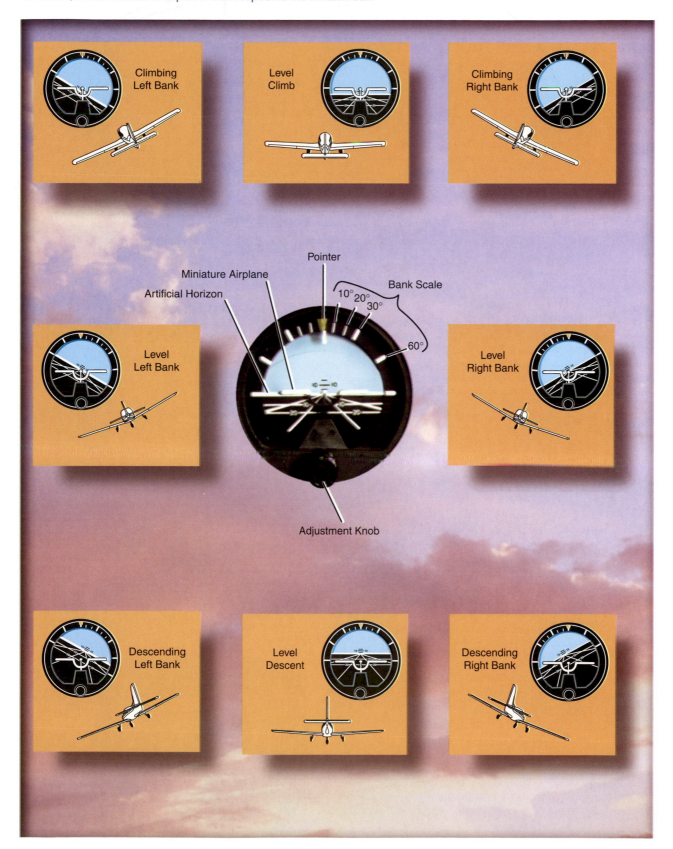

Prior to flight, you should set the miniature airplane symbol so that it is level with the horizon bar. Once properly adjusted, modern attitude indicators normally are very reliable as long as the correct vacuum pressure is maintained. Occasionally, however, attitude indicators fail gradually without providing obvious warning signals. Therefore, you should remember to periodically cross-check it with outside visual references and other flight instruments.

The miniature airplane is adjustable and should be set to match the level flight indication of the horizon bar.

HEADING INDICATOR

The heading indicator, also called a directional gyro (DG), senses airplane movement and displays heading based on a 360° azimuth, with the final zero omitted. In other words, 6 indicates 60°, 21 indicates 210°, and so on. When properly set, it is your primary source of heading information. Heading indicators in most training airplanes are referred to as "free" gyros. This means they have no automatic, north-seeking system built into them. For the heading indicator to display the correct heading, you must align it with the magnetic compass before flight. However, precession can cause the selected heading to drift from the set value. For this reason, you must regularly align the indicator with the magnetic compass. [Figure 2-87]

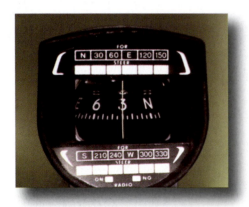

Figure 2-87. You should align the heading indicator (right) with the magnetic compass (left) before flight and check it at approximately 15-minute intervals during flight. When aligning the heading indicator while airborne, be certain you are in straight-and-level, unaccelerated flight, with the magnetic compass showing a steady indication.

Like most vacuum-powered instruments, the heading indicator may "tumble" during excessive pitch and roll conditions. If the indicator has tumbled, you must realign it with a known heading or with a stabilized indication from the magnetic compass.

MAGNETIC COMPASS

The magnetic compass was one of the first instruments to be installed in an airplane, and it is still the only direction seeking instrument in many airplanes. If you understand its limitations, the magnetic compass is a reliable source of heading information. [Figure 2-88]

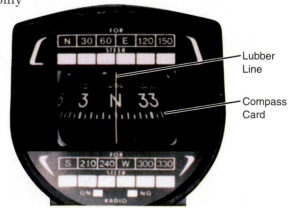

Lubber Line

Compass Card

Figure 2-88. The compass doesn't work on gyroscopic principles, but you will use it frequently to help correct for gyroscopic precession in the heading indicator.

D The Point System

As legend has it, sailors created the compass card in the early 14th century by attaching a magnetized needle or piece of lodestone to a card that depicted a compass rose. The accomplishment was a logical marriage of the direction seeking instrument, which is thought to have been invented around the 11th century, and the compass rose, which was developed much earlier. The compass rose is an outgrowth of the wind rose of ancient times, which may have been invented when Homer suggested 4 wind directions, now known as north, east, south, and west. By the 14th and 15th centuries, the rose evolved to contain 12 main directions, or points.

Eventually, the number of points increased to a total of 32. Of the 32, the original 4 wind directions were referred to as cardinal points. An additional 4 points, called intercardinal points, were placed between each cardinal heading at northeast, southeast, southwest, and northwest. Further divisions were provided by 8 combination directions which were named for the 2 directions between which they were positioned, with the cardinal point coming first, e.g. north-northwest. Finally, adding 16 additional "by-points" resulted in 32 total compass points. By-points were named for the nearest cardinal or intercardinal point and the next cardinal point in the direction of measurement, e.g. northwest by north.

The point system was widely used for quite some time, however it ultimately fell into disuse. Today's typical aircraft compass only retains the four cardinal directions in addition to the 360 degree divisions.

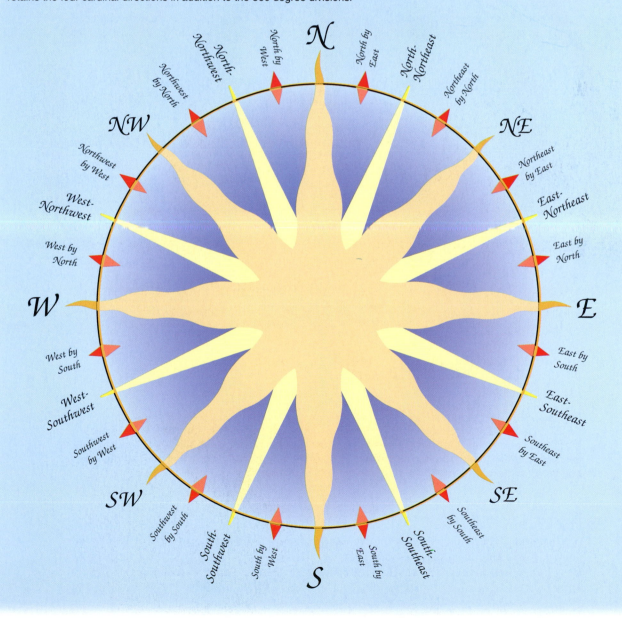

The magnetic compass is a self-contained unit which does not require electrical or suction power. To determine direction, the compass uses is a simple bar magnet with two poles. The bar magnet in the compass is mounted so it can pivot freely and align itself automatically with the earth's magnetic field. [Figure 2-89]

 Due to precession, the heading indicator must be aligned periodically with the magnetic compass.

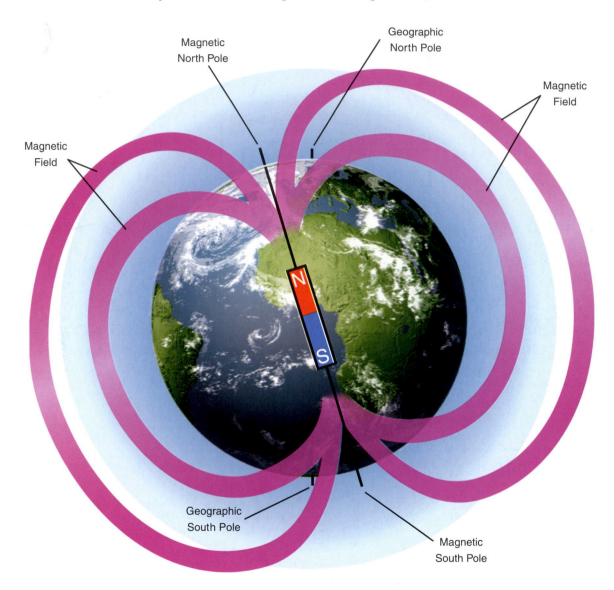

Figure 2-89. The geographic north and south poles form the axis for the earth's rotation. These positions are also referred to as true north and south. Another axis is formed by the magnetic north and south poles. Lines of magnetic force flow out from each pole in all directions, and eventually return to the opposite pole. A freely mounted bar magnet will align itself with the magnetic axis formed by the north/south magnetic field of the earth.

VARIATION

The angular difference between the true and magnetic poles at a given point is referred to as **variation**. Since most aviation charts are oriented to true north and the aircraft compass is oriented to magnetic north, you must convert a true direction to a magnetic direction by correcting for the variation. The amount of variation you need to apply is dependent upon your location on the earth's surface. [Figure 2-90]

Figure 2-90. Variation at this point in the western United States is 17°. Since the magnetic north pole is located to the east of the true north pole in relation to this point, the variation is easterly. When the magnetic pole falls to the west of the true pole, variation is westerly. Isogonic lines connect points where the variation is equal, while the agonic line defines the points where the variation is zero.

DEVIATION

Deviation refers to a compass error which occurs due to disturbances from magnetic fields produced by metals and electrical accessories within the airplane itself. Although it cannot be completely eliminated, deviation error can be decreased by manufacturer-installed compensating magnets located within the compass housing. The remaining error is recorded on a chart, called a compass correction card, which is mounted near the compass. Correction cards usually indicate whether the aircraft radios were on or off when the deviation was calculated. You should take the proper amount of deviation into account when you read the compass. [Figure 2-91]

 Deviation is the error caused by the magnetic fields of the airplane and its electronic equipment.

FOR (MH)	0°	30°	60°	90°	120°	150°	180°	210°	240°	270°	300°	330°
STEER (CH)	359°	30°	60°	88°	120°	152°	183°	212°	240°	268°	300°	329°
RADIO ON ✓							**RADIO OFF** ☐				

Figure 2-91. On this compass correction card, the deviation varies between 0° and 3°. For example, if you want to fly a magnetic heading (MH) of 060°, the compass heading (CH) also is 060°; to fly 180° magnetic, you must fly a compass heading of 183°.

COMPASS ERRORS

Although you can correct for variation and deviation, the compass is susceptible to other types of errors which, although predictable, can make it difficult to use. For example, the freedom of movement necessary for the compass to orient itself to magnetic north makes it sensitive to in-flight turbulence. In light turbulence, you may be able to use the compass by averaging the readings. For instance, if the compass swings between 030° to 060°, you can estimate an approximate heading of 045°. In heavier turbulence, however, the compass can be of very little use. Even in smooth air, additional errors can occur while you are turning or changing speed due to a phenomenon known as magnetic dip.

MAGNETIC DIP

When the bar magnet contained in the compass is pulled by the earth's magnetic field, it tends to point north and somewhat downward. The downward pull, called **magnetic dip**, is greatest near the poles and diminishes as you approach the equator. [Figure 2-92]

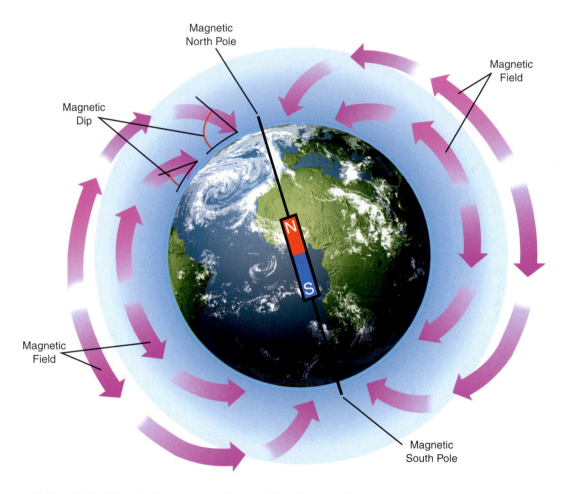

Figure 2-92. Although the compass is not subject to magnetic dip near the equator, as the compass moves closer to the poles errors resulting from magnetic dip increase gradually. Within approximately 300 miles of either magnetic pole, these errors are so great that use of the compass for navigation is impractical.

In order to minimize the tilting force on the bar magnet caused by magnetic dip, a weight is placed on the side nearest the equator. For aircraft that fly in the northern hemisphere, the weight is placed on the south end of the bar magnet. Unfortunately, the corrective weight, as well as magnetic dip itself, both contribute to acceleration and turning errors.

ACCELERATION ERROR

If you accelerate or decelerate an airplane on an easterly or westerly heading, an erroneous indication will occur. As you accelerate an airplane, inertia causes the compass weight on the south end of the bar magnet to lag slightly and turn the compass toward the north. During a deceleration, inertia causes the weight to move slightly ahead, which moves the compass toward a southerly heading even though no change of direction has taken place. The compass will return to its previous, and proper, heading once the acceleration or deceleration subsides.

 If you accelerate an airplane in the northern hemisphere, the compass shows a turn to the north; if you decelerate, it indicates a turn to the south. The error is most pronounced when flying on headings of east or west; it doesn't occur when you are flying directly on a north or south heading.

Acceleration error is more pronounced as you move closer to due east or west. The error doesn't occur when you are flying on a directly north or south heading because the bar magnet weight is in line with the direction of travel. In addition, these acceleration errors are valid only for the northern hemisphere. The effects are reversed in the southern hemisphere. The memory aid, ANDS (Accelerate North, Decelerate South), may help you recall how acceleration error affects the compass in the northern hemisphere. [Figure 2-93]

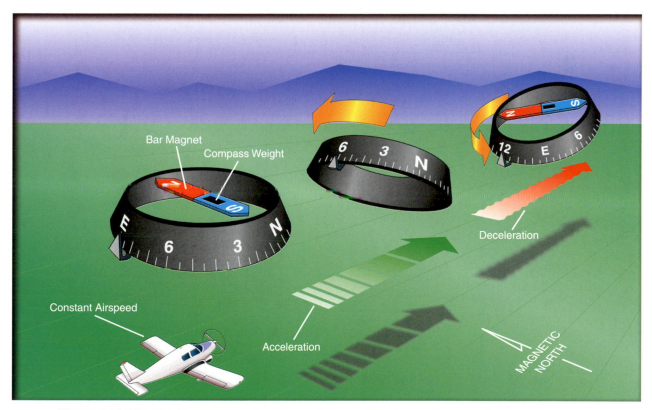

Figure 2-93. The acceleration error shown here is only valid in the northern hemisphere.

TURNING ERROR

Turning error is directly related to magnetic dip; the greater the dip, the greater the turning error. It is most pronounced when you are turning to or from headings of north or south. When you begin a turn from a heading of north, the compass initially indicates a turn in the opposite direction. When the turn is established, the compass begins to turn in the correct direction, but it lags behind the actual heading. The amount of lag decreases as the turn continues, then disappears as the airplane reaches a heading of east or west.

When turning from a heading of east or west to a heading of north, there is no error as you begin the turn. However, as the heading approaches north, the compass increasingly lags behind the airplane's actual heading. When you turn from a heading of south, the compass initially indicates a turn in the proper direction but leads the airplane's actual heading. This error also cancels out as the airplane reaches a heading of east or west. Turning from east or west to a heading of south causes the compass to move correctly at the start of a turn, but then it increasingly leads the actual heading as the airplane nears a southerly direction. [Figure 2-94]

 In the northern hemisphere, a magnetic compass will initially indicate a turn to the west if a right turn is entered from a heading of north. A left turn under the same circumstances will cause a magnetic compass to initially indicate a turn toward the east.

Figure 2-94. The left portion of the figure shows the initial tendency of the magnetic compass in a turn from a northerly heading. The initial turning error which occurs during turns from a southerly heading is shown on the right.

The amount of lead or lag is approximately equal to the latitude of the airplane. For example, if you are turning from a heading of south to a heading of west while flying at 40° north latitude, the compass will rapidly turn to a heading of 220° (180° + 40°). At the midpoint of the turn, the lead will decrease to approximately half (20°), and upon reaching a heading of west, it will be zero. As in acceleration errors, these lead and lag errors are only valid for flight in the northern hemisphere. Lead and lag errors in the southern hemisphere act in the opposite directions.

 Turning error causes the magnetic compass to lead or lag the actual magnetic heading of the airplane during turns.

COPING WITH COMPASS ERRORS

Due to its potential for errors, the magnetic compass is normally used as a backup source of heading information while the gyroscopic heading indicator is used as the primary heading reference. If your heading indicator fails and you understand the limitations of the magnetic compass, you should still be able to navigate properly. When you are referring to the compass for heading information, remember that it is accurate only when your airplane is in smooth air and in straight-and-level, unaccelerated flight.

 The magnetic compass provides accurate indications only when you are flying in smooth air and in straight-and-level, unaccelerated flight.

SUMMARY CHECKLIST

✓ The airspeed indicator, altimeter, and vertical speed indicator all use static pressure. The airspeed indicator is the only instrument which uses pitot pressure.

✓ At sea level, the standard atmosphere consists of a barometric pressure of 29.92 in. Hg. (1013.2 millibars) and a temperature of 15°C (59°F).

✓ In the lower atmosphere (below 36,000 feet), the standard pressure lapse rate for each 1,000 feet of altitude is approximately 1.00 in. Hg., and the standard temperature lapse rate is 2°C (3.5°F).

✓ The airspeed indicator is divided into color-coded arcs which define speed ranges for different phases of flight. The upper and lower limits of the arcs correspond to specific airspeed limitations, called V-speeds.

✓ V_A, or maneuvering speed, is the maximum speed at which you may apply full and abrupt control movement without the possibility of causing structural damage. Since V_A changes with aircraft weight, it is not depicted on the airspeed indicator.

✓ Regardless of altitude, the indicated airspeed at which a particular airplane stalls in a specific configuration remains the same.

✓ Indicated altitude is the altitude measured, and displayed, by your altimeter. Pressure altitude is the vertical distance above the standard datum plane, while density altitude corrects pressure altitude for nonstandard temperature. True altitude is the actual height of an object above mean sea level. Absolute altitude is the actual height of the airplane above the earth's surface over which it is flying.

✓ If you fly from an area of high pressure to an area of lower pressure without resetting your altimeter, the altimeter will indicate higher than the true altitude. True altitude will be higher than indicated altitude if you do not reset your altimeter when flying from a low pressure area to an area of high pressure.

✓ A one inch change in the altimeter setting equals 1,000 feet of indicated altitude change in the same direction.

✓ If atmospheric temperature is higher than standard, true altitude will be higher than your indicated altitude. In colder than standard temperatures, true altitude will be lower than indicated altitude.

✓ Trend information shows an immediate indication of an increase or decrease in the airplane's rate of climb or descent, while rate information shows you a stabilized rate of change.

✓ Blockage of the pitot tube only affects the airspeed indicator, but a clogged static system affects all three pitot-static instruments.

✓ Rigidity in space refers to the principle that a wheel with a heavily weighted rim spun rapidly will remain in a fixed position in the plane in which it is spinning.

✓ Precession causes slow drifting and minor erroneous indications in the gyroscopic instruments.

✓ The turn coordinator typically uses electrical power while an engine-driven vacuum pump is used to power the attitude and heading indicators.

✓ The turn coordinator provides an indication of turn direction and quality as well as a backup source of bank information in the event of attitude indicator failure.

✓ The attitude indicator uses an artificial horizon and miniature airplane to depict the position of your airplane in relation to the true horizon.

✓ Due to precession, the heading indicator must be aligned periodically with the magnetic compass. When aligning the heading indicator, be certain you are in straight-and-level, unaccelerated flight with the magnetic compass showing a steady indication.

✓ The magnetic compass shows a turn to the north if you accelerate an airplane in the northern hemisphere; if you decelerate, it indicates a turn to the south. The error doesn't occur when you are flying directly on a north or south heading.

✓ Turning error causes the magnetic compass to lead or lag the actual magnetic heading of the airplane during turns.

KEY TERMS

International Standard Atmosphere (ISA)

Standard Lapse Rates

Pitot Tube

Static Port

V-Speeds

Indicated Altitude

Pressure Altitude

Density Altitude

Calibrated Altitude

True Altitude

Absolute Altitude

Trend Information

Rate Information

Rigidity In Space

Precession

Vacuum (Suction) System

Standard-Rate Turn

Slip

Skid

Variation

Deviation

Magnetic Dip

QUESTIONS

1. What is the atmospheric pressure and temperature at sea level in a standard atmosphere?

2. Pitot pressure is used by which flight instrument(s)?

3. Referring to the airspeed indicator below, identify the V-speeds associated with the colored arcs.

4. Which important airspeed limitation changes with aircraft weight and is not depicted on the airspeed indicator.

Match the following types of altitude with the corresponding description.

5. Pressure Altitude

6. Density Altitude

7. True Altitude

8. Absolute Altitude

A. The height of the airplane above the earth's surface

B. The actual height of an object above mean sea level

C. The vertical distance above the standard datum plane

D. Pressure altitude corrected for non-standard temperature

9. You fly from an area of high pressure to an area of low pressure but do not reset your altimeter. If you maintain a consistent indicated altitude, will you be at your desired altitude? Why?

10. What will the effect be on the airspeed indicator if the static system becomes clogged, but the pitot system remains unobstructed? Why?

11. What type of movement is depicted by the attitude indicator, but not the turn coordinator?

12. True/False. If you accelerate an airplane in the northern hemisphere on a heading of east, your compass will indicate a turn to the south.

CHAPTER 3

AERODYNAMIC PRINCIPLES

Part I, Chapter 3 — Aerodynamic Principles

SECTION A
FOUR FORCES OF FLIGHT

The science of aerodynamics deals with the motion of air and the forces acting on bodies moving relative to the air. When you study aerodynamics, you are learning about why and how an airplane flies. Although aerodynamics is a complex subject, exploring the fundamental principles which govern flight can be an exciting and rewarding experience. The challenge to understand what makes an airplane fly begins with learning the four forces of flight.

During flight, the four forces acting on the airplane are lift, weight, thrust, and drag. **Lift** is the upward force created by the effect of airflow as it passes over and under the wing. The airplane is supported in flight by lift. **Weight**, which opposes lift, is caused by the downward pull of gravity. **Thrust** is the forward force which propels the airplane through the air. It varies with the amount of engine power being used. Opposing thrust is **drag**, which is a backward, or retarding, force which limits the speed of the airplane. In unaccelerated flight, the four forces are in equilibrium. Unaccelerated flight means that the airplane is maintaining a constant airspeed and is neither accelerating nor decelerating. [Figure 3-1]

The arrows which show the forces acting on an airplane are often called **vectors**. The magnitude of a vector is indicated by the arrow's length, while the direction is shown by the arrow's orientation. When two or more forces act on an object at the same time, they combine to create a resultant. [Figure 3-2]

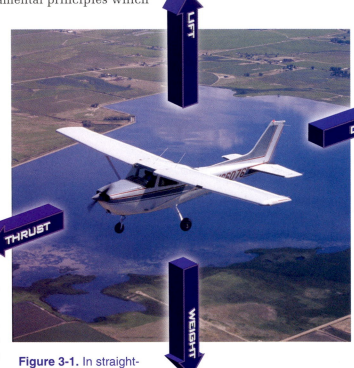

Figure 3-1. In straight-and-level, unaccelerated flight, lift is equal to and directly opposite weight and thrust is equal to and directly opposite drag. Notice that the arrows which represent the opposing forces are equal in length, but all four arrows are not the same length. This indicates that all four forces are not equal but that the opposing forces are equal to each other.

 The four forces acting on an airplane in flight are lift, weight, thrust, and drag. These forces are in equilibrium during unaccelerated flight.

Figure 3-2. When vertical and horizontal forces are applied, as shown on the left, the resultant acts in a diagonal direction. As shown on the right, the resultant of two opposing forces, which are equal in magnitude, is zero.

Resultant is Zero

LIFT

Lift is the key aerodynamic force. It is the force which opposes weight. In straight-and-level, un-accelerated flight, when weight and lift are equal, an airplane is in a state of equilibrium. If the other aerodynamic factors remain constant, the airplane neither gains nor loses altitude.

When an airplane is stationary on the ramp, it is also in equilibrium, but the aerodynamic forces are not a factor. In calm wind conditions, the atmosphere exerts equal pressure on the upper and lower surfaces of the wing. Movement of air about the airplane, particularly the wing, is necessary before the aerodynamic force of lift becomes effective. Knowledge of some of the basic principles of motion will help you to understand the force of lift.

 In straight-and-level, unaccelerated flight, lift equals weight and thrust equals drag.

NEWTON'S LAWS OF FORCE AND MOTION

In the 17th century, Sir Isaac Newton, a physicist and mathematician presented principles of motion which, today, help to explain the creation of lift by an airfoil. **Newton's three laws of motion** are as follows:

Newton's first law: A body at rest tends to remain at rest, and a body in motion tends to remain moving at the same speed and in the same direction. For example, an airplane at rest on the ramp will remain at rest unless a force is applied which is strong enough to overcome the airplane's inertia.

Newton's second law: When a body is acted upon by a constant force, its resulting acceleration is inversely proportional to the mass of the body and is directly proportional to the applied force. This law may be expressed by the formula: Force = mass × acceleration ($\mathbf{F} = m\mathbf{a}$).

Newton's third law: For every action there is an equal and opposite reaction. This principle applies whenever two things act upon each other, such as the air and the propeller, or the air and the wing of an airplane.

BERNOULLI'S PRINCIPLE

Daniel Bernoulli, a Swiss mathematician, expanded on Newton's ideas and further explored the motion of fluids in his 1783 publication *Hydrodynamics*. It was in this text that Bernoulli's equation, which describes the basic principle of airflow pressure differential, first appeared. **Bernoulli's principle**, simply stated, says, "as the velocity of a fluid (air) increases, its internal pressure decreases." Bernoulli's principle is derived from Newton's second law of motion which states the requirement of an unbalanced force (in this case, pressure) to produce an acceleration (velocity change).

One way you can visualize Bernoulli's principle is to imagine air flowing through a tube which is narrower in the middle than at the ends. This type of device is usually called a **venturi**. [Figure 3-3]

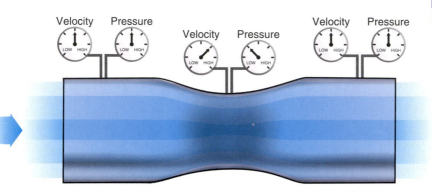

Figure 3-3. As the air enters the tube, it is traveling at a known velocity and pressure. When the airflow enters the narrow portion, the velocity increases and the pressure decreases. Then, as the airflow continues through the tube to the wider portion, both the velocity and pressure return to their original values. Throughout this process, the total energy of the airstream is conserved. An increase in velocity (kinetic energy) is accompanied by a decrease in static pressure (potential energy).

AIRFOILS

An **airfoil** is any surface, such as a wing, which provides aerodynamic force when it interacts with a moving stream of air. Some of the terms used to describe the wing, and the interaction of the airflow about it, are defined in figures 3-4 and 3-5.

Circulation of the airstream about the airfoil is an important factor in the generation of lift. Circulatory flow affects the pressure distribution on an airfoil. [Figure 3-6] The physical principles just discussed help explain the circulation of air around a wing and the pressure distribution on the wing's surface. A combination of the forces described by these principles create the total lift generated by an airfoil.

The airplane wing's shape is designed to take advantage of both Newton's laws and Bernoulli's principle. The greater curvature on the upper portion of an airfoil causes air to accelerate as it passes over the wing.

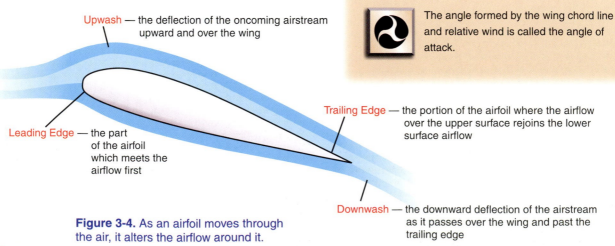

Upwash — the deflection of the oncoming airstream upward and over the wing

The angle formed by the wing chord line and relative wind is called the angle of attack.

Leading Edge — the part of the airfoil which meets the airflow first

Trailing Edge — the portion of the airfoil where the airflow over the upper surface rejoins the lower surface airflow

Downwash — the downward deflection of the airstream as it passes over the wing and past the trailing edge

Figure 3-4. As an airfoil moves through the air, it alters the airflow around it.

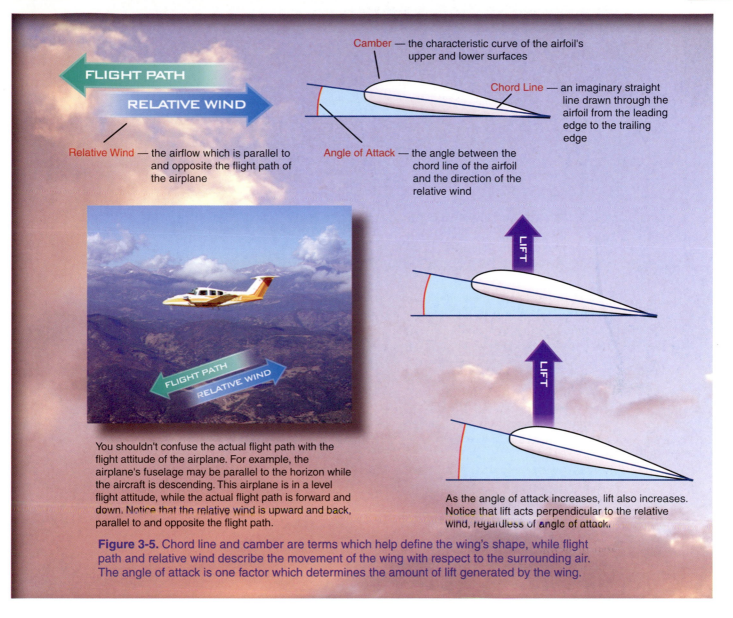

Camber — the characteristic curve of the airfoil's upper and lower surfaces

Chord Line — an imaginary straight line drawn through the airfoil from the leading edge to the trailing edge

FLIGHT PATH

RELATIVE WIND

Relative Wind — the airflow which is parallel to and opposite the flight path of the airplane

Angle of Attack — the angle between the chord line of the airfoil and the direction of the relative wind

FLIGHT PATH

RELATIVE WIND

LIFT

LIFT

You shouldn't confuse the actual flight path with the flight attitude of the airplane. For example, the airplane's fuselage may be parallel to the horizon while the aircraft is descending. This airplane is in a level flight attitude, while the actual flight path is forward and down. Notice that the relative wind is upward and back, parallel to and opposite the flight path.

As the angle of attack increases, lift also increases. Notice that lift acts perpendicular to the relative wind, regardless of angle of attack.

Figure 3-5. Chord line and camber are terms which help define the wing's shape, while flight path and relative wind describe the movement of the wing with respect to the surrounding air. The angle of attack is one factor which determines the amount of lift generated by the wing.

According to Bernoulli's theorem, the increase in speed of air on the top of an airfoil produces a drop in pressure and this lowered pressure is a component of total lift.

In addition to the lowered pressure, a downward-backward flow of air also is generated from the top surface of the wing. The reaction to this downwash results in an upward force on the wing which demonstrates Newton's third law of motion. This action/reaction

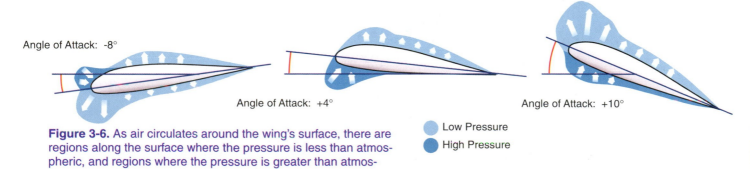

Angle of Attack: -8°

Angle of Attack: +4°

Angle of Attack: +10°

Low Pressure
High Pressure

Figure 3-6. As air circulates around the wing's surface, there are regions along the surface where the pressure is less than atmospheric, and regions where the pressure is greater than atmospheric. The specific pressure distribution varies with angle of attack.

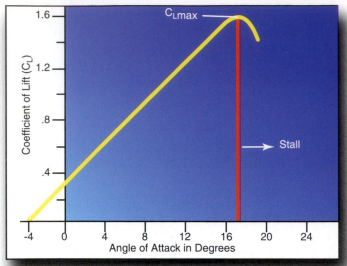

Figure 3-7. As angle of attack increases, C_L also increases. This continues to a point where C_L peaks. This point of maximum lift is called C_{Lmax}. In this example, C_{Lmax} occurs at about 17°. If the maximum lift angle is exceeded, lift decreases rapidly and the wing stalls.

principle also is apparent as the airstream strikes the lower surface of the wing when inclined at a small angle (the angle of attack) to its direction of motion. The air is forced downward and therefore causes an upward reaction resulting in positive lift.

 An airplane always stalls when the critical angle of attack is exceeded regardless of airspeed, flight attitude, or weight.

The **coefficient of lift** (C_L) is a way to measure lift as it relates to angle of attack. C_L is determined by wind tunnel tests and is based on airfoil design and angle of attack. Every airplane has an angle of attack where maximum lift occurs. [Figure 3-7]

STALLS

A **stall** is caused by the separation of airflow from the wing's upper surface. This results in a rapid decrease in lift. For a given airplane, a stall always occurs at the same angle, regardless of airspeed, flight attitude, or weight. This angle is the stalling or **critical angle of attack**. [Figure 3-8]

Stall characteristics vary with different airplanes. However, in training airplanes during most normal maneuvers, the onset of a stall is gradual. The first indications may be provided by a mushy feeling in the flight controls, a stall warning device, or a slight buffeting of the airplane. To recover from a stall, you must restore the smooth airflow by decreasing the angle of attack to a point below the critical angle of attack.

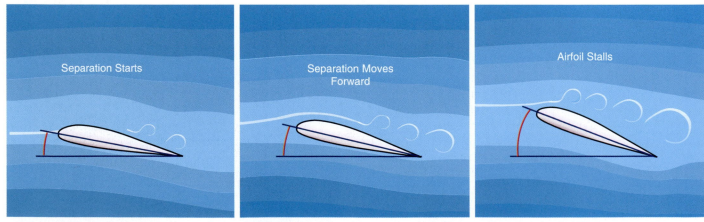

Figure 3-8. Increasing the angle of attack beyond C_{Lmax} causes progressive disruption of airflow from the upper surface of the wing. At first the airflow begins to separate at the trailing edge. As the angle of attack is further increased, the airflow separation progresses forward until the wing is fully stalled.

WING DESIGN FACTORS

Wing design is based on the anticipated use of the airplane, cost, and other factors. The main design considerations are wing planform, camber, aspect ratio, and total wing area.

Camber, as noted earlier, affects the difference in the velocity of the airflow between the upper and lower surfaces of the wing. If the upper camber increases and the lower camber remains the same, the velocity differential increases.

The Boundary Layer

Examining the boundary layer can lead to a better understanding of the cause of airflow separation from the wing. The boundary layer is a thin layer of air next to the surface of an airfoil which shows a reduction in speed due to the air's viscosity or stickiness. The boundary layer can be described as either laminar or turbulent based on the type of airflow. Laminar flow begins near the leading edge and consists of smooth laminations of air sliding over one another. At some point along the airfoil, this laminar layer transitions to a thicker turbulent flow with higher velocities.

Figure A depicts the development of the boundary layer on a flat plate. The velocity profiles can help you visualize the local velocity of the airstream in the boundary layer and provide a comparison between the laminar and turbulent airflow.

Proceeding back from the leading edge of the airfoil, pressure decreases with distance. This favorable pressure gradient (high to low) assists the flow of the boundary layer. At the point where the local velocity of the air at the surface is zero, the pressure gradient reverses and an adverse pressure gradient exists (low to high). As the angle of attack increases, the unfavorable pressure gradient grows longer, and the airflow begins to separate from the wing. [Figure B] When the airflow does not adhere to the surface near the leading edge, a stall occurs. The high velocity airflow of the turbulent boundary layer helps to prevent the airflow separation which can cause a stall.

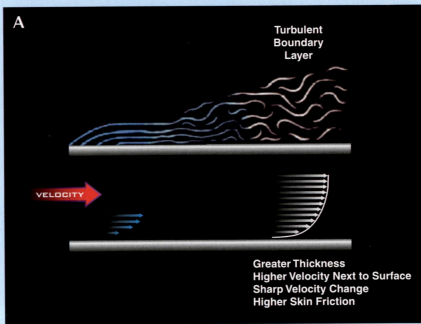

A

Turbulent Boundary Layer

VELOCITY

Greater Thickness
Higher Velocity Next to Surface
Sharp Velocity Change
Higher Skin Friction

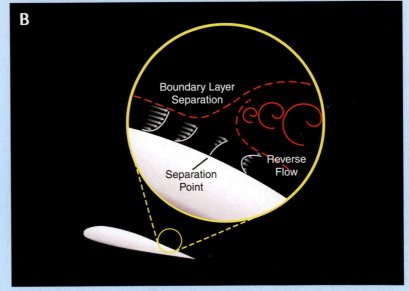

B

Boundary Layer Separation

Reverse Flow

Separation Point

Airfoil Design and Wind Tunnels

Orville and Wilbur Wright constructed a wind tunnel in 1901 and tested several hundred airfoil shapes to determine optimum performance before their aircraft was built. Today, aircraft designers use wind tunnels to test specific designs and organizations such as the National Aeronautics and Space Administration (NASA) use wind tunnels to perform research on the development of airfoil and aircraft shapes.

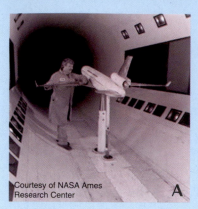

Courtesy of NASA Ames Research Center

A

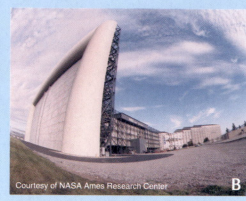

Courtesy of NASA Ames Research Center

B

Figure A shows a NASA researcher preparing a test of an MD-11 aircraft in a 12-foot pressure wind tunnel. One of the largest wind tunnels in the world measures 80 feet by 120 feet and is located at NASA's Ames Research Center in Silicon Valley, California. [Figure B]

There is, of course, a limit to the amount of camber which can be used. After a certain point, air will no longer flow smoothly over the airfoil. Once this happens, the lifting capacity diminishes. The ideal camber varies with the airplane's performance specifications, especially the speed range and the load-carrying requirements.

Aspect ratio is the relationship between the length and width of a wing. It is one of the primary factors in determining lift/drag characteristics. At a given angle of attack, a higher aspect ratio produces less drag for the same amount of lift. [Figure 3-9]

Wing area is the total surface area of the wings. Most wings don't produce a great amount of lift per square foot, so wing area must be sufficient to support the weight of the airplane. For example, in a training aircraft at normal operating speed, the wings produce only about 10.5 pounds of lift for each square foot of wing area. This means a wing area of 200 square feet is required to support an airplane weight of 2,100 pounds during straight-and-level flight.

Figure 3-9. Aspect ratio is the span of the wing, wingtip to wingtip, divided by its average chord. In general, the higher the aspect ratio, the higher the lifting efficiency of the wing. For example, gliders may have an aspect ratio of 20 to 30, while typical training aircraft have an aspect ratio of about 7 to 9.

Wing Area = 180 sq ft
Aspect Ratio = 7.2

5 ft Average Chord

36 ft Span

Wing Area = 100 sq ft
Aspect Ratio = 25

2 ft Average Chord

50 ft Span

$$\text{Aspect Ratio} = \frac{\text{Span}}{\text{Average Chord}}$$

Planform refers to the shape of the airplane's wing when viewed from above or below. Each planform design has advantages and disadvantages. [Figure 3-10]

The elliptical wing is ideal for flight at slow speeds since it provides a minimum of drag for a given aspect ratio. This type of planform is difficult to construct, though, and its stall characteristics are not as favorable as those of the rectangular wing.

The rectangular wing is not as efficient as the elliptical wing, but it has a tendency to stall first at the wing root which provides adequate stall warning and aileron effectiveness.

Tapering provides a decrease in drag and increase in lift which is most effective at high speeds. A highly tapered wing has a tendency to stall first slightly inboard of the wingtip. A good compromise on planform for low-speed aircraft is a combination of both rectangular and tapered configurations. The rectangular inboard section exhibits good stall characteristics and is cost effective. The tapered outboard portion allows for a reduction in weight and an increase in aspect ratio.

Sweptback wings, including delta wings, are efficient at high speeds but low-speed performance is degraded by this design.

Figure 3-10. Each planform design has its own specific aerodynamic characteristics.

The Swept Wing

Sweepback is an important design feature of high-speed air-craft. This characteristic allows the airplane to fly at higher speeds without reaching the critical Mach number. This is the speed at which the wing experiences supersonic airflow. Although high-speed performance is facilitated, sweepback degrades performance at low speeds. A significant part of the air velocity is flowing spanwise, not contributing to lift. This raises the stall speed and will also cause the wingtips to stall first.

By employing variable-sweep wings, the Grumman F-14 Tomcat changes its flying configuration to meet different aerodynamic and performance requirements during such operations as takeoff and landing or a high-speed air-to-air engagement. [Figure A]

A wing with forward sweep has the same effect on the airflow as a swept-back wing. Forward sweep also will reduce the critical Mach number over the wing. A forward-swept wing has the advantage of a spanwise flow directed inboard and does not have the problem of the wingtips stalling first as with aft-swept wings. Therefore, the forward-swept wing is more efficient at slow speeds. One drawback, though, is the tendency of the wing to twist more than a sweptback wing when high flight loads are applied, which can cause structural failure.

The Grumman Corporation's forward-swept wing research airplane, the X-29, uses high-tech composite construction which makes the wing lightweight and rigid to prevent twisting in flight. [Figure B]. Studies have shown that the X-29 is approximately 30% to 40% more efficient at producing lift than most conventional fighters with aft-swept wings.

A

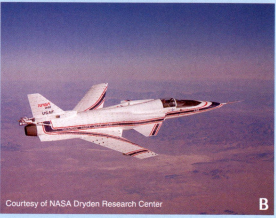

Courtesy of NASA Dryden Research Center

B

Once the design of the wing is determined, the wing must be mounted on the airplane. Usually it is attached to the fuselage with the chord line inclined upward at a slight angle, which is called the **angle of incidence**. [Figure 3-11]

When wing twist, or washout, is incorporated into the wing design, the wingtip has a lower angle of incidence than the wing root. Wing twist is used by airplane designers to prevent undesirable stall characteristics in some wing designs which have the tendency to stall first at the wingtips and then stall inward toward the root. This is an undesirable characteristic, since the disrupted airflow near the wingtip can reduce aileron effectiveness to such an extent that it may be impossible to control the airplane about its longitudinal axis. [Figure 3-12]

Longitudinal Axis

Angle of Incidence

Figure 3-11. Angle of incidence refers to the angle between the wing chord line and a line parallel to the longitudinal axis of the airplane.

Another method sometimes used to ensure positive control during the stall is installation of **stall strips**, which consist of two metal strips attached to the leading edge of each wing near the fuselage. These strips disrupt the airflow at high angles of attack, causing the wing area directly behind them to stall before the wingtips stall.

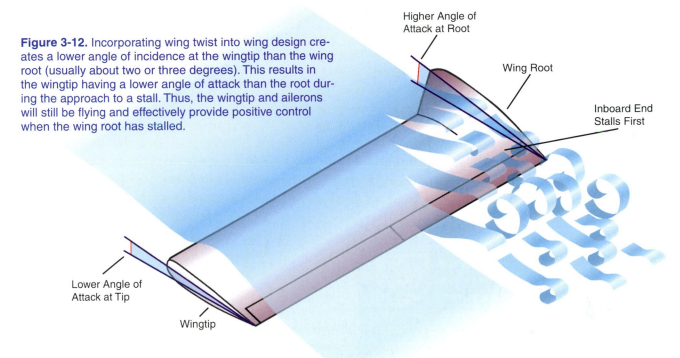

Figure 3-12. Incorporating wing twist into wing design creates a lower angle of incidence at the wingtip than the wing root (usually about two or three degrees). This results in the wingtip having a lower angle of attack than the root during the approach to a stall. Thus, the wingtip and ailerons will still be flying and effectively provide positive control when the wing root has stalled.

Higher Angle of Attack at Root

Wing Root

Inboard End Stalls First

Lower Angle of Attack at Tip

Wingtip

PILOT CONTROL OF LIFT

The amount of lift generated by an airplane is controlled by the pilot as well as determined by aircraft design factors. For example, you can change the angle of attack and the airspeed or you can change the shape of the wing by lowering the flaps. Anytime you do something to increase lift, drag also increases. Drag is always a by-product of lift.

CHANGING ANGLE OF ATTACK

You have direct control over angle of attack. During flight at normal operating speeds, if you increase the angle of attack, you increase lift. Anytime you change the pitch of the airplane during flight, you change the angle of attack of the wings. At the same time, you are changing the coefficient of lift.

CHANGING AIRSPEED

The faster the wing moves through the air, the greater the lift. Actually, lift is proportional to the square of the airplane's speed. For example, at 200 knots, an airplane has four times the lift of the same airplane traveling at 100 knots, if the angle of attack and other factors are constant. On the other hand, if the speed is reduced by one-half, lift is decreased to one-quarter of the previous value.

Although airspeed is an important factor in the production of lift, it is only one of several factors. The airspeed required to sustain an aircraft in flight depends on the flap position, the angle of attack, and the weight.

ANGLE OF ATTACK AND AIRSPEED

The relationship between angle of attack and airspeed in the production of lift is not as complex as it may seem. Angle of attack establishes the coefficient of lift for the airfoil.

At the same time, lift is proportional to the square of the airplane's speed. Since you can control both angle of attack and airspeed, you can control lift.

Total lift depends on the combined effects of airspeed and angle of attack. When speed decreases, you must increase the angle of attack to maintain the same amount of lift. Conversely, if you want to maintain the same amount of lift at a higher speed, you must decrease the angle of attack.

HIGH-LIFT DEVICES

High-lift devices are designed to increase the efficiency of the airfoil at low speeds. The most common high-lift device is the trailing-edge flap. When properly used, **flaps** increase the lifting efficiency of the wing and decrease stall speed. This allows you to fly at a reduced speed while maintaining sufficient control and lift for sustained flight. Remember, though, that when you retract the flaps, the stall speed increases.

The ability to fly at slow speeds is particularly important during the approach and landing phases. For example, an approach with full flaps permits you to fly at a fairly steep descent angle without gaining airspeed which allows the airplane to touch down at a slower speed. In addition, you can land near the approach end of the runway, even when there are obstacles along the approach path.

Flaps allow you to steepen the angle of descent on an approach without increasing airspeed.

In training airplanes, **configuration** normally refers to the position of the landing gear and flaps. When the gear and flaps are up, an airplane is in a clean configuration. If the gear is fixed rather than retractable, the airplane is considered to be in a clean configuration when the flaps are in the up position. During flight, you can change configuration by raising or lowering the gear, or by moving the flaps. Lowering the flaps affects the chord line and increases the angle of attack for the section of the wing where the flaps are attached. [Figure 3-13]

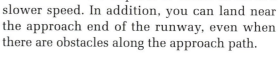

Figure 3-13. Flaps increase lift (and drag) by increasing the wing's effective camber and changing the chord line, which increases the angle of attack. In some cases, flaps also increase the area of the wing. Most flaps, when fully extended, form an angle of 35° to 40° relative to the wing.

There are several common types of flaps. The **plain flap** is attached to the wing by a hinge. When deflected downward, it increases the effective camber and changes the wing's chord line. Both of these factors increase the lifting capacity of the wing. [Figure 3-14]

Figure 3-14. Plain flap

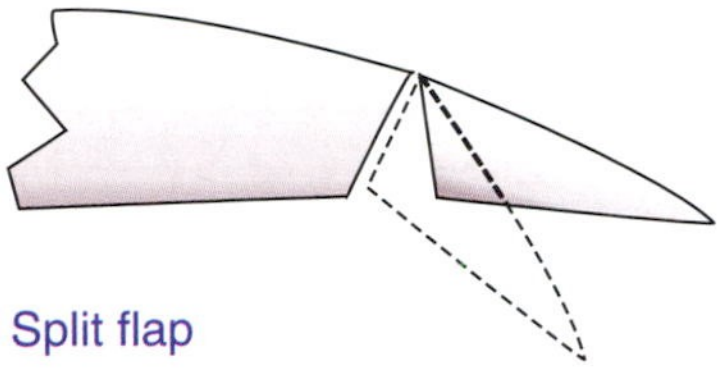

The **split flap** is hinged only to the lower portion of the wing. This type of flap also increases lift, but it produces greater drag than the plain flap because of the turbulent wake it causes. [Figure 3-15]

Figure 3-15. Split flap

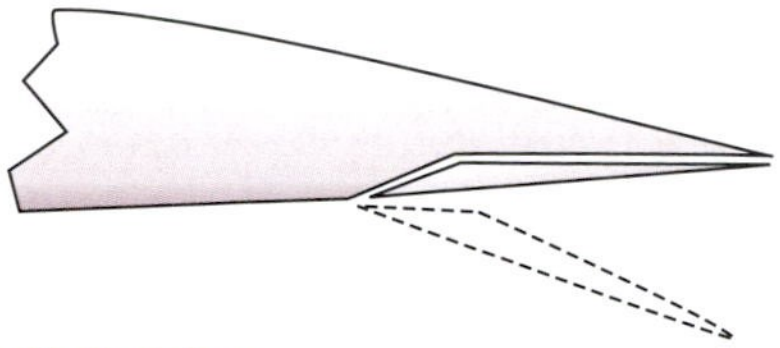

The **slotted flap** is similar to the plain flap. In addition to changing the wing's camber and chord line, it also allows a portion of the higher pressure air beneath the wing to travel through a slot. This increases the velocity of the airflow over the flap and provides additional lift. The high energy air from the slot accelerates the upper surface airflow and delays airflow separation to a higher angle of attack. [Figure 3-16]

Figure 3-16. Slotted flap

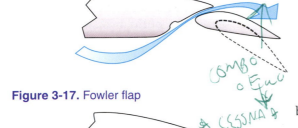

Another type of flap is the **Fowler flap**. It is attached to the wing by a track and roller system. When extended, the Fowler flap moves rearward as well as down. This rearward motion increases the total wing area, as well as the camber and chord line. [Figure 3-17]

Figure 3-17. Fowler flap

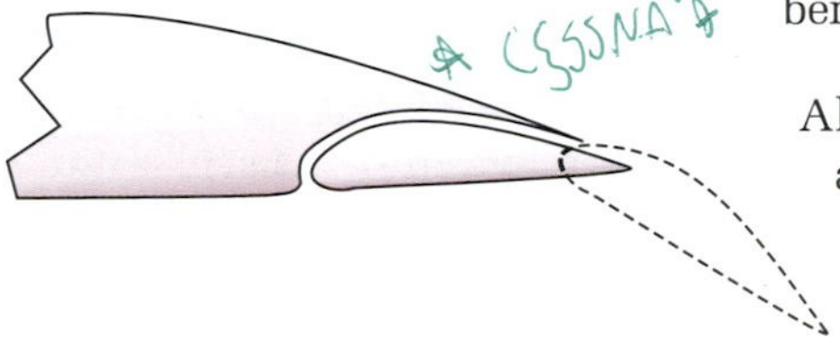

Although the amount of lift and drag created by a specific flap system varies, a few general observations can be made. As the flaps are extended, at first they will produce a relatively large amount of lift for a small increase in drag. However, once the flap extension reaches approximately the midpoint, this relationship reverses. Now, a significant increase in drag will occur for a relatively small increase in lift. Because of the large increase in drag beyond the half-flap position, most manufacturers limit the takeoff setting to half flaps or less.

Vortex Generators

Vortex generators are small airfoil-like surfaces on the wing which project vertically into the airstream. [Figure A] Vortices are formed at the tip of these generators just as they are on ordinary wingtips. These vortices add energy to the boundary layer (the layer of air next to the surface of the wing) to prevent airflow separation. This reduces stall speeds and can increase takeoff and landing performance. Although most commonly seen on high-speed aircraft, vortex generators also are used on some light general aviation aircraft.

Many animals, including bats, owls, beetles, flies, moths and even dolphins, have mechanisms for controlling lift and drag through control of the boundary layer. Blood vessels in the wings of a worker bee stabilize the membranes and increase the energy of the turbulent boundary layer flow. [Figure B]

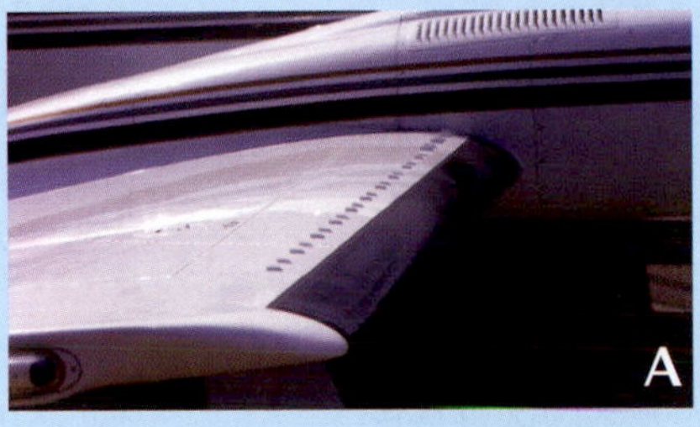

Many high-speed, high-performance airplanes employ high-lift devices to the leading edge of the wing to increase lift at slow speeds. Leading-edge flaps are used to increase the wing camber which provides additional lift. Fixed slots and movable slats conduct the flow of high energy air beneath the wing into the airflow on the upper surface of the wing which delays airflow separation to a higher angle of attack.

WEIGHT

Weight is the force of gravity which acts vertically through the center of the airplane toward the center of the earth. The weight of the airplane is not a constant. It varies with the equipment installed, passengers, cargo, and fuel load. During the course of a flight, the total weight of the airplane decreases as fuel is consumed. Additional weight reduction may also occur during some specialized flight activities, such as crop dusting, fire fighting, or sky diving flights.

THRUST

Thrust is the forward-acting force which opposes drag and propels the airplane. In most general aviation airplanes, this force is provided when the engine turns the propeller. The same physical principles involved in the generation of lift also apply when describing the force of thrust. As explained previously in this chapter, Newton's second law states that an unbalanced force, **F**, acting on a mass, m, will accelerate, **a**, the mass in the direction of the force ($\mathbf{F} = m\mathbf{a}$).

In the case of airplane thrust, the force is provided by the expansion of the burning gases in the engine which turns the propeller. A mass of air moves through the propeller, a rotating airfoil, and is accelerated opposite to the direction of the flight path. The equal and opposite reaction illustrated by Newton's third law is thrust, a force on the airplane in the direction of flight.

Figure 3-18. It is easy to visualize the creation of form drag by examining the airflow around a flat plate. Streamlining decreases form drag by reducing the airflow separation.

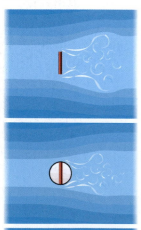

During straight-and-level, unaccelerated flight, the forces of thrust and drag are equal. You increase thrust by using the throttle to increase power. When you increase power, thrust exceeds drag, causing the airplane to accelerate. This acceleration, however, is accompanied by a corresponding increase in drag. The airplane continues to accelerate only while the force of thrust exceeds the force of drag. When drag again equals thrust, the airplane ceases to accelerate and maintains a constant airspeed. However, the new airspeed is higher than the previous one.

When you reduce thrust, the force of drag causes the airplane to decelerate. But as the airplane slows, drag diminishes. When drag has decreased enough to equal thrust, the airplane no longer decelerates. Once again, it maintains a constant airspeed. Now, however, the airspeed is slower than the one previously flown.

DRAG

Drag acts in opposition to the direction of flight, opposes the forward-acting force of thrust, and limits the forward speed of the airplane. Drag is broadly classified as either parasite or induced.

PARASITE DRAG

Parasite drag is caused by any aircraft surface which deflects or interferes with the smooth airflow around the airplane. Parasite drag normally is divided into three types: form drag, interference drag, and skin friction drag.

Figure 3-19. Design features such as wheel fairings and retractable landing gear can reduce both form and interference drag.

Form drag results from the turbulent wake caused by the separation of airflow from the surface of a structure. The amount of drag is related to both the size and shape of the structure which protrudes into the relative wind. [Figure 3-18]

Interference drag occurs when varied currents of air over an airplane meet and interact. Placing two objects adjacent to one another may produce turbulence 50% to 200% greater than the parts tested separately. An example of interference drag is the mixing of the air over structures such as wing and tail surface brace struts and landing gear struts. [Figure 3-19]

Skin friction drag is caused by the roughness of the airplane's surfaces. Even though these surfaces may appear smooth, under a microscope, they may be quite rough. A thin layer of air clings to these rough surfaces and creates small eddies which contribute to drag. [Figure 3-20]

Each type of parasite drag varies with the speed of the airplane. The combined effect of all parasite drag varies proportionately to the square of the airspeed. For example, a particular airplane at a constant altitude has four times as much parasite drag at 160 knots as it does at 80 knots. [Figure 3-21]

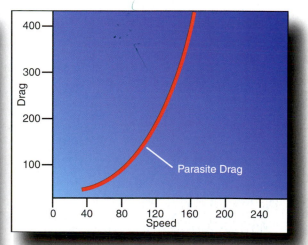

Figure 3-21. If airspeed is doubled, parasite drag increases fourfold. This is the same formula that applies to lift. Because of its rapid increase with increasing airspeed, parasite drag is predominant at high speeds. At low speeds, near a stall, parasite drag is at its low point.

Figure 3-20. Skin friction drag can be minimized by employing a glossy, flat finish to surfaces, and by eliminating protruding rivet heads, roughness, and other irregularities.

INDUCED DRAG

Induced drag is generated by the airflow circulation around the wing as it creates lift. The high pressure air beneath the wing joins the low pressure air above the wing at the trailing edge and wingtips. This causes a spiral or vortex which trails behind each wingtip whenever lift is being produced. These **wingtip vortices** have the effect of deflecting the airstream downward in the vicinity of the wing, creating an increase in downwash. Therefore, the wing operates in an *average* relative wind which is inclined downward and rearward near the wing. Because the lift produced by the wing is perpendicular to the relative wind, the lift is inclined aft by the same amount. The component of lift acting in a rearward direction is induced drag. [Figure 3-22]

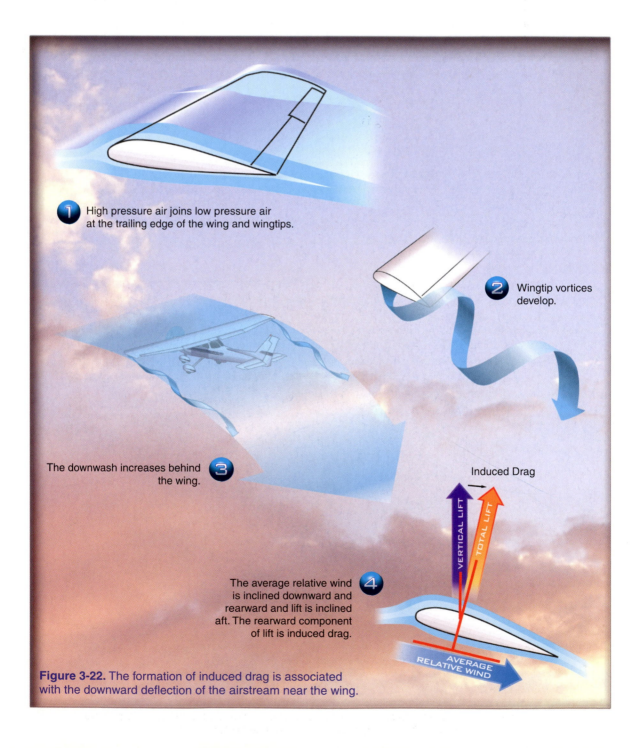

1 High pressure air joins low pressure air at the trailing edge of the wing and wingtips.

2 Wingtip vortices develop.

3 The downwash increases behind the wing.

Induced Drag

VERTICAL LIFT

TOTAL LIFT

4 The average relative wind is inclined downward and rearward and lift is inclined aft. The rearward component of lift is induced drag.

AVERAGE RELATIVE WIND

Figure 3-22. The formation of induced drag is associated with the downward deflection of the airstream near the wing.

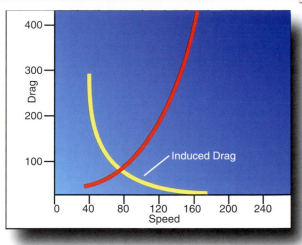

Figure 3-23. Induced drag is inversely proportional to the square of the speed. If speed is decreased by half, induced drag increases fourfold. It is the major cause of drag at reduced speeds near the stall; but, as speed increases, induced drag decreases.

As the air pressure differential increases with an increase in angle of attack, stronger vortices form and induced drag is increased. Since the wing usually is at a low angle of attack at high speed, and a high angle of attack at low speed, the relationship of induced drag to speed also can be plotted. [Figure 3-23]

TOTAL DRAG

Total drag for an airplane is the sum of parasite and induced drag. The total drag curve represents these combined forces and is plotted against airspeed. [Figure 3-24]

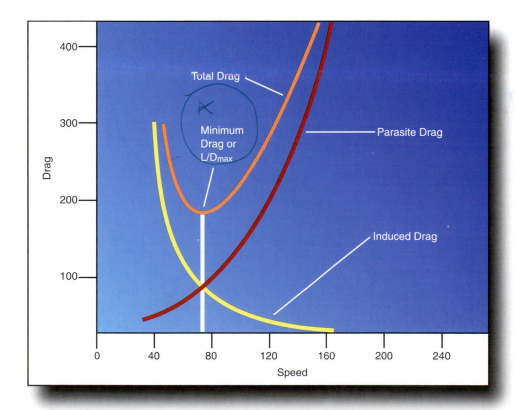

Figure 3-24. The low point on the total drag curve shows the airspeed at which drag is minimized. This point, where the lift-to-drag ratio is greatest, is referred to as L/D_{max}. At this speed, the total lift capacity of the airplane, when compared to the total drag of the airplane, is most favorable. This is important in airplane performance.

GROUND EFFECT

The phenomenon of **ground effect** is associated with the reduction of induced drag. During takeoffs or landings, when you are flying very close to the ground, the earth's surface actually alters the three-dimensional airflow pattern around the airplane. This causes a reduction in wingtip vortices and a decrease in upwash and downwash. Since ground effect restricts the downward deflection of the airstream, induced drag decreases. When the wing is at a height equal to its span, the decline in induced drag is only about 1.4%; when the wing is at a height equal to one-fourth its span, the loss of induced drag is about 24%. [Figure 3-25]

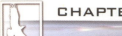
Ground effect is the result of the earth's surface altering the airflow patterns about the airplane. In ground effect, an airplane may become airborne before it reaches its recommended takeoff speed.

With the reduction of induced drag in ground effect, the amount of thrust required to produce lift is reduced. What this means is that your airplane is capable of lifting off at lower-than-normal speed. Although you might initially think that this is desirable, consider what happens as you climb out of ground effect. The power (thrust) required to sustain flight increases significantly as the normal airflow around the wing returns and induced drag is suddenly increased. If you attempt to climb out of ground effect before reaching the speed for normal climb, the airplane might sink back to the surface.

In ground effect, induced drag decreases and excess speed in the flare may cause floating when the aircraft is within one wingspan above the surface.

Ground effect is noticeable in the landing phase of flight, too, just before touchdown. Within one wingspan above the ground, the decrease in induced drag makes your airplane seem to float on the cushion of air beneath it. Because of this, power reduction usually is required during the flare to help the airplane land. Although all airplanes may experience ground effect, it is more noticeable in low-wing airplanes, simply because the wings are closer to the ground.

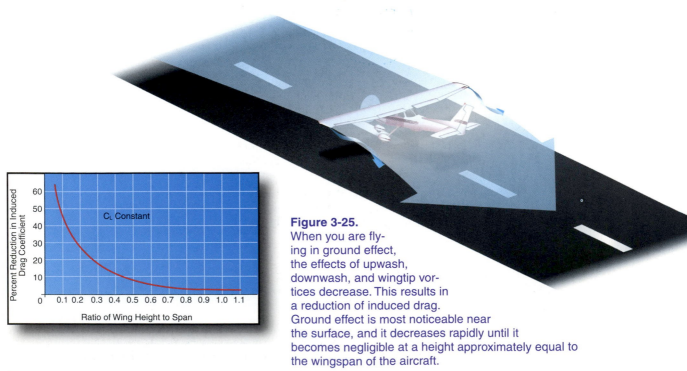

Figure 3-25.
When you are flying in ground effect, the effects of upwash, downwash, and wingtip vortices decrease. This results in a reduction of induced drag. Ground effect is most noticeable near the surface, and it decreases rapidly until it becomes negligible at a height approximately equal to the wingspan of the aircraft.

SUMMARY CHECKLIST

✓ During flight, the four forces acting on the airplane are lift, weight, thrust, and drag.

✓ The four forces are in equilibrium during unaccelerated flight.

✓ Lift is the upward force created by the effect of airflow as it passes over and under the wing.

✓ The airplane wing's shape is designed to take advantage of both Newton's laws and Bernoulli's principle.

✓ According to Bernoulli's principle, the increase in speed of air on the top of an airfoil produces a drop in pressure and this lowered pressure is a component of total lift.

✓ The reaction to downwash from the top surface of the wing and the airstream striking the wing's lower surface causes an upward reaction in positive lift according to Newton's third law of motion.

✓ Planform, camber, aspect ratio, and wing area are some of the design factors which affect a wing's lifting capability.

✓ A stall is caused by the separation of airflow from the wing's upper surface. For a given airplane, a stall always occurs at the critical angle of attack, regardless of airspeed, flight attitude, or weight.

✓ Total lift depends on the combined effects of airspeed and angle of attack. When speed decreases, you must increase the angle of attack to maintain the same amount of lift.

✓ Flaps increase lift (and drag) by increasing the wing's effective camber and changing the chord line which increases the angle of attack. Flap types include plain, split, slotted, and Fowler.

✓ Weight is the force of gravity which acts vertically through the center of the airplane toward the center of the earth.

✓ Thrust is the forward-acting force which opposes drag and propels the airplane.

✓ Drag acts in opposition to the direction of flight, opposes the forward-acting force of thrust, and limits the forward speed of the airplane.

✓ Parasite drag is caused by any aircraft surface which deflects or interferes with the smooth airflow around the airplane. Parasite drag normally is divided into three types: form drag, interference drag, and skin friction drag. If airspeed is doubled, parasite drag increases fourfold.

✓ Induced drag is generated by the airflow circulation around the wing as it creates lift. Induced drag increases with flight at slow airspeeds as the angle of attack increases.

✓ The phenomenon of ground effect occurs close to the ground where the earth's surface restricts the downward deflection of the airstream from the wing, decreasing induced drag.

KEY TERMS

Lift	Critical Angle of Attack
Weight	Aspect Ratio
Thrust	Wing Area
Drag	Planform
Vectors	Angle of Incidence
Newton's Three Laws of Motion	Stall Strips
Bernoulli's Principle	Flaps
Venturi	Configuration
Airfoil	Plain Flap
Leading Edge	Split Flap
Trailing Edge	Slotted Flap
Upwash	Fowler Flap
Downwash	Parasite Drag
Relative Wind	Form Drag
Camber	Interference Drag
Chord Line	Skin Friction Drag
Angle of Attack	Induced Drag
Coefficient of Lift	Wingtip Vortices
Stall	Ground Effect

QUESTIONS

1. Select the true statement(s) regarding the four forces of flight.

    a. During accelerated flight, thrust and drag are equal.
    b. The four forces are in equilibrium during unaccelerated flight.
    c. In straight-and-level unaccelerated flight, all four forces are equal in magnitude.

2. Refer to the following illustration and identify the aerodynamic terms associated with the airfoil.

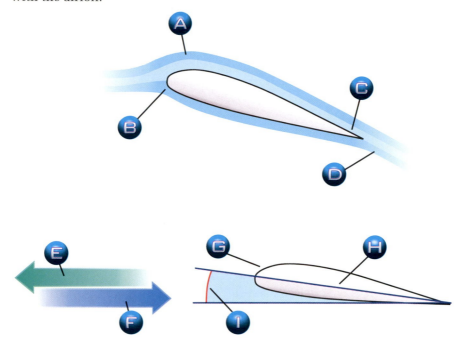

3. Describe how Newton's laws of motion and Bernoulli's principle explain the generation of lift by an airfoil.

4. True/False. As airspeed increases, the angle of attack at which an airfoil stalls also increases.

5. Determine the aspect ratio of the following planforms.

Wing Span = 196 ft
Average Chord = 28 ft

Wing Span = 35 ft
Average Chord = 5 ft

Wing Span = 37 ft
Average Chord = 11 ft

6. Identify three methods you can use to control lift during flight.

7. Will the wing's angle of attack increase or decrease when trailing edge flaps are lowered?

8. Is it more desirable for the wing root or wingtips to stall first and why?

9. List the three forms of parasite drag and provide examples of aircraft features which reduce parasite drag.

10. Explain why induced drag increases as airspeed decreases.

11. The reduction in induced drag due to ground effect is most noticeable when the airplane is within what distance from the earth's surface?

SECTION B
STABILITY

Although no airplane is completely stable, all airplanes must have desirable stability and handling characteristics. An inherently stable airplane is easy to fly and reduces pilot fatigue. This quality is essential throughout a wide range of flight conditions — during climbs, descents, turns, and at both high and low airspeeds. An aircraft's inherent stability also affects its ability to recover from stalls and spins. In fact, stability, maneuverability, and controllability are all interrelated design characteristics.

 An airplane said to be inherently stable will require less effort to control.

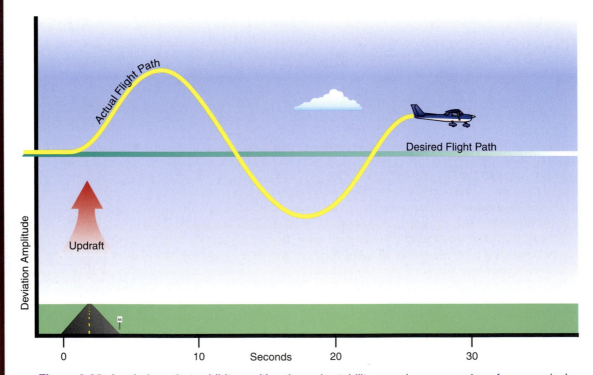

Figure 3-26. An airplane that exhibits positive dynamic stability experiences a series of progressively smaller oscillations after a disturbance, such as an updraft. The amount of time that it takes for the oscillations to cease is a measure of the degree of stability. After a significant disturbance, oscillations for typical light airplanes normally damp to half of the original deviation in 20 to 30 seconds.

Stability is the characteristic of an airplane in flight that causes it to return to a condition of equilibrium, or steady flight, after it is disturbed. For example, if you are flying a stable airplane that is disrupted while in straight-and-level flight, it has a tendency to return to the same attitude. The initial tendency to return to the position from which it was displaced is termed **positive static stability**. However, since the aircraft doesn't immediately return to the original position, but instead does so over a period of time through a series of successively smaller oscillations, the aircraft also displays **positive dynamic stability**. [Figure 3-26] Since an inherently stable platform is highly desirable in training aircraft, they are normally designed to possess both positive static and positive dynamic stability.

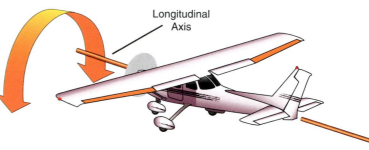

Maneuverability is the characteristic of an airplane that permits you to maneuver it easily and allows it to withstand the stress resulting from the maneuvers. An airplane's size, weight, flight control system, structural strength, and thrust determine its maneuverability. **Controllability** is the capability of an airplane to respond to your control inputs, especially with regard to attitude and flight path. Stability, maneuverability, and controllability all refer to movement of the aircraft about one or more of three axes of rotation.

THREE AXES OF FLIGHT

Since an aircraft operates in a three dimensional environment, aircraft movement takes place around one or more of three axes of rotation. They are called the **longitudinal**, **lateral**, and **vertical axes** of flight. The common reference point for the three axes is the airplane's **center of gravity (CG)**, which is the theoretical point where the entire weight of the airplane is considered to be concentrated. Since all three axes pass through this point, you can say that the airplane always moves about its CG, regardless of which axis is involved. The ailerons, elevator, and rudder create aerodynamic forces which cause the airplane to rotate about the three axes. [Figure 3-27]

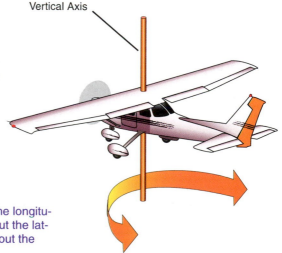

Figure 3-27. Ailerons control roll movement about the longitudinal axis; the elevator controls pitch movement about the lateral axis; and the rudder controls yaw movement about the vertical axis.

LONGITUDINAL AXIS

When you deflect the ailerons to begin a turn, they create an immediate rolling movement about the longitudinal axis. Since the ailerons always move in opposite directions, the aerodynamic shape of each wing and the associated production of lift is affected differently. [Figure 3-28] The rolling movement about the longitudinal axis will continue as long as the ailerons are deflected. To stop the roll, you must relax control pressure and return the ailerons to their original, or neutral, position. This is called neutralizing the controls.

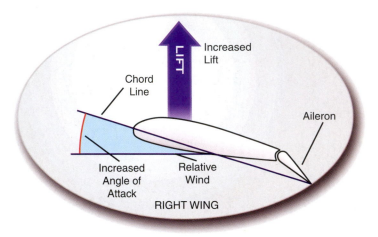

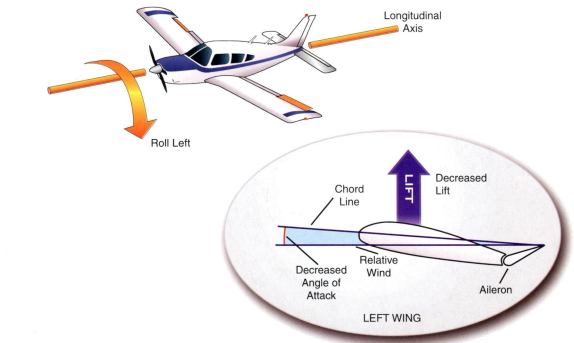

Figure 3-28. Deflected ailerons alter the chord line and change the effective camber of the outboard section of each wing. In this example, the angle of attack increases for the right wing, causing a corresponding increase in lift. At the same time, you can see that the left wing will lose some of its lift because of a decrease in its angle of attack. The airplane will roll to the left, because the right wing is producing more lift than the left wing.

LATERAL AXIS

Since the horizontal stabilizer is an airfoil, the action of the elevator (or stabilator) is quite similar to that of an aileron. Essentially, the chord line and effective camber of the stabilizer are changed by deflection of the elevator. Movement of the control wheel fore or aft causes motion about the lateral axis. Typically, this is referred to as an adjustment to pitch, or a change in pitch attitude. For example, when you move the control wheel forward, it causes movement about the lateral axis that decreases the airplane's pitch attitude. [Figure 3-29] A decrease in pitch attitude decreases the angle of attack. Conversely, an increase in pitch attitude increases the angle of attack.

Lateral Axis

Pitch Down

Figure 3-29. When you push forward on the control wheel, the elevator is lowered and the angle of attack of the stabilizer increases which causes it to produce more lift. The lifting force created by the stabilizer causes the airplane to pivot forward about its lateral axis.

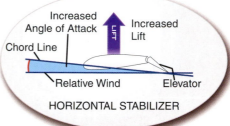

Increased Angle of Attack

Increased Lift

Chord Line

LIFT

Relative Wind

Elevator

HORIZONTAL STABILIZER

VERTICAL AXIS

When you apply pressure on the rudder pedals, the rudder deflects into the airstream. This produces an aerodynamic force that rotates the airplane about its vertical axis. This is referred to as yawing the airplane. The rudder may be displaced either to the left or right of center, depending on which rudder pedal you depress. [Figure 3-30]

Yaw movement about the vertical axis is produced by the rudder.

Figure 3-30. Since the vertical stabilizer also is an airfoil, deflection of the rudder alters the stabilizer's effective camber and chord line. In this case, left rudder pressure causes the rudder to move to the left. With a change in the chord line, the angle of attack is altered, generating an aerodynamic force toward the right side of the vertical fin. This causes the tail section to move to the right, and the nose of the airplane to yaw to the left.

Vertical Axis

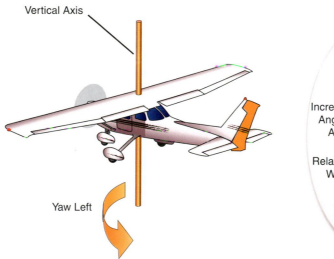

Yaw Left

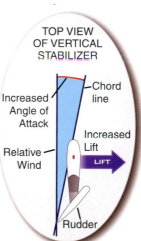

TOP VIEW OF VERTICAL STABILIZER

Chord line

Increased Angle of Attack

Increased Lift

Relative Wind

LIFT

Rudder

LONGITUDINAL STABILITY

The **longitudinal stability** of an airplane involves the pitching motion or tendency of the aircraft to move about its lateral axis. An airplane which is longitudinally stable will tend to return to its trimmed angle of attack after displacement. This is desirable because an airplane with this characteristic tends to resist either excessively nose-high or nose-low pitch attitudes. If an airplane is longitudinally unstable, it has the tendency to climb or dive until a stall or a steep dive develops. As a result, a longitudinally unstable airplane is very dangerous to fly.

BALANCE

An important consideration when designing a longitudinally stable airplane is the balance between the center of gravity and the center of pressure of the wing. The **center of pressure** is a point along the wing chord line where lift is considered to be concentrated.

For this reason, the center of pressure is sometimes referred to as the **center of lift**. On a typical cambered wing, this point along the chord line changes position with different flight attitudes. It moves forward as angle of attack increases and aft as angle of attack decreases. As a result, pitching tendencies created by the position of the center of pressure in relation to the CG vary.

 The longitudinal stability of an airplane is determined primarily by the location of the center of gravity in relation to the center of pressure (lift).

For example, with a high angle of attack and the center of pressure in a forward position (closer to the CG) the nose-down pitching tendency is decreased. The reverse is true as the angle of attack is decreased and the center of pressure moves further aft of the CG. [Figure 3-31]

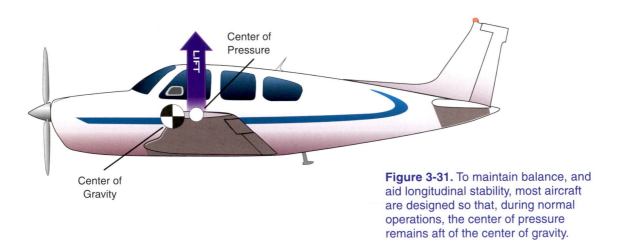

Figure 3-31. To maintain balance, and aid longitudinal stability, most aircraft are designed so that, during normal operations, the center of pressure remains aft of the center of gravity.

CENTER OF GRAVITY POSITION

The position of the center of gravity (CG), which is determined by the distribution of weight either by design or by the pilot, can also affect the longitudinal stability of an airplane. If the CG is too far forward, the airplane is very nose heavy; if the CG is too far aft, the airplane may become tail heavy. To achieve longitudinal stability, most airplanes are designed so they're slightly nose heavy. This is accomplished during the engineering and development phase by placing the center of gravity slightly forward of the center of pressure.

Your control over CG location is largely determined by what you put into the airplane, and where you put it. This includes the weight of items such as fuel, passengers, and baggage. For example, if you load heavy baggage into an aft baggage compartment, it might cause the CG to shift to an unfavorable position which can result in severe control problems. As you might expect, for an airplane to be controllable during flight, the CG must be located within a reasonable distance forward or aft of an optimum position. All airplanes have forward and aft limits for the position of the CG. The distance between these limits is the **CG range**. [Figure 3-32]

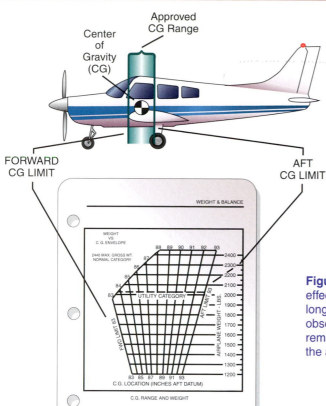

Figure 3-32. An airplane must be loaded so the effect of weight distribution does not adversely affect longitudinal balance. Loading limitations must be observed to ensure that the position of the CG remains within the approved range as published in the aircraft's pilot's operating handbook (POH).

When the CG is within the approved CG range, the airplane not only is controllable, but its longitudinal stability also is satisfactory. If the CG is located near the forward or aft limit of the approved CG range, a slight loss of longitudinal stability may be noticeable, but stabilator (or elevator) effectiveness is still adequate to control the airplane during all approved maneuvers. However, loading an aircraft in such a way as to move the CG too far forward or aft could result in a situation in which the capability of the stabilator (or elevator) to control the aircraft is exceeded.

CG TOO FAR FORWARD

If you load your airplane so the CG is forward of the forward CG limit, it will be too nose heavy. Although this tends to make the airplane seem stable, adverse side effects include longer takeoff distance and higher stalling speeds. The condition gets progressively worse as the CG moves to an extreme forward position. Eventually, stabilator (or elevator) effectiveness will be insufficient to lift the nose. [Figure 3-33]

Figure 3-33. If the CG is well forward of the approved CG range, stabilator (or elevator) effectiveness will be insufficient to exert the required tail-down force needed for a nose-high landing attitude. During landing, this may cause the nosewheel to strike the runway before the main gear.

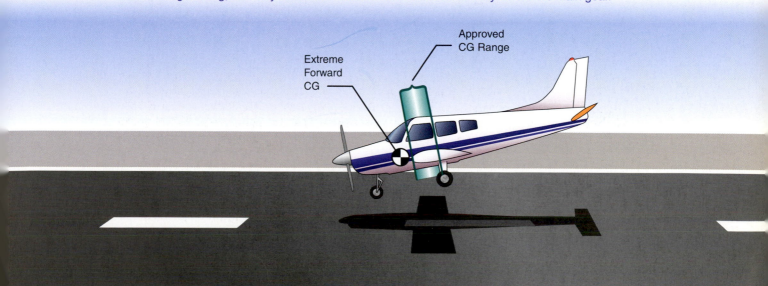

CG TOO FAR AFT

A CG located aft of the approved CG range is even more dangerous than a CG that is too far forward. With an aft CG, the airplane becomes tail heavy and very unstable in pitch, regardless of speed.

CG limits are established during initial testing and airworthiness certification. One of the criteria for determining the CG range in light airplanes is spin recovery capability. If the CG is within limits, a normal category airplane must demonstrate that it can be recovered from a one-turn spin; and a utility category airplane that is approved for spins must be recoverable from a fully developed spin. The aft CG limit is the most critical factor. As the CG moves aft, stabilator (or elevator) effectiveness decreases. When the CG is at the aft limit, stabilator effectiveness is adequate; but, when the CG is beyond the aft limit, the stabilator may be ineffective for stall or spin recovery. [Figure 3-34]

 An airplane loaded to its aft CG limit will be less stable at all speeds.

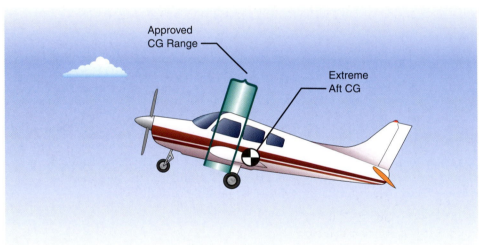

Figure 3-34. If the CG is too far aft, you will not have enough stabilator (or elevator) effectiveness to raise the tail and lower the nose of the airplane. As a result, you may be unable to recover from a stall or spin.

As a pilot, there are certain actions you can take to prevent an aft CG position. You can make sure the heaviest passengers and baggage, or cargo, are loaded as far forward as practical. Lighter passengers and baggage normally should be loaded in aft seats or compartments. The main thing you must do is follow the airplane manufacturer's loading recommendations in the POH. If you do this, your airplane will be loaded so the CG is within the approved range where longitudinal stability is adequate and, at the same time, where you can control the airplane during all approved maneuvers. Two important points to remember are that a CG beyond acceptable limits adversely affects longitudinal stability, and the most hazardous condition is an extreme aft CG position. You will learn more about the effects of adverse loading in the section on weight and balance in Chapter 8.

An airplane becomes progressively more difficult to control as the CG moves aft. If the CG is beyond the aft limit, it will be difficult to lower the nose to recover from a stall or spin.

HORIZONTAL STABILIZER

When the airplane is properly loaded, the CG remains forward of the center of pressure and the airplane is slightly nose heavy. The nose-heavy tendency is offset by the position of the horizontal stabilizer, which is designed with a negative angle of attack. This produces a downward force, or negative lift on the tail, to counteract the nose heaviness. The downward force is called the **tail-down force**, and is the balancing force in most flight conditions. [Figure 3-35]

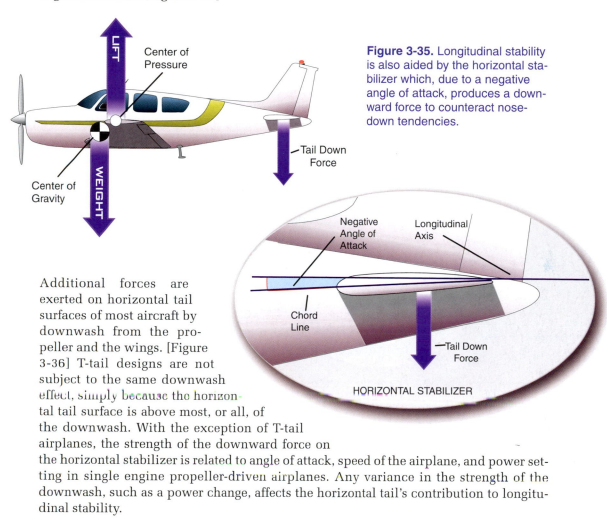

Figure 3-35. Longitudinal stability is also aided by the horizontal stabilizer which, due to a negative angle of attack, produces a downward force to counteract nose-down tendencies.

Additional forces are exerted on horizontal tail surfaces of most aircraft by downwash from the propeller and the wings. [Figure 3-36] T-tail designs are not subject to the same downwash effect, simply because the horizontal tail surface is above most, or all, of the downwash. With the exception of T-tail airplanes, the strength of the downward force on the horizontal stabilizer is related to angle of attack, speed of the airplane, and power setting in single engine propeller-driven airplanes. Any variance in the strength of the downwash, such as a power change, affects the horizontal tail's contribution to longitudinal stability.

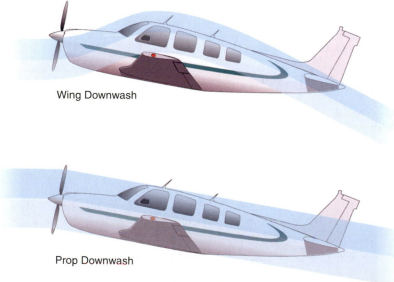

Figure 3-36. The downwash from the propeller and the wings passing over the horizontal stabilizer influences the longitudinal stability of the airplane.

The Canard Design

Although the tail-down force created by the horizontal stabilizer is excellent for longitudinal stability and balance, it is aerodynamically inefficient. The wings must support the negative lift created by the tail, and the negative angle of attack on the stabilizer increases drag. If an airplane design permitted two lifting surfaces, aerodynamic efficiency would be much greater.

A canard is a stabilizer that is located in front of the main wings. Canards are something like miniature forward wings. They were used in the pioneering days of aviation, most notably on the Wright Flyer, and are now reappearing on several original designs. The Beechcraft Starship (see photo) employs a variable sweep canard design. The canard provides longitudinal stability about the lateral axis by lifting the nose of the airplane.

Courtesy of Raytheon Aircraft

Since both the main wings and the canard produce positive lift, the design is aerodynamically efficient. A properly designed canard is also stall/spin resistant. The canard stalls at a lower angle of attack than the main wings. In doing so, the canard's angle of attack immediately decreases after it stalls. This breaks the stall and effectively returns the canard to a normal lift-producing angle of attack before the main wings have a chance to stall. Ailerons remain effective throughout the stall because they are attached to the main wings. In spite of its advantages, the canard design has limitations in total lift capability. Critical design conditions also must be met to maintain adequate longitudinal stability throughout the flight envelope.

POWER EFFECTS

If you reduce power during flight, a definite nose-down pitching tendency occurs due to the reduction of downwash from the wings and the propeller which reduces elevator effectiveness. Although this is a destabilizing factor, it is a desirable characteristic because it tends to result in a nose-down attitude during power reductions. The nose-down attitude helps you maintain, or regain, airspeed. Increasing power has the opposite effect. It causes increased downwash on the horizontal stabilizer which decreases its contribution to longitudinal stability and causes the nose of the airplane to rise.

A power reduction in airplanes, other than T-tails, will decrease the downwash on the horizontal stabilizer from the wings and propeller slipstream. This is what causes the nose to pitch down after a power reduction.

The influence of power on longitudinal stability also depends on the overall design of the airplane. Since power provides thrust, the alignment of thrust in relation to the longitudinal axis, the CG, the wings, and the stabilizer are all factors. The **thrustline** is determined by where the propeller is mounted and by the general direction in which thrust acts. In most light general aviation airplanes, the thrustline is parallel to the longitudinal axis and above the CG. This creates a slight pitching moment around the CG. If thrust is decreased, the pitching moment is reduced and the nose heaviness tends to decrease. An increase in thrust increases the pitching moment and increases nose heaviness. [Figure 3-37] Notice that these pitching tendencies are exactly the reverse of the pitching tendencies resulting from an increase or decrease in downwash. This thrustline design arrangement minimizes the destabilizing effects of power changes and improves longitudinal stability.

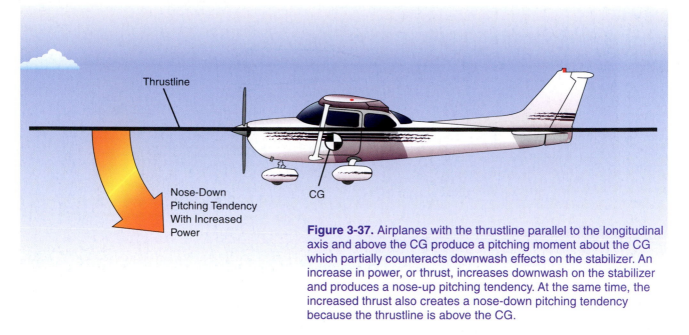

Thrustline

Nose-Down
Pitching Tendency
With Increased
Power

CG

Figure 3-37. Airplanes with the thrustline parallel to the longitudinal axis and above the CG produce a pitching moment about the CG which partially counteracts downwash effects on the stabilizer. An increase in power, or thrust, increases downwash on the stabilizer and produces a nose-up pitching tendency. At the same time, the increased thrust also creates a nose-down pitching tendency because the thrustline is above the CG.

High power settings combined with low airspeed produce a situation in which increased downwash and decreased airspeed reduce the overall stabilizing effect of the horizontal stabilizer. Additionally, the extension of high-lift devices, such as flaps, can increase downwash and its debilitating effects on longitudinal stability. Therefore, it is particularly important to maintain precise aircraft control during power-on approaches or go-arounds since longitudinal stability may be reduced.

LATERAL STABILITY

Stability about an airplane's longitudinal axis, which extends nose to tail, is called **lateral stability**. If one wing is lower than the opposite wing, lateral stability helps return the wings to a level attitude. This tendency to resist lateral, or roll, movement is aided by specific design characteristics. Four of the most common design features that influence lateral stability are weight distribution, dihedral, sweepback, and keel effect. Two of these, sweepback and keel effect, also help provide directional stability about the vertical axis.

You have no control over the design features that help maintain lateral stability, but you can control the distribution of weight and improve lateral stability. For example, most training airplanes have two fuel tanks, one inside each wing. Before you takeoff on a long flight, you normally fill both tanks. If you use fuel from only one tank, you will soon notice that the airplane wants to roll toward the wing with the full tank. The distribution of weight is uneven and lateral stability is affected. You can prevent the imbalance by switching tanks before a significant difference in weight can occur.

DIHEDRAL

The most common design for lateral stability is known as wing dihedral. **Dihedral** is the upward angle of the airplane's wings with respect to the horizontal. When you look at an airplane, dihedral makes the wings appear to form a spread-out V. Dihedral usually is just a few degrees.

If an airplane with dihedral enters an uncoordinated roll during gusty wind conditions, one wing will be elevated and the opposite wing will drop. This causes an immediate sideslip downward toward the low wing. Since the relative wind is now coming from the side, the low wing experiences an increased angle of attack while the high wing's angle

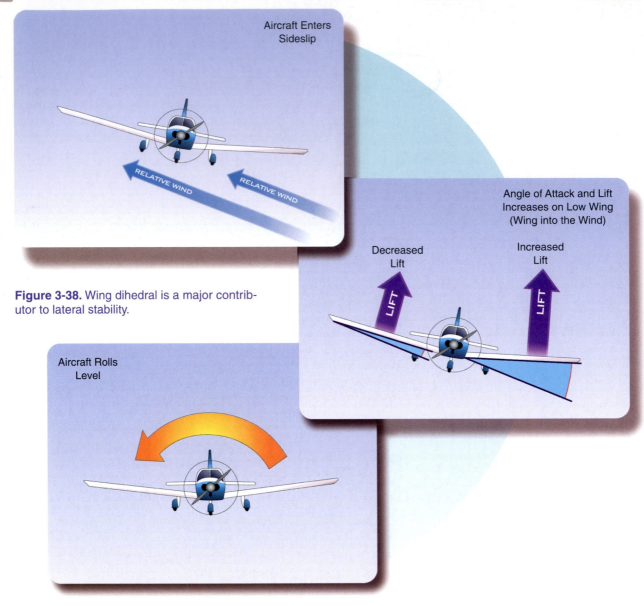

Figure 3-38. Wing dihedral is a major contributor to lateral stability.

of attack is reduced. The increased angle of attack on the low wing produces more lift for that wing and tends to roll the aircraft back toward a level flight attitude. [Figure 3-38]

The fuselage also is a contributor to lateral stability, although in varying degrees depending primarily on the placement of the wings. During a sideslip, airflow creates both an upwash and downwash as it passes around the fuselage just ahead of the wing. The upwash effect tends to roll a high-wing airplane toward the upright position, and therefore is a stabilizing factor. In a low-wing airplane, however, the downwash is destabilizing since it tends to contribute to a roll in the direction of the sideslip. [Figure 3-39] This effect produces a movement equivalent to 3° to 4° of negative dihedral in a typical low wing aircraft, while a high-wing aircraft may experience an effect approximating 2° to 3° of positive dihedral. This accounts for the greater dihedral normally found on most low-wing general aviation aircraft. [Figure 3-40]

From an operational standpoint, it's important to note that, in certain situations, the propeller slipstream can reduce the lateral stability of the airplane by reducing the effect of wing dihedral. At high power settings and low airspeeds, propwash increases

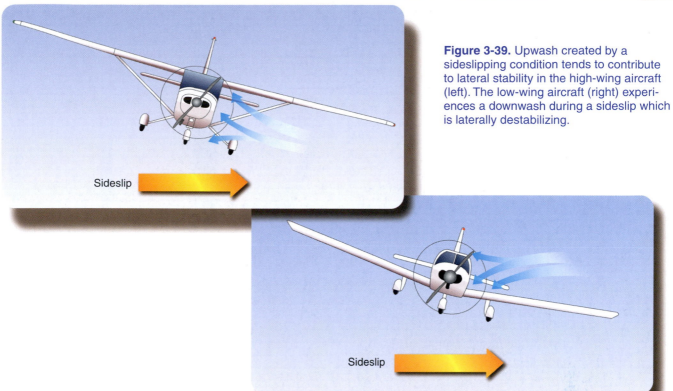

Figure 3-39. Upwash created by a sideslipping condition tends to contribute to lateral stability in the high-wing aircraft (left). The low-wing aircraft (right) experiences a downwash during a sideslip which is laterally destabilizing.

the effectiveness of the inboard sections of the wings which decreases the effect of dihedral, thereby reducing lateral stability. This warrants particular attention since high-power, low-airspeed conditions also contribute to a degradation of longitudinal stability.

SWEEPBACK

In many airplanes, the leading edges of the wings do not form right angles with the longitudinal axis. Instead, the wings are angled backward from the wing root to the wingtips. This design characteristic is referred to as wing sweep or **sweepback**. In high performance airplanes with pronounced sweepback, the design is used primarily to maintain the center of lift aft of the CG and reduce wave drag when operating at speeds

Figure 3-40. Since they are inherently more stable laterally, high-wing aircraft such as the Cessna 172 on the left are designed with less dihedral than the typical low-wing aircraft, as exhibited by the Beechcraft Bonanza on the right.

at or above the speed of sound, or Mach one. [Figure 3-41] In light training airplanes, the main purpose of sweepback design is to improve lateral stability.

Sweepback also may aid slightly in directional stability. If an airplane rotates about its vertical axis or yaws to the left, the right wing has less sweep and a slight increase in drag. The left wing has more sweep and less drag. This tends to force the airplane back into alignment with the relative wind.

KEEL EFFECT

Lateral stability also is provided by the vertical fin and side area of the fuselage reacting to the airflow very much like the keel of a ship. **Keel effect** is the steadying influence exerted by the side area of the fuselage and vertical stabilizer. [Figure 3-42]

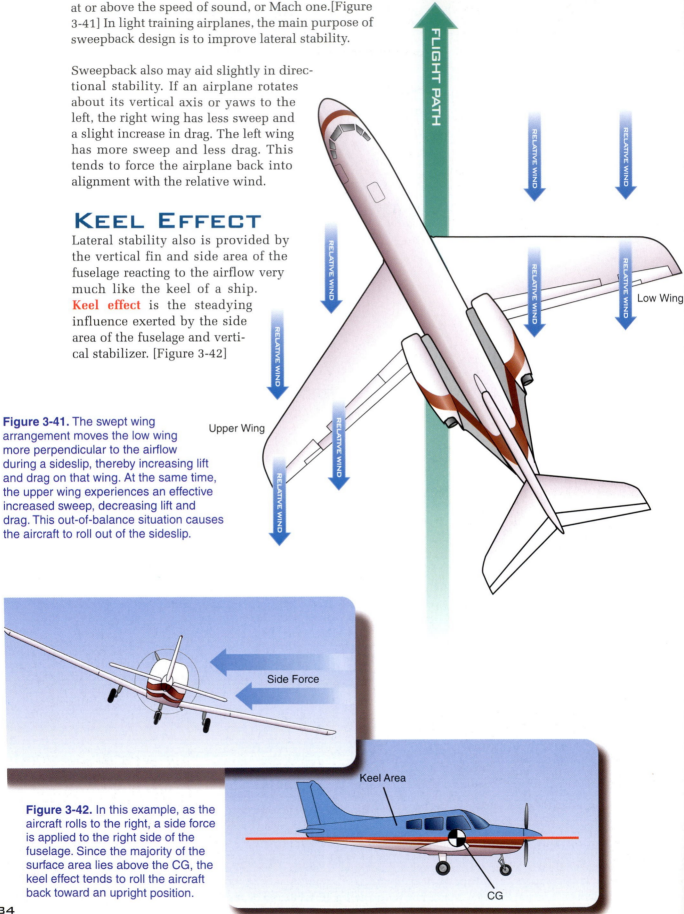

Figure 3-41. The swept wing arrangement moves the low wing more perpendicular to the airflow during a sideslip, thereby increasing lift and drag on that wing. At the same time, the upper wing experiences an effective increased sweep, decreasing lift and drag. This out-of-balance situation causes the aircraft to roll out of the sideslip.

Figure 3-42. In this example, as the aircraft rolls to the right, a side force is applied to the right side of the fuselage. Since the majority of the surface area lies above the CG, the keel effect tends to roll the aircraft back toward an upright position.

DIRECTIONAL STABILITY

Stability about the vertical axis is called **directional stability**. The primary contributor to directional stability is the vertical tail which causes an airplane in flight to act much like a weather vane. You can compare the pivot point on the weather vane to the center of gravity of the airplane. The nose of the airplane corresponds to the weather vane's arrowhead, and the vertical fin on the airplane acts like the tail of the weather vane. [Figure 3-43]

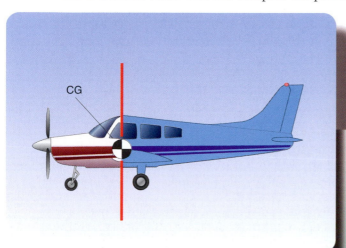

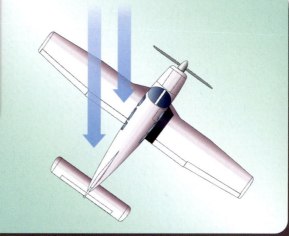

Figure 3-43. An airplane must have more surface area behind the CG than it has in front of it. When an airplane enters a sideslip, the greater surface area behind the CG helps keep the airplane aligned with the relative wind.

How Does a Flying Wing Maintain Directional Stability?

In most aircraft designs, the primary source of directional stability is the vertical tail. Aircraft designed without tail assemblies, such as flying wings, must somehow still maintain directional stability and control, but how is this possible?

A

Courtesy of Northrop Grumman

One of the most notable flying wing designs is employed by the U.S. Air Force B-2 *Stealth* bomber manufactured by Northrop Corporation. [Figure A] The B-2 uses a four-times redundant fly-by-wire flight control system that is controlled by approximately 200 computer processors. The actual flight controls are primarily located on the trailing edge of wing (fuselage). Yaw control is accomplished using "drag rudders" located near each wingtip. The drag rudders extend or retract independently to control the direction of nose movement. (Note the extended drag rudder on the left wing of the B-2 in figure A.) If both drag rudders are extended simultaneously, they act as speed brakes. Pitch and roll control is accomplished through the use of "elevons" located inboard of the drag rudders.

Although not employed on the B-2, some stability can be derived from bending the trailing edge of the wing upward. In addition, the tips of a swept wing can be twisted to a negative angle of attack to act as a horizontal tail.

B

Courtesy of Northrop Grumman

C

Courtesy of Northrop Grumman

Although the B-2 didn't fly until 1989, the flying wing concept is not new. In fact, the Northrop Corporation developed flying wing prototypes as early as the 1940's. These included the prop-powered B-35, first flown in 1946 [Figure B], and the jet-powered YB-49 which flew in 1947 [Figure C].

INTERACTION OF LATERAL AND DIRECTIONAL STABILITY

For ease-of-understanding, lateral and directional stability have been discussed separately up to this point. However, it is impossible to yaw an aircraft without also creating a rolling motion. This interaction between the lateral and directional stabilizing design elements can sometimes uncover some potentially undesirable side effects. Two of the most common are Dutch roll and spiral instability.

Dutch roll is a combination of rolling/yawing oscillations caused either by your control input or by wind gusts. Dutch roll will normally occur when the dihedral effects of an aircraft are more powerful than the directional stability. After a disturbance resulting in a yawing motion and sideslip, the dihedral effect will tend to roll the aircraft away from the direction of the initial yaw. However, due to weak directional stability, the rolling movement may overshoot the level position and reverse the sideslip. This motion continues to repeat, creating an oscillation that can be felt by the pilot as side-to-side wagging of the aircraft's tail. If Dutch roll tendency is not effectively dampened, it is considered objectionable.

The alternative to an airplane that exhibits Dutch roll tendencies is a design that has better directional stability than lateral stability. If directional stability is increased and lateral stability is decreased, the Dutch roll motion is adequately suppressed. However, this design arrangement tends to cause spiral instability.

Spiral instability is associated with airplanes that have strong directional stability in comparison with lateral stability. When an airplane susceptible to spiral instability is disturbed from a condition of equilibrium and a sideslip is introduced, the strong directional stability tends to yaw the airplane back into alignment with the relative wind. Due to the yaw back into the relative wind, the outside wing travels faster than the inside wing and, as a result, more lift is generated by the outside wing. The rolling moment increases the angle of bank, which increases the sideslip. The comparatively weak dihedral effect lags in restoring lateral stability and the yaw forces the nose of the airplane down while the angle of bank continues to increase, tightening the spiral. Spiral instability is normally easily overcome by the pilot. However, if left uncorrected, the motion could increase into a tight spiral dive, sometimes referred to as a graveyard spiral.

As you can see, even a well-designed airplane may have some undesirable characteristics. Generally, increased dihedral reduces spiral instability while an increased vertical tail surface increases spiral instability. Since Dutch roll is considered less tolerable than spiral instability, designers attempt to minimize the Dutch roll tendency. The compromise results in a small degree of spiral instability which generally is considered acceptable.

STALLS

The inherent stability of an airplane is particularly important as it relates to the aircraft's ability to recovery from stalls and spins (which can result from aggravated stalls). Familiarization with the causes and effects of stalls is especially important during flight at slow airspeeds, such as during takeoff and landing, where the margin above the stall speed is small.

It's important to understand the variables that affect stall development. As indicated earlier in this chapter, a stall will always occur when the maximum lift, or critical angle of attack (C_{Lmax}) is exceeded. If an airplane's speed is too slow, the required angle of attack to maintain lift may be exceeded, causing a stall. It's important to note, however, that the airspeed at which an aircraft may be stalled is not fixed. For example, although the extension of flaps increases drag, it also increases the wing's ability to produce lift, thereby reducing the stall speed.

Stall speed also can be affected by a number of other factors such as weight and environmental conditions. As aircraft weight increases, a higher angle of attack is required to maintain the same airspeed since some of the lift must be used to support the increased weight. This causes an increase in the aircraft's stall speed. The distribution of weight also affects the stall speed of an aircraft. For example, a forward CG creates a situation which requires the tail to produce more downforce to balance the aircraft. This, in turn, causes the wings to produce more lift than if the CG was located more rearward. So, you can see that a more forward CG also increases stall speed.

Any modification to the wing surface also can affect the stall speed of the aircraft. Although man-made high-lift devices can decrease stall speed, the opposite can occur due to natural factors. Snow, ice or frost accumulation on the wing's surface not only changes the shape of the wing, disrupting the airflow, but also increases weight and drag, all of which will increase stall speed.

Another environmental factor that can affect stall speed is turbulence. The unpredictable nature of turbulence encounters can significantly and suddenly cause an aircraft to stall at a higher airspeed than the same aircraft in stable conditions. This occurs when a vertical gust changes the direction of the relative wind and abruptly increases the angle of attack. During takeoff and landing operations in gusty conditions, an increase in airspeed usually is necessary in order to maintain a wide margin above stall.

TYPES OF STALLS

There are three basic types of stalls that will normally be practiced during training to familiarize you with stall recognition and recovery in particular flight regimes. **Power-off stalls** are practiced to simulate the conditions and aircraft configuration you will most likely encounter during a normal landing approach. **Power-on stalls** are normally encountered during takeoff, climb-out, and go-arounds when the pilot fails to maintain proper control due to premature flap retraction or excessive nose-high trim. To help you understand how stalls may occur at higher than normal stall speed, your instructor may demonstrate **accelerated stalls** and show you associated recovery techniques.

Most stalls are practiced while maintaining coordinated flight. However, uncoordinated, or crossed-control, inputs can be very dangerous when operating near a stall. One type of stall, sometimes referred to as the **crossed-control stall** is most likely to occur when a pilot tries to compensate for overshooting a runway during a turn from base to final while on landing approach. [Figure 3-44]

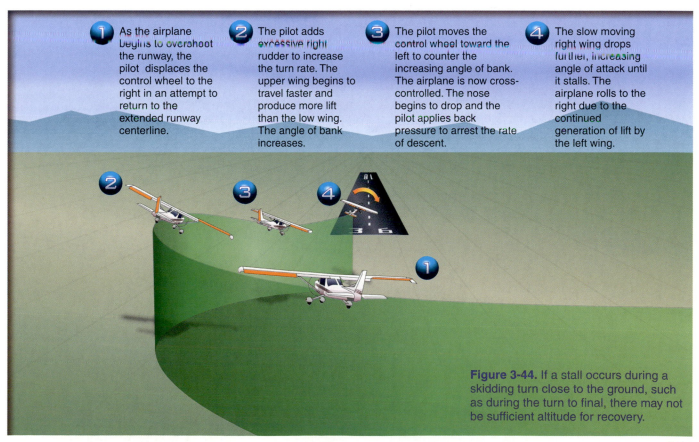

1 As the airplane begins to overshoot the runway, the pilot displaces the control wheel to the right in an attempt to return to the extended runway centerline.

2 The pilot adds excessive right rudder to increase the turn rate. The upper wing begins to travel faster and produce more lift than the low wing. The angle of bank increases.

3 The pilot moves the control wheel toward the left to counter the increasing angle of bank. The airplane is now cross-controlled. The nose begins to drop and the pilot applies back pressure to arrest the rate of descent.

4 The slow moving right wing drops further, increasing angle of attack until it stalls. The airplane rolls to the right due to the continued generation of lift by the left wing.

Figure 3-44. If a stall occurs during a skidding turn close to the ground, such as during the turn to final, there may not be sufficient altitude for recovery.

STALL RECOGNITION

There are a number of ways to recognize that a stall is imminent. Ideally, you should be able to detect the first signs of an impending stall and make appropriate corrections before it actually occurs. If you have a good understanding of the types of stalls, recognition is much easier. Recovery at the first indication of a stall is quite simple; but, if you allow the stalled condition to progress, recovery becomes more difficult.

A typical indication of a stall is a mushy feeling in the flight controls and less control effect as the aircraft's speed decreases. The reduction in control effectiveness is primarily due to reduced airflow over the flight control surfaces. In fixed-pitch propeller airplanes, a loss of revolutions per minute (r.p.m.) may be noticeable as you approach a stall in power-on conditions. Also, a reduction in the sound of air flowing along the fuselage is usually evident. Just before the stall occurs, buffeting, uncontrollable pitching, or vibrations may begin. Finally, your kinesthetic sense (ability to recognize changes in direction or speed) may also provide a warning of decreased speed or the beginning of a sinking feeling.

STALL RECOVERY

Your primary consideration after a stall occurs should be to regain positive control of the aircraft. If you do not recover promptly by reducing the angle of attack, a secondary stall and/or spin may result. A **secondary stall** is normally caused by poor stall recovery technique, such as attempting flight prior to attaining sufficient flying speed. If you encounter a secondary stall, you should apply normal stall recovery procedures. The following basic guidelines should be used to effect a proper stall recovery.

1. Decrease the angle of attack. Depending on of the type of aircraft, you may find that a different amount of forward pressure on the control wheel is required. Too little forward movement may not be enough to regain lift; too much may impose a negative load on the wing, hindering recovery.

2. Smoothly apply maximum allowable power. If you are not already at maximum allowable power, increase the throttle to minimize altitude loss and increase airspeed.

3. Adjust the power as required. As the airplane recovers, you should maintain coordinated flight while adjusting the power to a normal level.

You can usually prevent an accidental stall by knowing when you are most susceptible to a stall and recognizing the indicators of an impending stall. Unless you are practicing stalls and stall recoveries, don't wait for the stall to fully develop — apply stall recovery techniques at the first indication of an impending stall.

SPINS

The spin is one of the most complex of all flight maneuvers. A **spin** may be defined as an aggravated stall which results in the airplane descending in a helical, or corkscrew, path. Single-engine, normal category airplanes are prohibited from intentional spins. This is indicated by a placard with words such as "No acrobatic maneuvers, including spins, approved." However, during aircraft certification tests, normal category airplanes must demonstrate recovery from a one-turn spin or a three-second spin, whichever takes longer. The recovery must take place within one additional turn with normal control inputs. Since airplanes in the normal category have not been tested for more than one-turn/three second spins, their performance characteristics beyond these limits are unknown.

Acrobatic category airplanes must fully recover from fully developed spins within one and one-half additional turns. Certification in this category also requires six turns or three seconds, whichever takes longer, before the recovery control inputs are applied.

Utility category airplanes may be tested under the one-turn (normal) criteria or they may satisfy the six-turn (acrobatic) spin requirements. However, spins in utility category airplanes may be approved only with specific loading, such as a reduced weight and with a forward CG position. It is extremely important for you to understand all of the operating limitations for your airplane. Applicable limitations are placarded in the aircraft and/or included in the POH.

PRIMARY CAUSES

A stalled aircraft is a prerequisite for a spin. However, a properly executed stall is essentially a coordinated maneuver where both wings are equally or nearly equally stalled. In contrast, a spin is an uncoordinated maneuver with the wings unequally stalled. [Figure 3-45] In this case, the wing that is more completely stalled will often drop before the other, and the nose of the aircraft will yaw in the direction of the low wing.

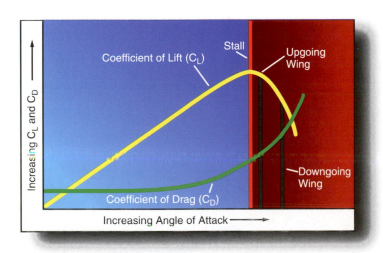

Figure 3-45. The relative coefficients of lift and drag for each wing during a spin are depicted in this graph. Note that the upgoing wing experiences more lift (or a lesser stalled condition) and less drag. The opposite wing is forced down and back due to less lift (more stall) and increased drag.

Typically, the cause of an inadvertent spin is exceeding the critical angle of attack while performing an uncoordinated maneuver. The lack of coordination is normally caused by either too much or not enough rudder control for the amount of aileron being used. The result is a crossed-control condition. If you do not initiate the stall recovery promptly, the airplane is more likely to enter a full stall that may develop into a spin. The spin that occurs from crossed-controlling usually results in rotation in the direction of the rudder being applied, regardless of which wing is raised. In a skidding turn, where both aileron and rudder are applied in the same direction, rotation will be in that direction. However, in a slipping turn, where opposite aileron is held against the rudder, the resultant spin will usually occur in the direction opposite the aileron that is being applied.

 To enter a spin, an airplane must first be stalled. Although both wings are in a stalled condition during a spin, one wing is stalled more than the other.

Coordinated use of the flight controls is important, especially during flight at slow air-speeds. Although most pilots are able to maintain coordination of the flight controls during routine maneuvers, this ability often deteriorates when distractions occur and their attention is divided between important tasks. Distractions that have caused problems include preoccupation with situations inside or outside the cockpit, maneuvering to avoid other aircraft, and maneuvering to clear obstacles during takeoffs, climbs, approaches, or landings. Because of this, you will be required to learn how to recognize and cope with these distractions by practicing "flight at slow airspeeds with realistic distractions" during your flight training. In addition, although you are not required to demonstrate flight proficiency in spins during private pilot training, you will need to exhibit knowledge of the situations where unintentional spins may occur, as well as the general spin recognition and recovery procedures for the airplane you use for your practical test.

TYPES OF SPINS

In general, there are three main types of spins. The most common is the upright, or **erect spin** which is characterized by a slightly nose down rolling and yawing motion in the same direction. In an **inverted spin**, the aircraft is spinning upside down with yaw and

Figure 3-46. A spin may be characterized as erect, inverted, or flat, depending on the roll and yaw motion of the aircraft.

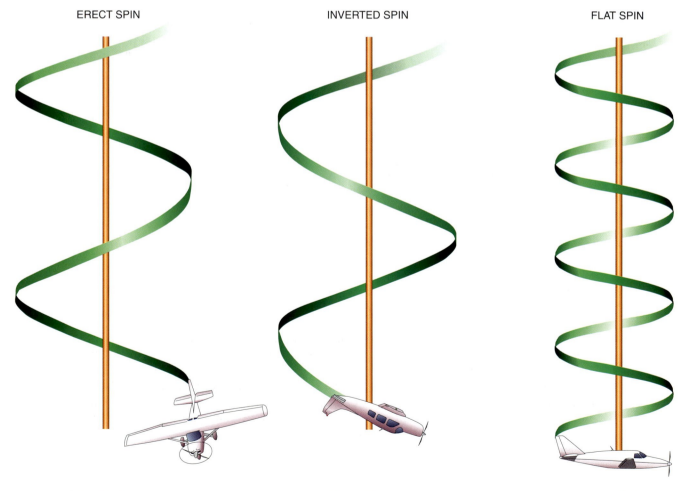

ERECT SPIN

INVERTED SPIN

FLAT SPIN

Roll and Yaw in
Same Direction

Roll and Yaw in
Opposite Directions

Yaw Only

STALL/SPIN ACCIDENT PREVENTION

During a recent four-year period, 171 stall/spin accidents occurred, 73 percent of which were fatal. By far the majority of the accidents were a result of unintentional stalls and spins that occurred close to the ground.

Are these accidents preventable? Consider that human error has been cited as a contributing factor in 90 to 95 percent of all stall/spin accidents, and the answer is a resounding yes. A review of related accident reports suggest that adhering to the following guidelines can help you avoid an accidental stall/spin.

- Pay attention to aircraft loading. An aircraft with an aft CG is more prone to stall/spin entry.

- Do not takeoff with snow, ice, or frost on the wings.

- If an emergency that requires a forced landing occurs immediately after takeoff, don't attempt to return to the runway. Select a suitable landing site straight ahead or slightly off to the side.

- Maintain coordinated flight as much as possible. Particularly avoid skidding turns near the ground.

- Use a somewhat higher than normal airspeed during takeoffs and landings in gusty winds.

- Always concentrate on flying the aircraft and avoid prolonged distractions.

roll occurring in opposite directions. Inverted spins are most likely to occur during aerobatic maneuvers. The third type of spin can be the most deadly. In a **flat spin**, the aircraft simply yaws about its vertical axis with a pitch attitude approximately level with the horizon. Although it sounds fairly benign, recovery is usually very difficult or impossible except in specialized aerobatic aircraft. Most general aviation aircraft are designed to prevent entry into flat spins provided the loading and CG location are within approved limits. [Figure 3-46]

WEIGHT AND BALANCE CONSIDERATIONS

Even minor weight and balance changes can affect an aircraft's spin characteristics. Heavier weights generally result in slow spin rates initially; but, as the spin progresses, heavier weights tend to cause an increasing spin rate and longer recovery time. Distribution of weight is even more significant. Forward center of gravity positions usually inhibit the high angles of attack necessary for a stall. Thus, an airplane with a forward CG tends to be more stall and spin resistant than an aircraft with an aft CG. In addition, spins with aft CG positions are more likely to become flat.

In a training airplane, the addition of a back seat passenger or a single suitcase to an aft baggage compartment can affect the CG enough to change the characteristics of a spin. In addition, any concentration of weight, or unbalanced weight distribution, that is particularly far from the CG is undesirable. This type of loading may occur with tip tanks or outboard wing tanks. If the fuel in these tanks becomes unbalanced, an asymmetrical condition exists. The worst asymmetric condition is full fuel in the wing on the outside of the spin and no fuel in the tanks on the inside of the turn. Once the spin is developed, the momentum (inertial force) makes recovery unlikely.

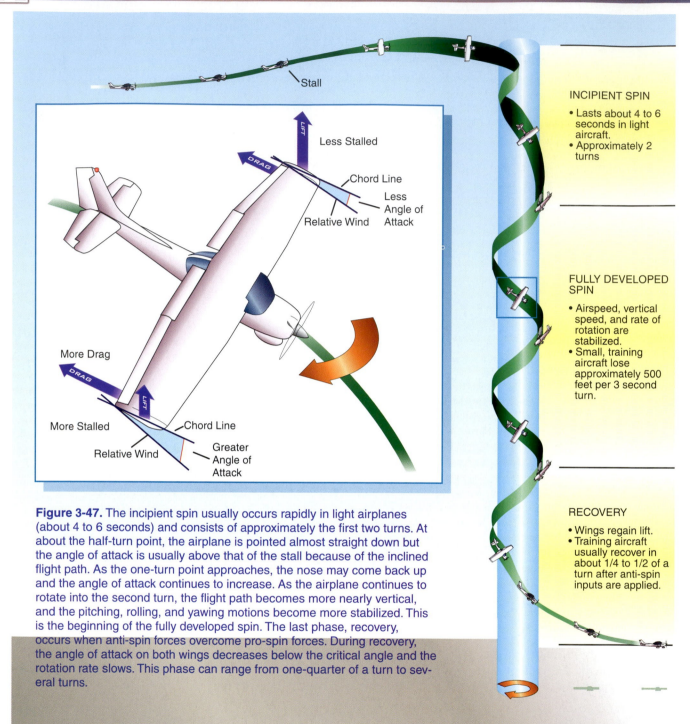

Stall

Less Stalled

LIFT

DRAG

Chord Line

Less
Angle of
Attack

Relative Wind

More Drag

DRAG

LIFT

More Stalled

Chord Line

Relative Wind

Greater
Angle of
Attack

INCIPIENT SPIN

• Lasts about 4 to 6
  seconds in light
  aircraft.
• Approximately 2
  turns

FULLY DEVELOPED
SPIN

• Airspeed, vertical
  speed, and rate of
  rotation are
  stabilized.
• Small, training
  aircraft lose
  approximately 500
  feet per 3 second
  turn.

RECOVERY

• Wings regain lift.
• Training aircraft
  usually recover in
  about 1/4 to 1/2 of a
  turn after anti-spin
  inputs are applied.

Figure 3-47. The incipient spin usually occurs rapidly in light airplanes (about 4 to 6 seconds) and consists of approximately the first two turns. At about the half-turn point, the airplane is pointed almost straight down but the angle of attack is usually above that of the stall because of the inclined flight path. As the one-turn point approaches, the nose may come back up and the angle of attack continues to increase. As the airplane continues to rotate into the second turn, the flight path becomes more nearly vertical, and the pitching, rolling, and yawing motions become more stabilized. This is the beginning of the fully developed spin. The last phase, recovery, occurs when anti-spin forces overcome pro-spin forces. During recovery, the angle of attack on both wings decreases below the critical angle and the rotation rate slows. This phase can range from one-quarter of a turn to several turns.

SPIN PHASES

Many different terms may be used to describe a spin. In light, training airplanes, a complete spin maneuver consists of three phases — incipient, fully developed, and recovery. The **incipient spin** is that portion of a spin from the time the airplane stalls and rotation starts until the spin is fully developed. The **fully developed spin** occurs after the incipient stage when the angular rotation rates, airspeed, and vertical speed are stabilized from turn to turn and the flight path is close to vertical. For this reason, the fully developed stage is often referred to as the steady-state portion of the spin. **Spin recovery** is the final stage of the spin and is the phase when the application of anti-spin forces result in a slowing and/or eventual cessation of rotation coupled with a decrease in angle of attack below C_{Lmax}. [Figure 3-47]

SPIN RECOVERY

While some characteristics of a spin are predictable, every airplane spins differently. In addition, the same airplane's spin behavior changes with variations in configuration, loading, and several other factors. Therefore, it's easy to understand why spin recovery techniques vary for different aircraft and why you must follow the recovery procedures outlined in the POH for your airplane. The following is a general recovery procedure for erect spins, but it should not be applied arbitrarily without regard for the manufacturer's recommendations.

1. Move the throttle to idle. This will eliminate thrust and minimize the loss of altitude.

2. Neutralize the ailerons.

3. Determine the direction of rotation. This is most easily and accurately accomplished by referencing the turn coordinator.

4. Apply full opposite rudder. Ensure that you apply the rudder opposite the direction of rotation.

5. Briskly apply elevator (or stabilator) forward to approximately the neutral position. Some aircraft require merely a relaxation of back pressure; others require full forward elevator (or stabilator) pressure.

6. As rotation stops (indicating the stall has been broken), neutralize the rudders. If you don't neutralize the rudders when rotation stops, you could enter a spin in the opposite direction.

7. Gradually apply aft elevator (or stabilator) to return to level flight. Applying the elevator too quickly may result in a secondary stall, and possibly another spin. Also, make sure you adhere to aircraft airspeed and load limits during the recovery from the dive.

Normally, the recovery from an incipient spin requires less time (and altitude) than the recovery from a fully developed spin. As a rule of thumb, small aircraft authorized for spins will lose approximately 500 feet of altitude per each 3-second turn and recover in 1/4 to 1/2 of a turn. More altitude will be lost and recoveries may be prolonged at higher altitudes due to the less dense air.

It should be clear that you, as an applicant for a private pilot certificate, are not required to demonstrate flight proficiency in spin entries or spin recovery techniques. Even though your flight instructor may demonstrate a spin at some point during your training, you should never intentionally enter a spin, even after you become certificated as a private pilot, unless you obtain additional training from an experienced instructor. The emphasis in stall/spin training for private pilots is awareness of conditions that could lead to an unintentional stall or spin and to provide you with some general recovery procedures.

SUMMARY CHECKLIST

✓ Most training aircraft are designed to display both positive static and positive dynamic stability.

✓ All aircraft movement takes place around the longitudinal, lateral, and vertical axes, all of which pass through the center of gravity.

✓ Longitudinal stability relates to movement about the airplane's lateral axis. Longitudinal stability is influenced by the relationship between the center of pressure and the center of gravity as well as the effects of power changes and the design of the horizontal stabilizer.

✓ Stability around the aircraft's longitudinal axis is referred to as lateral stability. Wing dihedral, sweepback, keel effect, and weight distribution are design features that affect an airplane's lateral stability.

✓ Directional stability, or stability about the vertical axis, of most aircraft is maintained by the vertical tail.

✓ Dutch roll is most likely to occur on aircraft with weak directional stability and strong lateral stability.

✓ Aircraft with strong directional stability and weak lateral stability are susceptible to spiral instability.

✓ A stall will always occur when the critical angle of attack, or C_{Lmax}, is exceeded. This can occur at any airspeed and in any configuration or attitude.

✓ A spin will not develop unless both wings are stalled. A normal, erect spin results in the airplane entering a nose-low autorotative descent with one wing stalled more than the other.

KEY TERMS

Stability

Positive Static Stability

Positive Dynamic Stability

Maneuverability

Controllability

Longitudinal Axis

Lateral Axis

Vertical Axis

Center of Gravity (CG)

Longitudinal Stability

Center of Pressure

Center of Lift

CG Range

Tail-Down Force

Thrustline

Lateral Stability

Dihedral

Sweepback

Keel Effect

Directional Stability

Dutch Roll

Spiral Instability

Power-Off Stalls

Power-On Stalls

Accelerated Stalls

Crossed-Control Stall

Secondary Stall

Spin

Erect Spin

Inverted Spin

Flat Spin

Incipient Spin

Fully Developed Spin

Spin Recovery

QUESTIONS

1. Referring to the airplane diagram below, identify the three axes of flight and the type of movement associated with each axis.

   Match the following control surface with the associated aircraft movement.

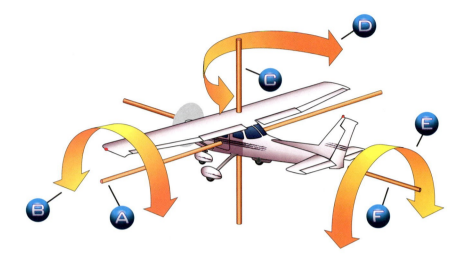

2. Roll movement   A. Elevator (or stabilator)

3. Pitch movement   B. Ailerons
       rudder is   *responsible for roll*
       resp.
4. Yaw movement   C. Rudder
       rudder is
       responsible for yaw
5. In relation to the center of gravity, in which direction would the center of pressure normally move as angle of attack is increased on a cambered wing?

6. What factors can affect the longitudinal stability of an airplane at high power settings and low airspeed?

7. Why are high wing aircraft normally designed with less dihedral than low wing aircraft?

8. Does the propwash resulting from high power settings increase or decrease the contribution of wing dihedral to the lateral stability of an airplane?

9. An aircraft with strong directional stability and weak lateral stability is prone to what type of undesirable side effect?

10. True/False. When landing in gusty winds, airspeed should be increased above normal to help guard against a stall.

11. List the basic guidelines for stall recovery.

12. Recall the general procedures for recovery from an erect spin.

SECTION C
AERODYNAMICS OF MANEUVERING FLIGHT

The extent to which an airplane can perform a variety of maneuvers is primarily a matter of design and a measure of its overall performance. Although aircraft design and performance may differ, the aerodynamic forces acting on any maneuvering aircraft are essentially the same. Understanding the aerodynamics of maneuvering flight can help you perform precise maneuvers while maintaining your airplane within its design limitations.

CLIMBING FLIGHT

The aerodynamic forces acting on an airplane established in a stabilized climb are in equilibrium; however, since the flight path is inclined, the relationship between these forces is altered. For example, the total force of weight no longer acts perpendicular to the flight path, but is comprised of two components. Although one component still acts 90° to the flight path, a rearward component of weight acts in the same direction as drag, opposing thrust. [Figure 3-48]

A transition from level flight into a climb normally combines a change in pitch attitude with an increase in power. If you attempt to climb just by pulling back on the control wheel to raise the nose of the airplane, momentum will cause a brief increase in altitude, but airspeed will soon decrease. The amount of thrust generated by the propeller for cruising flight at a given airspeed is not enough to maintain the same airspeed in a climb. Excess thrust, not excess lift, is necessary for a sustained climb. In fact, as the angle of climb steepens, thrust will not only oppose drag, but also will increasingly

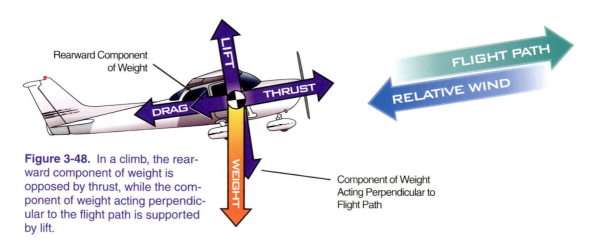

Figure 3-48. In a climb, the rearward component of weight is opposed by thrust, while the component of weight acting perpendicular to the flight path is supported by lift.

Rearward Component of Weight

Component of Weight Acting Perpendicular to Flight Path

When Is No Lift Required To Fly?

During a normal sustained climb, a component of weight is opposed by lift. However, in a true sustained vertical climb, such as the one performed by the General Dynamics F-16C pictured in figure A, the wings supply no vertical lift, and thrust is the only force opposing weight. Depending on an aircraft's thrust-to-weight ratio, a sustained vertical climb may be maintained under certain conditions. The thrust-to-weight ratio of the F-16 is approximately 1.1 to 1. In contrast, the thrust-to-weight ratio of the Boeing 747 [Figure B] is about 0.26 to 1.

replace lift as the force opposing weight. At the point where the climb becomes exactly vertical, weight and drag are opposed solely by thrust, and lift no longer acts to support the aircraft in flight.

LEFT-TURNING TENDENCIES

In addition to the basic aerodynamic forces present in a climb, a combination of physical and aerodynamic forces can contribute to a left-turning tendency in propeller-driven airplanes. The forces of torque, gyroscopic precession, asymmetrical thrust, and spiraling slipstream all work to create a left-turning tendency during high-power, low-airspeed flight conditions. A thorough understanding of left-turning tendencies will help you anticipate and correct for their effects.

 Torque effect is greatest at low airspeeds, high power settings, and high angles of attack.

TORQUE

You can understand **torque** most easily by remembering Newton's third law of motion: "For every action there is an equal and opposite reaction." In most airplanes with a single engine mounted on the front of the aircraft, the propeller rotates clockwise when viewed from the pilot's seat. The clockwise action of a spinning propeller causes a torque reaction, which tends to rotate the airplane counterclockwise about its longitudinal axis. [Figure 3-49]

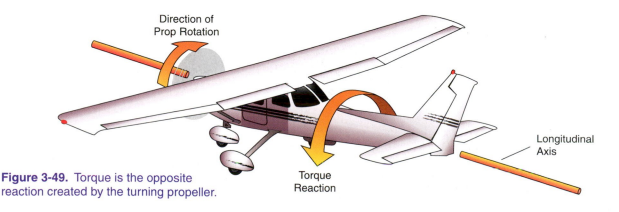

Figure 3-49. Torque is the opposite reaction created by the turning propeller.

Direction of Prop Rotation

Longitudinal Axis

Torque Reaction

GYROSCOPIC PRECESSION

The turning propeller of an airplane also exhibits characteristics of a gyroscope — rigidity in space and precession. The characteristic that produces a left-turning tendency is precession. **Gyroscopic precession** is the resultant reaction when a force is applied to the rim of a rotating disc. The reaction to a force applied to a gyro acts in the direction of rotation and approximately 90° ahead of the point where force is applied. You will experience the effects of precession only when the attitude of the aircraft is changed. [Figure 3-50]

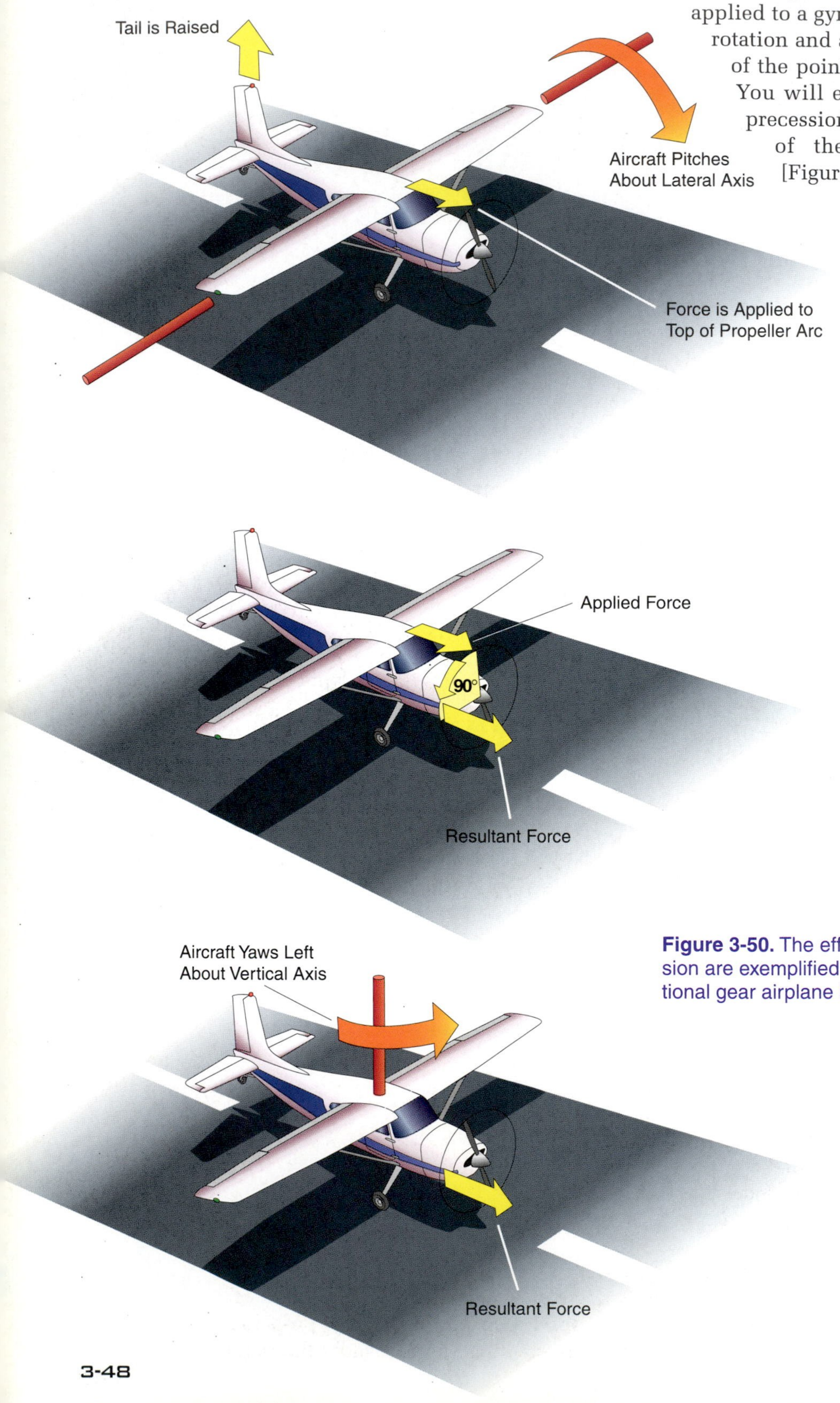

Tail is Raised

Aircraft Pitches About Lateral Axis

Force is Applied to Top of Propeller Arc

Applied Force

90°

Resultant Force

Aircraft Yaws Left About Vertical Axis

Resultant Force

Figure 3-50. The effects of gyroscopic precession are exemplified when the tail of a conventional gear airplane is raised during a takeoff.

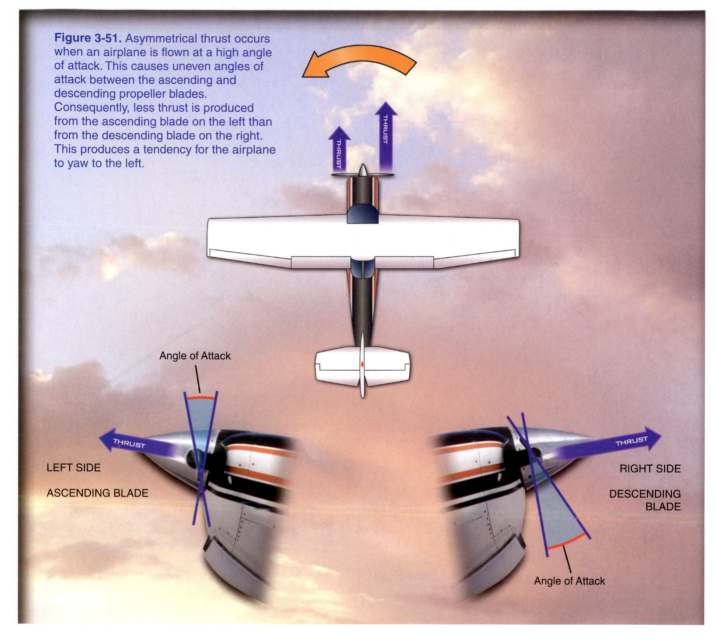

Figure 3-51. Asymmetrical thrust occurs when an airplane is flown at a high angle of attack. This causes uneven angles of attack between the ascending and descending propeller blades. Consequently, less thrust is produced from the ascending blade on the left than from the descending blade on the right. This produces a tendency for the airplane to yaw to the left.

THRUST

THRUST

Angle of Attack

THRUST

LEFT SIDE

ASCENDING BLADE

THRUST

RIGHT SIDE

DESCENDING BLADE

Angle of Attack

ASYMMETRICAL THRUST

When you are flying a propeller-driven airplane at a high angle of attack, the descending blade of the propeller takes a greater "bite" of air than the ascending blade on the other side. The greater bite is caused by a higher angle of attack for the descending blade, compared to the ascending blade. This creates the uneven, or **asymmetrical thrust,** which is known as P-factor. Since the descending blade is normally on the right side of the airplane (as viewed from the cockpit), **P-factor** makes an airplane yaw to the left about its vertical axis. [Figure 3-51]

 P-factor causes an airplane to yaw to the left when it is at high angles of attack. P-factor results from the descending propeller blade on the right producing more thrust than the ascending blade on the left.

You should remember that P-factor is most pronounced when the engine is operating at a high power setting, and when the airplane is flown at a high angle of attack. In level cruising flight, P-factor is not apparent, since both ascending and descending propeller blades are at nearly the same angle of attack, and are creating approximately the same amount of thrust.

SPIRALING SLIPSTREAM

As the propeller rotates, it produces a backward flow of air, or slipstream, which wraps around the airplane. This **spiraling slipstream** causes a change in airflow around the vertical stabilizer. Due to the direction of propeller rotation, the resultant slipstream strikes the left side of the vertical fin. The resulting sideward force yaws the airplane about its vertical axis, moving the nose to the left. [Figure 3-52]

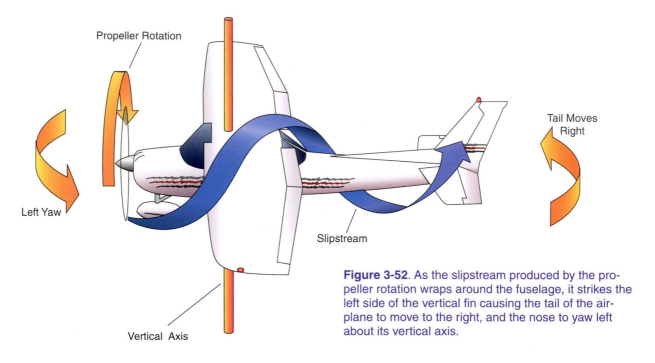

Propeller Rotation

Left Yaw

Tail Moves Right

Slipstream

Vertical Axis

Figure 3-52. As the slipstream produced by the propeller rotation wraps around the fuselage, it strikes the left side of the vertical fin causing the tail of the airplane to move to the right, and the nose to yaw left about its vertical axis.

AIRCRAFT DESIGN CONSIDERATIONS

Some aircraft manufacturers include design elements that help counteract left-turning tendencies and make the airplane easier to control. One such design places a small metal tab on the trailing edge of the rudder to help combat the effects of spiraling slipstream. The tab is bent to the left so that pressure from the passing airflow will push on the tab and force the rudder slightly to the right. The slight right-hand rudder displacement creates a yawing moment that opposes the left-turning tendency caused by spiraling slipstream. [Figure 3-53]

Figure 3-53. An adjustable metal trim tab is attached to the trailing edge of the rudder on this Cessna 172.

A horizontally canted engine also may be used to help counteract the left-turning tendency caused by spiraling slipstream. In this arrangement, the engine is turned slightly toward the right, effectively offsetting the airplane's thrustline and compensating for left yaw.

DESCENDING FLIGHT

In stabilized descending flight, aerodynamic forces are in equilibrium with the force of weight comprised of two components. One component of weight acts perpendicular to the flight path, while the other component of weight acts forward along the flight path. [Figure 3-54]

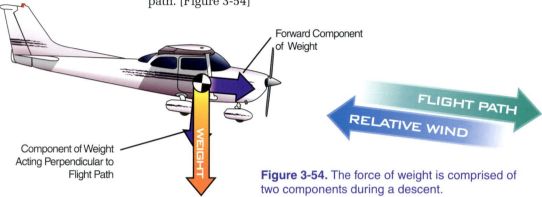

Figure 3-54. The force of weight is comprised of two components during a descent.

As the nose of the aircraft is lowered in the descent, the component of weight acting forward along the flight path increases and, assuming that power remains the same, an increase in speed occurs. Increasing airspeed results in an increase in parasite drag which works to balance the force of weight. Once speed is stabilized, the four forces of flight are once again in equilibrium. If the power is at idle, the force of thrust is removed and a larger component of weight must be allocated to counteract drag and maintain a constant airspeed. This is accomplished by lowering the nose of the airplane further. [Figure 3-55]

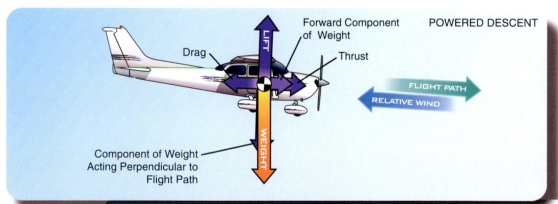

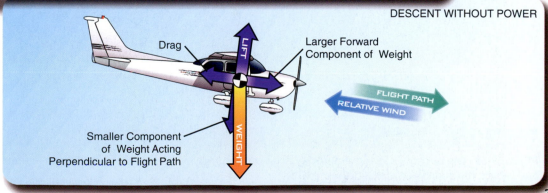

Figure 3-55. In a stabilized powered descent, four aerodynamic forces are in equilibrium. In a stabilized descent with the power at idle, three aerodynamic forces are in equilibrium with the forward component of weight equal to and opposite drag.

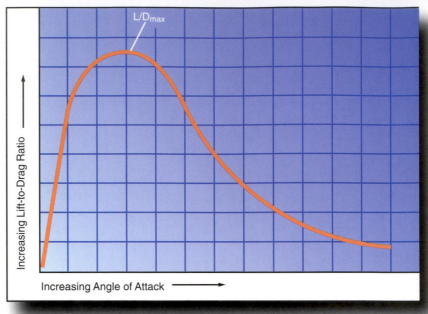

Figure 3-56. L/D_{max} is the specific angle of attack that generates the greatest lift with the least amount of corresponding drag.

Without the aid of power, your ability to control your rate of descent and flight path is somewhat limited. However, if you understand the glide characteristics of your airplane, you can maximize your chances of making a successful landing if a power failure should occur.

LIFT-TO-DRAG RATIO

The lift-to-drag ratio (L/D) can be used to measure the gliding efficiency of your airplane. The angle of attack resulting in the least drag on your airplane will give the **maximum lift-to-drag ratio** (L/D_{max}), the best glide angle, and the maximum gliding distance. [Figure 3-56]

GLIDE SPEED

At a given weight, L/D_{max} will correspond to a certain airspeed. This important performance speed is called the **best glide speed**. In most cases, it is the only speed that will give you the maximum gliding distance. In the event of an engine failure, maintaining the best glide speed is extremely important. Any speed, other than the best glide speed, creates more drag. If your airspeed is too high, parasite drag increases; and if you descend with too slow of an airspeed, induced drag increases. [Figure 3-57]

 If a power failure occurs after takeoff, immediately establish the proper gliding attitude and airspeed.

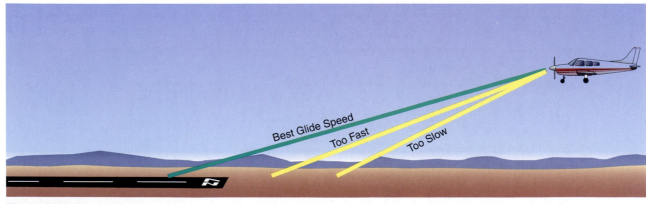

Figure 3-57. The best glide speed is normally achieved at L/D_{max}. Any deviation from best glide speed will increase drag and reduce the distance you can glide.

Trends in Lift-to-Drag Ratio

Improvements in aircraft design resulted in a general increase in maximum lift-to-drag ratios (L/D$_{max}$) between the years of 1920 to 1980. The higher aspect ratios that accompanied the emergence of the monoplane led to the relatively sharp rise in lift-to-drag ratios between World War I and World War II. You can see from the figure that there has been little change in L/D$_{max}$ since the 1940's. Any further increases in L/D$_{max}$ values will probably result from advances in structural materials that will allow significant reductions in drag and/or increased aspect ratio.

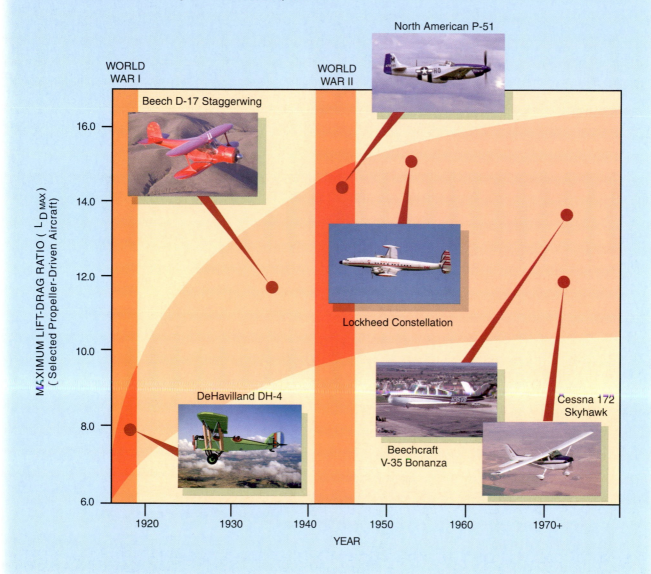

GLIDE RATIO

The **glide ratio** represents the distance an airplane will travel forward, without power, in relation to altitude loss. For example, a glide ratio of 10:1 means that an airplane will travel 10,000 feet of horizontal distance (approximately 1.6 n.m.) for every 1,000 feet of altitude lost in the descent. The best glide ratio of an aircraft is available only at the optimum angle of attack associated with L/D$_{max}$.

GLIDE ANGLE

During a descent, the angle between the actual glide path of your airplane and the horizon usually is called the **glide angle**. Your glide angle increases as drag increases, and

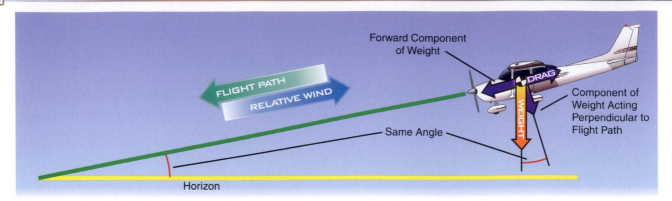

Figure 3-58. Notice that the angle between the component of weight acting perpendicular to the flight path and the resultant is the same as the angle between the flight path and the horizon. This is the glide angle of the airplane. To maintain a constant airspeed, any increase in drag must be offset by lowering the nose to increase the forward component of weight. This action increases the angle between the component of weight acting perpendicular to the flight path and the resultant vector, causing glide angle to increase.

decreases as drag decreases. Since a decreased glide angle, or a shallower glide, provides the greatest gliding distance, minimum drag normally produces the maximum glide distance. [Figure 3-58]

FACTORS AFFECTING THE GLIDE

In general, maintaining the best glide speed published by the manufacturer of your aircraft will assure an optimum glide. However, some factors may affect the efficiency of your glide. These factors include airplane weight, configuration, and wind.

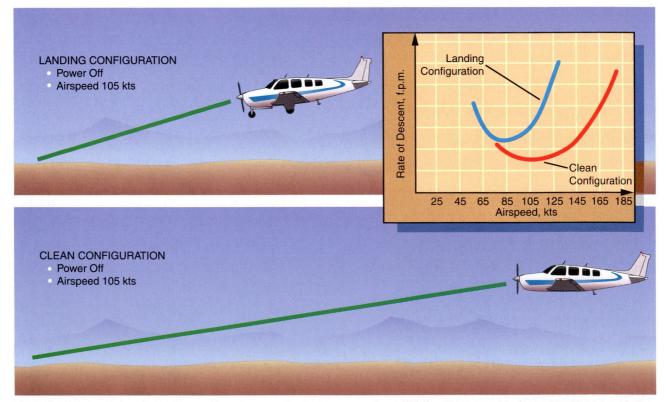

Figure 3-59. Any change in configuration will affect the glide performance of an airplane. A change in configuration that increases drag will result in a need for more weight to be allocated to counteract the increased drag. This lowering of the nose to maintain best glide speed will result in less distance covered over the ground for the same amount of altitude loss.

WEIGHT

Variations in weight do not affect the glide ratio of an airplane, however, there is a specific airspeed which is optimum for each weight. Two aerodynamically identical aircraft with different weights can glide the same distance from the same altitude. This can only be accomplished, however, if the heavier airplane flies at a higher airspeed than the airplane with the lighter load. Although the heavier airplane sinks faster and will reach the ground sooner, it will travel the same distance as the lighter airplane as long as the appropriate glide speed is maintained.

CONFIGURATION

Once you have established a state of equilibrium for a constant airspeed descent, the efficiency of the glide will be affected if you increase drag. For example, if you lower the landing gear, both parasite and total drag increase, which reduces the airplane's maximum lift-to-drag ratio and glide ratio. To maintain the airspeed you held before the landing gear was extended, you have to lower the nose of the airplane. [Figure 3-59]

WIND

A headwind will always reduce your glide range while a tailwind will always increase the distance you can glide. In light wind conditions you can normally use the best glide speed for no-wind conditions without a significant impact on your glide range. However, with a strong headwind or tailwind (winds greater than 25% of glide speed), best glide speed may not be found at L/D_{max}, and you will have to make adjustments to maximize your travel over the ground. [Figure 3-60]

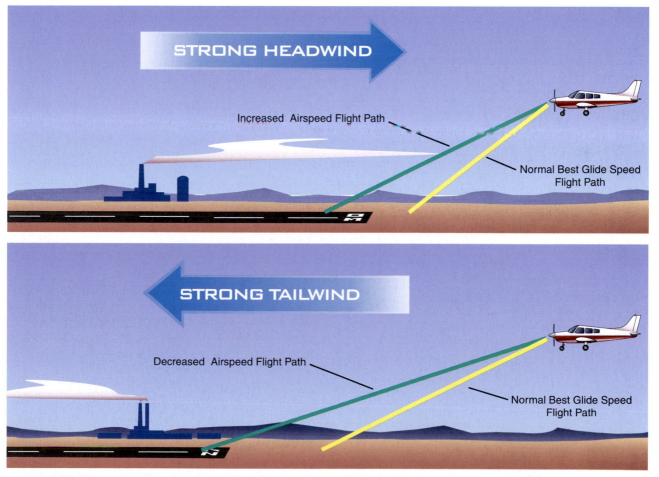

Figure 3-60. With a strong headwind, you will need to increase your normal best glide speed to obtain the maximum proportion of ground distance to altitude. A reduction in your normal best glide speed should be used to take advantage of strong tailwind conditions.

Comparing Glide Ratios

The glide ratio of an airplane is a matter of design. Some aircraft, such as high-speed military fighters, are designed with an emphasis on maneuverability. Their wings are generally short and have a low glide ratio. At the other end of the spectrum are aircraft, like gliders, that depend on a high glide ratio to stay airborne. Approximate glide ratios for a variety of aircraft are shown below.

9.1 : 1

11.5 : 1

12.2 : 1

23 : 1

TURNING FLIGHT

Before your airplane turns it must overcome inertia, or its tendency to continue in a straight line. You create the necessary turning force by using the ailerons to bank the airplane so that the direction of total lift is inclined. This is accomplished by dividing the force of lift so that one component of lift still acts vertically to oppose weight, while another acts horizontally. [Figure 3-61]

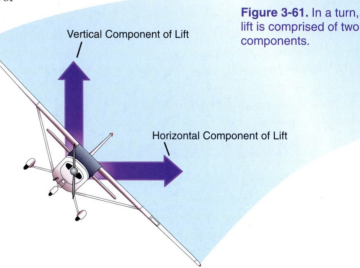

Figure 3-61. In a turn, lift is comprised of two components.

Vertical Component of Lift

Horizontal Component of Lift

The horizontal component of lift causes an airplane to turn.

To maintain altitude you will need to increase lift by increasing back pressure and, therefore, the angle of attack until the vertical component of lift equals weight. The horizontal component of lift creates a force directed inward toward the center of rotation which is known as **centripetal force**. It is this center-seeking force which causes the airplane to turn. Since centripetal force works against the tendency of the aircraft to continue in a straight line, inertia tends to oppose centripetal force toward the outside of the turn. This opposing impetus is referred to as **centrifugal force**. In reality, centrifugal force is not a true force; it is an apparent force that results from the effect of inertia during the turn. [Figure 3-62]

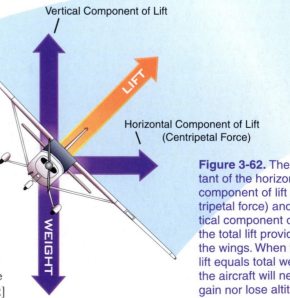

Vertical Component of Lift

LIFT

Horizontal Component of Lift
(Centripetal Force)

WEIGHT

Figure 3-62. The resultant of the horizontal component of lift (centripetal force) and the vertical component of lift is the total lift provided by the wings. When the total lift equals total weight, the aircraft will neither gain nor lose altitude while in the turn.

ADVERSE YAW

When you roll into a turn, the aileron on the inside of the turn is raised, and the aileron on the outside of the turn is lowered. The lowered aileron on the outside increases the angle of attack and produces more lift for that wing. Since induced drag is a by-product of lift, the outside wing also produces more drag than the inside wing. This causes a yawing tendency toward the outside of the turn, which is called **adverse yaw**. [Figure 3-63]

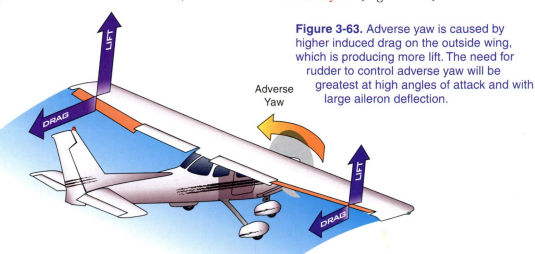

Figure 3-63. Adverse yaw is caused by higher induced drag on the outside wing, which is producing more lift. The need for rudder to control adverse yaw will be greatest at high angles of attack and with large aileron deflection.

The coordinated use of aileron and rudder helps compensate for adverse yaw. For example, when you enter a turn to the left, you should depress the left rudder pedal slightly. After you are established in the turn, and you neutralize the ailerons to prevent further roll, the tendency for adverse yaw is removed and rudder pressure can be relaxed. When you roll out of the turn, you should apply coordinated right aileron and rudder pressure to return to a wings-level attitude.

Proverse Yaw

On aircraft that don't exclusively employ ailerons as a means of roll control, adverse yaw may not be a factor. Some aircraft use spoilers as either the primary method of controlling roll, or as a complement to ailerons. Spoilers work by "spoiling" the lift on the wing in the direction of the desired roll. One side effect of using spoilers is the propensity for creating proverse yaw. As you might expect, proverse yaw is essentially the opposite of adverse yaw.

The Boeing 727 is fitted with 14 spoilers, 10 of which are used in flight to assist the two sets of ailerons in rolling the aircraft. During high-speed flight, the outboard set of ailerons is locked in a trim position, while the inboard ailerons and spoilers work to roll the aircraft.

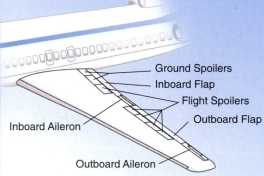

Ground Spoilers
Inboard Flap
Flight Spoilers
Outboard Flap
Inboard Aileron
Outboard Aileron

Although proverse yaw may be common to spoiler-equipped aircraft and may be considered a beneficial characteristic, spoilers are most suitable for use on high-speed aircraft. Since spoilers dump lift, they may not be desirable for training aircraft or other low-speed airplanes.

OVERBANKING TENDENCY

As you enter a turn and increase the angle of bank, you may notice the tendency of the airplane to continue rolling into a steeper bank, even though you neutralize the ailerons. This **overbanking tendency** is caused by additional lift on the outside, or raised, wing. Since the outside wing is traveling faster than the inside wing, it produces more lift and the airplane tends to roll beyond the desired bank angle. [Figure 3-64] To correct for overbanking tendency, you can use a small amount of opposite aileron, away from the turn, to maintain your desired angle of bank.

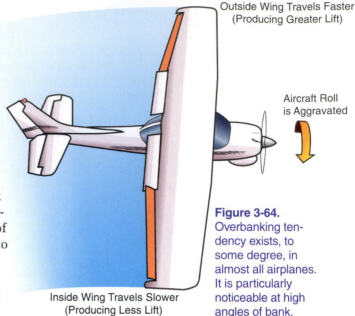

Outside Wing Travels Faster
(Producing Greater Lift)

Aircraft Roll
is Aggravated

Inside Wing Travels Slower
(Producing Less Lift)

Figure 3-64. Overbanking tendency exists, to some degree, in almost all airplanes. It is particularly noticeable at high angles of bank.

RATE AND RADIUS OF TURN

Two major components that define airplane performance during turning flight are rate and radius of turn. **Rate of turn** refers to the amount of time it takes for an airplane to turn a specified number of degrees. If flown at the same airspeed and angle of bank, every aircraft will turn at the same rate. If airspeed increases and the angle of bank remains the same, the rate of turn will decrease. Conversely, a constant airspeed coupled with an angle of bank increase will result in a faster rate of turn.

The amount of horizontal distance an aircraft uses to complete a turn is referred to as the **radius of turn**. Although the radius of turn is also dependent on an airplane's airspeed and angle of bank, the relationship is the opposite of rate of turn. For example, as an airplane's airspeed is increased with the angle of bank held constant, the radius of turn increases. On the other hand, if the angle of bank is increased and the airspeed remains the same, the radius of turn is decreased. [Figure 3-65]

LOAD FACTOR

If you attempt to improve turn performance by increasing angle of bank while maintaining airspeed, you should pay close attention to airplane limitations due to the effects of increasing load factor. **Load factor** is the ratio of the load supported by the airplane's wings to the actual weight of the aircraft and its contents. An airplane in cruising flight, while not accelerating in any direction, has a load factor of one. This one-G condition means the wings are supporting only the actual weight of the airplane and its contents. If the wings are supporting twice as much weight as the weight of the airplane and its contents, the load factor is two. You may be more familiar with the term "G-forces" as a way to describe flight loads caused by aircraft maneuvering. Since G-force increases commonly occur when pulling back on the control wheel to increase back pressure, the term "pulling G's" is sometimes used when referring to an increase in load factor. [Figure 3-66]

Figure 3-66. When a pilot pulls G's during aerobatic maneuvers in warm, humid conditions, the increased wing loading and decreased pressure above the wings can contribute to the formation of a distinctive condensation cloud.

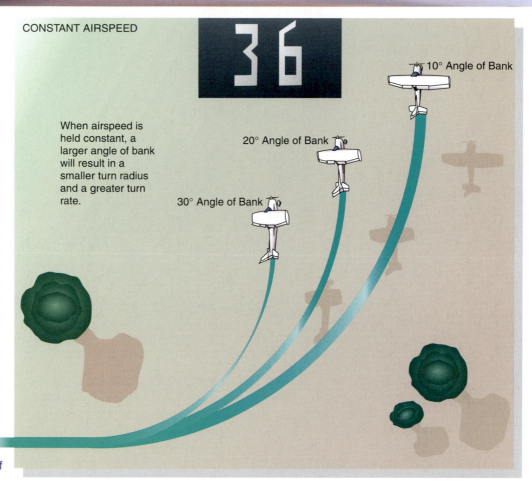

CONSTANT AIRSPEED

When airspeed is held constant, a larger angle of bank will result in a smaller turn radius and a greater turn rate.

10° Angle of Bank

20° Angle of Bank

30° Angle of Bank

Figure 3-65. Angle of bank and airspeed regulate the rate and radius of a turn.

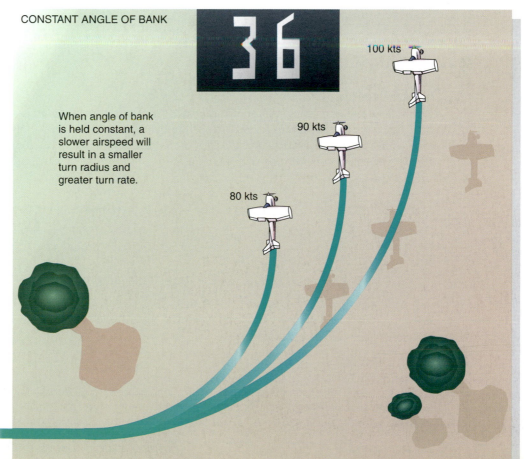

CONSTANT ANGLE OF BANK

When angle of bank is held constant, a slower airspeed will result in a smaller turn radius and greater turn rate.

100 kts

90 kts

80 kts

Figure 3-67. Riders on this rollercoaster experience a maximum load factor of 3.85G's.

As you enter a banked turn while riding on a rollercoaster, the forces you will experience are very similar to the forces which act on a turning airplane. On a rollercoaster, you can feel the resultant force created by the combination of centripetal force and inertia as an increase in seat pressure. This pressure is an increased positive load factor that causes you to feel heavier in the turn than when you are on a flat portion of the track. [Figure 3-67]

If you abruptly push the control wheel forward while flying, you would experience a sensation as if your weight suddenly decreased. This is caused by inertia attempting to keep your body moving forward while the aircraft is diving away from the original flight path. If the effects of inertia and centripetal force cancel each other out, you will experience a weightless sensation of zero G's. If inertia overcomes centripetal force, negative G-loading occurs.

It is important to note that a change in load factor can occur at any time due to either pilot input, or environmental conditions, such as turbulence. In rare instances, you may experience a rapid change in G-forces. For example, in extremely turbulent air, you might be subjected to a variety of G-forces including positive G's, negative G's, and side-ward, or transverse, G's.

LOAD FACTOR IN TURNS

In a turning airplane, you must compensate for the apparent increase in weight and loss of vertical lift, or you will lose altitude. You can do this by increasing the angle of attack with back pressure on the control wheel. The increase in angle of attack increases the total lift of the airplane and imposes additional loads which must be supported by the wings. [Figure 3-68]

 The load factor imposed on an airplane will increase as the angle of bank is increased.

Figure 3-68. During constant altitude turns, the relationship between load factor, or G's, and bank angle is the same for all airplanes. For example, with a 60° bank, two G's are required to maintain level flight. This means the airplane's wings must support twice the weight of the airplane and its contents, although the actual weight of the airplane does not increase.

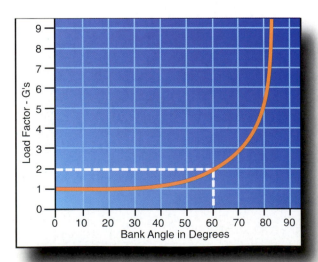

LOAD FACTOR AND STALL SPEED

The additional load factor incurred during constant altitude turns will also increase stall speed. [Figure 3-69] In fact, stall speed increases in proportion to the square root of the load factor. For example, if you are flying an airplane with a one-G stalling speed of 55 knots, the airplane will stall at twice that speed (110 knots) with a load factor of four G's. Stalls that occur with G-forces on an airplane are called **accelerated stalls**. An accelerated stall occurs at a speed higher than the normal one-G stall speed. These stalls demonstrate that the critical angle of attack, rather than airspeed, is the reason for a stall.

Figure 3-69. If you attempt to maintain altitude during a turn by increasing the angle of attack, the stall speed increases as the angle of bank increases. The percent of increase in stall speed is fairly moderate with shallow bank angles — less than 45°. However, once you increase the bank angle beyond 45°, the percent of increase in the stall speed rises rapidly. For example, in a 60°, constant-altitude bank, the stall speed increases by approximately 41%; a 75° bank increases stall speed by about 100%.

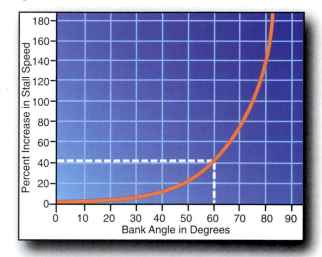

 Increasing the load factor will cause an airplane to stall at a higher speed.

HOW MANY G'S ARE TOO MANY?

From the files of the NTSB...
Aircraft: Pitts S-2A — destroyed
Crew: One — seriously injured
Narrative: The witness stated the pilot was performing aerobatic maneuvers. At the top of the loop (approx. 3,000 ft AGL), the aircraft remained inverted, power was reduced, and an inverted spin was entered. The aircraft remained in the inverted spin to water impact. The pilot does not recall the accident flight, but stated he had been having problems with G-loads and low blood pressure.

It is possible, even likely, that some aerobatic aircraft may be able to withstand more G's than the pilot. A particular pilot's G-tolerance is a function of many factors, including the intensity, duration, and direction of the G-forces. The main physical problems associated with G-forces are caused by basic changes within the cardiovascular system. Positive G's create a pooling of blood in the lower extremities of the body, impairing circulation and reducing blood pressure at head level. Continued or increased G-loading will result in a decrease of visual acuity, ultimately followed by unconsciousness, or blackout.

The human body is less tolerant of negative G's, which force blood into the head. Large amounts of sustained negative G's can result in uncomfortable symptoms such as facial pain and redout. Although some experienced aerobatic pilots may be able to withstand 7 or 8 positive G's before blackout occurs, most will be incapacitated by only -3G's. You can improve your G-tolerance by maintaining good physical conditioning and avoiding smoking, hyperventilation, and hypoxia. Most civil pilots, however, will not encounter G-forces of sufficient strength during normal flight to cause any major problems.

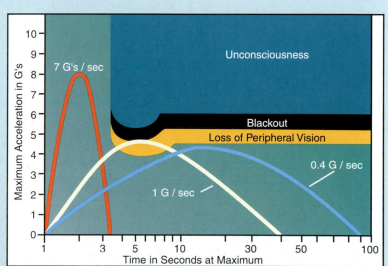

Calculating Maneuvering Speed

Maneuvering speed may only be provided by the airplane manufacturer at maximum weight. For other weights, you can mathematically determine the maneuvering speed using one of two methods.

METHOD 1

One method uses a formula which is based on limit load factor (n) and stall speed (V_S):

$$V_A = V_S \times \sqrt{n\ \text{limit}}$$

The above formula requires you to know the stall speed for the associated weight. This can be determined from the POH or by using the formula,

$$V_{S2} \div V_S = \sqrt{W_2 \div W_1}$$

OR

$$V_{S2} = V_S \times \sqrt{W_2 \div W_1}$$

Using these formulas and the following information (obtained from the POH), the V_A for a Cessna 172 at 1,800 pounds can be determined.

Given:
Limit load factor (n): 3.8G's
Maximum weight (W_1): 2,400 lbs.
Stall speed at maximum weight (V_S): 51 KCAS

First, determine the stall speed (V_{S2}) at 1,800 lbs.

$$V_{S2} = 51 \times \sqrt{1,800 \div 2,400}$$
$$V_{S2} = 51 \times \sqrt{.75}$$
$$V_{S2} = 51 \times .866 = 44.2\ \text{KCAS}$$

Next, use the maneuvering speed formula to determine V_{A2}.

$$V_{A2} = 44.2 \times \sqrt{3.8}$$
$$V_{A2} = 44.2 \times 1.95 = 86.2\ \text{KCAS}$$

METHOD 2

Another method allows you to determine V_A using the formula, V_A at maximum weight multiplied by the square root of the ratio of the actual weight (W_2) divided by the maximum weight (W_1):

$$V_{A2} = V_A \times \sqrt{W_2 \div W_1}$$

Using this method, and given the following data, can you determine the maneuvering speed for a Boeing 727 approaching to land at 122,000 lbs?

V_A at maximum landing weight: 200 KIAS
Maximum landing weight: 137,500 lbs.

ANSWER: The V_A associated with a 122,000 pound Boeing 727 is about 188 KIAS, calculated as follows:

$$V_{A2} = 200 \times \sqrt{122,000 \div 137,500}$$
$$V_{A2} = 200 \times \sqrt{.887}$$
$$V_{A2} = 200 \times .942 = 188\ \text{KIAS}$$

LIMIT LOAD FACTOR

The amount of stress, or load factor, that an airplane can withstand before structural damage or failure occurs is expressed as the airplane's **limit load factor**. Primarily a function of airplane design, an individual airplane's limit load factor is published in the pilot's operating handbook in terms of maximum positive or negative G's.

Most small general aviation airplanes weighing 12,500 pounds or less, and nine passenger seats or less, are certificated in the normal, utility, or acrobatic categories. The maximum limit load factor in the normal category is 3.8 positive G's, and 1.52 negative G's, which is sufficient for basic training maneuvers. An airplane certificated in the utility category may be used for several maneuvers requiring additional stress on the airframe. A limit of 4.4 positive G's or 1.76 negative G's is permitted in the utility category. An acrobatic category airplane may be flown in any flight attitude as long as its limit load factor does not exceed 6 positive G's or 3 negative G's. By adhering to proper loading techniques and flying within the limits listed in the pilot's operating handbook, you will avoid excessive loads on the airplane, and possible structural damage.

The POH for the airplane you are flying is your best source of load limit information. Some pilot operating handbooks publish a **V-g diagram** which graphically depicts the limit load factors for the associated airplane at a variety of airspeeds. [Figure 3-70]

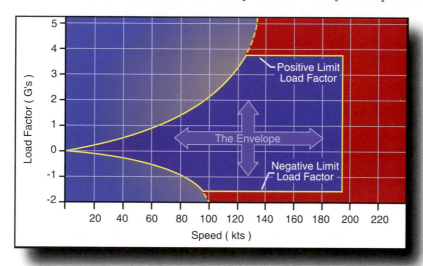

Figure 3-70. The V-g diagram depicts a specific aircraft's envelope, and is valid at a particular weight, configuration, and altitude. The diagram also assumes symmetrical wing loading.

MANEUVERING SPEED

An important airspeed related to load factors and stall speed is the **design maneuvering speed (V_A)**. V_A represents the maximum speed at which you can use full, abrupt control movement without overstressing the airframe. Any airspeed in excess of V_A can overstress the airframe during abrupt maneuvers or turbulence. The higher the airspeed, the greater the amount of excess load that can be imposed before a stall occurs. V_A is depicted on the V-g diagram where the stall curve meets the positive load limit. If you operate at or below maneuvering speed, and G-loading increases too far, the airplane will stall before you exceed the limit load factor, and potential damage to the airplane will be avoided. [Figure 3-71]

 V_A is defined as the design maneuvering speed.

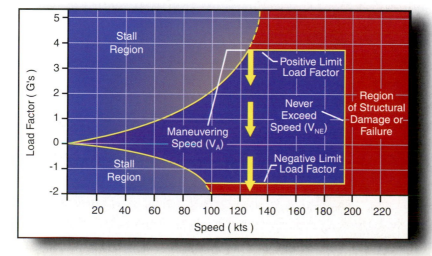

Figure 3-71. The V-g diagram shows that an increase in G-loading at speeds less than V_A will result in a stall before structural damage occurs. When operating at speeds above V_A, but below V_{NE}, structural damage or failure will not occur if limit load factors are not exceeded.

V_A normally is not marked on the airspeed indicator, since it may vary with total weight. V_A decreases as weight decreases since an aircraft operating at lighter weights is subject to more rapid acceleration from gusts and turbulence. The POH and/or a placard in the airplane are the best sources for determining V_A.

 The amount of excess load that can be imposed on an airframe depends on the aircraft's speed.

SUMMARY CHECKLIST

✓ In climbing flight, one component of weight acts perpendicular to the flight path, and another component of weight acts rearward, in the same direction as drag.

✓ Four left-turning tendencies associated with propeller-driven airplanes are torque, gyroscopic precession, asymmetrical thrust, and spiraling slipstream.

✓ During descending flight, one component of weight acts forward along the flight path, while another component acts perpendicular to the flight path.

✓ The least drag, best glide angle, and maximum gliding distance can be obtained by maintaining the angle of attack that corresponds to L/D_{max}.

✓ Changes in aircraft weight will not affect glide ratio, but a higher airspeed will have to be maintained in a heavier aircraft in order to cover the same distance over the ground.

✓ Centripetal force, which is created by the horizontal component of lift, is the center-seeking force that acts on a turning airplane.

✓ The effects of adverse yaw can be countered by maintaining a coordinated turn using rudder.

✓ Rate of turn increases and radius of turn decreases as angle of bank is increased in a constant airspeed turn. If angle of bank is held constant and airspeed is increased, turn rate will decrease and turn radius will increase.

✓ The ratio of the weight that the wings must support to the actual weight of the aircraft is termed load factor.

✓ Accelerated stalls occur when the critical angle of attack is exceeded at an airspeed higher than the one-G stall speed.

✓ The V-g diagram defines the airplane's envelope, which is bounded by the stall region, limit load factor, and V_{NE}.

KEY TERMS

Torque

Gyroscopic Precession

Asymmetrical Thrust

P-Factor

Spiraling Slipstream

Maximum Lift-to-Drag Ratio

Best Glide Speed

Glide Ratio

Glide Angle   Radius of Turn

Centripetal Force   Load Factor

Centrifugal Force   Accelerated Stalls

Adverse Yaw   Limit Load Factor

Overbanking Tendency   V-g Diagram

Rate of Turn   Design Maneuvering Speed (V_A)

QUESTIONS

1. Identify the aerodynamic force that opposes the rearward component of weight in a climb.

2. What relative airspeed, power, and angle of attack conditions produce the most noticeable left-turning tendencies common to single-engine, propeller-driven aircraft?

3. Name at least three design elements that can be used to help offset left-turning tendencies.

4. All else being equal, will two aerodynamically identical aircraft with different weights be able to glide the same distance over the ground? If so, how can this be accomplished and why?

5. What causes an airplane to turn?

6. If angle of bank and altitude are held constant, what can be done to increase the rate of turn?

Given a wings-level, 1G stall speed of 55 knots, use the chart provided to determine the stall speed under the following conditions:

7. Bank angle, 30°

8. Bank angle, 45°

9. Bank angle, 75°

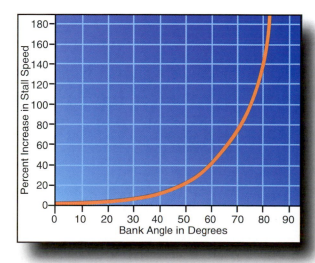

10. True/False. Maneuvering speed increases with a decrease in weight.

PART II
FLIGHT OPERATIONS

There is a feeling about an airport that no other piece of ground can have. No matter what the name of the country on whose land it lies, an airport is a place you can see and touch that leads to a reality that can only be thought and felt.

— Richard Bach

PART II

In the early days of aviation, there were few airplanes and even fewer airports. At the busiest airports, the amount of air traffic was negligible compared to today. As air traffic grew, pilots became aware of the increased potential for midair collisions; airports evolved to manage many aircraft at once; airspace designations were created to govern the operation of aircraft; and common radio procedures were established to enhance communication. Part II contains a broad range of information that you need to operate safely in today's complex flight environment. The rules and procedures which make it possible for thousands of aircraft to efficiently takeoff and land each day are examined in *The Flight Environment*. As you explore *Communication and Flight Information* you will discover how to effectively communicate with air traffic control and will learn about the various sources which provide you with information essential to flight operations.

CHAPTER 4

THE FLIGHT ENVIRONMENT

Part II, Chapter 4 — Flight Operations

Discovery Workshop — Flight Operations

SECTION A
SAFETY OF FLIGHT

Maintaining the safety of flight is your number one priority as a pilot. There are some safety issues which you must be aware of during every flight, such as collision avoidance and maintaining minimum safe altitudes. Other safety considerations only apply in certain situations; for example, taxiing in wind, flight over hazardous terrain, and effective exchange of flight controls with your instructor. Every flight is different and, as pilot in command, you need to consider the factors which can affect your flight and take the appropriate actions to ensure safety.

COLLISION AVOIDANCE

Learning **collision avoidance** procedures begins with your first flight. The risk of an in-flight collision exists for all pilots, but you can take action to avoid this type of accident. Studies show that the majority of midair collisions occur within five miles of an airport, during daylight hours, and in VFR conditions. You will hear the terms VFR and IFR used frequently in several different ways. If you are operating under **visual flight rules (VFR)**, you are governed by specific FARs which include minimum cloud clearance and visibility requirements, also referred to as weather minimums. In comparison, **instrument flight rules (IFR)** are rules which are established to govern flight operations in weather conditions below VFR weather minimums. The terms VFR and IFR also are used to define weather conditions. For example, visual meteorological conditions (VMC) are often referred to as VFR conditions, and instrument meteorological conditions (IMC) are sometimes called IFR conditions. In addition, the terms VFR and IFR can define the type of flight plan under which an aircraft is operating. It is possible for an aircraft to be on an IFR flight plan in VFR weather conditions.

Although there are many resources which can be used to avoid midair collisions in VFR conditions, including use of exterior lights, radio transmissions, and air traffic control services, the most important is your ability to effectively see and avoid other aircraft. Early detection of aircraft is crucial to avoiding a collision. For example, if your aircraft is flying at a speed of 150 knots on a head-on collision course with another aircraft also traveling at 150 knots, the closure rate is one quarter of a mile in the three seconds that is usually required for you or the other pilot to take action.

VISUAL SCANNING

To see and avoid other aircraft, you must develop an effective **visual scanning** pattern which is compatible with the function of your eyes. Two normal healthy eyes provide the average person with a field of vision of approximately 200°. However, the area in which the eye can focus sharply and perceive detail is a relatively narrow cone (usually only about 10° wide) directly in the center of the field of vision. Beyond this area, visual acuity decreases sharply in all directions. Since your eyes require time to focus on this

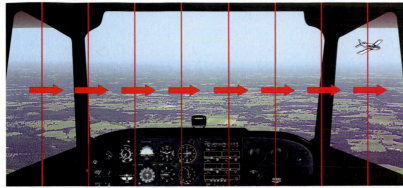

To scan using the side-to-side method, start at the far left of the windshield and make a methodical sweep to the right, pausing in each block of viewing area to focus your eyes.

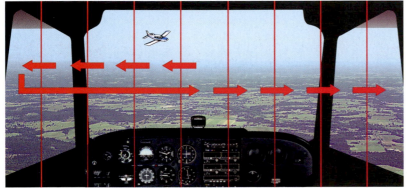

An alternative scanning method is to start in the center block of the windshield, move to the left, focusing in each block, then swing quickly to the center block after reaching the last block on the left and repeat this action to the right.

Figure 4-1. The block system of scanning involves dividing your viewing area (windshield) into segments, and then methodically scanning for traffic in each block of airspace in sequential order.

narrow viewing area, scanning is most effective when you use a series of short, regularly-spaced eye movements. This helps to bring successive areas of the sky into your central visual field. The FAA recommends that your eye movements not exceed 10°, and that you focus for at least one second on each segment of the sky. Be sure that the scan pattern you develop covers all of the sky that you can see from the cockpit, both horizontally and vertically. [Figure 4-1]

The most effective way to scan during daylight is through a series of short, regularly-spaced eye movements in 10° sectors.

The further objects are from your central visual field, the smaller the amount of detail that can be discerned. You may not notice objects in your peripheral vision unless there is some relative motion. An airplane on a converging course from one side does not have any relative motion unless there is a significant speed difference, and therefore, may not catch your attention. When scanning for traffic, you should be especially alert for an aircraft which shows no movement, since this indicates that it is most likely on a collision course with your airplane. If the other aircraft shows no lateral or vertical motion, but is increasing in size, take immediate evasive action.

If there is no apparent relative motion between another aircraft and yours, you are probably on a collision course.

As you scan, it may take several seconds for your eyes to refocus when switching from the instrument panel to distant objects outside the airplane. To counter eye fatigue, it helps to focus on exterior parts of the aircraft as a transition from inside to outside the cockpit.

A Visual Experiment

You can use this textbook to demonstrate the limitations of your visual field. Stand it on edge on a table and sit in a chair so your eyes are about 5 feet away. The width of the book represents an area approximately 10° wide. This is the relatively small area in which your eyes can focus sharply.

Now focus on the Guided Flight Discovery logo. Can you see the words Private Pilot Manual in the upper right corner? As long as you remain focused on the logo, you probably won't be able to see the printed title clearly even though you can tell something is there. [Figure A]

To discover the limitations of your peripheral vision, close your eyes and have a friend position his or her hand even with your ear and only two feet away. When you open your eyes, remain focused straight ahead. How well can you see your friend's hand when it is stationary? How about when it is moving up and down? This demonstration illustrates the difficulty in perceiving objects in your peripheral vision when there is no relative motion. [Figure B]

Sky conditions also have an effect on your ability to see traffic. In bright sunlight, a clean windshield and sunglasses can help you see objects more clearly. If the outside visibility is good, you have a better chance of spotting a hazard since haze or reduced visibility tends to make traffic and terrain features appear farther away than their actual distance. Another phenomenon which can occur in reduced visibility is called **empty field myopia**. When you are looking at a featureless sky that is devoid of objects, contrasting colors, or patterns, your eyes tend to focus at only 10 to 30 feet ahead. This means that spots on the windshield which are out of focus could appear to be airplanes, and distant traffic may go undetected. [Figure 4-2]

 In haze, air traffic and terrain features appear to be farther away than they actually are.

Figure 4-2. In addition to the effect of sky conditions, the contrast an aircraft has with its background is a factor in your ability to see it clearly. An aircraft below the horizon, silhouetted against a uniform landscape, has greater contrast with its environment than does a similar aircraft viewed against a cluttered background.

When you encounter traffic, remember that the other pilot may be occupied with tasks other than scanning and may not react in the manner that you anticipate. As you take evasive action, watch the other aircraft to see if it makes any unusual maneuvers and, if so, plan your reaction accordingly. You also should be aware that there may be more than one potential collision hazard in an area at the same time. The more time you spend on developing your scan in the early part of flight training, the more natural it will become later. The scanning techniques described here will help you see potential conflicts earlier and allow you to take the proper action to avoid a collision. Also, being familiar with the blind spots in your aircraft's design will improve your awareness of potential hazards.

BLIND SPOTS AND AIRCRAFT DESIGN

Airplanes, like automobiles, have problems associated with **blind spots**. In both high-wing and low-wing aircraft designs, portions of your view are blocked by the fuselage and wings. [Figure 4-3] This can make it difficult to see conflicting traffic. For example, in a high-wing airplane, your view is blocked as soon as you lower the wing to start a turn. Prior to beginning the turn, you can check the area for other aircraft by lifting the wing and looking in the direction of the turn.

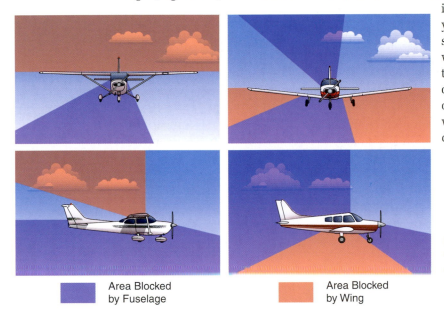

Area Blocked by Fuselage

Area Blocked by Wing

Figure 4-3. The portions of your view which are restricted depend on the design of the airplane.

In a high-wing airplane it is easy to see below the airplane, but difficult to see the area above the airplane. The reverse is true for low-wing airplanes. These blind spots can develop into a serious problem, particularly during the approach and landing phases of flight. A good way to reduce the possibility of a collision during extended climbs or descents is to make shallow S-turns and avoid climbing or descending at steep angles. [Figure 4-4]

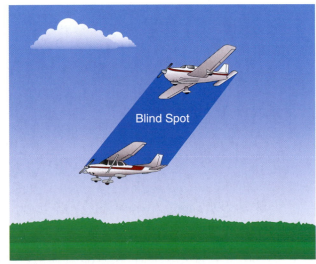

Blind Spot

Figure 4-4. When a high-wing airplane is below a low-wing airplane on approach to landing, both airplanes can easily remain out of sight of each other. Similar problems can occur during departures.

AIRPORT OPERATIONS

Any operation in the vicinity of an airport warrants extra caution. Even airports with control towers may be hazardous because of the large amount of air traffic. A controlled environment does not relieve you of the responsibility to see and avoid other aircraft. At airports without control towers, which are referred to as uncontrolled airports, sequencing to the airport is determined by the individual pilots, traffic advisories normally are not provided by air traffic control, and aircraft without radios may be operating in the area. These factors increase the potential for a collision if you are not vigilant.

To increase safety at airports, a voluntary program called **Operation Lights On** has been established by the FAA. Operation Lights On encourages you to use your landing lights during departures and approaches, both day and night, especially when operating within 10 miles of an airport, or in conditions of reduced visibility. It is recommended that you check your pilot's operating handbook for any limitations on the use of your aircraft lights.

In addition, your aircraft's anticollision lights are required to be on whenever the engines are running, day or night. However, anticollision lights need not be turned on when they might interfere with safety. For example, strobe lights should be turned off when their brightness might be detrimental to the vision of others.

MANEUVERS IN THE TRAINING AREA

It is important not only to maintain your scan, but to clear the area for traffic while practicing maneuvers. Your instructor will teach you to make **clearing turns** before performing maneuvers in the training, or practice, area. Clearing turns, which usually consist of at least a 180° change in direction, allow you to see areas blocked by blind spots and make it easier to maintain visual contact with other aircraft in the area.

 Prior to starting any maneuvers, make clearing turns and carefully scan the area for other aircraft.

RIGHT-OF-WAY RULES

The FARs state very clearly that the pilot in command is responsible for seeing and avoiding all traffic in visual flight conditions. To help avoid conflicting traffic situations, **right-of-way rules** have been established.

An aircraft in distress is one which requires immediate assistance due to a serious problem or emergency, and therefore, has the right-of-way over all other air traffic. If two aircraft are approaching each other head-on or nearly so, both aircraft will give way to the right. An overtaking aircraft must pass the slower aircraft to the right and stay well clear. When aircraft of the same category are converging, the aircraft to the other's right has the right-of-way. [Figure 4-5] The general rule regarding converging aircraft of different categories is that the least maneuverable aircraft usually has the right-of-way over all other air traffic. [Figure 4-6]

 An aircraft in distress has the right-of-way over all other aircraft.

 When two aircraft of the same category are converging, but not head-on, the aircraft to the left shall give way. If the aircraft are on a head-on collision course, both aircraft should give way to the right. See figure 4-5.

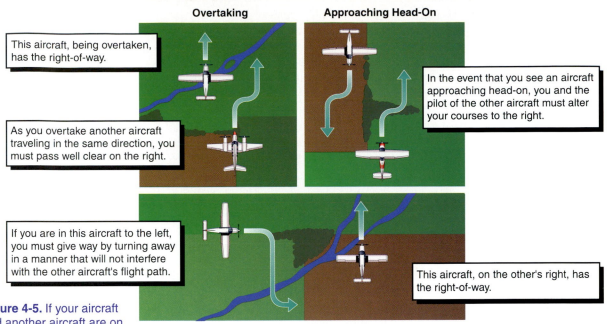

Overtaking

This aircraft, being overtaken, has the right-of-way.

As you overtake another aircraft traveling in the same direction, you must pass well clear on the right.

Approaching Head-On

In the event that you see an aircraft approaching head-on, you and the pilot of the other aircraft must alter your courses to the right.

If you are in this aircraft to the left, you must give way by turning away in a manner that will not interfere with the other aircraft's flight path.

This aircraft, on the other's right, has the right-of-way.

Converging

Figure 4-5. If your aircraft and another aircraft are on a collision course, both you and the other pilot should take the proper action to avoid each other. Primarily, there are three situations where right-of-way rules apply; converging with another aircraft, approaching another aircraft head-on, or overtaking another aircraft.

The least maneuverable aircraft normally has the right-of-way. For example, a glider has the right-of-way over an airship and an airship has the right-of-way over an airplane. See figure 4-6.

Figure 4-6. The FARs state that when aircraft of different categories are converging (except head-on or nearly so), a balloon has the right-of-way over all other aircraft. A glider has the right-of-way over any airship, airplane, or rotorcraft; and an airship has the right-of-way over any airplane or rotorcraft. Finally, an aircraft that is towing or refueling another aircraft has the right-of-way over all other engine-driven aircraft.

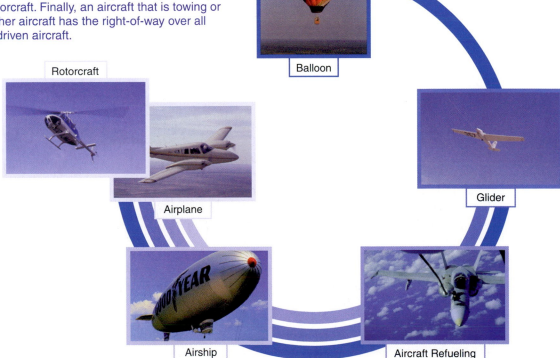

Rotorcraft

Balloon

Airplane

Glider

Airship

Aircraft Refueling

Right-of-way rules also apply to specific airport operations. An aircraft on final approach or an aircraft that is landing has the right-of-way over other aircraft in the traffic pattern and those on the ground. When two or more aircraft, which are preparing to land, enter the traffic pattern at the same time, the aircraft at the lowest altitude has the right-of-way. However, this is not intended to allow aircraft to enter the pattern below the specified traffic pattern altitude and disrupt or cut in front of those already established in the pattern.

 When two or more aircraft are approaching an airport for the purpose of landing, the right-of-way belongs to the aircraft at the lower altitude.

MINIMUM SAFE ALTITUDES

For safety reasons, the FARs specify minimum altitudes that you must maintain during flight. Maintaining **minimum safe altitudes** is required at all times except during takeoffs and landings.

Over a congested area, such as a city or metropolitan area, you are required to fly at least 1,000 feet above any obstacle within a horizontal radius of 2,000 feet of your aircraft. When flying over an uncongested area, you must fly at least 500 feet above the surface. Over sparsely populated or open water areas you cannot fly within 500 feet of any person, vessel, vehicle, or structure. The lowest altitude at which you can fly anywhere is one which allows an emergency landing without undue hazard to persons or property on the surface. Keep in mind that the altitudes specified in the FARs are *minimums*. A higher altitude will give you more time to troubleshoot any problems and choose a better landing site in the event of an engine failure. [Figure 4-7]

 The minimum safe altitude anywhere must allow an emergency landing, following an engine failure, without undue hazard to persons or property on the surface.

 Over a congested area, you are required to fly 1,000 feet above any obstacle within a horizontal radius of 2,000 feet of your aircraft.

 When flying over an uncongested area, you must fly at least 500 feet above the surface. Over sparsely populated or open water areas you cannot fly within 500 feet of any person, vessel, vehicle, or structure.

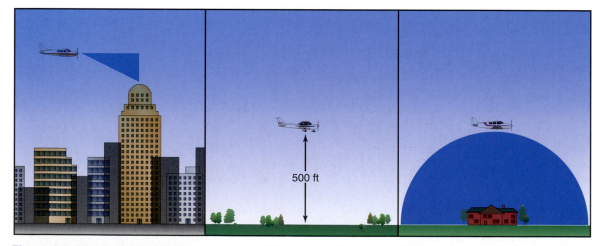

500 ft

Figure 4-7. Minimum safe altitudes over congested areas are based on obstruction clearance. A congested area may be a city, town, settlement, or an open air assembly of people. Obstacle clearance over uncongested and sparsely populated areas is reduced significantly.

LOW AND SLOW IS NO WAY TO GO

If you are involved in, or observe, an incident or situation that you feel compromises aviation safety, you can submit a report to the Aviation Safety Reporting System (ASRS). Your report will be analyzed to identify any aviation hazards which demand immediate action, and the appropriate FAA office or aviation authority is then contacted. In addition, the ASRS investigates the causes underlying a reported event, and incorporates each report into a database which provides information for research regarding aviation safety and human factors.

More than 300,000 reports have been submitted to ASRS. Each report is held in strict confidence and the FAA cannot use ASRS information in enforcement actions against those who submit reports. The following accounts are excerpts from reports submitted to the ASRS.

Flying over uninhabited terrain, I suddenly came upon a golf course, with houses and golfers on the course. Before I was able to analyze the situation, I passed low overhead of some golfers, maybe within 500 feet. Increased familiarity with the locale would have prevented this particular event.

I came upon a softball game taking place. . .I became too focused on the players and failed to realize how low and close to the field I was. Suddenly there was a row of trees ahead of me. I tried to climb but due to low airspeed, I struck one of the trees. I proceeded directly back to the airstrip with reduced elevator control.

These reports provide excellent examples of the importance of flying at a safe altitude and airspeed, as well as maintaining situational awareness. According to an annual safety report issued by the AOPA Flight Safety Foundation, low-level maneuvering was the number one cause of fatalities in single-engine, fixed-gear aircraft in 1996, surpassing weather-related fatal accidents.

FLIGHT OVER HAZARDOUS TERRAIN

Although it depends on where you learn to fly, mountain flying and flight over open water usually are beyond the scope of private pilot training. To safely operate over mountainous terrain or over open water, you need to obtain specialized training from an experienced instructor who is familiar with the area over which the flight will be conducted. Appropriate survival gear is an absolute necessity. Although it can be a rewarding experience, mountain flying, in particular, introduces numerous hazards for the inexperienced. Decreased aircraft performance at high altitudes, turbulence, rapidly changing weather, and difficulty in locating a forced landing site are just a few of the challenges facing you on a mountain flight.

TAXIING IN WIND

Another safety concern that you will be introduced to early in your flight training is the effect of wind during taxi operations. Strong winds passing over and around the wings and horizontal stabilizer during taxi can actually lift the airplane. In the most adverse conditions, it is possible for the airplane to flip or roll over.

Proper use of the aileron and elevator controls normally will counteract the wind and help you maintain control of your airplane. For example, if the wind is blowing

When taxiing in strong winds, proper use of the aileron and elevator controls will help you maintain control of your airplane. For example, when taxiing in a quartering headwind, hold the aileron up on the side from which the wind is blowing. In a quartering tailwind, position the aileron down on the side from which the wind is blowing. See figure 4-8.

The Hazards of Paradise

During an island-hopping flight in Hawaii, pilots face a unique challenge as rugged terrain gives way to an over-water adventure. [Figure A] As you fly over the Hawaiian landscape, you will encounter volcanoes, steep cliffs, rocky coastlines, and lush tropical forests. This varied terrain can create a number of concerns for pilots. Finding a place to land in the event of an engine failure may be difficult. Low clouds can obscure higher terrain and at times erupting volcanoes can produce ash and smoke which reduce visibility. In addition, mountainous terrain combined with onshore winds can produce turbulence and windshear.

Despite these obstacles, flying over the islands can be an exciting and rewarding experience if you are well prepared and receive flight training from an instructor familiar with the area.

In the event of an emergency over the islands, you can receive assistance quickly if you are communicating with an air traffic controller through the Island Reporting Service. This type of flight following requires you to make radio contact over designated checkpoints and report the estimated time to the next checkpoint. If a position report is not made, flight service will attempt to contact you. Search and rescue is alerted if contact is not made within 15 minutes.

Oahu, third largest of the Hawaiian Islands (with an area of 598 square miles), can be seen in this photograph taken from the space shuttle in orbit at an altitude of 166 nautical miles above the earth. [Figure B] Pearl Harbor, the city of Honolulu, and the Honolulu International Airport can be seen on the southern end of the island. Oahu was once made up of two immense volcanoes, but erosion has left the volcanoes as two parallel mountain ranges – Koolau to the northeast of Honolulu and Waianae to the northwest. Visible north of Honolulu, these mountains are separated by a rolling plateau crossed by deep gorges. Today there are no active volcanoes on Oahu, but there are many extinct craters, such as Diamond Head, which can be seen southeast of Honolulu.

—Honolulu International Airport

from the left front quarter, you should turn the yoke to the left which will hold the left aileron up to counteract the lifting tendency of the wind. When you turn while taxiing, the flow of air around the airplane changes direction, and you will have to compensate by altering the position of the control surfaces. In a tricycle-gear airplane, the elevator should be in a neutral position to prevent the wind from exerting any lifting force on the tail. [Figure 4-8]

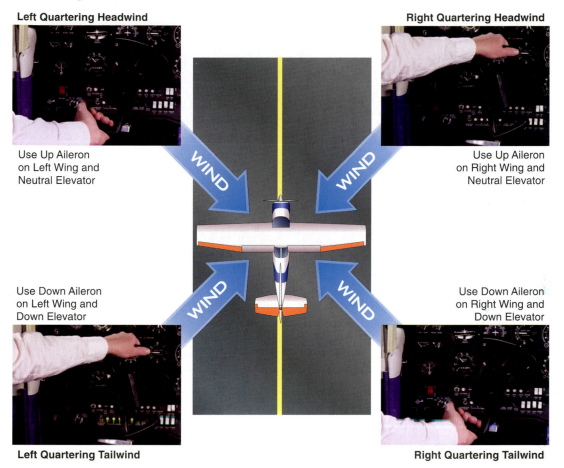

Left Quartering Headwind

Use Up Aileron on Left Wing and Neutral Elevator

Right Quartering Headwind

Use Up Aileron on Right Wing and Neutral Elevator

Use Down Aileron on Left Wing and Down Elevator

Use Down Aileron on Right Wing and Down Elevator

Left Quartering Tailwind

Right Quartering Tailwind

Figure 4-8. Your knowledge of proper control use during windy conditions will help you control the airplane while taxiing.

You will encounter some differences in taxiing tricycle-gear airplanes versus conventional-gear, or tailwheel, airplanes. The most critical situation exists when you are taxiing a tricycle-gear airplane with a high wing in a strong quartering tailwind. The high wing is susceptible to being lifted by the wind. In extreme conditions, a quartering tailwind can cause the airplane to nose over and flip on its back.

When taxiing a tailwheel airplane, you will position the ailerons the same as you do for a tricycle-gear airplane. However, to help keep the tailwheel on the ground,

 Generally, the most critical wind condition when taxiing a high-wing, tricycle-gear airplane is a quartering tailwind.

 When taxiing a tailwheel airplane, you should position the ailerons the same as you do for a tricycle-gear airplane. However, you should hold the elevator control aft (elevator up) in a headwind, and hold the elevator control forward (elevator down) in a tailwind.

hold the elevator control aft (elevator up) in a headwind, and in a tailwind, hold the elevator control forward (elevator down). [Figure 4-9]

Figure 4-9. Compared with tricycle-gear airplanes, in gusty and crosswind conditions, the tailwheel airplane has an increased tendency to weathervane into the wind due to the greater surface area behind the main gear. In addition, the location of the center of gravity behind the main wheels can cause the airplane to swerve further and further out of alignment once it is displaced.

POSITIVE EXCHANGE OF FLIGHT CONTROLS

Frequently during your flight training, it will be necessary for you to exchange the flight controls with your instructor. For example, your instructor normally will demonstrate a maneuver first, before passing the controls to you. To ensure that it is clear as to who has control of the aircraft, the FAA strongly recommends the use of a three-step process when exchanging the flight controls. During the preflight briefing, the following procedure to pass control of the aircraft should be reviewed.

PILOT **PASSING** CONTROL: *"You have the flight controls."*

PILOT **TAKING** CONTROL: *"I have the flight controls."*

PILOT **PASSING** CONTROL: *"You have the flight controls."*

The pilot passing the controls should continue to fly until the pilot taking the controls acknowledges the exchange by saying, *"I have the flight controls."* A visual check also is recommended to ensure that the other pilot actually has the controls. There may be times when your instructor desires to assume control of the aircraft from you. If this is necessary, your instructor should take the controls while informing you, *"I have the flight controls."*

SUMMARY CHECKLIST

✓ The majority of midair collisions occur during daylight hours, in VFR conditions, and within five miles of an airport.

✓ During daylight hours, the most effective way to scan is through a series of short, regularly-spaced eye movements in 10° sectors.

✓ You may not notice objects in your peripheral vision unless there is some relative motion.

✓ If there is no apparent relative motion between another aircraft and yours, you are probably on a collision course.

✓ Empty field myopia occurs when you are looking at a featureless sky that is devoid of objects, contrasting colors, or patterns and your eyes tend to focus at only 10 to 30 feet.

✓ Blind spots make it difficult to see conflicting traffic. In both high-wing and low-wing designs, portions of your view are blocked by the fuselage and wings.

✓ Operation Lights On encourages you to use your landing lights during departures and approaches, both day and night, especially when operating within 10 miles of an airport, or in conditions of reduced visibility.

✓ Clearing turns allow you to see areas blocked by blind spots and make it easier to maintain visual contact with other aircraft in the practice area.

✓ An aircraft in distress has the right-of-way over all other aircraft.

✓ Primarily, there are three situations where right-of-way rules apply; converging with another aircraft, approaching another aircraft head-on, or overtaking another aircraft.

✓ You must maintain minimum safe altitudes at all times except during takeoffs and landings.

✓ Mountain flying and flight over open water require specialized training from experienced instructors who are familiar with the area over which the flights will be conducted.

✓ While taxiing in wind, proper use of the aileron and elevator controls will help you maintain control of the airplane.

✓ To ensure that it is clear as to who has control of the aircraft, the FAA strongly recommends the use of a three-step process when exchanging the flight controls.

KEY TERMS

Collision Avoidance	Blind Spots
Visual Flight Rules (VFR)	Operation Lights On
Instrument Flight Rules (IFR)	Clearing Turns
Visual Scanning	Right-of-Way Rules
Empty Field Myopia	Minimum Safe Altitudes

QUESTIONS

1. What is the most effective method to scan for other aircraft and why?

2. True/False. When looking through haze, air traffic and terrain features are not as close as they appear.

3. Select the true statement regarding collision avoidance.

   A. Operating at an airport with a control tower relieves you of the responsibility to see and avoid other traffic.
   B. If there is no apparent relative motion between another aircraft and yours, you are probably on a collision course.
   C. Studies show that the majority of midair collisions occur during daylight hours, in IFR conditions, and within five miles of an airport.

Select the aircraft which has the right-of-way in each of the following illustrations.

4.

5.

6.

Match the minimum safe altitudes with the appropriate areas.

7. 1,000 feet above any obstacle within a horizontal radius of 2,000 feet of the aircraft

A. Uncongested areas

8. 500 feet above the surface

B. Sparsely populated or open water areas

9. Within 500 feet of any person, vessel, vehicle, or structure

C. Congested areas

10. Select the proper control positions for taxiing in the wind condition shown.

    A.   Yoke to the right, elevator control aft
    B.   Yoke to the left, elevator control neutral
    C.   Yoke to the right, elevator control neutral

11. Describe the recommended procedure to be used when it is necessary for you to exchange the flight controls with your instructor.

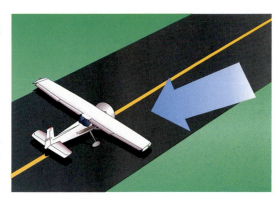

SECTION B
AIRPORTS

Each day, aircraft takeoff and land at private grass strips, busy international airports, and every type of field in between. Whether most of your flying is out of your local airport or you frequently journey to new destinations, an airport will never be unfamiliar territory once you learn the basic procedures for operating in the terminal environment. Regardless of your choice of airport, knowing how to determine the correct runway to use and understanding the markings on taxiways and runways is essential every time you fly. Night flying offers a new challenge as the airport is transformed by a myriad of lights designed to make aircraft operations safe and efficient in the darkness.

CONTROLLED AND UNCONTROLLED AIRPORTS

There are two types of airport environments that you will operate in — controlled and uncontrolled. A **controlled airport** has an operating control tower and is sometimes referred to as a tower airport. Since all aircraft in the vicinity, as well as those on the ground, are subject to instructions issued by **air traffic control (ATC)**, a two-way radio is required for you to operate in the controlled airport environment. At an **uncontrolled airport**, or nontower airport, control of VFR traffic is not exercised. Although you are not required to have a two-way radio, most pilots use radios to transmit their intentions to other pilots. You also are responsible for determining the active runway and how to enter and exit the traffic pattern. [Figure 4-10]

Figure 4-10. Air traffic controllers direct operations at controlled airports from the tower. At uncontrolled airports, you are responsible for determining the active or favored runway and following local procedures.

RUNWAY LAYOUT

Since airplanes are directly affected by wind during takeoffs and landings, **runways** are not arbitrarily placed by builders. If there is only one runway at an airport, it is normally positioned so that you can take off and land in the direction of the prevailing wind. If there is more than one runway, the main runway is aligned with the prevailing wind and the remaining runway or runways are placed so that they are aligned with other common wind directions.

The numbers that you see on runways also are not arbitrary, but correspond to a magnetic north reference. The runway's magnetic direction is rounded off to the nearest 10°, with the last zero omitted. A runway with a magnetic heading of 268° is rounded off to 270° and, with the zero dropped, becomes Runway 27. A runway with a magnetic heading of 088° becomes Runway 09. To further simplify runway numbers, any runway that is between the headings of 010° and 090° is designated with a single-digit runway number, so Runway 09 is marked as Runway 9. The number at the end of the runway corresponds to the direction that you are heading when taking off or landing on that runway. So, the numbers at each end of a runway are different because the runway designators are 180° apart. [Figure 4-11]

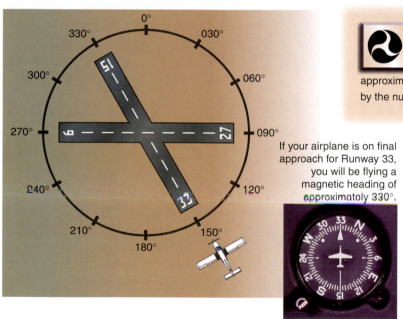

The runway's magnetic direction is rounded off to the nearest 10°, with the last zero omitted. For example, runways oriented approximately 090° and 270° magnetic are designated by the numbers 9 and 27. See figure 4-11.

If your airplane is on final approach for Runway 33, you will be flying a magnetic heading of approximately 330°.

Figure 4-11. A runway labeled 9 on one end is labeled 27 on the opposite end. The runway may be referred to as either 9 or 27, depending on the direction you are heading for takeoff or landing. You will use Runway 9 if you are taking off or landing to the east and Runway 27 if you are taking off or landing to the west.

At some airports, there may be two or three parallel runways with the same runway number. If there are two parallel runways, one is labeled the left runway and the other is the right; for example, 36L and 36R. If there is a third parallel runway, the one in the middle is the center runway and the respective runways are marked 36L, 36C, and 36R. [Figure 4-12]

Figure 4-12. At large airports with heavy air traffic, it is common to have parallel runways. When assigning runways for takeoffs and landings, air traffic controllers will refer to these runways as *"one-seven-left,"* and *"one-seven-right."*

Flying in Circles

Today, pilots take airports for granted. If you want to fly to Chicago for the weekend, there is no question that there will be not just one, but many airports available to you day and night, in and around this great city. It hasn't always been so simple. For example, the Wright Brothers flew for miles in some of their early aircraft but never went anywhere except in circles over crowds of excited onlookers.

The first airports were circular fields which allowed pilots to take-off and land in any direction. [Figure A] A white gravel circle 50 to 100 feet in diameter marked the middle of the airfield and distinguished it from a field used for livestock. A windsock was placed at the center of the circle. At some early airports, to help orient pilots, the name of the nearest town would be painted atop a nearby building. [Figure B]

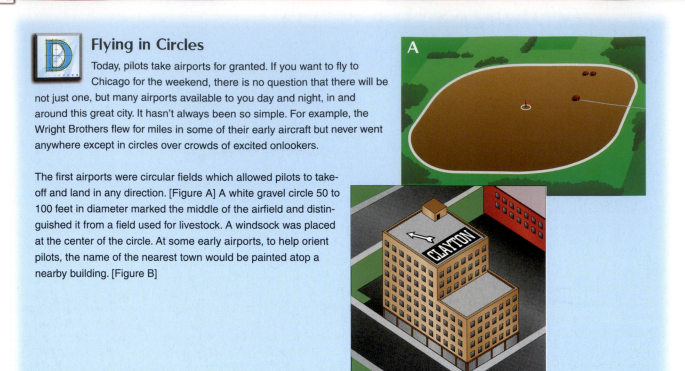

TRAFFIC PATTERN

Traffic patterns are established to ensure that air traffic flows into and out of an airport in an orderly manner. Although the direction and placement of the pattern, the altitude at which it is to be flown, and the procedures for entering and exiting the pattern may vary, a standard rectangular pattern with five named legs is used at most airports. [Figure 4-13] At controlled airports, you may be instructed to deviate from the standard pattern to keep traffic moving smoothly. Adhering to the rectangular traffic pattern procedures

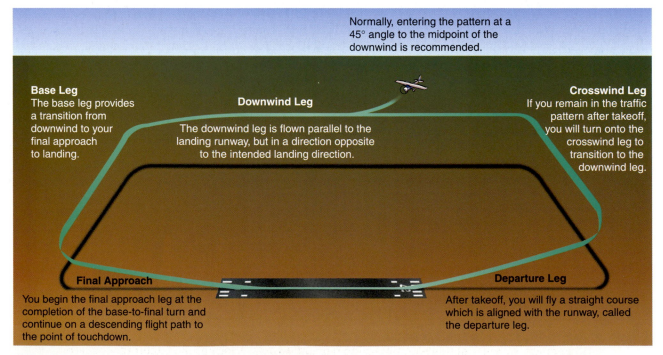

Normally, entering the pattern at a 45° angle to the midpoint of the downwind is recommended.

Base Leg
The base leg provides a transition from downwind to your final approach to landing.

Downwind Leg
The downwind leg is flown parallel to the landing runway, but in a direction opposite to the intended landing direction.

Crosswind Leg
If you remain in the traffic pattern after takeoff, you will turn onto the crosswind leg to transition to the downwind leg.

Final Approach
You begin the final approach leg at the completion of the base-to-final turn and continue on a descending flight path to the point of touchdown.

Departure Leg
After takeoff, you will fly a straight course which is aligned with the runway, called the departure leg.

Figure 4-13. The standard traffic pattern has five named legs; downwind, base, final, departure, and crosswind.

D Not Your Ordinary Traffic Pattern

In certain special situations, normal traffic pattern procedures have to be modified. An excellent example is management of traffic flow at the Experimental Aircraft Association (EAA) convention and airshow which occurs each year at Wittman Regional Airport in Oshkosh, Wisconsin. [Figure A] Over 11,000 aircraft fly into this airport during the convention, making Wittman the world's busiest airport during that time.

To enhance safety and minimize air traffic delays, the Special Air Traffic Management Program is in effect daily. You must obtain an arrival slot from the Computerized Voice Reservations System (CVRS) and you will then be issued a code which must be included in the remarks section of your flight plan. Specific procedures apply to both radio-equipped and no-radio VFR traffic, IFR traffic, and warbirds. Figure B is an example of the procedures which have been used to manage no-radio air traffic during the convention.

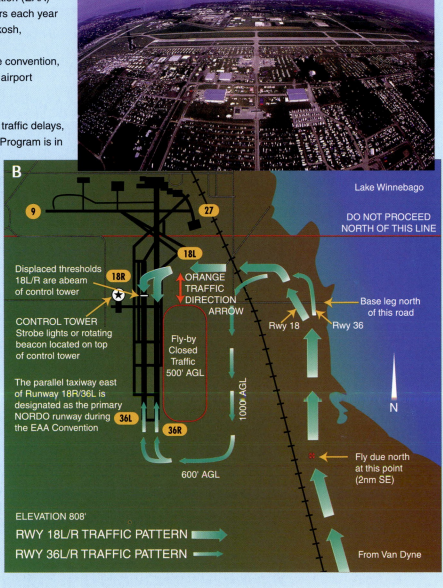

at uncontrolled airports increases safety by reducing the possibility of conflict between aircraft. As specified in FAR Part 91, turns should be made to the left in the traffic pattern unless right turns are indicated by visual marking on the airport, approved light signals, or the tower controller specifically directs otherwise. In addition, some terminal areas, such as Anchorage, Alaska, have unique traffic pattern procedures which are covered in FAR Part 93, Special Air Traffic Rules and Airport Traffic Patterns.

WIND DIRECTION INDICATORS

In most cases, you will want to take off and land into the wind. At a controlled airport, there are various methods of obtaining current airport information, including surface winds and the active runway, or runway in use. In addition, a controller will assign you a runway for takeoff or landing. At an uncontrolled airport, you must make the final decision as to which runway to use. Some uncontrolled airports have radio operators who are able to tell you the wind direction and speed, and advise you of the active or favored runway. Airports normally have a designated calm-wind runway which is used whenever the wind is 5 knots or less. However, you must still watch carefully for other traffic that may be using other runways. When approaching an unfamiliar uncontrolled airport, it is recommended that you overfly the airport at 500 to 1,000 feet above the traffic pattern altitude to observe the flow of traffic and to locate the wind direction indicator.

Of the two types of airport wind direction indicators, the most common is the **wind sock**. Used at both controlled and uncontrolled airports, the windsock may not be your initial source of wind information, but will provide you with the present wind conditions near the touchdown zone of the runway. The stronger the wind, the straighter the extension of the wind sock. Gusty conditions are indicated by back and forth movement of the wind sock.

Although you can determine the wind direction from a **wind tee**, wind intensity or gusty conditions are not indicated. The tail of the tee aligns itself like a weather vane into the wind, so you need to take off or land on the runway that most closely parallels the direction of the tee. The wind tee is not as common as the wind sock and in some cases, a wind sock and tee may be at the same location. If so, the tee may be manually aligned to show which runway is active.

A **tetrahedron** is a landing direction indicator, usually located near a wind direction indicator. The tetrahedron may swing around with the small end pointing into the wind, or it may be manually positioned to show landing direction. In either case, you are cautioned not to use it solely as a wind direction indicator, but to use it in conjunction with a wind sock. [Figure 4-14]

The wind sock aligns itself into the wind because the wind blows into the large end and out the small end. The small end of the wind sock points downwind.

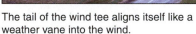

The tail of the wind tee aligns itself like a weather vane into the wind.

The tetrahedron may swing around with the small end pointing into the wind, or it may be manually positioned to show landing direction.

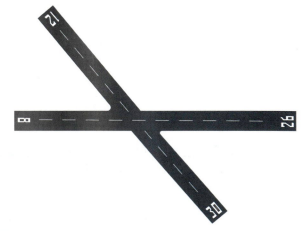

Figure 4-14. When possible, you should select the runway that is the closest to paralleling the direction of the wind. In this case, Runway 8 would be the logical choice for takeoff and landing into the wind.

SEGMENTED CIRCLE

When installed at uncontrolled airports, a wind or landing direction indicator usually is placed in the middle of a **segmented circle** at a central location on the airport. The segmented circle has a two-fold purpose. First, it helps to identify the location of the wind direction indicator. Second, there will be extensions on the segmented circle if the traffic pattern is other than left-hand traffic.

To indicate the direction you should turn in the traffic pattern for a given runway, the segmented circle uses L-shaped extensions which consist of landing strip indicators in conjunction with traffic pattern indicators. Landing strip indicators are installed in pairs to indicate the alignment of the runways. Traffic pattern indicators are aligned with the base leg of the pattern for the specific runway. You can think of the L as your base and final legs to the runway. If it is a right turn from base to final on the L, then you need to make a right-hand pattern on your approach. If right-hand turns are required for the approach, they normally will be used for departure as well. If there are no traffic pattern indicators, the runways all have left-hand traffic patterns. At night, overhead lights normally illuminate both the wind direction indicator and the segmented circle. [Figure 4-15]

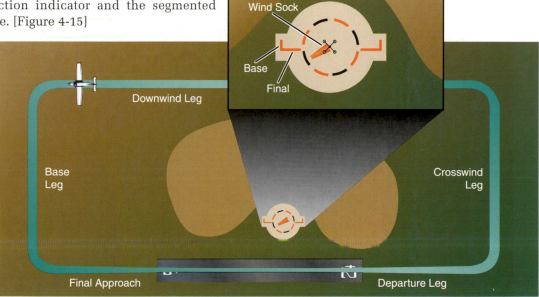

At an uncontrolled airport, you can determine landing direction by observing the wind direction indicator. The extensions on the segmented circle indicate whether a left-hand or right-hand pattern should be used for a given runway. See figure 4-15.

Figure 4-15. At this airport, the segmented circle with the wind sock is located on the north side of Runway 6/24. The wind sock shows that the wind is coming from the east-northeast and that Runway 6 should be the active runway. The L extension corresponding to Runway 6 shows a left turn from base to final indicating a left-hand pattern. Runway 24 has a right-hand pattern, since a right turn is required from base to final.

NOISE ABATEMENT PROCEDURES

The FAA, in conjunction with airport proprietors and community leaders, is now using **noise abatement procedures** to reduce the level of noise generated by aircraft departing over neighborhoods that are near airports. The airport authority may simply request that you use a designated runway, wind permitting. You also may be asked to restrict some of your operations, such as practicing landings, during certain time periods. There are at least three ways to determine the noise abatement procedures at an airport. First, if there is a control tower on the field, they will assign the preferred noise abatement runway to you. Second, you can check the *Airport/Facility Directory* for information on local procedures. The *Airport/Facility Directory* is a publication which contains a descriptive listing of all airports, heliports, and seaplane bases which are open to the public. Chapter 5 provides additional information about the features of the *Airport/Facility Directory*. Third, there may be information for you to read at the FBO, or even signs posted next to the runway that outline the appropriate procedures. [Figure 4-16]

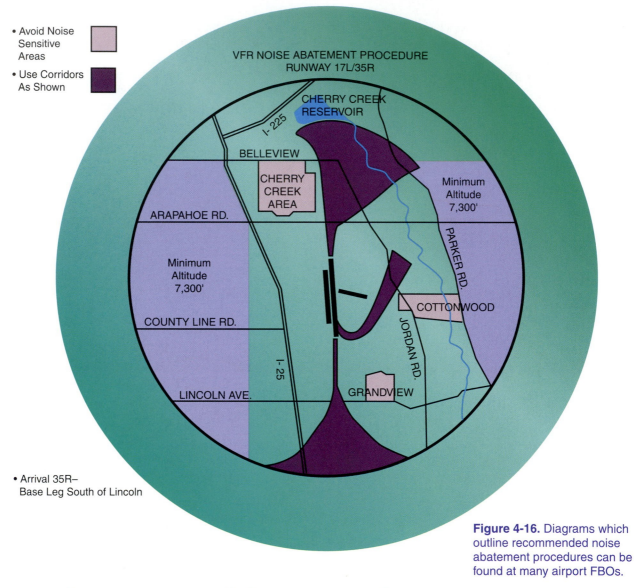

- Avoid Noise Sensitive Areas
- Use Corridors As Shown

- Arrival 35R–
Base Leg South of Lincoln

Figure 4-16. Diagrams which outline recommended noise abatement procedures can be found at many airport FBOs.

AIRPORT VISUAL AIDS

When you begin your flight training, the airport environment can seem confusing. However, just as you learn how to interpret traffic signals, road signs, and highway markings, you will soon become familiar with the visual aids at an airport that help you maintain orientation and keep traffic flowing smoothly.

RUNWAY MARKINGS

Runway markings vary between runways used solely for VFR operations and those used in conjunction with IFR operations. A visual runway usually is marked with only the runway number and a dashed white centerline. When flying instrument approaches, pilots can use the additional markings on IFR runways as references for landing. Instrument approach procedures allow pilots to navigate to the runway using only the flight instruments.

Lawn Mowers vs. Airplanes

Substantial research has been conducted to determine how aircraft noise affects individuals on the ground. Most noise studies use a common numeric measure of sound level referred to as a decibel. For example, rustling leaves emit an average noise level of 20 decibels, while a lawn mower produces approximately 98 decibels.

An aircraft can affect more people over a wider area than ground-based noise producers. A Cessna 172, on approach and at a distance of about 6,500 feet, produces a noise level of about 61 decibels. A Boeing 747 in the same position can emit noise close to 100 decibels.

Studies have found that people's perception of noise can vary with the frequency, rate, distance, level of background noise, and the change of the sound. For example, as little as a 10 decibel increase in intensity is heard by the human ear as a doubling of the loudness of the noise. Therefore, an increase in noise level from 20 decibels to 60 decibels is heard as a sound 16 times louder.

Typical Decibel (dBA) Values Encountered in Daily Life and Industry

Noise Producer	Approximate dBA
Rustling Leaves	20
Room in a Quiet Dwelling at Midnight	32
Window Air Conditioner	55
Conversational Speech	60
Cessna 172 (on approach at a distance of 6,500 feet)	61
Ringing Alarm Clock (at two feet)	80

Beginning of Hearing Damage If Prolonged Exposure Over 85 dBA

Noise Producer	Approximate dBA
Heavy City Traffic	92
Home Lawn Mower	98
Air Hammer	107
Boeing 747-200 (on approach at a distance of 6,500 feet)	95

Instrument approaches which use an electronic glide slope for guidance to the landing runway, such as the instrument landing system (ILS), are called precision approaches. Nonprecision approaches do not incorporate an electronic glideslope, and the corresponding runway markings vary accordingly.

When a visual runway is used in conjunction with a nonprecision instrument approach, threshold and aiming point markings are added. A precision instrument runway also includes touchdown zone markings. Occasionally, you may see threshold or aiming point markings on visual runways. [Figure 4-17]

1,000 ft Aiming Point Marking

Touchdown Zone Markings

Side Stripe

Threshold Markings

Visual

Nonprecision Instrument

Precision Instrument

Figure 4-17. The common types of runway markings for visual, precision, and nonprecision runways are shown here.

It is not uncommon to fly into an airport that has a runway with another type of marking called a **displaced threshold**. Usually, if the threshold is displaced, it is because of obstructions, such as trees, powerlines, or buildings off the end of the runway. This might prohibit you from making a normal descent and landing on the initial portion of the pavement. [Figure 4-18]

 On runways with a displaced threshold, the beginning portion of the landing zone is marked with a solid white line with white arrows leading up to it. Although the pavement leading up to a displaced threshold may not be used for landing, it may be available for taxiing, the landing rollout, and takeoffs. See figure 4-18.

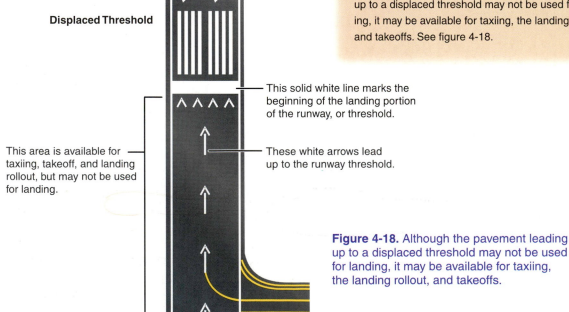

Displaced Threshold

This solid white line marks the beginning of the landing portion of the runway, or threshold.

These white arrows lead up to the runway threshold.

This area is available for taxiing, takeoff, and landing rollout, but may not be used for landing.

Figure 4-18. Although the pavement leading up to a displaced threshold may not be used for landing, it may be available for taxiing, the landing rollout, and takeoffs.

A **blast pad/stopway area**, sometimes referred to as an overrun, is different from the area preceding a displaced threshold because it cannot be used for landing, takeoff, or taxiing. The blast pad is an area where propeller or jet blast can dissipate without creating a hazard to others. The stopway area is paved so that, in the event of an aborted takeoff, an aircraft can use it to decelerate and come to a stop. [Figure 4-19]

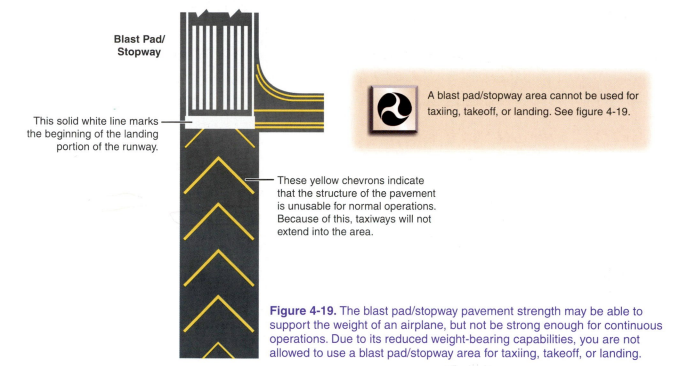

Blast Pad/ Stopway

This solid white line marks the beginning of the landing portion of the runway.

 A blast pad/stopway area cannot be used for taxiing, takeoff, or landing. See figure 4-19.

These yellow chevrons indicate that the structure of the pavement is unusable for normal operations. Because of this, taxiways will not extend into the area.

Figure 4-19. The blast pad/stopway pavement strength may be able to support the weight of an airplane, but not be strong enough for continuous operations. Due to its reduced weight-bearing capabilities, you are not allowed to use a blast pad/stopway area for taxiing, takeoff, or landing.

Sometimes construction, maintenance, or other activities require the threshold to be relocated temporarily. Methods of identifying the relocated threshold may vary but one common practice is to use a ten-foot wide white threshold bar across the width of the runway. A yellow X indicates that an entire runway or taxiway is closed. [Figure 4-20]

A closed runway or taxiway is marked by a yellow X. See figure 4-20.

A Notice to Airmen (NOTAM) may be issued to inform pilots of a runway closure. NOTAMs contain time-critical information which is of either a temporary nature or is not known far enough in advance to permit publication on aeronautical charts or other operational publications. In addition to runway closures or construction, NOTAMs can include changes in the status of navigational aids or instrument approach facilities, radar service availability, and other information essential to planned enroute, terminal, or landing operations.

Figure 4-20. Although the surface may appear to be usable, operations on a closed runway cannot be conducted safely.

Computer-Created Airport

The first airport in the world to be totally designed, built, and operated using computers is Denver International Airport (DIA). To create the runway, taxiway, and ramp configurations, computer models were used to analyze taxiing distances, fuel consumption rates, and arrival and departure patterns. Planners studied wind and weather pattern computer models to determine the most efficient airfield configuration. DIA's airfield design incorporates runways in every quadrant of the airport site. [Figure A]

To allow air traffic controllers to shift traffic quickly from one runway to another as the wind changes direction, the runways are arranged in a pinwheel which radiates from the central terminal area. To increase safety, no runway crosses another. This minimizes the potential for collisions. In addition, runway/taxiway lighting systems guide taxiing aircraft in times of low visibility by the use of lights imbedded in the concrete to form centerlines and stopbars at intersections.

The total area of DIA is 53 square miles, which is double the size of Manhattan Island, New York. The surface area of the runways, ramps, and taxiways included in the first design phase is equivalent to a single lane highway from Denver to Chicago. Air traffic controllers direct traffic from a 327-foot control tower with 16 panels of distortion-free glass (each weighing 11,000 pounds) in the tower cab. [Figure B]

DENVER   CHICAGO

TAXIWAY MARKINGS

The links between the airport parking areas and the runways are the **taxiways**. They are easily identified by a continuous yellow centerline stripe. At some airports, taxiway edge markings are used to define the edge of the taxiway and are normally used to separate the taxiway from pavement that is not intended for aircraft use. Runway holding position markings, or **hold lines**, which are located wherever the taxiway intersects a runway, keep aircraft clear of the runway in use.

At an uncontrolled airport, you should stop and check for traffic and cross the hold line only after ensuring that no one is on an approach to land. At a controlled airport, the controller may ask you to hold short of the runway for landing traffic. In this case, you should stop before the hold line and proceed only after you are cleared to do so by the controller, and you have checked for traffic. [Figure 4-21]

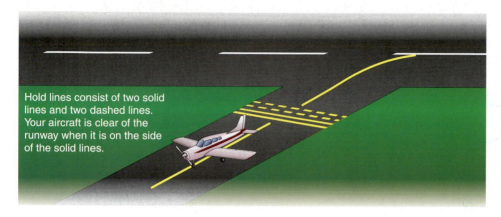

Hold lines consist of two solid lines and two dashed lines. Your aircraft is clear of the runway when it is on the side of the solid lines.

Figure 4-21. When exiting the runway, do not stop until you have cleared the hold line.

At airports equipped with an instrument landing system, it is possible for aircraft near the runway to interfere with the ILS signal. If this is the case, the hold line may be placed farther from the runway to prevent any interference, or you may find two hold lines for some runways. The one closest to the runway is the normal hold line, while the one farthest away is the ILS hold line. At other locations, only an ILS hold line may be used. [Figure 4-22]

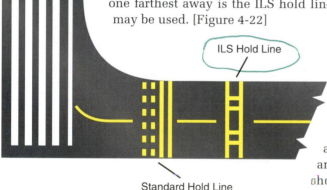

ILS Hold Line

Standard Hold Line

Figure 4-22. When ILS approaches are in progress, you may be asked by the controller to "... hold short of the ILS critical area."

RAMP AREA

The area where aircraft are parked and tied down is called the apron, or **ramp area**. The airport terminal and maintenance facilities are often located near the ramp area. You should be alert for fuel trucks driving on the ramp or in the process of refueling aircraft. Vehicle roadway markings are used to define a pathway for vehicles operating on, or crossing areas that also are intended for aircraft. In addition, you should be familiar with the standard **hand signals** used by ramp personnel for directing you during ground operations. [Figure 4-23]

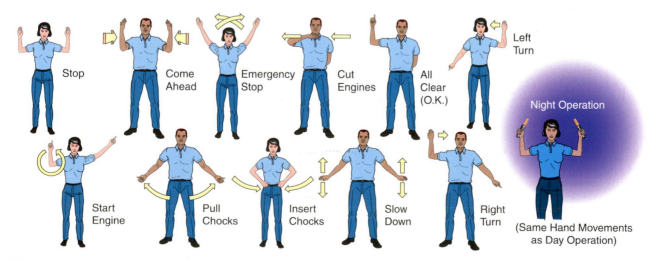

Stop   Come Ahead   Emergency Stop   Cut Engines   All Clear (O.K.)   Left Turn

Start Engine   Pull Chocks   Insert Chocks   Slow Down   Right Turn

Night Operation

(Same Hand Movements as Day Operation)

Figure 4-23. At many FBOs, ramp personnel will direct you to parking.

AIRPORT SIGNS

Major airports usually have complex taxi routes, multiple runways, and widely dispersed parking areas. In addition, vehicular traffic in certain areas may be quite heavy. As a result, most airfield signs are standardized to make it easy for you to identify taxi routes, mandatory holding positions, and boundaries for critical areas. [Figure 4-24] Another benefit, if you fly outside the United States, is that the U.S. standards are practically the same as ICAO specifications. The **International Civil Aviation Organization (ICAO)** is a specialized agency of the United Nations whose objective is to develop standard principles and techniques of international air navigation and to promote development of civil aviation. Specifications for airport signs include size, height, location, and illumination requirements. [Figure 4-25] Sometimes the installation of a sign is not practical so a surface-painted sign may be used. Surface painted signs may include directional guidance or location information. For example, the runway number may be painted on the taxiway pavement near the taxiway hold line.

STOP

Mandatory Instruction Signs denote an entrance to a runway, a critical area, or an area prohibited to aircraft. These signs are red with white letters or numbers. An example of a mandatory instruction sign is a runway holding position sign which is located at the holding position on taxiways that intersect a runway or on runways that intersect other runways.

Location Signs identify either the taxiway or runway where your aircraft is located. These signs are black with yellow inscriptions and a yellow border. Location signs also identify the runway boundary or ILS critical area for aircraft exiting the runway.

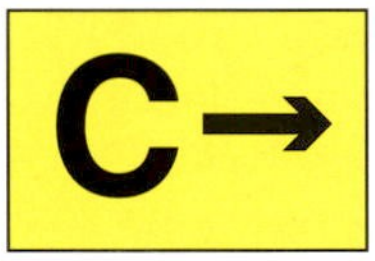

Direction Signs indicate directions of taxiways leading out of an intersection. They have black inscriptions on a yellow background and always contain arrows which show the approximate direction of turn.

Destination Signs indicate the general direction to a location on the airport, such as civil aviation areas, military areas, international areas, or FBOs. They have black inscriptions on a yellow background and always contain an arrow.

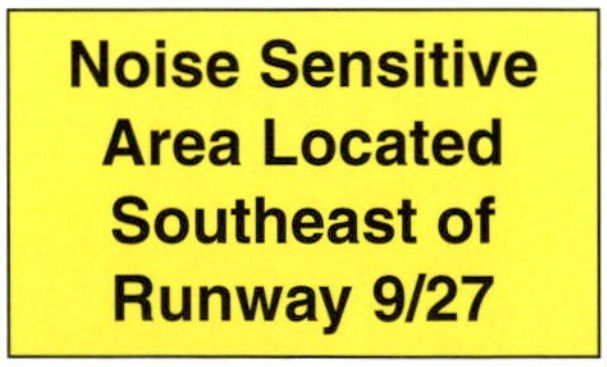

Noise Sensitive Area Located Southeast of Runway 9/27

Information Signs advise you of such things as areas that cannot be seen from the control tower, applicable radio frequencies, and noise abatement procedures. These signs use yellow backgrounds with black inscriptions.

3

Runway Distance Remaining Signs are used to provide distance remaining information to pilots during takeoff and landing operations. The signs are located along the sides of the runway, and the inscription consists of a white numeral on a black background. The signs indicate the distance remaining in thousands of feet. Runway distance remaining signs are recommended for runways used by turbojet aircraft.

Figure 4-24. There are six basic types of airport signs — mandatory, location, direction, destination, information, and runway distance remaining.

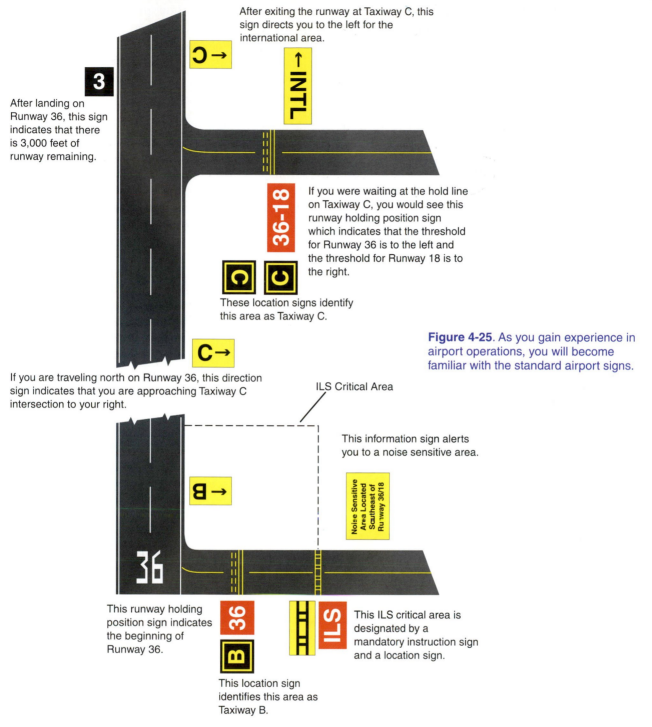

After exiting the runway at Taxiway C, this sign directs you to the left for the international area.

C→

↑ INTL

3

After landing on Runway 36, this sign indicates that there is 3,000 feet of runway remaining.

36-18

If you were waiting at the hold line on Taxiway C, you would see this runway holding position sign which indicates that the threshold for Runway 36 is to the left and the threshold for Runway 18 is to the right.

C   C

These location signs identify this area as Taxiway C.

C→

If you are traveling north on Runway 36, this direction sign indicates that you are approaching Taxiway C intersection to your right.

Figure 4-25. As you gain experience in airport operations, you will become familiar with the standard airport signs.

ILS Critical Area

This information sign alerts you to a noise sensitive area.

B→

Noise Sensitive Area Located Southeast of Runway 36/18

36

This runway holding position sign indicates the beginning of Runway 36.

36

B

This location sign identifies this area as Taxiway B.

ILS

This ILS critical area is designated by a mandatory instruction sign and a location sign.

RUNWAY INCURSION AVOIDANCE

The official definition of a runway incursion is "any occurrence at an airport involving an aircraft, vehicle, person, or object on the ground that creates a collision hazard or results in loss of separation with an aircraft taking off or intending to take off, landing, or intending to land." Runway incursions are primarily caused by errors associated with clearances, communication, airport surface movement, and positional awareness. There are several procedures that you can follow and precautions that you can take to avoid a runway incursion.

1. During your preflight planning, ensure that you have all the pertinent information regarding airport construction and lighting.

2. Complete as many checklist items as possible before taxi or while holding short.

3. Strive for clear and unambiguous pilot-controller communication. Read back (in full) all clearances involving active runway crossing, hold short, taxi into position, and hold instructions.

4. While taxiing, concentrate on your primary responsibilities. Don't become absorbed in other tasks, or conversation, while the aircraft is moving.

5. If unsure of your position on the airport, stop and ask for assistance. At a controlled airport, you can request progressive taxi instructions.

6. When possible, while in a run-up area or waiting for a clearance, position your aircraft so you can see landing aircraft.

7. Monitor the appropriate radio frequencies for information regarding other aircraft cleared onto your runway for takeoff or landing. Be alert for aircraft which may be on other frequencies or without radio communication.

8. After landing, stay on the tower frequency until instructed to change frequencies.

9. To help others see your aircraft during periods of reduced visibility or at night, use your exterior taxi/landing lights, when practical.

10. Report deteriorating or confusing airport markings, signs, and lighting to the airport operator or FAA officials. Also report confusing or erroneous airport diagrams and instructions.

11. Make sure you understand the required procedures if you fly into or out of an airport where LAHSO is in effect.

LAND AND HOLD SHORT OPERATIONS

Land and hold short operations (LAHSO) include landing and then holding short of an intersecting runway, taxiway, predetermined point, or an approach/departure flight path. A LAHSO clearance is an air traffic control tool used to increase airport capacity, maintain system efficiency, and enhance safety. LAHSO procedures are currently being used at over 200 airports in the United States. Specific knowledge-based training must be completed before any pilot can conduct LAHSO. In addition, student pilots conducting solo operations are not authorized to participate in LAHSO.

If you are trained and qualified to participate in LAHSO, you may accept or decline an ATC clearance to land and hold short. Acceptance of LAHSO indicates you fully understand the clearance, including all related procedures. This means, you can land safely in the available landing distance (ALD). As specified in FAR 91.103, before beginning a flight, each pilot in command shall become familiar with all available information concerning that flight, including runway lengths and takeoff and landing data for the conditions at airports of intended use. Information regarding the ALD for specific runways can be found in aeronautical publications such as the *Airport/Facility Directory.* [Figure 4-26]

NOTE: Refer to the NOTAM on page N-2 of this manual for further details on LAHSO. In addition, you should consult the Aeronautical Information Manual (AIM) for the latest LAHSO policies and procedures.

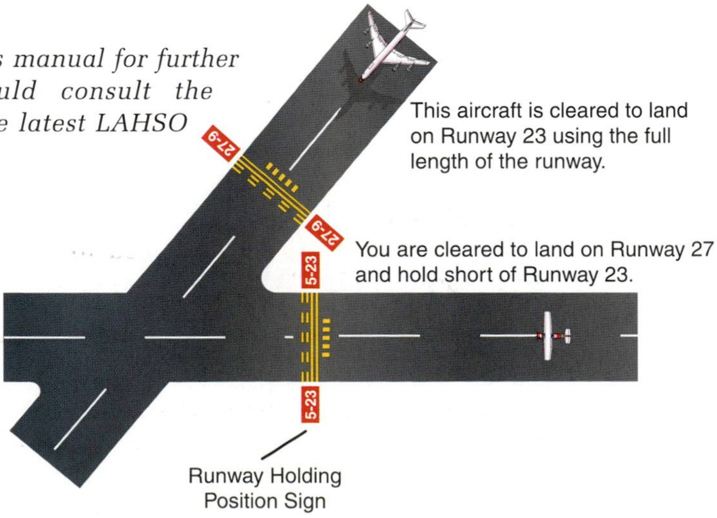

This aircraft is cleared to land on Runway 23 using the full length of the runway.

You are cleared to land on Runway 27 and hold short of Runway 23.

Figure 4-26. If you accept a LAHSO clearance, you should land and exit the runway at the first convenient taxiway before reaching the hold short line. If this is not possible, you must stop at the hold short point. It is crucial that you maintain situational awareness if you are participating in LAHSO.

Runway Holding Position Sign

A RUNWAY INCURSION TRAGEDY

From the files of the NTSB...

Aircraft: *McDonnell Douglas DC-9-82*
Cessna 441 Conquest

Injuries: *2 Fatal, 140 Uninjured*

Narrative: *During the takeoff roll on runway 30R, the MD-82, N954U, collided with the Cessna 441, N441KM, which was positioned on the runway waiting for takeoff clearance. The pilot of the Cessna acted on an apparently preconceived idea that he would use his arrival runway, runway 30R, for departure. After receiving taxi clearance to back-taxi into position and hold on runway 31, the pilot taxied into a position at an intersection of runway 30R, which was the assigned departure runway for the MD-82... Air traffic control personnel were not able to maintain visual contact with the Cessna after it taxied from the well-lighted ramp area into the runway/taxiway environment of the northeast portion of the airport.*

How can you prevent an accident like this from occurring? A thorough understanding of airport markings, signs, and lighting, as well as proper radio procedures are essential. In addition, maintaining an awareness of the current and impending situation is critical to flight safety. A breakdown in situational awareness can occur if you become overloaded with tasks. For example, trying to taxi, orient yourself at an unfamiliar airport, communicate on the radio, and prepare the airplane for takeoff may place too many demands on you.

To effectively manage your workload, you must plan ahead, prioritize tasks, recognize when you are becoming overloaded, and ask for assistance if needed. For example, at a controlled airport, if you are unfamiliar with the taxiway and runway layout, you can request progressive taxi instructions from ATC.

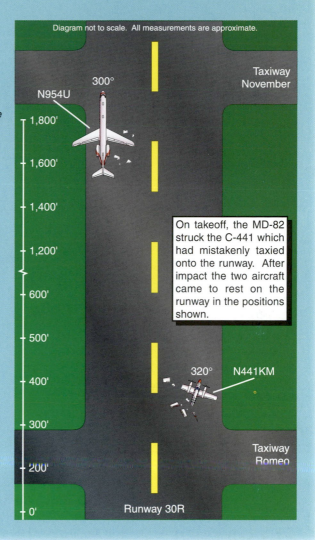

Diagram not to scale. All measurements are approximate.

On takeoff, the MD-82 struck the C-441 which had mistakenly taxied onto the runway. After impact the two aircraft came to rest on the runway in the positions shown.

AIRPORT LIGHTING

Your flying experiences will soon take you from flying only in the daytime to the new challenge of night flying. You will notice that airport lighting is similar from one airport to the next. To maintain continuity, airports that are lighted for nighttime operations use FAA-approved lighting systems and colors.

AIRPORT BEACON

At night, **airport beacons** are used to guide pilots to lighted airports. Airport beacons may be of the older rotating type, or the newer flashing variety which produces the same effect. These airport (and heliport) beacons are most effective from one to ten degrees above the horizon; however, you normally can see them at altitudes well above the ten

An airport's rotating beacon operated during daylight hours normally indicates that weather at the airport is below basic VFR minimums.

degree angle. If you maintain sufficient altitude, beacons can be seen at great distances in good visibility conditions. [Figure 4-27]

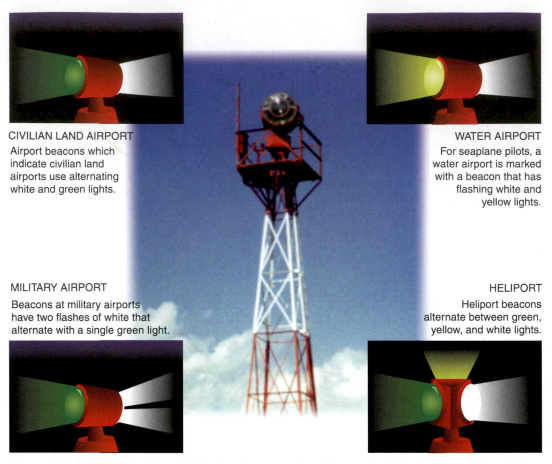

CIVILIAN LAND AIRPORT
Airport beacons which indicate civilian land airports use alternating white and green lights.

WATER AIRPORT
For seaplane pilots, a water airport is marked with a beacon that has flashing white and yellow lights.

MILITARY AIRPORT
Beacons at military airports have two flashes of white that alternate with a single green light.

HELIPORT
Heliport beacons alternate between green, yellow, and white lights.

Figure 4-27. The combination of light colors from an airport beacon indicates the type of airport. As a routine measure, you are not permitted to operate at military airports.

Generally, you will find that an airport's beacon is on from dusk until dawn. The beacon usually is not operating during the day unless the ceiling is less than 1,000 feet and/or the ground visibility is less than 3 statute miles, the normal VFR weather minimums. You should not rely solely on the operation of the airport beacon to indicate if weather conditions are below VFR minimums. These minimums will be discussed in greater detail in Section D.

 A military airport is identified by a rotating beacon which emits two quick, white flashes between green flashes.

VISUAL GLIDESLOPE INDICATORS

Visual glideslope indicators are light systems which indicate your position in relation to the desired glide path to the runway. The indicator lights are located on the side of a basic or instrument runway and can be used for day or night approaches. One of the most frequently used installations is the **visual approach slope indicator (VASI).**

VASI configurations vary and may have either 2 or 3 bars. Two-bar systems have near and far bars and may include 2, 4, or 12 light units. The VASI glide path provides safe obstruction clearance within 10° of the extended runway centerline out to 4 nautical miles from the threshold. You should not begin a descent using VASI until your aircraft is aligned with the runway. When landing at a controlled airport that has a VASI, regulations require you to remain on or above the glide path until a lower altitude is necessary for a safe landing. [Figure 4-28]

Above Glide Path

If both light bars are white, you are too high.

Below Glide Path

If you see red over red, you are below the glide path.

On Glide Path

If the far bar is red and the near bar is white, you are on the glide path. The memory aid "red over white you're all right," is helpful in recalling the correct sequence of lights.

Figure 4-28. The two-bar VASI shows whether or not you are on a glide path that will take you safely to the touchdown zone of the runway. The lights are either white or red, depending on the angle of your glide path, and may be visible from 20 miles at night.

 If you are landing at a controlled airport served by a VASI, regulations require that you maintain an altitude at or above the glide slope until a lower altitude is necessary for a safe landing.

 You will see white over white lights on the VASI if you are too high. Red over white indicates that you are on the glide path, and you are too low if the VASI shows red over red. See figure 4-28.

At larger airports, there may be a three-bar VASI system which incorporates two different glide paths. The lower glide path normally is set at three degrees, while the higher one usually is one-fourth of a degree above it. The higher glide path is used by certain transport category aircraft with high cockpits. This ensures that these aircraft will have sufficient altitude when crossing the threshold. If you encounter a three-bar VASI system, use the two lower bars as if it were a standard two-bar VASI.

A **tri-color VASI** uses a single light unit to project a three-color visual path. It has some similarity to the two-bar VASI because you will see a red light if you are too low. [Figure 4-29]

 An above glide slope indication from a tri-color VASI is an amber light. If you see a green light, you are on glide path, and a red light indicates that you are too low. See figure 4-29.

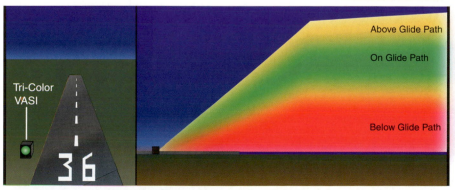

Above Glide Path

On Glide Path

Below Glide Path

Tri-Color VASI

If you see amber, you are too high.

If the light is green, you are on the glide path.

As you decend below the glide path, you may see dark amber during the transition from green light to red, so you should not be deceived into thinking that you are too high.

Figure 4-29. You should ensure that you have correctly identified the tri-color VASI since this single light source may be confused with other runway lighting.

Some airports may have a **pulsating approach slope indicator (PLASI)** which projects a two-color visual approach path into the final approach area. A pulsating red light indicates below glide path; above glide path is usually pulsating white; and the on-glide path indication is a steady white light. The useful range is about 4 miles during the day and up to 10 miles at night.

Another system is the **precision approach path indicator (PAPI)**. It has two or four lights installed in a single row instead of far and near bars. [Figure 4-30]

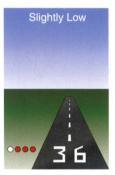 A below glide path indication from a pulsating approach slope indicator is a pulsating red light.

 A slightly high glide slope indication from a PAPI is three white lights and one red light. See figure 4-30.

High	Slightly High	On Glide Path	Slightly Low	Low

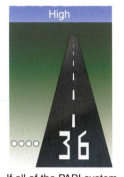 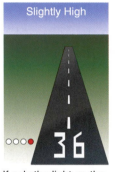 

If all of the PAPI system lights are white you are too high.

If only the light on the far right is red and the other three are white, you are slightly high.

When you are on the glide path, the two lights on the left are white and the two lights on the right are red.

If you are slightly low, only the light on the far left is white.

If you are below the glide path, all four of the lights are red.

Figure 4-30. The PAPI is normally located on the left side of the runway and can be seen up to 5 miles during the day and 20 miles at night.

APPROACH LIGHT SYSTEMS

Some airports have **approach lighting systems (ALS)** to help instrument pilots transition to visual references at the completion of an instrument approach. These light systems can begin as far away as 3,000 feet along the extended runway centerline, and normally include a combination of steady and flashing lights. The most complex systems are for precision instrument runways and usually have sequenced flashing lights that look like a ball of light traveling toward the runway at high speed. For nonprecision instrument runways, the approach lighting is simpler and, for VFR runways, the system may consist only of visual glideslope indicators. [Figure 4-31]

Figure 4-31. Approach light systems can aid you in locating the runway at night.

RUNWAY EDGE LIGHTS

Runway edge lights consist of a single row of white lights bordering each side of the runway and lights identifying the runway threshold. Runway edge lights can be classified according to three intensity levels. High intensity runway lights (HIRLs) are the brightest runway lights available. Medium intensity runway lights (MIRLs) and low intensity runway lights (LIRLs) are, as their names indicate, dimmer in intensity. At some airports, you will be able to adjust the intensity of the runway lights from your cockpit by using your radio transmitter. At others, the lights are preset or are adjusted by air traffic controllers.

Some runway edge lights incorporate yellow runway remaining lights on the last half of the runway (or last 2,000 feet of runway, whichever distance is less) to inform you of the amount of runway left. These lights are two-sided, so they appear white when viewed from the opposite end of the runway.

At night, there are three ways to determine where the runway begins. If the runway has a displaced threshold, there is a set of green lights on each side of the white threshold line to indicate the beginning of the landing portion of the runway. If the threshold is not displaced, the beginning of the runway pavement has a row of green lights across it. These lights are two-sided. If you were taking off or landing on the opposite end, they would appear red to mark the end of the usable portion of the runway.

Sometimes high intensity white strobe lights are placed on each side of the runway to mark the threshold. These are called **runway end identifier lights (REILs)** and can be used in conjunction with the green threshold lights.

IN-RUNWAY LIGHTING

Some precision approach runways have flush-mounted centerline, touchdown zone, and taxiway turnoff lighting. Viewed from the threshold, the runway centerline lighting system (RCLS) is white until the last 3,000 feet of the runway. From the 3,000-foot point to the 1,000-foot point, alternating red and white lights appear, with the last 1,000 feet of lights changing to red only. This system helps instrument pilots determine the amount of runway remaining in very low visibility situations.

Touchdown zone lighting (TDZL) consists of two rows of transverse light bars on either side of the runway centerline starting at 100 feet from the threshold and extending 3,000 feet or to the midpoint of the runway, whichever is less. Taxiway lead-off lights are alternating green and yellow lights which define the curved path of aircraft travel from the runway centerline to a point on the taxiway (normally the runway holding position or ILS critical area boundary).

TAXIWAY LIGHTING

As you taxi off the active runway, blue lights, lining both edges of the taxiway, guide you from the runway to the ramp area. Because they can be seen from any direction, they are said to be omnidirectional lights. At some airports, green taxiway centerline lights also may be installed. These lights are located along the taxiway centerline in both straight and curved portions of the taxi-way. They also may be located along designated taxiing paths in portions of runways and ramp areas. [Figure 4-32]

Blue ominidirectional lights identify the edge of the taxiway at night.

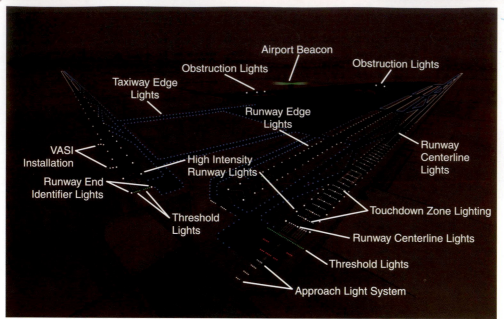

Figure 4-32. This pictorial summary shows the various types of airport marking and lighting typically found at large, controlled airports.

PILOT-CONTROLLED LIGHTING

Pilot-controlled lighting is the term used to describe systems that you can activate by keying the aircraft's microphone, or mike, on a specified radio frequency. For practical and economic reasons, the approach, runway, and taxiway lights at some unattended airports may be on a timer that will turn off the lights 15 minutes after they have been activated. Keep in mind that other types of airport lighting may be pilot controlled, not just approach and runway lighting. For example, VASI and REIL lights may be pilot controlled at some locations.

To activate three-step pilot-controlled lighting, you should key your mike seven times on the specified frequency to turn all the lights on at maximum intensity. If conditions dictate a lower intensity, key your mike five times for medium-intensity lighting and three times for the lowest intensity. For each adjustment, you must key the mike the required number of times within a period of five seconds. Remember though, using the lower intensity lighting on some installations may turn the REILs completely off. The *Airport/Facility Directory* contains a description of the type of pilot-controlled lighting available at individual airports.

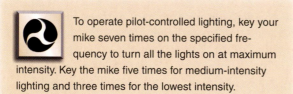

To operate pilot-controlled lighting, key your mike seven times on the specified frequency to turn all the lights on at maximum intensity. Key the mike five times for medium-intensity lighting and three times for the lowest intensity.

OBSTRUCTION LIGHTING

Obstruction lighting is used both on and off the airport, during the day and at night. The purpose of obstruction lighting is to give you advance warning of prominent structures such as towers, buildings and, sometimes, even powerlines. Bright red and high intensity white lights typically are used and flashing lights may be employed. Remember, there may be guy-wires extending from the top of a tower to the ground, so be sure that you are well clear of the obstruction.

SUMMARY CHECKLIST

✓ A two-way radio is required for you to operate in the controlled airport environment since all aircraft in the vicinity, as well as those on the ground, are subject to instructions issued from the control tower.

✓ Control of VFR traffic is not exercised at an uncontrolled airport.

✓ The number at the end of the runway corresponds to the magnetic direction that you are heading when taking off or landing on that runway.

✓ A standard rectangular pattern with five named legs is used at most airports to ensure that air traffic flows in an orderly manner.

✓ The most common wind direction indicator is the wind sock, which is used at both controlled and uncontrolled airports. It provides you with the present wind conditions near the touchdown zone of the runway.

✓ A tetrahedron is a landing direction indicator which may swing around with the small end pointing into the wind, or may be manually positioned to show landing direction.

✓ The segmented circle helps to identify the location of the wind direction indicator and employs landing strip indicators in conjunction with traffic pattern indicators to show traffic pattern turn direction for a given runway.

✓ Adhering to noise abatement procedures reduces the level of noise over neighborhoods that are near airports.

✓ A visual runway normally is marked only with the runway number and a dashed white centerline. When flying instrument approaches, pilots can use the additional markings on IFR runways, such as threshold markings, touchdown zone markings, and aiming point markings.

✓ Usually, a runway has a displaced threshold because of an obstruction off the end of the runway which might prohibit a normal descent and landing on the beginning portion of the pavement.

✓ A blast pad/stopway area is an area where propeller or jet blast can dissipate without creating a hazard to others.

✓ Taxiways normally have yellow centerline markings, and hold lines wherever they intersect with a runway.

✓ There are six basic types of airport signs — mandatory, location, direction, destination, information, and runway distance remaining.

✓ Airport beacons are used to guide pilots to lighted airports at night and may indicate when weather conditions are below VFR minimums during the day.

✓ The two-bar visual approach slope indicator (VASI) shows whether or not you are on a glide path that will take you safely to the touchdown zone of the runway.

✓ A variety of lighting systems, including approach light systems, runway edge lights, runway end identifier lights (REILs), in-runway lighting, and taxiway lighting are used at airports to aid pilots in identifying the airport environment at night and in low visibility conditions.

✓ Pilot-controlled lighting is the term used to describe systems that you can activate by keying the aircraft's microphone on a specified radio frequency.

KEY TERMS

Controlled Airport

Air Traffic Control (ATC)

Uncontrolled Airport

Runways

Traffic Patterns

Wind Sock

Wind Tee

Tetrahedron

Segmented Circle

Noise Abatement Procedures

Displaced Threshold

Blast Pad/Stopway Area

Taxiways

Hold Lines

Ramp Area

Hand Signals

International Civil Aviation Organization (ICAO)

Land and Hold Short Operations (LAHSO)

Airport Beacons

Visual Approach Slope Indicator (VASI)

Tri-Color VASI

Pulsating Approach Slope Indicator (PLASI)

Precision Approach Path Indicator (PAPI)

Approach Lighting Systems (ALS)

Runway Edge Lights

Runway End Identifier Lights (REILs)

Pilot-Controlled Lighting

QUESTIONS

1. Describe how runway numbers are determined.

2. Determine the proper runway and traffic pattern for landing.

   A. Left-hand traffic for Runway 36
   B. Left-hand traffic for Runway 4
   C. Right-hand traffic for Runway 22

3. Explain the purpose of a displaced threshold and the operating limitations associated with it.

4. What marking indicates a closed runway?

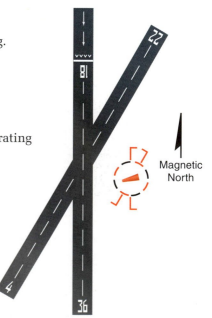

5. Which airplane is on the correct side of the hold line to be clear of the runway?

Match the following signs to their descriptions.

6. Direction Sign

7. Location Sign

8. Mandatory Instruction Sign

9. True/False. Runway incursions are primarily caused by errors associated with clearances, communications, airport surface movement, and positional awareness.

Match the following airport beacon light patterns to the appropriate airport.

10. White/White/Green   A. Civilian land airport

11. White/Green   B. Military airport

12. White/Yellow   C. Water airport

Match each illustration to the correct glideslope description.

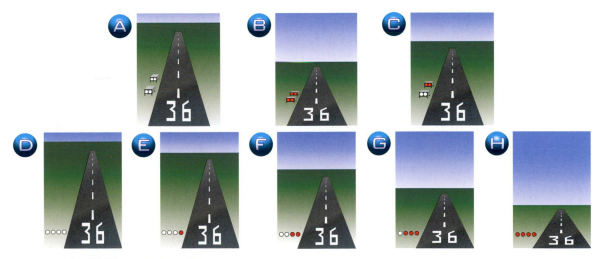

13. VASI, on glide path

14. PAPI, slightly high

15. PAPI, on glide path

16. VASI, low

17. Describe the procedure for activating three-step pilot-controlled lighting.

SECTION C
AERONAUTICAL CHARTS

Living with those maps and charts was absorbing and instructive. . . Some day I would like to write a piece about the fun of voyaging with maps without ever leaving home.
—Amelia Earhart, after planning one of her flights

Maps conjure up images of travel, adventure, and discovery. By exploring maps, you can journey to exotic locales without ever leaving the comfort of your home. For you, as a pilot, maps are essential in turning imaginary excursions into actual trips. **Aeronautical charts** are maps which provide a detailed portrayal of an area's topography and include aeronautical and navigational information. Before you learn about the specific features and symbology of aeronautical charts, you need to understand some basic concepts which apply to representations of the earth's surface on maps.

LATITUDE AND LONGITUDE

The largest circle which can be drawn on the surface of the earth, or any sphere, is referred to as a **great circle**. A great circle's plane must pass through the center of the earth dividing it into two equal parts. A **small circle** is formed on the surface of the earth by the intersection of a plane which does not pass through the center of the earth.

There are several reference lines, based on small and great circles, which are used to define locations on the earth's surface. For example, the equator forms a great circle. The equator is the imaginary line which circles the earth midway between the north and south poles. You can locate a position north or south of the equator by using **parallels**, or lines of **latitude**, which form small circles. As a reference point, the equator is labeled as 0° of latitude. The parallel lines north of the equator are numbered from 0° to 90°, with 90° north latitude positioned at the north pole. Parallels in the southern hemisphere also are numbered from 0° to 90°, with 90° south latitude representing the south pole.

Meridians, or lines of longitude, are imaginary lines which extend from the north to the south pole. [Figure 4-33] Since they connect the poles, lines of longitude always are given in a direction of true north and south. Just as the equator is designated 0° of latitude, the Prime Meridian, which passes through Greenwich, England, is labeled 0° of longitude.

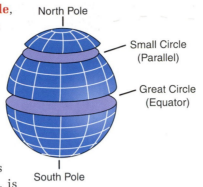

Figure 4-33. Reference lines of latitude and longitude form great and small circles on the earth's surface.

There are a total of 360° of longitude encompassing the earth, with 180° on the east side and 180° on the west side of the Prime Meridian. The line of 180° of longitude is on the opposite side of the earth from the Prime Meridian. The International Date Line approximately corresponds with the 180° line of longitude, although segments of the Date Line actually vary as much as 20°. When you locate a position east or west of the Prime Meridian, you will be determining a position in reference to a line of longitude. Most maps, including aeronautical charts, use a system based on latitude and longitude to reference the exact location of a point on the earth. [Figure 4-34]

 You can locate a position on an aeronautical chart by knowing its coordinates of latitude and longitude. See figure 4-34.

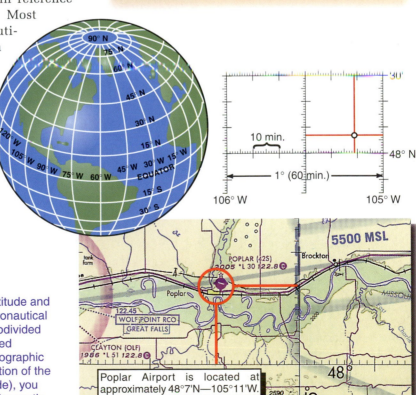

Figure 4-34. The lines of latitude and longitude are printed on aeronautical charts with each degree subdivided into 60 equal segments called minutes. By knowing the geographic coordinates (or the intersection of the lines of latitude and longitude), you can locate any position on the earth.

Poplar Airport is located at approximately 48°7'N—105°11'W.

PROJECTIONS

A globe is the most accurate reduced representation of earth, but obviously is not the most convenient navigation tool. To create a useful map or chart, a picture of the reduced-earth globe must be projected onto a flat surface. Since this is like pressing a section of orange peel on a flat surface, some distortion ultimately occurs in this process.

Projections are used for transferring a section of the earth's surface onto a flat chart. Two of the most common types of projections are the Mercator and the Lambert Conformal Conic. **Mercator projections** normally are used as wall charts. Distortion of landmasses on a Mercator chart increases with distance from the equator. [Figure 4-35] The **Lambert Conformal Conic projection** is frequently used to create aeronautical charts because it minimizes distortion. [Figure 4-36]

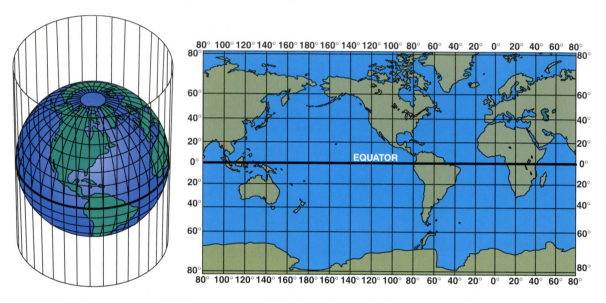

Figure 4-35. The extensive use of Mercator maps in classrooms has caused many mistaken ideas about the relative size of various landmasses. For example, Greenland is only 1/8 as large as South America.

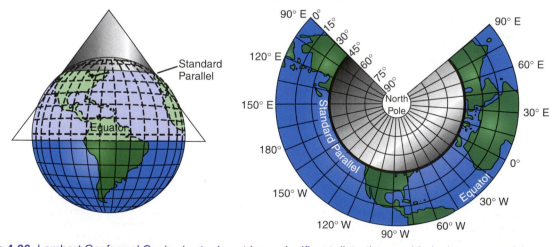

Figure 4-36. Lambert Conformal Conic charts do not have significant distortion provided a large area of the earth's surface is not shown. When you compare miles on a Lambert chart to actual miles on earth, the overall scale inaccuracies are small enough that you can consider them negligible on a single chart.

SECTIONAL CHARTS

The first aeronautical chart was a strip chart which covered the route from Kansas City, Missouri, to Moline, Illinois. Published in 1927, the same year that Lindbergh completed his historic transatlantic flight, it showed topographic features and airway beacons that were used for night navigation. Strip charts for other major routes were soon published but each chart only covered an area 80 miles wide. These charts were of little help if a pilot got lost, had to deviate, or needed to fly to a destination that was not located along a primary route. In 1930, area charts were developed which provided coverage for the entire United States by dividing the country into 87 sections. Today, these **sectional charts**, or sectionals, cover all of the 48 mainland states, plus Alaska, Hawaii, Puerto Rico, and the Virgin Islands. Published by the National Ocean Service (NOS), sectionals are the most commonly used chart for VFR flight. Each covers 6° to 8° of longitude and approximately 4° of latitude and is given the name of a primary city within its coverage.

The scale of a sectional chart is 1:500,000. This means that each inch on the sectional chart represents 500,000 actual inches. This translates to one inch on the sectional equaling approximately 7 nautical, or 8 statute, miles on the earth's surface. To choose a safe maneuvering or cruising altitude, you can refer to the contour lines, spot elevations, and color tints used to show terrain elevation on sectional charts. In addition, topographical information includes cities, towns, rivers, highways, railroads, and other distinctive landmarks which you can use as visual checkpoints. Along with airport depictions, sectionals also contain aeronautical information pertaining to navigation and communication facilities, as well as airspace and obstructions. Sectional charts are folded for easy handling, storage, and identification during flight. Most are printed on both sides in order to reduce the total number of charts required. [Figure 4-37]

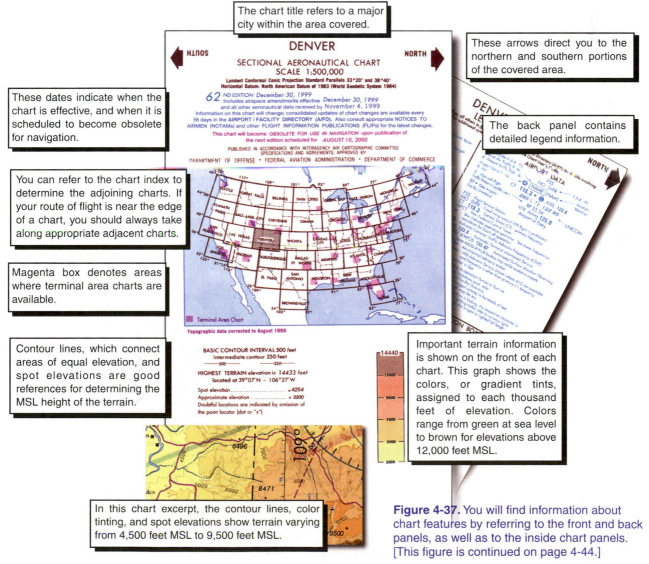

The chart title refers to a major city within the area covered.

These arrows direct you to the northern and southern portions of the covered area.

These dates indicate when the chart is effective, and when it is scheduled to become obsolete for navigation.

The back panel contains detailed legend information.

You can refer to the chart index to determine the adjoining charts. If your route of flight is near the edge of a chart, you should always take along appropriate adjacent charts.

Magenta box denotes areas where terminal area charts are available.

Contour lines, which connect areas of equal elevation, and spot elevations are good references for determining the MSL height of the terrain.

Important terrain information is shown on the front of each chart. This graph shows the colors, or gradient tints, assigned to each thousand feet of elevation. Colors range from green at sea level to brown for elevations above 12,000 feet MSL.

In this chart excerpt, the contour lines, color tinting, and spot elevations show terrain varying from 4,500 feet MSL to 9,500 feet MSL.

Figure 4-37. You will find information about chart features by referring to the front and back panels, as well as to the inside chart panels. [This figure is continued on page 4-44.]

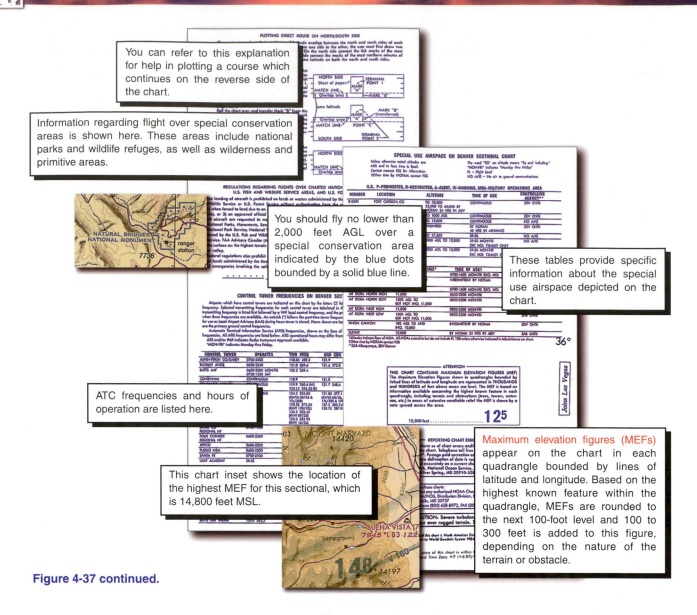

You can refer to this explanation for help in plotting a course which continues on the reverse side of the chart.

Information regarding flight over special conservation areas is shown here. These areas include national parks and wildlife refuges, as well as wilderness and primitive areas.

You should fly no lower than 2,000 feet AGL over a special conservation area indicated by the blue dots bounded by a solid blue line.

These tables provide specific information about the special use airspace depicted on the chart.

ATC frequencies and hours of operation are listed here.

This chart inset shows the location of the highest MEF for this sectional, which is 14,800 feet MSL.

Maximum elevation figures (MEFs) appear on the chart in each quadrangle bounded by lines of latitude and longitude. Based on the highest known feature within the quadrangle, MEFs are rounded to the next 100-foot level and 100 to 300 feet is added to this figure, depending on the nature of the terrain or obstacle.

Figure 4-37 continued.

Most sectionals are revised every 6 months, but some outside the 48 contiguous states are on an annual revision schedule. Changes in aeronautical data which could affect your flight might occur between chart revisions. For this reason, you should consult the *Airport/Facility Directory* prior to flight and review the "Aeronautical Chart Bulletin" section, as well as the *Notices to Airmen* publication. A discussion of these sources of flight information can be found in Chapter 5.

The terrain height is portrayed on sectional charts by contour lines and spot elevations. See figure 4-37.

You should fly no lower than 2,000 feet AGL over a special conservation area, such as a national park, or wildlife refuge. See figure 4-37.

From Clay to Computers

Maps made on clay tablets from Mesopotamia and maps created on mosaic tile from ancient Mediterranean cultures are the oldest surviving maps. The maps and charts of ancient Greece and Rome were designed on perishable parchment. The typical map commonly used today is printed on paper and folded accordion style into such a complex configuration that once opened, it seems as if it can never be refolded properly. Traditionally, aeronautical charts have been of this same ilk. However, with the aid of a global positioning system (GPS) receiver in your cockpit, computer software can transform your portable computer into an electronic moving map.

With this type of software, all the features of an aeronautical chart can be viewed on your laptop screen and the computer uses information from the GPS receiver to display your position. As you fly your course, the chart scrolls and your position is constantly updated.

WORLD AERONAUTICAL CHARTS

A **world aeronautical chart (WAC)** is similar to a sectional, but it uses a scale of 1:1,000,000. At this scale, approximately 14 nautical miles, or 16 statute miles, are represented by one inch on the map. The symbols are basically the same as those found on sectionals, but some of the detail is omitted due to the smaller scale. Most WAC charts are revised on a yearly basis. [Figure 4-38]

Figure 4-38. Pilots of high performance airplanes often use WAC charts since their aircraft operate at higher altitudes and airspeeds. WAC charts not only reduce the total number of charts needed, but also reduce the need to change charts frequently.

The chart effective date, as well as the expiration date, are shown here. Usually, the expiration date is keyed to the publication schedule of the next edition.

This WAC index shows the general area covered by each chart in the total network.

In addition to sectionals and WAC charts, terminal area charts and flyway planning charts provide detailed information for navigating at, and near, some of the busiest airports in the country. These charts are discussed in Section D of this chapter.

CHART SYMBOLOGY

The **legend** is your tool for deciphering symbols and decoding aeronautical chart information. Divided into seven categories, the legend describes symbology for airports, airport data, radio aids to navigation and communication boxes, airport traffic service and airspace information, obstructions, topographic information, and miscellaneous data. The sectional and WAC legends generally depict the same chart symbology.

AIRPORT SYMBOLS

There are thousands of airports identified by symbols on sectional charts. Since there is a wide variety of airport types, shapes, and sizes, several different airport diagrams are shown on sectional charts to help you picture the actual airport being illustrated. Civil, military, and private airports, as well as seaplane bases, heliports, and ultralight flight parks are depicted by unique symbology. A variety of symbols are used to provide you with information regarding the type and length of runways, and the airport services available at a particular airport. In addition, you can quickly identify airports with control towers as they are shown in blue, while nontower airports are magenta in color. [Figure 4-39]

 Tick marks extending from an airport symbol indicate that fuel is available and that the field is attended, at least during normal working hours. A star above the airport symbol indicates an airport beacon normally operates from sunset to sunrise. See figure 4-39.

Figure 4-39. Information provided in the legend will help answer questions you might have concerning a specific airport.

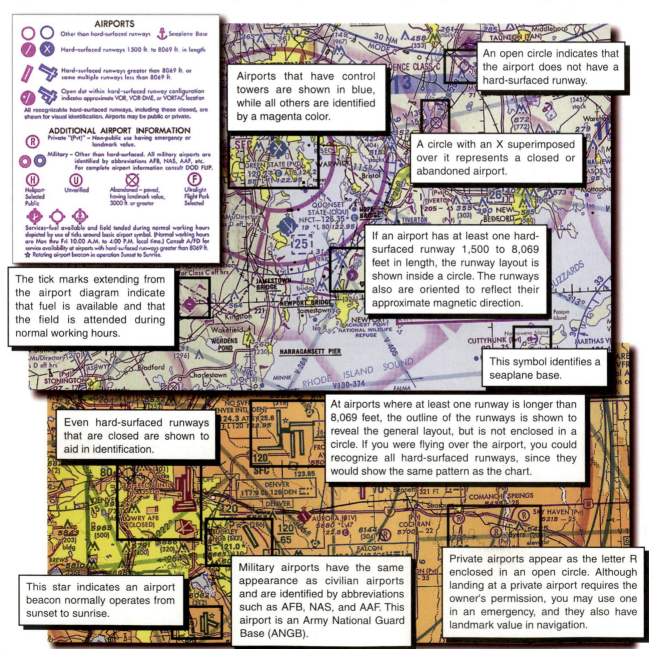

An open circle indicates that the airport does not have a hard-surfaced runway.

Airports that have control towers are shown in blue, while all others are identified by a magenta color.

A circle with an X superimposed over it represents a closed or abandoned airport.

If an airport has at least one hard-surfaced runway 1,500 to 8,069 feet in length, the runway layout is shown inside a circle. The runways also are oriented to reflect their approximate magnetic direction.

The tick marks extending from the airport diagram indicate that fuel is available and that the field is attended during normal working hours.

This symbol identifies a seaplane base.

Even hard-surfaced runways that are closed are shown to aid in identification.

At airports where at least one runway is longer than 8,069 feet, the outline of the runways is shown to reveal the general layout, but is not enclosed in a circle. If you were flying over the airport, you could recognize all hard-surfaced runways, since they would show the same pattern as the chart.

This star indicates an airport beacon normally operates from sunset to sunrise.

Military airports have the same appearance as civilian airports and are identified by abbreviations such as AFB, NAS, and AAF. This airport is an Army National Guard Base (ANGB).

Private airports appear as the letter R enclosed in an open circle. Although landing at a private airport requires the owner's permission, you may use one in an emergency, and they also have landmark value in navigation.

AIRPORT DATA

A second portion of the sectional legend explains the data printed near each individual airport. Airport data contains communication frequencies, including the common traffic advisory frequency (CTAF), and approximate length of the longest runway, as well as the availability of lighting and weather services. Chapter 5 provides additional details regarding the use of CTAF and other frequencies shown on the chart. In addition, the airport elevation is included as part of the airport data. The official **airport elevation** is defined as the highest part of usable runway surface, measured in feet above mean sea level. [Figure 4-40]

By referring to the airport data on sectional charts, you can determine what radio frequencies to use for communication at that airport. In addition, information such as longest runway length, airport lighting, and field elevation can be determined. See figure 4-40.

Figure 4-40. Airport data includes information such as communication frequencies, field elevation, airport lighting, and runway lengths.

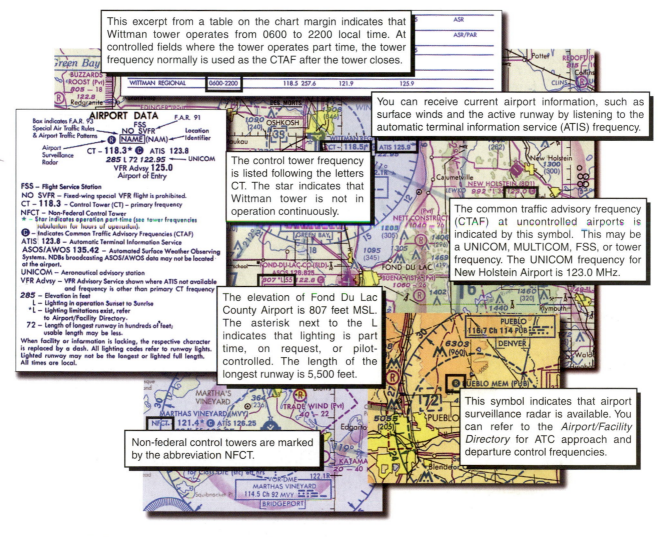

This excerpt from a table on the chart margin indicates that Wittman tower operates from 0600 to 2200 local time. At controlled fields where the tower operates part time, the tower frequency normally is used as the CTAF after the tower closes.

You can receive current airport information, such as surface winds and the active runway by listening to the automatic terminal information service (ATIS) frequency.

The control tower frequency is listed following the letters CT. The star indicates that Wittman tower is not in operation continuously.

The common traffic advisory frequency (CTAF) at uncontrolled airports is indicated by this symbol. This may be a UNICOM, MULTICOM, FSS, or tower frequency. The UNICOM frequency for New Holstein Airport is 123.0 MHz.

The elevation of Fond Du Lac County Airport is 807 feet MSL. The asterisk next to the L indicates that lighting is part time, on request, or pilot-controlled. The length of the longest runway is 5,500 feet.

This symbol indicates that airport surveillance radar is available. You can refer to the *Airport/Facility Directory* for ATC approach and departure control frequencies.

Non-federal control towers are marked by the abbreviation NFCT.

NAVIGATION AIDS

For cross-country planning and flight, you can refer to navigation and communication boxes for information concerning radio aids to navigation, or **navaids**, and flight service stations (FSSs) in the area. You will communicate with FSSs enroute to open and close

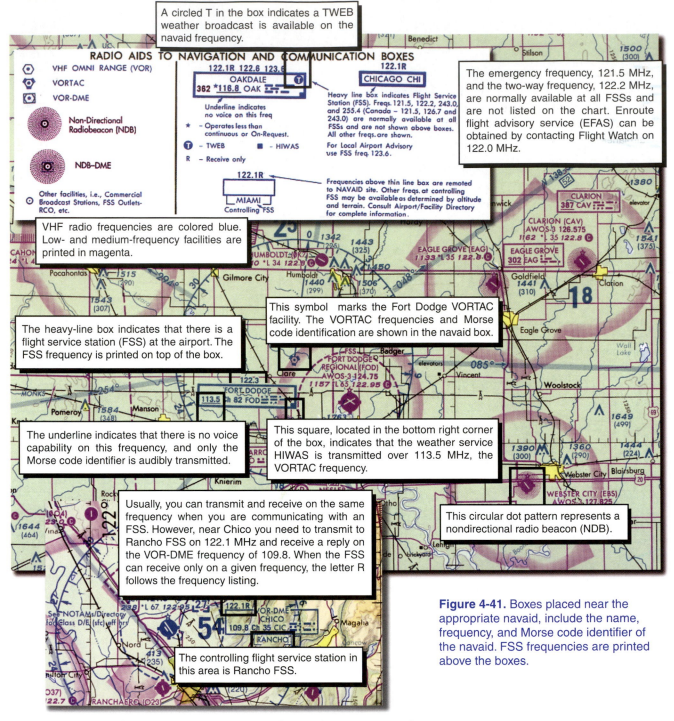

A circled T in the box indicates a TWEB weather broadcast is available on the navaid frequency.

The emergency frequency, 121.5 MHz, and the two-way frequency, 122.2 MHz, are normally available at all FSSs and are not listed on the chart. Enroute flight advisory service (EFAS) can be obtained by contacting Flight Watch on 122.0 MHz.

VHF radio frequencies are colored blue. Low- and medium-frequency facilities are printed in magenta.

This symbol marks the Fort Dodge VORTAC facility. The VORTAC frequencies and Morse code identification are shown in the navaid box.

The heavy-line box indicates that there is a flight service station (FSS) at the airport. The FSS frequency is printed on top of the box.

The underline indicates that there is no voice capability on this frequency, and only the Morse code identifier is audibly transmitted.

This square, located in the bottom right corner of the box, indicates that the weather service HIWAS is transmitted over 113.5 MHz, the VORTAC frequency.

Usually, you can transmit and receive on the same frequency when you are communicating with an FSS. However, near Chico you need to transmit to Rancho FSS on 122.1 MHz and receive a reply on the VOR-DME frequency of 109.8. When the FSS can receive only on a given frequency, the letter R follows the frequency listing.

This circular dot pattern represents a nondirectional radio beacon (NDB).

The controlling flight service station in this area is Rancho FSS.

Figure 4-41. Boxes placed near the appropriate navaid, include the name, frequency, and Morse code identifier of the navaid. FSS frequencies are printed above the boxes.

flight plans, obtain current weather information, or for assistance in emergency situations. Chapter 5 describes the services available at FSSs in greater detail and Chapter 9 provides information on the operation of navaids represented by chart symbols. [Figure 4-41]

A VORTAC navigational facility is depicted by a blue triangular symbol on aeronautical charts. See figure 4-41.

A square located in the bottom right corner of a communication box indicates that the weather service HIWAS is transmitted over the navaid frequency. See figure 4-41.

What Good is a Map If I Can't See the Ground?

Before aeronautical charts were available, many pilots flying airmail and cargo used road maps for navigation and when visibility was limited, they often followed the railroad tracks, which they called "hugging the UP," or Union Pacific. If weather conditions deteriorated drastically, pilots had to land their airplanes in fields and wait until conditions improved.

There are now charts specifically designed to allow instrument-rated pilots to fly in the clouds thanks to aviation pioneer Elrey B. Jeppesen. As an airmail pilot in the 1930s, Jeppesen began recording information about terrain heights, field lengths, airport layouts, lights, and obstacles in a little black notebook. [Figure A] The notes that he took eventually turned into a thriving business that provided pilots with enroute charts which depicted airways and navigation aids, as well as instrument approach procedure charts.

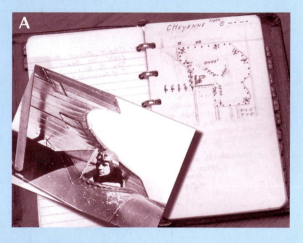

A

B

Although some of the symbols used on instrument charts are the same as those shown on VFR charts, instrument pilots operating in IFR conditions seldom have use for the visual landmarks which are featured on VFR charts. You can see that the same area depicted on a VFR chart appears much differently on an instrument chart. [Figure B]

TOPOGRAPHICAL INFORMATION AND OBSTRUCTIONS

The locations of natural and man-made features, such as lakes, rivers, railroads, roads, and highways are shown on sectional charts as reference points for navigation. [Figure 4-42] In addition to paying close attention to terrain features, you also must be aware of man-made obstructions to flight. While some structures may extend only several feet above the ground, others may rise more than 1,000 feet. [Figure 4-43] Sectional chart legends also define several miscellaneous symbols which depict areas of parachuting, glider, and ultralight activity, as well as visual check points which can be used to

identify your position to ATC. [Figure 4-44] You will continue your exploration of aeronautical chart information and symbols as you examine airspace dimensions and operating requirements in Section D of this chapter.

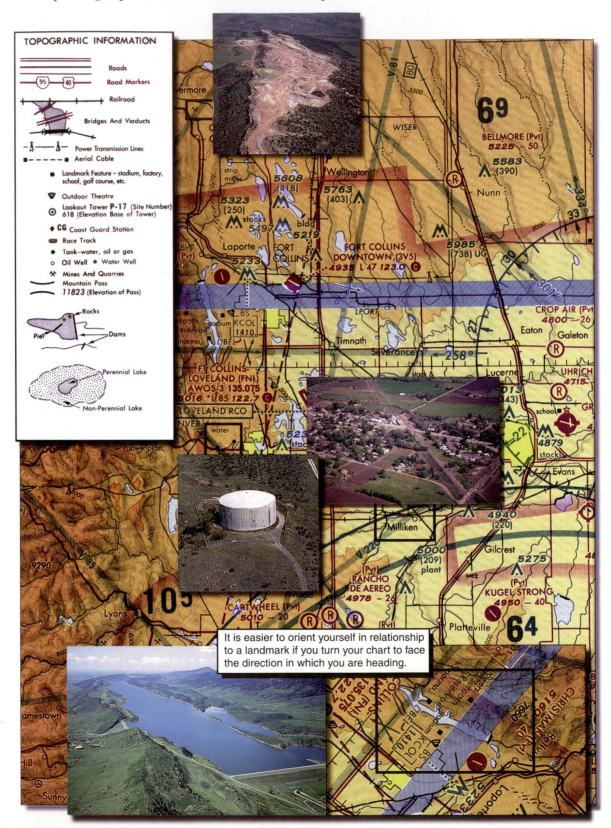

It is easier to orient yourself in relationship to a landmark if you turn your chart to face the direction in which you are heading.

Figure 4-42. During your flight training, you will become skilled at associating the symbol on the chart with the landmark as viewed from the airplane.

Figure 4-43. While obstructions can impose hazards to flight, they can be good references to identify your position.

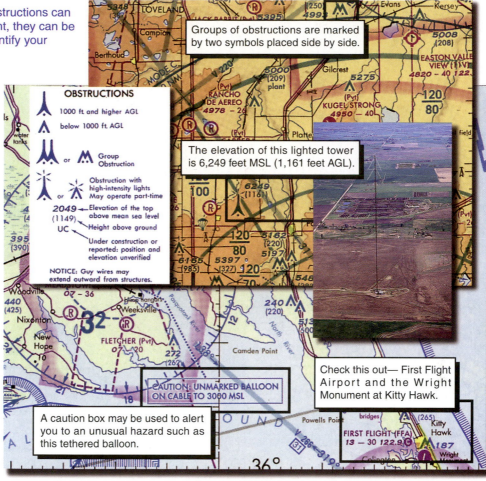

Groups of obstructions are marked by two symbols placed side by side.

The elevation of this lighted tower is 6,249 feet MSL (1,161 feet AGL).

Check this out— First Flight Airport and the Wright Monument at Kitty Hawk.

A caution box may be used to alert you to an unusual hazard such as this tethered balloon.

OBSTRUCTIONS

- 1000 ft. and higher AGL
- below 1000 ft. AGL
- or — Group Obstruction
- or — Obstruction with high-intensity lights May operate part-time
- 2049 — Elevation of the top above mean sea level
- (1149) — Height above ground
- UC — Under construction or reported: position and elevation unverified

NOTICE: Guy wires may extend outward from structures.

CAUTION: UNMARKED BALLOON ON CABLE TO 3000 MSL

The height of an obstruction is located next to the symbol and may be indicated by both an MSL and AGL altitude. By referring to terrain and obstruction heights, you can determine a safe cruising altitude. See figure 4-43.

At times, a caution box may alert you to a specific hazard depicted on a sectional chart. See figure 4-43.

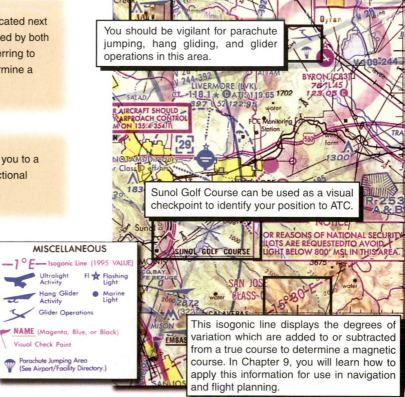

You should be vigilant for parachute jumping, hang gliding, and glider operations in this area.

Sunol Golf Course can be used as a visual checkpoint to identify your position to ATC.

MISCELLANEOUS

- —1° E— Isogonic Line (1995 VALUE)
- Ultralight Activity
- Hang Glider Activity
- Glider Operations
- Fl ★ Flashing Light
- ● Marine Light
- NAME (Magenta, Blue, or Black) Visual Check Point
- Parachute Jumping Area (See Airport/Facility Directory.)

Figure 4-44. This sectional chart excerpt depicts a variety of miscellaneous symbols in the area around San Francisco International Airport.

This isogonic line displays the degrees of variation which are added to or subtracted from a true course to determine a magnetic course. In Chapter 9, you will learn how to apply this information for use in navigation and flight planning.

What On Earth Am I Flying Over?

There are a wide variety of symbols and markings shown on aeronautical charts which are not identified on the chart legend. These symbols are defined in the *Aeronautical Chart Users Guide* published by the National Ocean Service (NOS). See if you can correctly identify the following symbols:

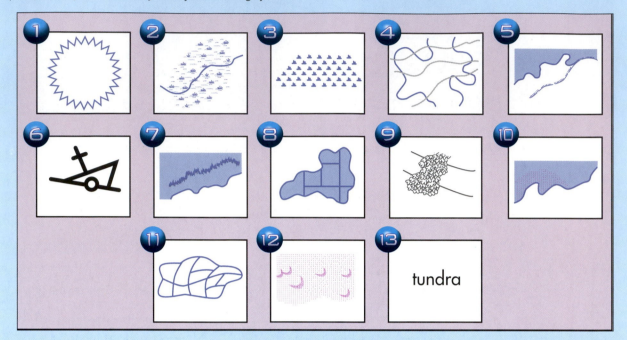

Answers: 1. high energy radiation areas; 2. swamps, marshes, and bogs; 3. rice paddies; 4. glaciers; 5. ice cliffs; 6. exposed ship wreck; 7. rocky or coral reefs; 8. fish ponds and hatcheries; 9. lava flows; 10. tidal flats exposed at low tide; 11. cranberry bog; 12. sand dunes; 13. tundra (an easy one)

SUMMARY CHECKLIST

✓ Aeronautical charts are maps which provide a detailed portrayal of an area's topography and include aeronautical and navigational information.

✓ There are several reference lines, based on great and small circles, which are used to define locations on the earth's surface.

✓ You can locate a position on an aeronautical chart by knowing its coordinates of latitude and longitude.

✓ Each sectional chart covers 6° to 8° of longitude and approximately 4° of latitude and is given the name of a primary city within its coverage.

✓ Maximum elevation figures (MEFs) are based on the highest known feature within a quadrangle bounded by lines of latitude and longitude.

✓ You should fly no lower than 2,000 feet AGL over a special conservation area, such as a national park or wildlife refuge.

✓ World aeronautical charts (WACs) use a scale of 1:1,000,000 and are commonly used by pilots of high performance aircraft.

✓ Divided into seven categories, the chart legend describes symbology for airports, airport data, radio aids to navigation and communication boxes, airport traffic service and airspace information, obstructions, topographic information, and miscellaneous data.

✓ Since there is a wide variety of airport types, shapes, and sizes, several types of airport diagrams are shown on sectional charts to help you picture the actual airport being illustrated.

✓ Tick marks extending from an airport diagram indicate that fuel is available and that the field is attended, at least during normal working hours.

✓ A star above the airport diagram indicates an airport beacon normally operates from sunset to sunrise.

✓ Airports with control towers are shown in blue, while all others are identified by a magenta color.

✓ By referring to the airport data on sectional charts, you can determine what radio frequencies to use for communication at a particular airport. In addition, information such as longest runway length, airport lighting, and field elevation can be determined.

✓ For cross-country planning and flight, refer to navigation and communication boxes for information concerning navaids and flight service stations (FSSs) in the area.

✓ Boxes placed near the appropriate navaid, include the name, frequency, and Morse code identifier of the navaid. FSS frequencies are printed above the boxes.

✓ With the help of contour lines, spot elevations, and the elevations of obstructions, you can choose a safe cruising altitude.

✓ The locations of natural and man-made features, such as lakes, rivers, railroads, roads, and highways are shown on charts as reference points for navigation.

✓ While obstructions can impose hazards to flight, they can be good references to identify your position.

KEY TERMS

Aeronautical Charts	Mercator Projection
Great Circle	Lambert Conformal Conic Projection
Small Circle	Sectional Charts
Parallels	Maximum Elevation Figures (MEFs)
Latitude	World Aeronautical Chart (WAC)
Meridians	Legend
Longitude	Airport Elevation
Prime Meridian	Navaids
Projections	

QUESTIONS

1. Determine the approximate latitude and longitude of Red Bluff Airport.

2. What is the minimum MSL altitude that you should fly over the area depicted in this chart excerpt?

Match the airport diagrams with their descriptions.

3. Hard-surfaced runways 1,500 feet to 8,069 feet in length

4. Private airport

5. Hard-surface runways greater that 8,069 feet in length

6. Seaplane base

7. Closed airport

8. True/False. Airports which have control towers are magenta on sectional charts.

Refer to this chart excerpt for questions 9 through 15.

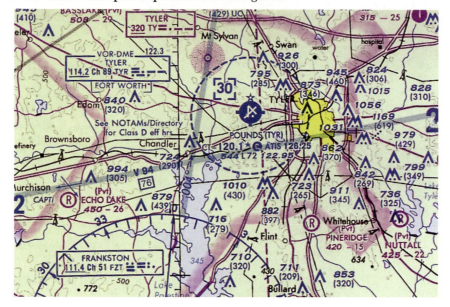

9. What is the control tower frequency for Pounds Airport?

10. What is the elevation of Pounds Airport?

11. True/False. Pounds Airport has full-time lighting.

12. What do the tick marks on the airport diagram indicate?

13. What does the star symbol above the airport diagram indicate?

14. Does the control tower at Pounds Airport operate full time?

15. You can use the frequency 122.3 located on top of the navaid box to communicate with what facility?

16. What is the height of the lighted obstruction?

    A. 1,125 feet MSL
    B. 1,467 feet AGL
    C. 2,049 feet AGL

SECTION D
AIRSPACE

Webster's dictionary defines **airspace** as "the portion of the atmosphere above a particular land area, especially above a nation." To efficiently manage the large amount of air traffic that traverses the sky each day, the atmosphere above the United States is divided into several sectors, or classes. In each airspace class, specific rules apply. For example, there are **VFR weather minimums** (minimum flight visibilities and distances from clouds) which you must maintain in each airspace class. In some areas, you are required to communicate with ATC and comply with pilot certification and aircraft equipment requirements. In addition to the primary classes, the airspace over the United States includes special use and other airspace areas where certain restrictions apply or specific ATC services are provided.

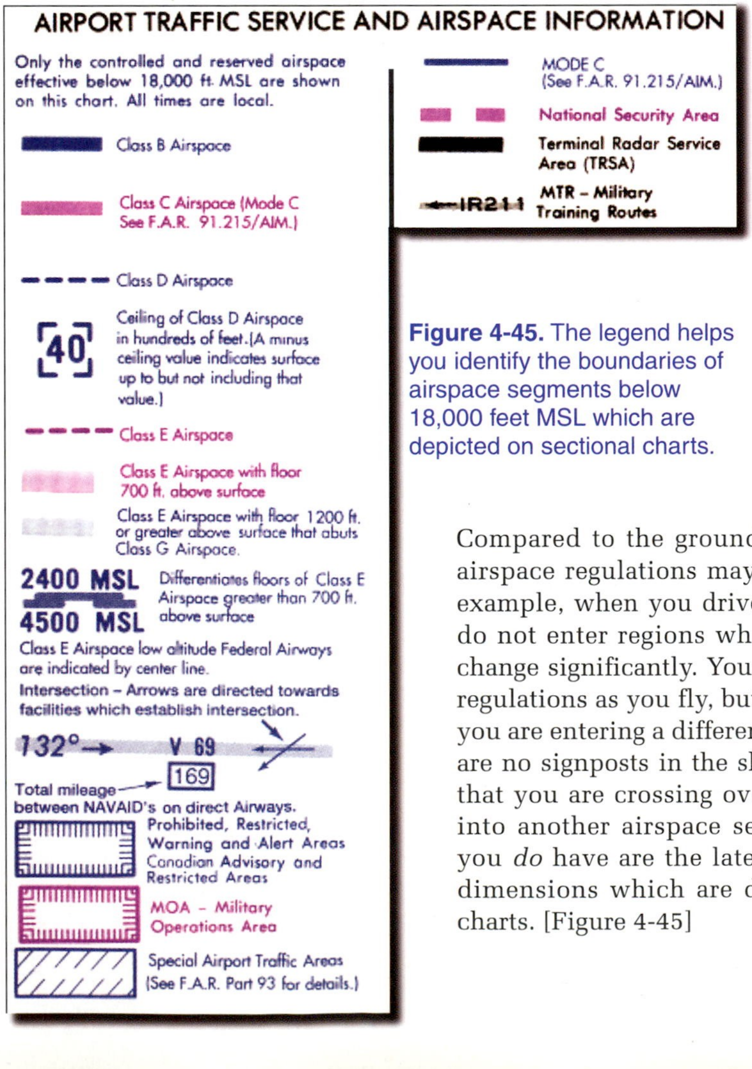

AIRPORT TRAFFIC SERVICE AND AIRSPACE INFORMATION

Only the controlled and reserved airspace effective below 18,000 ft. MSL are shown on this chart. All times are local.

Class B Airspace

Class C Airspace (Mode C See F.A.R. 91.215/AIM.)

Class D Airspace

[40] Ceiling of Class D Airspace in hundreds of feet. (A minus ceiling value indicates surface up to but not including that value.)

Class E Airspace

Class E Airspace with floor 700 ft. above surface

Class E Airspace with floor 1200 ft. or greater above surface that abuts Class G Airspace.

2400 MSL Differentiates floors of Class E
4500 MSL Airspace greater than 700 ft. above surface

Class E Airspace low altitude Federal Airways are indicated by center line.

Intersection – Arrows are directed towards facilities which establish intersection.

132° → V 69 ↘
[169]

Total mileage between NAVAID's on direct Airways.

Prohibited, Restricted, Warning and Alert Areas Canadian Advisory and Restricted Areas

MOA – Military Operations Area

Special Airport Traffic Areas (See F.A.R. Part 93 for details.)

MODE C (See F.A.R. 91.215/AIM.)

National Security Area

Terminal Radar Service Area (TRSA)

← IR211 MTR – Military Training Routes

Figure 4-45. The legend helps you identify the boundaries of airspace segments below 18,000 feet MSL which are depicted on sectional charts.

Compared to the ground-based rules of driving, airspace regulations may seem very unusual. For example, when you drive across the country, you do not enter regions where the rules of the road change significantly. You need to comply with the regulations as you fly, but how do you know when you are entering a different class of airspace? There are no signposts in the sky to alert you to the fact that you are crossing over an invisible boundary into another airspace sector. The signposts that you *do* have are the lateral and vertical airspace dimensions which are depicted on aeronautical charts. [Figure 4-45]

AIRSPACE CLASSIFICATIONS

Controlled airspace is a general term which covers five of the six classes of airspace; Class A, Class B, Class C, Class D, and Class E. While operating in controlled airspace, you are subject to certain operating rules, as well as pilot qualification and aircraft equipment requirements. Class G airspace is referred to as **uncontrolled airspace**. There is no airspace designation for Class F in the United States.

One of the primary functions of airspace classification is the separation of IFR and VFR traffic. The FARs prohibit noninstrument-rated pilots from flying when conditions are below the basic VFR weather minimums specified for each class of airspace. VFR cloud clearance and visibility requirements are designed to help you avoid flying into clouds, as well as to allow you to maintain adequate forward visibility to see and avoid other aircraft and navigate in flight. Keep in mind that, these values are legal minimums. You may need to establish higher personal minimums until you have acquired more practical experience. Your instructor can advise you in this area.

When the weather conditions deteriorate below VFR minimums, all aircraft in controlled airspace must be flown by instrument-rated pilots in accordance with IFR clearances issued by ATC. If you are an instrument-rated pilot on an IFR flight plan, you are not subject to any visibility or cloud clearance minimums, but ATC must issue a clearance allowing you to proceed through controlled airspace.

The following discussion of airspace follows a standard format which makes it easy to understand the features of each class of airspace. Following a general description of the airspace class and its operating requirements, a graphic illustrating the airspace dimensions is shown with the corresponding sectional chart depiction. In addition, a table lists the VFR weather minimums which apply to the airspace class and summarizes the operating requirements. For easy reference, a chart which combines the individual airspace class tables, and a diagram which depicts the relationships between each airspace class can be found at the end of this chapter.

Lateral distances and visibility figures are indicated in nautical or statute miles. When describing airspace dimensions, the term *floor* often is used to refer to the lowest altitude at which the airspace segment begins, and the term *ceiling* applies to the upper limit of the airspace. These boundaries, as well as the height of clouds are described as heights above ground level (AGL), above mean sea level (MSL), or as flight levels (FL). At 18,000 feet MSL and above, altitudes are prefaced by the letters FL meaning flight level, with the last two zeros omitted. For example, 35,000 feet is referenced as FL350.

CLASS G AIRSPACE (UNCONTROLLED)

Normally, ATC does not exercise control of air traffic in uncontrolled, or **Class G airspace**. You are not required to communicate with ATC when operating in Class G airspace unless a temporary control tower has been established. In the early days of aviation, all airspace was uncontrolled. Today, due to the need to coordinate the movement of a large amount of air

 Specific VFR weather minimums apply in Class G airspace below 1,200 feet AGL, between 1,200 feet AGL and 10,000 feet MSL, and above 10,000 feet MSL. The minimums which you must maintain in Class G airspace depend on whether you are operating during the day or at night. See figure 4-46.

traffic, the major portion of airspace that covers the contiguous U.S. is controlled and the amount of uncontrolled airspace has continued to decrease. [Figure 4-46]

Airspace Features	Class G
VFR Min. Vis. and Distance from Clouds 1,200 ft AGL or less (Regardless of MSL Altitude)	Day 1 s.m. Clear of Clouds Night 3 s.m. 500 ft Below 1,000 ft Above 2,000 ft Horizontal
VFR Minimum Visibility	**Below 10,000 ft MSL –** Day 1 s.m. Night 3 s.m. **At or Above 10,000 ft MSL –** 5 s.m. (above 1,200 ft AGL)
VFR Minimum Distance from Clouds	**Below 10,000 ft MSL –** 500 ft Below 1,000 ft Above 2,000 ft Horizontal (above 1,200 ft AGL) **At or Above 10,000 ft MSL –** 1,000 ft Below 1,000 ft Above 1 s.m. Horizontal (above 1,200 ft AGL)
Minimum Pilot Qualifications	Student Pilot Certificate
VFR Entry and Equipment Requirements	None
ATC Services	VFR Traffic Advisories on Request (workload permitting)

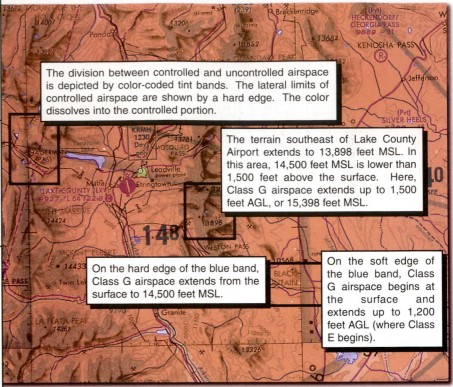

The division between controlled and uncontrolled airspace is depicted by color-coded tint bands. The lateral limits of controlled airspace are shown by a hard edge. The color dissolves into the controlled portion.

The terrain southeast of Lake County Airport extends to 13,898 feet MSL. In this area, 14,500 feet MSL is lower than 1,500 feet above the surface. Here, Class G airspace extends up to 1,500 feet AGL, or 15,398 feet MSL.

On the hard edge of the blue band, Class G airspace extends from the surface to 14,500 feet MSL.

On the soft edge of the blue band, Class G airspace begins at the surface and extends up to 1,200 feet AGL (where Class E begins).

Figure 4-46. Class G Dimensions — Class G airspace typically extends from the surface to the base of the overlying controlled airspace (Class E), which is normally 700 or 1,200 feet AGL. In some areas of the western U.S. and Alaska, Class G airspace may extend from the surface to 14,500 feet MSL. An exception to this rule occurs when 14,500 feet MSL is lower than 1,500 feet AGL. In that event, Class G airspace continues up to 1,500 feet above the surface.

 Class G airspace typically extends from the surface to 700 or 1,200 feet AGL. In some areas, Class G may extend from the surface to 14,500 feet MSL. See figure 4-46.

CONTROLLED AIRSPACE

The important thing to know about operating in controlled airspace is that you may be subject to air traffic control. As a routine measure, IFR flights are controlled from takeoff to touchdown, since they are permitted to operate in all kinds of weather. As a VFR pilot, your contact with ATC typically is limited to terminal areas. For example, when you take off or land at controlled airports, you must contact the control tower, and you often will use radar approach and departure control services.

Separation of air traffic is the primary function of ATC, and radar is one of the controller's principal tools. Because of this, the FARs require you to use your aircraft transponder (if your aircraft is so equipped) whenever you fly in controlled airspace.

A **transponder** is an electronic device aboard the airplane which enhances your aircraft's identity on an ATC radar screen. An air traffic controller may assign an individual code to your transponder to help distinguish your aircraft from others in the area. Transponders carry designations appropriate to their capabilities. For example, those used in general aviation have Mode A capability. Usually they can be set to any of 4,096 codes, and many are able to indicate, or encode, your altitude on the controller's radar screen. A Mode A transponder with altitude encoding equipment is referred to as having Mode C capability. Another type of transponder which uses advanced technology is the Mode S transponder, which also is compatible with Mode C altitude reporting equipment.

The FARs require that you have an operating transponder with Mode C capability in Class A airspace, Class B airspace, within 30 nautical miles of Class B primary airports, and in and above Class C airspace. In addition, you must have a Mode C transponder when flying at or above 10,000 feet MSL, excluding the airspace at and below 2,500 feet AGL. This requirement applies in all airspace (controlled or uncontrolled) within the 48 contiguous states and the District of Columbia. Transponders and radar are discussed in more detail in Chapter 5. [Figure 4-47]

 An operable 4,096-code transponder with Mode C capability is required while operating within Class A airspace, Class B airspace, within 30 nautical miles of Class B primary airports, and Class C airspace.

A transponder with Mode C capabilities is required above the dotted line.

Figure 4-47. You must have a transponder with Mode C capability to operate in the darker areas shown, as well as in Class C and B airspace segments. In addition, if your aircraft is equipped with a transponder, you must have it on while operating in all controlled airspace.

CLASS E AIRSPACE

The majority of your flying time will probably be spent in the controlled airspace designated as **Class E airspace**. There are no communication requirements to operate within Class E airspace, but you can request traffic advisory services which ATC provides on a workload-permitting basis. In Class E airspace, you cannot fly when the weather is below VFR minimums unless you are instrument rated, have filed an IFR flight plan, and have received a clearance from ATC.

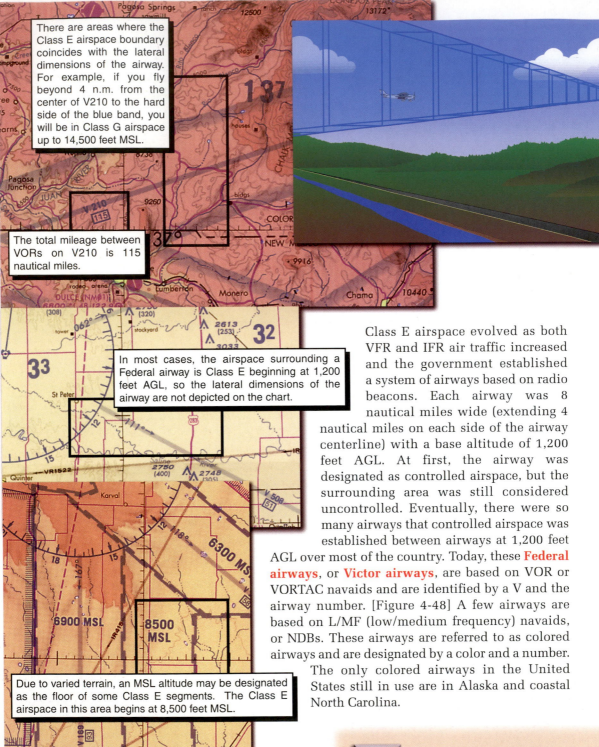

There are areas where the Class E airspace boundary coincides with the lateral dimensions of the airway. For example, if you fly beyond 4 n.m. from the center of V210 to the hard side of the blue band, you will be in Class G airspace up to 14,500 feet MSL.

The total mileage between VORs on V210 is 115 nautical miles.

In most cases, the airspace surrounding a Federal airway is Class E beginning at 1,200 feet AGL, so the lateral dimensions of the airway are not depicted on the chart.

Due to varied terrain, an MSL altitude may be designated as the floor of some Class E segments. The Class E airspace in this area begins at 8,500 feet MSL.

Class E airspace evolved as both VFR and IFR air traffic increased and the government established a system of airways based on radio beacons. Each airway was 8 nautical miles wide (extending 4 nautical miles on each side of the airway centerline) with a base altitude of 1,200 feet AGL. At first, the airway was designated as controlled airspace, but the surrounding area was still considered uncontrolled. Eventually, there were so many airways that controlled airspace was established between airways at 1,200 feet AGL over most of the country. Today, these **Federal airways**, or **Victor airways**, are based on VOR or VORTAC navaids and are identified by a V and the airway number. [Figure 4-48] A few airways are based on L/MF (low/medium frequency) navaids, or NDBs. These airways are referred to as colored airways and are designated by a color and a number. The only colored airways in the United States still in use are in Alaska and coastal North Carolina.

Figure 4-48. Class E Dimensions — Federal airways are usually 8 nautical miles wide, begin at 1,200 feet AGL, and extend up to, but not including, 18,000 feet MSL.

Class E airspace segments include Federal, or Victor, airways which usually extend to 4 nautical miles on each side of the airway centerline and, unless otherwise indicated, extend from 1,200 feet AGL up to, but not including, 18,000 feet MSL. See figure 4-48.

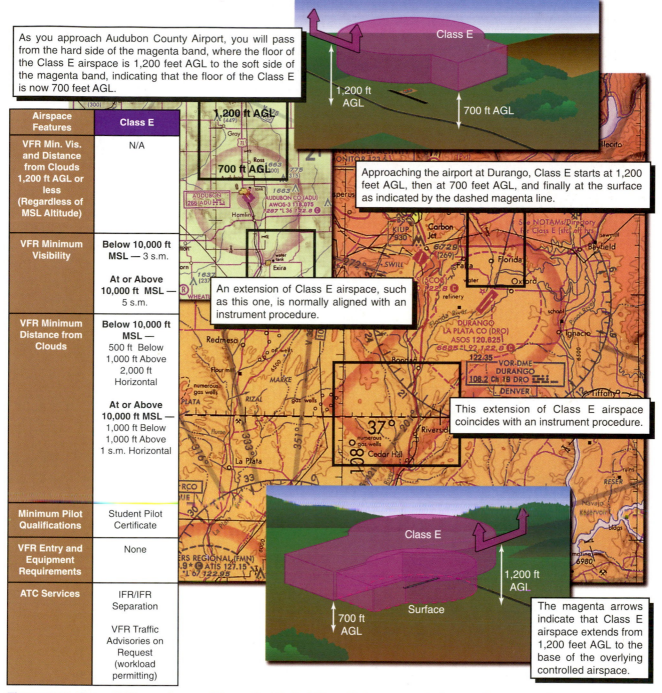

As you approach Audubon County Airport, you will pass from the hard side of the magenta band, where the floor of the Class E airspace is 1,200 feet AGL to the soft side of the magenta band, indicating that the floor of the Class E is now 700 feet AGL.

Class E

1,200 ft AGL

700 ft AGL

Approaching the airport at Durango, Class E starts at 1,200 feet AGL, then at 700 feet AGL, and finally at the surface as indicated by the dashed magenta line.

An extension of Class E airspace, such as this one, is normally aligned with an instrument procedure.

This extension of Class E airspace coincides with an instrument procedure.

Class E

1,200 ft AGL

Surface

700 ft AGL

The magenta arrows indicate that Class E airspace extends from 1,200 feet AGL to the base of the overlying controlled airspace.

Airspace Features	Class E
VFR Min. Vis. and Distance from Clouds 1,200 ft AGL or less (Regardless of MSL Altitude)	N/A
VFR Minimum Visibility	Below 10,000 ft MSL — 3 s.m.
	At or Above 10,000 ft MSL — 5 s.m.
VFR Minimum Distance from Clouds	Below 10,000 ft MSL — 500 ft Below 1,000 ft Above 2,000 ft Horizontal
	At or Above 10,000 ft MSL — 1,000 ft Below 1,000 ft Above 1 s.m. Horizontal
Minimum Pilot Qualifications	Student Pilot Certificate
VFR Entry and Equipment Requirements	None
ATC Services	IFR/IFR Separation VFR Traffic Advisories on Request (workload permitting)

Figure 4-49. Class E Dimensions — The vertical limit of Class E airspace encircling an airport extends up to the base of the overlying or adjacent controlled airspace. At airports where Class E begins at the surface, weather reporting services are provided by a weather observer or automatic weather observation equipment (ASOS or AWOS). At certain times this service may not be available, and the airspace will be designated as Class G.

To allow IFR traffic to remain in controlled airspace while transitioning from the enroute to the terminal environment, the base of Class E extends closer to the ground near many airports. At airports without control towers which have approved instrument approach procedures, Class E airspace begins either at 700 feet AGL or at the surface. [Figure 4-49]

Class E airspace consists of several different segments. The weather minimums that you must maintain while in each of these segments depend on whether you are operating at an altitude below 10,000 feet MSL, or at or above 10,000 feet MSL. See figure 4-49.

Another portion of Class E airspace extends from 14,500 feet MSL up to, but not including, the base of Class A airspace at 18,000 feet MSL. This Class E segment covers the 48 contiguous states, District of Columbia, Alaska, and the airspace out to 12 nautical miles from the coastlines. In addition, the airspace in these areas above FL600 is designated as Class E. The only exceptions are the airspace located over the Alaska peninsula west of 160°W longitude and the airspace below 1,500 feet AGL. [Figure 4-50]

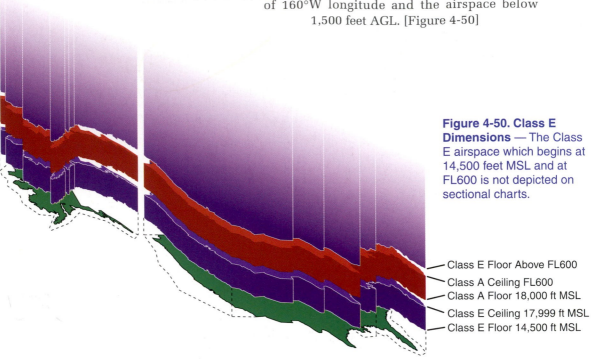

Figure 4-50. Class E Dimensions — The Class E airspace which begins at 14,500 feet MSL and at FL600 is not depicted on sectional charts.

Class E Floor Above FL600
Class A Ceiling FL600
Class A Floor 18,000 ft MSL
Class E Ceiling 17,999 ft MSL
Class E Floor 14,500 ft MSL

CLASS D AIRSPACE

An airport which has an operating control tower, but does not provide radar services as in Class B or C airspace, is surrounded by **Class D airspace**. The control tower provides sequencing and traffic advisories to VFR aircraft operating into and out of the airport, and IFR traffic separation. You must establish two-way radio communication with the tower prior to entering Class D airspace and maintain radio contact during all operations to, from, or on that airport. As a general rule, you should avoid Class D airspace except to take off or land at an airport within the area.

Airspace at an airport with a part-time control tower is classified as Class D airspace only when the associated tower is in operation.

The airspace at an airport with a part-time control tower is designated as Class D only when the tower is in operation. At airports where the tower operates part time, the airspace changes to Class E, or a combination of Class E and Class G when the tower is closed. For these airports, check the *Airport/Facility Directory* for the tower's hours of operation and the airspace designation.

In some Class D airspace areas, a satellite airport may be located within the airspace designated for the primary airport. If a control tower is in operation at the satellite airport, you should contact it for arrival and departure. When the satellite airport is a nontower field, you must establish contact with the primary airport's control tower. When departing a nontower satellite airport in Class D airspace, contact the controlling tower as soon as practicable after takeoff. To the maximum extent practical and consistent with safety, satellite airports have been excluded from Class D airspace. For instance, airspace may be carved out of a Class D area to allow traffic to arrive and depart from a nontower satellite airport. [Figure 4-51]

 The lateral dimensions of Class D airspace are based on the instrument procedures for which the controlled airspace is established. Class D airspace is depicted on a sectional chart by a blue segmented circle. See figure 4-51.

Airspace Features	Class D
VFR Min. Vis. and Distance from Clouds 1,200 ft AGL or less (Regardless of MSL Altitude)	N/A
VFR Minimum Visibility	3 Statute Miles
VFR Minimum Distance from Clouds	500 ft Below 1,000 ft Above 2,000 ft Horizontal
Minimum Pilot Qualifications	Student Pilot Certificate
VFR Entry and Equipment Requirements	Establish Radio Communication
ATC Services	IFR/IFR Separation VFR Traffic Advisories (workload permitting)

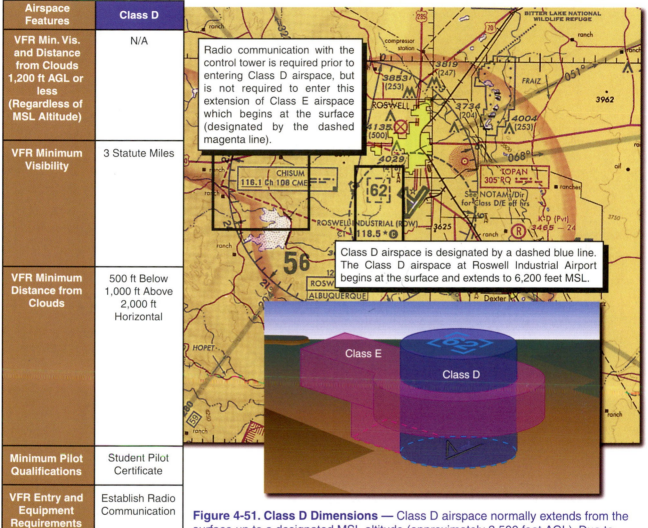

Radio communication with the control tower is required prior to entering Class D airspace, but is not required to enter this extension of Class E airspace which begins at the surface (designated by the dashed magenta line).

Class D airspace is designated by a dashed blue line. The Class D airspace at Roswell Industrial Airport begins at the surface and extends to 6,200 feet MSL.

Figure 4-51. Class D Dimensions — Class D airspace normally extends from the surface up to a designated MSL altitude (approximately 2,500 feet AGL). Due to requirements unique to each airport, extensions for instrument approaches and departures may be included.

 When operating at a nontower satellite airport within Class D airspace, you must establish contact with the primary airport's control tower.

 Unless otherwise authorized, you must establish two-way radio communication with the control tower prior to entering Class D airspace. In addition, while operating within Class D airspace, you must maintain at least 3 statute miles visibility and a distance 500 feet below, 1,000 feet above, and 2,000 feet horizontally from clouds. See figure 4-51.

Airspace Features	Class C
VFR Min. Vis. and Distance from Clouds 1,200 ft AGL or less (Regardless of MSL Altitude)	N/A
VFR Minimum Visibility	3 Statute Miles
VFR Minimum Distance from Clouds	500 ft Below 1,000 ft Above 2,000 ft Horizontal
Minimum Pilot Qualifications	Student Pilot Certificate
VFR Entry and Equipment Requirements	Establish Radio Communication Transponder with Mode C
ATC Services	IFR/IFR Separation IFR/VFR Separation VFR Traffic Advisories (workload permitting)

If you are flying into a satellite airport within Class C airspace, such as Somerville, you must be in contact with ATC while you are in the Class C airspace. The radar service provided to you will be discontinued early enough for you to change to the CTAF (122.9) at Somerville Airport. When departing a satellite airport, you should contact ATC as soon as practicable after takeoff.

The outer area associated with Class C airspace extends 10 n.m. beyond the shelf area. VFR pilots are not required to contact ATC prior to entering the outer area, but it is helpful to do so. For approach, departure, or overflights, ATC normally provides the same radar services in the outer area as it does within the Class C airspace.

Solid magenta circles represent the boundaries of Class C airspace. The shelf area of Grand Rapids Class C airspace extends from 2,000 feet MSL to 4,800 feet MSL.

The core area begins at the surface and extends to 4,800 feet MSL.

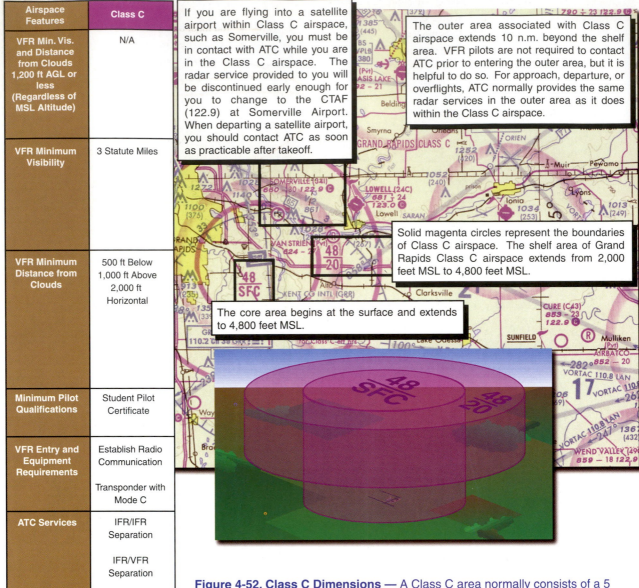

Figure 4-52. Class C Dimensions — A Class C area normally consists of a 5 nautical mile radius core area which extends from the surface to 4,000 feet above the elevation of the primary airport. A 10 nautical mile radius shelf area usually extends from 1,200 feet to 4,000 feet above the airport elevation. An outer area usually extends out to 20 nautical miles from the primary airport. Aeronautical charts depict the MSL altitudes which define the floor and ceiling of each segment of Class C airspace.

CLASS C AIRSPACE

Factors considered in designating controlled airspace include safety, users' needs, and the volume of air traffic. Because of these considerations, many busy airports are surrounded by **Class C airspace**. Within a Class C area, ATC provides radar service to all IFR and VFR aircraft, and participation in this service is mandatory. You will find that Class C areas usually have very similar dimensions from one location to another, although some may be modified to fit unique aspects of a particular airport's location.

 Class C airspace usually has similar dimensions from one airport to another although some areas may be modified to fit unique aspects of a specific airport environment. See figure 4-52.

Prior to entering Class C airspace, you must establish two-way communication with the

ATC facility having jurisdiction and maintain it while you are operating within the airspace. When you are departing the primary airport, you must maintain radio contact with ATC until you are clear of the area. In addition to the two-way radio requirement, all aircraft operating in a Class C area and in all airspace above it, from its ceiling up to 10,000 feet MSL within the lateral boundaries of that Class C area, must be equipped with an operable transponder with Mode C capability. Aircraft operating in the airspace beneath a Class C area are not required to have a Mode C transponder.

Keep in mind that ATC facilities may not operate full time at some Class C locations, so radar service may not be available at all times. If the ATC facility is closed, the operating rules for the Class C area are not in effect. Hours of operation for ATC facilities are listed in the *Airport/Facility Directory*. [Figure 4-52]

You must establish two-way radio communication with the ATC facility having jurisdiction over the area prior to entering Class C airspace.

While operating in Class C airspace, you must maintain at least 3 statute miles visibility and remain at least 500 feet below, 1,000 feet above, and 2,000 feet horizontally from clouds. See figure 4-52.

If you are operating out of a satellite airport within Class C airspace you should contact ATC as soon as practicable after takeoff.

CLASS B AIRSPACE

At some of the country's major airports, **Class B airspace** has been established to separate all arriving and departing traffic. While each Class B area usually is designated for a major terminal, it typically serves several airports in the area. A Class B area has different levels of airspace which are portrayed as a series of interconnected circular patterns around the airport. You may notice that it looks something like an upside-down wedding cake. Each Class B area is individually designed to serve the needs of the particular airport that it surrounds. Terrain, the amount and flow of air traffic, and the location of other airports all influence each design. Generally, you will find that Class B airspace surrounds the busiest airports in the country.

To operate within Class B airspace, your aircraft must have two-way radio communication capability and a Mode C transponder.

To operate within Class B airspace, your aircraft must have two-way radio communication capability and a transponder with Mode C. With certain exceptions, the transponder is required within 30 nautical miles of the Class B area's primary airport from the surface to 10,000 feet MSL. In addition, a VOR or TACAN is required for IFR operations.

In order to fly within Class B airspace, or to take off or land at an airport within that airspace, you must possess at least a private pilot certificate. In certain Class B areas, student pilots may be permitted to conduct flight operations by obtaining specified training and a logbook endorsement from a certificated flight instructor. However, student pilot operations are prohibited at designated major airports within the nation's busiest Class B areas. You should refer to FAR Part 91 for specific rules pertaining to student pilot operations within Class B airspace.

To operate in Class B airspace, you must be at least a private pilot or a student pilot with the appropriate logbook endorsement.

Prior to entering any part of Class B airspace, you are required to obtain a clearance from ATC on the appropriate frequency. You must advise ATC of your intended altitude and route of flight before departing an airport in a Class B area. ATC permission is required before you can fly through Class B airspace, even after a departure from an airport that is other than the primary airport. [Figure 4-53]

 The floor and ceiling of each layer of Class B airspace are denoted on a sectional chart by MSL altitudes. See figure 4-53.

It's a Tough Job, But Somebody Has to Do It.

A

Don't worry, you don't need to understand figure A to operate in the airspace system, but air traffic controllers do. The diagram is an excerpt from the FAA Order 7110.65 *Air Traffic Control* which is an operations handbook for ATC. Next time you are feeling overwhelmed with all the procedures that you have to know to fly in the airspace system, consider this; the ATC handbook covers over 1,100 topics ranging from radar separation, disseminating weather information, and IFR procedures to celestial navigation training, aircraft bomb threats, and derelict balloons.

Air traffic controllers are required to be familiar with the areas of the handbook which pertain to their operational responsibilities. For controllers at some of the busiest airports, those responsibilities may include handling a wide variety of situations and the ATC handbook helps a controller prepare for almost anything. For example, how does a controller direct a formation flight of two or more aircraft? According to the handbook, formation flights are to be treated as one aircraft. What about flyers who refuse to conform to the standard traffic pattern, such as birds? Controllers are instructed to issue advisory information on bird activity to include position, species or size of birds, course of flight, and altitude. [Figure B]

What about a more explosive situation? The ATC handbook has it covered. In the event of an emergency landing of an aircraft with explosive cargo on board, the handbook advises controllers to inform the pilot of the safest and least congested airport areas. ATC should then relay the explosive cargo information to the emergency equipment crew, the airport management, and the appropriate military agencies.

e. When takeoff direction is other than in subparagraph 6–20d—The departing aircraft takes off so that it is established on a course diverging by at least 45 degrees from the reciprocal of the final approach course *5 minutes* before the arriving aircraft is estimated at the airport or before it starts procedure turn. (See Figure 6–20[2] and Figure 6–20[3]).

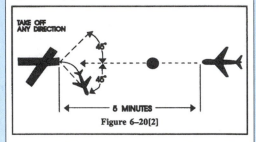

Figure 6–20[2]

Figure 6–20[3]

B

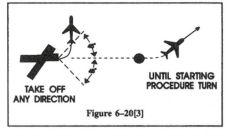

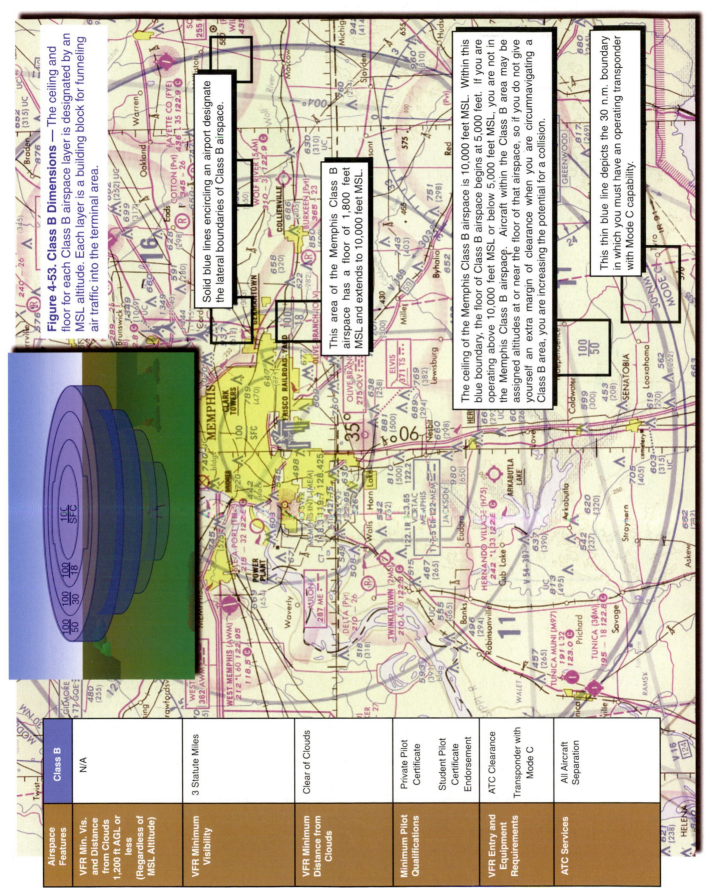

Figure 4-53. Class B Dimensions — The ceiling and floor for each Class B airspace layer is designated by an MSL altitude. Each layer is a building block for funneling air traffic into the terminal area.

Solid blue lines encircling an airport designate the lateral boundaries of Class B airspace.

This area of the Memphis Class B airspace has a floor of 1,800 feet MSL and extends to 10,000 feet MSL.

The ceiling of the Memphis Class B airspace is 10,000 feet MSL. Within this blue boundary, the floor of Class B airspace begins at 5,000 feet. If you are operating above 10,000 feet MSL or below 5,000 feet MSL, you are not in the Memphis Class B airspace. Aircraft within the Class B area may be assigned altitudes at or near the floor of that airspace, so if you do not give yourself an extra margin of clearance when you are circumnavigating a Class B area, you are increasing the potential for a collision.

This thin blue line depicts the 30 n.m. boundary in which you must have an operating transponder with Mode C capability.

Airspace Features	Class B	
VFR Min. Vis. and Distance from Clouds 1,200 ft AGL or less (Regardless of MSL Altitude)	N/A	
VFR Minimum Visibility	3 Statute Miles	
VFR Minimum Distance from Clouds	Clear of Clouds	
Minimum Pilot Qualifications	Private Pilot Certificate	Student Pilot Certificate Endorsement
VFR Entry and Equipment Requirements	ATC Clearance	Transponder with Mode C
ATC Services	All Aircraft Separation	

B Stands for Busy

What is the typical Class B airport like? Chicago O'Hare International Airport is an example of an airport that is surrounded by Class B airspace. For 30 years, O'Hare has been a commercial aviation giant, handling more passengers and aircraft operations than any airport in the world. O'Hare has 50 commercial, commuter, and cargo airlines and approximately 180,000 travelers pass through the airport each day. O'Hare handles over 900,000 flights a year, close to 2,500 a day. [Figure A]

O'Hare's International Terminal greets arriving passengers in 17 different languages, boasts 68 U.S. Custom booths and has the capacity to process 4,000 passengers each hour. Figure B shows the ranking of the world's busiest airports based on the number of passengers. Each U.S. airport included on this chart is surrounded by Class B airspace.

A   Courtesy of the Chicago Department of Aviation

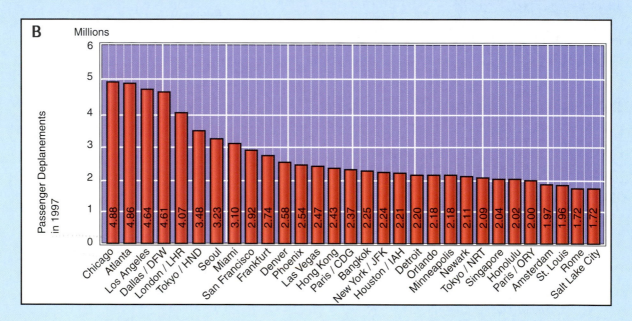

B   Millions

Passenger Deplanements in 1997

Chicago	4.88
Atlanta	4.86
Los Angeles	4.64
Dallas / DFW	4.61
London / LHR	4.07
Tokyo / HND	3.48
Seoul	3.23
Miami	3.10
San Francisco	2.92
Frankfurt	2.74
Denver	2.58
Phoenix	2.54
Las Vegas	2.47
Hong Kong	2.43
Paris / CDG	2.37
Bangkok	2.25
New York / JFK	2.24
Houston / IAH	2.21
Detroit	2.20
Orlando	2.18
Minneapolis	2.18
Newark	2.11
Tokyo / NRT	2.09
Singapore	2.04
Honolulu	2.02
Paris / ORY	2.00
Amsterdam	1.97
St. Louis	1.96
Rome	1.72
Salt Lake City	1.72

VFR TERMINAL AREA CHARTS

Whenever you are flying VFR in or around Class B airspace, **VFR terminal area charts** will help significantly with orientation and navigation. Terminal area charts show the lateral limits of the various sections of the Class B area on a larger scale (1:250,000) than sectional charts and give you a more detailed display of topographical features. Sectional charts display a blue border around Class B airspace to indicate the area covered by a VFR terminal area chart. [Figure 4-54]

The title block of the terminal area chart identifies its location.

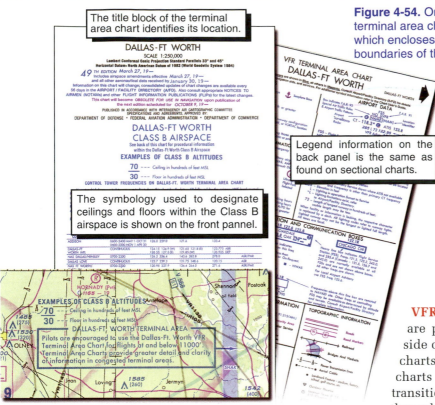

Figure 4-54. On sectional charts, the availability of a terminal area chart is indicated by a wide, blue band which encloses the Class B airspace and reflects the boundaries of the terminal area chart.

Legend information on the back panel is the same as found on sectional charts.

The symbology used to designate ceilings and floors within the Class B airspace is shown on the front pannel.

VFR flyway planning charts are published on the reverse side of some VFR terminal area charts. The flyway planning charts show VFR routes for transitioning around, under, and through Class B airspace. These routes are not intended to discourage requests for VFR operations, but are designed to help you avoid heavily congested areas, such as IFR arrival and departure routes. Flyway charts omit most of the terrain features and geographic information found on terminal area charts because they are for planning, not navigating. However, major landmarks are shown as visual aids to orientation. [Figure 4-55]

Prior to entering Class B airspace on a VFR transition route, you must obtain an ATC clearance. After receiving a clearance, you must fly the route as depicted at an ATC assigned altitude.

You can fly along a VFR flyway in the vicinity of Class B airspace without actually entering the airspace. An ATC clearance is not required to operate on a VFR flyway.

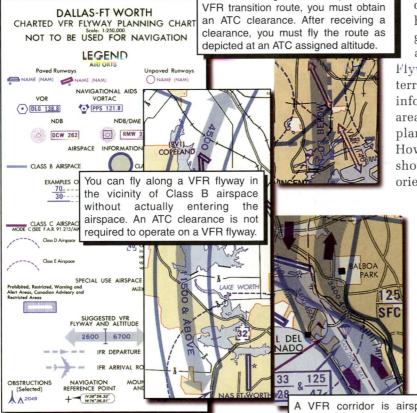

Figure 4-55. To help pilots navigate around and through Class B airspace, several types of VFR routes are used, including VFR flyways, VFR corridors, and VFR transition routes. Located on the reverse side of the terminal area chart, a flyway planning chart legend identifies the symbols used to depict VFR routes.

A VFR corridor is airspace with specific vertical and lateral boundaries, which allows you to fly through Class B airspace without a clearance from, or communication with, ATC.

TIME TO SLOW DOWN

. . . we were busy with checklists and passenger announcements, while changing to Tower frequency. [The] Tower cleared us for immediate takeoff, and even though we had not finished our checklists, I taxied our aircraft into position and started to advance the power for takeoff. . . After about 1,000 feet of takeoff roll, Tower canceled our takeoff clearance. . . [we] asked the Tower why we had our takeoff clearance canceled. . .the F/O said [that] we're not on the runway. At that point I realized we had started our takeoff roll on an active taxiway. — excerpt from an ASRS report

This excerpt is from one of 125 incident reports included in an ASRS study involving time-related problems experienced by air carrier and commuter crews. Time-related pressures may include pressure from ATC to expedite taxi for takeoff or to meet a restriction in clearance time, as well as pressure to keep on schedule when delays have occurred due to maintenance or weather. Any situation where a pilot's performance is degraded by a perceived or actual need to hurry or rush tasks is referred to by the ASRS as the hurry-up syndrome.

The ASRS study found that each time-pressure incident had a point where the error occurred and another point where the error actually resulted in an incident. Figure A shows that the majority of errors occurred during the pre-flight and taxi-out stages of flight.

Due to the increased amount of traffic and demands placed on you by ATC at busy airports, you may experience this hurry-up syndrome as you begin to operate in more complex airspace. To avoid errors caused by this rushed feeling, you need to take the time to prioritize tasks and defer nonessential tasks to low workload phases of flight. Strict adherence to checklists is essential, and if a procedure is interrupted for any reason, you should return to the beginning of that task.

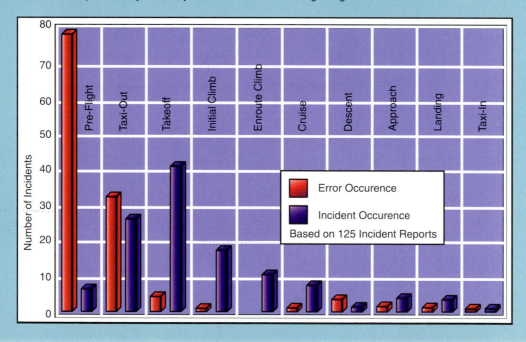

CLASS A AIRSPACE

The airspace extending from 18,000 feet MSL up to and including FL600 is defined as **Class A airspace**. It covers the majority of the contiguous states and Alaska, as well as the area extending 12 nautical miles out from the U.S. coast. To operate within Class A airspace, you must be instrument rated. In addition, your aircraft must be transponder equipped, operated under an IFR flight plan, and controlled directly by ATC. Because of the overall increase in speed of aircraft operating in Class A airspace and the corresponding increase of the closure rates between these aircraft, VFR flight is not allowed. Jet routes are designed to serve aircraft operations from the floor of Class A airspace up to and including FL450.

Within Class A airspace, you are required to set your altimeter to the standard setting of 29.92 in. Hg. so that all pilots are maintaining their assigned altitudes using the same altimeter reference. Altitudes within Class A airspace are expressed to ATC by using the term flight level (FL). [Figure 4-56]

Class A airspace extends from 18,000 feet MSL up to and including FL600. You must be instrument rated and be on an IFR flight plan to operate in Class A airspace.

Within Class A airspace, you are required to set your altimeter to the standard setting of 29.92 in. Hg.

Airspace Features	Class A
VFR Min. Vis. and Distance from Clouds 1,200 ft AGL or less (Regardless of MSL Altitude)	N/A
VFR Minimum Visibility	N/A
VFR Minimum Distance from Clouds	N/A
Minimum Pilot Qualifications	Instrument Rating
VFR Entry and Equipment Requirements	IFR Flight Plan and IFR Clearance Required
ATC Services	All Aircraft Separation

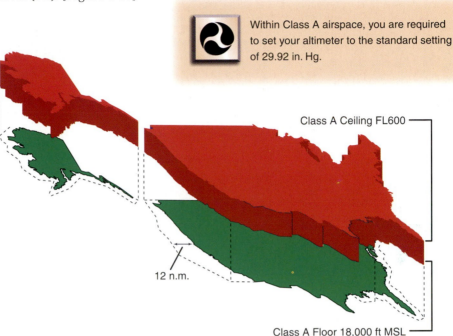

Class A Ceiling FL600

12 n.m.

Class A Floor 18,000 ft MSL

Figure 4-56. Class A dimensions — Class A airspace extends from 18,000 feet MSL up to and including FL600. It covers the majority of the contiguous U.S. and extends 12 nautical miles out from the U.S. coast. The dimensions of Class A airspace are not shown on sectional charts.

SPECIAL VFR

In addition to maintaining the VFR minimums already discussed, you may only operate within the areas of Class B, C, D, or E airspace which extend to the surface around an airport, when the ground visibility is at least 3 statute miles and the cloud ceiling is at least 1,000 feet AGL. If ground visibility is not reported, you can use flight visibility. When the weather is below these VFR minimums, and there is no conflicting IFR traffic, a **special VFR clearance** may be obtained from the ATC facility having jurisdiction over the affected airspace. A special VFR clearance

A special VFR clearance allows you to operate within the surface areas of Class B, C, D, or E airspace if the visibility is at least 1 statute mile and you can remain clear of clouds.

may allow you to enter, leave, or operate within most Class C and Class E surface areas and some Class B and Class C surface areas if the flight visibility is at least 1 statute mile and you can remain clear of clouds. At least 1 statute mile ground visibility is required for takeoff and landing, however, if ground visibility is not reported, you must have at least 1 statute mile flight visibility.

As a private pilot, you may obtain a special VFR clearance only during the daytime. Because of the difficulty in seeing clouds at night, special VFR is not permitted between sunset and sunrise unless you have a current instrument rating and the aircraft is equipped for instrument flight. At certain major airports, special VFR clearances are not issued to fixed-wing aircraft. [Figure 4-57]

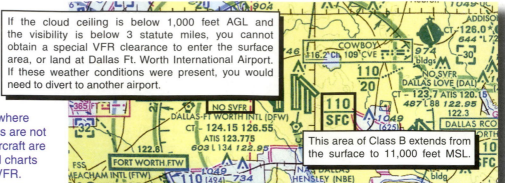

If the cloud ceiling is below 1,000 feet AGL and the visibility is below 3 statute miles, you cannot obtain a special VFR clearance to enter the surface area, or land at Dallas Ft. Worth International Airport. If these weather conditions were present, you would need to divert to another airport.

This area of Class B extends from the surface to 11,000 feet MSL.

Figure 4-57. Airports where special VFR clearances are not issued to fixed-wing aircraft are annotated on sectional charts with the phrase NO SVFR.

You may not operate under a special VFR clearance at night unless you are instrument rated and your aircraft is instrument equipped.

The phrase NO SVFR included with the airport data on a sectional chart indicates that special VFR clearances are not issued to fixed-wing aircraft.

PANIC SETS IN. . .

Imagine that you are on a cross-country flight. Everything has been progressing smoothly but as you scan the horizon, you notice some clouds up ahead. *"It must just be a high scattered layer,"* you say to yourself. *"Flight service didn't mention anything about low clouds."* As you proceed on course, you realize that the clouds are at your altitude. *"No problem,"* you think, *"I'll just drop down a little lower, stay underneath this weather until it clears up. The forecast for the airport was clear."* As you continue to descend lower and lower to avoid the clouds, visual references begin to disappear and the sky turns white. Panic sets in. . .

You have just attempted what many pilots refer to as "scud running" — trying to stay below the clouds while continuing into deteriorating weather conditions. When inexperienced, noninstrument-rated pilots find themselves in this situation, the outcome often is fatal.

NTSB statistics indicate that approximately 25% of all general aviation accidents are weather related, as well as nearly 40% of all fatal accidents. The NTSB cites "continued VFR flight into adverse weather/IMC" as the primary cause in many of these accidents. Inadvertent entry into instrument weather conditions can result in either flying into terrain or experiencing spatial disorientation.

How can you avoid an unplanned flight into instrument conditions? The first step is to define safe weather minimums for yourself and stick to them. Set conservative ceiling and visibility values which may be higher than those required by the FARs. Start with a thorough weather briefing prior to your flight and if there is any question about the conditions, don't go. Learn how to obtain weather information enroute so you can keep updated on changing conditions. If you do inadvertently enter IFR weather, maintain control of the airplane and make a 180° turn back to VFR conditions. If you cannot maintain VFR, do not let your pride keep you from contacting ATC or an FSS for assistance.

AIRSPEED LIMITATIONS

Since the airspace at lower altitudes, and especially in the vicinity of airports, tends to be congested, the FAA has established aircraft speed restrictions. In general, flights below 10,000 feet MSL are limited to a maximum indicated airspeed of 250 knots. When operating in Class C or D airspace, at or below 2,500 feet above the surface and within 4 nautical miles of the primary airport, you must not exceed 200 knots indicated airspeed. This 200-knot restriction also applies in airspace underlying a Class B area and in VFR corridors through Class B airspace.

SPECIAL USE AIRSPACE

Special use airspace is used to confine certain flight activities and to place limitations on aircraft operations which are not part of these activities. Special use airspace is divided into alert areas, military operations areas, warning areas, restricted areas, prohibited areas, controlled firing areas, and national security areas. [Figure 4-58]

SPECIAL USE AIRSPACE ON CHEYENNE SECTIONAL CHART

Unless otherwise noted altitudes are MSL and in feet; time is local.
Contact nearest FSS for information.
†Other time by NOTAM contact FSS

The word "TO" an altitude means "To and including."
"MON-FRI" indicates "Monday thru Friday"
FL – Flight Level
NO A/G – No air to ground communications

U.S. P–PROHIBITED, R–RESTRICTED, A–ALERT, W–WARNING, MOA–MILITARY OPERATIONS AREA

NUMBER	LOCATION	ALTITUDE	TIME OF USE	CONTROLLING AGENCY**
R-7001A	GUERNSEY, WY	TO BUT NOT INCL 8000	INTERMITTENT, 24 HRS IN ADVANCE BY NOTAM	ZDV CNTR
R-7001B	GUERNSEY, WY	8000 TO 23,500	INTERMITTENT, 24 HRS IN ADVANCE BY NOTAM	ZDV CNTR

**ZDV-Denver

MOA NAME	ALTITUDE OF USE*	TIME OF USE†	CONTROLLING AGENCY**
COUGAR A	100' AGL	0900-1600 TUE-SAT	ZDV CNTR
COUGAR B	10,000	0900-1600 TUE-SAT	ZDV CNTR
EDGEMONT A, B & C	12,000	INTERMITTENT BY NOTAM	ZDV CNTR
POWDER RIVER B	1000 AGL	INTERMITTENT BY NOTAM	ZDV CNTR
TILFORD	12,000	INTERMITTENT BY NOTAM	ZDV CNTR

*Altitudes indicate floor of MOA. All MOAs extend to but do not include FL 180 unless otherwise indicated in tabulation or on chart.
†Other time by NOTAM contact FSS
**ZDV-Denver

Figure 4-58. By referring to tables on each sectional chart, you can determine the altitudes, times of use, and controlling agencies for the special use airspace depicted on that specific chart.

ALERT AREAS

Areas shown on aeronautical charts to inform you of unusual types of aerial activities, such as parachute jumping, glider towing, or high concentrations of student pilot training are designated as **alert areas**. Pilots of participating aircraft and pilots transiting the area are equally responsible for collision avoidance, so you should be especially cautious when flying through alert areas. [Figure 4-59]

 Responsibility for collision avoidance in an alert area rests with all pilots.

Pilots are requested to avoid flight in the vicinity of the USAF Academy due to intensive student pilot training and parachute jumping from sunrise to sunset, seven days a week, surface to 17,500' MSL. Suggest flight east of I-25 at or above 9,000' MSL. For advisory information, contact Academy Tower on 124.15 MHz.

This alert area surrounding the U.S. Air Force Academy near Colorado Springs was established due to intensive student pilot training and parachute jumping.

Glider activity also exists in this area.

Check this out — the view from the top of Pikes Peak inspired Katherine Lee Bates to compose *America the Beautiful*.

Figure 4-59. Alert areas are designated by the letter A followed by a number.

MILITARY OPERATIONS AREAS

A **military operations area (MOA)** is a block of airspace in which military training and other military maneuvers are conducted. MOAs usually have specified floors and ceilings for containing military activities. VFR aircraft are not prevented from flying through active MOAs, but it is wise to avoid them when possible. Flight service stations within 100 nautical miles of an MOA are provided with information regarding the hours of operation. [Figure 4-60]

 While operating under VFR in an MOA, you should exercise extreme caution when military training activity is being conducted.

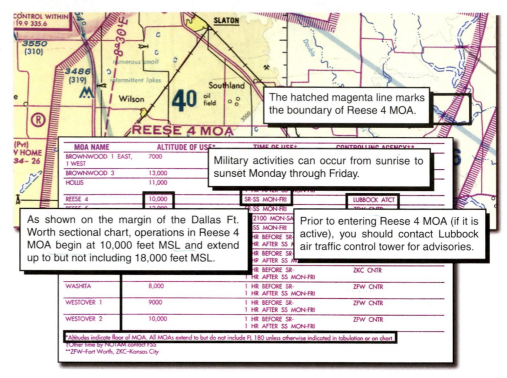

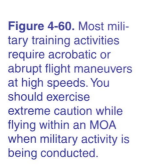

Figure 4-60. Most military training activities require acrobatic or abrupt flight maneuvers at high speeds. You should exercise extreme caution while flying within an MOA when military activity is being conducted.

The hatched magenta line marks the boundary of Reese 4 MOA.

Military activities can occur from sunrise to sunset Monday through Friday.

As shown on the margin of the Dallas Ft. Worth sectional chart, operations in Reese 4 MOA begin at 10,000 feet MSL and extend up to but not including 18,000 feet MSL.

Prior to entering Reese 4 MOA (if it is active), you should contact Lubbock air traffic control tower for advisories.

WARNING AREAS

A **warning area** is airspace of defined dimensions, extending from three nautical miles outward from the coast of the United States, that contains activity which may be hazardous to nonparticipating aircraft. Warning areas are depicted on aeronautical charts to caution nonparticipating pilots of the potential danger. A warning area may be located over domestic or international waters or both. [Figure 4-61]

 Warning areas often contain hazards such as aerial gunnery or guided missiles.

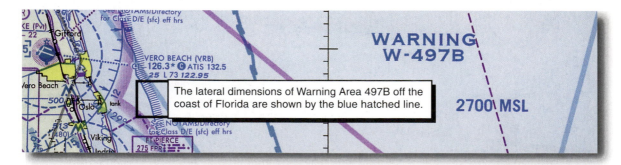

The lateral dimensions of Warning Area 497B off the coast of Florida are shown by the blue hatched line.

Figure 4-61. Hazards such as aerial gunnery and guided missiles may exist over the waters of warning areas.

RESTRICTED AREAS

Restricted areas often have invisible hazards to aircraft, such as artillery firing, aerial gunnery, or guided missiles. Permission to fly through restricted areas must be granted by the controlling agency. [Figure 4-62]

You must have the controlling agency's permission to fly through a restricted area.

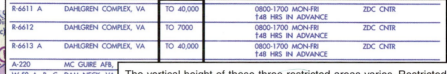

R-6611 A	DAHLGREN COMPLEX, VA	TO 40,000	0800-1700 MON-FRI †48 HRS IN ADVANCE	ZDC CNTR
R-6612	DAHLGREN COMPLEX, VA	TO 7000	0800-1700 MON-FRI †48 HRS IN ADVANCE	ZDC CNTR
R-6613 A	DAHLGREN COMPLEX, VA	TO 40,000	0800-1700 MON-FRI †48 HRS IN ADVANCE	ZDC CNTR
A-220	MC GUIRE AFB,			
W-50 A, B, C	DAM NECK, VA			

Figure 4-62. Although the dimensions of many restricted areas may be such that you can avoid them, extra caution is appropriate, even when you are flying near the area.

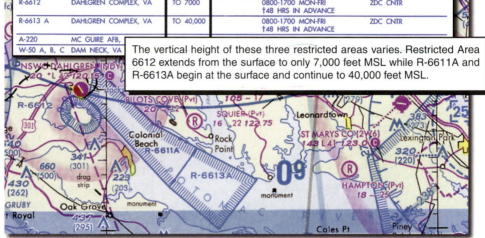

The vertical height of these three restricted areas varies. Restricted Area 6612 extends from the surface to only 7,000 feet MSL while R-6611A and R-6613A begin at the surface and continue to 40,000 feet MSL.

PROHIBITED AREAS

Prohibited areas are established for security or other reasons associated with national welfare and contain airspace within which the flight of aircraft is prohibited. You must obtain permission from the controlling agency to operate within a prohibited area. [Figure 4-63]

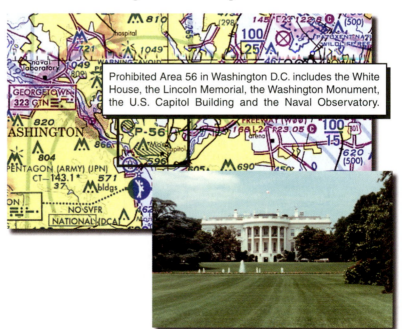

Prohibited Area 56 in Washington D.C. includes the White House, the Lincoln Memorial, the Washington Monument, the U.S. Capitol Building and the Naval Observatory.

Figure 4-63. Although the lateral dimensions of alert, warning, restricted, and prohibited areas are all shown on sectional charts by blue hatched lines, you can identify a prohibited area by the letter P followed by a number.

CONTROLLED FIRING AREAS

The distinguishing feature of a **controlled firing area** compared to other special use airspace, is that its activities are discontinued immediately when a spotter aircraft, radar, or ground lookout personnel determines an aircraft might be approaching the area. Since nonparticipating aircraft are not required to change their flight path, controlled firing areas are not depicted on aeronautical charts.

OTHER AIRSPACE AREAS

Other airspace areas mainly consist of national security areas, airport advisory areas and military training routes. Other segments in this category may be designated as temporary flight restrictions, flight limitations in proximity to space flight operations, and flight restrictions in proximity to the Presidential party. Parachute jump areas and terminal radar service areas (TRSAs) also are classified as other airspace areas.

NATIONAL SECURITY AREAS

National security areas (NSAs) are established at locations where there is a requirement for increased security and safety of ground facilities. You are requested to voluntarily avoid flying through an NSA. At times, flight through an NSA may be prohibited to provide a greater level of security and safety. A NOTAM is issued to advise you of any changes in an NSA's status. [Figure 4-64]

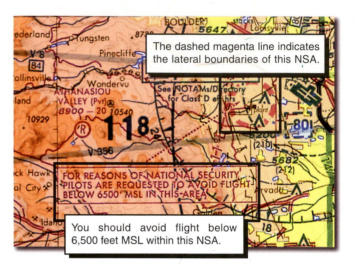

The dashed magenta line indicates the lateral boundaries of this NSA.

FOR REASONS OF NATIONAL SECURITY PILOTS ARE REQUESTED TO AVOID FLIGHT BELOW 6500' MSL IN THIS AREA.

You should avoid flight below 6,500 feet MSL within this NSA.

Figure 4-64. This NSA is established over Rocky Flats Environmental Technology Site located in Colorado.

AIRPORT ADVISORY AREAS

Airport advisory areas extend 10 statute miles from airports where there is a flight service station located on the field and no operating control tower. You normally will contact the FSS on the published CTAF frequency of 123.6 MHz prior to entering the airport advisory area. The FSS provides **local airport advisory service (LAA)**, which includes advisories on wind direction and velocity, favored runway, altimeter setting, and reported traffic within the area. [Figure 4-65]

Local airport advisory service (LAA) from the flight service station at Iliamna, Alaska is only available from May 1 through September 30.

Figure 4-65. In Alaska, several airport advisory areas operate on a seasonal basis.

MILITARY TRAINING ROUTES

Low-level, high-speed military training flights are conducted on **military training routes (MTRs)**. Generally, MTRs are established below 10,000 feet MSL for operations at speeds in excess of 250 knots. Routes at and below 1,500 feet AGL are designed to be flown under VFR; routes above 1,500 feet AGL are developed primarily to be flown under IFR. Although you are not restricted from flying through MTRs, you need to check with an

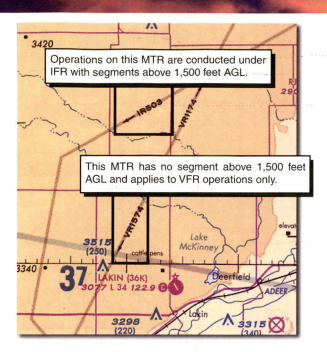

Operations on this MTR are conducted under IFR with segments above 1,500 feet AGL.

This MTR has no segment above 1,500 feet AGL and applies to VFR operations only.

FSS within 100 nautical miles to obtain the current information regarding MTR activity in your area. [Figure 4-66]

Military aircraft are normally operating at speeds in excess of 250 knots along MTRs.

MTRs are classified as VR or IR and are identified with a three or four number designation based on the type and altitude of the operations conducted on the specific route. See figure 4-66.

Figure 4-66. MTRs are classified as VR where VFR operations apply. Flights on routes marked IR are conducted in accordance with instrument flight rules regardless of the weather. MTRs with no segment above 1,500 feet AGL are identified by four numbers, while a three-number designation indicates that the MTR has one or more segments above 1,500 feet AGL.

TEMPORARY FLIGHT RESTRICTIONS

When necessary, **temporary flight restrictions** are imposed by the FAA to protect persons or property on the surface or in the air from a specific hazard or situation. The objectives are to provide a safe environment for rescue/relief operations and to prevent unsafe congestion of sightseeing or other aircraft above an incident or event which may generate high public interest. The FAA will issue a NOTAM designating the area in which a temporary restriction applies. Situations which warrant these restrictions include toxic spills, volcanic eruptions, nuclear incidents, aircraft hijackings, and forest fires.

For rescue/relief aircraft operations, the restricted airspace is normally limited to 2,000 feet above the surface within a 3 nautical mile radius. Incidents within Class B, C, or D airspace are handled through existing procedures, and usually do not require issuance of a NOTAM. In other cases, the FSS nearest the incident site normally is the coordination facility.

When a NOTAM is required, the format includes the facility establishing the temporary restriction, location, effective times, the area defined in statute miles, and the affected altitudes. The NOTAM also contains the FAA coordination facility, the reason for the restriction, the agency directing any relief activities, commercial telephone numbers, and other information considered appropriate by the issuing authority. [Figure 4-67]

Figure 4-67. A special edition of the Jacksonville sectional chart depicted temporary flight restriction areas established near Savannah, Georgia for the 1996 summer Olympic Games.

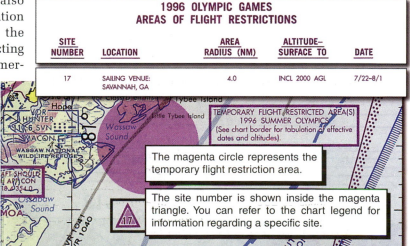

1996 OLYMPIC GAMES AREAS OF FLIGHT RESTRICTIONS

SITE NUMBER	LOCATION	AREA RADIUS (NM)	ALTITUDE– SURFACE TO	DATE
17	SAILING VENUE: SAVANNAH, GA	4.0	INCL 2000 AGL	7/22–8/1

TEMPORARY FLIGHT RESTRICTED AREA(S) 1996 SUMMER OLYMPICS (See chart border for tabulation of effective dates and altitudes).

The magenta circle represents the temporary flight restriction area.

The site number is shown inside the magenta triangle. You can refer to the chart legend for information regarding a specific site.

FLIGHT LIMITATIONS AND RESTRICTIONS

Flight limitations in proximity of space flight operations are designated by NOTAMs. These limitations provide protection for space flight crews and prevent costly delays. A NOTAM also may be issued to create flight restrictions in the proximity of the Presidential, and other, parties. This prevents aircraft operations over, or in the vicinity of, any area to be visited or traveled by the President, Vice President, or other public figure who may attract large numbers of people. When such NOTAMs are issued, they are considered to be regulatory. [Figure 4-68]

KENNEDY SPACE CENTER
FAR 91.143 SPACE OPERATIONS

ACTIVE: INTERMITTENT BY NOTAM
Listed under Melbourne (MLB)
(Launch minus 3 hrs - UFN)
(Recovery minus 3½ hrs - UFN)
ALTITUDES: Surface to unlimited
CONTACT: St Petersburg FSS 1-800-992-7433

You can contact St. Petersburg FSS for the current NOTAMs regarding flight limitations in this area.

CAUTION: UNMARKED BALLOON ON CABLE TO 15,000 MSL

Figure 4-68. FAR 91.143 refers to flight limitations in the proximity of space flight operations.

PARACHUTE JUMP AIRCRAFT AREAS

Parachute jump aircraft areas are tabulated in the *Airport/Facility Directory*. The busiest periods of activity are normally on weekends and holidays. Times of operation are local, and MSL altitudes are listed unless otherwise specified. [Figure 4-69]

This symbol represents a parachute jump area near Perry Airport.

Figure 4-69. Parachute jumping sites that have been used on a frequent basis and that have been in use for at least one year are depicted on sectional charts.

TERMINAL RADAR SERVICE AREAS

Terminal radar service areas (TRSAs) do not fit into any of the U.S. airspace classes. Originally part of the terminal radar program at selected airports, TRSAs have never been established as controlled airspace and, therefore, FAR Part 91 does not contain any rules for TRSA operations. By contacting approach control, you can receive radar services within a TRSA, but participation is not mandatory. [Figure 4-70]

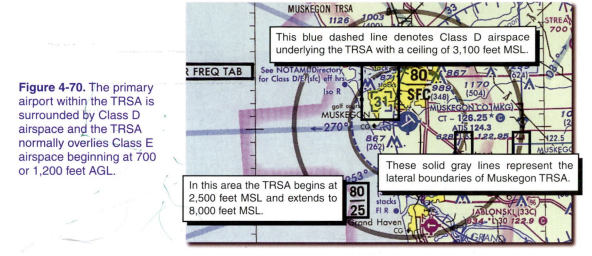

Figure 4-70. The primary airport within the TRSA is surrounded by Class D airspace and the TRSA normally overlies Class E airspace beginning at 700 or 1,200 feet AGL.

This blue dashed line denotes Class D airspace underlying the TRSA with a ceiling of 3,100 feet MSL.

In this area the TRSA begins at 2,500 feet MSL and extends to 8,000 feet MSL.

These solid gray lines represent the lateral boundaries of Muskegon TRSA.

EMERGENCY AIR TRAFFIC RULES

Emergency air traffic rules are established by the FAA immediately after determining that, without such action, the air traffic control system could not operate at the required level of safety and efficiency. If this happens, a NOTAM, which designates the applicable airspace, is issued to communicate information about the emergency rules governing flight operations and the use of navigation facilities. When a NOTAM is issued with this information, no one may operate an aircraft in conflict with it.

ADIZ

All aircraft entering domestic U.S. airspace from outside the country must provide identification prior to entry. **Air defense identification zones (ADIZs)** are established to facilitate this identification in the vicinity of U.S. international airspace boundaries. Generally, you must file an IFR or defense VFR (DVFR) flight plan for all operations that enter or exit an ADIZ. In addition, you are required to have an operating transponder with Mode C capability and a two-way radio to make periodic position reports. Failure to follow these rules may result in your aircraft being intercepted by U.S. security.

The Alaskan ADIZ, which lies along the coastal waters of Alaska has different operating rules than the contiguous U.S. ADIZs. If you are thinking about flying across any ADIZ, you should refer to the *Aeronautical Information Manual* or the *International Flight Information Manual* for detailed procedural information.

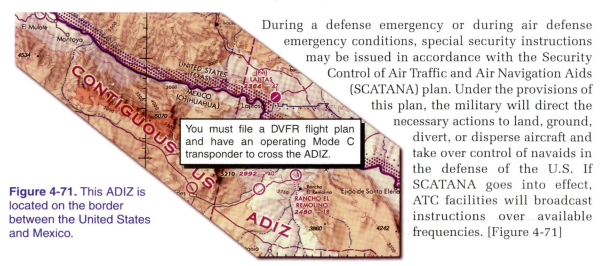

During a defense emergency or during air defense emergency conditions, special security instructions may be issued in accordance with the Security Control of Air Traffic and Air Navigation Aids (SCATANA) plan. Under the provisions of this plan, the military will direct the necessary actions to land, ground, divert, or disperse aircraft and take over control of navaids in the defense of the U.S. If SCATANA goes into effect, ATC facilities will broadcast instructions over available frequencies. [Figure 4-71]

You must file a DVFR flight plan and have an operating Mode C transponder to cross the ADIZ.

Figure 4-71. This ADIZ is located on the border between the United States and Mexico.

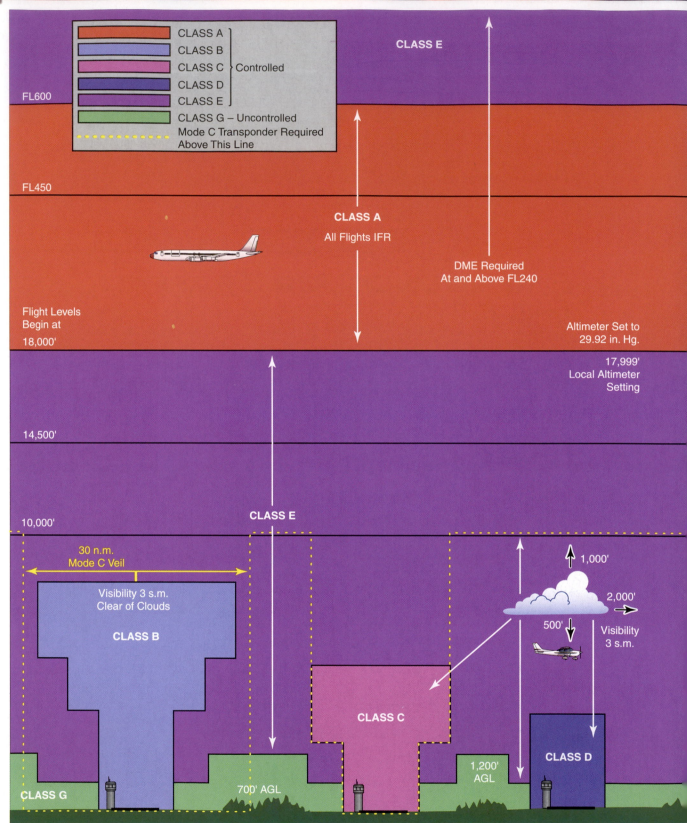

Now that you are familiar with the various classes of airspace, Chapter 5 will provide you with additional information regarding specific ATC services available and the radio procedures used to communicate with ATC in the airspace system. You can review the primary classes of airspace, their relationship to one another, and airspace operating requirements by referring to figures 4-72 and 4-73.

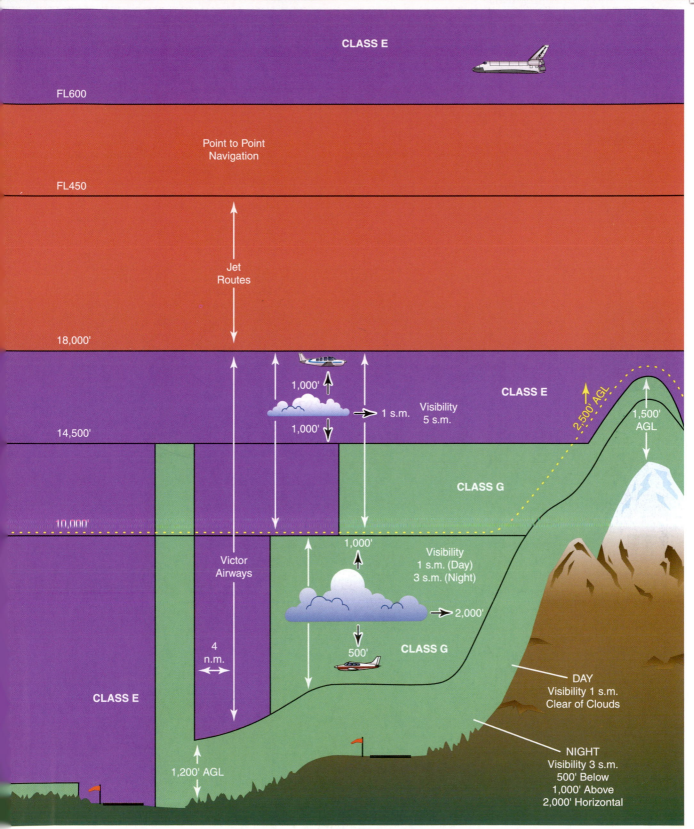

Figure 4-72. This diagram helps you to visualize how the various airspace areas interrelate. Distance measuring equipment (DME) is an instrument equipment requirement above FL240. You will learn more about DME in Chapter 9.

Airspace Features	Class A	Class B	Class C	Class D	Class E	Class G
VFR Min. Vis. and Distance from Clouds 1,200 ft AGL or less (Regardless of MSL Altitude)	N/A	N/A	N/A	N/A	N/A	Day 1 s.m. Clear of Clouds Night 3 s.m. 500 ft Below 1,000 ft Above 2,000 ft Horizontal
VFR Minimum Visibility	N/A	3 Statute Miles	3 Statute Miles	3 Statute Miles	Below 10,000 ft MSL – 3 s.m. At or Above 10,000 MSL – 5 s.m.	Below 10,000 ft MSL – Day 1 s.m. Night 3 s.m. At or Above 10,000 MSL – 5 s.m. (above 1,200 ft AGL)
VFR Minimum Distance from Clouds	N/A	Clear of Clouds	500 ft Below 1,000 ft Above 2,000 ft Horizontal	500 ft Below 1,000 ft Above 2,000 ft Horizontal	Below 10,000 ft MSL – 500 ft Below 1,000 ft Above 2,000 ft Horizontal At or Above 10,000 ft MSL – 1,000 ft Below 1,000 ft Above 1 s.m. Horizontal	Below 10,000 ft MSL – 500 ft Below 1,000 ft Above 2,000 ft Horizontal (above 1,200 ft AGL) At or Above 10,000 ft MSL – 1,000 ft Below 1,000 ft Above 1 s.m. Horizontal (above 1,200 ft AGL)
Minimum Pilot Qualifications	Instrument Rating	Private Pilot Certificate Student Pilot Certificate Endorsement	Student Pilot Certificate	Student Pilot Certificate	Student Pilot Certificate	Student Pilot Certificate
VFR Entry and Equipment Requirements	IFR Flight Plan and IFR Clearance Required	ATC Clearance Transponder with Mode C	Establish Radio Communication Transponder with Mode C	Establish Radio Communication	None	None
ATC Services	All Aircraft Separation	All Aircraft Separation	IFR/IFR Separation IFR/VFR Separation VFR Traffic Advisories (workload permitting)	IFR/IFR Separation VFR Traffic Advisories (workload permitting)	IFR/IFR Separation VFR Traffic Advisories on Request (workload permitting)	VFR Traffic Advisories on Request (workload permitting)

Figure 4-73. You can use this table as a quick reference for the VFR weather minimums and operating requirements of each class of airspace.

SUMMARY CHECKLIST

✓ In each class of airspace, you must maintain specific VFR weather minimums (minimum flight visibilities and distances from clouds).

✓ While operating in controlled airspace (Class A, Class B, Class C, Class D, and Class E) you are subject to certain operating rules, as well as pilot qualification and aircraft equipment requirements.

✓ ATC does not exercise control of air traffic in uncontrolled, or Class G, airspace.

✓ Class G airspace typically extends from the surface to 700 or 1,200 feet AGL. In some areas, Class G may extend from the surface to 14,500 feet MSL.

✓ A transponder is an electronic device aboard the airplane which enhances your aircraft's identity on an ATC radar screen.

✓ The FARs require that you have an operating transponder with Mode C capability when flying at or above 10,000 feet MSL (excluding the airspace at and below 2,500 feet AGL), in Class A airspace, Class B airspace, within 30 nautical miles of Class B primary airports, and in and above Class C airspace.

✓ There are no communication requirements to operate within Class E airspace, but you can request traffic advisory services which ATC provides on a workload-permitting basis.

✓ Federal airways are usually 8 nautical miles wide, begin at 1,200 feet AGL, and extend up to but not including 18,000 feet MSL.

✓ You must establish two-way radio communication with the tower prior to entering Class D airspace and maintain radio contact during all operations to, from, or on that airport.

✓ Prior to entering Class C airspace, you must establish two-way communication with the ATC facility having jurisdiction and maintain it while you are operating within the airspace. Within a Class C area, ATC provides radar service to all IFR and VFR aircraft.

✓ Located at some of the country's major airports, Class B airspace has different levels which are portrayed as a series of interconnected circular patterns around the airport.

✓ Prior to entering any part of Class B airspace, you are required to obtain a clearance from ATC.

✓ To operate in Class B airspace, you must be at least a private pilot or a student pilot with the appropriate logbook endorsement.

✓ Whenever you are flying VFR in or around Class B airspace, VFR terminal area charts will help significantly with orientation and navigation.

✓ VFR flyway planning charts, published on the reverse side of some VFR terminal area charts, show VFR routes for transitioning around, under, and through Class B airspace.

✓ To operate within Class A airspace, you must be instrument rated, and your aircraft must be transponder equipped, operated under an IFR flight plan, and controlled directly by ATC.

✓ A special VFR clearance must be obtained from ATC to operate within the surface areas of Class B, C, D, or E airspace when the ground visibility is less than 3 statute miles and the cloud ceiling is less than 1,000 feet AGL.

✓ Since the airspace at lower altitudes, and especially in the vicinity of airports, tends to be congested, the FAA has established aircraft speed restrictions.

✓ Alert areas are shown on aeronautical charts to inform you of unusual types of aerial activities, such as parachute jumping and glider towing, or high concentrations of student pilot training.

✓ A military operations area (MOA) is a block of airspace in which military training and other military maneuvers are conducted.

✓ Warning areas extend from three nautical miles outward from the coast of the United States and contain activity which may be hazardous to nonparticipating aircraft.

✓ Restricted areas often have invisible hazards to aircraft, such as artillery firing, aerial gunnery, or guided missiles. Permission to fly through restricted areas must be granted by the controlling agency.

✓ Prohibited areas are established for security or other reasons associated with the national welfare and contain airspace within which the flight of aircraft is prohibited.

✓ Activities within a controlled firing area are discontinued immediately when a spotter aircraft, radar, or ground lookout personnel determines an aircraft might be approaching the area.

✓ Airport advisory areas extend 10 statute miles from airports where there is an FSS located on the field and no operating control tower.

✓ Generally, military training routes (MTRs) are established below 10,000 feet MSL for operations at speeds in excess of 250 knots.

✓ Temporary flight restrictions are imposed by the FAA to protect persons or property on the surface or in the air from a specific hazard or situation.

✓ Emergency air traffic rules are established by the FAA immediately after determining that, without such action, the air traffic control system could not operate at the required level of safety and efficiency.

✓ Air defense identification zones (ADIZs) are established to facilitate identification of aircraft in the vicinity of U.S. international airspace boundaries.

KEY TERMS

Airspace	Class E Airspace
VFR Weather Minimums	Federal Airways
Controlled Airspace	Victor Airways
Uncontrolled Airspace	Class D Airspace
Class G Airspace	Class C Airspace
Transponder	Class B Airspace

VFR Terminal Area Charts

VFR Flyway Planning Charts

Class A Airspace

Special VFR Clearance

Special Use Airspace

Alert Area

Military Operations Area (MOA)

Warning Area

Restricted Area

Prohibited Area

Controlled Firing Area

National Security Area (NSA)

Other Airspace Areas

Airport Advisory Area

Local Airport Advisory Service (LAA)

Military Training Route (MTR)

Temporary Flight Restriction

Parachute Jump Aircraft Area

Terminal Radar Service Area (TRSA)

Air Defense Identification Zone (ADIZ)

QUESTIONS

1. If you are flying in the traffic pattern at 8,700 feet MSL during daylight hours, what minimum cloud clearance and visibility would you have to maintain at Questa 2 Airport?

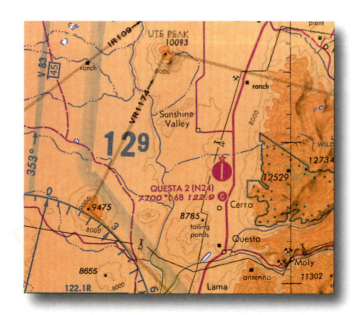

2. Select the true statement regarding transponder operation.

   A. To enter Class D airspace, you are required to have a Mode C transponder.
   B. You are required to have a Mode C transponder from 2,500 feet AGL up to and including 10,000 feet MSL.
   C. The FARs require that you have an operating Mode C transponder in Class B airspace and within 30 nautical miles of the Class B primary airport.

3. What minimum visibility and cloud clearance must you maintain if you are at the position shown by the airplane symbol at an altitude of 4,500 feet MSL.

4. Which airport has Class D airspace?

5. What is the floor and ceiling of the shelf area of Class C airspace that contains the airplane symbol?

6. True/False. You must obtain a clearance prior to operating within a 30 nautical mile radius from the primary airport in Class B airspace.

7. If your airplane is at 5,500 feet MSL in the position shown by the airplane symbol, what are your weather minimums?

8. Class A airspace begins at what altitude?

9. What is the maximum airspeed that you can fly below 10,000 feet MSL?

10. Explain when it would be necessary to request a special VFR clearance.

11. Which of these areas can you enter without permission from the controlling agency?

CHAPTER 5

COMMUNICATION AND FLIGHT INFORMATION

Part II, Chapter 5 — Communication and Flight Information

Discovery Workshop — Flight Operations

SECTION A
RADAR AND ATC SERVICES

Air traffic control began in the 1930's with a system that used teletype machines, wall-sized blackboards, large table maps, and markers representing airplanes. Controllers moved the markers across a map to estimate the positions of aircraft. Radar, developed during World War II, made possible the surveillance of traffic in the air, and was eventually adapted to the control of aircraft taxiing on the surface of large airports during low visibility. Although radar increased the capacity of the airspace system, ATC procedures were still labor-intensive. Controllers were required to spend 75% of their time in voice communication and in activities such as recording flight progress on paper strips. When radar was combined with computers and aircraft transponders, ATC services became substantially more effective.

RADAR

Radar (radio detection and ranging) uses a synchronized radio transmitter and receiver to emit radio waves and process their reflections for display. **Primary radar** is a ground-based system used by ATC which transmits radio waves in a narrow beam by a rotating antenna. When the radio waves strike your aircraft, some of the waves are reflected back to the antenna and processed to provide a display, or echo, which shows your aircraft's location on a radarscope. An electron beam (sweep) emanates from the center of the scope (a cathode ray tube) and rotates in the same direction as the radar antenna. The intensity of the sweep is too low to generate much light on the face of the tube until it reaches a point corresponding to your aircraft. At this point, the return echo is intensified to produce a blip of light which represents your aircraft.

The **range** of your aircraft (distance from the antenna) is determined by measuring the time it takes (at 186,000 miles per second) for the radio waves to reach your aircraft and then return to the receiving antenna. The **azimuth**, or angle of your aircraft from the radar site, is determined by the position of the rotating antenna when the reflected portion of the radio wave is received. It is measured clockwise from north in a horizontal plane. [Figure 5-1]

In spite of its capabilities, primary radar has some serious limitations. One of these is the bending of radar pulses, or anomalous propagation, which can be caused by atmospheric temperature inversions. If the radar beam is bent toward the ground, extraneous returns, known as ground clutter, may appear on the radarscope.

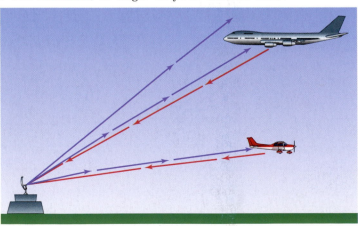

Figure 5-1. The radar antenna is designed to both transmit radio waves and receive the reflected signals.

It's All Light to Me

Radar uses radio waves (electromagnetic waves) which travel at 186,000 miles per second, commonly referred to as the speed of light. In fact, these waves are just a different frequency of light. When you listen to music, you perceive different frequencies of sound as different tones. The same concept applies to light. Different frequencies of visible light are perceived as different colors. For example, red light has a frequency of about 460 trillion (460×10^{12}) waves per second, while violet light has a frequency of approximately 710 trillion (710×10^{12}) waves per second.

Just as some sounds are too high- or too low-pitched for humans to hear, some frequencies are outside our range of vision. For example, gamma rays are transmitted at frequencies much higher than visible light — around a billion billion waves per second and long radio waves exist at low frequencies of approximately one wave per second. Radar uses light to "see" traffic. The radio waves used in ASR-9, a radar system commonly used by ATC facilities, have a frequency of 2.7 billion (2.7×10^{9}) waves per second. Waves per second are more commonly referred to as cycles per second or hertz. One gigahertz equals 1 billion hertz, therefore, ASR-9 has a frequency of 2.7 GHz (gigahertz).

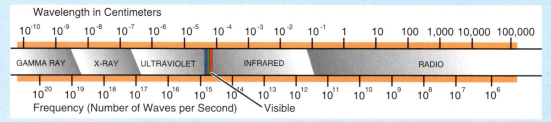

If the beam is bent upward, detection range is reduced. In addition, precipitation or heavy clouds can produce returns which can block out the display of aircraft. To help combat ground clutter and weather phenomena, devices called moving target indicators (MTIs) and moving target detectors (MTDs) eliminate slow-moving and stationary objects. Two of the most significant drawbacks to the primary radar system are its inability to easily identify an individual aircraft return and to display an aircraft's altitude.

The **air traffic control radar beacon system (ATCRBS)**, which sometimes is referred to as **secondary surveillance radar**, or simply secondary radar, overcomes most of the limitations of primary radar. Although ATCRBS is a separate system and capable of operating independently, ATC typically uses secondary and primary radar together. The ATCRBS incorporates three components in addition to primary radar; a decoder, an interrogator, and a transponder. [Figure 5-2]

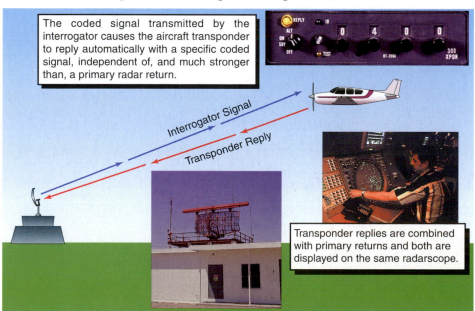

The coded signal transmitted by the interrogator causes the aircraft transponder to reply automatically with a specific coded signal, independent of, and much stronger than, a primary radar return.

Interrogator Signal

Transponder Reply

Transponder replies are combined with primary returns and both are displayed on the same radarscope.

Figure 5-2. The decoder, which is part of the ground equipment, enables a controller to assign a discrete transponder code to your aircraft and is designed to receive Mode C altitude information. Normally only one code will be assigned by the computer for your entire flight.

TRANSPONDER OPERATION

Since transponder returns are the basis for radar separation, regulations require that transponders be tested and inspected every 24 calendar months for operations in controlled airspace. To operate your transponder correctly, you need to become familiar with its features. [Figure 5-3] The function selector of a typical transponder has several positions, which usually include OFF, SBY (STANDBY), ON, ALT (ALTITUDE), and TST (TEST). You can set up to 4,096 four-digit codes on your transponder. The term **squawk** is used by the controller to assign your aircraft a code, as well as to indicate which transponder function you should select. [Figure 5-4]

The reply/monitor light illuminates when you select the test feature to show proper operation. It also flashes when the transponder is replying to interrogation signals or transmitting ident pulses.

 You may not use a transponder for operations in controlled airspace unless it has been tested and inspected within at least the preceding 24 calendar months.

The function selector turns the unit on or off and controls the mode of operation.

Figure 5-3. The ALT position selected on this transponder activates the Mode C altitude encoding feature. The number 1200 is the standard code for VFR operations.

Pressing the IDENT button causes the transponder return to blossom on the radar screen for a few seconds, allowing the controller to establish positive radar contact.

A typical transponder can be set to display any number between zero and seven. This gives a total of 4,096 possible codes.

Figure 5-4. Controllers use distinctive phraseology when referring to transponder operation.

Transponder Phraseology
"Squawk (Number)" Operate your transponder on designated code.
"Squawk Standby" Switch your transponder to STANDBY position.
"Stop Altitude Squawk" Turn off the automatic altitude reporting feature of your transponder.
"Squawk Altitude" Activate the automatic altitude reporting feature of your transponder.
"Ident" Press the IDENT feature of your transponder.
"Squawk (Number) and Ident" Operate your transponder on designated code and press the IDENT feature.
"Squawk Low/Normal" Operate your transponder on LOW or NORMAL, as specified. Transponder is operated in NORMAL position unless ATC specifies LOW. ON is used instead of NORMAL on some types of transponders, and many do not have a LOW position.
"Stop Squawk" Switch your transponder OFF.
"Squawk MAYDAY on 7700" Operate your transponder on code 7700.
"Squawk VFR" Operate your transponder on code 1200.

You should be careful to avoid codes 7500, 7600, and 7700 when you are making routine code changes on your transponder. Inadvertent selection of these codes may cause momentary false alarms at radar facilities. Code 7500 alerts ATC that an aircraft has been hijacked; 7600 is used after the failure of two-way radio communication; and 7700 is used for all other emergencies. For example, when switching from code 2700 to code 7200, switch first to 2200, then to 7200; do not switch to 7700 and then to 7200. This procedure also applies to code 7500 and all codes in the 7600 and 7700 series (7600-7677 and 7700-7777). [Figure 5-5]

 When making routine transponder code changes, you should avoid inadvertent selection of 7500, 7600, and 7700.

 The standard transponder code for VFR operations is 1200.

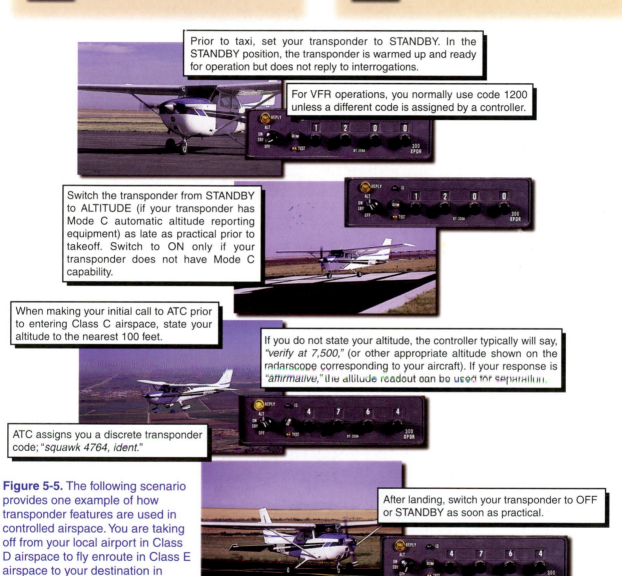

Prior to taxi, set your transponder to STANDBY. In the STANDBY position, the transponder is warmed up and ready for operation but does not reply to interrogations.

For VFR operations, you normally use code 1200 unless a different code is assigned by a controller.

Switch the transponder from STANDBY to ALTITUDE (if your transponder has Mode C automatic altitude reporting equipment) as late as practical prior to takeoff. Switch to ON only if your transponder does not have Mode C capability.

When making your initial call to ATC prior to entering Class C airspace, state your altitude to the nearest 100 feet.

If you do not state your altitude, the controller typically will say, "verify at 7,500," (or other appropriate altitude shown on the radarscope corresponding to your aircraft). If your response is "affirmative," the altitude readout can be used for separation.

ATC assigns you a discrete transponder code; "squawk 4764, ident."

After landing, switch your transponder to OFF or STANDBY as soon as practical.

Figure 5-5. The following scenario provides one example of how transponder features are used in controlled airspace. You are taking off from your local airport in Class D airspace to fly enroute in Class E airspace to your destination in Class C airspace.

In cases where your altitude readout differs significantly (300 feet or more) from your reported altitude, the controller will issue instructions such as, "Stop altitude squawk, altitude differs by 350 feet." This means you should turn off Mode C altitude reporting but continue to operate your transponder on Mode A. This could mean your Mode C equipment is not calibrated properly or you have an incorrect altimeter setting. The wrong altimeter setting has no direct effect on your Mode C readout, since the transponder is preset at 29.92. However, it would cause your actual altitude to vary from the one assigned by the controller. Be sure to verify that your altimeter setting is correct whenever the controller indicates your Mode C readout is invalid. If the controller subsequently needs your Mode C information, the phrase "squawk *altitude"* will be used. Occasionally, during flight, the controller may direct you to *"squawk standby"* for operational reasons.

FAA RADAR SYSTEMS

The FAA operates two basic radar systems; airport surveillance radar and air route surveillance radar. Both of these surveillance systems use primary and secondary radar returns, as well as sophisticated computers and software programs designed to give the controller additional information, such as aircraft speed and altitude.

AIRPORT SURVEILLANCE RADAR

The direction and coordination of IFR traffic within specific terminal areas is delegated to **airport surveillance radar (ASR)** facilities. Approach and departure control manage traffic at airports with ASR. This radar system is designed to provide relatively short-range coverage in the airport vicinity and to serve as an expeditious means of handling terminal area traffic. The ASR also can be used as an instrument approach aid. **Terminal radar approach control facilities (TRACONs)** provide radar and nonradar services at major airports. The primary responsibility of each TRACON is to ensure safe separation of aircraft transitioning from departure to cruise flight or from cruise to a landing approach.

Most ASR facilities throughout the country utilize a form of the **automated radar terminal system (ARTS)**. This system has several different configurations which depend on the computer equipment and software programs used. Usually the busiest terminals in the country have the most sophisticated computers and programs. The type of system installed is designated by a suffix of numbers and letters. For example, an ARTS-IIIA installation can detect, track, and predict primary, as well as secondary, radar returns.

On a controller's radar screen, ARTS equipment automatically provides a continuous display of an aircraft's position, altitude, groundspeed, and other pertinent information. This information is updated continuously as the aircraft progresses through the terminal area. To gain maximum benefit from the system, each aircraft in the area must be equipped with a Mode C transponder and its associated altitude encoding altimeter, although this is not an operational requirement. Direct altitude readouts eliminate the need for time-consuming verbal communication between controllers and pilots to verify altitude. This helps to increase the number of aircraft which may be handled by one controller at a given time. [Figure 5-6]

Primary Target

Aircraft ID

Groundspeed readout is 230 knots.

Mode C altitude readout is 15,100 feet MSL.

Aircraft is equipped with a traffic collision avoidance system (TCAS)

Figure 5-6. An ARTS-III radar display shows primary and secondary returns, as well as computer-generated alphanumerics. The alphanumeric data include the aircraft call sign, the altitude readout, and the groundspeed.

AIR ROUTE SURVEILLANCE RADAR

The long-range radar equipment used in controlled airspace to manage traffic is the **air route surveillance radar (ARSR)** system. There are approximately 100 ARSR facilities to relay traffic information to radar controllers throughout the country. Some of these facilities can detect only transponder-equipped aircraft and are referred to as beacon-only sites. Each air route surveillance radar site can monitor aircraft flying within a 200-mile radius of the antenna, although some stations can monitor aircraft as far away as 600 miles through the use of remote sites.

The direction and coordination of IFR traffic in the U.S. is assigned to **air route traffic control centers (ARTCCs)**. These centers are the authority for issuing IFR clearances and managing IFR traffic, however they also provide services to VFR pilots. Workload permitting, controllers will provide traffic advisories and course guidance, or vectors, if requested. Because of their extensive radar coverage, centers can be of assistance if you are lost and disoriented. [Figure 5-7]

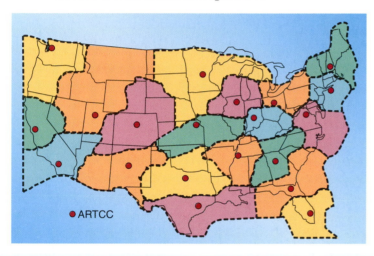

Figure 5-7. There are 20 ARTCCs established within the contiguous U.S. Each center is responsible for IFR traffic within its assigned geographical area.

Invisible Aircraft

The Lockheed F-117, or Stealth, fighter is designed to have little or no radar signature. Radar cross-section (RCS) and radar absorbent material (RAM) are the two features which play a vital role in the design of stealth aircraft. Reducing the amount of surface area, or RCS, of an aircraft can make it difficult for radar to detect. A computer program used to design the F-117 employed a shaping technique called faceting to transform the normally smooth surfaces of an aircraft into a series of triangular and trapezoidal segments which scatter radar waves and reflect very little back to the receiver. The radar cross section of a normal airplane is generally a minimum of 5 square meters. The F-117's RCS is between 0.001 and 0.01 meters which makes this airplane appear to be no larger than a small bird on a radarscope.

Radar absorbent material, which can be sprayed on, covers the entire skin of the aircraft and further reduces the reflection of radar waves. For peacetime operations, the F-117 carries large radar reflectors so it is visible to civilian ATC radar.

Courtesy of Lockheed Martin

VFR Radar Services

Radar services for VFR aircraft usually are available from any ATC radar facility. This includes ARTCCs, as well as ASR facilities in terminal areas. Traffic advisories, safety alerts, radar assistance, sequencing, and separation may be provided by ATC in radar areas, however, the types of services available depend on the facility.

Radar Traffic Information Service

ATC radar facilities routinely provide traffic information to IFR aircraft. As a pilot of a VFR aircraft, you may request **radar traffic information service**, also called **VFR radar advisory service**, which is intended to alert you to air traffic relevant to your flight. This service also is often referred to as **flight following**.

When giving traffic alerts, controllers reference traffic from your airplane as if it were a clock. For example, if a controller says, *"traffic at 11 o'clock,"* it means the traffic appears to the controller to be about 30° left of your nose. You should look for the traffic anywhere between the nose (12 o'clock) and left wing (9 o'clock) of your airplane. After you locate the traffic, tell the controller that you have the traffic *"in sight."* You should maintain visual contact with the traffic until it is no longer a factor. If you do not see the traffic, acknowledge the advisory by telling the controller *"negative contact."* [Figure 5-8]

Figure 5-8. A radar screen cannot adjust for the amount of wind correction you may be using to maintain your track over the ground. In this example, the controller thinks that the traffic is at your 11 o'clock position, but your wind correction angle places it at your 10 o'clock position.

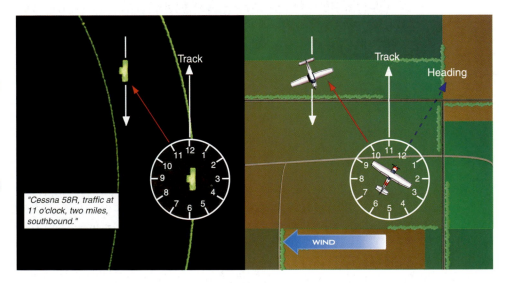

"Cessna 58R, traffic at 11 o'clock, two miles, southbound."

When you are operating in the radar environment, you should remember that the altitude of the reported traffic may not be known if the aircraft is not equipped with a Mode C transponder and the pilot is not in communication with ATC. Therefore, the traffic may be well above or below your flight path.

Controllers reference traffic from your airplane as if it were a clock. See figure 5-8. For example, if you are flying a heading of 090° and ATC states, *"traffic 3 o'clock, 2 miles westbound,"* you should look for the traffic to the south.

The basic purpose of VFR radar advisory service is to alert you to possible conflicting traffic, not to relieve you of your responsibility for collision avoidance. The controller's first responsibility is to serve the needs of aircraft flying on IFR flight plans. Many factors, such as limitations of radar, volume of traffic, controller workload, or frequency congestion, may prevent the controller from providing radar service to VFR pilots.

CONTROLLED FLIGHT INTO TERRAIN

Controlled flight into terrain (CFIT) defines a situation when an aircraft is flown into terrain or water with no prior awareness on the part of the pilot or crew of impending danger. Caused by lack of situational awareness, many CFIT accidents could be avoided through improved planning, understanding, and training.

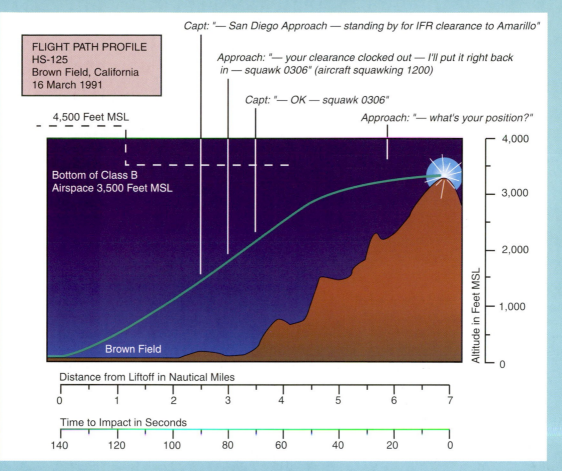

FLIGHT PATH PROFILE
HS-125
Brown Field, California
16 March 1991

Capt: "— San Diego Approach — standing by for IFR clearance to Amarillo"

Approach: "— your clearance clocked out — I'll put it right back in — squawk 0306" (aircraft squawking 1200)

Capt: "— OK — squawk 0306"

Approach: "— what's your position?"

4,500 Feet MSL

Bottom of Class B
Airspace 3,500 Feet MSL

Brown Field

Distance from Liftoff in Nautical Miles
0   1   2   3   4   5   6   7

Time to Impact in Seconds
140   120   100   80   60   40   20   0

Altitude in Feet MSL
4,000
3,000
2,000
1,000
0

At 1:45 a.m. on March 16, 1991, a Hawker jet (HS-125) crashed into the side of Otay Mountain located 8 nautical miles northeast of San Diego's Brown Field Municipal Airport. The crew of 2 and all 8 passengers perished. It was a clear moonless night when the jet departed Brown Field under VFR. Although they were unfamiliar with the area's terrain, the crew opted to stay below the San Diego Class B airspace until they could obtain an IFR clearance. Two minutes after departure and prior to obtaining the instrument clearance from San Diego approach control, the Hawker erupted into a fireball as it flew into the terrain at 3,300 feet MSL, only 72 feet from clearing the top of Otay Mountain.

Learning to effectively use your resources can help you to maintain situational awareness and prevent an accident like this from occurring. ATC radar services are a valuable resource and should be used to the maximum extent possible, especially in an unfamiliar area. Although use of ATC radar services can increase safety, you should not become complacent while under radar contact. Understand the limitations of these services and maintain situational awareness at all times. A thorough knowledge of the terrain along your route can be obtained by studying aeronautical charts, the *Airport/Facility Directory*, or other flight information publications. In addition, another pilot or passenger on board can be enlisted to help you monitor the terrain.

SAFETY ALERTS

ATC radar facilities issue safety alerts to aircraft under their control when, in the controller's judgment, safety may be compromised. For example, you may receive a **safety alert** if you are in unsafe proximity to terrain, obstructions, or another aircraft. If terrain or obstructions are involved, the controller will say, *". . . low altitude alert, check your altitude immediately."* If other traffic is involved, the controller may say, *". . . traffic alert, advise you turn right, heading 090 or climb to 8,000 immediately."* Safety alerts are not automatic, although an ARTS function called **minimum safe altitude warning (MSAW)** will alert the controller when an aircraft is in unsafe proximity to terrain or obstructions. You may request MSAW monitoring if your aircraft is Mode C equipped. Keep in mind that safety alerts are contingent on the capability of the controller to recognize unsafe situations, uncontrolled aircraft often are involved, and the primary method of detecting unsafe proximity is through Mode C altitude readouts.

RADAR ASSISTANCE TO VFR AIRCRAFT

ATC radar facilities may provide navigation service, or **vectors**, to VFR aircraft in certain situations on the basis that the navigational guidance information issued is advisory in nature and the job of flying the aircraft safely remains with the pilot. You may be given vectors if the controller suggests the vector and you agree, a special program has been established and vectoring service has been advertised, or in the controller's judgment the vector is necessary for air safety. If you are provided with radar vectors by ATC you should keep the controller advised of the weather conditions along your course. In many cases, controllers cannot determine if a vector will result in flight into instrument conditions.

TERMINAL VFR RADAR SERVICE

Terminal VFR radar service is a national program which extends the terminal radar services for IFR aircraft to VFR aircraft. The program has four types of service — basic radar service, terminal radar service area (TRSA) service, Class C service, and Class B service. The type of service provided at a given airport is published in the *Airport/Facility Directory*. Pilots operating under VFR are required to participate in Class B and C services. However, participation in basic and TRSA service, although encouraged, is voluntary for VFR pilots.

Basic radar service in the terminal radar program includes traffic advisories and limited vectoring to VFR aircraft.

Basic radar service for VFR aircraft includes safety alerts, traffic advisories, and limited radar vectoring. Sequencing also is available at certain terminal locations. The objective of sequencing is to adjust the flow of arriving IFR and VFR aircraft into the traffic pattern in a safe and orderly manner and to provide traffic advisories to departing VFR aircraft. Depending on the traffic conditions, you may use your own navigation to enter the pattern or approach control may provide you with routing or vectors for proper sequencing with other VFR and IFR traffic enroute to the airport. If you report having a preceding aircraft in sight, you may be instructed to follow that aircraft, however, you are not authorized to comply with any instructions issued to the preceding aircraft. When you are departing an airport which provides basic radar service, you should request radar traffic information by notifying ground control on initial contact. [Figure 5-9]

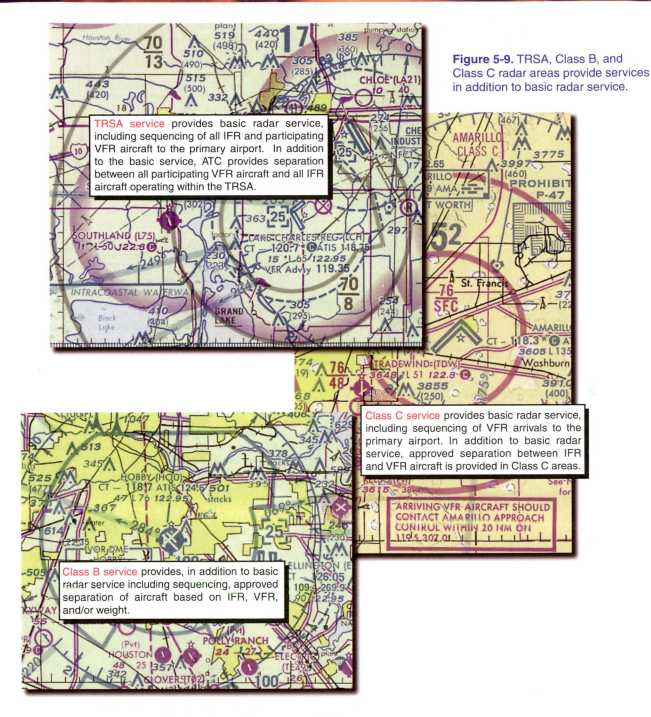

Figure 5-9. TRSA, Class B, and Class C radar areas provide services in addition to basic radar service.

TRSA service provides basic radar service, including sequencing of all IFR and participating VFR aircraft to the primary airport. In addition to the basic service, ATC provides separation between all participating VFR aircraft and all IFR aircraft operating within the TRSA.

Class C service provides basic radar service, including sequencing of VFR arrivals to the primary airport. In addition to basic radar service, approved separation between IFR and VFR aircraft is provided in Class C areas.

Class B service provides, in addition to basic radar service including sequencing, approved separation of aircraft based on IFR, VFR, and/or weight.

AUTOMATIC TERMINAL INFORMATION SERVICE

At busy airports, it would be difficult and time consuming for controllers to give every aircraft a separate airport advisory. To improve controller effectiveness and to reduce frequency congestion, **automatic terminal information service (ATIS)** is available in selected high activity terminal areas. ATIS is prerecorded and broadcast continuously on its own frequency. At larger airports, there may be one ATIS frequency for departing aircraft and another one for arriving aircraft. ATIS broadcasts are labeled with successive letters from the phonetic alphabet, such as Information Alpha or Information Bravo. Each new ATIS broadcast is identified by the next letter. You will find a complete listing of the phonetic alphabet in Section B. ATIS is updated when airport conditions change, or when any official weather is received, regardless of content change. Although, you may listen to the broadcast as many times as necessary, you may find it helpful to write down the ATIS information. [Figure 5-10]

 Automatic terminal information service (ATIS) is the continuous broadcast of noncontrol airport information at selected high activity terminal areas.

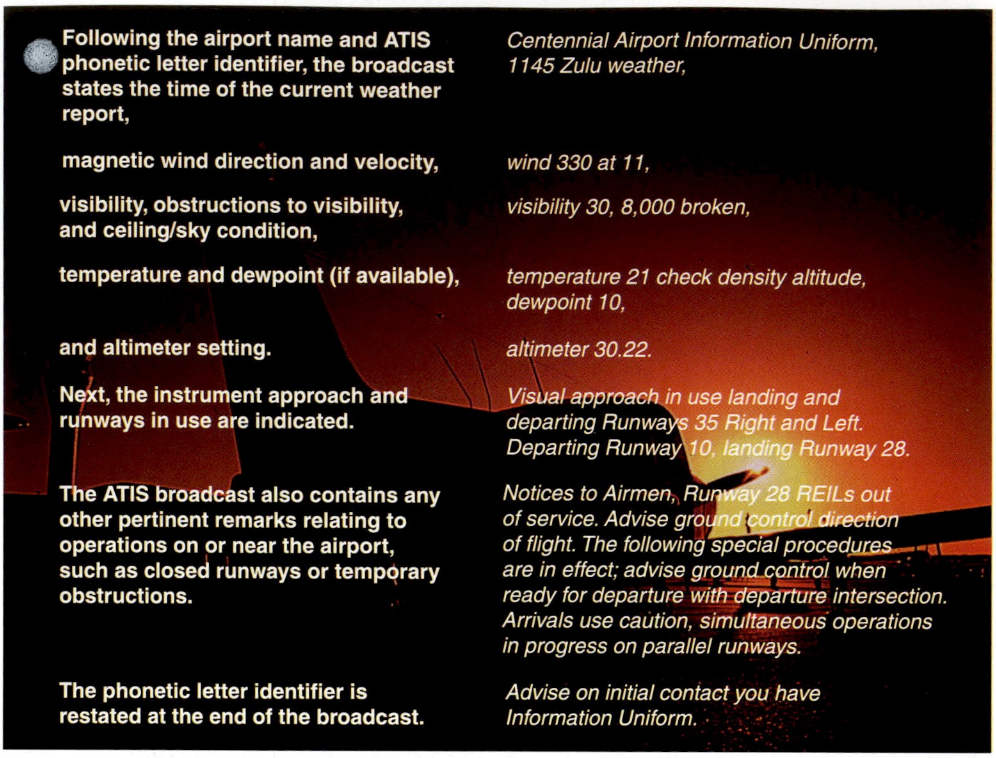

Following the airport name and ATIS phonetic letter identifier, the broadcast states the time of the current weather report,

Centennial Airport Information Uniform, 1145 Zulu weather,

magnetic wind direction and velocity,

wind 330 at 11,

visibility, obstructions to visibility, and ceiling/sky condition,

visibility 30, 8,000 broken,

temperature and dewpoint (if available),

temperature 21 check density altitude, dewpoint 10,

and altimeter setting.

altimeter 30.22.

Next, the instrument approach and runways in use are indicated.

Visual approach in use landing and departing Runways 35 Right and Left. Departing Runway 10, landing Runway 28.

The ATIS broadcast also contains any other pertinent remarks relating to operations on or near the airport, such as closed runways or temporary obstructions.

Notices to Airmen, Runway 28 REILs out of service. Advise ground control direction of flight. The following special procedures are in effect; advise ground control when ready for departure with departure intersection. Arrivals use caution, simultaneous operations in progress on parallel runways.

The phonetic letter identifier is restated at the end of the broadcast.

Advise on initial contact you have Information Uniform.

Figure 5-10. If the cloud ceiling is above 5,000 feet AGL and the visibility is more than 5 statute miles, inclusion of the ceiling/sky condition, visibility, and obstructions to vision in the ATIS message is optional.

ATC On Board

Using radar to locate air traffic is not a task which is exclusive to ATC. To aid in collision avoidance, air carriers, as well as many other aircraft use on-board radar systems. A traffic collision avoidance system (TCAS) creates a cylinder of monitored airspace around an aircraft. All transponder-equipped aircraft which enter this airspace are interrogated by the TCAS to determine bearing, distance, and altitude. The TCAS provides the crew with advance warning of potential conflict by both visual and aural cues so that appropriate evasive action can be taken and safe separation maintained.

Symbols on the TCAS display represent traffic within specific distances and altitudes of the TCAS-equipped aircraft. Displays also can indicate whether the traffic is climbing or descending. Most air carrier TCAS units issue resolution advisories (RAs) which command the crew to climb or descend to avoid conflicting traffic.

The general aviation version of TCAS is called TCAD (traffic collision avoidance device). This device receives all transponder replies in the local area and then presents altitude and distance of targets within the designated traffic shield on the display. TCAD is different from TCAS in that it does not provide the pilot with the relative bearing or clock position of the threat aircraft. If you fly an aircraft which is equipped with TCAD, you should use it as a supplemental tool to increase scanning effectiveness.

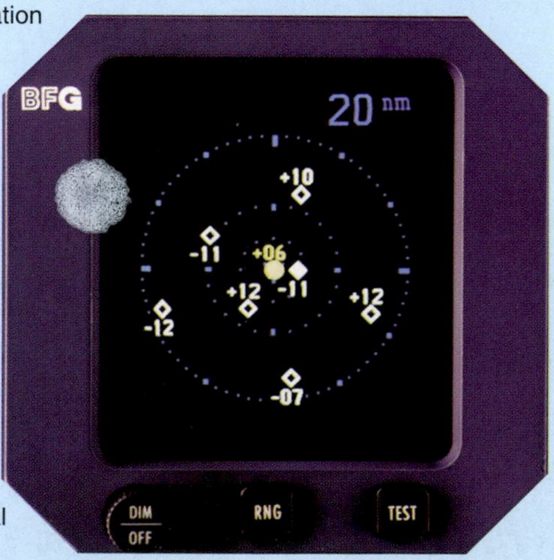

Courtesy of BFGoodrich Avionics Systems, Inc.

FLIGHT SERVICE STATIONS

Flight service stations (FSSs) are ATC facilities which provide a variety of services to pilots, including weather briefings, enroute communication, and VFR search and rescue services. In addition, FSSs assist lost aircraft and aircraft in emergency situations, relay ATC clearances, originate NOTAMs, broadcast aviation weather and airspace information, receive and process flight plans, and monitor navaids. [Figure 5-11]

Figure 5-11. Selected FSSs provide enroute weather service, take weather observations, issue airport advisories, and advise Customs and Immigration of transborder flights.

When you file a **flight plan** with an FSS prior to a cross-country flight, a record is made which includes your destination, route of flight, arrival time, and the number of people on board your aircraft. Once airborne, you open your flight plan so the FSS can keep track of your airplane's estimated arrival time. You must close your flight plan upon arrival at your destination. If you decide not to go to your original destination, or if you will be at least 15 minutes later than you had planned, inform the nearest FSS accordingly. If you have not closed or canceled your flight plan within 30 minutes after your estimated arrival time, the FSS initiates search and rescue procedures to find your aircraft. Although the FAA does not require pilots of VFR aircraft to file flight plans, it is strongly recommended since it will allow you to receive VFR flight search and rescue protection.

Search and rescue (SAR) is a lifesaving service provided through the combined efforts of federal and state agencies. ARTCCs and FSSs alert the SAR system when information is received from any source that an aircraft is in difficulty, overdue, or missing. Flight plan information is invaluable to SAR forces for search planning and for executing search efforts. It is a good idea to make occasional position reports to FSSs during your flight so in the event you do not arrive at your destination, the FSS has an idea of your last known position. Usually, the Civil Air Patrol (CAP), a civilian extension of the U.S. Air Force, assists in search and rescue operations. For more information on flight plans, SAR operations, or other emergency procedures, refer to the *Aeronautical Information Manual.*

If you get disoriented while on a cross-country flight, an FSS specialist may be able to locate your aircraft with a **VHF direction finder (VHF/DF)**. The only aircraft equipment required for VHF direction finding assistance is an operable VHF transmitter and receiver. The FSS specialist will ask you to key your microphone while the direction finding equipment homes in on your radio signal. The specialist can determine your location from the FSS and then give you headings to guide you to an airport or provide other assistance. This service is often referred to as a DF steer. [Figure 5-12]

Figure 5-12. The VHF/DF display indicates your direction, but not your distance from the ground station. Many air traffic control towers also have direction finding equipment. Towers and FSSs with DF service are listed in the *Airport/Facility Directory.*

 The letters VHF/DF appearing in an *Airport/Facility Directory* airport listing indicate that the FSS has direction finding equipment.

At times, you will talk to an FSS on one frequency while listening for a response over the frequency used for a navaid (commonly a VOR) in the area. Whenever you initiate contact with an FSS, give the name of the facility followed by *"radio,"* such as *"Prescott Radio."* If you are listening for a response over a VOR frequency, identify the VOR to the FSS. Consider this example: *"Albuquerque Radio, Piper 8852 Papa, receiving Corona VOR."* If contact is initiated in this manner, the FSS specialist, who can respond over several VOR frequencies, knows which frequency to use in answering your call. You will become more familiar with radio procedures as you explore Section B of this chapter.

 To use VHF/DF facilities for assistance in locating your aircraft's position, you must have a VHF transmitter and receiver.

SUMMARY CHECKLIST

✓ Radar (radio detection and ranging) is a system which uses a synchronized radio transmitter and receiver to emit radio waves and process their reflections for display.

✓ Primary radar is a ground-based system used by ATC which transmits radio waves in a narrow beam by a rotating antenna. When the radio waves strike your aircraft, they are reflected back to the antenna and processed to provide a display, or echo, which shows your aircraft's location on a radarscope.

✓ The range of your aircraft is determined by measuring the time it takes for the radio waves to reach your aircraft and then return to the receiving antenna.

✓ The azimuth, or angle of your aircraft from the radar site, is measured clockwise from north in a horizontal plane.

✓ Some of the limitations of primary radar are the bending of radar pulses (anomalous propagation), blocking of radar returns by precipitation or heavy clouds, and its inability to easily identify an individual aircraft return and display an aircraft's altitude.

✓ The ATCRBS which sometimes is referred to as secondary surveillance radar, or simply secondary radar, consists of three main components in addition to primary radar; a decoder, an interrogator, and a transponder.

✓ The FARs require that your transponder be tested and inspected every 24 calendar months for operations in controlled airspace.

✓ The term squawk is used by the controller to assign a four-digit code, as well as to indicate which transponder function you should select.

✓ Airport surveillance radar (ASR) facilities are designed to provide relatively short-range coverage in the airport vicinity and to serve as an expeditious means of handling terminal area traffic.

✓ ARTS equipment automatically provides a continuous display of an aircraft's position, altitude, groundspeed, and other pertinent information.

✓ The primary responsibility of terminal radar approach control facilities (TRACONs) is to ensure safe separation of aircraft transitioning from departure to cruise flight or from cruise to a landing approach.

✓ Air route surveillance radar (ARSR) is the long-range radar equipment used in controlled airspace to manage traffic.

✓ Workload permitting, air route traffic control centers (ARTCCs) will provide traffic advisories and course guidance, or vectors to VFR aircraft on request.

✓ When giving traffic alerts, controllers reference traffic from your airplane as if it were a clock.

✓ Safety alerts are issued when an aircraft is in unsafe proximity to terrain, obstructions, or other aircraft.

✓ Terminal VFR radar service includes basic radar service, terminal radar service area (TRSA) service, Class C service, and Class B service.

✓ Basic radar service for VFR aircraft includes safety alerts, traffic advisories, and limited radar vectoring. Sequencing also is available at certain terminal locations.

✓ To improve controller effectiveness and to reduce frequency congestion, automatic terminal information service (ATIS) is available in selected high activity terminal areas.

✓ Flight service stations (FSSs) are ATC facilities which provide a variety of services to pilots, including weather briefings, enroute communication, VFR search and rescue services, processing of flight plans, and assisting lost aircraft and aircraft in emergency situations.

✓ When you file a flight plan with an FSS prior to a cross-country, a record is made which includes your destination, route of flight, arrival time, and number of people on board your aircraft.

✓ If you get disoriented while on a cross-country flight, an FSS specialist may be able to locate you with a VHF direction finder.

KEY TERMS

Radar

Primary Radar

Range

Azimuth

Air Traffic Control Radar Beacon System (ATCRBS)

Secondary Surveillance Radar

Squawk

Airport Surveillance Radar (ASR)

Terminal Radar Approach Control Facility (TRACON)

Automated Radar Terminal System (ARTS)

Air Route Surveillance Radar (ARSR)

Air Route Traffic Control Centers (ARTCCs)

Radar Traffic Information Service

VFR Radar Advisory Service

Flight Following

Safety Alert

Minimum Safe Altitude Warning (MSAW)

Vectors

Terminal VFR Radar Service

Basic Radar Service

TRSA Service

Class C Service

Class B Service

Automatic Terminal Information Service (ATIS)

Flight Service Station (FSS)

Flight Plan

Search and Rescue (SAR)

VHF Direction Finder (VHF/DF)

QUESTIONS

1. Describe the limitations of primary radar.

2. In addition to those required for primary radar, what are the three components required for secondary radar?

Match the following transponder instructions from ATC to the appropriate actions.

3. *"Stop Altitude Squawk"*

4. *"Stop Squawk"*

5. *"Squawk VFR"*

6. *"Squawk MAYDAY on 7700."*

A. Select code 7700.

B. Select code 1200.

C. Turn off automatic altitude reporting.

D. Turn transponder off.

7. True/False. If your radio is inoperative, you should squawk code 7500 on your transponder.

8. What is the long-range radar system used in controlled airspace?

    A. Airport surveillance radar (ASR)
    B. Air route surveillance radar (ARSR)
    C. Traffic collision avoidance system (TCAS)

9. ATC gives you the following traffic advisory: *". . .traffic at two o'clock, three miles, westbound."* Refer to the illustration to the right. Which traffic position corresponds to the advisory?

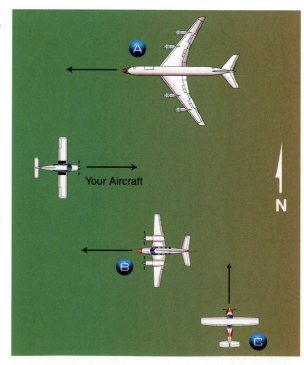

10. You are on a heading of north and receive the following traffic advisory from departure control: *". . . traffic at ten o'clock, three miles, eastbound."* Where should you look for this traffic?

    A. Off the right wingtip
    B. Ahead of the left wingtip
    C. Slightly left of the nose

11. When does ATC issue a safety alert?

12. Which services are included in basic radar service for VFR aircraft?

    A. Separation, limited radar vectoring, and traffic advisories
    B. Safety alerts, traffic advisories, sequencing, and separation
    C. Safety alerts, traffic advisories, and limited radar vectoring

13. What is the term used for the continuous broadcast of current conditions and weather information at selected high activity terminal areas?

14. What aircraft equipment is necessary for you to use VHF/DF facilities for assistance in locating your position?

SECTION B
RADIO PROCEDURES

Twenty-seven hours after Charles Lindbergh took off in *The Spirit of St. Louis* from New York's Curtiss Field, he spotted several fishing boats. When a fisherman appeared at a porthole of the first boat, Lindbergh circled low, closed down the throttle, leaned out the window and shouted, *"Which way is Ireland?"*

If today's extensive radar and communication network had been in operation during the golden age of aviation, Lindbergh would have had a much better chance of pinpointing his position. For example, ATC facilities monitoring *The Spirit of St. Louis* on their radar screens could have instantly replied to a radio inquiry. Today, *"Which way is Ireland?"* would sound out of place transmitted over an aircraft radio. To make communication with ATC as effective as possible, specific radio procedures and terminology have been developed. Nearly any service you obtain during flight requires radio contact, so you need to learn this unique way of communicating.

VHF COMMUNICATION EQUIPMENT

Communication radios in general aviation aircraft use a portion of the **very high frequency (VHF)** range, which includes the frequencies between 118.0 megahertz (MHz) and 135.975 MHz. Communication radios are classified according to the number of channels they were designed to accommodate. A 360-channel radio uses 50 kHz (.05 MHz) spacing between channels, such as 118.05, 118.10, 118.15, 118.20. A 720-channel radio doubles the frequencies available by using 25 kHz (.025 MHz) spacing, such as 118.025, 118.050, 118.075, 118.100. Since communication radios usually combine a transmitter and receiver, they are called **transceivers**. [Figure 5-13]

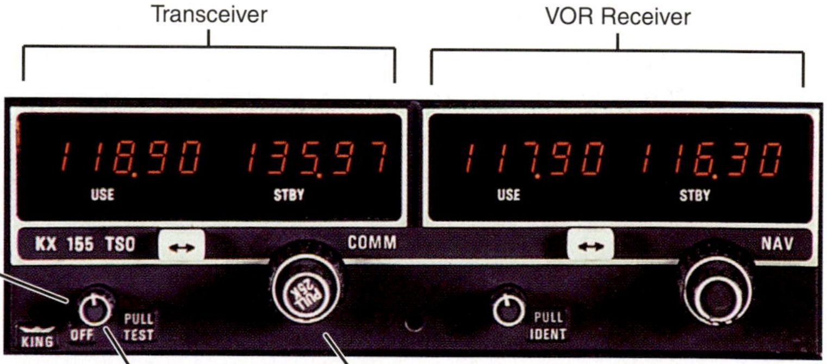

You can adjust the volume with the **on/off/volume control**. If you want to adjust the volume when no one is talking on the frequency, pull the control knob and turn the squelch control until you hear background noise. Then, adjust the volume and turn the squelch down to remove the background noise.

Figure 5-13. Most VHF radios have both communication and VOR navigation receiver capability in one unit. Use of the VOR receiver for navigation is discussed in Chapter 9.

The **squelch control** adjusts how strong a received signal has to be for you to hear the audio. Turning the squelch up increases the reception range and allows you to receive weaker signals.

To change from one frequency to another, use the **frequency selector** and check the display to verify that the correct frequency has been set in the transceiver. On this transceiver, pulling the frequency selector knob allows you to select .025 MHz fractions for communication frequencies.

Birth of the Intercom

During the 1940's the Stearman, a tandem seat, open cockpit biplane was one of the primary military trainers. [Figure A] A rigid tube, called a gosport tube, leading from the instructor's forward cockpit to the student's cockpit in back provided the primary communication between the instructor and pilot. The instructor wore a rubber mask fitted with a flexible hose which connected to the gosport tube. When the instructor spoke into the mask, the sound traveled through the tube to ear pieces connected to the student's cloth helmet. Although the communication was only one way, the instructor could see the student by using a mirror mounted to the underside of the Stearman's upper wing.

For civilian aircraft, many manufacturers offered portable speaking tubes which provided two-way communication. [Figure B] Today, closed cockpits, headsets, and aircraft radio intercom systems make it fairly easy for instructors and students to hear each other during flight lessons.

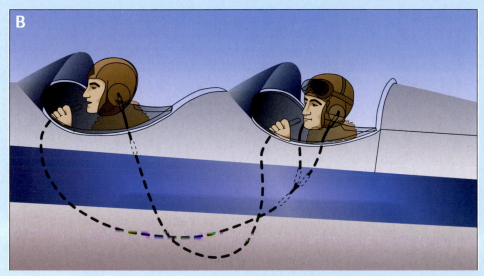

To receive full ATC services, a 720-channel transceiver is a necessity, particularly in busy terminal areas. If you only have 360-channel capability, you can still operate in most areas, but delays can be expected and some services may not be available. Occasionally, you may encounter transceivers with only 90, 100, or 180 channels, so you should ensure that the frequency capability will be adequate for the type of facilities you plan to contact.

VHF antennas usually are the bent whip rods or plastic-encapsulated blade types that are mounted on top of the cabin. [Figure 5-14] The range of VHF transmissions is limited to **line of sight**, meaning that obstructions such as buildings, terrain, or the curvature of the earth block the radio waves. [Figure 5-15]

Figure 5-14. Normally, a VHF antenna is installed for each transceiver in the airplane. An airplane equipped with two transceivers usually has a microphone selector switch for the respective radios, so a second microphone is not required.

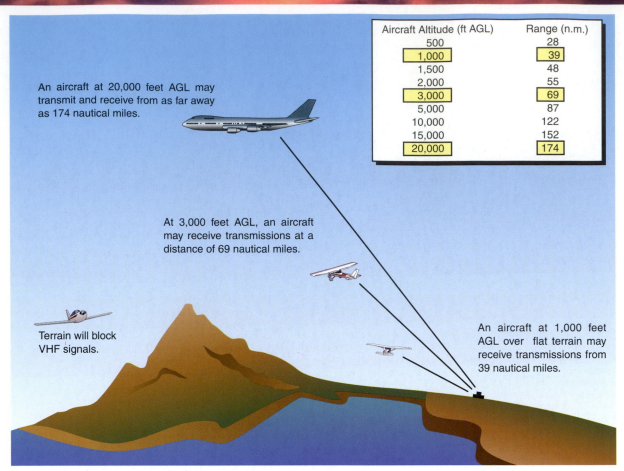

Figure 5-15. Since VHF radio signals are limited to line of sight, aircraft flying at higher altitudes are able to transmit and receive at greater distances.

USING THE RADIO

When you are using the radio, it is important to speak in a professional manner which ensures that others understand the message you are trying to convey. Slang, CB jargon, and incorrect radio procedures can compromise your safety and the safety of others. Radio transmissions should be as brief as possible to help avoid frequency congestion. Before you depress the microphone button (key the mike), think of what you will say and listen for a few moments to make sure that someone else is not already talking or waiting for a response. You should state who you are, where you are, and what type of service you are requesting. Any other information may be excessive, especially in busy terminal areas.

When you are ready to talk, hold the mike very close to your lips. Then, key the mike and speak into it in a normal, conversational tone. It may take a few moments for the facility you have called to respond. If you do not receive any response, try again. If there is no sound coming from your speaker, check your radio to see if it is working properly. Make sure the mike is not stuck in the transmitting position, since this can block other transmissions and disrupt communications for an extended period of time.

PHONETIC ALPHABET

It would be difficult for pilots to speak all of the languages which could be involved in international flight. Therefore, the English language is recommended by the International Civil Aviation Organization (ICAO) for international air/ground communication. In countries where English is not the official language, ICAO member states have agreed to make English available upon request. ICAO also has adopted a

Molecules in Motion

If you have been flying, by now you are probably familiar with the hissing noise heard on your radio receiver with the squelch open and the volume up. Where does this noise come from? You may have theorized that the hiss is atmospheric noise, picked up by the antenna and processed by the receiver, but at VHF frequencies there normally is almost no atmospheric noise present for the receiver to pick up. In fact, if the antenna were removed from the receiver, the noise would still be there.

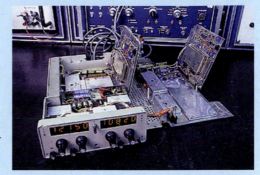

The noise is generated in the receiver by the molecular motion of the materials that make up the electrical components. Although the noise produced by molecular motion is extremely weak, the sensitivity of the VHF receiver is so great that it amplifies the noise enough to make it audible. If the amplification was reduced to remove the hiss, the receiver would be unable to pick up the very weak stations which are heard as a mixture of station and noise.

phonetic alphabet to be used in radio transmissions. When you identify your aircraft during initial contact with ATC or other facilities, you will use the phonetic alphabet as a routine measure. The phonetic equivalents for single letters also should be used to spell out difficult words or groups of letters. [Figure 5-16]

ICAO Phonetic Alphabet

A	Alfa	(**Al**-fah)	· —	N	November	(No-**vem**-ber)	— ·
B	Bravo	(**Brah**-voh)	— · · ·	O	Oscar	(**Oss**-cah)	— — —
C	Charlie	(**Char**-lee) or	— · — ·	P	Papa	(Pah-**pah**)	· — — ·
		(**Shar**-lee)		Q	Quebec	(Keh-**beck**)	— — · —
D	Delta	(**Dell**-tah)	— · ·	R	Romeo	(**Row**-me-oh)	· — ·
E	Echo	(**Eck**-oh)	·	S	Sierra	(See-**air**-rah)	· · ·
F	Foxtrot	(**Foks**-trot)	· · — ·	T	Tango	(**Tang**-oh)	—
G	Golf	(Golf)	— — ·	U	Uniform	(**You**-nee-form) or	· · —
H	Hotel	(Hoh-**tell**)	· · · ·			(**Oo**-nee-form)	
I	India	(**In**-dee-ah)	· ·	V	Victor	(**Vik**-tah)	· · · —
J	Juliett	(**Jew**-lee-ett)	· — — —	W	Whiskey	(**Wlss**-key)	· — —
K	Kilo	(**Key**-loh)	— · —	X	X-ray	(**Ecks**-ray)	— · · —
L	Lima	(**Lee**-mah)	· — · ·	Y	Yankee	(**Yang**-key)	— · — —
M	Mike	(Mike)	— —	Z	Zulu	(**Zoo**-loo)	— — · ·

Figure 5-16. Since letters such as B, C, D, and E have similar sounds, they can easily be mistaken for one another, especially during radio transmissions. The phonetic alphabet was developed to avoid misunderstandings of this type. The associated Morse code also is helpful when tuning and identifying navigation facilities, which typically use three-letter identifiers.

USING NUMBERS ON THE RADIO

When you transmit or receive numbers over the radio, each number is spoken the same way you are used to saying it, with the exception of the number nine. It is spoken as *"niner"* to distinguish it from the German word *"nein,"* which means no. To reduce confusion, certain sets of numbers are spoken as individual digits. When you state radio frequencies, the decimal is pronounced as *"point,"* but the decimal is dropped when you state an altimeter setting.

In the U.S., each aircraft is identified by a registration number which is painted on the outside of the airplane. Registration numbers usually are a combination of five letters and numbers. They are sometimes referred to as the tail number, or N-number, because all U.S.-registered aircraft have an N preceding the number. On initial callups to ATC or other facilities, you should state the name of the facility you are calling and then give your aircraft type, model, or manufacturer and registration number. If you state the manufacturer's name or model, you may drop the N prefix of the registration. [Figure 5-17]

 The correct method of stating 4,500 feet MSL is *"four thousand five hundred."* See figure 5-17.

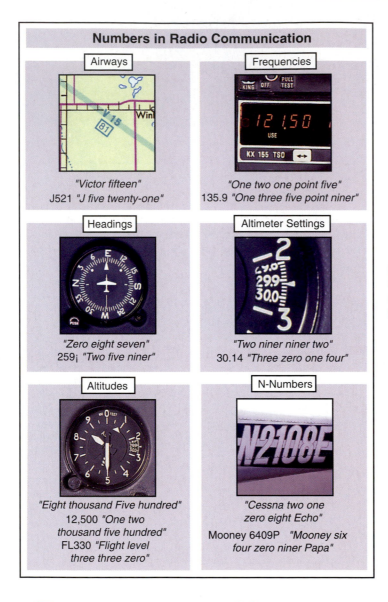

Numbers in Radio Communication

Airways
"Victor fifteen"
J521 *"J five twenty-one"*

Frequencies
"One two one point five"
135.9 *"One three five point niner"*

Headings
"Zero eight seven"
259¡ *"Two five niner"*

Altimeter Settings
"Two niner niner two"
30.14 *"Three zero one four"*

Altitudes
"Eight thousand Five hundred"
12,500 *"One two thousand five hundred"*
FL330 *"Flight level three three zero"*

N-Numbers
"Cessna two one zero eight Echo"
Mooney 6409P *"Mooney six four zero niner Papa"*

Figure 5-17. By studying these examples, you will become more familiar with the correct pronunciation of numbers.

COORDINATED UNIVERSAL TIME

Since a flight may cross several time zones, it would be confusing to estimate the arrival time at your destination using only the local time at the departure airport. To overcome this problem, aviation uses the 24-hour clock system, along with an international standard called **coordinated universal time (UTC)**. The 24-hour clock eliminates the need for a.m. and p.m. designations, since the 24 hours of the day are numbered consecutively. For instance, 9 a.m. becomes 0900 hours; 1 p.m. becomes 1300 hours, and so on.

Coordinated universal time, which is referred to as **Zulu time** in aviation, places the entire world on one time standard. When a given time is expressed in UTC, or Zulu, it is the time at the 0° line of longitude which passes through Greenwich, England. All of the 24 time zones around the world are based on this reference. In the United States, you add hours to convert local time to Zulu time and, to convert Zulu time to local time, you subtract hours. [Figure 5-18]

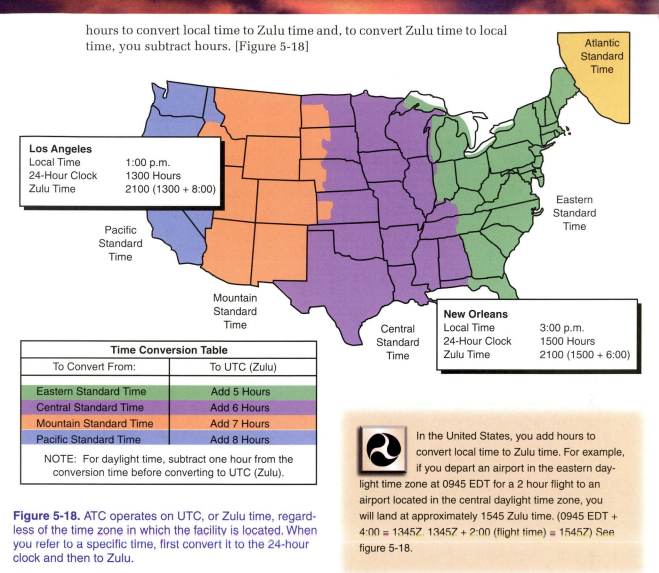

Los Angeles
Local Time	1:00 p.m.
24-Hour Clock	1300 Hours
Zulu Time	2100 (1300 + 8:00)

Pacific Standard Time

Mountain Standard Time

Central Standard Time

New Orleans
Local Time	3:00 p.m.
24-Hour Clock	1500 Hours
Zulu Time	2100 (1500 + 6:00)

Atlantic Standard Time

Eastern Standard Time

Time Conversion Table	
To Convert From:	To UTC (Zulu)
Eastern Standard Time	Add 5 Hours
Central Standard Time	Add 6 Hours
Mountain Standard Time	Add 7 Hours
Pacific Standard Time	Add 8 Hours

NOTE: For daylight time, subtract one hour from the conversion time before converting to UTC (Zulu).

Figure 5-18. ATC operates on UTC, or Zulu time, regardless of the time zone in which the facility is located. When you refer to a specific time, first convert it to the 24-hour clock and then to Zulu.

In the United States, you add hours to convert local time to Zulu time. For example, if you depart an airport in the eastern daylight time zone at 0945 EDT for a 2 hour flight to an airport located in the central daylight time zone, you will land at approximately 1545 Zulu time. (0945 EDT + 4:00 = 1345Z, 1345Z + 2:00 (flight time) = 1545Z) See figure 5-18.

COMMON TRAFFIC ADVISORY FREQUENCY

To increase safety at airports without operating control towers, it is important that all radio-equipped aircraft transmit and receive traffic information on a common frequency. You can broadcast your position and intentions to other aircraft in the area on the **common traffic advisory frequency (CTAF)**. At many airports you can receive airport advisories, and activate pilot-controlled lighting on the designated CTAF. Common traffic advisory frequencies are listed in the *Airport/Facility Directory,* indicated on aeronautical charts, and may be obtained from the nearest FSS. The three methods of broadcasting your intentions, as well as receiving airport and traffic information at uncontrolled airports are communication with a UNICOM operator, contacting an FSS on the field, or by making a self-announce broadcast.

UNICOM

An aeronautical advisory station, or **UNICOM** is a privately owned air/ground communication station which transmits on a limited number of frequencies. Announcing your position and intentions is standard procedure at airports where the designated CTAF is a UNICOM. In addition, you can request an airport advisory from the UNICOM operator.

These advisories usually include information such as wind direction and speed, favored runway, and known traffic. Since UNICOMs are privately operated, you also can request other information or services, such as refueling.

AIRPORT ADVISORY AREAS

Local airport advisory service (LAA) is provided at selected uncontrolled airports that have an FSS on the field. The airport advisory area extends out to 10 statute miles from the primary airport. An FSS with a designated CTAF (normally 123.6 MHz) may provide wind direction and velocity, favored or designated runway, altimeter setting, known traffic, NOTAMs, airport taxi routes, airport traffic pattern information, and instrument approach procedures. You should establish two-way communication before transmitting outbound/inbound intentions or requesting an advisory. For example, transmit *"Homer Radio, Cessna 78564"* and then wait for a reply before providing the FSS with any further information. When departing the airport, advise the FSS of your aircraft type, full identification number, type of flight intended (VFR or IFR), and the planned destination or direction of flight.

 Prior to entering an airport advisory area, you should contact the local FSS for airport and traffic advisories.

SELF-ANNOUNCE PROCEDURE

If your flight takes you to an airport that does not have a tower, an FSS, or a UNICOM, the CTAF is the **MULTICOM** frequency, 122.9 MHz. The purpose of MULTICOM is to provide an air-to-air communication frequency for pilots to self-announce their position and intentions.

The **self-announce procedure** also is used if an airport has a tower and it is temporarily closed, or operated on a part-time basis and there is no FSS on the airport, or the FSS is closed. In these situations, you broadcast your proposed flight activity or ground operation on the designated CTAF to alert other traffic in the area of your intentions. [Figure 5-19]

When you are landing at an airport with a part-time tower and the tower is not in operation, you should monitor airport traffic and announce your position and intentions on the designated CTAF.

Facility at Airport	Frequency to Use
UNICOM (No Tower or FSS)	Communicate with UNICOM station on published CTAF; 122.7, 122.725, 122.8, 122.975, or 123.0.
No Tower in Operation, FSS Open	Communicate with FSS on CTAF.
No Tower, FSS, or UNICOM	Self-announce on MULTI–COM frequency 122.9.
Tower or FSS Not in Operation	Self-announce on CTAF.

Figure 5-19. The principal concept of a common traffic advisory frequency (CTAF) is to provide a method for pilots to communicate with each other at uncontrolled airports.

CTAF PROCEDURES

Although they may vary with the type of airport and facility, you should be familiar with recommended CTAF procedures. When using a CTAF, make your initial call when you are 10 miles from the airport. You should also report entering the downwind, base, and final legs of the traffic pattern, and when exiting the runway. During departure, you should monitor and communicate on the CTAF from the time you start the engine, during taxi, and until 10 miles from the airport unless the FARs or local procedures require otherwise. In addition, if you are performing other operations at altitudes used by arriving or departing aircraft, such as practicing maneuvers, or if you are enroute over the area, you should monitor the CTAF or communicate your intentions within 10 miles of the airport. [Figure 5-20]

The recommended communication procedure when using a CTAF is to transmit your intentions when you are 10 miles out and give position reports in the traffic pattern.

"Front Range UNICOM, Cessna 50826, Corporate Air, taxiing to Runway 26, request wind and traffic information, Front Range."

"Front Range traffic, Cessna 50826, departing Runway 26, departing the pattern to the south, Front Range."

"Front Range UNICOM, Cessna 50826, 10 miles south, descending through 7,500, landing Front Range, request wind and runway information, Front Range."

"Front Range traffic, Cessna 50826 entering downwind for Runway 26, full stop, Front Range."

Figure 5-20. If you broadcast your position at specified locations, it is much easier for other pilots to establish and maintain visual contact with your aircraft. Since there may be other uncontrolled airports within reception range using the same frequency, it is helpful to repeat the name of the airport at the end of your transmission.

ATC FACILITIES AT CONTROLLED AIRPORTS

As you approach a controlled airport you establish communication with a control tower, or approach control at a radar facility. Your initial callup to ATC should include the name of the facility you are trying to contact, your full aircraft identification, the type of message to follow or request if it is short. An example of an initial callup is, *"Great Falls Tower, Cessna 8458 Romeo."* If your message is short, you also may include your request, as well as your position and altitude with the callup. At times, controllers may ask you to *"stand by,"* which means that they will get back to you as soon as they can. [Figure 5-21]

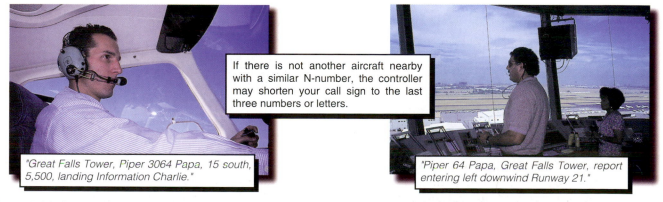

If there is not another aircraft nearby with a similar N-number, the controller may shorten your call sign to the last three numbers or letters.

"Great Falls Tower, Piper 3064 Papa, 15 south, 5,500, landing Information Charlie."

"Piper 64 Papa, Great Falls Tower, report entering left downwind Runway 21."

Figure 5-21. Shortening your aircraft call sign reduces the amount of air time needed for further transmissions. You should not shorten your call sign until the controller does so first.

An **air traffic control clearance** is an authorization by ATC for you to proceed under specified traffic conditions within controlled airspace. Its purpose is to prevent collisions between known aircraft. If you receive an ATC clearance and do not hear all of it or do not understand it, ask the controller to *"say again"* and the controller will repeat the last message. You also can ask the controller to *"speak slower"* and the controller will repeat the previous transmission more slowly. At times, you or the controller may repeat the transmission to verify that it was heard correctly. The response in these situations usually is, *"that is correct."* The use of the word *"over"* indicates that your transmission is complete and that you expect a response. On subsequent contacts, the ground station name and the word *"over"* may be omitted if the message requires an obvious reply and there is no danger of misunderstanding.

An air traffic clearance is an authorization by ATC for you to proceed under specified traffic conditions within controlled airspace.

If a controller contacts you with a request, you should acknowledge it and quickly restate any instructions given to reduce the possibility of a misunderstanding. For example, if asked to turn right to a heading of 210°, you should respond with, *"Cessna 58 Romeo, roger, turn right heading 210."*

If you are asked to contact the same controller on a different frequency, the controller will say, *"Cessna 58 Romeo, change to my frequency, 123.4."* In this situation, you can abbreviate your callup by saying, *"Cessna 58 Romeo on 123.4."* At times, such as when you are flying into Class B or C airspace, you may talk to a succession of controllers on different frequencies. Each controller will hand you off to the next controller by telling you when to change to the next frequency and what frequency to use. Before changing frequencies, you should verify that you heard the new frequency correctly with a readback such as, *"Cessna 58 Romeo, roger, contact tower 118.3."* Since the two controllers have already coordinated the hand-off, the tower will be expecting your call.

As a student pilot, you can request additional assistance from ATC simply by identifying yourself as a student pilot. For example, assume you are approaching a controlled field with heavy traffic and you are unfamiliar with the airport. In this situation, you should make your initial callup as follows: *"Centennial Tower, Cessna 8458 Romeo, student pilot."* This procedure is not mandatory, but it does alert controllers so they can give you extra assistance and consideration, if needed. In addition, identifying yourself as a student may be advantageous when you self-announce your position over the CTAF at uncontrolled fields.

RADAR FACILITIES

To operate within a large terminal area with radar services, you need to be familiar with a number of ATC functions which are necessary to coordinate departures and arrivals. The following scenario covers the various ATC functions in the normal order that you would use them. The airport used in these examples is Phoenix Sky Harbor International Airport, which serves Phoenix, Arizona. This is the primary airport within the Phoenix Class B airspace.

DEPARTURE PROCEDURES

At controlled airports, you must receive permission from ATC to taxi to the active runway and subsequently be cleared for takeoff. You can expect more complex departure procedures at larger airports due to heavier traffic and more ATC services. Before contacting ground control, you usually listen to the ATIS recording which includes current airport information, such as the altimeter setting and active runway.

CLEARANCE DELIVERY

The clearance delivery facility is established at busy airports primarily for ATC to relay IFR clearances to departing IFR traffic. However, when the ATIS message so indicates, you should contact **clearance delivery** prior to taxiing. Your call should include your N-number and aircraft type, and you should also specify that you are VFR and have listened to the current ATIS. Finally, identify your destination or direction of flight. This allows departure controllers to improve traffic coordination. Clearance delivery may provide detailed departure instructions and then instruct you to contact ground control.

GROUND CONTROL

Ground control is an ATC function for directing the movement of aircraft and other vehicles on the airport surface. Before leaving the parking area, you must receive a clearance from ground control to taxi to the active runway. At busy airports, you may be instructed to wait in a holding area near the runway. At unfamiliar airports, you can request a **progressive taxi**, which means a controller will provide you with precise taxi instructions or will direct you in stages as you proceed along the taxi route. [Figure 5-22]

ATIS — *"Phoenix Sky Harbor Airport, Information Foxtrot, 1656 Zulu. Wind 280 at 8, visibility 10, 15,000 scattered, temperature 33, dewpoint 3, altimeter 29.81. Runway 26 in use. Arrivals from the north expect the north runway. Arrivals from the south expect the south runway. Simultaneous approaches in use. Expect visual Runway 26 Right approach or visual approach Runway 26 Left. Clearance delivery frequency is 118.1. VFR aircraft state location and destination. Ground traffic on the north complex use frequency 119.75. On the south complex use frequency 132.55. Aircraft at terminals 2 and 3 contact ground prior to pushback. Notices to Airmen, 90-foot crane located south of Runway 8R/26L. Advise on initial contact, you have Information Foxtrot."*

Clearance Delivery — Contact Phoenix Sky Harbor's clearance delivery on a frequency of 118.1 MHz.

"Sky Harbor Clearance Delivery, Piper 8252 Sierra, Information Delta, VFR to the southwest."

The controller gives you a departure clearance, which includes a heading and an altitude, as well as a transponder code and the departure control frequency.

"Piper 8252 Sierra, after departure, fly heading 250, climb and maintain 4,500 feet, squawk 3504, departure frequency will be 123.7, contact ground control 121.9 when ready to taxi."

You should write down the clearance, then read it back to the controller to ensure that you heard everything correctly.

Ground Control — Contact Phoenix Sky Harbor's ground control on a frequency of 121.9 MHz.

"Phoenix Sky Harbor Ground, Piper 8252 Sierra, at the general aviation ramp, ready to taxi to Runway 26 Right for departure."

A clearance to *"taxi to"* your assigned takeoff runway authorizes you to cross any runways (except the active runway) intersecting your taxi route, but not to taxi onto the departure runway.

"Piper 52 Sierra, taxi to Runway 26 Right."

Figure 5-22. If you are asked to *"hold short"* of a runway, you must read back the hold short clearance to the controller, stop at the hold lines preceding the runway, check for traffic, and continue only after cleared to do so.

CONTROL TOWER

After completing the before-takeoff checklist at the departure runway, you normally switch to the control tower frequency for takeoff clearance. When you receive takeoff clearance, make a final check for traffic before you taxi onto the runway. You may be asked to *"...taxi into position*

 A clearance to *"taxi to"* your assigned takeoff runway authorizes you to cross any runways intersecting your taxi route, but not to taxi on to the departure runway.

and hold." This means that you may position yourself on the runway for takeoff while waiting for another aircraft to clear the runway. Usually, you can expect to be cleared for take-off after the other aircraft is clear.

DEPARTURE CONTROL

After takeoff, contact **departure control** and a controller will advise if you are in radar contact. The term **radar contact** means your aircraft has been radar identified and flight following will be provided. If you receive flight following, the controller is observing the progress of your aircraft while you provide your own navigation. [Figure 5-23]

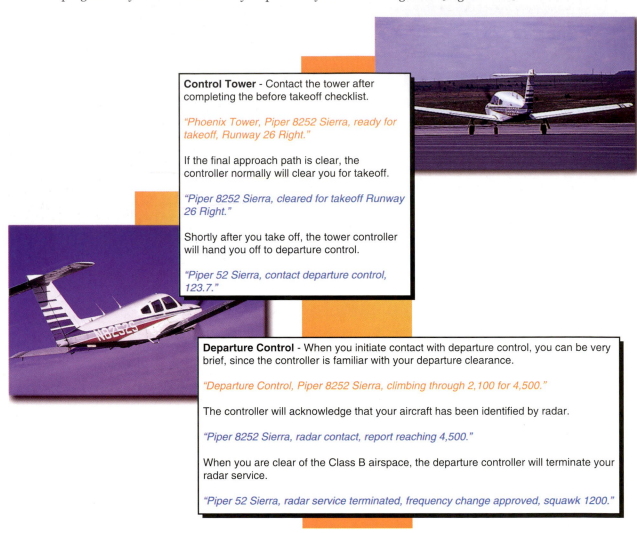

Control Tower - Contact the tower after completing the before takeoff checklist.

"Phoenix Tower, Piper 8252 Sierra, ready for takeoff, Runway 26 Right."

If the final approach path is clear, the controller normally will clear you for takeoff.

"Piper 8252 Sierra, cleared for takeoff Runway 26 Right."

Shortly after you take off, the tower controller will hand you off to departure control.

"Piper 52 Sierra, contact departure control, 123.7."

Departure Control - When you initiate contact with departure control, you can be very brief, since the controller is familiar with your departure clearance.

"Departure Control, Piper 8252 Sierra, climbing through 2,100 for 4,500."

The controller will acknowledge that your aircraft has been identified by radar.

"Piper 8252 Sierra, radar contact, report reaching 4,500."

When you are clear of the Class B airspace, the departure controller will terminate your radar service.

"Piper 52 Sierra, radar service terminated, frequency change approved, squawk 1200."

Figure 5-23. During departure, terrain, and obstruction clearance remains your responsibility until the controller begins to provide navigational guidance in the form of radar vectors.

ARRIVAL PROCEDURES

Approach control is the ATC function which provides separation and sequencing of inbound aircraft, and traffic advisories or safety alerts when necessary. Approach control frequencies are published on sectional charts and broadcast over ATIS. At large terminals, expect different frequencies for approach control, depending on your arrival sector. On initial contact, ATC routinely provides you with wind, runway, and altimeter information unless you indicate

After landing at a controlled airport, you should contact ground control when advised to do so by the tower.

that you have received the ATIS or you use the phrase *"have numbers."* The phrase, have numbers means you have received only wind, runway, and altimeter information, but does not indicate that you have listened to ATIS. [Figure 5-24]

Approach Control - When you return to Phoenix, listen to the current ATIS as soon as you can receive it. While you are still outside of the Class B airspace, contact approach control over a designated visual checkpoint or other prominent landmark.

"Phoenix Sky Harbor Approach, Piper 8252 Sierra, over Avondale, with Golf, at 4,500, landing."

Usually, approach control provides a transponder code and asks you to ident.

"Piper 8252 Sierra, squawk 3550 and ident."

The controller acknowledges that your aircraft is in radar contact and gives you a clearance to proceed.

"Piper 52 Sierra, radar contact, 15 miles west of Phoenix Sky Harbor Airport, cleared to operate in the Class B airspace, turn right, expect heading 080 for a left downwind to Runway 26 Left."

At the appropriate time, the approach controller will hand you off to the tower controller.

"Piper 52 Sierra, contact tower on 120.9"

Control Tower - After contacting the tower, continue your approach and follow any other instructions given to you by the tower controller. At tower-controlled airports, you cannot land without permission.

"Piper 52 Sierra, cleared to land Runway 26 Left."

During your roll-out, the tower gives you instructions for clearing the runway.

"Piper 52 Sierra, turn left on the next available taxiway and contact ground, point niner."

There are occasions when controllers issue time-critical instructions such as, *"Piper 52 Sierra, expedite your turnoff at the next available taxiway."* You may acknowledge these with *"wilco," "affirmative,"* or *"negative,"* as appropriate, preceded by your call sign.

Ground control, on 121.9 MHz, provides a taxi clearance to the parking area. You should not switch to ground control before the tower instructs you to do so.

Figure 5-24. You should respond immediately to time-critical requests by ATC. If, at any time, you are given an instruction that is beyond the capabilities of your airplane, is not safe to follow, or would cause you to violate an FAR, you must inform the controller that you are *"unable"* to comply with the directions. The controller should then give you an amended clearance with instructions that you can follow without compromise.

There may be times when you want to stay in the traffic pattern to practice landings. You should advise approach control or the tower on initial contact that you will be *". . . remaining in the pattern."* The tower controller may ask you to *". . . make closed traffic . . ."* This means you should remain in the traffic pattern unless you are otherwise instructed. During your last time around the pattern, request a *"full-stop"* landing.

LOST COMMUNICATION PROCEDURES

As you are aware, establishing two-way radio communication with the control tower is required before you enter Class D airspace. If your communication radios become inoperative, it is still possible to land at an airport with an operating control tower by following **lost communication procedures**. If you believe that your radio has failed, set your transponder to code 7600. If you are in an area of radar coverage, the code 7600 will alert ATC of your radio failure. [Figure 5-25]

If you are unable to contact ATC:

- Ensure that you are using the correct frequency. Try a different frequency for the ATC facility, if available.

- Check the volume and squelch on your transceiver.

- Check the switch position on your audio control panel.

- Verify that your mike is properly plugged into the jack. If you are wearing headsets, ensure that both the speaker and mike plugs are in the jacks all the way.

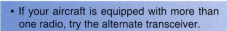

- Try the hand held mike if you are using headsets.

Figure 5-25. If you are unable to make contact with ATC, you can follow several steps to determine if your radio is inoperative. In the event of radio failure, it may be more convenient to land at an uncontrolled airport nearby.

- If your aircraft is equipped with more than one radio, try the alternate transceiver.

- If it is within range, call the last ATC facility with which you had contact to request assistance.

If after taking these steps, you still are unable to contact ATC, follow the lost communication procedures.

Formation Communication

Have you ever thought about how photographers capture all those aircraft in flight that you see throughout the pages of this and other textbooks? Most of the photos are taken during formation flights. A formation flight is comprised of a lead aircraft and one or more wingmen flying in close proximity with totally coordinated movements. In a flight of two, the wingman uses the lead as a fixed frame of reference to maintain a specific position.

Although the pilots who so skillfully entertain us at airshows make formation flying look easy, it is much more difficult than it appears. Learning to safely fly in formation takes extensive

training and experience. In addition to the tremendous flying abilities and concentration involved, formation pilots must be skilled communicators. Prior to each flight, the pilots discuss and clearly define objectives for the mission. A typical preflight briefing covers everything from engine start and taxi procedures to radio failure and emergencies.

Effective communication during a formation flight is essential. Pilots use the air-to-air frequency 122.75, and to avoid frequency congestion, a strict format is used. The lead is responsible for traffic avoidance, navigation, and ATC communication. An example of an initial callup made by the lead to a control tower is, *"Centennial Tower, Cessna 6319 Lima, flight of two."*

If neither your transmitter nor your receiver is working, you need to remain outside or above the Class D airspace until you have determined the direction and flow of traffic. Then, join the airport traffic pattern and maintain visual contact with the tower to receive light signals. During the daytime, you should acknowledge tower transmissions or light signals by rocking your wings and at night by blinking your landing light or navigation lights. [Figure 5-26]

 If your aircraft radio fails when landing at a controlled airport, you should observe the traffic flow, enter the pattern, and look for a light signal from the control tower.

 Each color or color combination of light signal has a specific meaning for an aircraft in flight or on the airport surface. For example, after a communication failure, a steady green light signal from the control tower indicates that you are cleared to land. See figure 5-26.

Figure 5-26. In the event of a radio failure, a tower controller can provide light signals to your aircraft. Each color or color combination has a specific meaning for an aircraft in flight, or on the airport surface.

COLOR AND TYPE OF SIGNAL	MEANING	
	On the Ground	In Flight
Steady Green	Cleared for takeoff	Cleared to land
Flashing Green	Cleared to taxi	Return for landing (to be followed by steady green at proper time)
Steady Red	Stop	Give way to other aircraft and continue circling
Flashing Red	Taxi clear of landing area (runway) in use	Airport unsafe — do not land
Flashing White	Return to starting point on airport	(No assigned meaning)
Alternating Red and Green	Exercise extreme caution	Exercise extreme caution

It is possible for only your radio transmitter or receiver to fail. For example, if you are fairly certain that only the receiver is inoperative, you should remain outside or above the Class D airspace until you have determined the direction and flow of traffic. Then, advise the tower of your aircraft type, position, altitude, intention to land, and request to be controlled by light signals. When you are approximately three to five miles away from the airport, advise the tower of your position and join the traffic pattern. Watch the tower for light signals, and if you fly a complete pattern, self-announce your position when you are on downwind and/or turning base.

If only your transmitter is inoperative, follow the same procedure that you would when the receiver is not working, but do not self-announce your intentions. Monitor the airport frequency for landing or traffic information, and look for a light signal which may be addressed to your aircraft.

EMERGENCY PROCEDURES

An emergency can be either a distress or an urgency condition. The *Aeronautical Information Manual* defines **distress** as a condition of being threatened by serious and/or imminent danger and of requiring immediate assistance, such as fire, mechanical failure, or structural failure. You are experiencing an **urgency** situation the moment you become doubtful about your position, fuel endurance, weather, or any other condition which could adversely affect flight safety. If you become apprehensive about your safety for any reason, you should request assistance immediately. Do not wait until the situation has developed into a distress condition.

The frequency of 121.5 MHz is used across the country for transmitting emergency messages. Although range is limited to line-of-sight, 121.5 MHz is guarded by military towers, most civil towers, FSSs, and radar facilities. In a distress situation, using the word MAYDAY commands radio silence on the frequency in use. When you hear the words PAN-PAN, the urgency situation in progress has priority over all other communication and warns other stations not to interfere with these transmissions.

Radar-equipped ATC facilities can provide radar assistance and navigation service to you within an area of radar coverage. Changing your transponder code to 7700 triggers an alarm, or special indication, at all radar facility control positions. Although you may not be sure if your aircraft is within radar coverage, it is a good idea to squawk 7700 to alert any ATC facility which may be in the area. If you are under radar control and in contact with ATC, continue squawking the code assigned, unless instructed otherwise. [Figure 5-27]

Figure 5-27. If you are in distress, your initial communication and any subsequent transmissions should begin with the word MAYDAY repeated three times. PAN-PAN should be used in the same manner for an urgency situation. Following this, you need to provide information about your situation and the assistance that you require.

Emergency Message	
Distress or Urgency	"MAYDAY, MAYDAY, MAYDAY (or PAN-PAN, PAN-PAN, PAN-PAN),
Name of station addressed	Denver Radio,
Identification and type of aircraft	5674R Cessna 172,
Nature of distress or urgency	trapped above overcast,
Weather	marginal VFR,
Your intentions and request	request radar vectors to nearest VFR airport,
Present position and heading	Newberg VOR, heading 253°,
Altitude	6,500,
Fuel remaining in hours and minutes	estimate 30 minutes fuel remaining,
Number of people aboard	three people aboard,
Any other useful information	squawking 7700."

DON'T LET PRIDE BE YOUR GUIDE

In 1990, Avianca Airlines Flight 052 crashed into a residential area near Long Island, New York after running out of fuel. There were 73 fatalities including the 8 crew members. The NTSB determined that in addition to mismanagement of the airplane's fuel load, the accident was caused by the crew's failure to communicate an emergency fuel state to ATC before fuel exhaustion occurred.

At JFK International Airport, Flight 052 was placed into a holding pattern three times by ATC. Although, the crew stated that they needed priority, they also indicated that they could remain in the holding pattern for at least five minutes. During a poorly executed ILS approach, the Captain elected to go-around and at this time finally stated to the First Officer to *"tell them we are in an emergency."* As the aircraft was being vectored around for a second approach, the First Officer radioed, *"We just lost two engines and we need priority please."*

Although a long chain of events led to this accident, this tragedy could have been prevented if the crew of Flight 052 would have properly alerted ATC to their situation by declaring a fuel emergency prior to being instructed to enter the holding pattern. Although you may be hesitant to admit an error, you should never let pride or fear of repercussions get in the way of notifying ATC in the event of an emergency situation.

As discussed in Section A, VHF/DF equipment has been used for many years to locate lost aircraft or to guide aircraft to areas of good weather. At most DF-equipped airports, DF instrument approaches may be given to pilots, especially when a pilot has a limited amount of flight experience. These approaches are for emergency use only and are not issued in IFR conditions unless a distress or urgency situation has been declared. In VFR weather conditions, you can request a practice DF approach.

If you are lost, keep in mind, the **Five C's — climb, communicate, confess, comply, and conserve**. Climb for better radio and navaid reception, as well as increased radar and DF coverage. Communicate with any available facility using frequencies shown on your sectional chart or in the *Airport/Facility Directory*. Confess that you are lost when contacting ATC or another ground facility, and if your situation is threatening, clearly explain your problem, using the emergency frequency 121.5 MHz, if necessary. Then, comply with assistance instructions, and consider reducing your power setting to conserve fuel. In addition, ensure that the mixture is leaned properly to extend your range and endurance.

Emergency locator transmitters (ELTs) are emergency signaling devices developed as a means of locating downed aircraft. Required for most general aviation airplanes, these electronic, battery-operated transmitters emit a distinctive audio tone on 121.5 MHz (VHF) and 243.0 MHz (UHF). If armed and subjected to crash-generated forces, ELTs are designed to activate automatically. The transmitters should operate continuously for at least 48 hours over a wide range of temperatures. A properly installed and maintained ELT can expedite search and rescue operations and save lives. [Figure 5-28]

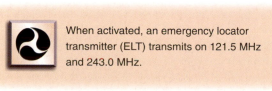

When activated, an emergency locator transmitter (ELT) transmits on 121.5 MHz and 243.0 MHz.

Figure 5-28. Most aircraft are designed to provide pilot access to the ELT. If necessary after a crash landing, you can manually activate the ELT.

You are encouraged to monitor 121.5 MHz while you are flying to assist in identifying ELT transmissions. If you do hear an ELT, report your position to the nearest ATC facility the first and last time you hear the signal, as well as indicate your position and cruising altitude at maximum signal strength.

A false ELT signal can lead to expensive and frustrating searches, as well as interfere with genuine emergency transmissions and hinder or prevent the timely location of crash sites. Many cases of activation have occurred unintentionally as a result of aerobatics, hard landings, movement by ground crews, and aircraft maintenance. You can minimize ELT false alarms by monitoring 121.5 MHz during flight, prior to engine shut down, and after maintenance.

ELT false alarms can be minimized by monitoring 121.5 MHz during flight, prior to engine shut down, and after maintenance.

ELTs must be tested and maintained according to the manufacturer's instructions. The FARs require that the ELT battery be replaced, or recharged if the battery is rechargeable, after one-half of the battery's useful life, or when the transmitter has been in use for more than one cumulative hour. ELTs should be tested in a screened room to

The battery in an emergency locator transmitter (ELT) must be replaced, or recharged if the battery is rechargeable, after one-half of its useful life. An ELT may be tested during the first five minutes after the hour.

prevent broadcast of signals, but when this cannot be done, you can conduct ELT testing in your aircraft only during the first five minutes after the hour, and for no longer than three audible sweeps. Airborne tests of ELTs are not allowed.

SUMMARY CHECKLIST

✓ Communication radios in general aviation aircraft use a portion of the very high frequency (VHF) range, which includes the frequencies between 118.0 MHz and 135.975 MHz.

✓ The range of VHF transmissions is limited to line of sight, which means that obstructions such as buildings, terrain, or the curvature of the earth block radio waves.

✓ An initial callup to ATC or another facility should include who you are, where you are, and what type of service you are requesting.

✓ The ICAO has adopted a phonetic alphabet to be used in radio transmissions.

✓ Aviation uses the 24-hour clock system and coordinated universal time (UTC), or Zulu time, which places the entire world on one time standard.

✓ To increase safety at airports without operating control towers, it is important that all radio-equipped aircraft transmit and receive traffic information on a common traffic advisory frequency (CTAF).

✓ An aeronautical advisory station, or UNICOM is a privately owned air/ground communication station which transmits on a limited number of frequencies.

✓ The purpose of MULTICOM is to provide an air-to-air communication frequency for pilots to self-announce their position and intentions at airports which do not have a tower, an FSS, or UNICOM.

✓ Your initial callup to ATC should include the name of the facility you are trying to contact, your full aircraft identification, the type of message to follow or request if it is short.

✓ An air traffic control clearance is an authorization by ATC for you to proceed under specified traffic conditions within controlled airspace.

✓ Ground control is an ATC function for directing the movement of aircraft and other vehicles on the airport surface.

✓ The term radar contact means your aircraft has been radar identified and flight following will be provided.

✓ Approach control is the ATC function that provides separation and sequencing of inbound aircraft, as well as traffic advisories and safety alerts when necessary.

✓ To land at a tower-controlled airport if your communication radios become inoperative, set your transponder to code 7600, and follow the lost communication procedures.

✓ In the event of a radio failure, a tower controller can provide light signals to direct your aircraft.

✓ If armed and subjected to crash-generated forces, ELTs are designed to automatically emit a distinctive audio tone on 121.5 MHz (VHF) and 243.0 MHz (UHF).

✓ The FARs require that the ELT battery must be replaced, or recharged if the battery is rechargeable, after one-half of the battery's useful life, or if the transmitter has been used for more than one cumulative hour.

KEY TERMS

Very High Frequency (VHF)	Clearance Delivery
Transceivers	Ground Control
Line of Sight	Progressive Taxi
Phonetic Alphabet	Departure Control
N-Number	Radar Contact
Coordinated Universal Time (UTC)	Approach Control
Zulu Time	Lost Communication Procedures
Common Traffic Advisory Frequency (CTAF)	Distress
UNICOM	Urgency
MULTICOM	Five C's — Climb, Communicate, Confess, Comply, and Conserve
Self-Announce Procedure	Emergency Locator Transmitter (ELT)
Air Traffic Control Clearance	

QUESTIONS

1. Select the VHF frequency range used for aircraft communication radios.

   A. 118.0 to 135.975 kHz
   B. 118.0 to 135.975 MHz
   C. 108.0 to 135.975 MHz

2. Using the phonetic alphabet, write out the pronunciation of the following aircraft call sign: Cessna 649SP.

Refer to the time conversion table on page 5-23 to answer questions 3 and 4.

3. If you depart an airport in the central standard time zone at 1:00 p.m. and arrive in a city on the west coast two hours later, what is your arrival time in Zulu?

4. If you fly from a city in the pacific daylight time zone to a city in the central daylight time zone, and you leave at 0700 PDT with an estimated time enroute of three hours, what is your estimated time of arrival in Zulu?

5. What are the three methods of broadcasting your intentions and receiving airport information at uncontrolled airports?

6. When transmitting on a CTAF, how many miles from the airport should you normally make your initial contact?

7. True/False. If ATC gives you a clearance that compromises your safety or would cause you to violate a regulation, you should comply with it.

8. Select the actions that you would take to comply with the following ATC clearance: *"Cessna 52 Sierra, taxi to Runway 26 Right."*

   A. Taxi onto Runway 26 Right.
   B. Taxi to Runway 26 Right, crossing any runways intersecting your taxi route, except the active runway.
   C. Taxi to Runway 26 Right, but hold short at any runways intersecting your taxi route until cleared to proceed by ground control.

9. Describe the lost communication procedure used for landing at a Class D airspace primary airport.

Match the frequencies to appropriate use.

10. 121.5   A. Emergency Frequency

11. 122.9   B. UNICOM

12. 122.8   C. MULTICOM

13. How often must the ELT battery be replaced or recharged if the battery is rechargeable?

SECTION C
SOURCES OF FLIGHT INFORMATION

Your destination is Greater Green River Inter Galactic Spaceport. After asking around your local airport, you determine that not one of your pilot friends or acquaintances has ventured into this small airport, located not in the outer reaches of the galaxy, but in the southwest corner of Wyoming. Although the airport is depicted on your sectional, without any additional information, you feel as if you are voyaging into uncharted territory. What will you find as you touchdown on the Spaceport's dirt strip? It has been a long time since you flew into an uncontrolled airport. What are the procedures for entering the traffic pattern and announcing your intentions? You would like to plan the trip by using navaids. Are any of the VORs shut down for maintenance? These and many other questions can be answered by using sources of flight information.

AIRPORT/FACILITY DIRECTORY

Published by the National Ocean Service (NOS), the ***Airport/Facility Directory*** **(A/FD)** contains a descriptive listing of all airports, heliports, and seaplane bases which are open to the public. The *Airport/Facility Directory* is divided into seven volumes, each of which covers a specific region of the contiguous United States, as well as Puerto Rico and the U. S. Virgin Islands. The entire directory is reissued every 56 days and is designed to be used in conjunction with aeronautical charts. [Figure 5-29]

Figure 5-29. The effective dates of the A/FD are shown on the cover of each volume. Supplements to the A/FD cover airports in Alaska and the Pacific.

To help you interpret the abundance of information in an A/FD airport listing, there is a **directory legend** in the front of each

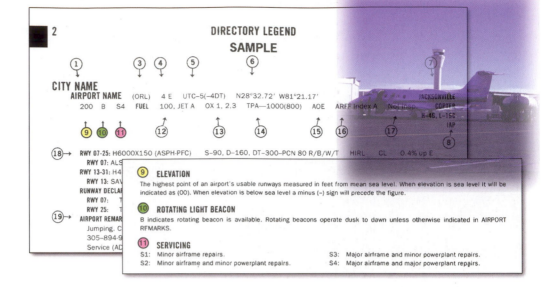

Figure 5-30. The directory legend provides a detailed explanation of each of the items which can be found in airport information listings.

regional volume. [Figure 5-30] The airports presented in the A/FD are listed alphabetically by state, and then by the city associated with the airport. [Figure 5-31]

Airport listings in the *Airport/Facility Directory* include the airport location, availability and type of radar services, as well as communication and navigation frequencies. The designation "Rgt tfc." indicates that the runway has right-hand traffic. See figure 5-31.

Figure 5-31. Each airport listing contains information regarding runways, communication and navigation facilities, weather data sources, airspace, and airport services.

This code indicates that major airframe and powerplant repairs are available at the airport.

The location of the airport is three nautical miles southwest of the city.

To convert UTC, or Zulu time, to local time, you need to subtract 6 hours (5 hours daylight savings time).

The airport elevation is 957 feet MSL.

Runway 5/23 is 6,501 feet long, 150 feet wide, is composed of asphalt, and grooved.

You should fly a right-hand traffic pattern when landing on Runway 13R.

Runway 5 has runway end identifier lights (REIL) and a visual approach slope indicator (VASI).

The airport appears on the Omaha sectional chart.

The remote communications outlet (RCO) located at the airport is an unmanned facility which extends the service range of Fort Dodge FSS.

The airport provides Class C airspace radar services including sequencing, traffic advisories, and safety alerts.

If you are approaching the airport from the west for landing on Runway 31, you should contact approach control on 135.2 MHz.

DES MOINES
DES MOINES INTL (DSM) 3 SW UTC–6(–5DT)   OMAHA
957 B S4 FUEL 100LL, JET A OX 1, 2, 3, 4   H–1E, 3G, L–11C
RWY 13L–31R: H9001X150 (ASPH–GRVD)   S–133, D–1   IAP
RWY 13L: MALSR. VASI(V4L)—GA 3.0° TCH 56'. Arresting device.
RWY 31R: MALSR. PAPI(P4L)—GA 3.0° TCH 56'. Road. Rgt tfc. Arresting device. 0.8%
RWY 05–23: H6501X150 (ASPH–GRVD)   S–133, D–169, DT–285   MIRL
RWY 05: REIL. VASI(V4L)—GA 3.0° TC
RWY 23: REIL. VASI(V4L)—GA 3.0° TC
RWY 13R–31L: H3202X100 (ASPH)   S–
RWY 13R: REIL. Rgt tfc.   RWY 31L
                                                        18, 1997. Taxiway M weight
                                                        ation of explosives by civil
                                                        or. Rubber supported arresting
          of Rwy 13L and Rwy 31R, 1250' in from thlds of Rwy 05 and Rwy 23 may be in
          during military ops. Twr has limited visibility on Twy D between Twy D–5 and
          D–8. Ramps weight restricted to 60,000 lbs. fixed-base operator. Men and equipment working adjacent all
          surfaces Apr–Oct Mon–Fri 1330–2230Z‡. mowing ops. Flight Notification Service (ADCUS) avbl, Mon–Fri
          1430–2300Z‡. For Sat, Sun Holidays and ngt customs svc, make appointments Mon–Fri 1430–2300Z‡. At least
          3 hr advance notice required. NOTE: See Land and Hold Short Operations Section.
WEATHER DATA SOURCES: ASOS (515) 287–1012. LLWAS.
COMMUNICATIONS: ATIS 119.55 (515) 287–3180   UNICOM 122.95
FORT DODGE FSS (FOD) TF 1–800–WX–BRIEF. NOTAM FILE DSM.
RCO 122.65 (FORT DODGE FSS)
Ⓡ APP/DEP CON: 123.9 (306°–127° Rwy 13–31) (049°–231° Rwy 05–23) 135.2 (127°–306° Rwy 13–31) (231°–049°
     Rwy 05–23) 118.6 Utilized as APCH secondary freq, all sectors.
     TOWER 118.3   GND CON 121.9   CLNC DEL 134.15
AIRSPACE: CLASS C svc ctc APP CON.
RADIO AIDS TO NAVIGATION: NOTAM FILE DSM.
     (H) VORTACW 117.5   DSM   Chan 122   N41°26.26' W9
     FOREM NDB (LOM) 344   DS   N41°28.93' W93°34.85'
     ILS 110.3   I–DSM   Rwy 31R   LOM FOREM NDB.
     ILS 108.7   I–VGU   Rwy 13L
     ILS/DME 111.5   I–DWW   Chan 52   Rwy 05.   Localizer only.
     ASR

Caution: Rising Terrain

Operations at some airports create unique concerns for pilots due to surrounding terrain, obstacles, or complex approach and departure procedures. The FARs require pilots in command of air carriers to meet special qualifications to take off and land at certain airports. Within 12 calendar months prior to operating at an airport which requires special qualifications, a pilot must have completed a takeoff and landing at that airport or have used approved visual training aids, such as Airport Qualification Charts. These charts provide photos of the airport, graphic and textual descriptions of the surrounding terrain and obstacles, as well as typical weather conditions and other unique airport information of concern to pilots.

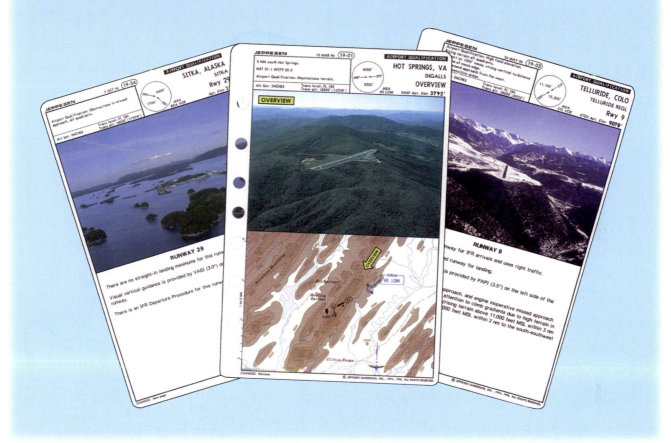

In addition to the airport listings, several other A/FD sections contain information essential to VFR flight operations, such as Special Notices, Land and Hold Short Operations, FAA and NWS Telephone Numbers, VOR Receiver Checkpoints, Parachute Jumping Areas, and the Aeronautical Chart Bulletin. Miscellaneous information in the A/FD includes the address and phone number for each Flight Standards District Office (FSDO) in the region, a map showing stations that provide enroute flight advisory service, and a key for decoding TAF and METAR printed weather reports.

You can refer to the *Airport/Facility Directory* for information regarding parachute jumping and glider operations.

The A/FD also contains information of special interest to IFR pilots such as a regional list of sector frequencies for ARTCCs, as well as preferred IFR routes. Some A/FDs provide information on tower enroute control service between adjacent approach control facilities. [Figure 5-32]

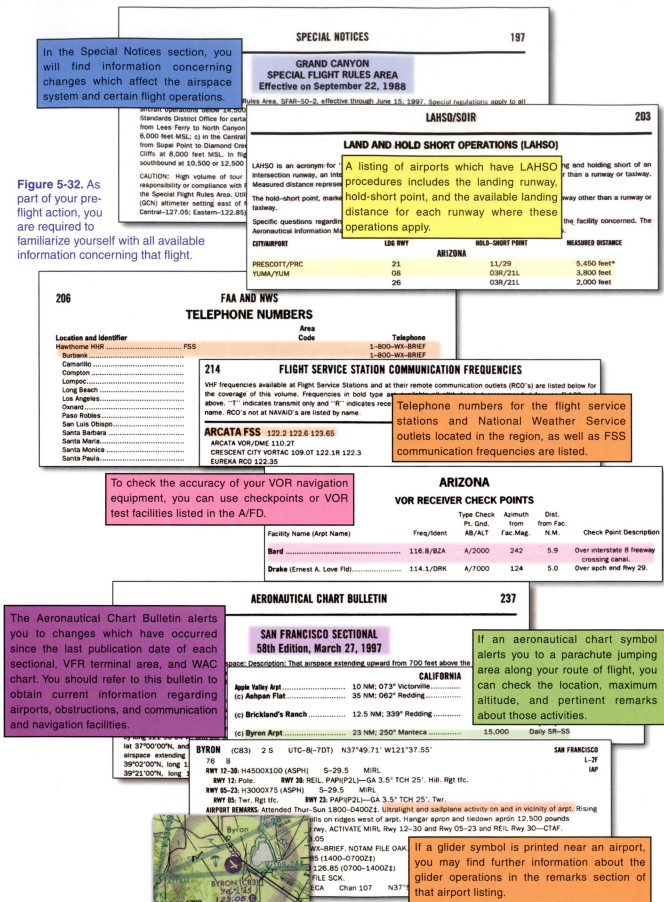

In the Special Notices section, you will find information concerning changes which affect the airspace system and certain flight operations.

SPECIAL NOTICES 197

**GRAND CANYON
SPECIAL FLIGHT RULES AREA**
Effective on September 22, 1988

Rules Area, SFAR–50–2, effective through June 15, 1997. Special regulations apply to all

aircraft operations below 14,500
Standards District Office for certa
from Lees Ferry to North Canyon
6,000 feet MSL; c) in the Central
from Supai Point to Diamond Cree
Cliffs at 8,000 feet MSL. In flig
southbound at 10,500 or 12,500

CAUTION: High volume of tour
responsibility or compliance with F
the Special Flight Rules Area. Util
(GCN) altimeter setting east of N
Central–127.05; Eastern–122.85)

Figure 5-32. As part of your pre-flight action, you are required to familiarize yourself with all available information concerning that flight.

LAHSO/SOIR 203

LAND AND HOLD SHORT OPERATIONS (LAHSO)

LAHSO is an acronym for '   ng and holding short of an
intersection runway, an inte   r than a runway or taxiway.
Measured distance represe

The hold–short point, marke   way other than a runway or
taxiway.

Specific questions regardin   e facility concerned. The
Aeronautical Information Ma

A listing of airports which have LAHSO procedures includes the landing runway, hold-short point, and the available landing distance for each runway where these operations apply.

CITY/AIRPORT	LDG RWY	HOLD–SHORT POINT	MEASURED DISTANCE
		ARIZONA	
PRESCOTT/PRC	21	11/29	5,450 feet*
YUMA/YUM	08	03R/21L	3,800 feet
	26	03R/21L	2,000 feet

206   **FAA AND NWS
TELEPHONE NUMBERS**

Location and Identifier	Area Code	Telephone
Hawthorne HHR .... FSS		1–800–WX–BRIEF
Burbank		1–800–WX–BRIEF
Camarillo		
Compton		
Lompoc.........................		
Long Beach		
Los Angeles		
Oxnard		
Paso Robles		
San Luis Obispo		
Santa Barbara		
Santa Maria		
Santa Monica		
Santa Paula		

214   **FLIGHT SERVICE STATION COMMUNICATION FREQUENCIES**

VHF frequencies available at Flight Service Stations and at their remote communication outlets (RCO's) are listed below for the coverage of this volume. Frequencies in bold type are available all altitudes but recommended for use above. ''T'' indicates transmit only and ''R'' indicates rece   name. RCO's not at NAVAID's are listed by name.

ARCATA FSS 122.2 122.6 123.65
ARCATA VOR/DME 110.2T
CRESCENT CITY VORTAC 109.0T 122.1R 122.3
EUREKA RCO 122.35

Telephone numbers for the flight service stations and National Weather Service outlets located in the region, as well as FSS communication frequencies are listed.

To check the accuracy of your VOR navigation equipment, you can use checkpoints or VOR test facilities listed in the A/FD.

ARIZONA

VOR RECEIVER CHECK POINTS

Facility Name (Arpt Name)	Freq/Ident	Type Check Pt. Gnd. AB/ALT	Azimuth from Fac.Mag.	Dist. from Fac. N.M.	Check Point Description
Bard	116.8/BZA	A/2000	242	5.9	Over interstate 8 freeway crossing canal.
Drake (Ernest A. Love Fld).........	114.1/DRK	A/7000	124	5.0	Over apch end Rwy 29.

AERONAUTICAL CHART BULLETIN 237

The Aeronautical Chart Bulletin alerts you to changes which have occurred since the last publication date of each sectional, VFR terminal area, and WAC chart. You should refer to this bulletin to obtain current information regarding airports, obstructions, and communication and navigation facilities.

**SAN FRANCISCO SECTIONAL
58th Edition, March 27, 1997**

space: Description: That airspace extending upward from 700 feet above the

		CALIFORNIA
Apple Valley Arpt.........................	10 NM; 073° Victorville............	
(c) Ashpan Flat.........................	35 NM; 062° Redding...............	
(c) Brickland's Ranch...............	12.5 NM; 339° Redding............	
(c) Byron Arpt.........................	23 NM; 250° Manteca.............	15,000 Daily SR–SS

If an aeronautical chart symbol alerts you to a parachute jumping area along your route of flight, you can check the location, maximum altitude, and pertinent remarks about those activities.

by long 121 08 04 a
lat 37°00'00"N, and
airspace extending
39°02'00"N, long 1
39°21'00"N, long

BYRON   (C83)   2 S   UTC–8(–7DT)   N37°49.71' W121°37.55'   **SAN FRANCISCO**
   76   B   **L–2F**
RWY 12–30: H4500X100 (ASPH)   S–29.5   MIRL   **IAP**
   RWY 12: Pole.   RWY 30: REIL. PAPI(P2L)—GA 3.5° TCH 25'. Hill. Rgt tfc.
RWY 05–23: H3000X75 (ASPH)   S–29.5   MIRL
   RWY 05: Twr. Rgt tfc.   RWY 23: PAPI(P2L)—GA 3.5° TCH 25'. Twr.
AIRPORT REMARKS: Attended Thur–Sun 1800–0400Z‡. Ultralight and sailplane activity on and in vicinity of arpt. Rising
                                        hills on ridges west of arpt. Hangar apron and tiedown apron 12,500 pounds
                                        rwy. ACTIVATE MIRL Rwy 12–30 and Rwy 05–23 and REIL Rwy 30–CTAF.
3.05   WX–BRIEF. NOTAM FILE OAK.
85 (1400–0700Z‡)
126.85 (0700–1400Z‡)
FILE SCK.
ECA   Chan 107   N37°5

If a glider symbol is printed near an airport, you may find further information about the glider operations in the remarks section of that airport listing.

FEDERAL AVIATION REGULATIONS

The Code of Federal Regulations (CFR) contains the official text of public regulations issued by the agencies of the Federal government. The Code is divided into 50 titles by subject matter, such as Agriculture, Energy, Labor, Postal Service, and Transportation. The Federal Aviation Regulations (FARs) can be found under subject title 14, Aeronautics and Space. The FARs are broken down into numbered parts and then sections which refer to a specific regulation. In government documents, a regulation is referred to by the CFR subject title number (14 CFR section 91.3). You normally will see the same regulation referred to as FAR 91.3. [Figure 5-33]

FAR Part 1 — Definitions and Abbreviations

FAR Part 43 — Maintenance, Preventive Maintenance, Rebuilding, and Alteration

FAR Part 61 — Certification: Pilots and Flight Instructors

FAR Part 67 — Medical Standards and Certification

FAR Part 71 — Designation of Federal Airways, Area Low Routes, Controlled Airspace, Reporting Points, Jet Routes, Area High Routes

FAR Part 73 — Special Use Airspace

FAR Part 91 — General Operating and Flight Rules

FAR Part 97 — Standard Instrument Approach Procedures

FAR Part 119 — Certification: Air Carriers and Commercial Operators

FAR Part 121 — Operating Requirements: Domestic, Flag, and Supplemental Operations

FAR Part 125 — Certification and Operations: Airplanes Having a Seating Capacity of 20 or More Passengers or a Maximum Payload Capacity of 6,000 Pounds or More

FAR Part 135 — Operating Requirements: Commuter and On-Demand Operations

FAR Part 141— Pilot Schools

FAR Part 142 — Training Centers

HMR 175 — Hazardous Materials Regulations (HMR) – Carriage by Aircraft

NTSB 830 — Rules Pertaining to the Notification and Reporting of Aircraft Accidents or Incidents and Overdue Aircraft, and Preservation of Aircraft Wreckage, Mail, Cargo, and Records

SFAR — Special Federal Aviation Regulations

Figure 5-33. There are several FAR Parts which cover subjects ranging from aircraft certification and maintenance to pilot medical standards and flight rules. The FAR Parts which pilots use most are shown here.

The *Federal Register* contains **Notices of Proposed Rulemaking (NPRMs)** which inform pilots of pending regulation changes. The publication of NPRMs allows interested parties enough time to comment on the proposal and present ideas which may influence the final rule. In addition, you often can determine the intent behind a regulation by reviewing the preamble to the final rule.

AERONAUTICAL INFORMATION MANUAL

Your official guide to basic flight information and ATC procedures is the *Aeronautical Information Manual* **(AIM)**. The AIM is revised several times a year, and it furnishes a detailed description of the national airspace system, including the procedures necessary to conduct flight operations in the United States. The AIM also includes items of special interest to pilots, such as medical facts and other flight safety information. [Figure 5-34]

Chapter 1
Navigation Aids

The AIM describes the capabilities, components, and procedures required for the use of each type of navaid. It also contains a discussion of radar services and procedures, as well as information regarding radar's capabilities and limitations.

Chapter 2
Aeronautical Lighting and Other Airport Visual Aids

A comprehensive description of the many types of airport lighting and marking aids can be found in this chapter.

Chapter 3
Airspace

This chapter covers the various forms of controlled, uncontrolled, special use , and other airspace areas including airspace dimensions, weather minimums, and operating requirements of each airspace class. VFR cruising altitudes also are outlined.

Chapter 4
Air Traffic Control

A discussion of the air traffic control system includes a description of facilities and services, such as air route traffic control centers, control towers, and flight service stations. In addition, a discussion is devoted to radio communication phraseology and techniques.

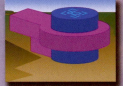

Chapter 5
Air Traffic Procedures

This chapter covers preflight, departure, enroute, and arrival procedures, as well as pilot/ controller roles and respon-sibilities and national security procedures.

Each new issue of the AIM provides an explanation of major changes. The areas that have been revised are indicated by solid bars in the margins aligned with the appropriate text.

Chapter 6
Emergency Procedures

In this chapter you can find descriptions of emergency services, as well as the procedures to be used in distress and urgency situations, and during two-way radio communication failure.

Chapter 7
Safety of Flight

Numerous weather services available for your preflight and enroute operations are detailed in this chapter. Altimeter settings, wake tur-bulence avoidance, and potential flight hazards, as well as safety, accident, and hazard reporting procedures are discussed.

Chapter 8
Medical Facts for Pilots

Aviation physiology, including fitness for flight, the effects of altitude, and vision in flight are discussed here.

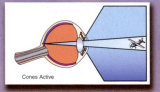

Chapter 9
Aeronautical Charts and Related Publications

The AIM provides a list of the various aeronautical charts and publications available from the government.

Pilot/Controller Glossary

This glossary is intended to promote a common understanding of the terms used in the air traffic control system. International terms which differ from the FAA definitions are listed after their U.S. equivalents.

LANDING AREA- Any locality either on land, water. or structures, including airports/heliports and intermediate landing fields, which is used, or intended to be used, for the landing and takeoff of aircraft whether or not facilities are provided for the shelter, servicing, or for receiving or discharging passengers or cargo.
(See ICAO term LANDING AREA).
LANDING AREA [ICAO]- That part of a movement area intended for the landing or takeoff of aircraft.

2-1-5. IN-RUNWAY LIGHTING
Touchdown zone lights and runway centerline lights are installed on some precision approach runways to facilitate landing under adverse visibility conditions. Land and hold short lights are installed on some runways which are approved for land and hold short operations (LAHSO) to indicate the hold-short point. Taxiway lead-off lights may be added to expedite movement of aircraft from the runway.

Figure 5-34. The AIM's comprehensive table of contents and alphabetical index help you locate specific subjects.

BREAKING THE RULES

There are several types of FAA enforcement actions which may be taken if a pilot violates a regulation. These actions range from warning notices and letters of correction to reexamination or certificate action. In more serious cases, the FAA may pursue emergency actions, civil penalties, or even criminal actions.

Although an enforcement action by the FAA is a substantial deterrent to violating a regulation, the most compelling reason to adhere to the FARs is to preserve flight safety. The consequence of breaking the rules is often an accident. It is your responsibility as pilot in command to understand the current FARs, and you must make the decision to follow them. Some pilots exhibit an anti-authority attitude which causes them to regard regulations as unnecessary. When these pilots choose to disregard regulations such as currency requirements, weather minimums, and minimum safe altitudes, the outcome is often tragic.

NOTICES TO AIRMEN

Often, changes in aeronautical information are not known far enough in advance to be included in the most recent aeronautical charts or *Airport/Facility Directory*. The National Notices to Airmen System provides you with time-critical flight planning information. Each notice is categorized as a NOTAM(D), a NOTAM(L), or an FDC NOTAM.

NOTAM(D) (distant NOTAM) information is disseminated for all navigational facilities which are part of the U.S. airspace system, all public use airports, seaplane bases, and heliports listed in the A/FD. The complete NOTAM(D) file is maintained in a computer database at the National Weather Message Switching Center (WMSC) in Atlanta, Georgia. Most air traffic facilities, primarily FSSs, have access to the entire database of NOTAM(D)s, which remain available for the duration of their validity, or until published.

NOTAM(L)s (local NOTAMs) are distributed locally and contain information, such as taxiway closures, personnel and equipment near or crossing runways, and airport rotating beacon and lighting aid outages. A separate file of local NOTAMs is maintained at each FSS for facilities in the area. NOTAM(L) information for other FSS areas must be specifically requested directly from the FSS that has responsibility for the airport concerned. [Figure 5-35]

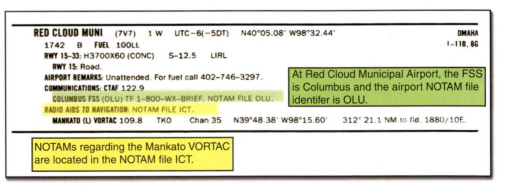

Figure 5-35.
Airport/Facility Directory listings include the associated FSS and NOTAM file identifiers.

FDC NOTAMs, issued by the National Flight Data Center, contain regulatory information such as temporary flight restrictions or amendments to instrument approach procedures and other current aeronautical charts. FDC NOTAMs are available through all air traffic facilities with telecommunications access.

The **Notices to Airmen publication (NTAP)** is issued every 28 days and contains all current NOTAM(D)s and FDC NOTAMs (except FDC NOTAMs for temporary flight restrictions) available for publication. Federal airway changes, which are identified as Center Area NOTAMs, are included with the NOTAM(D) listing. Published NOTAM(D) information is not provided during pilot briefings unless requested. Data of a permanent nature are sometimes printed in the NOTAM publication as an interim step prior to publication on the appropriate aeronautical chart or in the A/FD. [Figure 5-36]

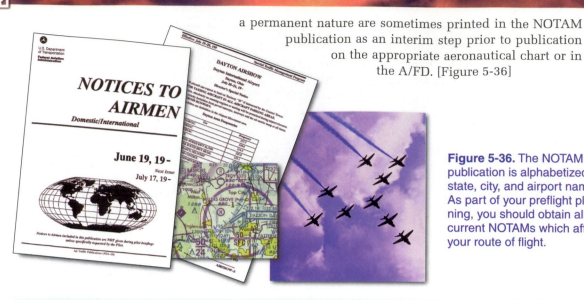

Figure 5-36. The NOTAM publication is alphabetized by state, city, and airport name. As part of your preflight planning, you should obtain all the current NOTAMs which affect your route of flight.

Extra, Extra — Read All About It!

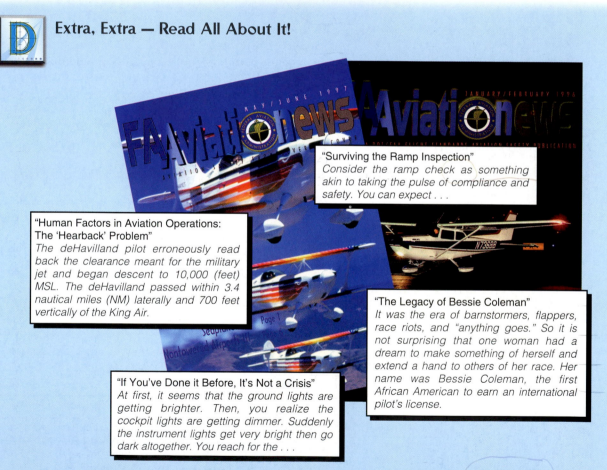

"Surviving the Ramp Inspection"
Consider the ramp check as something akin to taking the pulse of compliance and safety. You can expect . . .

"Human Factors in Aviation Operations: The 'Hearback' Problem"
The deHavilland pilot erroneously read back the clearance meant for the military jet and began descent to 10,000 (feet) MSL. The deHavilland passed within 3.4 nautical miles (NM) laterally and 700 feet vertically of the King Air.

"The Legacy of Bessie Coleman"
It was the era of barnstormers, flappers, race riots, and "anything goes." So it is not surprising that one woman had a dream to make something of herself and extend a hand to others of her race. Her name was Bessie Coleman, the first African American to earn an international pilot's license.

"If You've Done it Before, It's Not a Crisis"
At first, it seems that the ground lights are getting brighter. Then, you realize the cockpit lights are getting dimmer. Suddenly the instrument lights get very bright then go dark altogether. You reach for the . . .

The preceding excerpts were taken from the magazine, *FAA Aviation News.* This publication contains a wide variety of articles on subjects ranging from human factors and accident investigation to regulations and aviation history. *FAA Aviation News* provides up-to-date information on technology, FARs, and procedures which affect the safe operation of aircraft. Although based on current FAA policy and rule interpretation, the information in *FAA Aviation News* is not regulatory, but is published in the interest of safety.

You can obtain a subscription to *FAA Aviation News* through the U.S. Government Printing Office or access their website at **www.faa.gov/avr/news/newshome.htm.**

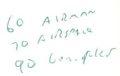

ADVISORY CIRCULARS

By issuing **advisory circulars (ACs)** the FAA has developed a systematic means of providing pilots with nonregulatory guidance and information in a variety of subject areas. ACs also explain methods for complying with FARs. Unless incorporated into a regulation by reference, the contents of an AC are not binding. [Figure 5-37]

60 Airmen
70 Airspace
90 Complex

Advisory Circular

U.S. Department of Transportation

Federal Aviation Administration

As advisory circulars are revised, a letter suffix is added to the identification number. For example, the subsequent version of this AC would be numbered 00-24C.

The subject of an advisory circular is identified in the heading.

Subject:	THUNDERSTORMS	Date:	1/20/83	AC No:	00-24B
		Initiated by:	AFO-260	Change:	

1. PURPOSE. This advisory circular describes the hazards of thunderstorms to aviation and offers guidance to help prevent accidents caused by thunderstorms.

00 General

00-24B Thunderstorms

70 Airspace

70/7460-1H Obstruction Marking and Lighting

20 Aircraft

20-27D Certification and Operation of Amateur-Built Aircraft

90 Air Traffic Control and General Operating Rules

91-13C Cold Weather Operation of Aircraft

60 Airmen

61-9B Pilot Transition Courses for Complex Single-Engine and Light Twin-Engine Airplanes

150 Airports

150/5340-18C Standards for Airport Sign Systems

If a series of circulars exists for a given subject, the general area of information is subdivided into specific areas. For example, within the 150 series pertaining to airports, the number 5340 designates the specific subject area of airport visual aids.

Figure 5-37. Advisory circulars are divided into a variety of subjects, and are identified by numbers corresponding to the different Part numbers of the FARs.

You can order ACs through the Department of Transportation, U.S. Government Printing Office. Some ACs are free and others are available at cost. The *Advisory Circular Checklist* (AC-00-2) provides you with pricing and ordering information and is periodically revised and reissued to inform you of the current status of ACs.

 Advisory circulars are divided into a variety of subjects, and are identified by numbers corresponding to the different Part numbers of the FARs. For example, ACs specifically related to airmen are issued under 60. Airspace information is contained in ACs issued under 70, while air traffic control and general operations can be found under 90.

 FAA advisory circulars (some free, others at cost) are available to all pilots and can be ordered from the U.S. Government Printing Office.

JEPPESEN INFORMATION SERVICES

Many commercial publishers offer information for pilots which is comparable to that found in government sources. For example, Jeppesen publishes both a printed and CD ROM version of the FAR/AIM, each of which is revised annually. In addition, **Jeppesen Information Services** provide revision subscriptions for several flight information publications including the *Jeppesen AIM, Jeppesen FARs for Pilots*, the *Jeppesen Airport Directory*, *JeppGuide,* and the *GPS/LORAN Coordinate Directory*. The AIM, FARs, airport directory, and *JeppGuide* are printed in loose-leaf format for ease of revision.

JEPPESEN FARs FOR PILOTS

By subscribing to the FARs service, you receive updates to the regulations every 16 weeks and as regulations are amended. The FARs service includes the Parts most commonly used by pilots, including the Hazardous Materials Regulations (HMR), National Transportation Safety Board (NTSB) Part 830, and current Special FARs. [Figure 5-38]

Figure 5-38. The revised paragraphs, which are actually amendments to the regulations, are clearly indicated by arrows or brackets in the margin of the affected pages.

JEPPESEN AIM

The *Jeppesen AIM* service provides revisions upon receiving any changes and contains the information published in the government edition, including the Pilot/Controller Glossary, as well as Tables and Codes and Entry Requirements. Because of the comprehensive coverage of the material and the frequency of revision, FAR Part 135.81 authorizes air taxi and commercial operators to use the *Jeppesen AIM* as a substitute for the government edition.

JEPPESEN AIRPORT DIRECTORY AND JEPPGUIDE

The *Jeppesen Airport Directory* service includes a choice of regional coverages or full U.S. coverage updated twice a year. To avoid duplication of diagrams on IFR approach charts, only VFR airport diagrams are published in these directories. However, pertinent airport data are included for both IFR and VFR airports. When appropriate, general operational information, airport remarks, fixed base operator (FBO) services, car rental services, and lodging and restaurant availability are noted. Airports within each state are listed by city name, followed by the airport name, when different. The *JeppGuide* depicts one airport per page and provides diagrams for both VFR and IFR airports. [Figure 5-39]

Figure 5-39. In addition to airport data, *JeppGuide* provides extensive, detailed listings of FBO services, including availability of restaurants at the airport and nearby, fuel services, repair facilities, credit card acceptance, lodging, and rental cars.

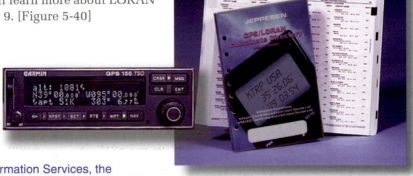

GPS/LORAN COORDINATE DIRECTORY

An important reference document for users of GPS and LORAN equipment, this directory contains coordinates for all public-use airports, navaids, and waypoints within the contiguous 48 states. Airports are arranged by state, city, and airport name. An FAA identifier is included, as well as the airport reference point (ARP) coordinates. The ARP is usually located in the center of the airport. Waypoints are listed by name, and airports and navaids are listed by name and three-letter identifier. Each listing is indicated by an edge-marked tab. You will learn more about LORAN and GPS navigation in Chapter 9. [Figure 5-40]

Figure 5-40. Unlike the other Jeppesen Information Services, the *GPS/LORAN Coordinate Directory* is published in a bound book (5-1/2″ × 8-1/2″). It is updated and reissued on the FAA's 56-day cycle.

ELECTRONIC FLIGHT PUBLICATIONS

You can access a variety of flight information by using a modem-equipped personal computer and the appropriate software or Internet service. The government uses electronic bulletin boards and world wide web sites to make flight publications and information updates more readily accessible to the general aviation community. For example, the FAA Home Page contains information on various aviation subjects and links to other home pages, such as FedWorld Information Network. Through FedWorld, you can access and order government publications, such as advisory circulars, FARs, practical test standards, and the *Federal Register*. [Figure 5-41]

Figure 5-41. You can access the FAA Home Page at **http://www.faa.gov**.

SUMMARY CHECKLIST

✓ The *Airport/Facility Directory* contains a descriptive listing of all airports, heliports, and seaplane bases which are open to the public.

✓ The *Aeronautical Information Manual* (AIM) contains basic flight information, a detailed description of the national airspace system, ATC procedures, and other items of special interest to pilots, such as medical facts and other flight safety information.

✓ NOTAM(D)s are disseminated for all navigational facilities which are part of the U.S. airspace system, all public use airports, seaplane bases, and heliports listed in the A/FD.

✓ NOTAM(L)s, which are locally distributed, contain information such as taxiway closures, personnel and equipment near or crossing runways, and airport rotating beacon and lighting aid outages.

✓ FDC NOTAMs, which are issued by the National Flight Data Center, contain regulatory information such as temporary flight restrictions or amendments to instrument approach procedures and other current aeronautical charts.

✓ The Notices to Airmen publication is issued every 28 days and contains all current NOTAM(D)s and FDC NOTAMs (except FDC NOTAMs for temporary flight restrictions) available for publication.

✓ Advisory circulars (ACs) provide you with nonregulatory guidance and information in a variety of subject areas. ACs also explain methods for complying with the FARs.

✓ Jeppesen Information Services provide revisions for the *Jeppesen AIM, Jeppesen FARs for Pilots*, the *Jeppesen Airport Directory, JeppGuide,* and the *GPS/LORAN Coordinate Directory.*

KEY TERMS

Airport/Facility Directory (A/FD)	NOTAM(D)
Directory Legend	NOTAM(L)
Federal Register	FDC NOTAM
Notice of Proposed Rulemaking (NPRM)	Notices to Airmen Publication (NTAP)
Aeronautical Information Manual (AIM)	Advisory Circulars (ACs)
	Jeppesen Information Services

QUESTIONS

Refer to the Airport/Facility Directory excerpt to answer questions 1 through 9.

```
NORTH PLATTE REGIONAL AIRPORT LEE BIRD FLD    (LBF)   3 E   UTC-6(-5DT)                    OMAHA
        N41°07.56' W100°41.23'                                                            H-1D, L-11A
  2778    B    S4    FUEL 100LL, JET A    OX 4    ARFF Index Ltd.                               IAP
  RWY 12L-30R: H8000X150 (CONC-GRVD)      S-75, D-110, DT-190      HIRL
    RWY 12L: VASI(V4L)—GA 3.0° TCH 55'.          RWY 30R: MALSR. Rgt tfc.
  RWY 12R-30L: H4925X100 (ASPH)      S-42, D-58, DT-106      MIRL
    RWY 12R: Rgt tfc.    RWY 30L: Tree.
  RWY 17-35: H4436X100 (ASPH)      S-28, D-48, DT-86      MIRL
    RWY 17: Road.          RWY 35: REIL. VASI(V4L)—GA 3.0° TCH 41'. Thld dsplcd 234'. Berm.
  AIRPORT REMARKS: Attended 1200-0500Z‡. 5 foot dike 100' from approach end Rwy 35. Waterfowl and deer on and
    in the vicinity of the arpt. PPR 24 hours for unscheduled air carrier ops with more than 30 passenger seats call
    arpt manager 308-532-1900. ACTIVATE HIRL Rwy 12L-30R, MIRL Rwy 17-35, VASI Rwy 12L and Rwy 35,
    MALSR Rwy 30R and REIL Rwy 35—CTAF. For MIRL Rwy 12R-30L ctc arpt manager 308-532-1900.
  WEATHER DATA SOURCES: ASOS 118.425 (308) 534-1617.
  COMMUNICATIONS: CTAF/UNICOM 123.0
    COLUMBUS FSS (OLU) TF 1-800-WX-BRIEF. NOTAM FILE LBF.
    LEE BIRD RCO 122.5 (COLUMBUS FSS)
  Ⓡ DENVER CENTER APP/DEP CON 132.7    OLNO DEL 133.7
  RADIO AIDS TO NAVIGATION: NOTAM FILE LBF.
    (L) VORTACW 117.4    LBF    Chan 121    N41°02.92' W100°44.83'    019° 5 4 NM to fld. 3050/11E.
    PANBE NDB (LOM) 416    LB    N41°04.10' W100°34.35'    295° 6.3 NM to fld. Unmonitored.
    ILS 111.5    I-LBF    Rwy 30R    LOM PANBE NDB. LOM and MM unmonitored.
```

1. What is the distance and direction of Lee Bird Field from the city?

2. What is the airport elevation?

3. How many feet long and wide is the longest runway at Lee Bird Field?

4. What type of servicing is available at Lee Bird Field?

    A. Minor airframe and minor powerplant repairs
    B. Major airframe and minor powerplant repairs
    C. Major airframe and major powerplant repairs

5. Select the correct traffic patterns for the runways at Lee Bird Field.

    A. Left-hand for all runways
    B. Left-hand for Runways 12L and 30R and right-hand for all other runways
    C. Right-hand for Runways 30R and 12R and left-hand for all other runways

6. True/False. The UNICOM frequency for Lee Bird Field is 122.5.

7. If you land at Lee Bird Field at 2:15 p.m. local standard time, what is your arrival time in Zulu?

8. What flight service station should you contact to obtain a weather briefing at Lee Bird Field?

9. What NOTAM file is designated for Lee Bird Field?

10. Select the information which you can obtain by referencing the *Aeronautical Information Manual* (AIM).

    A. The official text of regulations issued by the agencies of the Federal government
    B. ATC procedures, a description of the airspace system, and flight safety information
    C. Information regarding specific airports, including runway lengths, communication frequencies, and airport services

11. Explain the differences between NOTAM(L)s, NOTAM(D)s, and FDC NOTAMs.

12. What is the primary source document for identifying and ordering advisory circulars?

PART III
AVIATION WEATHER

Know the signs of the sky and you will far the happier be.

— Benjamin Franklin

PART III

It is one of the largest variables affecting any flight, yet its fickle nature is one of the things that makes flying so challenging and exciting. It, of course, is the atmosphere and the weather which occurs within it. The information in Part III will provide you with the tools necessary to ensure that your flights in the ever-changing atmosphere are safe and enjoyable. In *Meteorology for Pilots*, you will discover how weather forms and how its hazards can affect aircraft operations. In *Graphic Reports and Forecasts*, you will unlock the mystery of how meteorologists formulate weather forecasts. Then, you will see how those forecasts, and the current weather on which they are based, is presented and disseminated to pilots.

CHAPTER 6

METEOROLOGY FOR PILOTS

Part III, Chapter 6   Meteorology for Pilots

Discovery Workshop — Aviation Weather

SECTION A
BASIC WEATHER THEORY

Weather and flying are inextricably linked. You cannot take to the air without being affected by the environment through which you are flying. In order to determine the impact of weather on your flight, you will need to evaluate day-to-day elements like clouds, wind, and rain. To do so, a fundamental understanding of the atmosphere and its dynamic nature is essential.

THE ATMOSPHERE

The **atmosphere** is a remarkable mixture of life-giving gases surrounding our planet. Without the atmosphere, there would be no clouds, oceans, or protection from the sun's intense rays. Though this protective blanket is essential to life on earth, it is extraordinarily thin — nearly 99% of the atmosphere exists within 30 kilometers (about 100,000 feet) of the surface. That's roughly equivalent to a piece of paper wrapped around a beach ball. [Figure 6-1]

Figure 6-1. When viewed from space, the most dense part of the earth's atmosphere is seen as a thin blue area near the surface.

Why is the Sky Blue?

As sunlight passes through the air, the wavelengths of light are scattered by the molecules of atmospheric gases. The degree to which a particular color of light is scattered is a function of its wavelength. Colors with short wavelengths such as blue, green, and violet are scattered more than others and, consequently, enter the eye from a variety of angles. Since the human eye is more sensitive to the wavelength associated with blue, it seems as if blue light is coming from all directions, hence the predominant color of the sky. [Figure A]

Of course, the shade of blue can vary widely from one day to the next. In general, the lighter the shade of blue, the more likely that contaminants are present in the air. When relatively large particles, such as dust, become suspended in the atmosphere, all the wavelengths of light will be scattered. The effect on the human eye is such that the sky appears to become milky white, or hazy. [Figure B]

ATMOSPHERIC LEVELS

There is no specific upper limit to the atmosphere; it simply thins to a point where it fades away into empty space. As you progress outward from the earth's surface, the atmosphere displays different properties, including a fluctuating distribution of temperatures. These temperature variances are the most common basis for classifying the atmosphere into layers, or spheres.

The **troposphere** (from the Greek word, trope, meaning "turn" or "change") is the layer extending from the surface to an average altitude of about 36,000 feet. Above the troposphere is the **tropopause** (a level, not a layer) which acts as a lid to confine most of the water vapor, and the associated weather, to the troposphere. Above the tropopause are three more atmospheric layers. The first is the **stratosphere**, which has much the same composition as the troposphere and extends to a height of approximately 160,000 feet. Above the stratosphere are the **mesosphere** and **thermosphere**, which have little practical influence over weather. [Figure 6-2]

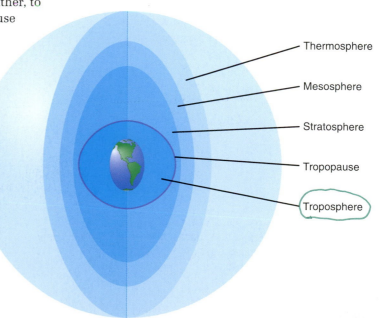

Thermosphere

Mesosphere

Stratosphere

Tropopause

Troposphere

Figure 6-2. The height of the troposphere (and tropopause) varies with the season and location over the globe. The tropopause is lower near the poles and in the winter; it is higher near the equator and in the summer. Note that the layer depths around the globe have been greatly exaggerated for clarity.

LOOKING AT THE WORLD THROUGH GRAY COLORED GLASSES

In the presence of bright glare, a good pair of sunglasses can usually improve visual acuity, reduce fatigue, and help your dark adaptation later in the day. There are, however, some things you should consider when selecting and wearing sunglasses. For example, sunglasses should be a neutral gray color in order to allow the widest spectrum of light to reach the eye. A green lens, for example, will tend to wash out any object colored green. This of course can be critical if a particular cockpit display uses green as a primary color. A neutral gray lens, on the other hand, filters out equal amounts of all colors, and provides you with the truest representation of the entire light spectrum. [Figure A]

In addition, you should understand that your depth of field is reduced when wearing sunglasses. This is analogous to a camera lens. As the aperture of the lens is opened to allow more light in (similar to the eye's iris opening as sunglasses are donned) objects will remain focused to a lesser depth. [Figure B] As you can imagine, this can be of particular importance in the landing pattern.

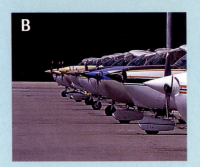

COMPOSITION OF THE ATMOSPHERE

If you could capture a cubic foot of atmosphere and analyze it, you would find it is composed of about 78% nitrogen and 21% oxygen. The remaining 1% is made up of several other gases, primarily argon and carbon dioxide. This cubic foot of atmosphere would also contain anywhere from almost zero to about 4% water vapor by volume. This relatively small amount of water vapor is responsible for major changes in the weather. [Figure 6-3]

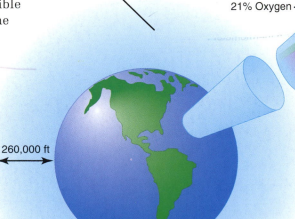

Atmosphere

78% Nitrogen
1% Other Gases
21% Oxygen

260,000 ft

Figure 6-3. The atmosphere is a mixture of gases that exists in fairly uniform proportions up to approximately 260,000 feet above the earth.

ATMOSPHERIC CIRCULATION

Atmospheric **circulation** may be considered simply to be the movement of air relative to the earth's surface. Since the atmosphere is fixed to the earth by gravity and rotates with the earth, there would be no circulation were it not for forces which upset the atmosphere's equilibrium. The dynamic nature of the atmosphere is due, in a large part, to unequal temperatures at the earth's surface.

TEMPERATURE

As the earth rotates about the sun, the length of time and the angle at which sunlight strikes a particular portion of the earth's surface changes. Over the course of a year, this variance in solar energy is the reason we experience seasons. In general, however, the most direct rays of the sun strike the earth in the vicinity of the equator while the poles receive the least direct light and energy from the sun. [Figure 6-4]

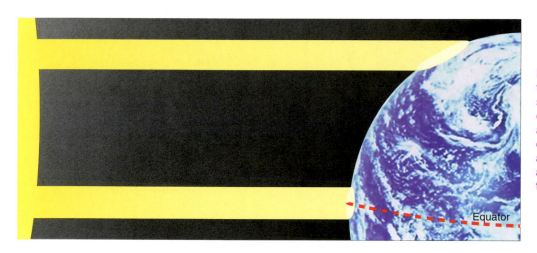

Equator

Figure 6-4. Although the same amounts of solar energy strike the earth at the equator and near the pole, the energy is spread over a much larger surface area near the pole than at the equator.

 2,000 Degrees Cooler in the Shade

In the upper reaches of the atmosphere, the air temperature can approach 1500°F, yet, if a thermometer were shielded from the sun, it would display a temperature close to absolute zero (-459.67°F). How is this possible? The apparent paradox stems from the meaning of air temperature and how it is measured. Normally, a thermometer measures temperature by displaying the average kinetic energy of the air molecules striking the thermometer's bulb. Although the few molecules in the thin upper atmosphere are moving at speeds corresponding to a very high temperature, the traditional method of measuring temperature doesn't work well because there simply aren't enough molecules to heat an object (such as a thermometer's bulb). Temperatures at extremely high altitudes are more closely related to radiation gain and loss between the portion of an object facing the sun and the opposite side. The harsh environment requires that space suits be designed to keep astronauts comfortable even when the difference between sun and shade could be the equivalent of nearly 2000°!

Courtesy of NASA Ames Home Page (image no. AS11-44-6557).

CONVECTION

To compensate for heating inequities, heat is transported, or circulated, from one latitude to another. When air is heated, its molecules spread apart. As the air expands, it becomes less dense and lighter than the surrounding air. As air cools, the molecules become packed more closely together, making it denser and heavier than warm air. As a result, the cool, heavy air tends to sink and replace warmer, rising air. This circulation process is known as **convection**.

To understand how convection contributes to atmospheric circulation, it is easiest to start with a simplified example. In this convection-only model, a stationary earth uniformly covered with water is warmed by energy radiating from the sun positioned directly over the equator. This solar energy strikes equatorial regions in much greater concentrations, resulting in much higher temperatures than at the poles. As a result, cold, dense air from the poles sinks and flows toward the equator, where it displaces rising air that is warmer and less dense. [Figure 6-5]

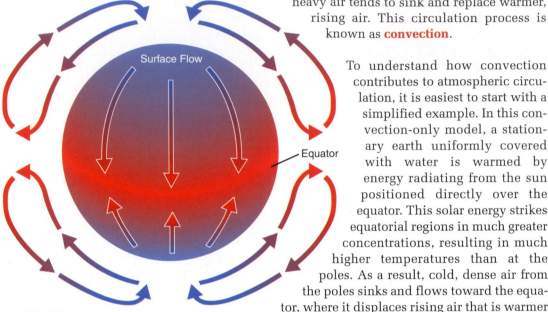

Figure 6-5. If the earth did not rotate, a huge convective circulation pattern would develop as air flowed from the poles to the equator and back again.

THREE-CELL CIRCULATION PATTERN

Of course, the earth doesn't stand still in space. As the earth rotates, the single-cell circulation breaks up into three cells. The air still rises at the equator and flows toward the poles aloft, but that branch of the circulation reaches only about 30° latitude where the air sinks. This cell is called the Hadley Cell for an 18th century scientist who first proposed the model of general circulation. The Ferrel cell, which forms between 30° and 60° latitude, bears the name of another researcher of general circulation. The cell which exists between 60° and the poles is aptly referred to as the Polar cell. This resulting wind circulation is more involved, but much more realistic. [Figure 6-6]

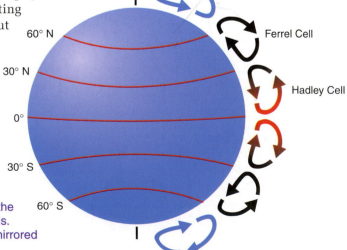

Figure 6-6. In the three-cell circulation model, three cells per hemisphere distribute heat energy. In the Hadley cell, warm air rises and moves toward the poles. At approximately 30° latitude the air cools enough to sink back to the surface. Some of this air moves poleward until, at about 60° latitude, it meets cooler air migrating from the poles. The two air masses of different temperatures are forced upward creating the circulation associated with the Ferrel and Polar cells. Note that the northern hemisphere cell pattern is mirrored south of the equator.

ATMOSPHERIC PRESSURE

The unequal heating of the surface not only modifies air density and creates circulation patterns, it also causes changes in pressure. This is one of the main reasons for differences in altimeter settings between weather reporting stations. Meteorologists plot these pressure readings on weather maps and connect points of equal pressure with lines called isobars. Isobars are measured in millibars and are usually drawn at four-millibar intervals. The resulting pattern reveals the **pressure gradient**, or change in pressure over distance. When isobars are spread widely apart, the gradient is considered to be weak, while closely spaced isobars indicate a strong gradient. Isobars also help to identify pressure systems, which are classified as highs, lows, ridges, troughs, and cols. A **high** is a center of high pressure surrounded on all sides by lower pressure. Conversely, a **low** is an area of low pressure surrounded by higher pressure. A **ridge** is an elongated area of high pressure, while a **trough** is an elongated area of low pressure. A **col** can designate either a neutral area between two highs and two lows, or the intersection of a ridge and a trough. [Figure 6-7]

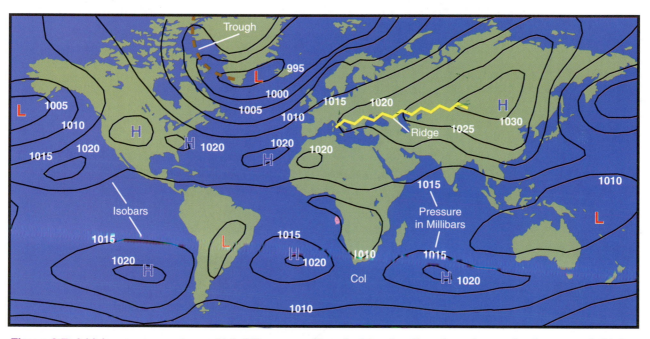

Figure 6-7. A high pressure center, or high (H), on a weather chart is a location where the sea level pressure is high compared to the surrounding pressure. Similarly, a low pressure center, or low (L), is a roughly circular area with a lower sea level pressure in the center as compared to the surrounding region. Isobars are analogous to contour lines on a topographical chart.

Air generally flows from the cool, dense air of highs into the warm, less dense air of lows. The speed of the resulting wind depends on the strength of the pressure gradient. A strong gradient tends to produce strong wind, while a weak gradient results in lighter winds. The force behind this movement is caused by the pressure gradient and is referred to as pressure gradient force. If **pressure gradient force** were the only force affecting the movement of air, wind would always blow directly from the higher pressure area to the lower pressure area. However, as soon as the air begins to move, it is deflected by a phenomenon known as Coriolis force.

 Variations in altimeter settings between weather reporting points are primarily caused by the unequal heating of the earth's surface.

CORIOLIS FORCE

Coriolis force, named after the French scientist who first described it in 1835, affects all objects moving freely across the face of the earth. Essentially, things such as ocean currents and airplane flight paths, which would otherwise follow a straight line, end up tracing a curved path due to the earth's rotation. [Figure 6-8]

A man stands on the edge of a spinning merry-go-round.

A ball is thrown to the man by a person standing on the opposite side of the merry-go-round.

Figure 6-8. Coriolis force explains why a ball thrown across a spinning merry-go-round appears to curve away from the intended target.

To an outside observer, the ball travels in a straight line after it is thrown.

To the people on the merry-go-round, the ball seems to curve away from the intended path, missing the target.

The outside observer realizes that the ball is not actually deflected; rather, the thrower and catcher change positions during the time it takes the ball to travel across the merry-go-round.

Since the earth rotates only once every 24 hours, the effect of Coriolis force is much weaker than what was displayed in the merry-go-round example in figure 6-8. In fact, Coriolis is only significant when an object such as a parcel of air moves over a large distance (several hundred miles or more). The amount of deflection produced by Coriolis force also varies with latitude. It is zero at the equator and increases toward the poles. [Figure 6-9] In the northern hemisphere, any deviation will be to the right of its intended path while the opposite will occur in the southern hemisphere. In addition, the magnitude of the curve caused by Coriolis force varies with the speed of the moving object — the greater the speed, the greater the deviation.

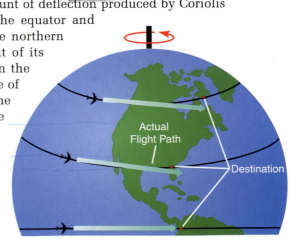

Figure 6-9. An airplane traveling either east or west directly above the equator will not experience any deviation from its intended flight path due to the effects of Coriolis force. Closer to the poles, the effects of Coriolis force become increasingly apparent.

FRICTIONAL FORCE

Pressure gradient and Coriolis forces work in combination to create wind. Pressure gradient force causes air to move from high pressure areas to low pressure areas. As the air begins to move, Coriolis force deflects it to the right in the northern hemisphere. This results in a clockwise flow around a high pressure area. The deflection continues until pressure gradient force and Coriolis force are in balance, and the wind flows roughly parallel to the isobars. As the air flows into a low pressure area, it moves counterclockwise around the low. This generally holds true for upper air winds. However, within about 2,000 feet of the ground, friction caused by the earth's surface slows the moving air. This **frictional force** reduces the Coriolis force. Since the pressure gradient force is now greater than Coriolis force, the wind is diverted from its path along the isobars toward the lower pressure. [Figure 6-10]

 Friction causes wind to shift directions when near the earth's surface.

Figure 6-10. As surface friction retards the airflow, Coriolis force is weakened. This allows pressure gradient force to shift the airflow toward areas of lower pressure, causing the wind to blow at an angle across the isobars.

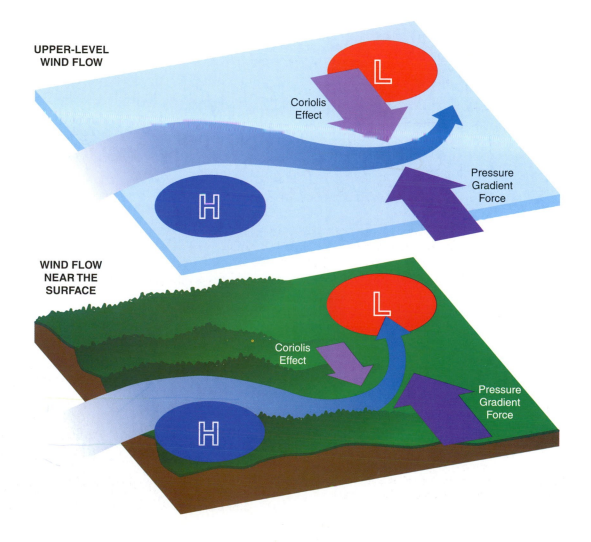

GLOBAL WIND PATTERNS

As tropical air rises and flows northward, it is deflected to the right by Coriolis. Around 30° north, the flow is eastward, causing air to pile up (converge) at this latitude. This creates a semi-permanent high pressure area. At the surface, air flows back toward the equator where an area of low pressure exists. This low-level southerly flow is deflected to the west creating the northeast trade winds, named for the steady winds provided to ships sailing to the New World. The low-level air flowing northward from the high pressure at 30° also is deflected to the right by Coriolis. This creates the prevailing westerlies common to the middle latitudes. The cold polar air which flows southward from an area of high pressure is deflected to the right to create the polar easterlies. As this cold air meets the relatively warmer air from the prevailing westerlies, a semi-permanent low pressure area is formed around 60° north latitude. The line separating the airmasses in this region is called the polar front. [Figure 6-11]

Figure 6-11. The three-cell circulation pattern produces areas of high pressure near 30° latitude and the poles; areas of low pressure exist over the equator and at approximately 60° latitude. Note that the associated wind pattern in the southern hemisphere is a mirror image of the pattern north of the equator.

The Last Great Aviation Record

By landing their balloon, dubbed the *Double Eagle II*, on French soil in August 1978, Maxie Anderson, Ben Abruzzo, and Larry Newman completed the first successful crossing of the Atlantic Ocean by a manned balloon. The pilots and their craft accomplished what had eluded people for nearly 200 years. Three years later, Abruzzo and Newman were joined by Ron Clark and Rocky Aoki when they flew the *Double Eagle 5* across the Pacific Ocean.

The most logical next step — circumnavigating the globe in a balloon — has proven to be another difficult, but not impossible, endeavor. Although several attempts were made in the early 1990s, the competition intensified in the last half of the decade. The magnitude of the challenge made the design and construction of a balloon that could make the trip an achievement in itself. The successful balloon had to be thinner than a piece of paper, yet strong enough to support a crew capsule weighing several tons while withstanding hurricane force winds.

Regardless of the design of the craft, a round-the-world attempt can triumph or fail as quickly as the winds can change. One balloon was even shot down by a Belarussian helicopter gunship on September 12, 1995. Several other attempts were made between 1996 and 1999 in various balloons such as the *Solo Challenger, Solo Spirit, Breitling Orbiter, Global Hilton, ICO Global Challenger*, and *Cable and Wireless*.

On March 1, 1999, the *Breitling Orbiter 3* was launched from Chateaux d'Oeux, Switzerland with crewmembers Bertrand Piccard and Brian Jones on board. As the *Orbiter* passed over Central America, cabin temperature dropped to 46° F, causing breathing problems for the crew. They became demoralized as the voyage dragged on and the winds refused to cooperate, yet they continued to make progress. Finally, the winds began to pick up over the Atlantic and they sailed past the meridian that marked the finish of the first complete circumnavigation of the world in a balloon. The *Orbiter 3* landed at 1:02 a.m. near the Oasis of Mut in Egypt on March 21, 1999, after 19 days, 21 hours, and 55 minutes in the air. The last great aviation record was achieved.

LOCAL WIND PATTERNS

Although global wind patterns influence the earth's overall weather, local wind patterns may be of greater practical importance to you as a pilot since they usually cause significant changes in the weather of a particular area. These localized wind patterns are caused by terrain variations such as mountains, valleys, and water. The force behind these winds — cool air replacing warm air — is the same as it is for global wind patterns, but on a much smaller scale.

 Convective circulation patterns associated with sea breezes are caused by cool, dense air moving inland from over the water.

SEA BREEZE

Since land surfaces warm or cool more rapidly than water surfaces, land is usually warmer than water during the day. This creates the **sea breeze**, which is a wind that blows from cool water to warmer land. As afternoon heating increases, the sea breeze can reach speeds of 10 to 20 knots. [Figure 6-12]

Figure 6-12. During the day, a low-level sea breeze flows from sea to land due to the pressure gradient caused by the temperature differential between the land mass and the water. A well-developed sea breeze exists between 1,500 and 3,000 feet AGL. A return flow forms above the sea breeze due to the reversal of the pressure gradient.

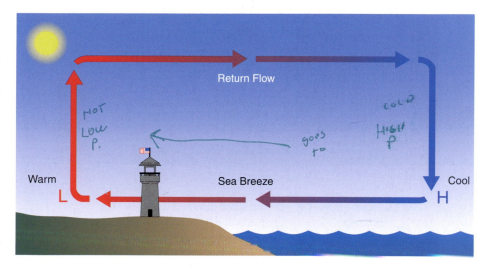

LAND BREEZE

At night, land cools faster than water, and a **land breeze** blows from the cooler land to the warmer water. The pressure gradients are essentially a reversal of what occurs during the day, however, since the temperature contrasts are smaller at night, the land breeze is generally weaker than the sea breeze. [Figure 6-13]

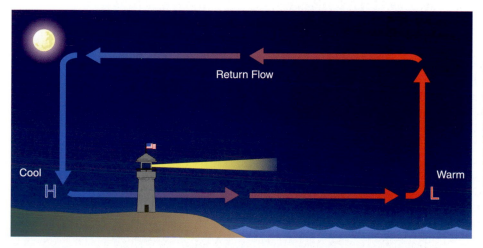

Figure 6-13. The land breeze, which flows offshore, is capped by a weaker onshore return flow. The land breeze can reach an altitude of 1,000 to 2,000 feet AGL and extend between 5 and 100 n.m. inland, depending on the conditions and the location.

VALLEY BREEZE

As mountain slopes are warmed by the sun during the day, the adjacent air also is heated. Since the heated air is less dense than the air at the same altitude over the valley, an upslope flow known as a **valley breeze** is created. Typical valley breezes reach speeds of between 5 and 20 knots with the maximum winds occurring a few hundred feet above the surface. [Figure 6-14]

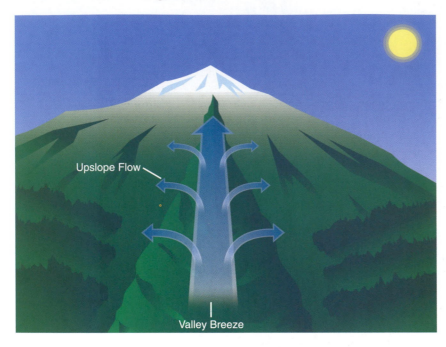

Upslope Flow

Valley Breeze

Figure 6-14. At low levels, air typically flows up the valley and up the warm slopes during the day.

MOUNTAIN BREEZE

At night, the high terrain cools off and eventually becomes cooler than the air over the valley. The pressure gradient reverses and a downslope flow, or **mountain breeze** develops. Prior to sunrise, speeds of 5 to 15 knots are common with greater speeds at the mouth of the valley, sometimes exceeding 25 knots. [Figure 6-15]

Figure 6-15. As the ground cools at night, air flows down the slope and away from the higher terrain.

Downslope Flow

Mountain Breeze

KATABATIC WINDS

Technically, any downslope wind can be classified as a **katabatic wind**. However, in many cases, the term katabatic is used to refer to downwind flows which are stronger than mountain breezes. Katabatic winds can be either warm or cold and some are even given special names in areas where they are particularly severe.

COLD DOWNSLOPE WINDS

When large ice and snow fields accumulate in mountainous terrain, the overlying air becomes extremely cold and a shallow dome of high pressure forms. This pressure gradient force pushes the cold air through gaps in the mountains. Although the air may be warmed during its descent, it's still colder than the air it displaces. If the wind is confined to a narrow canyon it can dramatically increase in velocity. Combined with the force of gravity, some winds can reach speeds in excess of 100 knots. [Figure 6-16] Cold downslope winds which occasionally occur around the world include the *bora* in Croatia, the *mistral* in the Rhone Valley of France, and the *Columbia Gorge wind* in the northwestern United States.

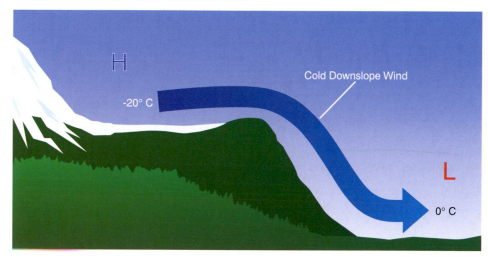

Figure 6-16. A cold downslope wind can become quite strong as it flows downhill from snow-covered plateaus or steep mountain slopes.

WARM DOWNSLOPE WINDS

When a warm airmass moves across a mountain range at high levels, it often forms a trough of low pressure on the downwind, or lee, side which causes a downslope wind to develop. As the air descends the lee side, it is compressed, which results in an increase in temperature. The warmer wind can raise temperatures over 20° in an hour. Wind speed is typically 20 to 50 knots although, in extreme cases, speeds can reach nearly 100 knots. [Figure 6-17] Well-known winds of this type include the *Chinook*, which occurs along the eastern slopes of the Rocky Mountains, the *foehn* in the Alps, and the *Santa Ana* in southern California.

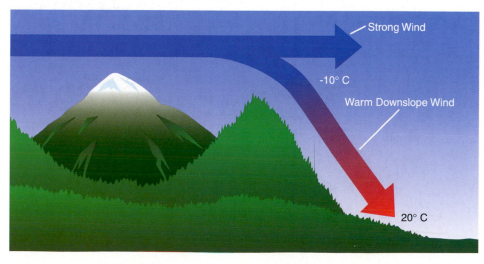

Figure 6-17. A fast-moving wind down a mountain slope will warm as it descends, sometimes dramatically raising the temperature at the base of the mountain.

SUMMARY CHECKLIST

✓ The troposphere is the atmospheric layer extending from the surface to an average altitude of about 36,000 feet. Above the troposphere is the stratosphere, mesosphere, and the thermosphere.

✓ Because of heating inequities, heat is transported, or circulated, from one latitude to another by a process known as convection.

✓ In the three-cell circulation model, the Hadley, Ferrel, and Polar cells generate predictable wind patterns and distribute heat energy.

✓ Pressure readings on weather maps connect points of equal pressure with lines called isobars. When isobars are spread widely apart, the pressure gradient is considered to be weak, while closely spaced isobars indicate a strong gradient.

✓ A high is a center of high pressure surrounded on all sides by lower pressure. Conversely, a low is an area of low pressure surrounded by higher pressure.

✓ A ridge is an elongated area of high pressure, while a trough is an elongated area of low pressure. A col can designate either a neutral area between two highs and two lows, or the intersection of a ridge and a trough.

✓ Coriolis force causes all free-moving objects to trace a curved path due to the earth's rotation. In the northern hemisphere, the deviation will be to the right of its intended path while the opposite will occur in the southern hemisphere.

✓ Frictional force causes a wind to shift directions when near the earth's surface.

✓ A sea breeze blows from the cool water to the warmer land during the day. At night, a land breeze blows from the cooler land to the warmer water.

✓ A cold downslope wind flows downhill from snow-covered plateaus or steep mountain slopes.

✓ Warm, downslope winds sometimes dramatically raise the temperature at the base of the mountain.

KEY TERMS

Atmosphere	Pressure Gradient
Troposphere	High
Tropopause	Low
Stratosphere	Ridge
Mesosphere	Trough
Thermosphere	Col
Circulation	Pressure Gradient Force
Convection	Coriolis Force
Isobars	Frictional Force

Sea Breeze   Mountain Breeze

Land Breeze   Katabatic Wind

Valley Breeze

QUESTIONS

1. Identify the four major layers of the atmosphere depicted in the accompanying illustration.

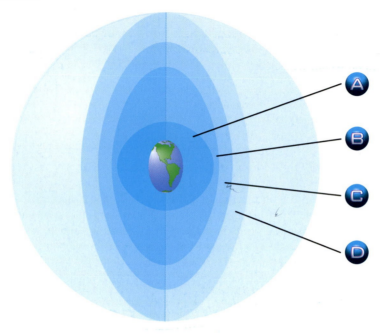

2. Which layer of the atmosphere contains most of the earth's weather?

3. Describe the atmospheric convection process.

4. What is the primary cause of changing altimeter settings between weather reporting points?

5. True/False. Closely spaced isobars on a weather map is an indicator of light surface winds.

6. What three factors affect the amount of deflection caused by Coriolis force?

7. Describe how frictional force causes wind to shift near the earth's surface.

Match the following types of breezes with the most appropriate descriptor.

8. Sea Breeze   A. Occurs at night as land cools faster than water

9. Land Breeze   B. Occurs during the day as the sun warms mountain slopes

10. Valley Breeze   C. Occurs at night as the high terrain cools (relative to air over the valley)

11. Mountain Breeze   D. Occurs during the day as the sun warms the land

SECTION B
WEATHER PATTERNS

It was a stormy night in late October 1743 when Benjamin Franklin ventured outside hoping to catch a glimpse of a lunar eclipse. Although he never saw it, he learned later that clear skies in Boston the same night had given a friend an unobstructed view of the rare occurrence. His friend also related that the day following the eclipse, the weather took a turn for the worse. This prompted Franklin to study weather reports in an effort to document the storm's movement. His subsequent findings led to a more complete understanding of weather patterns. Since then, much more has been learned about the nature of the atmosphere and the weather it produces. A good grasp of these atmospheric principles can help you evaluate weather conditions prior to and during your flights.

ATMOSPHERIC STABILITY

Stability is the atmosphere's resistance to vertical motion. A stable atmosphere does not necessarily prevent air from moving vertically, but it does make that movement more difficult. In most cases, the vertical motions present in a stable environment are very small, resulting in a generally smooth airflow. In an unstable atmosphere, convection is the rule. The air rises because it is warmer than its surroundings. In comparison with vertical motions in a stable environment, unstable vertical movements are large, and the airflow is turbulent. This instability can lead to significant cloud development, turbulence, and hazardous weather.

 Stability of an airmass is decreased by warming from below.

Air that moves upward expands due to lower atmospheric pressure. When air moves downward, it is compressed by the increased pressure at lower altitudes. As the pressure of a given portion of air changes, so does its temperature. The temperature change is caused by a process known as **adiabatic heating** or **adiabatic cooling**, which is a change in the temperature of dry air during expansion or compression.

The adiabatic process takes place in all upward and downward moving air. When air rises into an area of lower pressure, it expands to a larger volume. As the molecules of air expand, the temperature of the air lowers. As a result, when a parcel of air rises, pressure decreases, volume increases, and temperature decreases. When air descends, the opposite is true. The rate at which temperature decreases with an increase in altitude is referred to as its **lapse rate**. As you ascend through the atmosphere, the **average** rate of temperature change is 2°C (3.5°F) per 1,000 feet.

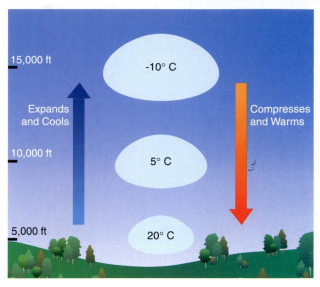

Figure 6-18. As long as a parcel of air remains unsaturated, it will expand and cool at a rate of 3°C per 1,000 feet. As the air descends, it will compress and warm at the same rate.

Since water vapor is lighter than air, moisture decreases air density, causing it to rise. Conversely, as moisture decreases, air becomes denser and tends to sink. Since moist air cools at a slower rate, it's generally less stable than dry air since the moist air must rise higher before its temperature cools to that of the surrounding air. The dry adiabatic lapse rate (unsaturated air) is 3°C (5.4°F) per 1,000 feet. [Figure 6-18] The moist adiabatic lapse rate varies from 1.1°C to 2.8°C (2°F to 5°F) per 1,000 feet.

Overall, the combined effects of temperature and moisture determine the stability of the air and, to a large extent, the type of weather produced. The greatest instability occurs when the air is both warm and moist. Tropical weather, with its almost daily thunderstorm activity, is a perfect example of weather that occurs in very unstable air. Air that is both cool and dry resists vertical movement and is very stable. A good example of this can be found in arctic regions in winter, where stable conditions often result in very cold, generally clear weather.

The actual lapse rate can be used to determine the stability of the atmosphere.

TEMPERATURE INVERSIONS

Although temperature usually decreases with an increase in altitude, the reverse is sometimes true. When temperature increases with altitude, a **temperature inversion** exists. Inversions are usually confined to fairly shallow layers and may occur near the surface or at higher altitudes. They act as a lid for weather and pollutants. Below the inversion, visibility is often restricted by fog, haze, smoke, and low clouds. Temperature inversions occur in stable air with little or no wind and turbulence. [Figure 6-19]

A smooth, stable layer of air and a temperature increase with altitude are features of a temperature inversion. Visibility in an inversion is usually poor due to trapped pollutants. In addition, high humidity beneath a low-level temperature inversion can contribute to the formation of fog, haze, or low clouds.

Figure 6-19. Visibility is often very poor in a temperature inversion.

One of the most familiar types of inversions is the one that forms near the ground on cool, clear nights when the wind is calm. As the ground cools, it lowers the temperature of the adjacent air. If this process of terrestrial radiation continues, the air within a few hundred feet of the surface may become cooler than the air above it. An inversion can also occur when cool air is forced under warm air, or when warm air spreads over cold. Both of these are called frontal inversions.

 A surface-based temperature inversion is often produced by terrestrial radiation on clear, cool nights when the air is relatively calm.

Smoke Plumes and Atmospheric Stability

What can you tell about the changing stability of the atmosphere from smoke patterns? From the typical temperature inversion in the early morning, through the reversal of the vertical temperature profile around mid-day, to the reappearance of the temperature inversion in the evening, the stability of the atmosphere changes. Coupled with a steady breeze, these changes produce characteristic patterns as shown in the accompanying illustration.

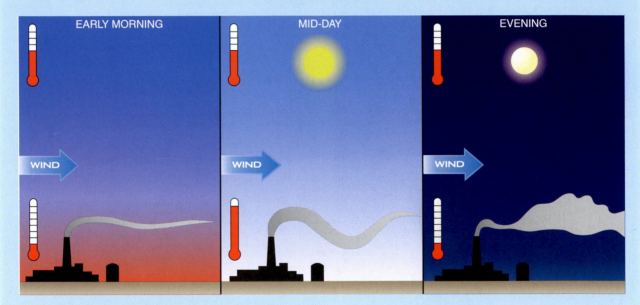

MOISTURE

Even over tropical rain forests, moisture only accounts for a small percentage of the total volume of the atmosphere. Despite this small amount of moisture, water vapor is still responsible for many of the flight hazards encountered in aviation operations. Generally speaking, if the air is very moist, poor, or even severe weather can occur; if the air is dry, the weather usually will be good.

CHANGE OF STATE

Water is present in the atmosphere in three states: solid, liquid, and gas. All three states are found within the temperature ranges normally encountered in the atmosphere, and the change from one to another happens readily. Changes in state occur through the processes of evaporation, condensation, sublimation, deposition, melting, and freezing. As water changes from one physical state to another, an exchange of heat takes place.

Every physical process of weather is accompanied by a heat exchange.

Evaporation is the changing of liquid water to invisible water vapor. As water vapor forms, heat is absorbed from the nearest available source. For example, as perspiration evaporates from your body, you feel cooler because some of your body heat has been absorbed by the water vapor. This heat exchange is known as the latent heat of evaporation. The reverse of evaporation is **condensation**. It occurs when water vapor changes to a liquid, as when water drops form on a cool glass on a warm day. When condensation takes place, the heat absorbed by water vapor during evaporation is released. The heat released is referred to as the latent heat of condensation, and is an important factor in cloud development.

Sublimation is the changing of ice directly to water vapor, while the transformation of water vapor to ice is known as **deposition**. In both cases, the liquid state is bypassed. The changes from ice to water and water to ice are well known to most everyone as **melting** and **freezing**, respectively. The heat exchange which occurs during melting and freezing is small and has relatively little effect on weather. [Figure 6-20]

Water vapor is added to the atmosphere by evaporation and sublimation.

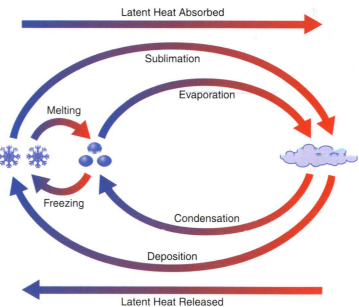

Figure 6-20. The diagram shows the changes of state of water and the latent heat absorbed or released. The latent heat energy involved in the ice-to-water change is only about 17% of the latent heat required in the water-to-vapor change.

HUMIDITY

Humidity simply refers to moisture in the air. For example, on warm, muggy days when you perspire freely, the air is said to be humid. **Relative humidity** is the actual amount of moisture in the air compared to the total amount that could be present at that temperature. It's important to remember that relative humidity tells you nothing about the actual amount of water vapor in the air. For example, at the same 100% relative humidity levels, air at -4°F in Alaska only has about one twentieth of the water vapor as 68°F air in Florida.

The amount of moisture in the air depends on air temperature.

DEWPOINT

Dewpoint is the temperature at which air reaches a state where it can hold no more water. When the dewpoint is reached, the air contains 100% of the moisture it can hold at that temperature, and it is said to be **saturated**. Note that both relative humidity and dewpoint relate moisture to temperature, two inseparable features of our weather. [Figure 6-21]

32°C Temperature
10°C Dewpoint
26% Relative Humidity

-5°C Temperature
-5°C Dewpoint
100% Relative Humidity

Figure 6-21. Does the air in the photo on the right contain more or less moisture than the one on the left? Remember, relative humidity is not indicative of the amount of water vapor in the air. Although the air in the photo on the right is saturated, the higher temperature and dewpoint in the scene on the left means that the air over the desert can and, in this case, does hold more moisture.

When warm, moist air begins to rise in a convective current, clouds often form at the altitude where its temperature and dewpoint reach the same value. When lifted, unsaturated air cools at about 5.4°F per 1,000 feet, and the dewpoint temperature decreases at about 1°F per 1,000 feet. Therefore, the temperature and dewpoint converge at 4.4°F per 1,000 feet. You can use these values to estimate cloud bases. For example, if the surface temperature is 80°F and the surface dewpoint is 62°F, the spread is 18°F. This difference, divided by the rate that the temperature approaches the dewpoint (4.4°F), will help you judge the approximate height of the base of the clouds in thousands of feet (18 ÷ 4.4 = 4 or 4,000 feet AGL).

Dewpoint is the temperature to which air must be cooled to become saturated.

You can calculate cloud bases by using the following formula:

$$\frac{\text{Temperature (°F)} - \text{Dewpoint (°F)}}{4.4 \ (\text{F°})} \times 1,000$$

DEW AND FROST

On cool, still nights, surface features and objects may cool to a temperature below the dewpoint of the surrounding air. Water vapor then condenses out of the air in the form of **dew**, which explains why grass is often moist in the early morning. **Frost** forms when water vapor changes directly to ice on a surface that is below freezing. From late fall through early spring, you may frequently encounter frost on your airplane in the early morning.

Frost forms when the temperature of the collecting surface is at or below the dewpoint of the surrounding air and the dewpoint is below freezing.

If frost is not removed from the wings before flight, it may spoil the smooth airflow over the wings, decrease lift, and increase drag, preventing the aircraft from becoming airborne at normal takeoff speed.

Freezing Above Freezing

How is it possible for frost to form on the ground when the thermometer reads 40°F (4°C)? Since ice doesn't form at temperatures above freezing, the object on which frost forms must be below 32°F (0°C). At night, in particular, variations in temperature can occur over very short distances. As night falls, heat is lost from the ground at a faster rate than the air several feet above it. This rapid cooling decreases the temperature immediately above the ground, possibly below freezing,

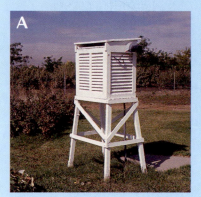

even though the temperature at the level of a thermometer located in a standard instrument shelter 6 feet above the surface is greater than 32°F. [Figure A] This can result in frost forming on the ground even though the minimum reported overnight temperature never dropped below freezing.[Figure B]

Frost can pose a serious hazard during takeoffs. It interferes with the smooth airflow over the wings and can cause early airflow separation, resulting in a loss of lift. It also increases drag and, when combined with the loss of lift, may prevent the aircraft from becoming airborne. Always remove all frost from the aircraft surfaces before flight.

CLOUDS

As air cools to its saturation point, the processes of condensation and sublimation change invisible water vapor into states that are readily seen. Most commonly, this visible moisture takes the form of clouds or fog. Clouds are composed of very small droplets of water or, if the temperature is low enough, ice crystals. The droplets condense or sublimate on very small particles of solid matter in the air. These particles, called **condensation nuclei**, can be dust, salt from evaporating sea spray, or products of combustion. When clouds form near the surface, they are referred to as fog. [Figure 6-22]

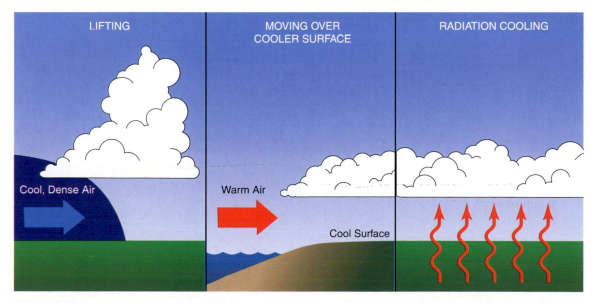

Figure 6-22. Air can be cooled by lifting, by moving over a cooler surface, or by cooling from the underlying surface. Depending upon the temperature of the air, water vapor may condense into visible water droplets or sublimate into snow.

Clouds and fog usually form as soon as the air becomes saturated. You can anticipate the formation of fog or very low clouds by monitoring the difference between surface temperature and dewpoint, usually referred to as the **temperature/dewpoint spread**. When the spread reaches 4°F (2°C) and continues to decrease, the air is nearing the saturation point, increasing the probability of fog and low clouds.

Clouds, fog, or dew always form when water vapor condenses.

A small and decreasing temperature/dewpoint spread indicates conditions are favorable for the formation of fog.

TYPES OF CLOUDS

Clouds are your weather signposts in the sky. They provide a visible indication of the processes occurring in the atmosphere. To the astute observer, they give valuable information about current and future conditions. Clouds are divided into four basic groups, or families, depending upon their characteristics and the altitudes where they occur. Clouds are classified as low, middle, high, and clouds with vertical development.

In general, clouds are named using Latin words. Sheet-like clouds are referred to as *stratus* (meaning "layer"); *cumulus* translates as "heap" and refers to puffy clouds; *cirrus* ("ringlet") is used to designate wispy clouds; and rain clouds contain the prefix or suffix *nimbus* which means "violent rain."

Clouds are grouped by families according to their altitudes (height range).

The term *nimbus* describes clouds which produce rain.

LOW CLOUDS

Low clouds extend from near the surface to about 6,500 feet AGL. Low clouds usually consist almost entirely of water but sometimes may contain supercooled water which can create an icing hazard for aircraft. Types of low clouds include **stratus**, **stratocumulus**, and **nimbostratus**. [Figure 6-23]

LOW CLOUDS

Courtesy of Peter F. Lester

Figure 6-23. Low clouds are found at altitudes extending from the surface to about 6,500 feet AGL.

Stratus Clouds
Stratus clouds are layered clouds that form in stable air near the surface due to cooling from below. Stratus clouds have a gray, uniform appearance and generally cover a wide area. Although turbulence in these clouds is low, they usually restrict visual flying due to low ceilings and visibility. Icing conditions are possible if temperatures are at or near freezing. Stratus clouds may form when moist stable air is lifted up sloping terrain, or when warm rain evaporates as it falls through cool air.

Nimbostratus Clouds
Nimbostratus clouds are gray or black clouds that can be more than several thousand of feet thick, contain large quantities of moisture, and produce widespread areas of rain or snow. If temperatures are near or below freezing, they may create heavy aircraft icing.

Stratocumulus Clouds
Stratocumulus clouds are white, puffy clouds that form as stable air is lifted. They often form as a stratus layer breaks up or as cumulus clouds spread out.

Stratus clouds form when moist, stable air flows upslope.

FOG

Technically, fog is a low cloud which has its base within 50 feet of the ground. If the fog is less than 20 feet deep, it is called **ground fog**. Fog is classified according to the way it forms. **Radiation fog** forms over low-lying, fairly flat surfaces on clear, calm, humid nights. As the surface cools by radiation, the adjacent air also is cooled to its dewpoint. Radiation fog usually occurs

Figure 6-24. Radiation fog is often found in river valleys where cool air pools and moisture is abundant.

in stable air associated with a high pressure system. As early morning temperatures increase, the fog begins to lift and usually "burns off" by mid-morning. If higher cloud layers form over the fog, visibility will improve more slowly. [Figure 6-24]

Advection fog is caused when a low layer of warm, moist air moves over a cooler surface. It is most common under cloudy skies along coastlines where wind transports air from the warm water to the cooler land. Winds up to about 15 knots will intensify the fog. Above 15 knots, turbulence creates a mixing of the air, and it usually lifts sufficiently to form low stratus clouds. **Upslope fog** forms when moist, stable air is forced up a sloping land mass. Like advection fog, upslope fog can form in moderate to strong winds and under cloudy skies.

Radiation fog forms in moist air over low, flat areas on clear, calm nights.

Advection and upslope fog require wind for formation. Both types of fog commonly occur along coastlines where sea breezes transport air from warm water to the cooler land surfaces.

Steam fog, which is often called sea smoke, occurs as cold, dry air moves over comparatively warmer water. The warm water evaporates and rises upward resembling rising smoke. It is composed entirely of water droplets that often freeze quickly and

Low-level turbulence and aircraft icing are associated with steam fog.

fall back into the water as ice particles. This can produce an icing hazard to aircraft. In addition, aircraft may experience low-level turbulence in steam fog since it forms in relatively unstable air. [Figure 6-25]

Figure 6-25. A type of steam fog occurs daily over the thermal pools in Yellowstone National Park.

MIDDLE CLOUDS

Middle clouds have bases that range from about 6,500 to 20,000 feet AGL. They are composed of water, ice crystals, or supercooled water, and may contain moderate turbulence and potentially severe icing. **Altostratus** and **altocumulus** are classified as middle clouds. [Figure 6-26]

MIDDLE CLOUDS

Courtesy of Peter F. Lester

Altostratus Clouds
Altostratus clouds are flat, dense clouds that cover a wide area. They are a uniform gray or gray-white in color. Although they produce minimal turbulence, they may produce moderate aircraft icing.

Figure 6-26. Middle clouds are found at altitudes extending from 6,500 feet to 20,000 feet AGL.

Altocumulus Clouds
Altocumulus clouds are gray or white, patchy clouds of uniform appearance that often form when altostratus clouds start to break up. They usually extend over a wide area, produce light turbulence, and may contain supercooled water droplets.

HIGH CLOUDS

High clouds have bases beginning above 20,000 feet AGL. They are generally white to light gray in color and form in stable air. They are composed mainly of ice crystals and seldom pose a serious turbulence or icing hazard. The three basic types of high clouds are called **cirrus**, **cirrostratus**, and **cirrocumulus**. [Figure 6-27]

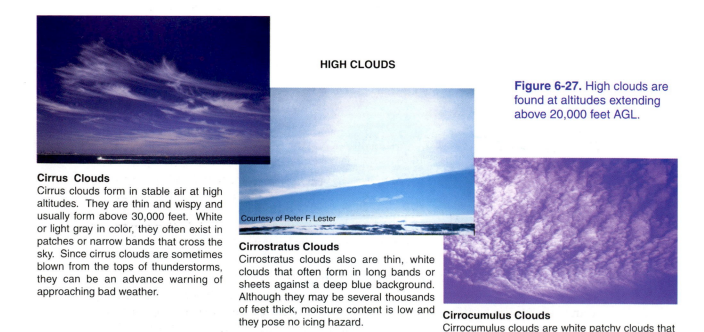

HIGH CLOUDS

Figure 6-27. High clouds are found at altitudes extending above 20,000 feet AGL.

Courtesy of Peter F. Lester

Cirrus Clouds
Cirrus clouds form in stable air at high altitudes. They are thin and wispy and usually form above 30,000 feet. White or light gray in color, they often exist in patches or narrow bands that cross the sky. Since cirrus clouds are sometimes blown from the tops of thunderstorms, they can be an advance warning of approaching bad weather.

Cirrostratus Clouds
Cirrostratus clouds also are thin, white clouds that often form in long bands or sheets against a deep blue background. Although they may be several thousands of feet thick, moisture content is low and they pose no icing hazard.

Cirrocumulus Clouds
Cirrocumulus clouds are white patchy clouds that look like cotton. They form as a result of shallow convective currents at high altitude and may produce light turbulence.

CLOUDS WITH VERTICAL DEVELOPMENT

Cumulus clouds are puffy white clouds with flat bases which may start off as harmless fair weather clouds and build vertically into **towering cumulus** or even giant **cumulonimbus** clouds. The bases of clouds with vertical development are found at altitudes associated with low to middle clouds, and their tops extend into the altitudes associated with high clouds. Frequently, these cloud types are obscured by other cloud formations. When this happens, they are said to be **embedded**. [Figure 6-28]

**CLOUDS WITH
VERTICAL DEVELOPMENT**

Cumulus Clouds
Cumulus clouds form in convective currents resulting from the heating of the earth's surface. They usually have flat bottoms and dome-shaped tops. Widley spaced cumulus clouds that form in fairly clear skies are called fair weather cumulus and indicate a shallow layer of instability. You can expect turbulence, but little icing and precipitation.

Towering Cumulus
Towering cumulus clouds look like large mounds of cotton with billowing cauliflower tops. Their color may vary from brilliant white at the top to gray near the bottom. Towering cumulus clouds indicate a fairly deep area of unstable air. They contain moderate to heavy turbulence with icing and often develop into thunderstorms.

Cumulonimbus Clouds
Cumulonimbus clouds, which are more commonly called thunderstorms, are large, vertically developed clouds that form in very unstable air. They are gray-white to black in color and contain large amounts of moisture. Many flying hazards are linked with cumulonimbus clouds.

Figure 6-28. Clouds with vertical development, also known as cumuliform clouds, are indicative of some instability.

 Vertical cloud development and turbulence result from the lifting of unstable air.

PRECIPITATION

Precipitation can be defined as any form of particles, whether liquid or solid, that fall from the atmosphere. Whether it reaches the ground or evaporates before it reaches the surface, precipitation contributes to many aviation weather problems. It can reduce visibility, affect engine performance, increase braking distance, and cause dramatic shifts in wind direction and velocity. Under the right conditions, precipitation can freeze on contact, affecting airflow over aircraft wings and control surfaces.

PRECIPITATION CAUSES

Although a cloud usually forms when the atmosphere is saturated, it doesn't necessarily mean that the cloud will produce precipitation. For precipitation to occur, water or ice particles must grow in size until they can no longer be supported by the atmosphere. There are three ways by which precipitation-size particles can be produced. In the condensation/deposition method, water droplets or ice crystals simply continue to grow

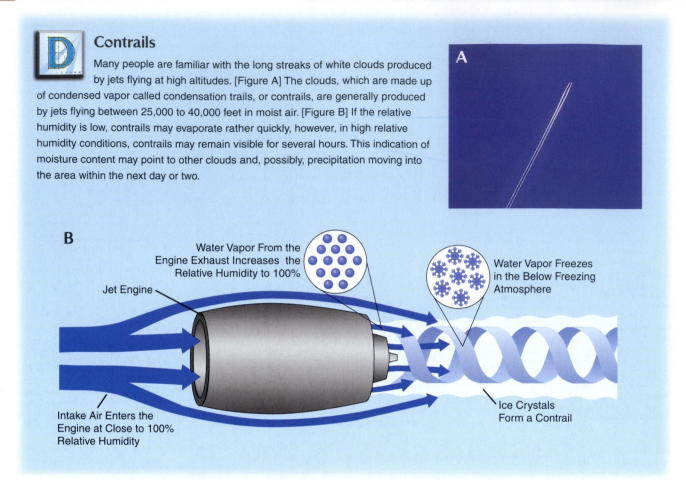

Contrails

Many people are familiar with the long streaks of white clouds produced by jets flying at high altitudes. [Figure A] The clouds, which are made up of condensed vapor called condensation trails, or contrails, are generally produced by jets flying between 25,000 to 40,000 feet in moist air. [Figure B] If the relative humidity is low, contrails may evaporate rather quickly, however, in high relative humidity conditions, contrails may remain visible for several hours. This indication of moisture content may point to other clouds and, possibly, precipitation moving into the area within the next day or two.

A

B

Water Vapor From the Engine Exhaust Increases the Relative Humidity to 100%

Jet Engine

Water Vapor Freezes in the Below Freezing Atmosphere

Intake Air Enters the Engine at Close to 100% Relative Humidity

Ice Crystals Form a Contrail

by the same processes as they were initially formed until they are large enough to fall out of the cloud. The second process, known as coalescence, generally occurs when the initial cloud water droplets are of different sizes. The larger drops fall faster, growing as they collide and capture the smaller ones.

The first two processes, while important, are usually too slow to allow much precipitation to fall within the normal lifetime of a rain cloud. A more efficient ice-crystal process occurs primarily in the middle to high latitudes where the clouds can extend upward into areas well below freezing. These clouds not only contain ice crystals, but also water droplets. Although it may seem contradictory, water droplets can exist in temperatures below freezing. In fact, studies show that, depending on the conditions, these **supercooled water droplets** can stay in a liquid form in temperatures as low as -40°C. During the ice-crystal process, water vapor given up by the evaporating water droplets causes the ice crystals to grow to precipitation-sized particles in a relatively short time period.

TYPES OF PRECIPITATION

As they fall, snowflakes and raindrops may change into other types of precipitation depending on the atmospheric conditions beneath the cloud. In addition to snow and rain, falling moisture also can take the form of drizzle, ice pellets, or hail.

DRIZZLE AND RAIN

Drizzle is distinguished by very small droplets (less than 0.02 inches in diameter). It is commonly associated with fog or low stratus clouds. Falling drops of liquid precipitation is considered to be rain when it is 0.02 inches in diameter or greater. Rain generally falls at a relatively steady rate and stops gradually. Rain showers refer to liquid precipi-

What Shape are Raindrops?

Of the three illustrations to the right, which do you think most closely resembles an actual raindrop? Most people pick drop B. Did you? Well, contrary to popular conception, raindrops don't look like tears. Their real shape depends on the size of the drop. A raindrop will take the shape shown as drop A when it is less than about 0.08 inches (2 mm) in diameter. Larger drops tend to be shaped like drop C.

Figure 6-29. Streaks of rain which evaporate before reaching the ground are known as virga.

tation which starts, changes intensity, and stops suddenly. The largest drops and greatest short-term precipitation amounts typically occur with rain showers associated with cumulus clouds and thunderstorms. At times, falling rain may never reach the ground due to rapid evaporation. The smaller the drops become, the slower their rate of fall, hence the appearance of rain streaks hanging in the air. These streams of evaporating precipitation are called **virga**. [Figure 6-29]

When warm rain or drizzle falls through a layer of cooler air near the surface, evaporation from the falling precipitation may saturate the cool air, causing **precipitation-induced fog** to form. This fog can be very dense, and usually does not clear until the rain moves out of the area.

Freezing drizzle and freezing rain maintain the same general characteristics as described above except that they freeze upon contact with the ground or other objects such as power lines, trees, or aircraft. Freezing rain can produce black ice (clear ice on black pavement). Since it's difficult to distinguish, black ice can be a serious hazard to aircraft ground operations.

ICE PELLETS AND HAIL

If rain falls through a temperature inversion, it may freeze as it passes through the underlying colder air, striking the ground as **ice pellets**. In some cases, water droplets that freeze in clouds with strong upward currents may grow in size as they collide with other freezing water droplets. Eventually they become too large for air currents to support, and they fall as **hail**. Hailstones can grow to more than five inches in diameter with weights of more than one and one-half pounds.

Ice pellets at the surface are an indication of a temperature inversion and freezing rain at a higher altitude.

SNOW

Snow is precipitation composed of ice crystals. Snow and snow showers are distinguished in the same way as rain showers. Snow grains are the solid equivalent of drizzle. They are very small, white, opaque particles of ice. They are different from ice pellets in that they are flatter and they neither shatter nor bounce when they strike the ground. Ice crystals that descend from cirrus clouds are called cirrus **fallstreaks**, or mare's tails. [Figure 6-30]

Figure 6-30. Fallstreaks behave similar to virga. The ice particles change from ice into vapor (sublimate) as they fall.

AIRMASSES

An **airmass** is a large body of air with fairly uniform temperature and moisture content. It may be several hundred miles across and usually forms where air remains stationary, or nearly so, for at least several days. During this time, the airmass takes on the temperature and moisture properties of the underlying surface.

SOURCE REGIONS

The area where an airmass acquires the properties of temperature and moisture that determine its stability is called its **source region**. An ideal source region is a large area with fairly uniform geography and temperature. A source region is usually located where air tends to stagnate. The best areas for airmass development are in the regions where atmospheric circulation has caused the buildup of semipermanent areas of high pressure. This often occurs in snow and ice covered polar regions, over tropical oceans, and in the vicinity of large deserts. The middle latitudes are poor source regions because of the strong westerly winds and the continual mixing of tropical and polar airmasses.

CLASSIFICATIONS

Airmasses are classified according to the regions where they originate. They are generally divided into polar or tropical to identify their temperature characteristics, and continental or maritime to identify their moisture content. A continental polar airmass, for example, originates over a polar land mass and contains cold, dry, and stable air. A stable airmass generally exhibits widespread stratiform clouds, restricted visibility, smooth air, and steady rain or drizzle. A maritime tropical airmass originates over water and contains warm, moist, and unstable air. The instability associated with a warm airmass

Figure 6-31. Airmass source regions surround North America. As airmasses move out of their source regions, they often converge and give birth to the continent's major weather systems.

tends to result in the formation of cumuliform clouds with showers, turbulence, and good surface visibility. [Figure 6-31]

MODIFICATION

As an airmass moves out of its source region, it is modified by the temperature and moisture of the area over which it moves. The degree to which an airmass is changed depends on several factors including its speed, the nature of the region it moves over, the depth of the airmass, and the temperature difference between the airmass and the new surface.

WARMING FROM BELOW

As an airmass moves over a warmer surface, its lower layers are heated and vertical movement of the air develops. Depending on temperature and moisture levels, this can result in extreme instability. [Figure 6-32]

 Stable air is generally smooth with layered or stratiform clouds. Visibility is usually restricted, with widespread areas of clouds and steady rain or drizzle.

Moist unstable air causes the formation of cumuliform clouds, showers, turbulence, and good surface visibility.

Figure 6-32. The Great Lakes do much to modify continental polar airmasses moving out of Canada. In early winter, the lakes heat and moisten air near the surface, creating very unstable air. This often results in large quantities of lake-effect snows over the Great Lakes and on the lee shores.

COOLING FROM BELOW

When an airmass flows over a cooler surface, its lower layers are cooled and vertical movement is inhibited. As a result, the stability of the air is increased. If the air is cooled to its dewpoint, low clouds or fog may form. This cooling from below creates a temperature inversion and may result in low ceilings and visibility for long periods of time. [Figure 6-33]

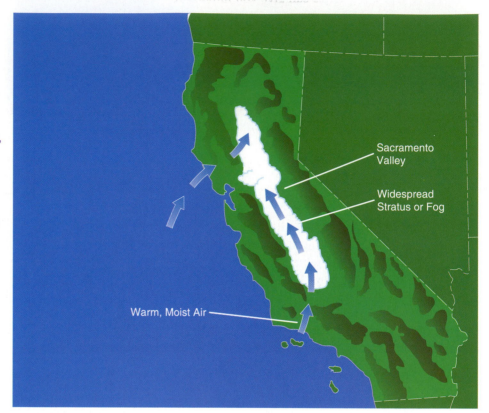

Figure 6-33. In winter months, warm, moist Pacific air flows into the Sacramento Valley of California and is cooled from below. As its temperature drops, its stability increases. Prolonged cooling causes the air to cool to its dewpoint, often resulting in widespread stratus clouds or fog which may persist for weeks.

Sacramento Valley

Widespread Stratus or Fog

Warm, Moist Air

FRONTS

When an airmass moves out of its source region, it comes in contact with other airmasses that have different moisture and temperature characteristics. The boundary between airmasses is called a **front**. Since the weather along a front often presents a serious hazard to flying, you need to have a thorough understanding of the associated weather.

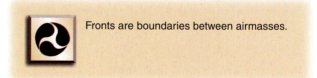

Fronts are boundaries between airmasses.

TYPES OF FRONTS

Fronts are named according to the temperature of the advancing air relative to the temperature of the air it is replacing. A **cold front** is one where cold air is moving to displace warmer air. In a **warm front**, warm air is replacing cold air. A **stationary front** has no movement. Cold fronts are usually fast moving and often catch up to and merge with a slower moving warm front. When cold and warm fronts merge, they create an **occluded front**.

FRONTAL DISCONTINUITIES

In weather terminology, frontal discontinuities refer to the comparatively rapid changes in the meteorological characteristics of an airmass. When you cross a front, you move from one airmass into another airmass with different properties. The changes between the two may be very abrupt, indicating a narrow frontal zone. On the other hand, the changes may occur gradually, indicating a wide and, perhaps diffused frontal zone. These changes can give you important cues to the location and intensity of the front.

TEMPERATURE

Temperature is one of the most easily recognized discontinuities across a front. At the surface, the temperature change is usually very noticeable and may be quite abrupt in a fast-moving front. With a slow-moving front, it usually is less pronounced. When you are flying through a front, you can observe the temperature change on the outside air temperature gauge. However, the change may be less abrupt at middle and high altitudes than it is at the surface.

One of the most easily recognized discontinuities across a front is the change in temperature.

WIND

The most reliable indications that you are crossing a front are a change in wind direction and, less frequently, wind speed. Although the exact new direction of the wind is difficult to predict, the wind always shifts to the right in the northern hemisphere. When you are flying through a front at low to middle altitudes, you will always need to correct to the right in order to maintain your original ground track.

When you are flying across a front, you will notice a change in wind direction. Wind speed may also change.

PRESSURE

As a front approaches, atmospheric pressure usually decreases, with the area of lowest pressure lying directly over the front. Pressure changes on the warm side of the front generally occur more slowly than on the cold side. When you approach a front toward the cool air, pressure drops slowly until you cross the front, then rises quickly. When you are crossing toward the warm air, pressure drops abruptly over the front and then rises slowly. The important thing to remember is that you should update your altimeter setting as soon as possible after crossing a front.

FRONTAL WEATHER

The type and intensity of frontal weather depend on several factors. Some of these factors are the availability of moisture, the stability of the air being lifted, and the speed of the frontal movement. Other factors include the slope of the front and the moisture and temperature variations between the two fronts. Although some frontal weather can be very severe and hazardous, other fronts produce relatively calm weather.

COLD FRONTS

A cold front separates an advancing mass of cold, dense, and stable air from an area of warm, lighter, and unstable air. Because of its greater density, the cold air moves along

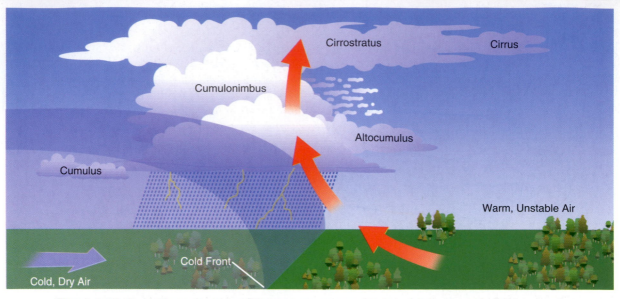

Figure 6-34. Cumuliform clouds and showers are common in the vicinity of cold fronts.

TYPICAL COLD FRONT WEATHER			
	Prior to Passage	**During Passage**	**After Passage**
Clouds	• Cirriform • Towering cumulus and/or cumulonimbus	• Towering cumulus and/or cumulonimbus	• Cumulus
Precipitation	• Showers	• Heavy showers • Possible hail, lightning, and thunder	• Slowly decreasing showers
Visibility	• Fair in haze	• Poor	• Good
Wind	• SSW	• Variable and gusty	• WNW
Temperature	• Warm	• Suddenly cooler	• Continued cooler
Dewpoint	• High	• Rapidly dropping	• Continued drop
Pressure	• Falling	• Bottoms out, then rises rapidly	• Rising

the surface and forces the less dense, warm air upward. In the northern hemisphere, cold fronts are usually oriented in a northeast to southwest line and may be several hundred miles long. Movement is usually in an easterly direction. A depiction of the typical cold front and a summary of its associated weather is shown in figure 6-34.

FAST-MOVING COLD FRONTS

Fast-moving cold fronts are pushed along by intense high pressure systems located well behind the front. Surface friction acts to slow the movement of the front, causing the leading edge of the front to bulge out and to steepen the front's slope. These fronts are particularly hazardous because of the steep slope and wide differences in moisture and temperature between the two airmasses.

SLOW-MOVING COLD FRONTS

The leading edge of a slow-moving cold front is much shallower than that of a fast-moving front. This produces clouds which extend far behind the surface front. A slow-moving cold front meeting stable air usually causes a broad area of stratus clouds to form behind the front. When a slow-moving cold front meets unstable air, large numbers of vertical clouds often form at and just behind the front. Fair weather cumulus clouds are often present in the cold air, well behind the surface front.

 Steady precipitation with little turbulence usually precedes a warm front.

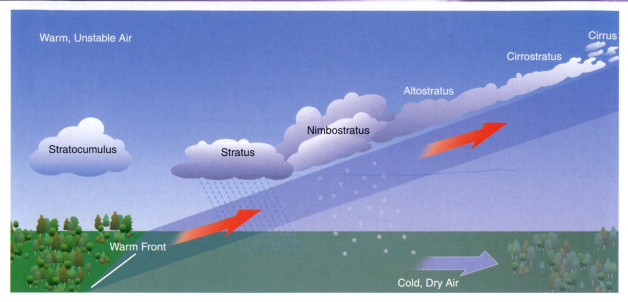

Figure 6-35. Although stratus clouds usually extend out ahead of a slow-moving warm front, cumulus clouds sometimes develop along and ahead of the surface front if the air is unstable.

TYPICAL WARM FRONT WEATHER			
	Prior to Passage	**During Passage**	**After Passage**
Clouds	• Cirriform • Stratiform • Fog • Possible cumulonimbus in the summer	• Stratiform	• Stratocumulus • Possible cumulonimbus in the summer
Precipitation	• Light-to-moderate rain, drizzle, sleet, or snow	• Drizzle, if any	• Rain or showers, if any
Visibility	• Poor	• Poor, but improving	• Fair in haze
Wind	• SSE	• Variable	• SSW
Temperature	• Cold to cool	• Rising steadily	• Warming, then steady
Dewpoint	• Rising steadily	• Steady	• Rising, then steady
Pressure	• Falling	• Becoming steady	• Slight rise, then falling

WARM FRONTS

Warm fronts occur when warm air overtakes and replaces cooler air. They usually move at much slower speeds than cold fronts. The slope of a warm front is very gradual, and the warm air may extend up over the cool air for several hundred miles ahead of the front. A depiction of the typical warm front and a summary of its associated weather is shown in figure 6-35.

STATIONARY FRONTS

When the opposing forces of two airmasses are relatively balanced, the front that separates them may remain stationary and influence local flying conditions for several days. The weather in a stationary front is usually a mixture of that found in both warm and cold fronts.

OCCLUDED FRONTS

A frontal occlusion occurs when a fast-moving cold front catches up to a slow-moving warm front. The difference in temperature within each frontal system is a major factor that influences which type of front and weather are created. A **cold front occlusion** develops when the fast-moving cold front is colder than the air ahead of the slow-moving warm front. In this case, the cold air replaces the cool air at the surface and forces the warm front aloft. A **warm front occlusion** takes place when the air ahead of the slow-moving warm front is colder than the air within the fast-moving cold front. In this case, the cold front rides up over the warm front, forcing the cold front aloft. A depiction of the typical warm and cold front occlusions and a summary of their associated weather is shown in figure 6-36.

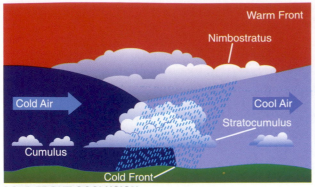

COLD FRONT OCCLUSION

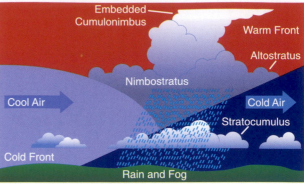

WARM FRONT OCCLUSION

Figure 6-36. When the air being lifted by a cold front occlusion is moist and stable, the weather will be a mixture of that found in both a warm and a cold front. When the air being lifted by a warm front occlusion is moist and unstable, the weather will be more severe than that found in a cold front occlusion.

TYPICAL OCCLUDED FRONT WEATHER			
	Prior to Passage	**During Passage**	**After Passage**
Clouds	• Cirriform • Stratiform	• Nimbostratus • Possible towering cumulus and/or cumulonimbus	• Nimbostratus • Altostratus • Possible cumulus
Precipitation	• Light-to-heavy precipitation	• Light-to-heavy precipitation	• Light-to-moderate precipitation, then clearing
Visibility	• Poor	• Poor	• Improving
Wind	• SE to S	• Variable	• W to NW
Temperature	• Cold Occlusion: Cold to Cool • Warm Occlusion: Cold	• Cold Occlusion: Falling • Warm Occlusion: Rising	• Cold Occlusion: Colder • Warm Occlusion: Milder
Dewpoint	• Steady	• Slight drop	• Rising, then steady
Pressure	• Falling	• Becoming steady	• Slight drop; however, may rise after passage of warm occlusion

SUMMARY CHECKLIST

✓ Stability is the atmosphere's resistance to vertical motion.

✓ The rate at which temperature decreases with an increase in altitude is referred to as its lapse rate. As you ascend in the atmosphere, temperature decreases at an average rate of 2°C (3.5°F) per 1,000 feet.

✓ When temperature increases with altitude, a temperature inversion exists.

✓ Evaporation is the changing of liquid water to invisible water vapor. Condensation occurs when water vapor changes to a liquid. Sublimation is the changing of ice directly to water vapor, while the transformation of water vapor to ice is known as deposition. In both cases, the liquid state is bypassed.

✓ Relative humidity is the actual amount of moisture in the air compared to the total amount that could be present at that temperature.

✓ The temperature at which air reaches a state where it can hold no more water is called the dewpoint.

✓ Frost forms on aircraft when the temperature of the collecting surface is at or below the dewpoint of the surrounding air and the dewpoint is below freezing. If frost is not removed from the wings before flight, it may decrease lift and increase drag to a point which seriously compromises safety.

✓ When the temperature/dewpoint spread reaches 4°F (2°C) and continues to decrease, the air is nearing the saturation point and the probability of fog and low clouds forming increases.

✓ Since they normally form below 6,500 feet AGL, stratus, stratocumulus, and nimbostratus are classified as low clouds. Altostratus and altocumulus are classified as middle clouds and have bases that range from about 6,500 to 20,000 feet AGL. High clouds have bases beginning at altitudes above 20,000 feet AGL. The three basic types of high clouds are called cirrus, cirrostratus, and cirrocumulus. Extensive vertical development is characteristic of cumulus, towering cumulus, and cumulonimbus clouds.

✓ Fog is a low cloud which has its base within 50 feet of the ground. If the fog is less than 20 feet deep, it is called ground fog.

✓ Although a cloud usually forms when the atmosphere is saturated, it doesn't necessarily mean that the cloud will produce precipitation. For precipitation to occur, water or ice particles must grow in size until they can no longer be supported by the atmosphere.

✓ As they fall, snowflakes and raindrops may change into other types of precipitation depending on the atmospheric conditions beneath the cloud. In addition to snow and rain, falling moisture also can take the form of drizzle, ice pellets, or hail.

✓ An airmass is a large body of air with fairly uniform temperature and moisture content. As an airmass moves, it is modified by the temperature and moisture of the area over which it moves.

✓ Stable air is generally smooth with layered or stratiform clouds. Visibility is usually restricted, with widespread areas of clouds and steady rain or drizzle. Moist unstable air causes the formation of cumuliform clouds, showers, turbulence, and good surface visibility.

✓ A cold front is one where cold air is moving to displace warmer air. In a warm front, warm air is replacing cold air. A stationary front has no movement. When cold and warm fronts merge, they create an occluded front.

✓ Frontal discontinuities refer to the comparatively rapid changes in the meteorological characteristics of an airmass. When you cross a front, you move from one airmass into another and will normally experience changes in temperature, pressure, and wind.

KEY TERMS

Stability	Temperature Inversion
Adiabatic Heating	Evaporation
Adiabatic Cooling	Condensation
Lapse Rate	Sublimation

Melting

Freezing

Deposition

Humidity

Relative Humidity

Dewpoint

Saturated

Dew

Frost

Condensation Nuclei

Temperature/Dewpoint Spread

Stratus

Stratocumulus

Nimbostratus

Fog

Radiation Fog

Ground Fog

Advection Fog

Upslope Fog

Steam Fog

Altostratus

Altocumulus

Cirrus

Cirrostratus

Cirrocumulus

Embedded

Cumulus

Towering Cumulus

Cumulonimbus

Precipitation

Supercooled Water Droplets

Virga

Precipitation-Induced Fog

Ice Pellets

Hail

Fallstreaks

Airmass

Source Region

Front

Cold Front

Warm Front

Stationary Front

Occluded Front

Cold Front Occlusion

Warm Front Occlusion

QUESTIONS

1. What is the average rate of temperature change associated with a change in altitude?

2. Describe the pressure and temperature changes which take place in ascending and descending air.

3. What two processes add water vapor to the atmosphere?

4. At what height above the ground would you expect to find the base of the clouds if the surface temperature is 65°F and the surface dewpoint is 56°F?

5. Identify the clouds in the following photos.

6. True/False. Advection fog normally occurs when the wind is calm.

7. What must happen for a cloud to precipitate?

8. What is the difference between rain and rain showers?

9. Describe the weather characteristics of a stable airmass.

Match the following fronts with the weather characteristics you would expect to see as the front approaches.

10. Warm Front

11. Cold Front

12. Occluded Front

A. Nimbostratus clouds, light-to-heavy precipitation, poor visibility in precipitation, steady dewpoint

B. Stratus clouds, fog, light-to-moderate rain, poor visibility, steadily rising dewpoint

C. Towering cumulus clouds, short periods of showers, fair visibility in haze, high dewpoint

SECTION C
WEATHER HAZARDS

After brewing for several days, severe weather exploded over the central plains of the United States on April 3 and 4, 1974. The churning atmosphere created huge areas of thunderstorms and spawned 127 tornadoes, some containing winds in excess of 260 miles per hour. When it was over, 315 people in 11 states were killed and 6,142 were injured. Of course, the magnitude of destruction resulting from this single weather occurrence is rare. Nonetheless, the atmosphere continues to produce hazardous weather on a near daily basis. You can avoid the worst of nature's fury by combining a thorough understanding of its characteristics with a healthy respect for its power.

THUNDERSTORMS

Thunderstorms are arguably the single greatest threat to aircraft operations. They may contain strong wind gusts, icing, hail, driving rain, lightning, and sometimes tornadoes. Before a thunderstorm capable of exhibiting these hazards can develop, three conditions must be present — air that has a tendency toward instability, some type of lifting action, and relatively high moisture content. The lifting action may be provided by several factors, such as rising terrain (orographic lifting), fronts, or heating of the earth's surface (convection).

 Thunderstorm formation requires unstable conditions, a lifting force, and high moisture levels.

TYPES OF THUNDERSTORMS

While all thunderstorms usually have similar physical features, they are generally classified as one of two types depending on the intensity of the conditions occurring within them. The scattered thunderstorms which are common during summer afternoons, or in coastal areas at night, are frequently described as **airmass thunderstorms**. They are relatively short-lived storms which rarely produce large hail or strong winds. On the other hand, violent thunderstorms with wind gusts of 50 knots or more, hail 3/4 inches in diameter or larger, and/or tornadoes are referred to as **severe thunderstorms**.

A thunderstorm may exist as a single cell, supercell, or, if combined with others, in a multicell form. A **single-cell** thunderstorm lasts less than one hour. In contrast, a **supercell** severe thunderstorm may last two hours. A **multicell** storm is a compact cluster of thunderstorms. It is usually composed of airmass thunderstorms in different stages of development. These cells interact to cause the duration of the cluster to be much longer than any individual cell. In some cases, thunderstorms may form in a line, called a

squall line. While it often forms 50 to 300 miles ahead of a fast-moving cold front, the existence of a front is not necessary for a squall line to form. This continuous line of non-frontal thunderstorms can range in distance from about one hundred to several hundred miles in length. [Figure 6-37] Depending on the degree of instability, thunderstorms along a squall line may be ordinary multi-cell, supercell, or a mixture of storms. The most severe weather conditions, such as destructive winds, heavy hail, and tornadoes are generally associated with squall lines.

The terminology, **frontal thunderstorms** is sometimes used to refer to storms which are associated with frontal activity. Those which occur with a warm front are often obscured by stratiform clouds. When there is showery precipitation near a warm front, thunderstorms should be expected. In a cold front, the cumulonimbus clouds are often visible in a continuous line parallel to the frontal surface. Depending on the conditions, thunderstorms also may be present in an occluded front.

Courtesy of NASA

Figure 6-37. A squall line is clearly visible in this photograph from space.

 A squall line is a non-frontal band of thunderstorms that often produces the most intense weather hazards for aircraft.

LIFE CYCLE

About fifty years ago it was discovered that thunderstorms progress through three definite stages — cumulus, mature, and dissipating. Certain characteristics, such as cloud shape, air current direction, and precipitation intensity, are associated with each stage. [Figure 6-38]

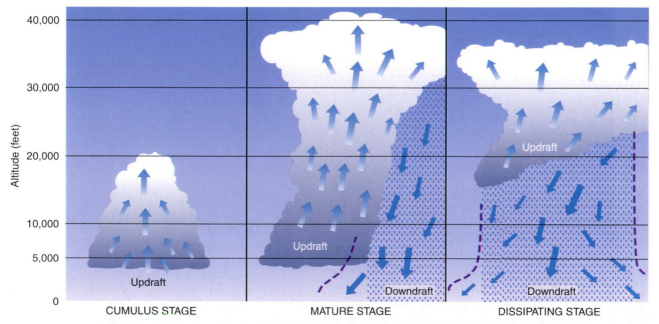

Figure 6-38. These distinctive cloud shapes signal the stages of a thunderstorm. In some cases, other weather phenomena may prevent you from seeing these characteristic shapes.

CUMULUS STAGE

In the **cumulus stage**, a lifting action initiates the vertical movement of air. As the air rises and cools to its dewpoint, water vapor condenses into small water droplets or ice crystals. If sufficient moisture is present, heat released by the condensing vapor provides energy for continued vertical growth of the cloud. Because of strong updrafts, precipitation usually does not fall. Instead, the water drops or ice crystals rise and fall within the cloud, growing larger with each cycle. Updrafts as great as 3,000 feet per minute (f.p.m.) may begin near the surface and extend well above the cloud top. During the cumulus stage, the convective circulation grows rapidly into a towering cumulus (TCU) cloud which typically grows to 20,000 feet in height and 3 to 5 miles in diameter. The cloud reaches the mature stage in about 15 minutes. [Figure 6-39]

 The cumulus stage is characterized by continuous updrafts.

Figure 6-39. Towering cumulus clouds are characteristic of the cumulus stage of an airmass thunderstorm. Although not every cumulus cloud develops into a thunderstorm, all thunderstorms begin at the cumulus stage. If a convective cloud reaches the cumulonimbus stage, it should be considered a thunderstorm, whether or not any other evidence of thunderstorm activity is present.

MATURE STAGE

As the drops in the cloud grow too large to be supported by the updrafts, precipitation begins to fall. This creates a downward motion in the surrounding air and signals the beginning of the **mature stage**. The circulation of the thunderstorm cell is organized in this, the storm's most violent stage. The relatively warm updraft and the cool, precipitation-induced downdraft exist side by side, causing severe turbulence. At the surface, the down-rushing air spreads outward, producing a sharp drop in temperature, a rise in pressure, and strong, gusty surface winds. The leading edge of this wind is referred to as a **gust front**. As the thunderstorm advances, a rolling, turbulent, circular-shaped cloud may form at the lower leading edge of the cloud. This is called the **roll cloud**. The gust front and roll cloud are generally associated with large multicell and supercell thunderstorms. [Figure 6-40]

Figure 6-40. A gust front is the sharp boundary found on the edge of the pool of cold air that is fed by the downdrafts and spreads out below a thunderstorm.

Figure 6-41. A cumulonimbus cloud indicates that the thunderstorm has reached at least the mature stage.

Courtesy of National Center for Atmospheric Research/University Corporation for Atmospheric Research/National Science Foundation

The top of the mature cell can reach as high as 40,000 feet. [Figure 6-41] The highest portion of the cloud may develop a cirriform appearance because of the very cold temperatures and the strong stability of atmosphere above it. As the vertical motions slow near the top of the storm, the cloud spreads out horizontally, forming the well-known anvil shape. The anvil top is an indicator of upper-level winds and points in the approximate direction of the storm's movement.

 Thunderstorms reach the greatest intensity during the mature stage which is signaled by the beginning of precipitation.

An exception to the model of the mature thunderstorm sometimes occurs in arid regions. In these areas, lightning and thunder may occur, but the precipitation often evaporates before reaching the ground, creating virga. Below the virga, an invisible downdraft will often continue to the ground below. This combination of gusty winds, lack of precipitation reaching the ground, and lightning is often the cause of forest fires.

DISSIPATING STAGE

Fifteen to thirty minutes after it reaches the mature stage, the single-cell airmass thunderstorm reaches the **dissipating stage**. As the storm develops, more and more air aloft is disturbed by the falling drops. Eventually, the downdrafts begin to spread out within the cell, taking the place of the weakening updrafts. Because upward movement is necessary for condensation and the release of the latent energy, the entire thunderstorm begins to weaken. When the cell becomes an area of predominant downdrafts, it takes on a stratiform appearance, gradually dissipating. Because the anvil top is an ice cloud, it often lasts longer than the rest of the cell.

 A dissipating thunderstorm is characterized by downdrafts.

Occasionally, a severe thunderstorm does not dissipate in the typical manner. If winds become markedly stronger with altitude, the upper portion of the cloud may be "tilted,"

Inside a Thunderstorm

On July 27, 1959, U.S. Marine Corps Lieutenant Colonel William H. Rankin was forced to eject from his jet at 47,000 feet. Generally, most people would be incapacitated by the low atmospheric pressure at that altitude. However, Lt. Col. Rankin was not so lucky. He remained conscious as he descended into a well-developed severe thunderstorm. Although it should have taken him only 10 minutes to pass through the storm, the updrafts kept him inside the cloud for 40 minutes. During that time he battled for survival in temperatures as low as -57°C (-71°F), all the while being pelted with hailstones, blinded by lightning, deafened by thunder, and soaked by driving rain. At one point, the rain was so torrential that Lt. Col. Rankin thought he might survive everything else only to be drowned. To this day, he may be the only person ever to have survived such an ordeal.

Figure 6-42. In a severe thunderstorm, upper-level winds may tilt the up- and downdrafts. This usually causes the precipitation to fall through the downdrafts rather than through the updrafts, as in an airmass thunderstorm. Since the updrafts can remain strong for a longer period of time, the life of the storm may be extended, sometimes by several hours.

or blown downwind. In this case, precipitation falls through only a small portion of the rising air, or it may fall completely outside the cloud. As a result, the updrafts may continue to maintain their strength, prolonging the mature stage. [Figure 6-42]

THUNDERSTORM HAZARDS

The weather hazards associated with thunderstorms are not confined to the cloud itself. For example, you can encounter turbulence in clear conditions as far as 20 miles from the storm. You can think of a cumulonimbus cloud as the visible part of a widespread system of turbulence and other weather hazards.

TURBULENCE

Thunderstorm turbulence develops when air currents change direction or velocity rapidly over a short distance. The magnitude of the turbulence depends on the differences between the two air currents. Within the thunderstorm's

 Severe turbulence often exists in a cumulonimbus cloud, the most turbulent of all clouds.

cumulonimbus cloud, the strongest turbulence occurs in the zone between the updrafts and downdrafts. Near the surface, there is a low-level area of turbulence which develops as the downdrafts spread out at the surface. These create a **shear zone** between the surrounding air and the cooler air of the downdraft. The resulting area of gusty winds and turbulence can extend outward for many miles from the center of the storm.

LIGHTNING

Lightning is always associated with thunderstorms and can occur in several forms including in-cloud, cloud-to-cloud, cloud-to-ground, and occasionally, between the cloud and clear air. Regardless of the type, a lightning discharge involves a voltage difference between both ends of the lightning stroke of about 300,000 volts per foot. Air along the discharge channel is heated to more than 50,000°F causing a rapid expansion of air and the production of a shock wave that you eventually hear as thunder. For all its power, lightning rarely causes crew injury or substantial damage to aircraft structures. However, lightning can cause temporary loss of vision, puncture the aircraft skin, or damage electronic navigation and communications equipment. [Figure 6-43]

Lightning is always associated with thunderstorms.

Figure 6-43. The typical thunderstorm generates three to four lightning discharges per minute.

HAIL

Hail can occur at all altitudes within or outside a thunderstorm. You can encounter it in flight, even when no hail is reaching the surface. In addition, large hailstones have been encountered in clear air several miles downwind from a thunderstorm. While any hail can be dangerous, large hail with diameters in excess of 3/4 inches can inflict enormous damage to aircraft. [Figure 6-44]

Figure 6-44. Hail can cause significant damage to aircraft.

TORNADOES

Funnel clouds are violent, spinning columns of air which descend from the base of a cloud. Wind speeds within them may exceed 200 knots. If a funnel cloud reaches the earth's surface, it is referred to as a **tornado**. [Figure 6-45] If it touches down over water, it is called a **waterspout**.

Figure 6-45. A severe thunderstorm's rotational circulation pattern is conducive to producing extremely powerful tornadoes.

TURBULENCE

In addition to turbulence in and near thunderstorms, three other categories of turbulence affect aviation operations: Low-level turbulence, clear air turbulence, and mountain wave turbulence. The effects of turbulence can vary from occasional light bumps to severe jolts which can cause personal injury to occupants and/or structural damage to the airplane. If you enter turbulence or expect that you will encounter it during flight, slow the airplane to maneuvering speed or less, attempt to maintain a level flight attitude, and accept variations in altitude. If you encounter turbulent or gusty conditions during an approach to a landing, you should consider flying a power-on approach at an airspeed slightly above the normal approach speed.

 If you encounter turbulence during flight, establish maneuvering speed and try to maintain a level flight attitude.

LOW-LEVEL TURBULENCE

While **low-level turbulence (LLT)** is often defined as turbulence below 15,000 feet MSL, most low-level turbulence originates due to surface heating or friction within a few thousand feet of the ground. LLT includes mechanical turbulence, convective turbulence, frontal turbulence, and wake turbulence.

MECHANICAL TURBULENCE

When obstacles such as buildings or rough terrain interfere with the normal wind flow, turbulence develops. This phenomenon, referred to as **mechanical turbulence**, is often experienced in the traffic pattern when the wind forms eddies as it blows around hangars, stands of trees, or other obstructions. [Figure 6-46] As the winds grow stronger, mechanical turbulence extends to greater heights. For example, when surface winds are 50 knots or greater, significant turbulence due to surface effects can reach altitudes in excess of 3,000 feet AGL.

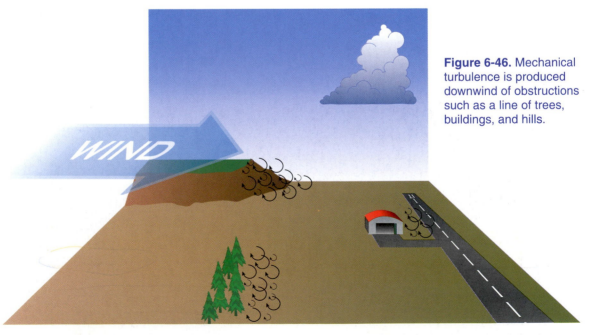

Figure 6-46. Mechanical turbulence is produced downwind of obstructions such as a line of trees, buildings, and hills.

Mechanical turbulence also occurs when strong winds flow nearly perpendicular to steep hills or mountain ridges. In comparison with turbulence over flat ground, the relatively larger size of the hills produce greater turbulence. In addition, steep hillsides generally produce stronger turbulence because the sharp slope encourages the wind flow to separate from the surface. Steep slopes on either side of a valley can produce particularly dangerous turbulence for aircraft operations. [Figure 6-47]

Figure 6-47. Winds moving across a gentle sloping valley (left) produce winds which generally follow the valley contour. In a very narrow canyon with strong crosswinds (right), conditions may be significantly different. In this case, turbulence or downward motions occur on the downwind side of the valley. Additionally, airflow at the bottom of a narrow canyon can be turbulent due to sharp bends and limited space.

CONVECTIVE TURBULENCE

Convective turbulence, which is also referred to as thermal turbulence, is typically a daytime phenomena which occurs over land in fair weather. It is caused by currents, or thermals, which develop in air heated by contact with the warm surface below. This heating can occur when cold air is moved horizontally over a warmer surface or when the ground is heated by the sun. When the air is moist, the currents may be marked by build-ups of cumulus cloud formations.

 When sufficient moisture is present, towering cumulus clouds indicate the presence of convective turbulence.

With typical upward gusts ranging from 200 to 2,000 f.p.m., thermals are used to great advantage by glider pilots to gain altitude. However, as the pilot of a powered aircraft, you may find the continuous bumpiness produced by thermals undesirable. In some cases, you can find relief by climbing into the **capping stable layer** which begins at the top of the convective layer. This can sometimes be identified by a layer of cumulus clouds, haze, or dust. [Figure 6-48]

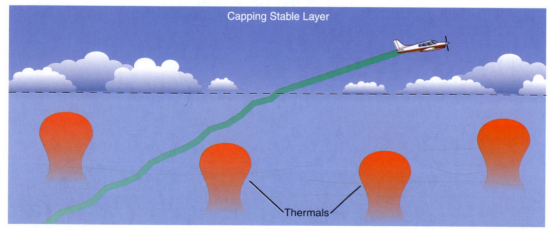

Capping Stable Layer

Thermals

Figure 6-48. By climbing into the capping stable layer, you may be able to find relief from convective turbulence. The height of the capping layer is typically a few thousand feet above the ground, although it can exceed 10,000 feet AGL over the desert in the summer.

Hurricane Hunters

When most city inhabitants flee from a hurricane, others are headed in the opposite direction, flying right into the eye of the storm! Some call them crazy, but to the people who make the journey, it's not only exciting and fascinating, but it's also necessary.

Whenever a hurricane threatens the country, Air Force Reserve Lockheed WC-130s and two National Oceanic and Atmospheric Administration (NOAA) Lockheed WP-3D aircraft weave their way into the heart of the storm. While both types of airplanes are used to gather data for forecasters, the NOAA WP-3Ds also carry scientists who conduct hurricane research.

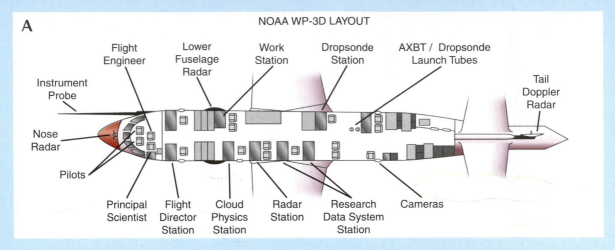

A — NOAA WP-3D LAYOUT

NOAA has flown the heavily instrumented WP-3Ds since 1975. [Figure A] While inside the hurricane, scientists gather information such as temperature, pressure, wind speed and direction, and humidity. For information on other portions of the storm, scientists launch weather instruments, called dropsondes, through the airplane's floor. As the devices parachute through the clouds, they radio back meteorological data. Scientists also can launch another instrument package, called an AXBT, which floats on the ocean's surface to collect more data. Information gathered by scientists is sent to the Hurricane Center in Miami, Florida via satellite links. In one instance, observations made by hurricane hunters resulted in an upgraded forecast credited with saving 10,000 lives.

B — Eye

Certainly, flying into a hurricane is not routine; however, thorough planning, weather radar, and constant crew coordination combine to make most flights relatively uneventful. In heavy turbulence, the pilot flying the airplane only tries to maintain wings level. Few, if any, corrections are made for altitude deviations. The flight engineer, sitting behind the two pilots, monitors the instruments and manipulates the four throttles. The pilot-not-flying backs up both the pilot and flight engineer. The worst of the turbulence is in the wall of the eye, but once established inside the eye, it's smooth enough for crewmembers to sip coffee while gazing down on the churning ocean 5,000 feet below. [Figure B]

FRONTAL TURBULENCE

Frontal turbulence occurs in the narrow zone just ahead of a fast-moving cold front where updrafts can reach 1,000 f.p.m. When combined with convection and strong winds across the front, these updrafts can produce significant turbulence. Over flat ground, any front moving at a speed of 30 knots or more will generate at least a moderate amount of turbulence. A front moving over rough terrain will produce moderate or greater turbulence, regardless of its speed.

WAKE TURBULENCE

Whenever an airplane generates lift, air spills over the wingtips from the high pressure areas below the wings to the low pressure areas above them. This flow causes rapidly rotating whirlpools of air called wingtip vortices, or **wake turbulence**. The intensity of the turbulence depends on aircraft weight, speed, and configuration.

Wingtip vortices are created when an airplane generates lift.

The greatest wake turbulence danger is produced by large, heavy aircraft operating at low speeds, high angles of attack, and in a clean configuration. Since these conditions are most closely duplicated on takeoff and landing, you should be alert for wake turbulence near airports used by large airplanes. In fact, wingtip vortices from large commercial jets can induce uncontrollable roll rates in smaller aircraft. Although wake turbulence settles, it persists in the air for several minutes, depending on wind conditions. In light winds of three to seven knots, the vortices may stay in the touchdown area, sink into your takeoff or landing path, or drift over a parallel runway. The most dangerous condition for landing is a light, quartering tailwind. It can move the upwind vortex of a landing aircraft over the runway and forward into the touchdown zone.

The greatest vortex strength occurs when the generating aircraft is heavy, slow, and in a clean configuration.

Wingtip vortices tend to sink below the flight path of the aircraft which generated them. They are most hazardous during light, quartering tailwind conditions.

If you are in a small aircraft approaching to land behind a large aircraft, controllers must ensure adequate separation. However, if you accept a clearance to follow an aircraft you have in sight, the responsibility for wake turbulence avoidance is transferred from the controller to you. On takeoff, controllers will sequence you to provide an interval behind departing heavy aircraft. Although you may waive these time intervals, this is not a wise decision. [Figure 6-49]

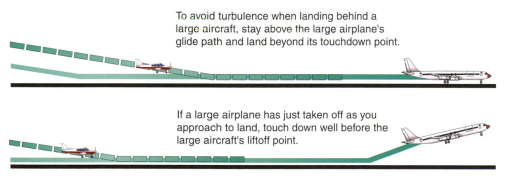

To avoid turbulence when landing behind a large aircraft, stay above the large airplane's glide path and land beyond its touchdown point.

If a large airplane has just taken off as you approach to land, touch down well before the large aircraft's liftoff point.

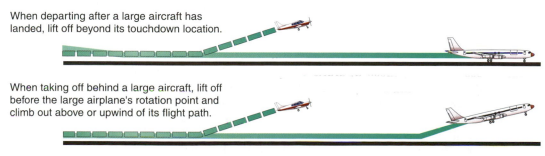

When departing after a large aircraft has landed, lift off beyond its touchdown location.

When taking off behind a large aircraft, lift off before the large airplane's rotation point and climb out above or upwind of its flight path.

Figure 6-49. Maintaining a safe distance from large aircraft can be critical. Research has shown that a vortex has the potential to "bounce" twice as high as the wingspan of the generating aircraft.

TAKEOFF THRUST

Figure 6-50. Hurricane force winds can be encountered over 200 feet behind a jet using takeoff power.

Jet engine blast is a related hazard. It can damage or even overturn a small airplane if it is encountered at close range. To avoid excessive jet blast, you must stay several hundred feet behind a jet with its engines operating, even when it is at idle thrust. [Figure 6-50]

CLEAR AIR TURBULENCE

Clear air turbulence (CAT) is commonly thought of as a high altitude phenomenon. It usually is encountered above 15,000 feet, however, it can take place at any altitude and is often present with no visual warning. While its name suggests that it cannot occur except in clear skies, CAT can also be present in nonconvective clouds. Clear air turbulence may be caused by the interaction of layers of air with differing wind speeds, convective currents, or obstructions to normal wind flow. It often develops in or near the **jet stream**, which is a narrow band of high altitude winds near the tropopause. CAT tends to be found in thin layers, typically less than 2,000 feet deep, a few tens of miles wide and more than 50 miles long. CAT often occurs in sudden bursts as aircraft intersect thin, sloping turbulent layers. [Figure 6-51]

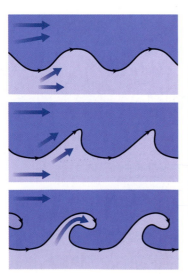

Figure 6-51. Clear air turbulence can form when a layer of air slides over the top of another, relatively slower moving layer. Eventually, the difference in speed may cause waves and, in some cases, distinctive clouds to form.

Dust Devils

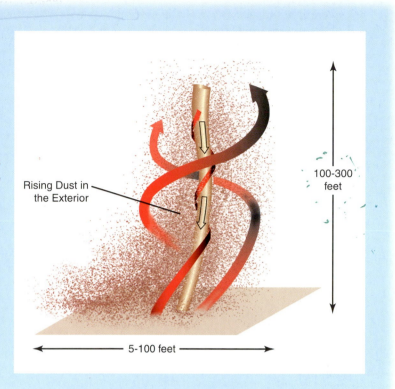

While it may look like a twister, the whirling column of dust you see on warm summer days doesn't come anywhere near producing the violence associated with a tornado. Widely known as dust devils, the whirlwinds form as heated air rises in thermals due to convection. Occasionally, strong winds become partially blocked by an obstruction, such as a stand of trees or a small hill. Air sweeping around the sides of the obstruction causes eddies to form downwind. This causes the thermal to rotate, stretch vertically, and shrink horizontally. You see the same effect when a figure skater pulls his or her arms toward the body, increasing the rate of rotation.

Once formed, dust devils move in the direction of the average wind in the layer which they occupy. Normally, they don't inflict much damage but, with wind speeds of up 50 knots, dust devils can still be a threat to aircraft operations.

Rising Dust in the Exterior

100-300 feet

5-100 feet

MOUNTAIN WAVE TURBULENCE

When stable air crosses a mountain barrier, the airflow is smooth on the windward side. Wind flow across the barrier is laminar — that is, it tends to flow in layers. The barrier may set up waves, called **mountain waves**. Mountain wave turbulence is possible as the stable air moves across a ridge and the wind is 40 knots or greater. The wave pattern may extend 100 miles or more downwind, and the crests may extend well above the highest peaks. Below the crest of each wave is an area of rotary circulation, or **rotor**, which forms below the mountain peaks. Both the rotor and the waves can create violent turbulence. [Figure 6-52]

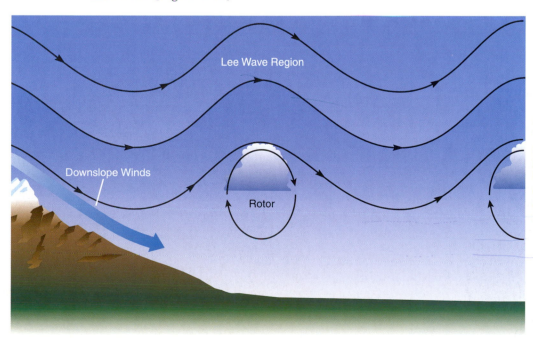

Lee Wave Region

Downslope Winds

Rotor

Figure 6-52. Mountain waves can create significant turbulence particularly along the lee slopes of the mountain, below the first lee wave trough, and in the rotor.

If sufficient moisture is present, characteristic clouds will warn you of the mountain wave. A rotor cloud (sometimes called a roll cloud) may form in the rotors. The crests of the waves may be marked by lens-shaped, or lenticular, clouds. Although they may contain winds of 50 knots or more, they may appear stationary because they form in updrafts and dissipate in downdrafts. Because of this, they are sometimes referred to as standing lenticulars. Another cloud, which may signal the presence of mountain wave turbulence, is called a cap cloud. In some instances, cap clouds may obscure the mountain peaks.[Figure 6-53]

Mountain wave turbulence can be anticipated when the winds across a ridge are 40 knots or more, and the air is stable.

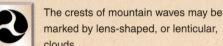
The crests of mountain waves may be marked by lens-shaped, or lenticular, clouds.

Figure 6-53. Cap, roll, and lenticular clouds can signal the presence of mountain wave activity.

You should anticipate some mountain wave activity whenever the wind is in excess of 25 knots and is blowing roughly perpendicular to mountain ridges. As wind speed increases, so does the associated turbulence. When conditions indicate a possible mountain wave, recommended cruising altitudes are at least 3,000 to 5,000 feet above the peaks. You should climb to the selected altitude while approximately 100 miles from the range, depending on wind and aircraft performance. Approach the ridge from a 45° angle to permit a safer retreat if turbulence becomes too severe. If winds at the planned flight altitude exceed 30 knots, the FAA recommends against flight over mountainous areas in small aircraft. Since local conditions and aircraft performance vary widely, you should consider scheduling a thorough checkout by a qualified flight instructor if you plan on flying in mountainous terrain.

Although they may appear stationary, standing lenticular clouds may contain winds of 50 knots or more.

WIND SHEAR

Wind shear is a sudden, drastic shift in wind speed and/or direction that may occur at any altitude in a vertical or horizontal plane. It can subject your aircraft to sudden updrafts, downdrafts, or extreme horizontal wind components, causing loss of lift or violent changes in vertical speeds or altitudes. Wind shear can

Wind shear often exists near the surface when there is a frontal system, thunderstorm, or temperature inversion with strong upper-level winds in the area. Wind shear is also associated with clear air turbulence.

Wind shear may occur during a low-level temperature inversion when cold, still surface air is covered by warmer air which contains winds of 25 knots or more at 2,000 to 4,000 feet above the surface.

 Wind shear can exist at any altitude and may occur in all directions.

be associated with convective precipitation, a jet stream, or a frontal zone. Wind shear also can materialize during a low-level temperature inversion when cold, still surface air is covered by warmer air which contains winds of 25 knots or more at 2,000 to 4,000 feet above the surface.

Generally, wind shear is most often associated with convective precipitation. While not all precipitation-induced downdrafts are associated with critical wind shears, one such downdraft, known as a **microburst**, is one of the most dangerous sources of wind shear. Microburst wind shear normally occurs over horizontal distances of one nautical mile or less and vertical distances of less than 1,000 feet. The typical microburst seldom lasts longer than 15 minutes with an average peak wind speed of about 25 knots. While winds in excess of 100 knots are possible, the average microburst will produce a headwind change of approximately 45 knots. The downdrafts within a microburst can be as strong as 6,000 f.p.m. The intense downdrafts and wind shifts make the microburst particularly dangerous, especially when encountered close to the ground. [Figure 6-54]

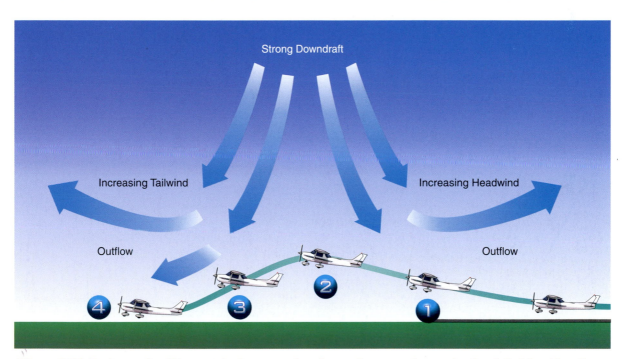

Figure 6-54. During a takeoff into a microburst, an aircraft experiences an increasing headwind (position 1), followed by a decreasing headwind and downdraft (position 2), and finally a tailwind (position 3). The area between positions 2 and 3 will produce the most severe downdrafts and, together with the tailwind, may result in an uncontrollable descent and impact with the ground (position 4).

LOW-LEVEL WIND SHEAR ALERT SYSTEM

To help detect hazardous wind shear associated with microbursts, **low-level wind shear alert systems (LLWAS)** have been installed at many airports. The LLWAS uses a system of anemometers placed at strategic locations around the airport to detect variances in the wind readings. Many systems operate by sending individual anemometer readings

ZERO TO DEADLY IN TWELVE MINUTES

It was a typical August day in Texas. The forecast called for the standard isolated or widely scattered rain showers and thunderstorms when the Lockheed L-1011 departed Fort Lauderdale, Florida enroute to Dallas/Fort Worth. By the time Flight 191 approached its destination, thunderstorms had built up east of the airport. While the flightcrew concentrated on avoiding the well-developed cells, a small area of rain showers began to show up on radar just north of the airport and on the approach path to Runway 17L. As the L-1011 skirted north, air traffic control sequenced a Lear 25 behind a Boeing 727 already on the approach to Runway 17L. Both aircraft flew through some rain and turbulence, but landed safely at the airport, which was in good weather.

As Flight 191 became stabilized on the approach, the small rain shower had grown considerably — in only 12 minutes. A rain-shaft was plainly visible below the 6,000-foot base, but the area around the storm was clear. Soon after the first officer piloted the L-1011 into the rain, an increasing headwind caused Flight 191 to balloon above the approach glideslope. The captain, who had nearly 30,000 flight hours, recognized the classic first sign of wind shear and began to issue warnings and instructions to the first officer. Quickly after encountering the headwind, the jet was buffeted by a downdraft which caused the airplane to lose 44 knots of indicated airspeed in 10 seconds. Then, in one short second, Flight 191 was hit with intense gusts which turned the airplane nearly sideways and caused its airspeed to drop from 140 knots to 120 knots. In the next 13 seconds, the L-1011 was hit with six changes in vertical wind direction causing load factor to vary from negative 0.3 to a positive 2.0 G's. At this point, the captain called for a go-around, but it was too late — the huge jet was already out-of-control. Although the crew fought valiantly to effect a recovery, the storm refused to relent. The airplane struck the ground at a speed of about 170 knots, bounced once, then came back to earth on a highway and skidded to a stop near the northern edge of the airport. The crash killed 134 of the 165 people on board the airplane and one on the ground.

In its report, the National Transportation Safety Board (NTSB) stated the probable causes of the accident as: "the flightcrew's decision to initiate and continue the approach into a cumulonimbus cloud which they observed to contain visible lightning, the lack of specific guidelines, procedures, and training for avoiding and escape from low-altitude wind shear, and the lack of defini-tive, real-time wind shear information. This resulted in the aircraft's encounter at low altitude with a microburst-induced, severe wind shear from a rapidly developing thunderstorm located on the final approach course."

What can be learned from this tragedy? The NTSB may have answered that question best when it said, "The circumstances of this accident indicate that there is an apparent lack of appreciation on the part of some, and perhaps many, flightcrews of the need to avoid thunderstorms and to appraise the position and severity of the storms pessimistically and cautiously."

every 10 seconds to a central computer which evaluates the wind differences across the airport. A wind shear alert is usually issued if one reading differs from the mean by at least 15 knots. If you are arriving or departing from an airport equipped with LLWAS, you will be advised by air traffic controllers if an alert is posted. You also will be provided with wind velocities at two or more of the sensors.

TERMINAL DOPPLER WEATHER RADAR

In addition to LLWAS, **terminal Doppler weather radar (TDWR)** systems are being installed at airports with high wind shear potential. These radar systems use a more powerful and narrower radar beam than conventional radar. The TDWR can provide a clearer, more detailed picture of thunderstorms which allows for better probability of predicting the presence of wind shear.

IN-FLIGHT VISUAL INDICATIONS

In areas not covered by LLWAS or TDWR, you may only be able to predict the presence of wind shear using visual indications. In humid climates where the bases of convective clouds tend to be low, wet microbursts are associated with a visible rainshaft. In the drier climates of the deserts and mountains of the western United States, the higher thunder-storm cloud bases result in the evaporation of the rainshaft producing a dry microburst. The only visible indications under these conditions may be virga at the cloud base and a dust ring on the ground. It's important to note that since downdrafts can spread horizontally across the ground, low-level wind shear may be found beyond the boundaries of the visible rainshaft. You should avoid any area which you suspect could contain a wind shear hazard.

ICING

Ice can build up on any exposed surface of an aircraft during flights in areas of visible moisture, when the temperature of the aircraft surface is 0°C or colder. Aircraft are affected by structural ice in a number of ways: thrust is reduced, drag and weight is increased, and lift is decreased. These effects combine to increase stall speed and reduce overall aircraft performance. In extreme cases, it can take as little as 5 minutes for 2 to 3 inches of ice to accumulate on the leading edge of the airfoil. Some aircraft may experience as much as a 50 percent decrease in lift after the build-up of only 1/2 inch of ice. There are three general types of ice — rime, clear, and a mixture of the two.

Visible moisture is necessary for structural icing to form. Freezing rain usually produces the highest rate of ice accumulation.

Rime ice normally is encountered in stratus clouds and results from instantaneous freezing of tiny supercooled water droplets striking the aircraft surface. It has an opaque appearance caused by air being trapped in the water droplets as they freeze. Rime ice is particularly hazardous due to its ability to change the shape of an airfoil and destroy its lift. Since rime ice freezes instantly, it builds up on the leading edge of airfoils, but it does not flow back following the basic curvature of the wing and tail surfaces. Rime ice normally forms in temperatures between -15°C and -20°C.

Clear ice may develop in areas of large supercooled water droplets which are in cumulus clouds or in freezing rain beneath a warm front inversion. The highest accumulation rate generally occurs in freezing rain. When the droplets flow over the aircraft structure and slowly freeze, they can glaze the aircraft's surfaces. Clear ice is the most serious form of ice because it adheres tenaciously to the aircraft and is difficult to remove. The formation of clear ice is likely when temperatures are between 0°C to -10°C. **Mixed ice** is possible in visible moisture between -10°C and -15°C.

Looking for Ice!

Artificial icing facilities such as wind tunnels or airborne spray tankers provide a unique capability to test and evaluate aircraft systems in an authentic, yet controlled icing environment. One such facility in use is the U.S. Army Helicopter Icing Spray System (HISS), which is installed in a modified JCH-47C Chinook helicopter. Flying ahead of another aircraft, the helicopter produces a spray cloud in flight. In figure A, a DH-6 Twin Otter airplane is shown flying behind a Chinook equipped with a HISS.

A

Courtesy of NASA Lewis Research Center

B
Courtesy of NASA Lewis Research Center

The DH-6 is used to conduct icing research including the characterization of icing clouds and the aerodynamic effects of icing. To make the ice accumulations more readily visible, a dye is mixed with the water. This can be seen as the yellow-green ice on the DH-6 shown in figure B.

RESTRICTIONS TO VISIBILITY

Particles which can absorb, scatter, and reflect light are always present in the atmosphere. The fact that the amount of particles in the air varies considerably explains why visibility is better on some days than others. Restrictions to visibility can take many forms, the most common of which are haze, smoke, smog, and dust.

HAZE

Haze is caused by a concentration of very fine dry particles. Individually, they are invisible to the naked eye, but in sufficient numbers, can restrict your visibility. Haze particles may be composed of a variety of substances, such as salt or dust particles. It occurs in stable atmospheric conditions with relatively light winds. Haze is usually no more than a few thousand feet thick, but it may occasionally extend to 15,000 feet. Visibility above the haze layer is usually good; however, visibility through the haze can be very poor. Dark objects tend to be bluish, while bright objects, like the sun or distant lights, have a dirty yellow or reddish hue.

SMOKE

Smoke is the suspension of combustion particles in air. The impact of smoke on visibility is determined by the amount of smoke produced, wind velocity, diffusion by turbulence, and distance from the source. You can often identify smoke by a reddish sky as the sun rises or sets, and an orange-colored sky when the sun is well above the horizon. When smoke travels distances of 25 miles or more, large particles fall out and the smoke tends to become more evenly distributed, giving the sky a grayish or bluish appearance, similar to haze.

SMOG

Smog, which is a combination of fog and smoke, can spread very poor visibility over a large area. In some geographical areas, topographical barriers, such as mountains, may combine with stable air to trap pollutants. This results in a build-up of smog, further reducing visibility.

DUST

Dust refers to fine particles of soil suspended in the air. When the soil is loose, the winds are strong, and the atmosphere is unstable, dust may be blown for hundreds of miles. Dust gives a tan or gray tinge to distant objects while the sun may appear as colorless, or with a yellow hue. Blowing dust is common in areas where dry land farming is extensive, such as the Texas panhandle.

VOLCANIC ASH

While lava from volcanoes generally threatens areas only in the immediate vicinity of the volcano, the ash cloud can affect a much more widespread area. **Volcanic ash**, which consists of gases, dust, and ash from a volcanic eruption, can spread around the world and remain the stratosphere for months or longer. [Figure 6-55] Due to its highly abrasive characteristics, volcanic ash can pit the aircraft windscreens and landing lights to the point they are rendered useless. Under severe conditions, the ash can clog pitot-static and ventilation systems as well as damage aircraft control surfaces. Piston aircraft are less likely than jet aircraft to lose power due to ingestion of volcanic ash, but severe damage is possible, especially if the volcanic cloud is only a few hours old.

An ash cloud may not be easily distinguishable from ordinary clouds when approached from a distance. However, if you suspect that you are in the vicinity of an ash cloud you should attempt to stay upwind. If you inadvertently enter a volcanic ash cloud you should not attempt to fly straight through or climb out of the cloud since ash cloud may be hundreds of miles wide and extend to great heights. You should reduce power to a minimum, altitude permitting, and reverse course to escape the cloud.

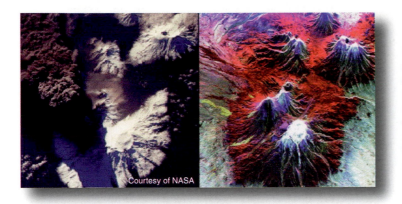

Courtesy of NASA

Figure 6-55. These images show the same eruption of the Kliuchevskoi volcano in Kamchatka, Russia. On the left is a photo taken by Space Shuttle astronauts as the Shuttle Endeavor passed over the site. The radar image on the right shows how radar can see through the ash and smoke to reveal the land underneath.

SUMMARY CHECKLIST

✓ Airmass thunderstorms are relatively short-lived storms which rarely produce large hail or strong winds. Severe thunderstorms contain wind gusts of 50 knots or more, hail 3/4 inch in diameter or larger, and/or tornadoes.

✓ The life of a thunderstorm passes through three distinct stages. The cumulus stage is characterized by continuous updrafts. When precipitation begins to fall, the thunderstorm has reached the mature stage. As the storm dies during the dissipating stage, updrafts weaken and downdrafts become predominant.

✓ Some weather hazards associated with thunderstorms, such as turbulence, lightning, and hail are not confined to the cloud itself.

✓ If you encounter turbulence during flight, you should establish maneuvering speed and try to maintain a level flight attitude.

✓ Mechanical turbulence is often experienced in the traffic pattern when wind forms eddies as it blows over hangars, stands of trees, or other obstructions.

✓ When sufficient moisture is present, cumulus cloud build-ups indicate the presence of convective turbulence.

✓ Wingtip vortices are created when an airplane generates lift. The greatest vortex strength occurs when the generating aircraft is heavy, slow, and in a clean configuration.

✓ Mountain wave turbulence can be anticipated when the winds across a ridge are 40 knots or more, and the air is stable. The crests of mountain waves may be marked by lens-shaped, or lenticular, clouds.

✓ Wind shear can exist at any altitude and may occur in a vertical or horizontal direction. A microburst is one of the most dangerous sources of wind shear.

✓ The three types of structural ice are rime, clear, and mixed.

✓ Volcanic ash clouds may be hundreds of miles wide and thousands of feet thick.

KEY TERMS

Airmass Thunderstorms

Severe Thunderstorms

Single-Cell

Supercell

Multicell

Squall Line

Frontal Thunderstorms

Cumulus Stage

Mature Stage

Gust Front

Roll Cloud

Dissipating Stage

Shear Zone

Tornado

Waterspout

Low-Level Turbulence (LLT)

Mechanical Turbulence

Convective Turbulence

Capping Stable Layer

Frontal Turbulence

Wake Turbulence

Jet Engine Blast

Clear Air Turbulence (CAT)

Jet Stream

Mountain Waves

Rotor

Wind Shear

Microburst

Low-Level Wind Shear Alert
Systems (LLWAS)

Terminal Doppler Weather Radar
(TDWR)

Rime Ice

Clear Ice

Mixed Ice

Haze

Smoke

Smog

Dust

Volcanic Ash

QUESTIONS

1. What are the three basic ingredients needed for the formation of a thunderstorm?

2. What causes the thunderstorm's anvil to form? What can it tell you about the thunderstorm's movement?

3. Recall the general procedures you should use when encountering turbulence in flight.

4. True/False. Cumulus clouds indicate the presence of mechanical turbulence.

5. What is the most dangerous condition for landing with respect to wingtip vortices?

6. What technique should be used to avoid wake turbulence during takeoff behind a large aircraft?
    A. Climb on the flight path of the preceding aircraft
    B. Climb below the flight path of the preceding aircraft
    C. Climb above the flight path of the preceding aircraft

7. What kind of turbulence is indicated by the presence of rotor, cap, and lenticular clouds?

8. Discuss the in-flight visual indications of possible wind shear.

Match the following types of structural icing with its characteristic.

9. Clear   A. Occurs in temperatures between -10°C and -15°C

10. Rime   B. Develops in an area of large supercooled water droplets

11. Mixed   C. Normally is encountered in stratus clouds

12. What is the recommended course of action if you inadvertently enter a volcanic ash cloud?
    A. Reverse course
    B. Attempt to climb up and out of the cloud
    C. Continue straight ahead to exit on the opposite side

CHAPTER 7

INTERPRETING WEATHER DATA

Part III, Chapter 7 — Interpreting Weather Data

SECTION A
THE FORECASTING PROCESS

Can you accurately predict the future? Most people would answer, "No," but ask a meteorologist and the response may different. It's true that weather forecasts are not always totally precise, however, a strong case can be made that scientists' ability to decipher atmospheric clues and produce a reasonably accurate forecast has been rapidly improving. In fact, weather prognosticators can now produce a seven-day outlook which is, on average, as accurate as a two-day forecast was in 1975. The desire for dependable predictions has led to the creation of a multi-millon-dollar-a-year industry which provides forecasts to everyone from weekend gardeners to major airlines. These forecasts, on which thousands of decisions are based every day, are generated through an elaborate process involving individual observers and complex computer programs.

FORECASTING METHODS

Predicting the weather can be accomplished through a multitude of methods with wide variances in accuracy. Some methods are best suited for short-term forecasts while others are more adequate for making long-range predictions. The methods may be used alone, or in combination, to create a picture of future weather conditions.

PERSISTENCE FORECAST

With very little meteorological information or knowledge of weather theory you can still make a weather forecast by simply looking out the window. The **persistence method** of forecasting involves simply predicting that the weather you are experiencing at the moment will continue to prevail. For example, if you wake up in the morning to brilliant sunshine, it would be reasonable for you to predict that it will remain sunny for the remainder of the morning. As you might expect, these types of forecasts are usually only accurate over a short period of time, such as a few hours.

TREND FORECAST

The **trend forecast** employs the assumption that weather systems which are moving in one direction and speed will continue to do so in the absence of any other intervening circumstances. For example, suppose a cold front is moving toward an airport at 30

D Is it True?

They are referred to as rules of thumb, folklore, and wives tales. Whatever you call them, they are as much a part of our culture as they are a method to predict the weather. Although many are pure myth, others have a measure of validity. Can you tell which is which?

A. When the dew is on the grass,
Rain will never come to pass.
When grass is dry at morning light,
Look for rain before the night.

B. The farther the sight, the nearer the rain.

C. Telephone wires hum and whine when a weather change is due.

D. Rainbow in the morning,
Sailor take warning;
Rainbow toward night,
Sailor's delight.

E. When a dog eats grass, it is a sign of rain.

F. When leaves show their backs, it will rain.

G. When squirrels lay in a big store of nuts, look for a hard winter.

Answers:

A. As the saying goes: "never say never." Even so, this piece of wisdom is essentially true.

B. This is true near large bodies of water. The mixing of the atmosphere due to instability coupled with the lack of evaporation contributes to relatively clear air, hence the ability to see far away objects.

C. This rule of thumb is also somewhat accurate. Cold, dry air tends to tighten the wires, making them hum. Typically, this will occur as cold air, and the associated storms, move into an area.

D. Although there are variations to this theme, this particular saying holds true. Since storms in North America generally move from west to east, a morning rainbow would indicate that the storm is still to the west. A rainbow seen in the evening would have to be to the east, meaning the storm has already passed.

E. Depending on the age of the dog, this could be true. Older dogs with rheumatism may experience more discomfort with the lowering atmospheric pressure and increasing humidity accompanying an approaching storm system. To relieve the pain, a dog may try to induce vomiting by eating grass.

F. Tree leaves tend to grow in a pattern according to the prevailing wind. Therefore, when a non-prevailing wind blows, such as that associated with a storm, the light-colored undersides of the leaves are exposed, making this a generally true statement.

G. Many people believe this to be true; however, squirrels simply collect all the nuts they can. If they amass more nuts in one year than another, it is probably only because of an increase in availability.

miles per hour. If the front is sixty miles away, you could predict that the front will begin to pass over the airport in two hours. This type of forecasting is typically used to predict events which will occur over the next few hours. Trend forecasting is often used to produce what is sometimes referred to as nowcasts.

CLIMATOLOGICAL FORECAST

Weather predictions also can be made by basing the outlook on the average weather (climatology) in a region. For example, historical records indicate there is, on average, less than one day of rain a month during the summer in San Francisco, California. Using the **climatological forecast** method, a meteorologist could confidently predict a remote chance of rain during next year's July fourth weekend in San Francisco. This type of forecasting is usually only reliable in areas and at times which enjoy little change in day-to-day weather conditions.

ANALOGUE FORECAST

Combining historical information with other prevailing weather elements can help refine a forecast. The **analogue forecast** compares the features of a current weather chart with those of a similar chart from the past. The weather conditions produced as a result of the historical chart can be used as a guide to predicting what will occur in the future. Unfortunately, regardless of how close two situations seem, there is rarely, if ever, an instance where everything is exactly the same. Despite these limitations, the analogue method can be used to predict things such as minimum and maximum temperatures. For example, a meteorologist can statistically correlate the minimum temperature on a particular date with other local weather factors such as humidity, wind, and cloud cover. Then, the forecaster can use the relationships in combination with current weather data to predict the minimum temperature for the day.

METEOROLOGICAL FORECAST

A **meteorological forecast** is generally more accurate than many other methods because it uses the forecaster's scientific knowledge of atmospheric processes to generate a weather prediction. In many cases, an experienced meteorologist can produce an accurate 6- to 12-hour forecast simply by analyzing a variety of weather charts and other data.

NUMERICAL WEATHER PREDICTION

Increased forecast accuracy can be accomplished using powerful computers and complex software. This process, known as **numerical weather prediction**, uses mathematical equations which relate atmospheric conditions with other variables. The system of equations is referred to as a numerical prediction model and represents the physical laws which govern the behavior of the atmosphere. The computer applies the model to the current atmospheric conditions to develop a forecast for the very near future (5 to 10 minutes). The resulting forecast in fed back into the computer to generate a prediction for the following 5 to 10 minutes. This process is repeated over and over again until a prediction for the next day or two has been developed. These forecasts are an integral part of today's overall weather data compilation and processing system.

COMPILING AND PROCESSING WEATHER DATA

Predicting weather conditions begins with an analysis of present and past conditions. From the compilation of the weather data until a final forecast is disseminated, the information is passed among various agencies for processing, analysis, and creation of weather charts, graphics, and text. [Figure 7-1]

Can a Butterfly Influence the Weather?

In a North American forest, a butterfly flaps its wings. Three months later, a typhoon hammers the Mariana Islands. Are these seemingly dissimilar events related?

The answers may be found by investigating the Butterfly Effect, which is technically known as "sensitive dependence on initial conditions." This effect is based on chaos theory, a relatively new science which began in the early 1960s with a mathematician and atmospheric scientist named Edward Lorenz. One winter's day in 1961, the former Army Air Corps weather forecaster made a discovery which seemed to verify what he had suspected for some time. While reexamining a particular forecast, the scientist decided to reenter numbers into a computer from a previous printout. However, instead of starting at the beginning, Lorenz entered the initial conditions as shown in the middle of the earlier printout. A few minutes later the computer produced a new prediction, which Lorenz expected to be exactly the same as the former. The scientist was shocked to observe that the forecast diverged rapidly from the existing pattern. Comparing the two, Lorenz found that the patterns began to grow apart until the three-month forecasts bore no resemblance to each other. What went wrong? The program was the same and the computer was operating perfectly. The only variable seemed to be

the numbers Lorenz had used to initialize the computer on the second run. Further investigation revealed that, although the computer was calculating numbers to six decimal places, the printout only indicated three. Conventional thinking up to this point in time would say that a seemingly inconsequential difference in starting points should have very little effect, even over the long run. It would be like small puffs of wind — they should cancel each other out, or fade away before they have any real impact on large-scale things such as global weather patterns.

The theory of minuscule variations having no perceptible effect on large-scale systems had been relied on in the past for describing the motions of stars, planets, and comets. Many scientists thought it should work for calculating the movements of weather systems or even the development of an individual cloud. Lorenz didn't see it the same way. He concluded that small atmospheric disturbances can have large-scale effects on weather systems. So, in effect, you can change the weather. Yet, you

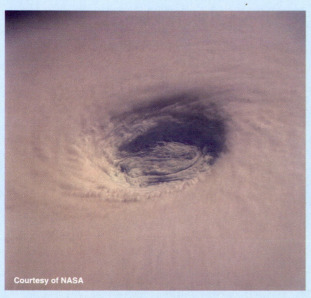

Courtesy of NASA

would never know what the weather would have been if you hadn't introduced a small disturbance. It is analogous to a blackjack dealer shuffling a deck of cards one more time. It will most certainly change your luck, but you will not know whether it is for the better or not. The effects of chaos theory on our ability to predict the weather are far reaching. Since all conditions affecting a forecast can never really be known, a forecast will diverge further and further from what really occurs as time progresses. Even with improving technology, a denser network of observing stations, and near perfect computer models, the effects suggested by chaos theory may ultimately limit the accuracy of forecasts.

OBSERVATIONS

Standardization of observation procedures is maintained by the World Meteorological Organization, a United Nations agency consisting of over 130 nations.

Figure 7-1. The forecasts you use to plan your flights are the result of the coordinated interaction of several agencies.

Courtesy of NOAA / DOC

At Sea
Hundreds of ships and weather buoys provide surface weather data.

On Land
Weather conditions are observed and recorded at over 10,000 land-based stations. Airports generally take an observation on an hourly basis, while other stations record the weather four times a day. In addition to standard readings such as temperature, pressure, and relative humidity, advanced weather radar systems gather additional information about precipitation and wind.

In the Sky
Upper-air data are chiefly provided by radiosondes attached to weather balloons, aircraft, and satellites.

COMMUNICATION

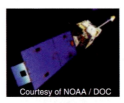
Courtesy of NOAA / DOC

Observations are transmitted by telephone, computer, or satellite to a communication substation for subsequent relay to three World Meteorological Centers.

World Meteorological Centers

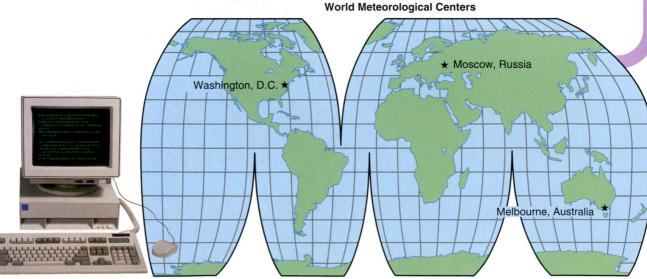

★ Moscow, Russia

Washington, D.C. ★

Melbourne, Australia ★

PROCESSING

From the World Meteorological Centers, weather information is transmitted to meteorological centers in each participating country, including the National Centers for Environmental Prediction (NCEP) in Camp Springs, Maryland.

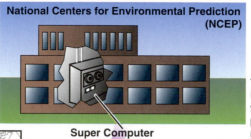

National Centers for Environmental Prediction (NCEP)

Super Computer

The NCEP is the focus of the United States' weather forecasting. Analyzing data, preparing charts and printed reports, and developing forecasts on a national and worldwide level are accomplished at the NCEP.

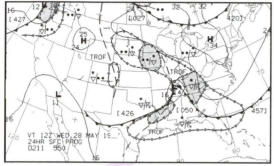

Most of the reports and forecasts are produced with the aid of NCEP's super computer which can perform over 2 billion operations per second. The NCEP generates approximately 20,000 different kinds of textual products and 6,000 graphic images.

```
FD KWBC 151640
BASED ON 151200Z DATA
VALID 151800Z FOR USE 1700-2100Z TEMPS NEG ABV 24000

FT    3000  6000   9000   12000   18000   24000   30000   34000   39000

ALA                2420   2635-08 2535-18 2444-30 245945  246755  246862
AMA         2714   2725+00 2625-04 2531-15 2542-27 265842  256352  256762
DEN                2321-04 2532-08 2434-19 2441-31 235347  236056  236262
HLC         1707-01 2113-03 2219-07 2330-17 2435-30 244145  244854  245561
MKC  0507   2006+03 2215-01 2322-06 2338-17 2348-29 236143  237252  238160
STL  2113   2325+07 2332+02 2339-04 2356-16 2373-27 239440  730649  731960
```

DISSEMINATION

Information produced by the NCEP is sent to National Weather Service facilities across the country as well as other public and private agencies worldwide.

Currently, the National Weather Service is undergoing a major modernization and reorganization. When complete, the streamlined network will consist of nearly 120 Weather Forecast Offices (WFOs), each equipped with a modern NEXRAD radar facility (below).

Private Agency

FSS

WFO

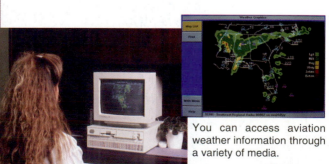

You can access aviation weather information through a variety of media.

FORECASTING ACCURACY AND LIMITATIONS

Despite advances in forecasting methods, especially with the aid of computers, there are limits to the accuracy of predictions. To some degree, this is due to the large distances between weather reporting stations and the length of time between weather reports. Also, the atmosphere occasionally does not behave exactly like computer models think it should. These flawed computer predictions are one of the primary reasons a predicted day of sunshine turns out to be rainy.

Usually, forecasters can accurately predict the occurrence of large-scale weather events such as cold waves and significant storms several days in advance. On the other hand, smaller, more short-term weather phenomena such as tornadoes and some types of wind shear are much more difficult to predict. Regardless of the type of weather, the further ahead in time the forecast is, the less accurate it becomes. [Figure 7-2]

Figure 7-2. Although the accuracy of weather forecasts continues to improve, long-term forecasts are still relatively unreliable.

12 HOURS OR LESS

Predictions of weather occurring within this time period are the most accurate. Nevertheless, severe localized storms normally can only be forecast an hour or less in advance.

UP TO 48 HOURS

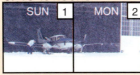

Major changes to daily weather can be predicted relatively accurately. The ability of meteorologists to predict weather as much as two days in advance has progressed rapidly over the past several years. For example, predictions of sea level pressure are nearly twice as accurate now as they were in the 1970s.

5 DAY FORECASTS

Weather events such as large storms or major heat waves can be accurately forecast up to 5 days in advance. Five-day forecasts are as precise as 3-day forecasts were 10 years ago.

10 DAY FORECASTS

Forecasters can do a fairly good job of estimating the average precipitation and temperatures up to 10 days ahead. Typically, the forecast temperatures are slightly more reliable than the precipitation estimates.

MONTHLY AND SEASONAL FORECASTS

Generally, only odds can be provided for expected temperatures and precipitation during these extended periods. For example, a meteorologist may predict that the west coast of the United States will have a 60 percent chance of a cooler-than-normal spring.

SUMMARY CHECKLIST

✓ Predicting that the weather you are experiencing at the moment will continue to prevail is referred to as the persistence method of forecasting.

✓ The trend forecast assumes that weather systems which are moving in one direction and speed will continue to do so in the absence of any other intervening circumstances.

✓ Climatological forecasts are based on the average weather in a region.

✓ The analogue forecast uses past weather patterns as a guide to predict what will occur in the future.

✓ A meteorological forecast uses the forecaster's scientific knowledge of the atmosphere and its processes to generate a weather prediction.

✓ Numerical weather prediction develops a forecast using mathematical equations which relate atmospheric conditions with other variables.

✓ Weather conditions are observed and recorded worldwide several times a day. Observations are subsequently relayed to three World Meteorological Centers, where the data are transmitted to meteorological centers in each participating country, including the National Centers for Environmental Prediction (NCEP) in the United States.

✓ Information produced by the NCEP is sent to National Weather Service (NWS) facilities across the country as well as other public and private agencies worldwide.

✓ Of all forecasts, short-term predictions are generally the most accurate.

KEY TERMS

Persistence Method	Analogue Forecast
Trend Forecast	Meteorological Forecast
Climatological Forecast	Numerical Weather Prediction

QUESTIONS

1. True/False. A persistence forecast assumes that weather systems will continue to move in the same direction and speed, unless some unexpected force intervenes.

2. Is the trend forecast more accurate for long or short periods of time?

3. How does numerical weather prediction develop a forecast?

4. Normally, how often do airports record a weather observation?

    A. Every hour
    B. Every 4 hours
    C. Every 12 hours

5. What type of weather events can be accurately predicted four days in advance?

SECTION B
PRINTED REPORTS AND FORECASTS

An ongoing restructuring of the National Weather Service (NWS) combined with the rapid expansion of the air transportation industry is changing the way weather information is gathered and disseminated. While the proliferation of electronic media has generally increased the availability of weather data, you may find that access to weather briefers and NWS meteorologists to interpret the data may not always be readily available. Consequently, a solid understanding of how to decipher the multitude of printed reports and forecasts can be more important than ever.

PRINTED WEATHER REPORTS

In general, a weather report is a record of observed atmospheric conditions at a certain location at a particular point in time. A variety of reports is used to disseminate information gathered by trained observers, radar systems, and other pilots. The types of reports you are likely to encounter include aviation routine weather reports, radar weather reports, and pilot weather reports.

AVIATION ROUTINE WEATHER REPORT

An **aviation routine weather report (METAR)** is an observation of surface weather which is reported in a standard format. While the METAR code has been adopted worldwide, each country is allowed to make modifications or exceptions to the code. Usually this is done to accommodate local procedures or particular units of measure. The following discussion covers the elements as reported in a METAR originating from an observation in the United States. [Figure 7-3]

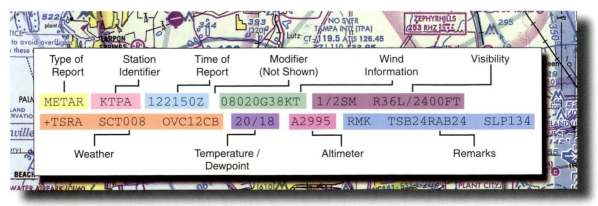

Figure 7-3. Although the content may vary somewhat, a typical METAR contains several distinct elements. If an element cannot be observed at the time of the report, it will be omitted.

TYPE OF REPORT
METAR KTPA...

The two types of reports are the METAR, which is taken every hour, and the **non-routine (special) aviation weather report (SPECI)**. The SPECI weather observation is an unscheduled report indicating a significant change in one or more elements.

STATION IDENTIFIER
METAR **KTPA** 122150Z...

Each reporting station is listed by its four-letter International Civil Aviation Organization (ICAO) identifier. In the contiguous 48 states, the letter K precedes the three-letter domestic location identifier. For example, the domestic identifier for Tampa International Airport is TPA, and the ICAO identifier is KTPA. In other areas of the world, the first two letters indicate the region, country, or state. Alaska identifiers begin with PA, for Hawaii, they begin with PH, and for Canada, the prefixes are CU, CW, CY, and CZ. You can decode station identifiers using the *Airport/Facility Directory* or a list which is usually available at an FSS or NWS office.

TIME OF REPORT
...KTPA **122150Z** 08020G38KT...

The date (day of the month) and time of the observation follows the station identifier. The time is given in UTC, or Zulu, as indicated by a Z following the time. The report in the example was issued on the 12th of the month at 2150Z.

MODIFIER
When a METAR is created by a totally automated weather observation station, the modifier AUTO follows the date/time element (e.g., ...251955Z AUTO 30008KT...). These stations are classified by the type of sensor equipment used to make the observations, and AO1 or AO2 will be noted in the remarks section of the report. An automated weather reporting station without a precipitation discriminator (which can determine the difference between liquid and frozen/freezing precipitation) is indicated by an AO1 in the remarks section of the METAR. An AO2 indicates that automated observing equipment with a precipitation discriminator was used to take the observation.

The modifier COR is used to indicate a corrected METAR and replaces a previously disseminated report. When the abbreviation COR is used in a report from an automated facility, the station type designator, AO1 or AO2, is removed from the remarks section. If a modifier is not included in the METAR (as in the example), it signifies that the observation was taken at a manual station or that manual input occurred at an automated station.

WIND INFORMATION
...122150Z **08020G38KT** 1/2SM R36L/2400FT...

The wind direction and speed are reported in a five digit group, or six digits if the speed is over 99 knots. The first three digits represent the direction from which the wind is blowing, in reference to true north. The letters VRB are used if the direction is variable.

The next two (or three) digits show the speed in knots (KT). Calm winds are reported as 00000KT. Gusty winds are reported with a G, followed by the highest gust. In the example, wind was

Winds are reported in reference to true north.

reported to be from 080° true at 20 knots with gusts to 38 knots.

If the wind direction varies 60 degrees or more and the speed is above 6 knots, a variable group follows the wind group. The extremes of wind direction are shown separated by a V. For example, if the wind is blowing from 020°, varying to 090°, it is reported as 020V090. [Figure 7-4]

As shown in figure 7-4, wind gusts are reported using a G followed by the highest gust.

CODED METAR DATA	EXPLANATIONS
00000KT	Wind calm
20014KT	Wind from 200° at 14 knots
15010G25KT	Wind from 150° at 10 knots, gusts to 25 knots
VRB04KT	Wind variable in direction at 4 knots
210103G130KT	Wind from 210° at 103 knots with gusts to 130 knots

Figure 7-4. This figure shows several examples of wind information as it appears on the METAR. The decoded wind direction, speed, and character are shown to the right.

Wind and the Aurora Borealis

The ancient Greeks called it "blood rain"; the Germans named it "heaven light"; and the Eskimos referred to it as "sky dwellers." Today, the colorful, luminous displays in poleward regions are called the Aurora Borealis (Northern Lights) and Aurora Australis (Southern Lights). Generally, Auroral activity occurs approximately 80 to 120 km above the earth's surface. The multi-hued shafts of light are most common during the spring and fall above 65 degrees north and south latitude.

Scientific explanations for the flickering lights have varied widely. In the 19th century, some researchers suspected that the myriad of colored lights was caused by sunlight reflecting off the ice caps and snow fields. Others suggested that the lights were caused by dust from meteorites burning up in the atmosphere. Finally, in 1887, Olof Birklelnad, a Norwegian physicist discovered that the Northern and Southern Lights were actually caused by a constant stream of charged particles produced by the sun — the solar wind. As these particles approach the earth, they are magnetically attracted to the polar regions where they interact with nitrogen and oxygen atoms in the upper atmosphere. During this process, a reaction takes place which results in surplus energy being released in the form of visible light. Blues and purples are produced when particles collide with nitrogen atoms; red and greenish-yellow flashes are visible when particles interact with oxygen atoms.

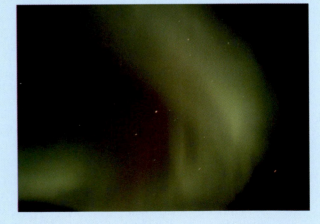

VISIBILITY

...08020G38KT **1/2SM R36L/2400FT** +TSRA...

Prevailing visibility is the greatest distance an observer can see and identify objects through at least half of the horizon. When the prevailing visibility varies from one area of the sky to another, the visibility in the majority of the sky is reported. If visibility varies significantly, the observer can report individual sector visibility in the remarks section of the METAR. [Figure 7-5]

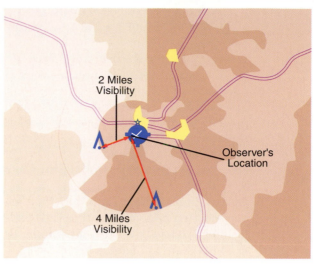

Figure 7-5. Prevailing visibility is determined by identifying distinctive objects, such as a tower or smokestack, which are at a known distance. At night, observers use lighted objects to determine visibility. In the example shown, the prevailing visibility is 4 miles since the visibility in the majority of the sky is 4 miles or greater.

Visibility is reported in statute miles (SM). For example, 1/2SM indicates one-half statute mile and 4SM would be used to report 4 statute miles. At times, **runway visual range (RVR)** may be reported following prevailing visibility. RVR, in contrast to prevailing visibility, is based on what a pilot in a moving aircraft should see when looking down the runway. RVR is designated with an R, followed by the runway number, a slant (/), and the visual range in feet (FT). In the example, R36L/2400FT means Runway 36 Left visual range is 2,400 feet. Variable RVR is shown as the lowest and highest visual range values separated by a V. Outside the United States, RVR is normally reported in meters.

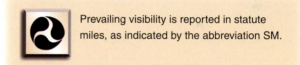

Prevailing visibility is reported in statute miles, as indicated by the abbreviation SM.

WEATHER

Weather or obstructions to vision which are present at the time of the observation are reported immediately after the visibility in the following order: intensity or proximity, descriptor, precipitation, obstruction to visibility, and any other weather phenomena. The intensity or proximity and/or descriptor are used to qualify the precipitation, obscuration, or other weather phenomena.

QUALIFIER AND DESCRIPTOR
...1/2SM R36L/2400FT **+TS**RA SCT008 OVC12CB 20/18...

Intensity or proximity of precipitation is shown immediately prior to the precipitation codes. The indicated intensity applies only to the first type of precipitation reported. Intensity levels are shown as light (–), moderate (no sign), or heavy (+). In the example, the precipitation was reported as heavy.

Weather obscurations occurring in the vicinity (between 5 and 10 statute miles) of the airport are shown by the letters VC. For precipitation, VC applies within 10 statute miles of the observation point. VC will not appear if an intensity qualifier is reported.

DESCRIPTOR CODES	
TS – Thunderstorm	DR – Low Drifting
SH – Shower(s)	MI – Shallow
FZ – Freezing	BC – Patches
BL – Blowing	PR – Partial

A description of the precipitation or obscurations is reported as a two-letter code. Only one descriptor is used for each type of precipitation or obscuration. In the example, a thunderstorm (TS) was reported.

WEATHER PHENOMENA

...1/2SM R36L/2400FT +TS**RA** SCT008 OVC12CB...

Weather phenomena covers eight types of precipitation, eight kinds of obscurations, as well as five, rather uncommon, weather events. Up to three types of precipitation can be coded in a single grouping of present weather conditions. When more than one is reported, they are shown in order of decreasing dominance. In the example, rain (RA) has been observed in connection with the thunderstorm.

Obscurations, which limit visibility, are shown after any reported precipitation. Fog (FG) is listed when the visibility is less than 5/8 statute mile. However, if the visibility were to increase to between 5/8 and 6 statute miles, the code for mist (BR) would be used. Shallow fog (MIFG), patches of fog (BCFG), or partial fog (PRFG) may be coded with prevailing visibility of 7 statute miles or greater. Following the obscurations, other weather phenomena may be listed when they occur.

WEATHER PHENOMENA CODES

Precipitation

RA — Rain	GR — Hail (> 1/4")
DZ — Drizzle	GS — Small Hail/Snow Pellets
SN — Snow	SG — Snow Grains
IC — Ice Crystals	PL — Ice Pellets

Obstructions to Visibility

FG — Fog	PY — Spray
BR — Mist	SA — Sand
FU — Smoke	DU — Dust
HZ — Haze	VA — Volcanic Ash

Other Weather Phenomena

SQ — Squall	SS — Sandstorm
DS — Duststorm	PO — Dust/Sand Whirls
FC — Funnel Cloud/Tornado/Waterspout	

SKY CONDITION

The sky condition groups describe the amount of clouds, if any, their heights and, in some cases, their type. In addition, a vertical visibility may be reported if the height of the clouds cannot be determined due to an obscuration.

AMOUNT

...+TSRA **SCT**008 **OVC**12CB 20/18...

The amount of clouds covering the sky is reported in eighths, or octas, of sky cover. Each layer of clouds is described using a code which corresponds to the octas of sky coverage. If the sky is clear, it is designated by SKC in a manual report and CLR in an automated report. FEW is used when cloud coverage is 1/8 to 2/8 of the sky. However, any amount less than 1/8 can also be reported as FEW. Scattered clouds, which cover 3/8 to 4/8 of the sky, are shown by SCT. Broken clouds, covering 5/8 to 7/8 of the sky, are designated by BKN, while an overcast sky is reported as OVC. In the example, there was a layer of scattered clouds (SCT) and an overcast layer (OVC).

The sky cover condition for a cloud layer represents total sky coverage, which includes any lower layers of clouds. In other words, when considering a layer of clouds, the observer must add the amount of sky covered by that layer to the amount of sky covered by all lower layers to determine the reported sky coverage for the layer being considered. [Figure 7-6]

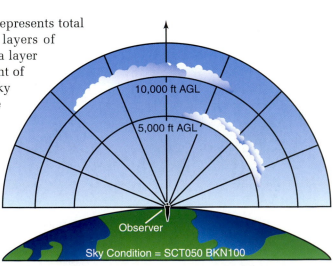

Figure 7-6. Note that the upper layer is reported as broken, even though that layer by itself covers less than 5/8 of the horizon. If the total coverage did not exceed 4/8, the upper layer would be reported as scattered.

HEIGHT, TYPE, AND VERTICAL VISIBILITY
...+TSRA SCT**008** OVC**12CB** 20/18...

The height of clouds or the vertical visibility into obscuring phenomena is reported with three digits in hundreds of feet above ground level (AGL). To determine the cloud height, add two zeros to the number given in the report. When more than one layer is present, the layers are reported in ascending order. Automated stations can only report a maximum of three layers at 12,000 feet AGL and below. Human observers can report up to six layers of clouds at any altitude. In the example, the scattered layer was at 800 feet AGL and the overcast layer was at 1,200 feet AGL.

In a manual report, a cloud type may be included if towering cumulus clouds (TCU) or cumulonimbus clouds (CB) are present. The code follows the height of their reported base. In the example, the base of the reported cumulonimbus clouds was at 1,200 feet AGL.

When more than half of the sky is covered by clouds, a ceiling exists. By definition, a **ceiling** is the AGL height of the lowest layer of clouds that is reported as broken or overcast, or the vertical visibility into an obscuration, such as fog or haze. Human observers may rely simply on their experience and knowledge of cloud formations to determine ceiling heights, or they may combine their experience with the help of reports from pilots, balloons, or other instruments. You can use the ceiling, combined with the visibility, to determine if VFR flight conditions exist. For example, if you are planning a VFR departure from a controlled airport (without a special VFR clearance), you must ensure that conditions of at least 1,000 feet and 3 statute miles visibility exist.

A ceiling is the lowest broken or overcast layer, or vertical visibility into an obstruction.

In controlled airspace, VFR conditions exist with a visibility of at least 3 statute miles and a ceiling of 1,000 feet or more.

Cloud Packing

Observations and reports of cloud layers may not always be accurate, particularly when differentiating between scattered and broken layers. Cumulus clouds, for example, may appear to be more closely packed together near the horizon than directly overhead. This illusion occurs because the observer cannot see the gaps between the clouds. This causes

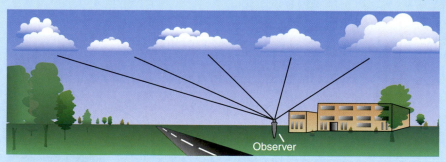

the cloud layer to seem more continuous than is really the case. Since observers do not take cloud packing into account, a pilot looking down through the same cloud layer may see it as scattered, while the observer reported it as broken.

Unlike clouds, an obscuration does not have a definite base. An obscuration can be caused by phenomena such as fog, haze, or smoke which extend from the surface to an indeterminable height. In these instances, a total obscuration is shown with a VV followed by three digits indicating the vertical visibility in hundreds of feet. For example, VV006 describes an indefinite ceiling at 600 feet AGL. Obscurations which do not cover the entire sky may be reported in the remarks section of the METAR.

Cloud heights or the vertical visibility into an obscuration are reported with three digits in hundreds of feet.

TEMPERATURE AND DEWPOINT

...SCT008 OVC12CB **20/18** A2995...

The observed air temperature and dewpoint (in degrees Celsius) are listed immediately following the sky condition. In the example, the temperature and dewpoint were reported as 20°C and 18°C, respectively. Temperatures below 0° Celsius are prefixed with an M to indicate minus. For instance 10°C below zero would be shown as M10. Temperature and dewpoint readings to the nearest 1/10°C may be included in the remarks section of the METAR.

ALTIMETER

...20/18 **A2995** RMK TSB24RAB24 SLP134

The altimeter setting is reported in inches of mercury in a four-digit group prefaced by an A. In the example, the altimeter setting was reported as 29.95 in. Hg.

REMARKS

...A2995 **RMK TSB24RAB24 SLP134**

Certain remarks are included to report weather considered significant to aircraft operations. The types of information that may be included are wind data, variable visibility, beginning and ending times of a particular weather phenomena, pressure information, and precise temperature/dewpoint readings. The start

The beginning of the remarks section is indicated by the code RMK. The remarks section reports weather considered significant to aircraft operations. See figure 7-7 for examples of coded remarks.

of the remarks section is identified by the code, RMK. The beginning of an event is shown by a B, followed by the time in minutes after the hour. If the event ended before the observation, the ending time in minutes past the hour is noted by an E. In the example, a thunderstorm began at 24 minutes past the hour (TSB24). Rain associated with the thunderstorm also began at 24 minutes past the hour (RAB24). Additionally, the sea level pressure (SLP) was 1013.4 millibars, or hectoPascals (hPa). A hectopascal is the metric equivalent of a millibar (1 mb = 1 hPa). Examples of other coded remarks are shown in figure 7-7.

CODED DATA	EXPLANATIONS	
A02	Automated station with precipitation discriminator	
PK WND 20032/25	Peak wind from 200° at 32 knots, 25 minutes past the hour	
VIS 3/4V1 1/2	Prevailing visibility variable 3/4 to 1 and 1/2 miles	
FRQ LTG NE	Frequent lightning to the northeast	
FZDZB45	Freezing drizzle began at 45 minutes past the hour	*Since the first digit after the T is a 0, it indicates that the temperature is positive; the dewpoint in this example is negative since the fifth digit is a 1.
RAE42SNB42	Rain ended and snow began at 42 minutes past the hour	
PRESFR	Pressure falling rapidly	
SLP045	Sea level pressure in millibars (hPa), 1004.5 mb (hPa)	
T00081016	Temperature/dewpoint in tenths °C, .8 °C/–1.6 °C*	

Figure 7-7. Examples of coded remarks are shown in the left column, with the corresponding explanations on the right.

RADAR WEATHER REPORTS

General areas of precipitation, especially thunderstorms, are observed by radar on a routine basis. Most radar stations issue routine **radar weather reports (SDs)** thirty-five minutes past each hour, with intervening special reports as required.

A radar weather report not only defines the areas of precipitation, but also provides information on the type, intensity, and intensity trend. In addition, these reports normally include movement (direction and speed) of the precipitation areas, as well as maximum height. If the base is considered significant, it may also be reported. All heights in an SD are reported in hundreds of feet MSL. [Figure 7-8]

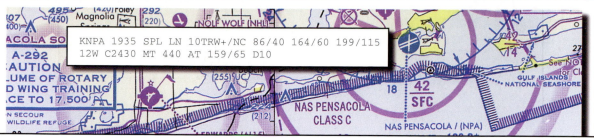

```
KNPA 1935 SPL LN 10TRW+/NC 86/40 164/60 199/115
12W C2430 MT 440 AT 159/65 D10
```

Translation:
Naval Air Station, Pensacola, Florida (KNPA) Special (SPL) Radar Weather Report at 1935Z (1935)...a line of echoes (LN), 10/10 coverage (10), thunderstorm (T), intense rain showers (RW+), no change in intensity (NC)...the center of the line extends from 86°at 40 n.m. (86/40) to 164° at 60 n.m. (164/60) to 199° at 115 n.m. (199/115)...the line is 12 n.m. wide (12W)...the thunderstorm cells are moving from 240° at 30 kts (C2430)...the maximum top (MT) is 44,000 feet MSL (440) at 159° at 65 n.m. (159/65) from KNPA...the diameter of the thunderstorm is 10 n.m. (D10). **Note:** To determine the thunderstorm location using a map, plot the center points on a map and connect the points with a straight line. Since the storm is reported to be 12 miles wide, it extends 6 n.m. either side of your plotted line.

Figure 7-8. Radar weather reports are useful in determining areas of severe weather. When the clouds extend to high levels, thunderstorms and the associated hazards are likely.

PILOT WEATHER REPORTS

Pilot weather reports (PIREPs) often confirm such information as the height of bases and tops of cloud layers, in-flight visibility, icing conditions, wind shear, and turbulence. When significant conditions are reported or forecast, ATC facilities are required to solicit PIREPs. However, anytime you encounter unexpected weather conditions, you are encouraged to make a pilot report. If you make a PIREP, the ATC facility or the FSS can add your report to the distribution system, and it can be used to brief other pilots or to provide in-flight advisories. [Figure 7-9]

 PIREPs use a standard format, as shown in figure 7-9. Note that altitudes are given in hundreds of feet above mean sea level (MSL).

Figure 7-9. PIREPs are made up of several elements, as indicated by the form shown on the right side of this figure. The left portion provides a sample PIREP and its plain-language translation. Notice that MSL altitudes are used. Although PIREPs should be complete and concise, you should not be overly concerned with strict format or terminology. The important thing is to forward the report so other pilots can benefit from your observation. Further information relating to the coding and interpretation of PIREPs is contained in the *Aeronautical Information Manual*.

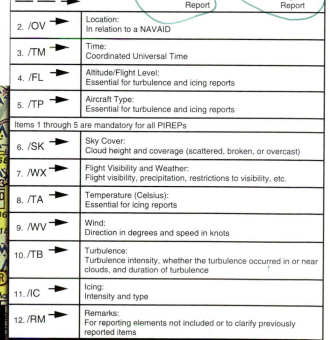

```
UA/OV OKC 063015/TM 1522/FL 080/TP C172/TA
-04/WV 245040/TB LGT 055-075/RM IN CLR
```

PIREP FORM	
Pilot Weather Report	= Space Symbol
3-Letter SA Identifier	1. UA → Routine Report UUA → Urgent Report
→	
2. /OV →	Location: In relation to a NAVAID
3. /TM →	Time: Coordinated Universal Time
4. /FL →	Altitude/Flight Level: Essential for turbulence and icing reports
5. /TP →	Aircraft Type: Essential for turbulence and icing reports
Items 1 through 5 are mandatory for all PIREPs	
6. /SK →	Sky Cover: Cloud height and coverage (scattered, broken, or overcast)
7. /WX →	Flight Visibility and Weather: Flight visibility, precipitation, restrictions to visibility, etc.
8. /TA →	Temperature (Celsius): Essential for icing reports
9. /WV →	Wind: Direction in degrees and speed in knots
10. /TB →	Turbulence: Turbulence intensity, whether the turbulence occurred in or near clouds, and duration of turbulence
11. /IC →	Icing: Intensity and type
12. /RM →	Remarks: For reporting elements not included or to clarify previously reported items

Translation:
Routine pilot report (UA)...15 n.m. on the 063° radial from the Will Rogers VOR (OV OKC 063015)...at 1522Z (TM 1522)...at 8,000 feet MSL (FL 080)...type of aircraft is a Cessna 172 (TP C172) ...outside air temperature is -4 °C (TA -04)...wind is from 245° at 40 kts (WV 245040)...light turbulence between 5,500 feet MSL and 7,500 feet MSL (TB LGT 055-075)...the aircraft is in clear skies (RM IN CLR).

PRINTED WEATHER FORECASTS

Many of the reports of observed weather conditions are used to develop forecasts of future conditions. Every day, Weather Forecast Offices (WFOs) prepare over 2,000 forecasts for specific airports, over 900 route forecasts, and a variety of other forecasts for flight planning purposes. The printed forecasts with which you need to become familiar include the terminal aerodrome forecast, aviation area forecast, and the winds and temperatures aloft forecast.

TERMINAL AERODROME FORECAST

One of your best sources for an estimate of what the weather will be in the future at a specific airport is the **terminal aerodrome forecast (TAF)**. TAFs normally are valid for a 24-hour period and are scheduled four times a day at 0000Z, 0600Z, 1200Z, and 1800Z. Each TAF contains these elements: type, location, issuance date and time, valid date and time, and the forecast. [Figure 7-10]

TAFs usually are valid for a 24-hour period and are scheduled four times a day. TAF codes are similar to those used in METARs. You should be familiar with the abbreviations and codes contained in the following discussion.

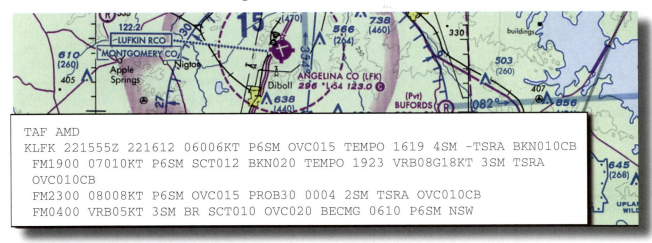

```
TAF AMD
KLFK 221555Z 221612 06006KT P6SM OVC015 TEMPO 1619 4SM -TSRA BKN010CB
 FM1900 07010KT P6SM SCT012 BKN020 TEMPO 1923 VRB08G18KT 3SM TSRA
OVC010CB
 FM2300 08008KT P6SM OVC015 PROB30 0004 2SM TSRA OVC010CB
 FM0400 VRB05KT 3SM BR SCT010 OVC020 BECMG 0610 P6SM NSW
```

Figure 7-10. With a few exceptions, the codes used in the TAF are similar to those used in the METAR.

TYPE OF FORECAST

TAF AMD

KLFK...

The TAF normally is a routine forecast. However, an amended TAF (TAF AMD) may be issued when the current TAF no longer represents the expected weather. TAF or TAF AMD appears in a header line prior to the text of the forecast. The abbreviations COR and RTD indicate a corrected and delayed TAF, respectively. The example depicts an amended TAF.

STATION IDENTIFIER AND ISSUANCE DATE/TIME

TAF AMD

KLFK 221555Z 221612...

The four-letter ICAO location identifier code is the same as that used for the METAR/SPECI. The first two numbers of the date/time group represent the day of the month, and the next four digits are the Zulu time that the forecast was issued. The example TAF is a forecast for Angelina County Airport (KLFK) which was issued on the 22nd day of the month at 1555Z.

VALID PERIOD
...221555Z **221612** 06006KT...

Normally, the forecast is valid for 24 hours. The first two digits represent the valid date. Next is the beginning hour of the valid time in Zulu, and the last two digits are the ending hour. The forecast for Angelina County Airport is valid from 1600Z on the 22nd of the month to 1200Z the next day. Since the TAF in the example was amended, the valid period is less than 24 hours. At an airport that is open part time, amendments are not issued after closing time. If an airport closes at 0500Z, for instance, the TAF may include a statement such as, NIL AMD NOT SKED AFT 0500Z. When part-time airports are closed, the word NIL appears in place of the forecast for those locations.

FORECAST
...221612 **06006KT P6SM OVC015** TEMPO 1619 4SM −TSRA BKN010CB...

The body of the TAF contains codes for forecast wind, visibility, weather, and sky condition in much the same format as the METAR/SPECI. Weather, including obstructions to visibility, is added to the forecast only when it is significant to aviation. In a TAF, expected visibilities greater than 6 statute miles are forecast using a P (plus). In the example, the winds are predicted to be from 060° at 6 knots, visibility is expected to be greater than 6 statute miles, and an overcast cloud layer is forecast at 1,500 feet AGL.

In a TAF, predicted low-level wind shear not associated with convective activity may be included using the code, WS, followed by a three digit height (up to and including 2,000 feet AGL), a slant (/), and the winds at the height indicated. For instance, WS015/30045KT indicates that low-level wind shear is expected at 1,500 feet with winds from 300° at 45 knots.

FORECAST CHANGE GROUPS
...FM1900 07010KT P6SM SCT012 BKN020...
...FM2300 08008KT P6SM OVC015...
...FM0400 VRB05KT 3SM BR SCT010 OVC020 BECMG 0610 P6SM NSW

When a significant permanent change to the weather conditions is expected during the valid time, a change group is used. If a rapid change, usually within one hour, is expected, the code for from (FM) is used with the time of change. The conditions listed following the FM will continue until the next change group or the end of the valid time of the TAF. In the example, the first forecast change group indicates that from 1900Z, the wind will be from 070° at 10 knots, the visibility will be greater than 6 statute miles, and cloud layers are expected to be scattered at 1,200 feet and broken at 2,000 feet.

A more gradual change in the weather, taking about two hours, is coded as BECMG, followed by beginning and ending times of the change period. The gradual change is expected to occur at an unspecified time within this time period. All items, except for the changing conditions shown in the BECMG group, are carried over from the previous time group. In the last line of the example, a gradual change in conditions is expected to occur between 0600Z and 1000Z. Sometime during this period, visibility is predicted to improve to greater than 6 miles with no significant weather (NSW). The NSW code is used only after a time period in which significant weather was forecast. NSW only appears in BECMG or TEMPO groups.

TEMPORARY CONDITIONS

...KLFK 221555Z 221612 06006KT P6SM OVC015 **TEMPO 1619 4SM -TSRA BKN010CB**
  FM1900 07010KT P6SM SCT012 BKN020 **TEMPO 1923 VRB08G18KT 3SM TSRA**
  OVC010CB...

Wind, visibility, weather, or sky conditions that are expected to last less than an hour at a time are described in a temporary (TEMPO) group, followed by beginning and ending times. The first TEMPO group in the example predicts that, between 1600Z and 1900Z, visibility is expected to be reduced to 4 statute miles in light rain associated with a thunderstorm. A broken layer of cumulonimbus clouds with bases at 1,000 feet is also predicted to occur. It's important to remember that these conditions only modify the previous forecast, and are expected to last for periods of less than one hour at a time.

 Cumulonimbus (CB) is the only type of cloud included in the TAF.

PROBABILITY FORECAST

...FM2300 08008KT P6SM OVC015 **PROB30 0004 2SM TSRA OVC010CB**
  FM0400 VRB05KT 3SM BR SCT010 OVC020...

TAFs may include the probability of thunderstorms or precipitation events with the associated wind, visibility, and sky conditions. A PROB group is used when the probability of occurrence is between 30 and 49 percent. The percentage is followed by the beginning and ending time of the period during which the thunderstorm or precipitation is expected. In the example, there is a 30 percent chance of a thunderstorm with moderate rain and 2 statute miles visibility between 0000Z and 0400Z. In addition, a 30 percent probability of an overcast layer of cumulonimbus clouds with bases at 1,000 feet AGL also is expected to occur during the four-hour time period.

AVIATION AREA FORECAST

An **aviation area forecast (FA)** covers general weather conditions over a wide region and is a good source of information for enroute weather. It also helps you determine the conditions at airports which do not have terminal aerodrome forecasts. FAs are issued three times a day in the 48 contiguous states, and amended as required. NWS offices issue FAs for Hawaii and Alaska; however, the Alaska FA uses a different format. An additional specialized FA may be issued for the Gulf of Mexico by the National Hurricane Center in Miami, Florida. [Figure 7-11]

 You should refer to the area forecast to determine forecast weather conditions between reporting stations and over several states. The area forecast is helpful in determining weather at airports which do not have TAFs.

COMMUNICATIONS AND PRODUCT HEADERS

The FA consists of several sections: a communications and product header section, a precautionary statement section, and two weather sections: a synopsis section, and a VFR clouds and weather section. Each area forecast covers an 18-hour period. [Figure 7-12]

In the heading SLCC FA 141045, the SLC identifies the Salt Lake City forecast area, C indicates the product contains a clouds and weather forecast, FA means area forecast, and 141045 tells you this forecast was issued on the 14th day of the month at 1045Z. Since these forecasts are rounded to the nearest full hour, the valid time for the report begins at 1100Z. The synopsis is valid until 18 hours later, which is shown as the 15th at 0500Z. The clouds and weather section forecast is valid for a 12-hour period, until 2300Z on the 14th. The outlook portion is valid for 6 hours following the forecast, from 2300Z on the 14th to 0500 on the 15th. The last line of the header lists the states that are included in the Salt Lake City forecast area.

Amendments to FAs are issued whenever the weather significantly improves or deteriorates based on the judgment of the forecaster. An amended FA is identified by the contraction AMD in the header along with the time of the amended forecast. When an FA is corrected, the contraction COR appears in the heading, also with the time of the correction.

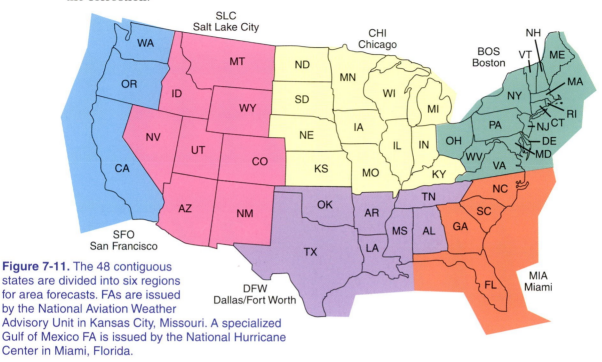

Figure 7-11. The 48 contiguous states are divided into six regions for area forecasts. FAs are issued by the National Aviation Weather Advisory Unit in Kansas City, Missouri. A specialized Gulf of Mexico FA is issued by the National Hurricane Center in Miami, Florida.

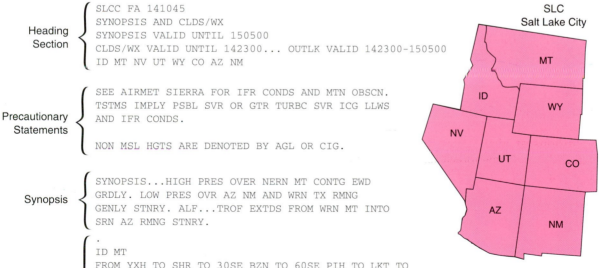

Heading Section
```
SLCC FA 141045
SYNOPSIS AND CLDS/WX
SYNOPSIS VALID UNTIL 150500
CLDS/WX VALID UNTIL 142300... OUTLK VALID 142300-150500
ID MT NV UT WY CO AZ NM
```

Precautionary Statements
```
SEE AIRMET SIERRA FOR IFR CONDS AND MTN OBSCN.
TSTMS IMPLY PSBL SVR OR GTR TURBC SVR ICG LLWS
AND IFR CONDS.

NON MSL HGTS ARE DENOTED BY AGL OR CIG.
```

Synopsis
```
SYNOPSIS...HIGH PRES OVER NERN MT CONTG EWD
GRDLY. LOW PRES OVR AZ NM AND WRN TX RMNG
GENLY STNRY. ALF...TROF EXTDS FROM WRN MT INTO
SRN AZ RMNG STNRY.
```

VFR Clouds and Weather
```
.
ID MT
FROM YXH TO SHR TO 30SE BZN TO 60SE PIH TO LKT TO
YXC TO YXH.
70-90 SCT-BKN 120-150. WDLY SCT RW-. TOPS SHWRS 180.
OTLK...VFR
RMNDR AREA...100-120. ISOLD RW- MNLY ERN PTNS AREA.
OTLK...VFR
.
UT NV NM AZ
80 SCT-BKN 150-200. WDLY SCT RW-/TRW-. CB TOPS 450.
OTLK...VFR
.
WY CO
FROM BZN TO GCC TO LBL TO DVC TO RKS TO BZN.
70-90 BKN-OVC 200. OCNL VSBY 3R-F. AFT 20Z WDLY SCT
TRW-. CB TOPS 450. OTLK...MVFR CIG RW.
```

Figure 7-12. The area forecast has several sections, beginning with a communications and product header, which identifies the area and provides the valid times. Area forecasts contain standard abbreviations and word contractions. The information in this sample forecast is interpreted in the accompanying paragraphs.

PRECAUTIONARY STATEMENTS

Following the headers are three precautionary statements which are part of all FAs. The first statement alerts you to check the latest AIRMET Sierra, which describes areas of mountain obscuration which may be forecast for the area. The next statement is a reminder that thunderstorms imply possible severe or greater turbulence, severe icing, low-level wind shear, and instrument conditions. Therefore, when thunderstorms are forecast, these hazards are not included in the body of the FA. The third statement points out that heights which are not MSL are noted by the letters AGL (above ground level) or CIG (ceiling). All heights are expressed in hundreds of feet.

SYNOPSIS

The synopsis is a brief description of the location and movement of fronts, pressure systems, and circulation patterns in the FA area over an 18-hour period. When appropriate, forecasters may use terms describing ceilings and visibilities, strong winds, or other phenomena. In the example, high pressure over northeastern Montana will continue moving gradually eastward. A low pressure system over Arizona, New Mexico, and western Texas will remain generally stationary. Aloft (ALF), a trough of low pressure extending from western Montana into southern Arizona is expected to remain stationary.

VFR CLOUDS AND WEATHER

The VFR clouds and weather portion is usually several paragraphs long, and broken down by states or geographical regions. It describes clouds and weather which could affect VFR operations over an area of 3,000 square miles or more. The forecast is valid for 12 hours, and is followed by a 6-hour categorical outlook (18 hours in Alaska).

When the surface visibility is expected to be 6 statute miles or less, the visibility and obstructions to vision are included in the forecast. When precipitation, thunderstorms, and sustained winds of 20 knots or greater are forecast, they will be included in this section. The term OCNL (occasional) is used when there is a 50% or greater probability of cloud or visibility conditions which could affect VFR flight. The percentage of an area covered by showers or thunderstorms is indicated by the terms ISOLD (isolated, meaning single cells), WDLY SCT (widely scattered, less than 25% of the area), SCT or AREAS (25% to 54% of the area), and NMRS or WDSPRD (numerous or widespread, 55% or more of the area). In addition, the term ISOLD is sometimes used to describe areas of ceilings or visibilities which are less than 3,000 square miles.

The outlook follows the main body of the forecast, and gives a general description of the expected weather, using the terms VFR, IFR, or MVFR (marginal VFR). Ceilings less than 1,000 feet and/or visibility less than 3 miles is considered IFR. Marginal VFR areas are those with ceilings from 1,000 to 3,000 feet and/or visibility between 3 and 5 statute miles. Abbreviations are used to describe the causes of IFR or MVFR weather.

In the example shown in figure 7-12, an area of coverage for the specific forecast is identified using three-letter designators. This area extends from Bozeman, Montana, to Gillette, Wyoming, to Liberal, Kansas, to Dove Creek, Wyoming, to Rock Springs, Wyoming, and back to Bozeman. A broken to overcast cloud layer begins between 7,000 and 9,000 feet MSL, with tops extending to 20,000 feet. Since visibility and wind information is omitted, the visibility is expected to be greater than 6 statute miles, and the wind less than 20 knots. However, the visibility (VSBY) is forecast to be occasionally 3 miles in light rain and fog (3R-F). After 2000Z, widely scattered thunderstorms with light rain showers are expected, with cumulonimbus (CB) cloud tops to 45,000 feet. The 6-hour categorical outlook covers the period from 2300Z on the 14th to 0500 on the 15th. The forecast is for marginal VFR weather due to ceilings (CIG) and rain showers (RW).

WINDS AND TEMPERATURES ALOFT FORECAST

A **winds and temperatures aloft forecast (FD)** provides an estimate of wind direction in relation to true north, wind speed in knots, and the temperature in degrees Celsius for selected altitudes. Depending on the station elevation, winds and temperatures are usually forecast for nine levels between 3,000 and 39,000 feet. [Figure 7-13]

In a winds and temperatures aloft forecast, winds are given in true direction and speed is shown in knots.

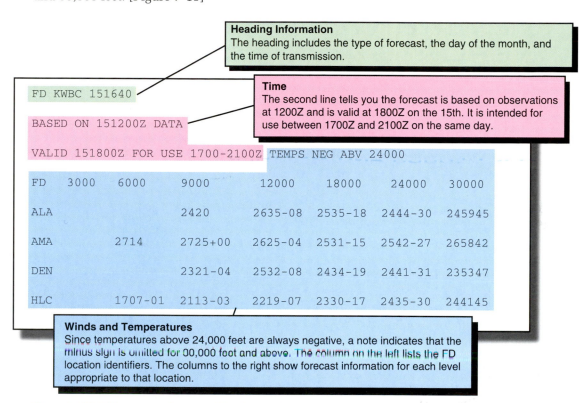

Heading Information
The heading includes the type of forecast, the day of the month, and the time of transmission.

Time
The second line tells you the forecast is based on observations at 1200Z and is valid at 1800Z on the 15th. It is intended for use between 1700Z and 2100Z on the same day.

```
FD KWBC 151640

BASED ON 151200Z DATA

VALID 151800Z FOR USE 1700-2100Z TEMPS NEG ABV 24000

FD    3000    6000    9000    12000    18000    24000    30000

ALA                   2420    2635-08  2535-18  2444-30  245945

AMA           2714    2725+00  2625-04  2531-15  2542-27  265842

DEN                   2321-04  2532-08  2434-19  2441-31  235347

HLC           1707-01 2113-03  2219-07  2330-17  2435-30  244145
```

Winds and Temperatures
Since temperatures above 24,000 feet are always negative, a note indicates that the minus sign is omitted for 00,000 foot and above. The column on the left lists the FD location identifiers. The columns to the right show forecast information for each level appropriate to that location.

Figure 7-13. This excerpt from an FD shows winds only to the 30,000-foot level. As stated in the report, all temperatures above 24,000 feet are negative.

The FD does not include levels within 1,500 feet of the station elevation, and temperatures are not forecast for the 3,000-foot level or for a level within 2,500 feet of the station elevation. At Denver (DEN), for example, the forecast for the lower two levels is omitted, since the station elevation at Denver is over 5,000 feet.

The presentation of wind information in the body of the FD is similar to other reports and forecasts. The first two numbers indicate the true direction from which the wind is blowing. For example, 2635-08 indicates the wind is from 260° at 35 knots and the temperature is −8°C. Quite often you must interpolate between the two levels. For instance, if you plan to fly near Hill City (HLC) at 7,500 feet, you must interpolate. Referring to figure 7-13, since your planned flight altitude is midway between 6,000 and 9,000 feet, a good estimate of the wind at 7,500 feet is 190° at 10 knots with a temperature of −2°C.

Wind direction and speed information on an FD is shown by a four-digit code. The first two digits are the wind direction in tens of degrees. Wind speed is shown by the second two digits. The last two digits indicate the temperature in degrees Celsius. All temperatures above 24,000 feet are negative.

Wind speeds between 100 and 199 knots are encoded so direction and speed can be represented by four digits. This is done by adding 50 to the two-digit wind direction and subtracting 100 from the velocity. For example, a wind of 270° at 101 knots is encoded as 7701 (27 + 50 = 77 for wind direction, and 101 − 100 = 01 for wind speed). A code of 9900 indicates light and variable winds (less than five knots).

 To decode a forecast of winds between 100 and 199 knots, subtract 50 from the two-digit direction code and multiply by 10. Then, add 100 to the two-digit wind speed code. If the code 9900 is used, it means the winds are light and variable.

SEVERE WEATHER REPORTS AND FORECASTS

While much weather gathering activity is concerned with routine reports and forecasts, considerable effort is also devoted to monitoring and reporting severe weather conditions. The National Hurricane Center in Miami, Florida issues hurricane advisories, while the National Severe Storms Forecast Center in Kansas City, Missouri issues special reports and forecasts for other severe weather conditions. These include convective outlooks, severe weather watch bulletins, AIRMETs, SIGMETs, and convective SIGMETs.

 ARE YOU UNDER THE WEATHER?

Do you get headaches or experience sleeplessness when a thunderstorm passes overhead? If so, you might be surprised to learn that an overabundance of positive ions could be the cause. Although scientists still do not fully understand why concentrations of positive and negative ions build inside thunderstorms, the electrical charge is known to be the cause of lightning, and is suspected to have a physical effect on some people.

Inhaling large amounts of air containing positive ions seems to stimulate the production of a powerful hormone known as serotonin. As the level of serotonin grows, it has an increasing effect on the area of the brain which controls mood, nerves, and sleep. In some cases, the surplus of positive ions can promote adrenaline production. This initially results in a burst of energy, but quickly leads to a feeling of exhaustion, putting you "under the weather."

HURRICANE ADVISORY

When a hurricane is located at least 300 nautical miles offshore, but threatens a coast line, a **hurricane advisory (WH)** is issued. The WH gives the location of the storm center, its expected movement, and the maximum winds in and near the storm center. It does not contain specific ceilings, visibilities, and weather hazards. As needed, those details will be reported in area forecasts, terminal aerodrome forecasts, and in-flight advisories. [Figure 7-14]

Courtesy of NASA

Figure 7-14. Hurricane Elena, shown in this space shuttle orbiter photograph, eventually reached landfall near Gulfport, Mississippi in 1985. Its associated 110 mile per hour winds likely would have been reported in a WH when it was still over 300 n.m. offshore.

CONVECTIVE OUTLOOK

The **convective outlook (AC)** forecasts general thunderstorm activity for the next 24-hour period. ACs describe areas in which there is a risk of severe thunderstorms. Severe thunderstorm criteria include winds equal to or greater than 50 knots at the surface or hail equal to or greater than 3/4 inch in diameter, or tornadoes. Convective outlooks are useful for planning flights within the forecast period.

SEVERE WEATHER WATCH BULLETIN

A **severe weather watch bulletin (WW)** defines areas of possible severe thunderstorms or tornadoes. WWs are issued on an unscheduled basis and are updated as required. Since severe weather forecasts and reports may affect the general public, as well as pilots, they are widely disseminated through all available media. When it becomes evident that no severe weather will develop or that storms have subsided, cancellation bulletins will be issued.

To alert forecasters and weather briefers that a severe weather watch bulletin is being issued, a preliminary message, called an **alert severe weather watch (AWW)** is sent. Each AWW is numbered sequentially beginning with the first of January each year. [Figure 7-15]

Figure 7-15. AWW in the header identifies this report as a severe weather forecast alert. This message warns of possible tornado activity in Nebraska and defines the watch area. Hail and high winds also are possible. A detailed severe weather watch bulletin (WW) immediately follows the alert message.

AIRMET

AIRMET is an acronym for airman's meteorological information. **AIRMETs (WAs)** are issued every 6 hours with amendments issued, as necessary, for weather phenomena which are of operational interest to all aircraft. These weather conditions are potentially

 AIRMETs warn of weather conditions which are particularly hazardous to small, single-engine aircraft.

hazardous to light aircraft or aircraft having limited capability because of lack of equipment, instrumentation, or pilot qualifications. AIRMETs are issued for moderate icing, moderate turbulence, sustained winds of 30 knots or more at the surface, ceilings less than 1,000 feet and/or visibility less than 3 miles affecting over 50 percent of an area at any one time, and extensive mountain obscurement. AIRMETs use the identifier Sierra for IFR conditions and mountain obscuration, Tango for turbulence, strong surface winds, and low-level wind shear, and Zulu for icing and freezing levels. After the first issuance of the day, AIRMETs are numbered sequentially for easier identification.

What are the Odds?

On any given day, the weather can be completely different in towns located only 20 miles apart. On average, however, the amount of rain, thunderstorms, hail, and other weather phenomena will probably be relatively uniform in that region. What are the odds that your area of the country will experience a thunderstorm today? Climatic data will not tell you for sure, but it can give you an idea of how much severe weather you can expect over the next year.

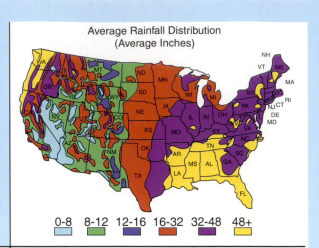

Average Rainfall Distribution
(Average Inches)

0-8 8-12 12-16 16-32 32-48 48+

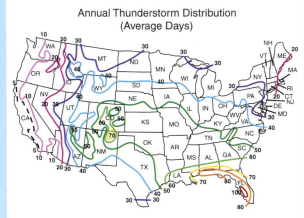

Annual Thunderstorm Distribution
(Average Days)

Annual Hail Distribution
(Average Days)

SIGMET

SIGMETs (WSs) are issued for hazardous weather (other than convective activity) which is considered significant to all aircraft. SIGMET (significant meteorological information) criteria include severe icing, severe or extreme turbulence, duststorms, sandstorms, volcanic eruptions and volcanic ash lowering visibility to less than three miles. [Figure 7-16]

 SIGMETs warn of weather hazards, such as severe icing, which concern all aircraft.

Courtesy of NASA

Figure 7-16. SIGMETs are issued for weather phenomena such as duststorms. This duststorm in the northern Sahara desert was photographed from the space shuttle orbiter.

SIGMETs are issued whether or not the conditions were included in the area forecast. Excluding those designators reserved for scheduled AIRMETs, SIGMETs use consecutive alphanumeric designators November through Yankee. [Figure 7-17]

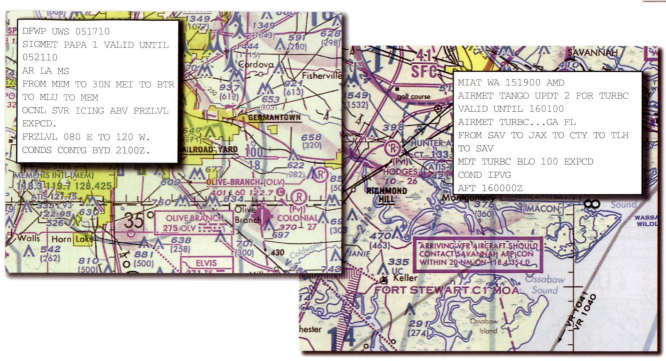

```
DFWP UWS 051710
SIGMET PAPA 1 VALID UNTIL
052110
AR LA MS
FROM MEM TO 30N MEI TO BTR
TO MLU TO MEM
OCNL SVR ICING ABV FRZLVL
EXPCD.
FRZLVL 080 E TO 120 W.
CONDS CONTG BYD 2100Z.
```

```
MIAT WA 151900 AMD
AIRMET TANGO UPDT 2 FOR TURBC
VALID UNTIL 160100
AIRMET TURBC...GA FL
FROM SAV TO JAX TO CTY TO TLH
TO SAV
MDT TURBC BLO 100 EXPCD
COND IPVG
AFT 160000Z
```

Figure 7-17. The first issuance of a SIGMET, as shown on the left, is labeled UWS (Urgent Weather SIGMET). PAPA 1 means it is the first issuance for a SIGMET phenomenon; PAPA 2 would be the second issuance for the same phenomenon. In the example on the right, AMD means this is an amended AIRMET of the phenomenon (moderate turbulence) identified as TANGO. The alphanumeric designator stays with the phenomenon even when it moves across the country.

CONVECTIVE SIGMET

Convective SIGMETs (WSTs) are issued for hazardous convective weather which is significant to the safety of all aircraft. Since they always imply severe or greater turbulence, severe icing, and low-level wind shear, these items are not specified in the advisory. WSTs include any of the following phenomena: tornadoes, lines of thunderstorms, thunderstorms over a wide area, embedded thunderstorms, hail greater than or equal to 3/4 inch in diameter, and/or wind gusts to 50 knots or greater. A WST consists of either an observation and a forecast or simply a forecast. [Figure 7-18]

Convective SIGMETs warn of weather hazards including tornadoes, embedded thunderstorms, and hail 3/4 inch or greater in diameter.

Figure 7-18. Convective SIGMETs are issued for clusters of thunderstorms. This photograph, taken from the space shuttle orbiter, displays a variety of weather elements including overshooting thunderstorm tops, squall lines, and areas of probable high-speed downdrafts or microbursts.

Courtesy of NASA

Convective SIGMETs are issued for the eastern (E), central (C), and western (W) United States. Individual convective SIGMETs are numbered sequentially for each area (01-99) each day. A convective SIGMET will usually be issued only for the area where the bulk of observations and forecast conditions are located. Bulletins are issued 55 minutes past each hour unless a special update bulletin is required. A SIGMET forecast is valid for 2 hours from the time of issuance or until it is superseded by the next hourly issuance. If the criteria for a convective SIGMET is not met at the issuance time, the message, CONVECTIVE SIGMET...NONE is sent. [Figure 7-19]

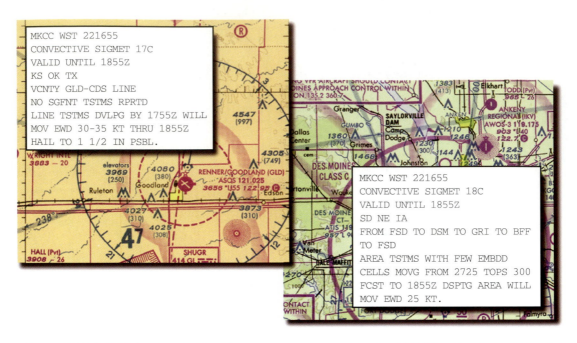

MKCC WST 221655
CONVECTIVE SIGMET 17C
VALID UNTIL 1855Z
KS OK TX
VCNTY GLD-CDS LINE
NO SGFNT TSTMS RPRTD
LINE TSTMS DVLPG BY 1755Z WILL
MOV EWD 30-35 KT THRU 1855Z
HAIL TO 1 1/2 IN PSBL.

MKCC WST 221655
CONVECTIVE SIGMET 18C
VALID UNTIL 1855Z
SD NE IA
FROM FSD TO DSM TO GRI TO BFF
TO FSD
AREA TSTMS WITH FEW EMBDD
CELLS MOVG FROM 2725 TOPS 300
FCST TO 1855Z DSPTG AREA WILL
MOV EWD 25 KT.

Figure 7-19. WST in the header identifies these reports as convective SIGMETs. The designators 17C and 18C indicate they are consecutive issuances for the central U.S. One forecasts a line of thunderstorms with possible hail, while the other forecasts embedded thunderstorms over a large area.

SUMMARY CHECKLIST

✓ An aviation routine weather report (METAR), is an observation of surface weather which typically contains 10 or more separate elements in a standard format.

✓ When a significant change in one or more elements occurs, a non-routine aviation weather report (SPECI) is issued.

✓ Prevailing visibility is the greatest distance an observer can see and identify objects through at least half of the horizon.

✓ Runway visual range (RVR) is based on what a pilot in a moving aircraft should see when looking down the runway. If included in a METAR, RVR will be reported following prevailing visibility.

✓ A ceiling is the height above ground level of the lowest layer of clouds aloft which is reported as broken or overcast, or the vertical visibility into an obscuration.

✓ Radar weather reports (SDs) define general areas of precipitation, particularly thunderstorms.

✓ Pilot weather reports (PIREPs) include information such as the height of bases and tops of cloud layers, in-flight visibility, icing conditions, wind shear, and turbulence.

✓ A prediction of what the weather will be in the future at a specific airport is contained in the associated terminal aerodrome forecast (TAF).

✓ An aviation area forecast (FA) can not only provide a good source of information for enroute weather, but it can also help you determine the conditions at airports which do not have terminal aerodrome forecasts.

✓ An estimate of wind direction in relation to true north, wind speed in knots, and the temperature in degrees Celsius for selected altitudes can be found in the winds and temperatures aloft forecast (FD).

✓ A convective outlook (AC) forecasts general thunderstorm activity for the next 24-hour period.

✓ Areas of possible severe thunderstorms or tornadoes are defined by a severe weather watch bulletin (WW).

✓ AIRMETs are issued every 6 hours with amendments issued, as necessary, for weather phenomena which are potentially hazardous to light aircraft. AIRMETs are issued for moderate icing, moderate turbulence, sustained winds of 30 knots or more at the surface, ceilings less than 1,000 feet and/or visibility less than 3 miles affecting over 50 percent of an area at any one time, and extensive mountain obscurement.

✓ SIGMETs are issued for hazardous weather such as severe icing, severe and extreme turbulence, duststorms, sandstorms, volcanic eruptions, and volcanic ash lowering visibility to less than three miles.

✓ Existing or forecast hazardous convective weather, which is significant to the safety of all aircraft, is contained in convective SIGMETs (WSTs).

KEY TERMS

Aviation Routine Weather Report (METAR)

Non-Routine (Special) Aviation Weather Report (SPECI)

Prevailing Visibility

Runway Visual Range (RVR)

Ceiling

Radar Weather Report (SD)

Pilot Weather Report (PIREP)

Terminal Aerodrome Forecast (TAF)

Aviation Area Forecast (FA)

Winds And Temperatures Aloft Forecast (FD)

Hurricane Advisory (WH)

Convective Outlook (AC)

Severe Weather Watch Bulletin (WW)

Alert Severe Weather Watch (AWW)

AIRMET (WA)

SIGMET (WS)

Convective SIGMET (WST)

QUESTIONS

1. What is the difference between prevailing visibility and runway visual range?

2. In a METAR, what is meant by a + sign immediately preceding a precipitation code?

   A. Light intensity
   B. Heavy intensity
   C. Moderate intensity

3. If a METAR reported a sky condition of BKN008, what altitude were the bases of the clouds at the time of the observation? How much of the sky was covered?

4. Decode the following METAR (KHOU = William P. Hobby Airport).

   METAR KHOU 221853Z 17009KT 2SM -TSRA SCT004 BKN009 OVC015 21/20
      A3004 RMK TSB12 SLP170 T02060196

5. True/False. Altitudes given in PIREPs are in feet MSL.

6. Normally, how long are TAFs valid?

   A. 12 hours
   B. 24 hours
   C. 48 hours

7. In a TAF, what does the code BECMG 0305 indicate?

8. Decode the following TAF (KPIT = Pittsburgh International Airport).

   TAF
   KPIT 091730Z 091818 22020KT 3SM -SHRA BKN020
      FM2030 30015G25KT 3SM SHRA OVC015 TEMPO 2022 1/2SM TSRA OVC008CB
      FM0100 27008KT 5SM -SHRA BKN020 OVC040 PROB40 0407 27008KT 1SM -RA
      FM1000 22010KT 5SM -SHRA OVC020 BECOMG 1315 20010KT P6SM NSW

9. If an aviation area forecast (FA) predicted marginal VFR conditions along your route of flight, what ceiling and visibility conditions should you expect?

10. The winds and temperatures at your flight altitude are forecast as 1825-02. You plan to fly a true heading of 360° and a true airspeed of 130 knots. What groundspeed can you expect? What will be the outside air temperature?

11. Select the weather phenomena which can initiate the issuance of an AIRMET.

    A. Light icing
    B. Extensive mountain obscurment
    C. Sustained winds of 25 knots or more at the surface

12. True/False. A line of thunderstorms will usually prompt the issuance of a SIGMET (WS).

SECTION C
GRAPHIC WEATHER PRODUCTS

You can develop a more complete picture of the weather which will affect your flights by combining the information contained in printed weather reports and forecasts with a graphic portrayal of the current and predicted weather. These graphic weather products use information gathered from ground observations, weather radar, satellites, and other sources to give you a pictorial view of large-scale weather patterns and trends.

GRAPHIC REPORTS

Reports of observed weather are graphically depicted in a number of products. These include the surface analysis chart, weather depiction chart, radar summary chart, and satellite weather pictures.

SURFACE ANALYSIS CHART

The **surface analysis chart**, also referred to as a surface weather analysis chart, shows weather conditions as of the valid time shown on the chart. [Figure 7-20] By reviewing this chart, you can get a picture of atmospheric pressure patterns at the earth's surface.

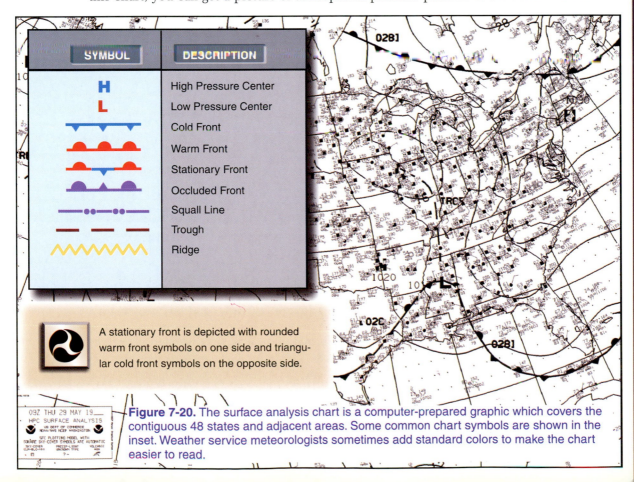

SYMBOL	DESCRIPTION
H	High Pressure Center
L	Low Pressure Center
	Cold Front
	Warm Front
	Stationary Front
	Occluded Front
	Squall Line
	Trough
	Ridge

A stationary front is depicted with rounded warm front symbols on one side and triangular cold front symbols on the opposite side.

09Z THU 29 MAY 19___
HPC SURFACE ANALYSIS
US DEPT OF COMMERCE
NOAA/NWS NCEP WASHINGTON

SFC PLOTTING MODEL WITH
SQUARE SKY-COVER SYMBOLS ARE AUTOMATIC

Figure 7-20. The surface analysis chart is a computer-prepared graphic which covers the contiguous 48 states and adjacent areas. Some common chart symbols are shown in the inset. Weather service meteorologists sometimes add standard colors to make the chart easier to read.

More importantly, you also can see the locations of high and low pressure systems and associated fronts. This chart is transmitted every three hours.

The surface analysis chart also provides surface weather observations for a large number of reporting points throughout the United States. Each of these points is illustrated by a **station model**. Round station symbols depict stations where observations are taken by human observers. Square station symbols indicate automated sites. Other models, which appear over water, display information gathered by ships, buoys, and offshore oil platforms. [Figure 7-21]

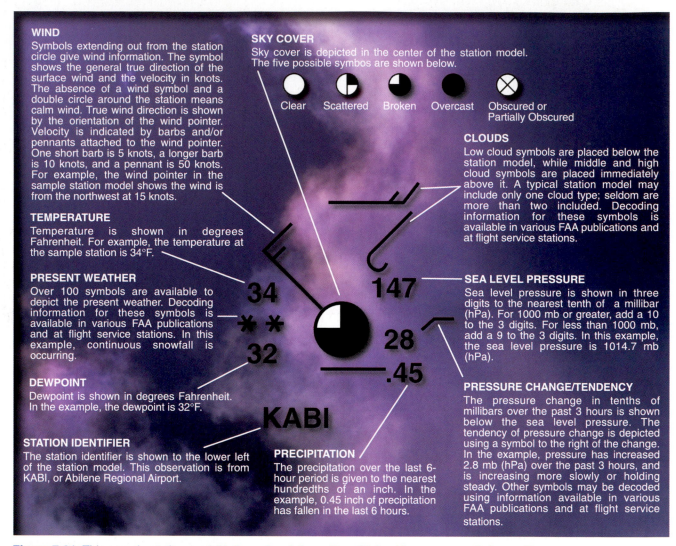

WIND

Symbols extending out from the station circle give wind information. The symbol shows the general true direction of the surface wind and the velocity in knots. The absence of a wind symbol and a double circle around the station means calm wind. True wind direction is shown by the orientation of the wind pointer. Velocity is indicated by barbs and/or pennants attached to the wind pointer. One short barb is 5 knots, a longer barb is 10 knots, and a pennant is 50 knots. For example, the wind pointer in the sample station model shows the wind is from the northwest at 15 knots.

TEMPERATURE

Temperature is shown in degrees Fahrenheit. For example, the temperature at the sample station is 34°F.

PRESENT WEATHER

Over 100 symbols are available to depict the present weather. Decoding information for these symbols is available in various FAA publications and at flight service stations. In this example, continuous snowfall is occurring.

DEWPOINT

Dewpoint is shown in degrees Fahrenheit. In the example, the dewpoint is 32°F.

STATION IDENTIFIER

The station identifier is shown to the lower left of the station model. This observation is from KABI, or Abilene Regional Airport.

SKY COVER

Sky cover is depicted in the center of the station model. The five possible symbos are shown below.

Clear   Scattered   Broken   Overcast   Obscured or Partially Obscured

CLOUDS

Low cloud symbols are placed below the station model, while middle and high cloud symbols are placed immediately above it. A typical station model may include only one cloud type; seldom are more than two included. Decoding information for these symbols is available in various FAA publications and at flight service stations.

SEA LEVEL PRESSURE

Sea level pressure is shown in three digits to the nearest tenth of a millibar (hPa). For 1000 mb or greater, add a 10 to the 3 digits. For less than 1000 mb, add a 9 to the 3 digits. In this example, the sea level pressure is 1014.7 mb (hPa).

PRESSURE CHANGE/TENDENCY

The pressure change in tenths of millibars over the past 3 hours is shown below the sea level pressure. The tendency of pressure change is depicted using a symbol to the right of the change. In the example, pressure has increased 2.8 mb (hPa) over the past 3 hours, and is increasing more slowly or holding steady. Other symbols may be decoded using information available in various FAA publications and at flight service stations.

PRECIPITATION

The precipitation over the last 6-hour period is given to the nearest hundredths of an inch. In the example, 0.45 inch of precipitation has fallen in the last 6 hours.

Figure 7-21. This sample station model is based on information obtained from a manual observation.

WEATHER DEPICTION CHART

The **weather depiction chart** provides an overview of favorable and adverse weather conditions for the chart time and is an excellent resource to help you determine general weather conditions during flight planning. Information plotted on this chart is derived from aviation routine weather reports (METARs). Like the surface chart, the weather depiction chart is prepared and transmitted by computer every three hours, and is valid at the time of the plotted data. Unlike the surface chart, pressure patterns and wind information are not provided; however, simplified station models are included. These station models are depicted as circles; a bracket symbol (]) to the right of the circle indicates an observation made by an automated station. [Figure 7-22]

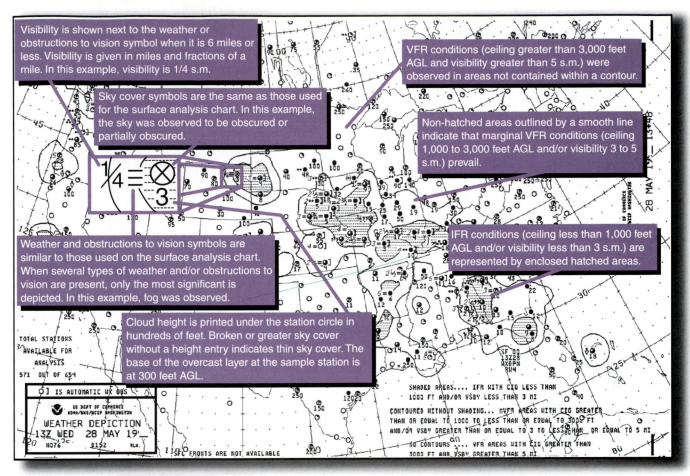

Visibility is shown next to the weather or obstructions to vision symbol when it is 6 miles or less. Visibility is given in miles and fractions of a mile. In this example, visibility is 1/4 s.m.

Sky cover symbols are the same as those used for the surface analysis chart. In this example, the sky was observed to be obscured or partially obscured.

VFR conditions (ceiling greater than 3,000 feet AGL and visibility greater than 5 s.m.) were observed in areas not contained within a contour.

Non-hatched areas outlined by a smooth line indicate that marginal VFR conditions (ceiling 1,000 to 3,000 feet AGL and/or visibility 3 to 5 s.m.) prevail.

IFR conditions (ceiling less than 1,000 feet AGL and/or visibility less than 3 s.m.) are represented by enclosed hatched areas.

Weather and obstructions to vision symbols are similar to those used on the surface analysis chart. When several types of weather and/or obstructions to vision are present, only the most significant is depicted. In this example, fog was observed.

Cloud height is printed under the station circle in hundreds of feet. Broken or greater sky cover without a height entry indicates thin sky cover. The base of the overcast layer at the sample station is at 300 feet AGL.

Figure 7-22. The weather depiction chart can give you a bird's-eye view of areas of adverse weather. However, the weather depiction chart may not completely represent the total enroute conditions because of variations in terrain and possible weather occurring between reporting stations.

 As shown in figure 7-22, a station circle on a weather depiction chart shows the visibility, cloud height or ceiling, and weather and/or obstructions to vision.

 For flight planning, the weather depiction chart is most useful for determining general weather conditions and quickly locating areas of adverse weather.

RADAR SUMMARY CHART

The computer-generated radar summary chart, which is produced 35 minutes past each hour, graphically depicts a collection of radar weather reports (SDs). The information for both products is gathered by special weather radar systems. These sys-

 As shown in figure 7-23, radar summary charts depict the location of precipitation, as well as direction and speed of movement of radar returns.

tems search for precipitation by transmitting pulses of radar energy in a specific direction with a rotating antenna. When the signals encounter precipitation, they are reflected back to the antenna. The reflected signals, also called echoes, are then presented on a radar display which shows the strength and location of the radar return. The radar summary chart uses this data to depict the location, size, shape, and intensity of returns, as well as the intensity trend and direction of movement. In addition, the chart shows lines and cells of hazardous thunderstorms as well as echo heights of the tops and bases of precipitation areas. [Figure 7-23]

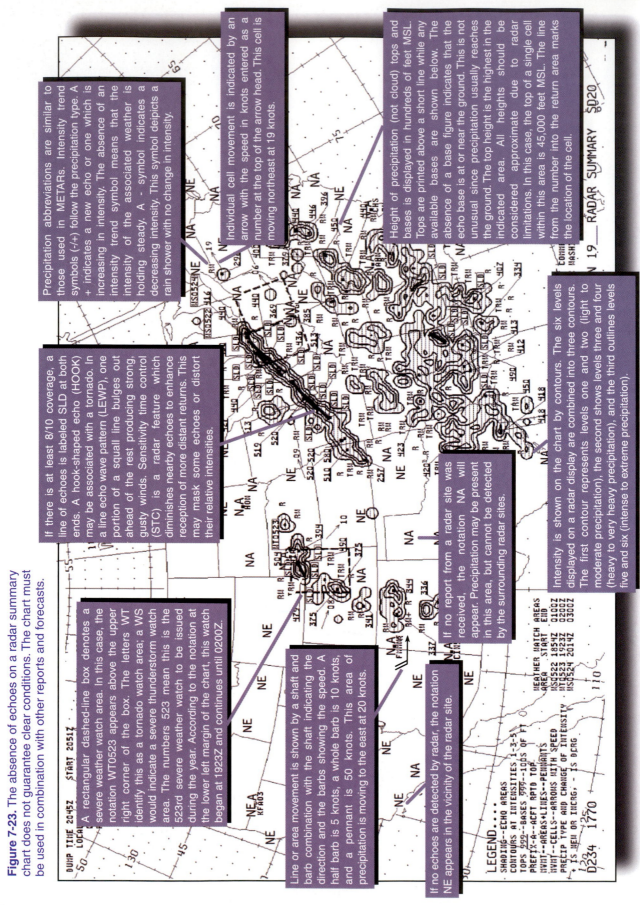

Figure 7-23. The absence of echoes on a radar summary chart does not guarantee clear conditions. The chart must be used in combination with other reports and forecasts.

Precipitation abbreviations are similar to those used in METARs. Intensity trend symbols (-/+) follow the precipitation type. A + indicates a new echo or one which is increasing in intensity. The absence of an intensity trend symbol means that the intensity of the associated weather is holding steady. A - symbol indicates a decreasing intensity. This symbol depicts a rain shower with no change in intensity.

Individual cell movement is indicated by an arrow with the speed in knots entered as a number at the top of the arrow head. This cell is moving northeast at 19 knots.

Height of precipitation (not cloud) tops and bases is displayed in hundreds of feet MSL. Tops are printed above a short line while any available bases are shown below. The absence of a base figure indicates that the echo base is at or near the ground. This is not unusual since precipitation usually reaches the ground. The top height is the highest in the indicated area. All heights should be considered approximate due to radar limitations. In this case, the top of a single cell within this area is 45,000 feet MSL. The line from the number into the return area marks the location of the cell.

If there is at least 8/10 coverage, a line of echoes is labeled SLD at both ends. A hook-shaped echo (HOOK) may be associated with a tornado. In a line echo wave pattern (LEWP), one portion of a squall line bulges out ahead of the rest producing strong, gusty winds. Sensitivity time control (STC) is a radar feature which diminishes nearby echoes to enhance reception of more distant returns. This may mask some echoes or distort their relative intensities.

If no report from a radar site was received, the notation NA will appear. Precipitation may be present in this area, but cannot be detected by the surrounding radar sites.

Intensity is shown on the chart by contours. The six levels displayed on a radar display are combined into three contours. The first contour represents levels one and two (light to moderate precipitation), the second shows levels three and four (heavy to very heavy precipitation), and the third outlines levels five and six (intense to extreme precipitation).

A rectangular dashed-line box denotes a severe weather watch area. In this case, the notation WT0523 appears above the upper right corner of the box. The letters WT identify this as a tornado watch area; a WS would indicate a severe thunderstorm watch area. The numbers 523 mean this is the 523rd severe weather watch to be issued during the year. According to the notation at the lower left margin of the chart, this watch began at 1923Z and continues until 0200Z.

Line or area movement is shown by a shaft and barb combination with the shaft indicating the direction and the barbs showing the speed. A half barb is 5 knots, a whole barb is 10 knots, and a pennant is 50 knots. This area of precipitation is moving to the east at 20 knots.

If no echoes are detected by radar, the notation NE appears in the vicinity of the radar site.

While the radar summary chart is a valuable preflight planning tool, it has certain limitations. Since radar only detects precipitation, either in frozen or liquid form, it does not detect all cloud formations. For instance, fog is not displayed, and actual cloud tops may be higher or lower than the precipitation returns indicate. Also, you should keep in mind that the radar summary chart is an observation of conditions that existed at the valid time. Since thunderstorms develop rapidly, you should examine other weather sources for current and forecast conditions that may affect your flight. [Figure 7-24]

Courtesy of NASA

Figure 7-24. Thunderstorms, such as this single cell storm, can develop quickly and, therefore, may not be depicted on the radar summary chart.

Individual thunderstorm cells as well as lines of thunderstorms are depicted on radar summary charts. Since radar only reflects precipitation, it does not detect cloud formations.

Radar That Sees the Future

While conventional weather radar has always been a powerful tool for detecting hazardous weather, the advent of Doppler weather surveillance radar has increased the capabilities of ground-based radar even more. As part of an ongoing modernization effort by the NWS, FAA, and DOD, the new radar, also known as NEXRAD, is quickly replacing old 1950's technology systems. When installation is completed, the 164 NEXRAD radar sites, each similar to the one shown in figure A, will cover the entire United States and its island territories from Puerto Rico to Guam.

The principle advantage of Doppler radar is that it can detect movement using the principle that radar signals reflected from a moving object undergo a change in frequency related to the speed of the object toward or away from the radar antenna. NEXRAD uses this information to calculate the speed and direction of storm movement. This can be particularly useful for identifying conditions which can eventually lead to severe weather. For example, NEXRAD can not only detect a tornado, but it can also provide weather observers with the direction and speed of the tornado, all before the tornado even reaches the ground. [Figure B] NEXRAD's timeliness, accuracy, and capability for improving forecasts is already contributing to improved public awareness and safety, both on the ground and in the air.

Winds blowing away from radar are shown in blue. The lightest blue indicates winds of 50 knots.

Green indicates winds blowing toward radar. The lightest green shows winds of 50 knots.

A red circle indicates an area where strong winds are blowing in opposite directions, possibly causing a tornado.

Grand Island

Lincoln

SATELLITE WEATHER PICTURES

Some of the most recognizable weather products come from satellites. Specialized weather satellites not only generate photos, but also record temperatures, humidities, wind speeds, and water vapor locations. Two types of images are available from weather satellites — visible and infrared (IR). Visible pictures are used primarily to determine the presence of clouds as well as the cloud shape and texture. IR photos depict the heat radiation emitted by the various cloud tops and the earth's surface. The difference in temperature between clouds can be used to determine cloud height. For example, since cold temperatures show up as light gray or white, the brightest white areas on an IR satellite photo depict the highest clouds. Both types of photos are transmitted every 30 minutes except for nighttime when visible photos are not available. [Figure 7-25]

Figure 7-25. A visible satellite picture is shown on the left. An infrared photo of the same area at the same time is shown on the right.

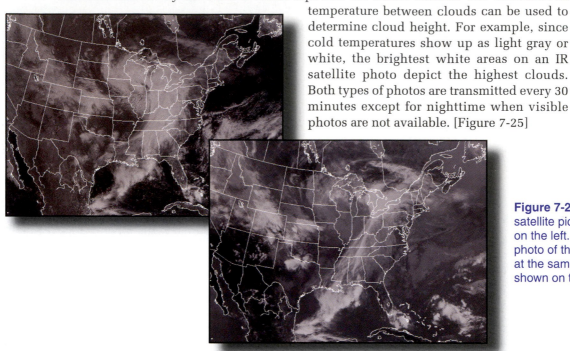

Eyes in the Sky

Weather satellites are positioned at different heights and different orbits to achieve the best possible coverage. Two geostationary operational environmental satellites (GOES) orbit the earth west-to-east at an altitude of 22,238 miles above the equator. The speed of the satellites is such that they match that of the earth. This allows the GOES satellites to remain in the same position over the earth, thus the term geostationary. GOES satellites provide weather observers and forecasters with a broad view from the African coast to beyond the International Date Line, and from Canada south to the tip of South America. [Figure A]

For imagery poleward of about 50 degrees latitude, two NOAA TIROS satellites are used. These spacecraft orbit the north and south poles about 530 miles above the earth. [Figure B] The high resolution pictures produced by these satellites are essential to weather personnel in Canada and Alaska.

A

Equator

GOES Satellites

B

Equator

TIROS Satellite

GRAPHIC FORECASTS

Graphically formatted forecasts for a variety of weather elements are available for several time periods in the future. These products include U.S. low-level significant weather prog charts, severe weather outlook charts, and forecast winds and temperatures aloft charts.

U.S. LOW-LEVEL SIGNIFICANT WEATHER PROG CHART

The **U.S. low-level significant weather prog (prognostic) chart** is valid from the surface up to the 400-millibar pressure level (24,000 feet). It is designed to help you plan your flights to avoid areas of low visibilities and ceilings as well as regions where turbulence and icing may exist. [Figure 7-26]

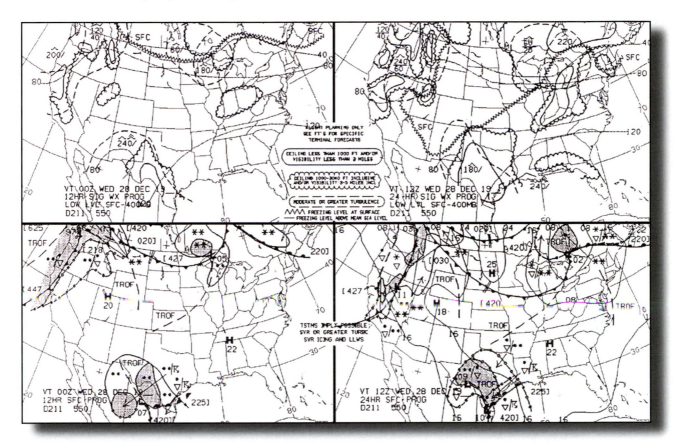

Figure 7-26. A low-level prog chart, which consists of four panels, is issued at 0000Z, 0600Z, 1200Z, and 1800Z. The two lower panels are 12- and 24-hour forecasts of surface weather conditions, while the two upper panels are 12- and 24-hour forecasts of weather between the surface and 24,000 feet. Legend information is included between the two upper panels.

Low-level prog charts are issued four times each day with the valid time printed on the lower margin of each panel. Since the two panels on the left forecast the weather 12 hours from the issue time and the two panels on the right forecast 24 hours ahead, you can compare the two sets of panels to determine the changes expected to take place between the two time frames.

 In addition to helping you avoid areas of significant turbulence, the information contained on the low-level significant weather prog chart helps you avoid areas where temperatures are conducive to aircraft icing.

SIGNIFICANT WEATHER PANELS

The upper panels show areas of nonconvective turbulence and freezing levels as well as IFR and marginal VFR (MVFR) weather. Although the definitions of the ceiling and visibility categories for this chart are the same as the weather depiction chart, the symbols for portraying IFR and MVFR are different.

Areas of forecast nonconvective moderate or greater turbulence are shown using a heavy dashed contour line. Numbers within these areas give the height of the turbulence in hundreds of feet MSL. Figures below a line show the expected base, while figures above a line represent the top of the turbulence. Since thunderstorms always imply moderate or greater turbulence, areas of possible thunderstorm turbulence are not outlined.

Forecast **freezing levels** are also depicted on the significant weather panels. Freezing level height contours for the highest freezing level are drawn at 4,000-foot intervals with dashed lines. These contours are labeled in hundreds of feet MSL. A zig-zag line labeled SFC shows the surface location of the freezing level.

SURFACE PROG PANELS

The two lower panels are the surface prog panels. They contain standard symbols for fronts and pressure centers. In addition, areas of forecast precipitation, as well as thunderstorms, are outlined. [Figure 7-27]

 As shown in figure 7-26, symbols used to define areas of IFR, MVFR, VFR, and moderate or greater turbulence, as well as the forecast altitude of the freezing level, are depicted in the legend between the two upper panels of the low-level significant weather prog chart.

On the low-level significant weather prog chart, frontal progress is shown with an arrow pointing in the direction of movement. A number near the arrowhead indicates the speed in knots.

Symbol	Meaning	Symbol	Meaning	Symbol	Meaning
(showery precip symbol)	Showery precipitation (thunderstorms/rain-showers) covering half or more of the area.	(rain shower symbol)	Rain Shower	(severe turbulence symbol)	Severe Turbulence
(continuous precip symbol)	Continuous precipitation (rain) covering half or more of the area.	(snow shower symbol)	Snow Shower	(moderate icing symbol)	Moderate Icing
(showery snow symbol)	Showery precipitation (snow showers) covering less than half of the area.	(thunderstorm symbol)	Thunderstorms	(severe icing symbol)	Severe Icing
		(freezing rain symbol)	Freezing Rain	●	Rain
(intermittent drizzle symbol)	Intermittent precipitation (drizzle) covering less than half of the area.	(tropical storm symbol)	Tropical Storm	✳	Snow
		(hurricane symbol)	Hurricane (Typhoon)	,	Drizzle
		(moderate turbulence symbol)	Moderate Turbulence		

 As shown in figure 7-27, turbulence is depicted on the low-level significant weather prog chart with a peaked symbol. Underneath the symbol, figures indicate the top and base of the turbulence.

Figure 7-27. An area which is expected to have continuous or intermittent precipitation is enclosed by a solid circle. If only showers are expected, the area is enclosed with a dot-dash pattern. A shaded area indicates that precipitation covers one-half or more of the area. Unique symbols indicate precipitation type and the manner in which it occurs. In the case of drizzle, rain, and snow, a single symbol is used to indicate intermittent conditions while a pair of symbols denotes continuous precipitation.

"THE CAPTAIN HAS TURNED OFF THE SEAT BELT SIGN..."
From the Files of the NTSB...

Aircraft: *Boeing 767-200*

Crew and Passengers: *211*

Narrative: *While in normal cruise flight, the flight crew was advised by ARTCC personnel that other aircraft were experiencing occasional severe turbulence at FL 370 [37,000 feet] along their route of flight. A descent was made to FL 330 [33,000 feet] to avoid turbulence. Later, as the aircraft was cruising at FL 330 with the seat belt sign off, it encountered "severe chop with severe turbulence, in clear air." One flight attendant and two passengers were injured during the turbulence encounter. The aircraft continued to its destination without further incident.*

As the incident cited above demonstrates, encounters with turbulence can occur at any time, without warning. Not only is turbulence capable of inflicting substantial damage to aircraft, but it also can have a wide range of effects on the human body, including motion sickness, fatigue, and broken bones. While a tight seat belt can help, some of the physiological affects of turbulence only can be averted by moving out of the turbulent air.

While weather reports and forecasts can alert you to areas of turbulence, simply avoiding those areas will not guarantee you a smooth flight. This is not to say that turbulence reports and forecasts have no value. On the contrary, PIREPs and other weather sources have undoubtedly prevented many a personal injury and/or overstressed aircraft. Anytime you encounter turbulence you should report your encounters with turbulence as soon as possible using the criteria shown in the accompanying table.

TURBULENCE REPORTING CRITERIA TABLE				
INTENSITY	**Light** ∧	**Moderate** ∧	**Severe** ∧	**Extreme**
AIRCRAFT REACTION	Turbulence that momentarily causes slight, erratic changes in altitude and/or attitude (pitch, roll, yaw); report as light turbulence. OR Turbulence that causes slight, rapid, and somewhat rhythmic bumpiness without appreciable changes in altitude or attitude; report as light chop.	Turbulence that is similar to light turbulence but of greater intensity. Changes in altitude and/or attitude occur but the aircraft remains in positive control at all times. It usually causes variations in indicated airspeed; report as moderate turbulence. OR Turbulence that is similar to light chop but of greater intensity. It causes rapid bumps or jolts without appreciable changes in aircraft altitude or attitude; report as moderate chop.	Turbulence that causes large abrupt changes in altitude and/or attitude. It usually causes large variations in indicated airspeed. Aircraft may be momentarily out of control; report as severe turbulence.	Turbulence in which the aircraft is violently tossed about and is practically impossible to control. It may cause structural damage; report as extreme turbulence.
REACTION INSIDE AIRCRAFT	Occupants may feel a slight strain against seat belts or shoulder straps. Unsecured objects may be displaced slightly. Food service may be conducted and little or no difficulty is encountered in walking.	Occupants feel definite strains against seat belts or shoulder straps. Unsecured objects are dislodged. Food service and walking is difficult.	Occupants are forced violently against seat belts or shoulder straps. Unsecured objects are tossed about. Food service and walking are impossible.	REPORTING TERMS: Occasional — Less than 1/3 of the time Intermittent — 1/3 to 2/3 of the time Continuous — More than 2/3 of the time

NOTE: High level turbulence (normally above 15,000 feet MSL) not associated with cumuliform clouds, including thunderstorms, should be reported as CAT (clear air turbulence) preceded by the intensity, or light to moderate chop.

SEVERE WEATHER OUTLOOK CHART

The two-panel **severe weather outlook chart** is a 48-hour forecast for thunderstorm activity. The left panel depicts the outlook for general thunderstorm activity and severe thunderstorms for the first 24-hour period beginning at 1200Z. A line with an arrowhead depicts forecast general thunderstorm activity. When facing in the direction of the arrow, thunderstorm activity is expected to the right of the line. If an area is labeled APCHG, it means that the general thunderstorm activity may approach severe intensity. Hatched areas indicate possible severe thunderstorms with an associated risk factor. For example, the notation SLGT indicates that there is a slight (2 to 5 percent coverage) risk of severe thunderstorms occurring during the forecast period. The other possible risk categories include moderate (6 to 10 percent coverage) and high (more than 10 percent coverage). The right panel of this computer-prepared chart provides a forecast for the next day beginning at 1200Z. This outlook is for the possibility of severe thunderstorms only, and does not include an associated risk factor. [Figure 7-28]

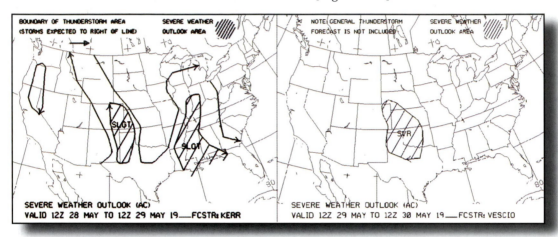

Figure 7-28. The severe weather outlook chart is issued every morning at about 0800Z.

FORECAST WINDS AND TEMPERATURES ALOFT CHART

Forecast winds and temperatures aloft charts (FD) are 12-hour forecasts valid at 0000Z and 1200Z daily. The charts contain eight panels, each of which corresponds to a forecast level — 6,000; 9,000; 12,000; 18,000; 24,000; 30,000; 34,000; and 39,000 feet MSL. Predicted winds are shown using an arrow emanating from the station circle to show direction to within 10 degrees. The second digit of the wind direction is printed at the end of the arrow to help you pinpoint the forecast direction. Pennants and/or barbs at the end of the arrow depict forecast wind speed in much the same way as on the surface analysis chart. When calm or light and variable winds are expected, the arrow is eliminated and a 99 is entered below the station circle. Predicted temperatures are shown as whole degrees Celsius near the station circle. [Figure 7-29]

Figure 7-29. The panel on the bottom is for 6,000 feet. The panel on the top is for the same forecast period, but at 39,000 feet. All altitudes below 18,000 feet are in true altitude while those above are in pressure altitude.

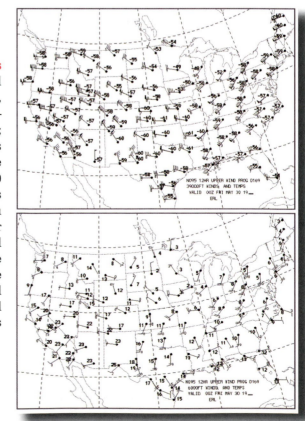

VOLCANIC ASH FORECAST AND DISPERSION CHART

As volcanic eruptions are reported, a **volcanic ash forecast transport and dispersion chart (VAFTAD)** is created. The chart is developed, with input from National Meteorological Center forecasts, using a model which focuses on hazards to aircraft flight operations with emphasis on the ash cloud location. The concentration of volcanic ash is forecast over 6- and 12-hour time intervals, beginning 6 hours following the eruption. The VAFTAD uses four panels in a column for each valid time period. The top three panels in a column reflect the ash location and relative concentrations for an atmospheric layer. The bottom panel in a column shows the total ash concentrations from the surface up to 55,000 feet (FL 550). [Figure 7-30] The VAFTAD chart is designed specifically for flight planning purposes only; it is not intended to take the place of SIGMETs regarding volcanic eruptions and ash.

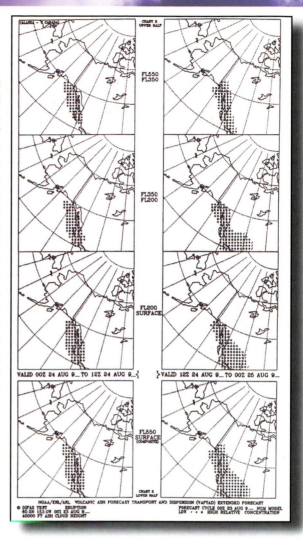

Figure 7-30. This VAFTAD shows the panels associated with the 24- and 36-hour valid times. Ash concentration is depicted as low (/), moderate (+), or high (■).

SUMMARY CHECKLIST

✓ To get a picture of atmospheric pressure patterns at the earth's surface, you can refer to the surface analysis chart.

✓ The surface analysis chart provides information obtained from surface weather observations for a large number of reporting points throughout the United States.

✓ The weather depiction chart is particularly useful during the preflight planning process for determining general weather conditions and areas of IFR and MVFR weather.

✓ The radar summary chart shows the location, size, shape, and intensity of areas of precipitation, as well as the intensity trend and direction of movement. Although the chart plots the location of lines and cells of hazardous thunderstorms, it does not show cloud formations.

✓ Both visible and infrared (IR) imagery are available from weather satellites. The visible picture is used generally to indicate the presence of clouds as well as the cloud shape and texture. IR photos, which depict the heat radiation emitted by the various cloud tops and the earth's surface, can be used to determine cloud height.

✓ The U.S. low-level significant weather prog chart can not only help you avoid areas of significant turbulence, but it also can provide you with information to help you avoid areas where temperatures are conducive to aircraft icing. The chart is valid from the surface up to 24,000 feet.

✓ The upper panels of the low-level significant weather prog chart show areas of non-convective turbulence, and freezing levels as well as areas of IFR, marginal VFR, and VFR weather. The surface prog panels, contained in the lower portion of the chart, use standard symbols for fronts and pressure centers.

✓ The severe weather outlook chart is a two-panel chart which forecasts thunderstorm activity over the next 48 hours. The left panel depicts the outlook for general thunderstorm activity and severe thunderstorms for the first 24-hour period beginning at 1200Z. The right panel of the severe weather outlook chart provides a forecast for the next day beginning at 1200Z.

✓ The forecast winds and temperatures aloft chart contains eight panels, each of which corresponds to a forecast level — 6,000; 9,000; 12,000; 18,000; 24,000; 30,000; 34,000; and 39,000 feet MSL. The chart is issued at 1200Z or 0000Z and is valid for a 12-hour forecast period.

✓ The volcanic ash forecast transport and dispersion chart (VAFTAD) forecasts the concentration of volcanic ash over 6- and 12-hour time intervals, beginning 6 hours following a volcanic eruption. The VAFTAD chart is not intended to take the place of SIGMETs regarding volcanic eruptions; it is designed specifically for flight planning purposes.

KEY TERMS

Surface Analysis Chart	Freezing Levels
Station Model	Severe Weather Outlook Chart
Weather Depiction Chart	Forecast Winds And Temperatures Aloft Chart (FD)
Radar Summary Chart	
U.S. Low-Level Significant Weather Prog Chart	Volcanic Ash Forecast Transport And Dispersion Chart (VAFTAD)

QUESTIONS

1. What is the significance of a square station model on a surface analysis chart?

2. What ceiling and visibility can you expect to encounter in the shaded areas of a weather depiction chart?

Refer to the excerpt from the radar summary chart to answer questions 3 through 5.

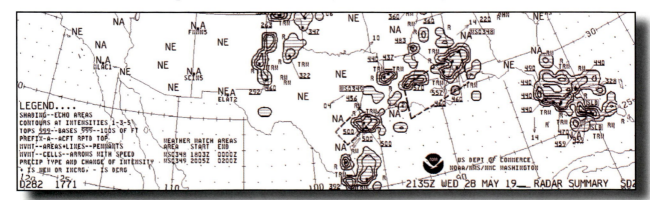

3. What time does weather watch WS0349 expire?

4. At what altitude are the highest tops of the echoes in southeastern Texas?

5. What speed and general direction is the cell in southeastern Texas moving?

6. Primarily, what can be ascertained by examining visible and infrared satellite weather pictures?

7. To what altitude is the U.S. low-level significant weather prog chart valid?

   A. 12,000 feet
   B. 18,000 feet
   C. 24,000 feet

8. On the excerpt from the low-level surface prog chart shown below, what does the symbol in southern California indicate?

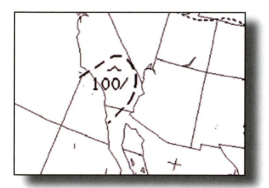

9. What chart should you refer to for a forecast of general thunderstorm activity?

10. What wind speed and direction is forecast over New York, New York in the excerpt from the forecast winds aloft chart shown below? What is the associated forecast temperature?

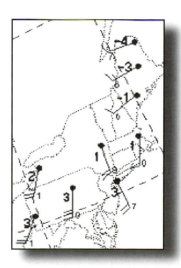

SECTION D
SOURCES OF WEATHER INFORMATION

Mark Twain once said, "If you don't like the weather in New England, just wait a few minutes." Whether you are flying in New England or not, the fickle nature of the weather requires that you familiarize yourself with the current and forecast conditions prior to your flights. Fortunately, in the information age, the sources of weather information are almost as varied as the weather itself. Although they can overlap somewhat, the places you turn to for weather data can be divided between those you can use for preflight planning and those available to you for use during flight.

PREFLIGHT WEATHER SOURCES

For VFR flights, federal regulations only require that you gather weather reports and forecasts if you plan on departing the airport vicinity. Nevertheless, it is a good idea to familiarize yourself with the current and expected weather anytime you take to the skies. Preflight weather information sources include Flight Service Station (FSS) and National Weather Service (NWS) telephone briefers, the telephone information briefing service, the direct user access terminal system, the internet, and a multitude of commercial vendors.

FLIGHT SERVICE STATION

Flight service stations are your primary source for preflight weather information. You can obtain a **preflight weather briefing** from an FSS, or a newer automated FSS (AFSS), 24 hours a day by calling the toll free number, 1-800-WX BRIEF. In areas not served by an FSS/AFSS, National Weather Service facilities may provide pilot weather briefings. Telephone numbers for NWS facilities and additional numbers for FSSs/AFSSs may be found in the *Airport/Facility Directory* (A/FD) or the U.S. Government section of the telephone directory under Department of Transportation, Federal Aviation Administration, or Department of Commerce, National Weather Service.

PREFLIGHT WEATHER BRIEFING

When you request a briefing, you should identify yourself as a pilot and supply the briefer with the following background information: type of flight planned (VFR or IFR), aircraft number or your name, aircraft type, departure airport, route of flight, destination, flight altitude(s), estimated time of departure (ETD), and estimated time enroute (ETE).

The briefer can then proceed directly with the briefing and concentrate on the weather affecting your flight. It helps to save your questions until the end of the briefing. This allows the briefer to present the information logically and lessens the chance that items will be overlooked.

When you contact a weather briefer, identify yourself as a pilot flying VFR and provide the briefer with your aircraft number or your name, type of aircraft, intended route, destination, and other relevant background data for the flight.

While pilot weather briefers do not actually predict the weather, they do translate and interpret reports and forecasts into terms that describe the weather conditions you can expect along your route of flight and at your destination. You can request one of three types of preflight weather briefings — standard, abbreviated, or outlook.

STANDARD BRIEFING

You should request a **standard briefing** when you are planning a trip and have not obtained preliminary weather or a previous briefing. This is the most complete weather briefing, and assumes you have no familiarity with the overall weather picture. When you request a standard briefing, the briefer automatically provides certain types of information in sequence, if applicable to your proposed flight. [Figure 7-31]

 The standard briefing provides the most complete information concerning weather for your flight. When you request a standard briefing, the weather briefer assumes you have not received any preliminary information.

1. **ADVERSE CONDITIONS** — This includes the type of information that might influence you to alter your proposed route or cancel the flight altogether. Examples include such things as hazardous weather or airport closures.

2. **VFR FLIGHT NOT RECOMMENDED** — If the flight service briefer indicates that VFR flight is not recommended, it means that, in the briefer's judgment, it is doubtful that you can complete the flight under VFR. Although the final decision to conduct the flight rests with you, this advisory should be taken seriously.

3. **SYNOPSIS** — The briefer will provide you with a broad overview of the major weather systems or airmasses that affect the proposed flight.

4. **CURRENT CONDITIONS** — This information is a rundown of existing conditions, including pertinent hourly, pilot, and radar weather reports. Unless you request otherwise, this item is omitted if your proposed departure time is more than two hours in the future.

5. **ENROUTE FORECAST** — The briefer will summarize the forecast conditions along your proposed route in a logical order from departure through descent for landing.

6. **DESTINATION FORECAST** — The briefer will provide the forecast for your destination at your estimated time of arrival (ETA). In addition, any significant changes predicted for an hour before or after your ETA will be included.

7. **WINDS AND TEMPERATURES ALOFT**—You will be given a summary of forecast winds for your route. If necessary, the briefer will interpolate wind direction and speed between levels and stations for your planned cruising altitude(s). Temperature information will be provided on request.

8. **NOTICES TO AIRMEN** — The briefer will supply NOTAM information pertinent to your proposed route of flight. However, information which has already been published in the *Notices to Airmen* publication will only be provided on request.

9. **ATC DELAYS**— You will be advised of any known air traffic control delays that might affect your proposed flight.

10. **OTHER INFORMATION** — Upon request, the briefer will provide you with other information such as approximate density altitude data, MOA and MTR activity within 100 n.m. of the flight plan area, ATC services and rules, as well as customs and immigration procedures.

Figure 7-31. The first three items of a standard briefing may be combined in any order when, in the briefer's opinion, it will help describe conditions more clearly.

ABBREVIATED BRIEFING

When you need only one or two specific items or would like to update weather information from a previous briefing or other weather sources, you should request an **abbreviated briefing**. Provide the briefer with the source of the prior information including the time you received it, as well as any other pertinent background information. This allows the briefer to limit the conversation to information you did not receive, plus any significant changes in weather conditions. Usually, the sequence of information will follow that of the standard briefing. If you request only one or two items, you still will be advised if adverse conditions are present or forecast.

 Request an abbreviated briefing to update weather information from mass dissemination sources, e.g. telephone information briefing service, or an earlier briefing.

OUTLOOK BRIEFING

If your proposed departure time is six or more hours away you should request an **outlook briefing**. An outlook briefing will provide you with forecast information appropriate to your proposed flight in order to help you make an initial judgment about the feasibility of your flight. The outlook briefing is designed for planning purposes only; as your departure time draws near, you will need to request either a standard or abbreviated briefing to obtain current conditions and the latest forecasts.

 You should request an outlook briefing when your proposed departure is six or more hours in the future.

TELEPHONE INFORMATION BRIEFING SERVICE

When calling an AFSS, you will hear an informational recording telling you how to directly access a weather briefer or additional services. Using a TOUCH-TONE® phone, you can normally connect to one such service, called the **telephone information briefing service (TIBS)**. This service provides a continuous recording of area and/or route meteorological briefings, airspace procedures, and special aviation-oriented announcements. Depending on demand, other information such as METARs and TAFs also may be included. TIBS is designed to be a preliminary briefing tool, and can be very useful in determining the overall feasibility of your proposed flight. TIBS is not intended, however, to replace an individual briefing from an FSS or NWS specialist. If you need more detailed information than TIBS supplies, the AFSS system allows you to transfer directly to a briefer.

DIRECT USER ACCESS TERMINAL SYSTEM

The FAA-funded **direct user access terminal system (DUATS)**, allows pilots with a current medical certificate to receive weather briefings and file flight plans directly via a personal computer and modem. You can access DUATS using a toll-free number in the 48 contiguous United States. The current providers of DUATS and their associated phone numbers are listed in the *Aeronautical Information Manual*.

PRIVATE INDUSTRY SOURCES

Prior to World War II, the U.S. Weather Bureau (the equivalent of today's National Weather Service) was the lone disseminator of weather data. Now, in addition to government sources, there also are over 100 companies in the 200 million-dollar-a-year business of providing weather information to the aviation industry. The services and products, as well as their associated costs, vary from one company to another. Jeppesen's JeppFax service is an example of a commercially provided source of weather information. JeppFax provides weather information ranging from airport and route briefings to real-time radar maps to anyone with a telephone and fax machine.

THE INTERNET

A wealth of weather information, some of which is directed toward aviation, is available at a variety of internet sites. You can locate many of the sites by using one of the variety of internet search engines. Some of the home pages are comprehensive while others can be somewhat sketchy and may provide less than up-to-date information. Consequently, you should exercise caution when accessing weather information on the internet. One source of accurate information can be obtained on the NWS internet site at: www.nws.noaa.gov. [Figure 7-32]

Figure 7-32. You can access a multitude of current weather products via the NWS internet home page.

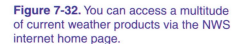

IN-FLIGHT WEATHER SOURCES

Since forecasting is an inexact science, weather conditions can change rapidly and unexpectedly in the course of a few hours. This often necessitates updating your weather information while in-flight. In these cases, you can obtain weather updates from FSSs, transcribed weather broadcasts, the hazardous in-flight weather advisory service, the enroute flight advisory service, ARTCC, and automated weather observing systems.

FLIGHT SERVICE STATIONS

Although some may think of it primarily as a preflight tool, the FSS/AFSS can also provide valuable information during flight. Typically, you should contact an FSS/AFSS when you need to update a previous briefing. After establishing contact, you should specify the type of briefing you want as well as appropriate background information similar to what you supplied your preflight briefer. If conditions along your route warrant, the specialist may direct you to other sources for further in-flight information.

ENROUTE FLIGHT ADVISORY SERVICE

A service specifically designed to provide timely enroute weather information upon pilot request is referred to as the **enroute flight advisory service (EFAS)**, or **Flight Watch**. EFAS will provide you with weather advisories tailored to your type of flight, route, and cruising altitude. EFAS can be one of your best sources for current weather information along your route of flight since EFAS

EFAS facilities provide actual weather information, including any thunderstorm activity which might affect your route.

"OKAY, HOUSTON, WE'VE HAD A PROBLEM HERE."

A

At 55 hours, 46 minutes after liftoff (shown in figure A), astronaut Jim Lovell wrapped up a 49-minute TV broadcast from Apollo 13 with the words, "This is the crew of Apollo 13 wishing everybody there a nice evening, and we're ready to close out our inspection of *Aquarius* [the lunar module] and get back for a pleasant evening in *Odyssey* [the command module]. Good night." Nine minutes later, the #2 oxygen tank blew up, also causing the failure of the #1 tank (the damage to the command module can be seen in figure B). The crippling explosion was accompanied by a sharp bang and vibration as well as the illumination of master caution and warning lights. After proceeding through the appropriate procedures, command module pilot Jack Swigert keyed his mike and informed Mission Control, "Okay, Houston, we've had a problem here."

Thus began one of the remarkable achievements in the history of flight. Stranded 200,000 miles from home with a loss of the normal source of electricity and water in the command module, the crew of Apollo 13 soon realized that the problems which they faced were beyond their ability to solve with the resources available aboard the spacecraft. Without help from the ground, the astronauts knew that they would never make it home alive. Apollo 13's ground controllers did not let them down. Using the powerful computers and sophisticated simulators at their disposal, the engineers and scientists feverishly worked to solve the formidable tasks of navigation and reentry.

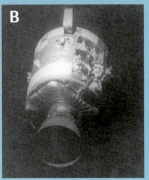
B

Ultimately, the coordinated effort of Apollo 13's crew and ground controllers yielded success. On the afternoon of April, 17, 1970, nearly three days after the explosion, *Odyssey* splashed down in the Pacific Ocean near Samoa on a triumphant return to earth, an event which most certainly would not have occurred without the effective use of resources by all of the people involved. [Figure C]

Although most pilots may never venture into space, many may still be faced with a situation which requires a timely decision and appropriate action. While the confines of the cockpit may not provide the information necessary to make a fully informed decision, all pilots should remember that there are a variety of resources available just for the asking.

C

Photos and emblem courtesy of NASA

facilities are not only a central collection and distribution point for PIREPs, but also because they are equipped to directly access weather radar displays. The radar can be particularly valuable in identifying areas of possible thunderstorm activity along your route.

You can usually contact an EFAS specialist from 6 A.M. to 10 P.M. anywhere in the conterminous U.S. and Puerto Rico. The common EFAS frequency, 122.0 MHz, is established for pilots of aircraft flying between 5,000 feet AGL and 17,500 feet MSL. Different discrete frequencies are allocated for each ARTCC area for

The frequency for EFAS (Flight Watch) below 18,000 feet MSL is 122.0 MHz.

operations above 18,000 feet MSL. The *Airport/Facility Directory* contains a chart depicting the locations and associated frequencies of EFAS facilities.

Since EFAS facilities usually serve large geographic regions through remote communications outlets (RCOs), you should make your initial callup using the name of the ARTCC serving the area. This allows the briefer to use the RCO which will provide the best communications coverage. After the ARTCC identifier, use the EFAS call sign, Flight Watch, followed by your aircraft identification and the name of the VOR nearest your position. For example, "*Denver Flight Watch, Cherokee 141FS, Casper VOR.*" Since sectional charts do not show EFAS outlets or parent facilities, there may be times when you will not know your EFAS area. In these situations, you can make your initial callup as follows: "*Flight Watch, Cherokee 141FS, Casper VOR.*" The briefer will then respond with the name of the controlling facility.

Although EFAS is normally based in an AFSS, you should confine your EFAS requests to weather information along your route of flight. EFAS is not intended for matters relating to flight plans, position reports, preflight briefings, or to obtain weather reports or forecasts unrelated to your flight. For these items, you should contact FSS/AFSS personnel on other published frequencies.

TRANSCRIBED WEATHER BROADCAST

The **transcribed weather broadcast (TWEB)**, is transmitted continuously over selected low frequency NDBs and/or VORs. You can determine which NDBs and VORs have a TWEB capability by referencing the associated sectional chart. [Figure 7-33] The information in a TWEB varies with the type of recording equipment that is available. Generally, the broadcast includes route-oriented data with specially prepared National Weather Service forecasts, in-flight advisories, winds aloft, and preselected information such as weather reports, NOTAMs and special notices.

Figure 7-33. On a sectional chart, a T in the upper right corner of a navaid box indicates TWEB capability.

At some locations, the information is only broadcast over the local VOR and is limited to items such as the hourly weather for the parent station and up to five adjacent stations, local NOTAM information, the TAF for the parent station, and potentially hazardous conditions. Typically, TWEBs are used for in-flight information purposes, however, at some locations, telephone access to the recording is available, providing an additional source of preflight information. Telephone numbers for this service, called TEL-TWEB, are listed in the *Airport/Facility Directory*.

 TWEB recordings are broadcast over selected NDBs and/or VORs. The recorded messages typically provide a variety of information including specific route forecasts and winds aloft information.

HAZARDOUS IN-FLIGHT WEATHER ADVISORY SERVICE

A program for broadcasting hazardous weather information on a continuous basis over selected VORs is called **hazardous in-flight weather advisory service (HIWAS)**. The broadcasts include advisories such as AIRMETs, SIGMETs, convective SIGMETs, and urgent PIREPs. When a HIWAS is updated, ARTCC and terminal facilities will broadcast an alert on all but emergency frequencies. The alert will provide the type and number of the updated advisory and the frequencies to which you can tune for complete information. Sectional chart notations depict the VORs which have HIWAS capability. In addition, a note in the *Airport/Facility Directory* indicates if a particular VOR is HIWAS-equipped. [Figure 7-34]

Figure 7-34. HIWAS availability is indicated on a sectional chart using a solid square in the lower right corner of the associated navaid box.

CENTER WEATHER ADVISORIES

A **center weather advisory (CWA)** is an unscheduled weather advisory issued by an ARTCC to alert pilots of existing or anticipated adverse weather conditions within the next two hours. A CWA may be initiated when a SIGMET has not been issued but, based on current PIREPs, conditions meet those criteria. Additionally, a CWA may be issued to supplement an existing in-flight advisory as well as any conditions which currently or will soon adversely affect the safe flow of traffic within the ARTCC area of responsibility.

Air Route Traffic Control Centers broadcast CWAs as well as SIGMETs, Convective SIGMETs, and AWWs once on all but emergency frequencies when any part of the area described is within 150 miles of the airspace under the ARTCC jurisdiction. In terminal areas, local control and approach control may limit these broadcasts to weather occurring within 50 miles of the airspace under their jurisdiction. These broadcasts contain the advisory identification and a brief description of the weather activity and general area affected.

WEATHER RADAR SERVICES

The NWS operates a nationwide network of weather radar sites which not only provides real-time information for printed and graphic weather products, but also furnishes EFAS and AFSS specialists with data they can use for in-flight advisories. Since weather radar can detect coverage, intensity, and movement of precipitation, an EFAS or AFSS specialist may be able to provide you with suggested routing around areas of hazardous weather. It is important to remember, however, that simply avoiding areas highlighted by weather radar does not guarantee clear weather radar conditions.

Airborne Weather Radar

Weather radar information obtained from ground-based sources is adequate for many users, however, for high performance aircraft, a real-time source of weather data in the cockpit can prove extremely useful. Weather radar units installed in aircraft work in much the same way as ground-based radar facilities. That is, pulses of energy transmitted into the atmosphere travel until they hit either a solid object or liquid water. The reflection off these objects is picked up by the antenna from which it was transmitted. The resulting weather picture is displayed on a monitor in either a monochrome or color format. The color displays are useful for indicating different degrees of precipitation severity. For example, a radar unit might use green to indicate light showers, yellow to show moderate rainfall, and red to depict heavy precipitation.

Aircraft weather radar units generally use one of two frequency ranges — X-band and C-band. X-band systems, which are more common in general aviation aircraft, transmit a frequency (9,333 gigahertz) which causes the energy to be reflected by very small amounts of precipitation. Due to the high amount of reflected energy, systems using an X-band frequency provide a higher resolution and see farther than C-band radars. A drawback to the X-band systems is that very little energy can pass through one storm to detect another which may be behind the first. The C-band frequency (5.44 gigahertz) can penetrate further into a storm, providing a more complete picture of the storm system. This capability makes C-band weather radar systems better for penetration into known areas of precipitation. Consequently, C-band radars are more likely to be found on large commercial aircraft.

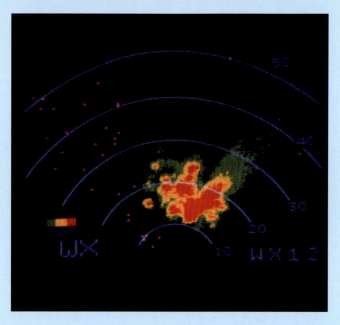

As a pilot, you should be aware that aircraft weather radar is prone to many of the same limitations as ground-based systems. That is, weather radar cannot detect water vapor, lightning, or wind shear. Training and experience as well as other on-board equipment and surface resources are all important tools for enhancing your mental picture of the weather which lies ahead.

AUTOMATED WEATHER REPORTING SYSTEMS

Technological advances over the past several years has made it practical to automate many surface weather observation tasks. Currently, the FAA operates the automated weather observing system while the NWS has fielded the automated surface observing system. Although their complexity and capabilities vary, both systems are primarily designed to provide weather information for aviation applications.

AUTOMATED WEATHER OBSERVING SYSTEM

First manufactured in 1979, the **automated weather observing system (AWOS)** was developed for the FAA and was the first widely installed automated weather data gathering system at U.S. airports. Installation of AWOS is continuing, particularly at airports without control towers. The AWOS uses various sensors, a voice synthesizer, and a radio transmitter to provide real-time weather data. Currently there are four types of AWOS. An AWOS-A only reports altimeter setting while an AWOS-1 also measures and reports wind speed, direction and gusts, temperature, and dew point. AWOS-2 provides visibility information in addition to everything reported by an AWOS-1. The most capable system, the AWOS-3, also includes cloud and ceiling data.

The AWOS transmits over a discrete VHF frequency or the voice portion of a navaid. The transmissions can usually be received within 25 n.m. of the site, at or above 3,000 feet AGL. Most units transmit a 20- to 30-second weather message updated each minute. AWOS sites and the associated frequencies are noted on aeronautical charts as well as in the *Airport/Facility Directory*. The A/FD also lists a phone number if telephone access is available.

AUTOMATED SURFACE OBSERVATION SYSTEM

The **automated surface observation system (ASOS)** is the primary surface weather observing system in the United States. The effort to install ASOS began in 1991 and will continue until nearly 1,700 are installed at airports across the U.S. [Figure 7-35] Using an array of sensors, computers, and digitized voice communications, ASOS provides continuous minute-by-minute observations. The ASOS measures and reports the same elements as an AWOS-3 as well as variable cloud height, variable visibility, rapid pressure changes, precipitation type, intensity, accumulation, and beginning and ending times. The ASOS is also capable of measuring wind shifts and peak winds. Some ASOS stations can determine the difference between liquid precipitation and frozen or freezing precipitation. If the station has this capability, it is designated as an AO2. Otherwise, it carries an AO1 designation.

ASOS broadcast over discrete VHF frequencies or the voice portion of VORs. These weather report transmissions are designed to be receivable up to 25 n.m. from the site and to a maximum of 10,000 feet AGL. Locations and frequencies are annotated on aeronautical charts and listed in the *Airport/Facility Directory*. As with AWOS, ASOS may be accessed via telephone using telephone numbers listed in the A/FD.

Figure 7-35. When installation of ASOS stations, such as this one, is complete, they will be the primary source of U.S. weather observations.

SUMMARY CHECKLIST

✓ You can obtain a preflight weather briefing from an FSS/AFSS 24 hours a day by calling the toll free number, 1-800-WX BRIEF. When you contact a weather briefer, identify yourself as a pilot flying VFR and provide the briefer with your aircraft number and other relevant background data for the flight.

✓ When you are planning a trip and have not obtained preliminary weather or a previous briefing, you should request a standard briefing.

✓ You should request an abbreviated briefing when you need only one or two specific items or would like to update weather information from a previous briefing or other weather sources.

✓ An outlook briefing will provide you with forecast information appropriate to the proposed flight to help you make an initial judgment about the feasibility of your flight.

✓ The telephone information briefing service (TIBS) provides a continuous recording of area and/or route meteorological briefings, airspace procedures, and special aviation-oriented announcements.

✓ You can receive weather briefings and file flight plans directly via a personal computer and modem using the direct user access terminal system (DUATS).

✓ Transcribed weather broadcasts (TWEBs), which are transmitted continuously over selected NDBs and/or VORs, include route-oriented data with specially prepared National Weather Service forecasts, in-flight advisories, winds aloft, and preselected information such as weather reports.

✓ Hazardous in-flight weather advisory service (HIWAS) broadcasts, which include advisories such as AIRMETs, SIGMETs, convective SIGMETs, and urgent PIREPs, are transmitted on a continuous basis over selected VORs.

✓ An unscheduled weather advisory issued by an ARTCC to alert pilots of existing or anticipated adverse weather conditions within the next two hours is called a center weather advisory (CWA).

✓ When flying below 18,000 feet MSL, you can contact the enroute flight advisory service (EFAS) on 122.0 MHz for real-time weather information, including any thunderstorm activity which might affect your route.

✓ The two types of automated weather observation systems currently in use are the automated weather observing system (AWOS) and the automated surface observing system (ASOS).

KEY TERMS

Preflight Weather Briefing

Standard Briefing

Abbreviated Briefing

Outlook Briefing

Telephone Information Briefing
Service (TIBS)

Direct User Access Terminal System
(DUATS)

Transcribed Weather Broadcast
(TWEB)

Hazardous In-Flight Weather
Advisory Service (HIWAS)

Center Weather Advisory (CWA)

Enroute Flight Advisory Service
(EFAS)

Flight Watch

Automated Weather Observing
System (AWOS)

Automated Surface Observation
System (ASOS)

QUESTIONS

1. What information should you provide a preflight weather briefer?

2. Explain the difference between standard, abbreviated, and outlook briefings.

3. True/False. The telephone information briefing service (TIBS) replaces the need for an individual briefing from an FSS or NWS specialist.

4. What type of recorded in-flight weather advisory provides specific route forecasts and winds aloft information over selected NDBs and VORs?

   A. EFAS
   B. TWEB
   C. HIWAS

5. Recall two sources you can use to obtain HIWAS frequencies.

6. What service is provided by EFAS?

   A. Preflight briefings
   B. Closing flight plans
   C. Hazardous weather advisories

7. When flying below 18,000 feet MSL, what frequency should you use to contact EFAS?

8. Which type of automated weather observation system can determine precipitation intensity?

PART IV
PERFORMANCE AND NAVIGATION

SUCCESS FOUR FLIGHTS THURSDAY MORNING ALL AGAINST TWENTY ONE MILE WIND STARTED FROM LEVEL WITH ENGINE POWER ALONE AVERAGE SPEED THROUGH AIR THIRTY ONE MILES LONGEST 59 SECONDS INFORM PRESS HOME CHRISTMAS

OREVELLE WRIGHT

— Telegram message received by Orville Wright's father. Note the telegrapher's misspelling of Orville's name.

PART IV

The preflight preparations for a space mission are complex and detailed. Without dozens of technicians and engineers calculating performance and navigation data, successful spaceflight would be virtually impossible. While the preflight preparations of general aviation pilots are less visible, they are no less important. Part IV introduces techniques which not only reduce your workload in the air, but also result in a safer, more enjoyable flight. *Airplane Performance* will show you how to get the most out of your airplane, whether that means the most speed or the most economy, the shortest takeoffs or the longest range. In *Navigation* you will learn to find your way from place to place using some of the latest technology, as well as the old and reliable techniques that will never go out of date.

CHAPTER 8

AIRPLANE PERFORMANCE

Part IV, Chapter 8 — Airplane Performance

SECTION A
PREDICTING PERFORMANCE

To describe the effectiveness of an aircraft in the jobs it was designed to accomplish, we use the term **performance**. Different designs emphasize speed, maneuverability, load-carrying capability, or the ability to handle short, rough fields. Aircraft designers usually try to accentuate specific performance characteristics at the expense of others. For instance, a competitive aerobatic plane is extremely maneuverable, but has virtually no payload capability other than the pilot. On the other hand, a design optimized for cross-country cargo hauling will sacrifice maneuverability for payload, stability, and economy of operation. [Figure 8-1]

Your ability to predict the performance of an airplane is extremely important. It allows you to determine how much runway you need for takeoff, if you can safely clear obstacles in your departure path, how long it will take you to reach a destination, the quantity of fuel required, and how much runway you will need for landing. Aircraft manufacturers provide much of this information in **performance charts**, usually located in the Performance section of the POH.

Aerobatic Aircraft – This aerobatic airplane is designed for maneuverability and agility.

Fighter Aircraft – The F-16 was designed for vertical penetration, maneuverability, and quick acceleration.

Airliner – The airlines require their aircraft to have the ability to haul a large payload economically and in all weather conditions at a moderate speed.

Agricultural Aircraft – Aircraft designed for agricultural operations must be capable of flying at low altitudes and carrying large loads of chemicals.

General Aviation Trainer – A training aircraft is engineered to be relatively stable with average speed and endurance characteristics.

Figure 8-1. Different kinds of performance are emphasized in the variety of aircraft designs.

AIRCRAFT PERFORMANCE AND DESIGN

In developing performance charts, airplane manufacturers make certain assumptions about the condition of the airplane and ability of the pilot. The pilot is expected to follow normal checklist procedures and to perform each of the required tasks correctly and at the appropriate time. Manufacturers also assume the airplane to be in good condition, with a properly tuned engine and all systems operating normally.

With the aid of these assumptions, the manufacturer develops performance data for the airplane based on actual flight tests. Rather than test the airplane under each and every condition shown on the performance charts, manufacturers evaluate specific flight test data and mathematically derive the remaining information. This data is provided for your use in the form of tables and graphs in the POH.

 ## Flight Testing and Test Pilots

Flight testing is the process of gathering information which will accurately describe the performance of a particular type of airplane. This information can then be used to predict the capabilities of the aircraft.

Test pilots specialize in many different kinds of flight testing. Experimental test pilots fly research aircraft to gather information that will be used to improve aircraft designs. Engineering test pilots evaluate newly designed and experimental aircraft, determine how well they comply with design standards, and make recommendations for improvements. Production test pilots fly new aircraft as they come off assembly lines to make sure they are airworthy and ready to turn over to customers. Test pilots for the airlines not only check airplanes after major overhauls to be sure they are ready to return to service, but also test new aircraft to make sure they are up to standards before the airline accepts them from the manufacturer.

Courtesy of NASA Dryden Flight Research Center

Experimental test pilot Milt Thompson, shown in the accompanying photo, made 14 flights in the X-15 research airplane. He gathered data on aerodynamics, thermodynamics, rocket propulsion, flight controls, and the physiological aspects of high speed, high altitude flight.

TEST PILOT GIVES FREE LESSON!

Here is your chance to learn from veteran experimental test pilot Scott Crossfield as he makes the second-ever dead stick (engine out) landing in the North American F-100.

I called Edwards and declared an emergency. All airborne planes in the vicinity were warned away. I held the ailing F-100 on course, dropping swiftly, lining up for a dead stick landing. I flared out and touched down smoothly. It was in fact one of the best landings I ever made. I then proceeded to violate a cardinal rule of aviation: never try tricks with a compromised airplane. I had already achieved the exceptional, now I would end it with a flourish. I would snake the stricken F-100 right up the ramp and bring it to a stop immediately in front of the NACA hangar . . .

According to the F-100 handbook, the hydraulic brake system was good for three "cycles" (pumps on the brake) engine out. The F-100 was moving at about 15 mph when I turned up the ramp. I hit the brakes once, twice, three times, the plane slowed but not enough. I hit the brakes a fourth time — and my foot went clear to the floorboards. The hydraulic fluid was exhausted. The F-100 rolled on, straight between the yawning hangar doors!

The NACA hangar was then crowded with expensive research tools — the Skyrocket . . . the X-3, X-4, and X-5. Yet somehow, my plane, refusing to halt, squeezed by them all and bored steadily on toward the side wall of the hangar.

Courtesy of NASA Dryden Flight Research Center

The nose of the F-100 crunched through the corrugated aluminum, punching out an eight-inch steel I-beam. I was lucky.

—Scott Crossfield, *Always Another Dawn*

Even test pilots need to stay within limits — and that includes personal limits as well as those of the aircraft. Although a superb pilot and fully aware of his situation, Scott Crossfield gave in to the urge to show off a little — with nearly catastrophic results. No matter how skilled you may become, your attitude as pilot in command will often determine the safety of the flight.

CHART PRESENTATIONS

To be a well-informed pilot, you need to know how to find and interpret published performance information, as well as how to operate the aircraft within the performance limitations imposed by aircraft design and atmospheric conditions. Keep in mind that all performance charts apply to specific aircraft, and the ones you see in this section are only samples. Since performance data can vary significantly between similar models, or even from one model year to the next, you should only refer to the POH for the particular airplane you intend to fly.

Performance charts generally present their information in either table or graph format. The table format usually contains several notes which require you to make adjustments for various conditions which are not accounted for in the body of the chart. Graph presentations usually incorporate more variables, reducing the required adjustments. To get as close to stated performance as possible, you must follow all of the chart procedures and conditions. [Figure 8-2]

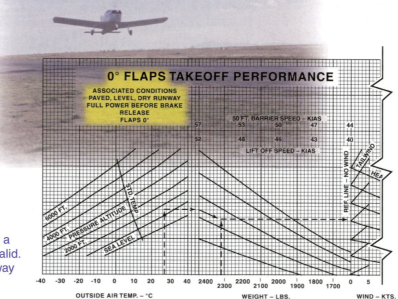

TAKEOFF DISTANCE
MAXIMUM WEIGHT 2400 LBS

SHORT FIELD

CONDITIONS:

Flaps 10°
Full Throttle Prior to Brake Release
Paved, Level, Dry Runway
Zero Wind

NOTES:
1. Short field technique as specified in Section 4.
2. Prior to takeoff from fields above 3000 feet elevation, the mixture should be leaned to give maximum RPM in a full throttle, static runup.
3. Decrease distances 10% for each 9 knots headwind. For operation with tailwinds up to 10 knots, increase distances by 10% for each 2 knots.
4. For operation on a dry, grass runway, increase distances by 15% of the "ground roll" figure.

WEIGHT LBS	TAKEOFF SPEED KIAS		PRESS ALT FT	0°C		10°C		20°C		30°C		40°C	
	LIFT OFF	AT 50 FT		GRND ROLL FT	TOTAL FT TO CLEAR 50 FT OBS	GRND ROLL FT	TOTAL FT TO CLEAR 50 FT OBS	GRND ROLL FT	TOTAL FT TO CLEAR 50 FT OBS	GRND ROLL FT	TOTAL FT TO CLEAR 50 FT OBS	GRND ROLL FT	TOTAL FT TO CLEAR 50 FT OBS
2400	51	56	S. L.	795	1460	860	1570	925	1685	995	1810	1065	1945
			1000	875	1605	940	1725	1015	1860	1090	2000	1170	2155
			2000	960	1770	1035	1910	1115	2060	1200	2220	1290	2395
			3000	1055	1960	1140	2120	1230	2295	1325	2480	1425	2685
			4000	1165	2185	1260	2365	1355	2570	1465	2790	1575	3030
			5000	1285	2445	1390	2660	1500	2895	1620	3160	1745	3455
			6000	1425	2755	1540	3015	1665	3300	1800	3620	1940	3990
			7000	1580	3140	1710	3450	1850	3805	2000	4220	–	–
			8000	1755	3615	1905	4015	2060	4480	–	–	–	–

0° FLAPS TAKEOFF PERFORMANCE

ASSOCIATED CONDITIONS
PAVED, LEVEL, DRY RUNWAY
FULL POWER BEFORE BRAKE RELEASE
FLAPS 0°

Figure 8-2. Both tables and graphs specify a set of conditions under which the chart is valid. As shown, these include flap position, runway type and condition, and application of full power prior to brake release.

TABLE FORMAT

Using the table is straightforward. Find the row and column that most closely match the conditions, and read the appropriate values. The table only gives data for a series of specified values, but you can determine values for conditions which are not shown directly by interpolation. Interpolation is the process of finding an unknown value between two known values. [Figure 8-3]

TAKEOFF DISTANCE
MAXIMUM WEIGHT 2400 LBS

CONDITIONS:
Flaps 10°
Full Throttle Prior to Brake Release
Paved, Level, Dry Runway
Zero Wind

WEIGHT LBS	TAKEOFF SPEED KIAS		PRESS ALT FT	0°C		10°C		20°C		30°C		40°C	
	LIFT OFF	AT 50 FT		GRND ROLL FT	TOTAL FT TO CLEAR 50 FT OBS	GRND ROLL FT	TOTAL FT TO CLEAR 50 FT OBS	GRND ROLL FT	TOTAL FT TO CLEAR 50 FT OBS	GRND ROLL FT	TOTAL FT TO CLEAR 50 FT OBS	GRND ROLL FT	TOTAL FT TO CLEAR 50 FT OBS
2400	51	56	S. L.	795	1460	860	1570	925	1685	995	1810	1065	1945
			1000	875	1605	940	1725	1015	1860	1090	2000	1170	2155
			2000	960	1770	1035	1910	1115	2060	1200	2220	1290	2395
			3000	1055	1960	1140	2120	1230	2295	1325	2480	1425	2685
			4000	1165	2185	1260	2365	1355	2570	1465	2790	1575	3030
			5000	1285	2445	1390	2660	1500	2895	1620	3160	1745	3455
			6000	1425	2755	1540	3015	1665	3300	1800	3620	1940	3990
			7000	1580	3140	1710	3450	1850	3805	2000	4220	–	–
			8000	1755	3615	1905	4015	2060	4480	–	–	–	–

 1 Looking at the sample takeoff chart, you can see that the given pressure altitude of 1,500 feet falls between the 1,000- and 2,000-foot pressure altitude values.

 2 This means if the outside air temperature is 30°C, your ground roll distance will fall between 1,090 and 1,200 feet.

 3 To solve for ground roll, interpolation is necessary. You must first compute the differences between the known values.

 4 The 1,500-foot airport pressure is 50% of the way between 1,000 and 2,000 feet. Therefore, the ground roll also is 50% of the way between 1,090 and 1,200 feet. The answer then, is 1,145 (110-foot difference x .5 + 1,090 feet = 1,145 feet).

Figure 8-3. Since the table only gives data for 1,000 and 2,000 feet, finding the ground roll for a pressure altitude of 1,500 feet requires interpolation. Interpolation could also be used to find a value for an intermediate temperature.

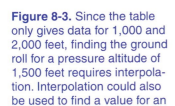

	Pressure Altitude	Ground Roll
	2,000 feet	1,200 feet
	-1,000 feet	1,090 feet
Difference	1,000 feet	110 feet

In practice, pilots often round off values from tables to the more conservative figure. Using values that reflect slightly more adverse circumstances provides a reasonable estimate of performance data, and gives a modest margin of safety.

GRAPH FORMAT

Performance graphs come in many arrangements and configurations, but all are designed to make the process of compensating for several variables fast and accurate. Since a graphic chart has more variables built into it, you must use extra care when determining performance values. You may be tempted to estimate where two lines meet on the chart. This can lead to substantial errors, and with charts that incorporate several sequential steps, a small error at the beginning can lead to a much larger error in the final result.

FACTORS AFFECTING AIRCRAFT PERFORMANCE

Two factors affecting aircraft performance are the weight of the airplane and the wind. Since wings must generate lift in direct proportion to the weight they carry, any increase in weight carries a corresponding penalty in performance, because energy used for lift is unavailable for thrust. Likewise, since it takes more energy to accelerate a heavy airplane to takeoff speed, or to slow it down after landing, runway requirements are greater at heavier weights. The motion of the air itself (wind) can be a help or a hindrance. Airplanes taking off or landing into a strong wind have reduced ground rolls. In cruising flight, the groundspeed and time en route vary depending on the direction and speed of the wind. The wind is an important consideration in planning fuel requirements, since fuel consumption is proportional to flight time.

Atmospheric conditions can decrease air density, increasing the apparent altitude. As pressure decreases, there are fewer air molecules in a given volume, so air density decreases. Because air expands when heated, a cubic foot of air on a hot day will contain fewer air molecules than the same cubic foot of air on a cooler day. Also, air containing water vapor is less dense than dry air.

Since aircraft performance diminishes with altitude, it follows that decreases in air density due to temperature, pressure, or humidity will also reduce performance. For example, when the air is less dense, wings must move through the air faster to develop enough lift for takeoff, resulting in a longer takeoff roll. Lower air density also reduces engine power, since the engine must take in a larger volume of air to get enough air molecules for combustion. Since the propeller works on the same principle as the wings, propeller efficiency also drops. Although lower air density also reduces drag, this results in a relatively minor performance benefit. Decreased air density affects performance in all flight regimes, but the effects are most apparent during takeoff and climb.

When altitude is corrected for nonstandard pressure, the result is pressure altitude. **Density altitude** is the term for pressure altitude that has been corrected for nonstandard temperature. At standard temperatures, pressure altitude and density altitude are the same. On a hot day the density altitude at an airport may be 2,000 or 3,000 feet higher than the field elevation, and as a result, your airplane will perform as though the airport were at the higher elevation. Density altitude differs from field elevation whenever temperature differs from standard conditions, which is most of the time. If you know the field elevation, altimeter setting, and temperature, you can use a chart to find density altitude. [Figure 8-4]

Pressure altitude and density altitude are equal only at standard temperature.

Low atmospheric pressure, high temperature, and high humidity all result in decreased air density and a corresponding increase in density altitude.

As density altitude increases, engine power output, propeller efficiency, and aerodynamic lift all decrease.

Humidity usually has a relatively small effect on performance, so it is ordinarily disregarded in density altitude computations. Even so, when humidity is very high, engine horsepower may be reduced by as much as 7%, and an airplane's total takeoff and climb performance may be reduced by as much as 10%.

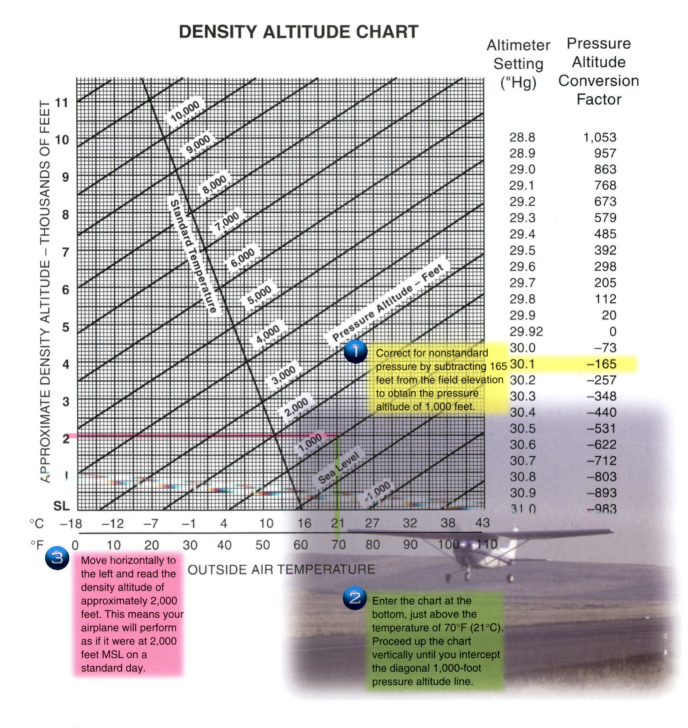

DENSITY ALTITUDE CHART

Altimeter Setting ("Hg)	Pressure Altitude Conversion Factor
28.8	1,053
28.9	957
29.0	863
29.1	768
29.2	673
29.3	579
29.4	485
29.5	392
29.6	298
29.7	205
29.8	112
29.9	20
29.92	0
30.0	−73
30.1	−165
30.2	−257
30.3	−348
30.4	−440
30.5	−531
30.6	−622
30.7	−712
30.8	−803
30.9	−893
31.0	−983

① Correct for nonstandard pressure by subtracting 165 feet from the field elevation to obtain the pressure altitude of 1,000 feet.

③ Move horizontally to the left and read the density altitude of approximately 2,000 feet. This means your airplane will perform as if it were at 2,000 feet MSL on a standard day.

OUTSIDE AIR TEMPERATURE

② Enter the chart at the bottom, just above the temperature of 70°F (21°C). Proceed up the chart vertically until you intercept the diagonal 1,000-foot pressure altitude line.

Figure 8-4. The primary reason for computing density altitude is to help determine aircraft performance. For a field elevation of 1,165 feet MSL, a temperature of 70°F (21°C), and an altimeter setting of 30.10 in. Hg. the density altitude is almost 2,000 feet.

Both density altitude and pressure altitude calculations may be solved using a density altitude chart. See figure 8-4.

 Two and a Half Miles High and Still on the Ground

Lake County Airport, located in Leadville, Colorado has a field elevation of 9,927 feet. Therefore, the standard temperature is 24°F (−4°C). This means that even with the temperature at freezing (+32°F, or 0°C), the density altitude is more than 500 feet above the field elevation.

On a typical summer afternoon, with a low barometric pressure and a temperature of 78°F (26°C), the density altitude at Lake County Airport can get as high as 14,000 feet, more than 4,000 feet above field elevation. Since this altitude is near the service ceiling of many common airplanes, performance may be dangerously degraded.

Many performance charts do not require you to compute density altitude. Instead, compensation is built into the performance chart itself. All you do is apply the correct pressure altitude and temperature. If the chart you are using does not ask you for these variables, you should compute density altitude before using it.

TAKEOFF AND LANDING PERFORMANCE

In addition to density altitude, takeoff performance depends on several factors you can measure or calculate in advance, such as aircraft weight, wind, and runway conditions. Most of these factors also affect landing distances. Under some conditions, takeoff may be impossible within the limits of the available runway.

 High density altitude will reduce aircraft takeoff performance.

AIRCRAFT WEIGHT AND CONFIGURATION

To generate sufficient lift for flight, a heavily loaded airplane must accelerate to a higher speed than the same airplane with a light load. Since acceleration will also be slower, the airplane may need significantly more runway for takeoff. You can readily see the effect of weight in the takeoff distance chart. [Figure 8-5]

TAKEOFF DISTANCE

CONDITIONS:
Flaps 10°
Full Throttle Prior to Brake Release
Paved, Level, Dry Runway
Zero Wind

NOTES:
1. Short field technique as specified in Section 4.
2. Prior to takeoff from fields above 3000 feet elevation, the mixture should be leaned to give maximum RPM in a full throttle, static runup.
3. Decrease distances 10% for each 9 knots headwind. For operation with tailwinds up to 10 knots, increase distances by 10% for each 2 knots.
4. For operation on a dry, grass runway, increase distances by 15% of the "ground roll" figure.

WEIGHT LBS	TAKEOFF SPEED KIAS LIFT OFF	TAKEOFF SPEED KIAS AT 50 FT	PRESS ALT FT	0°C GRND ROLL FT	0°C TOTAL FT TO CLEAR 50 FT OBS	10°C GRND ROLL FT	10°C TOTAL FT TO CLEAR 50 FT OBS	20°C GRND ROLL FT	20°C TOTAL FT TO CLEAR 50 FT OBS	30°C GRND ROLL FT	30°C TOTAL FT TO CLEAR 50 FT OBS	40°C GRND ROLL FT	40°C TOTAL FT TO CLEAR 50 FT OBS
2400	51	56	S.L.	795	1460	860	1570	925	1685	995	1810	1065	1945
			1000	875	1605	940	1725	1015	1860	1090	2000	1170	2155
			2000	960	1770	1035	1910	1115	2060	1200	2220	1290	2395
			3000	1055	1960	1140	2120	1230	2295	1325	2480	1425	2685
			4000	1165	2185	1260	2365	1355	2570	1465	2790	1575	3030
			5000	1285	2445	1390	2660	1500	2895	1620	3160	1745	3455
			6000	1425	2755	1540	3015	1665	3300	1800	3620	1940	3990
			7000	1580	3140	1710	3450	1850	3805	2000	4220	–	–
			8000	1755	3615	1905	4015	2060	4480	–	–	–	–
2200	49	54	S.L.	650	1195	700	1280	750	1375	805	1470	865	1575
			1000	710	1310	765	1405	825	1510	885	1615	950	1735
			2000	780	1440	840	1545	905	1660	975	1785	1045	1915
			3000	855	1585	925	1705	995	1835	1070	1975	1150	2130
			4000	945	1750	1020	1890	1100	2040	1180	2200	1270	2375
			5000	1040	1945	1125	2105	1210	2275	1305	2465	1405	2665
			6000	1150	2170	1240	2355	1340	2555	1445	2775	1555	3020
			7000	1270	2440	1375	2655	1485	2890	1605	3155	1730	3450
			8000	1410	2760	1525	3015	1650	3305	1785	3630	1925	4005
2000	46	51	S.L.	525	970	565	1035	605	1110	650	1185	606	1265
			1000	570	1060	615	1135	665	1215	710	1295	765	1385
			2000	625	1160	675	1240	725	1330	780	1425	840	1525
			3000	690	1270	740	1365	800	1465	860	1570	920	1685
			4000	755	1400	815	1500	880	1615	945	1735	1015	1865
			5000	830	1545	900	1660	970	1790	1040	1925	1120	2070
			6000	920	1710	990	1845	1070	1990	1150	2145	1235	2315
			7000	1015	1900	1095	2055	1180	2225	1275	2405	1370	2605
			8000	1125	2125	1215	2305	1310	2500	1410	2715	1520	2950

Figure 8-5. Increased weight results in an increased ground roll.

If you find you will be unable to safely take off at a particular airport at the airplane's proposed weight, you should consider reducing the weight of the airplane, perhaps by carrying less fuel. Consulting the takeoff performance charts in the POH will tell you how much difference a weight reduction would make in the takeoff roll, and you may find that you would be able to safely take off at that airport with a lower total weight. If you are in doubt, it might be best to delay your takeoff for more favorable density altitude or wind conditions.

Since stall speed is also affected by weight, approach and landing speeds will be higher in a heavily loaded airplane. After touchdown, the ground roll will be longer in a heavily loaded airplane due to the additional kinetic energy that must be dissipated by the brakes and wheels.

In most airplanes, the aerodynamic configuration can be changed to enhance takeoff and landing performance. While large aircraft employ a wide variety of devices, most training aircraft simply use wing flaps. Many high performance light airplanes partially extend the flaps on takeoff to provide greater lift at low speeds. Flaps are used during landing approaches to steepen the glide path and to permit lower touchdown speeds. Your use of flaps on landing approach will vary with field conditions and length. Normally, the use of flaps and a lower indicated approach speed are desirable when landing on a short runway or soft runway surface, such as grass.

SURFACE WINDS

Takeoff and landing distances are influenced by both the speed and direction of surface winds. Since a headwind reduces the amount of speed the airplane must gain to attain flying speed, it reduces ground roll. During landing, a headwind reduces the groundspeed at touchdown, so the landing roll will also be shorter. Because surface winds will not always be exactly aligned with the runway in use, you need a method of determining what portion of the wind is acting along the runway and what portion is acting across it. The headwind component refers to that portion of the wind which acts straight down the runway toward the airplane. The crosswind component is the portion of the wind which acts perpendicular to the runway. Most airplanes have a maximum demonstrated crosswind component stated in the POH. You can easily compute headwind and crosswind components by using a wind component chart. [Figure 8-6]

Figure 8-6. This example shows how to find the headwind and crosswind components for a wind from 060° at 20 knots when using Runway 3. When you use a wind component chart, remember that both the runway number and surface winds are given in magnetic direction.

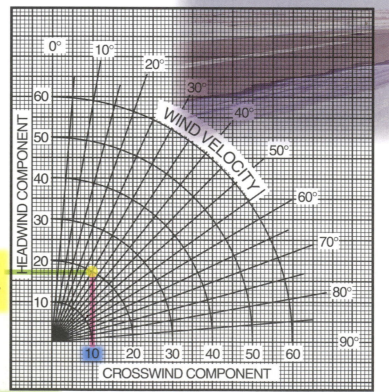

1. Determine the angle between the runway and the wind. (60° − 30° = 30°)

2. Find the point where the wind angle line and the wind velocity arc meet.

3. Look to the left to find the headwind component of 17 knots.

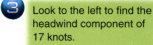

4. Find the crosswind component by following the vertical lines down to the bottom of the chart.

5. The crosswind component is 10 knots.

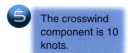

The **tailwind component** is the portion of the wind which acts directly on the tail of the airplane. Attempting to take off with a tailwind component (downwind) adds much more ground roll than the same amount of headwind would reduce it. For example, if you look at Note 3 on the chart in figure 8-5, you will see that taking off in this airplane with

Headwind and crosswind components are computed by using a crosswind component graph. See figure 8-6.

a 9 knot headwind reduces ground roll by 10%, but taking off with a 9 knot tailwind increases the ground roll by 45%. Tailwind components have a similar effect on landing distances. Another insidious effect of downwind landings is the pilot's perception of speed over the ground. Because of the greater groundspeed compared to normal approach speeds, some pilots unconsciously slow to a speed that looks right outside the cockpit, but that actually may be dangerously close to the stall speed.

RUNWAY GRADIENT AND SURFACE

Runway conditions relating to aircraft performance data generally specify a paved and level runway with a smooth, dry surface. If any of these conditions are different for the runway you use, you need to adjust the takeoff and landing distances using the methods described in the chart notes.

The **runway gradient**, or **slope**, refers to the amount of change in runway height over its length. Gradient is usually expressed as a percentage. For example, a gradient of 2 % means the runway height changes 2 feet for each 100 feet of runway length (100 × 2% = 2). A positive gradient indicates the height of the runway increases, while a negative value means it decreases. A positive gradient is unfavorable for takeoff, because the airplane must take off uphill. Since landing uphill reduces the ground roll, a positive gradient is desirable for landing. A negative gradient has the opposite effect on both takeoffs and landings. Runway slope is listed in the *Airport/Facility Directory* when it is 3/10 of 1% or more. [Figure 8-7]

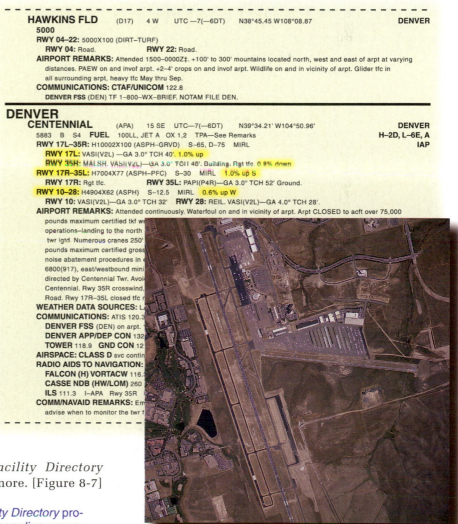

Figure 8-7. The *Airport/Facility Directory* provides pilots with information regarding runway gradient.

Generally, any runway surface that is not hard, smooth, and dry will increase the takeoff roll. This is due to the inability of the tires to roll smoothly along the runway. For example, on runways that are muddy, or covered with grass or snow, the tires may sink slightly into the ground. This reduces the airplane's acceleration, sometimes to the extent that it may be impossible to accelerate to takeoff speed.

The condition of the runway surface also affects the landing roll and braking. **Braking effectiveness** refers to how much braking power you can apply without skidding the tires. For the most part, it depends on the amount of friction between the tires and the runway. Braking effectiveness is considered normal on a dry runway, but if the runway is wet, less friction is available and your landing roll-out will increase. In some cases, you may lose braking effectiveness because of **hydroplaning**, which happens when a thin layer of water separates the tires from the runway. [Figure 8-8]

Figure 8-8. Exercise caution when operating on a wet runway because of the potential for hydroplaning.

Braking effectiveness also may be completely lost on ice-covered runways. If you must operate in conditions where braking effectiveness is reduced, be sure the runway length is adequate and surface wind is favorable. Although mud, grass, and snow may reduce the friction between tires and the runway, in some cases they may reduce the landing roll. This is because they act as obstructions to the tires.

TAKEOFF AND LANDING PERFORMANCE CHARTS

Most manufacturers supply charts for determining takeoff and landing performance. The use of a table for determining takeoff performance is shown in figure 8-9. Determining landing distance from a graph is explained in figure 8-10.

Figure 8-9. The length of the takeoff roll in this example is based on a pressure altitude of 2,000 feet, calm winds, a temperature of 30° C, a flap setting of 10°, an aircraft weight of 2,400 pounds, and a paved, level, and dry runway. The ground roll distance is 1,200 feet, and the total distance to clear a 50-foot obstacle is 2,220 feet.

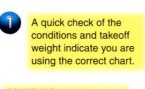

① A quick check of the conditions and takeoff weight indicate you are using the correct chart.

TAKEOFF DISTANCE
MAXIMUM WEIGHT 2400 LBS

SHORT FIELD

CONDITIONS:
Flaps 10°
Full Throttle Prior to Brake Release
Paved, Level, Dry Runway
Zero Wind

WEIGHT LBS	TAKEOFF SPEED KIAS		PRESS ALT FT	0°C		10°C		20°C		30°C		40°C	
	LIFT OFF	AT 50 FT		GRND ROLL FT	TOTAL FT TO CLEAR 50 FT OBS	GRND ROLL FT	TOTAL FT TO CLEAR 50 FT OBS	GRND ROLL FT	TOTAL FT TO CLEAR 50 FT OBS	GRND ROLL FT	TOTAL FT TO CLEAR 50 FT OBS	GRND ROLL FT	TOTAL FT TO CLEAR 50 FT OBS
2400	51	56	S.L.	795	1460	860	1570	925	1685	995	1810	1065	1945
			1000	875	1605	940	1725	1015	1860	1090	2000	1170	2155
			2000	960	1770	1035	1910	1115	2060	1200	2220	1290	2395
			3000	1055	1960	1140	2120	1230	2295	1325	2480	1425	2685
			4000	1165	2185	1260	2365	1355	2570	1465	2790	1575	3030
			5000	1285	2445	1390	2660	1500	2895	1620	3160	1745	3455
			6000	1425	2755	1540	3015	1665	3300	1800	3620	1940	3990
			7000	1580	3140	1710	3450	1850	3805	2000	4220	–	–
			8000	1755	3615	1905	4015	2060	4480	–	–	–	–

② Note the takeoff speed of 51 knots and the speed of 56 knots shortly after takeoff at 50 feet.

③ Enter the tabular data of the pressure altitude of 2,000 feet. Proceed horizontally to the column for 30°C. The ground roll distance is 1,200 feet, and the total distance to clear a 50-foot obstacle is 2,220 feet.

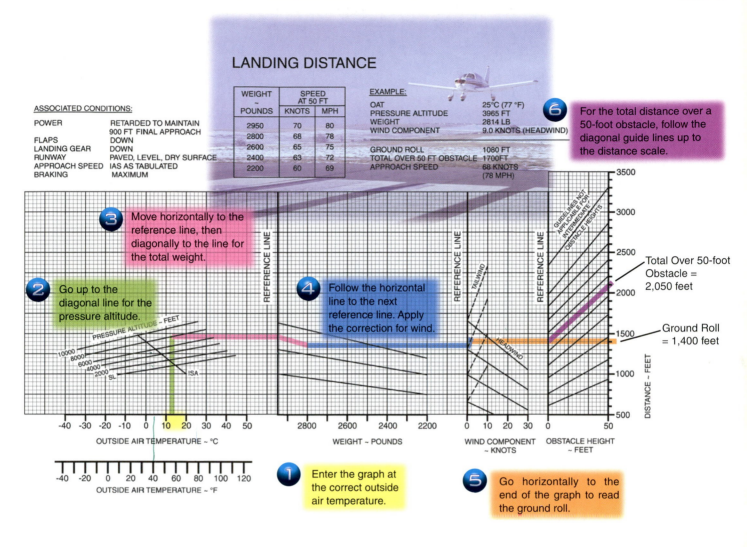

LANDING DISTANCE

WEIGHT ~ POUNDS	SPEED AT 50 FT	
	KNOTS	MPH
2950	70	80
2800	68	78
2600	65	75
2400	63	72
2200	60	69

ASSOCIATED CONDITIONS:

POWER	RETARDED TO MAINTAIN 900 FT FINAL APPROACH
FLAPS	DOWN
LANDING GEAR	DOWN
RUNWAY	PAVED, LEVEL, DRY SURFACE
APPROACH SPEED	IAS AS TABULATED
BRAKING	MAXIMUM

EXAMPLE:

OAT	25°C (77 °F)
PRESSURE ALTITUDE	3965 FT
WEIGHT	2814 LB
WIND COMPONENT	9.0 KNOTS (HEADWIND)
GROUND ROLL	1080 FT
TOTAL OVER 50 FT OBSTACLE	1700FT
APPROACH SPEED	68 KNOTS (78 MPH)

6 For the total distance over a 50-foot obstacle, follow the diagonal guide lines up to the distance scale.

3 Move horizontally to the reference line, then diagonally to the line for the total weight.

2 Go up to the diagonal line for the pressure altitude.

4 Follow the horizontal line to the next reference line. Apply the correction for wind.

Total Over 50-foot Obstacle = 2,050 feet

Ground Roll = 1,400 feet

1 Enter the graph at the correct outside air temperature.

5 Go horizontally to the end of the graph to read the ground roll.

Figure 8-10. This example shows that 2,050 feet is required to land over a 50-foot obstacle with a 2 knot tailwind, at a pressure altitude of 8,000 feet, a temperature of 13°C, and a weight of 2,800 pounds. The ground roll distance is 1,400 feet.

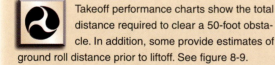

Takeoff performance charts show the total distance required to clear a 50-foot obstacle. In addition, some provide estimates of ground roll distance prior to liftoff. See figure 8-9.

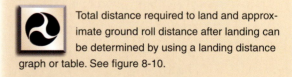

Total distance required to land and approximate ground roll distance after landing can be determined by using a landing distance graph or table. See figure 8-10.

Some pilot's operating handbooks recommend specific **approach airspeeds** for various flap settings and aircraft weights. In general, these recommended airspeeds should be used regardless of temperature and altitude combinations. As you recall, operating at higher density altitudes will result in higher than indicated true airspeeds. This is important to remember when landing at airports at higher elevations than those to which you have become accustomed. If you do not monitor the airspeed indicator, the higher groundspeed could lead you to slow to a dangerously low airspeed. This effect is similar to the downwind landing situation described earlier.

CLIMB PERFORMANCE

Most of the factors affecting takeoff performance also affect the climb capability of an aircraft. The pilot's operating handbook for the airplane lists airspeeds for a variety of climbing flight conditions. Two of the most important are the **best angle-of-climb airspeed** (V_X), and the **best rate-of-climb airspeed** (V_Y). [Figure 8-11]

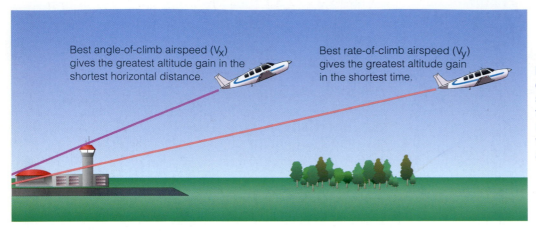

Best angle-of-climb airspeed (V_x) gives the greatest altitude gain in the shortest horizontal distance.

Best rate-of-climb airspeed (V_y) gives the greatest altitude gain in the shortest time.

Figure 8-11. Best angle-of-climb airspeed (V_x) results in a steeper climb path, although the airplane takes longer to reach the same altitude than it would at the best rate-of-climb airspeed (V_y).

CLIMB SPEEDS

The best angle-of-climb airspeed (V_x) is normally used for obstacle clearance immediately after takeoff. Because of the increased pitch attitude at V_X, your forward visibility is limited. Best angle-of-climb speed should be used anytime you need to gain the maximum amount of altitude in the minimum horizontal distance.

The best angle-of-climb airspeed (V_x) provides the greatest gain in altitude in the shortest distance during climb after takeoff.

Normally, you use best rate-of-climb (V_Y) after you have cleared all obstacles during departure. Best rate-of-climb speed gives the greatest altitude gain in a given time. After traffic pattern departure, you may use a cruise climb when climbing to cruising altitude. You can also use cruise climb during the enroute portion of a flight to climb to a higher altitude. **Cruise climb speed** is generally higher than V_X or V_Y, and the rate of climb is lower. In addition to better engine cooling and improved forward visibility, faster climb speeds provide better cross-country speeds, cutting down the total time enroute. [Figure 8-12]

The best rate-of-climb airspeed (V_y) provides the greatest gain in altitude over a period of time.

Before an airplane can climb, it must have a reserve of power or thrust. At any given speed, more power is required for a sustained climb than for unaccelerated level flight. Since propeller-driven airplanes lose power and thrust with increasing altitude, both the best angle-of-climb and best rate-of-climb speeds change as you climb. When the airplane is unable to climb any further, it has reached its **absolute ceiling**. Another important altitude, known as the **service ceiling**, refers to the altitude where a single-engine airplane is able to maintain a maximum climb of only 100 feet per minute. This altitude is more commonly used than absolute ceiling, since it represents the airplane's practical ceiling. [Figure 8-13]

Normal Cruise Climb

Best Angle of Climb

Courtesy of Paul Bowen

Figure 8-12. Climb airspeeds vary between aircraft. For example, the Cessna 172 has a normal cruise climb speed of 75-85 knots, however the pilot's operating handbook recommends 59 knots for the best angle-of-climb airspeed. The high-performance Pilatus PC-12 has a normal cruise climb airspeed of 125 knots and a best angle-of-climb speed of 110 knots.

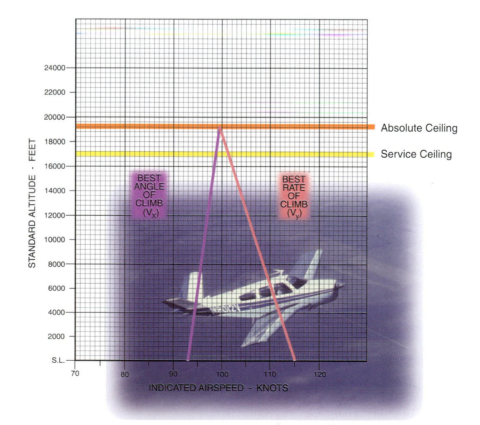

Absolute Ceiling

Service Ceiling

BEST ANGLE OF CLIMB (V_x)

BEST RATE OF CLIMB (V_y)

STANDARD ALTITUDE - FEET

INDICATED AIRSPEED - KNOTS

Figure 8-13. As altitude increases, the speed for best angle-of-climb increases, and the speed for best rate-of-climb decreases. The point at which these two speeds meet is the absolute ceiling of the airplane.

CLIMB PERFORMANCE CHARTS

Climb performance data included in the pilot's operating handbook provides the approximate performance that can be expected under various conditions. Many pilot's operating handbooks provide time, fuel, and distance-to-climb data. [Figure 8-14]

 Verify that you have the proper chart and the conditions specified on the chart are met.

TIME, FUEL, AND DISTANCE TO CLIMB

MAXIMUM RATE OF CLIMB

CONDITIONS:
Flaps Up
Full Throttle
Standard Temperature

 A check of the notes, however, indicates that you must add an additional 1.1 gallons of fuel for the engine start, taxi, and takeoff allowances.

NOTES:
1. Add 1.1 gallons of fuel for engine start, taxi and takeoff allowances.
2. Mixture leaned above 3000 feet for maximum RPM.
3. Increase time, fuel and distance by 10% for each 10° above standard temperature.
4. Distances shown are based on zero wind.

 Determine the time, fuel, and distance credits to be applied for departing an airport located at 2,000 feet.

WEIGHT LBS	PRESSURE ALTITUDE FT	TEMP °C	CLIMB SPEED KIAS	RATE OF CLIMB FPM	FROM SEA LEVEL		
					TIME MIN	FUEL USED GALLONS	DISTANCE NM
2400	S. L.	15	76	700	0	0.0	0
	1000	13	76	655	1	0.3	2
	2000	11	75	610	3	0.6	4
	3000	9	75	560	5	1.0	6
	4000	7	74	515	7	1.4	9
	5000	5	74	470	9	1.7	11
	6000	3	73	425	11	2.2	14
	7000	1	72	375	14	2.6	18
	8000	-1	72	330	17	3.1	22
	9000	-3	71	285	20	3.6	26
	10,000	-5	71	240	24	4.2	32
	11,000	-7	70	190	29	4.9	38
	12,000	-9	70	145	35	5.8	47

 Read the time, fuel, and distance to climb to 8,000 feet.

 After you subtract the credits, the net values are 14 minutes, 2.5 gallons, and 18 miles.

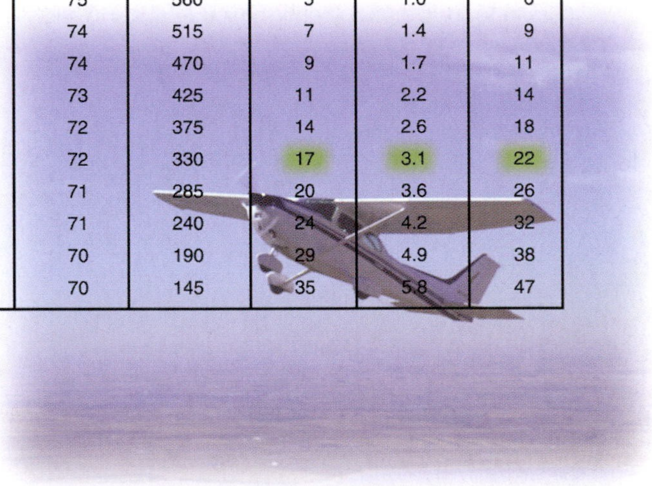

 The values to climb from 2,000 feet to 8,000 feet are a total of 14 minutes, 3.6 gallons, and 18 miles.

Figure 8-14. The time, fuel, and distance-to-climb table is a little different from other performance tables since it is used in two stages. First, determine the time, fuel, and distance to climb from sea level to cruising altitude. Then, subtract the amount of time, fuel, and distance required to climb to the altitude of your departure point, since you have essentially already climbed to that altitude. This example shows how you would use the chart to plan a climb from an airport with an elevation of 2,000 feet to a cruising altitude of 8,000 feet.

The type of climb performance information provided in figure 8-14 is helpful in preflight planning. It permits accurate estimates of three important factors affecting the climb segment of a flight: time, fuel, and distance. A climb performance graph allows you to determine the best rate of climb using temperature and pressure altitude. [Figure 8-15]

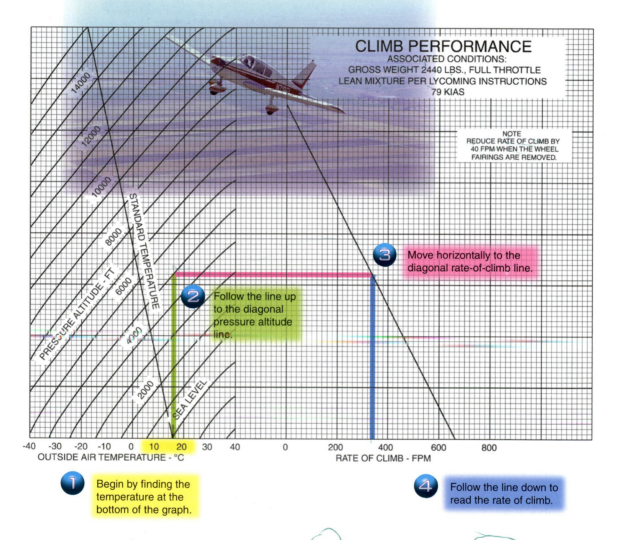

Figure 8-15. With an outside air temperature of 16°C and a pressure altitude of 5,000 feet, you can expect a rate of climb of 340 feet per minute. As shown at the top of the graph, the climb performance values were calculated with a gross weight of 2,440 pounds, full throttle, 79 knots indicated airspeed, and the use of proper leaning procedures.

A high density altitude decreases engine performance, aerodynamic lift, and propeller efficiency with a resulting reduction in climb performance.

Time-to-Climb Record

On January 23, 1996, Bruce Bohannon climbed from sea level to 33,800 feet MSL in one hour flat, simultaneously setting new time-to-climb, altitude in horizontal flight, and absolute altitude records in the Aeroshell Special Formula One racing plane. He broke the previous time-to-climb to 9,000 meters record for this class of aircraft set two years before by astronaut and general aviation pilot Robert "Hoot" Gibson. Incidentally, Gibson set his record in the same airplane.

The aircraft uses the same basic Continental O-200 engine widely used in light airplanes like the Cessna 150, but it also has sophisticated engine control and nitrous oxide injection systems. The airplane used 5.8 gallons of 100LL avgas and 20 pounds of nitrous oxide on the record flight. To obtain maximum performance, the cylinder temperatures were kept at 600°F. Piston walls begin to melt at 605°F.

Courtesy of Anita Infante via Shell Oil Products

Bruce Bohannon also set a new time-to-climb record in the Exxon Flyin' Tiger on July 30, 2000 at Airventure 2000. In just 17 minutes, and 37 seconds Bruce and the Exxon Flyin' Tiger reached 30,000 feet.

CRUISE PERFORMANCE

The manufacturers of today's light airplanes provide cruise performance charts to indicate rate of fuel consumption, true airspeed, range, and endurance. They will give you a close approximation of the performance you can expect at different altitudes and power settings. Any deviation from the specific information upon which the chart computations are based will affect the accuracy of the results. For example, many cruise performance charts are based on standard atmospheric conditions with zero wind. During flight planning, you must compensate for nonstandard conditions, and use flight times that take into account the effects of predicted winds. You should remember that wind has a significant effect on the distance an aircraft can fly, but no effect on its rate of fuel consumption or the total time it can remain aloft.

In selecting your **cruising speed**, you usually want to cover the distance to be traveled in the shortest period of time, but there are many other factors that might influence your decision. There may be times when you want to use the minimum amount of fuel, or stay aloft for the greatest period of time. If you understand the trade-offs you make between time, power, fuel consumption, range, and speed, you will be able to make choices that maximize the pleasure and utility you get from flying.

PERFORMANCE SPEEDS

In addition to the selection of cruising speeds provided in the charts, there are some specific power settings and speeds that result in maximum performance. Three important speeds are maximum level flight speed, maximum endurance speed, and maximum range speed. These speeds have been determined by the manufacturer, and balance the combination of available power, fuel economy, lift and drag to obtain the best possible performance for the situation described.

In level flight, the maximum speed of the airplane is limited by the amount of power produced by the engine and the total drag generated by the airplane. If thrust exceeds total drag when you apply power, the airplane accelerates. When the force of total drag equals

What Is the Power Curve?

More correctly called the power-required curve, it shows the amount of power necessary to maintain level flight at airspeeds throughout the aircraft performance envelope. The left end of the curve is the stall speed. Flight at low airspeeds requires a high angle of attack, and a great deal of power is required to overcome the resulting induced drag. As airspeed increases, the wing generates more lift with less induced drag, and less power is needed for level flight until, at the low point of the graph, the highest efficiency is reached. This is the point where the airplane will maintain level flight with the least amount of power. As speed increases past this point, the additional power is being used to overcome increased parasite drag.

You may hear other pilots talk about operating on the back side of the power curve. This refers to the curve to the left of the low point, where any reduction in airspeed requires an increase in power to maintain level flight. Through the majority of the graph (the front side of the curve) a decrease in airspeed means that less power is needed for level flight. Flying on the back side of the curve is discouraged, since a reduction in speed may demand more power than the engine can supply, or an unplanned drop in power could result in an involuntary descent. Since these speeds are relatively close to the stall, even minor engine trouble could leave you with two choices: descend or stall. You should try to avoid situations where you are dependent on engine power to prevent a stall.

the force of full thrust, the airplane is flying at its **maximum level flight speed**. [Figure 8-16]

Figure 8-16. The curved power-required line shows the amount of power necessary to maintain level flight at various speeds. The power-available line is also curved, since power available in the typical single-engine airplane is a function of airspeed. The point at which these two curves cross is where the forces of thrust and drag are in balance and where maximum level flight speed occurs.

The **maximum range speed** lets you travel the greatest distance for a given amount of fuel. You can think of it as getting the most miles per gallon out of the airplane. This speed is determined by considering the speed and rate of fuel consumption at a given power setting. The setting which yields the greatest distance traveled per gallon of fuel burned is the

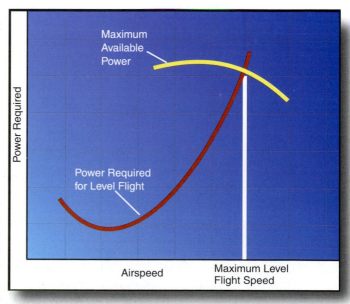

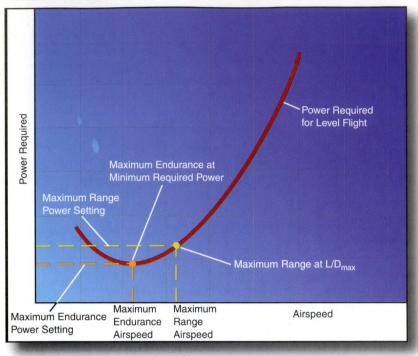

power setting which provides maximum range speed. This speed produces the minimum total drag with enough lift to maintain altitude. It is where the lift-to-drag ratio is greatest, and is referred to as L/D_{max}. The speed and power setting which allows the airplane to remain aloft for the longest possible time is called the **maximum endurance speed**. It uses the minimum amount of power necessary to maintain level flight, and may be thought of as the speed that provides the most hours per gallon. [Figure 8-17]

Figure 8-17. Maximum endurance speed occurs at the lowest point on the power-required curve. This is the speed and the lowest power setting which will sustain an airplane in steady, level flight. Maximum range speed is a higher airspeed that minimizes total drag.

USING CRUISE PERFORMANCE CHARTS

Cruise performance charts vary considerably. A cruise performance table used to determine fuel flow, fuel consumption, true airspeed, and manifold pressure is shown in figure 8-18.

Figure 8-18. An airplane flying at a pressure altitude of 8,000 feet, at standard temperature, and a power setting of 2,450 r.p.m., should achieve approximately 161 knots true airspeed and a fuel consumption rate of 11.5 gallons per hour.

CRUISE POWER SETTINGS
65% MAXIMUM CONTINUOUS POWER (OR FULL THROTTLE)
2800 POUNDS

PRESS ALT.	IOAT		ENGINE SPEED	MAN PRESS	FUEL FLOW PER ENGINE		TAS		IOAT		ENGINE SPEED	MAN PRESS	FUEL FLOW PER ENGINE		TAS		IOAT		ENGINE SPEED	MAN PRESS	FUEL FLOW PER ENGINE		TAS	
	ISA –20 °C (–36 °F)								STANDARD DAY (ISA)								ISA + 20 °C (+36 °F)							
FEET	°F	°C	RPM	IN HG	PSI	GPH	KTS	MPH	°F	°C	RPM	IN HG	PSI	GPH	KTS	MPH	°F	°C	RPM	IN HG	PSI	GPH	KTS	MPH
SL	27	-3	2450	20.7	6.6	11.5	147	169	63	17	2450	21.2	6.6	11.5	150	173	99	37	2450	21.8	6.6	11.5	153	176
2000	19	-7	2450	20.4	6.6	11.5	149	171	55	13	2450	21.0	6.6	11.5	153	176	91	33	2450	21.5	6.6	11.5	156	180
4000	12	-11	2450	20.1	6.6	11.5	152	175	48	9	2450	20.7	6.6	11.5	156	180	84	29	2450	21.3	6.6	11.5	159	183
6000	5	-15	2450	19.8	6.6	11.5	155	178	41	5	2450	20.4	6.6	11.5	158	182	79	26	2450	21.0	6.6	11.5	161	185
8000	-2	-19	2450	19.5	6.6	11.5	157	181	36	2	2450	20.2	6.6	11.5	161	185	72	22	2450	20.8	6.6	11.5	164	189
10000	-8	-22	2450	19.2	6.6	11.5	160	184	28	-2	2450	19.9	6.6	11.5	163	188	64	18	2450	20.3	6.5	11.4	166	191
12000	-15	-26	2450	18.8	6.4	11.3	162	186	21	-6	2450	18.8	6.1	10.9	163	188	57	14	2450	18.8	5.9	10.6	163	188
14000	-22	-30	2450	17.4	5.8	10.5	159	183	14	-10	2450	17.4	5.6	10.1	160	184	50	10	2450	17.4	5.4	9.8	160	184
16000	-29	-34	2450	16.1	5.3	9.7	156	180	7	-14	2450	16.1	5.1	9.4	156	180	43	6	2450	16.1	4.9	9.1	155	178

NOTES: 1. Full throttle manifold pressure settings are approximate.
2. Shaded area represents operation with full throttle.

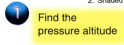 Find the pressure altitude

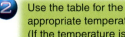 Use the table for the appropriate temperature. (If the temperature is between the given values, use interpolation.)

 Read the true airspeed and fuel consumption for your chosen power setting.

A range graph is used to determine aircraft range based on specific conditions. In the range graph shown in figure 8-19, you can determine horsepower combinations and expected range in nautical miles for various temperatures and pressure altitudes. This particular graph shows range with or without reserves.

 Cruise performance tables are used to calculate manifold pressure, fuel flow, fuel consumption, and true airspeed. See figure 8-18.

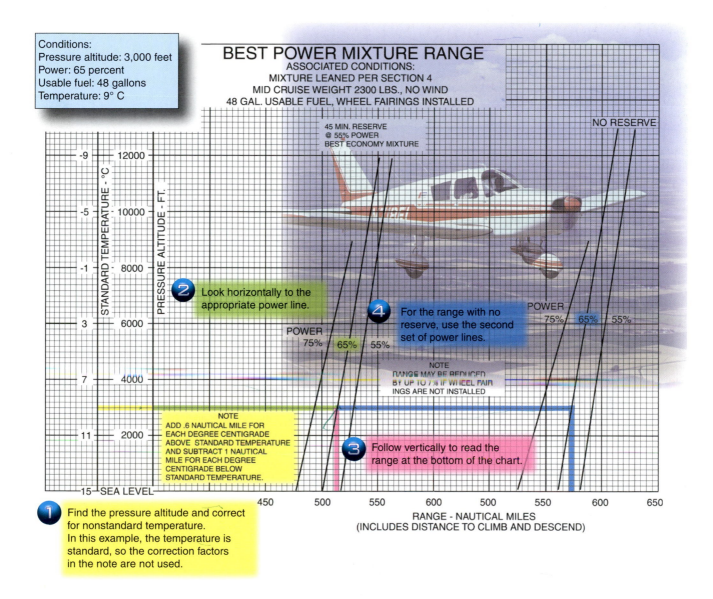

Conditions:
Pressure altitude: 3,000 feet
Power: 65 percent
Usable fuel: 48 gallons
Temperature: 9° C

BEST POWER MIXTURE RANGE
ASSOCIATED CONDITIONS:
MIXTURE LEANED PER SECTION 4
MID CRUISE WEIGHT 2300 LBS., NO WIND
48 GAL. USABLE FUEL, WHEEL FAIRINGS INSTALLED

45 MIN. RESERVE
@ 55% POWER
BEST ECONOMY MIXTURE

NO RESERVE

2 Look horizontally to the appropriate power line.

4 For the range with no reserve, use the second set of power lines.

POWER 75% 65% 55%

POWER 75% 65% 55%

NOTE
RANGE MAY BE REDUCED BY UP TO 7% IF WHEEL FAIRINGS ARE NOT INSTALLED

NOTE
ADD .6 NAUTICAL MILE FOR EACH DEGREE CENTIGRADE ABOVE STANDARD TEMPERATURE AND SUBTRACT 1 NAUTICAL MILE FOR EACH DEGREE CENTIGRADE BELOW STANDARD TEMPERATURE.

3 Follow vertically to read the range at the bottom of the chart.

1 Find the pressure altitude and correct for nonstandard temperature. In this example, the temperature is standard, so the correction factors in the note are not used.

RANGE - NAUTICAL MILES
(INCLUDES DISTANCE TO CLIMB AND DESCEND)

Figure 8-19. At standard temperature and a pressure altitude of 3,000 feet, using 65% power in an aircraft with 48 gallons of usable fuel, you can expect a range of 512 nautical miles with normal reserves, or 573 nautical miles with no reserve.

To determine the amount of power for various altitude/r.p.m. combinations, you should consult either an engine or cruise performance chart. Formats vary, but a typical chart is shown in figure 8-20.

Figure 8-20. Engine performance charts are helpful in calculating the engine speed required for a specific cruise power setting. At a pressure altitude of 5,000 feet and an outside air temperature of 16°C, approximately 2,620 r.p.m. must be used to obtain 75% power. At 75%, best power fuel flow is 10.0 g.p.h. and best economy fuel flow is 8.5 g.p.h.

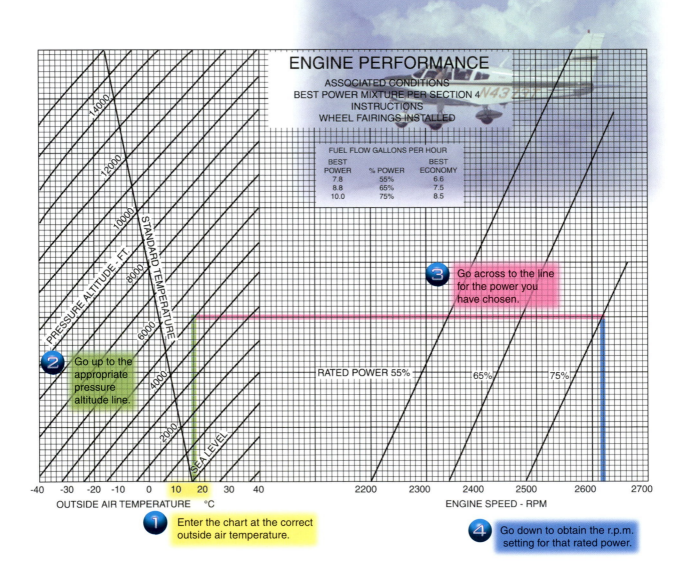

ENGINE PERFORMANCE

ASSOCIATED CONDITIONS
BEST POWER MIXTURE PER SECTION 4
INSTRUCTIONS
WHEEL FAIRINGS INSTALLED

FUEL FLOW GALLONS PER HOUR

BEST POWER	% POWER	BEST ECONOMY
7.8	55%	6.6
8.8	65%	7.5
10.0	75%	8.5

3 Go across to the line for the power you have chosen.

2 Go up to the appropriate pressure altitude line.

RATED POWER 55%   65%   75%

1 Enter the chart at the correct outside air temperature.

4 Go down to obtain the r.p.m. setting for that rated power.

OUTSIDE AIR TEMPERATURE   °C

ENGINE SPEED - RPM

SUMMARY CHECKLIST

✓ The pilot's operating handbook presents numerous charts which allow you to predict the airplane's performance accurately. They pertain to the takeoff, climb, cruise, descent, and landing phases of flight.

✓ Density altitude, wind, and runway conditions can greatly affect airplane performance.

✓ Takeoff performance depends mainly upon factors that can be measured or calculated in advance, such as density altitude, pressure altitude, temperature, wind, aircraft weight, and runway gradient or surface.

✓ You can easily break down wind direction and speed into headwind and crosswind components by using a wind component chart.

✓ Best angle-of-climb airspeed (V_x) is used to gain the most altitude in the shortest horizontal distance.

✓ The best rate-of-climb airspeed (V_y) gives the maximum altitude gain in the least amount of time.

✓ Typically, a normal or cruise climb airspeed is used when climbing for prolonged periods of time.

✓ Climb performance data is included in the POH to provide you with an idea of the approximate performance that can be expected under various conditions.

✓ When choosing a cruising speed, you should consider fuel consumption, range, and the effects of winds.

KEY TERMS

Performance	Approach Airspeeds
Performance Charts	Best Angle-of-Climb Airspeed (V_x)
Interpolation	Best Rate-of-Climb Airspeed (V_y)
Density Altitude	Cruise Climb Speed
Headwind Component	Absolute Ceiling
Crosswind Component	Service Ceiling
Tailwind Component	Cruising Speed
Runway Gradient	Maximum Level Flight Speed
Runway Slope	Maximum Range Speed
Braking Effectiveness	Maximum Endurance Speed
Hydroplaning	

QUESTIONS

1. Where can you normally find the performance charts for your airplane?

2. Describe how density altitude affects aircraft performance.

3. True/False. Takeoff performance depends mainly upon factors that can be measured or calculated in advance, such as density altitude, pressure altitude, temperature, wind, aircraft weight, and runway gradient or surface.

4. Refer to the wind component chart shown below to determine the headwind and crosswind component for a departure on Runway 18 with a reported wind of 210° at 20 knots.

WIND COMPONENTS

NOTE:
Maximum demonstrated crosswind velocity is 15 knots (not a limitation).

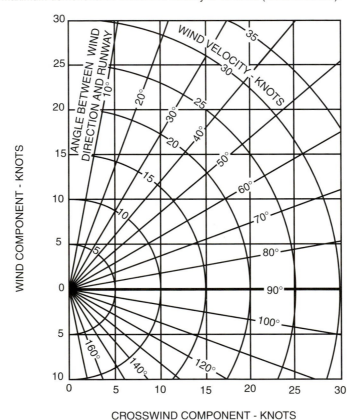

5. What is the runway gradient?

A. The material used to surface the runway
B. The amount of change in runway height over its length
C. The direction of the runway as it relates to magnetic north

6. Use the chart shown below and the following conditions to determine the ground roll and distance necessary to clear a 50-foot obstacle.

Conditions:
Pressure Altitude:	6,000 feet
Temperature:	20°C
Flaps:	10°
Runway:	Paved, level, and dry
Wind:	Calm
Weight:	2,400 pounds

TAKEOFF DISTANCE
MAXIMUM WEIGHT 2400 LBS

SHORT FIELD

CONDITIONS:
Flaps 10°
Full Throttle Prior to Brake Release
Paved, Level, Dry Runway
Zero Wind

NOTES:
1. Short field technique as specified in Section 4.
2. Prior to takeoff from fields above 3000 feet elevation, the mixture should be leaned to give maximum RPM in a full throttle, static runup.
3. Decrease distances 10% for each 9 knots headwind. For operation with tailwinds up to 10 knots, increase distances by 10% for each 2 knots.
4. For operation on a dry, grass runway, increase distances by 15% of the "ground roll" figure.

WEIGHT LBS	TAKEOFF SPEED KIAS		PRESS ALT FT	0°C		10°C		20°C		30°C		40°C	
	LIFT OFF	AT 50 FT		GRND ROLL FT	TOTAL FT TO CLEAR 50 FT OBS	GRND ROLL FT	TOTAL FT TO CLEAR 50 FT OBS	GRND ROLL FT	TOTAL FT TO CLEAR 50 FT OBS	GRND ROLL FT	TOTAL FT TO CLEAR 50 FT OBS	GRND ROLL FT	TOTAL FT TO CLEAR 50 FT OBS
2400	51	56	S. L.	795	1460	860	1570	925	1685	995	1810	1065	1945
			1000	875	1605	940	1725	1015	1860	1090	2000	1170	2155
			2000	960	1770	1035	1910	1115	2060	1200	2220	1290	2395
			3000	1055	1960	1140	2120	1230	2295	1325	2480	1425	2685
			4000	1165	2185	1260	2365	1355	2570	1465	2790	1575	3030
			5000	1285	2445	1390	2660	1500	2895	1620	3160	1745	3455
			6000	1425	2755	1540	3015	1665	3300	1800	3620	1940	3990
			7000	1580	3140	1710	3450	1850	3805	2000	4220	–	–
			8000	1755	3615	1905	4015	2060	4480	–	–	–	–

7. True/False. As altitude increases, the best angle-of-climb speed will decrease, and the best rate-of-climb speed will increase.

8. Name the three important factors affecting the climb segment of a flight.

9. Select the items which would be found on a cruise performance chart.

A. Time, fuel, and distance to climb
B. Fuel consumption and true airspeed at various power settings
C. Power required for level flight, including maximum level flight speed and L/D$_{max}$

10. From the following range graph, determine the expected range in nautical miles with and without reserve.

Pressure Altitude: 4,000 feet
Standard Temperature
75% Power
48 Gallons Usable Fuel

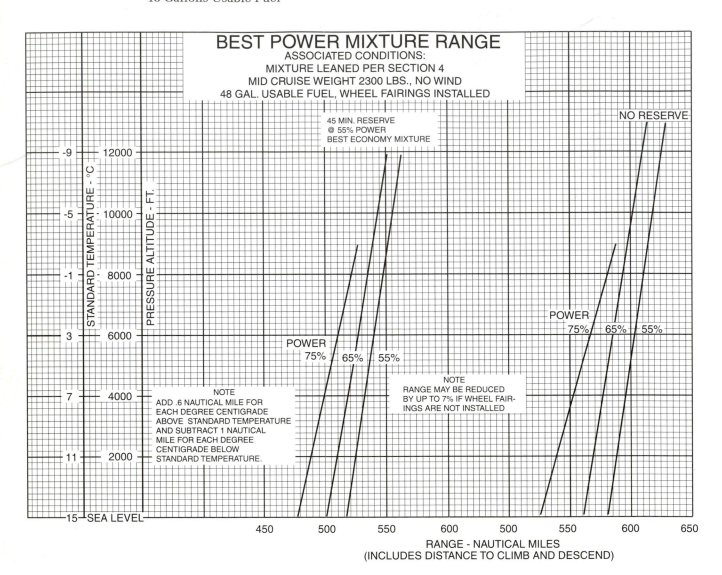

11. True/False. Landing weight is not a factor that must be considered during an approach.

SECTION B
WEIGHT AND BALANCE

The earliest airplanes could barely lift the pilot and enough fuel for a few minutes of flight. Many could not even manage to get airborne at all on a warm day! Although aircraft performance capabilities continue to improve, pilots still need to keep weight within safe limits, and balance the loads carried to maintain control of the airplane. [Figure 8-21]

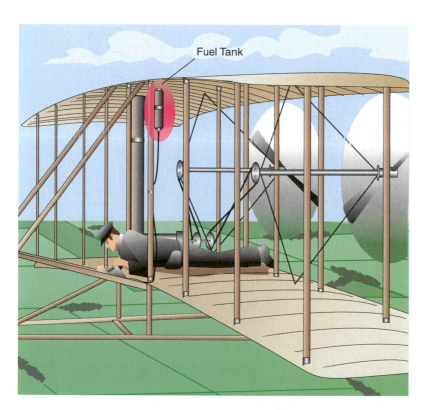

Fuel Tank

Figure 8-21. The first Wright Flyer could carry the pilot and a few ounces of fuel — if the headwind was at least 11 miles per hour.

IMPORTANCE OF WEIGHT

Almost every aspect of performance is influenced by the weight of the aircraft and its contents. For example, compared to a properly loaded airplane, an overweight airplane has a longer takeoff run, higher takeoff speed, reduced angle and rate of climb, reduced cruising speed, shorter range, higher stalling speed, and longer landing roll. Loading an aircraft too heavily can dangerously decrease its performance, and increase the risk of structural damage if you encounter turbulence or make a hard landing, or even when maneuvering. As you might expect, a severely overloaded airplane will not fly at all.

Aircraft manufacturers do extensive testing to establish safe limits for aircraft loading. Such limits may include maximum takeoff and landing weights. These weights are approved by the FAA during initial airworthiness certification, and are established as operating limitations after consideration of factors such as performance, structural strength, and type of operation.

IMPORTANCE OF BALANCE

In addition to checking weight, you need to know that the aircraft is balanced within approved limits. It's not just a matter of how much you put into the plane, but where you put it. You can check the balance condition of an airplane by locating its **center of gravity** (CG), which is the imaginary point where the aircraft would balance if suspended. [Figure 8-22] The location of this point is critical to an airplane's stability and elevator (or stabilator) effectiveness. Improper balance of the airplane's load can result in serious control problems. You can avoid these problems by taking the time to determine the location of the CG before each flight and then making sure it is within the limits provided by the manufacturer. The **CG limits** are the forward and aft center of gravity locations within which the aircraft must be operated at a given weight.

Figure 8-22. The center of gravity is the imaginary balance point of the aircraft.

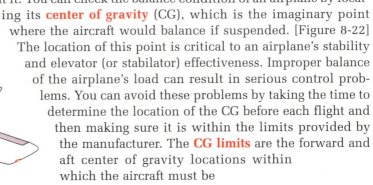

[Figure 8-23] Also called the CG envelope or range, The CG limits are established by the manufacturer. Many aircraft are certificated in more than one category, and will have different CG limits depending on the category in which the airplane is operated. If the CG is located within these limits, the airplane can be flown safely. If it is located outside these limits, you will need to rearrange fuel, passengers, or cargo in order to move the CG within acceptable limits. It's also important to maintain this distribution of weight during flight, since any movement of passengers or cargo will change the location of the CG.

Utility Category CG Range

Normal Category CG Range

Figure 8-23. This airplane is certificated in the normal category, and is permitted a maximum weight of 2,300 pounds when operated in the green-tinted CG range. The same airplane may be operated in the utility category if the total weight is kept under 2,000 pounds and the CG is kept within the narrower, yellow-tinted range.

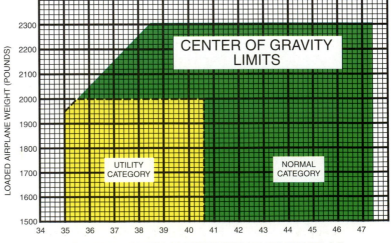

Supersonic Balancing Act

The supersonic Concorde must keep its CG within certain limits in spite of flight attendants moving heavy serving carts and people walking around inside it. Added to that is the problem that the center of lift of the wings moves back several feet as the plane nears the speed of sound, so the CG must be shifted along with it. To do this, a system of pumps and fuel lines moves fuel between the fore and aft fuselage fuel tanks.

WEIGHT AND BALANCE TERMS

Fortunately, the concepts and terms for weight and balance are straightforward and sensible. Some of the terms may be familiar to you from science classes, but as a pilot you will need to know their precise meanings in the aviation context.

REFERENCE DATUM

The center of gravity limits usually are specified in inches from a **reference datum**. This is an imaginary vertical plane from which all horizontal distances are measured for balance purposes. Common locations are the nose of the airplane, the engine firewall, the leading edge of the wing, or even somewhere in space ahead of the airplane. The location of the datum is established by the manufacturer and is defined in the POH or in the airplane's weight and balance papers. [Figure 8-24]

TERMS DESCRIBING THE EMPTY AIRPLANE

Basic empty weight includes the weight of the standard airplane, optional equipment, unusable fuel, and full operating fluids including full engine oil. The **unusable fuel** is the small amount of fuel in the tanks that cannot be safely used in flight or drained on the ground. Older airplanes might use the term **licensed empty weight**, which is similar to basic empty weight except that it does not include full engine oil. Instead, it only counts the weight of undrainable oil. You can obtain basic empty weight by simply adding the weight of the oil to the licensed empty weight.

The weight of the empty airplane may change many times during its lifetime as equipment is installed and removed. This equipment could include new instruments, radios, wheel fairings, engine accessories, or other modifications. Anything that significantly changes

The datum is 66.25 inches ahead of the wing's leading edge.

The datum is at the front face of the firewall.

The datum is 109.7 inches ahead of the center of the main gear.

Figure 8-24. Although the datum is different in each of these airplanes, it is used in the same way for weight and balance calculations.

Basic empty weight includes the weight of the standard airplane, optional equipment, unusable fuel, and full operating fluids including full engine oil.

the weight or center of gravity must be documented by a mechanic in the aircraft weight and balance papers. This could be something as minor as a new antenna, or as major as removing the landing gear and installing floats. As a pilot, you should be sure you are always using the most recent weight and balance information for your calculations.

I *Hate* It When That Happens...

Some airplanes have a tail stand, a temporary support to hold up the rear fuselage during loading. When the back of the airplane is loaded before the front, it can rock back on its tail before enough weight can be loaded in front to balance things out. Installing the stand keeps the airplane level until the load is balanced. But sometimes people forget to prop up the tail, and...

Courtesy of USAF Air Mobility Command Museum

TERMS DESCRIBING THE LOADED AIRPLANE

Ramp weight is the term used to describe the airplane loaded for flight prior to engine start. Subtracting the fuel burned during engine start, runup, and taxi, yields the **takeoff weight**. This is the weight of the airplane just before you release the brakes to begin the takeoff roll. **Landing weight** is the takeoff weight minus the fuel burned enroute. To determine an airplane's **useful load**, either prior to engine start or at takeoff, you must subtract the basic empty weight from ramp weight or takeoff weight respectively. The useful load includes the weight of the flight crew and usable fuel, as well as any passengers, baggage, and cargo. **Payload** is the term used for the weight of only the passengers, baggage, and cargo. Adding the weight of the flight crew and usable fuel to the payload is another way to determine useful load. Some POHs may refer to total weight or gross weight which are general terms used to describe the weight of the airplane and everything carried in it.

Aircraft manufacturers try to build some mission flexibility into their designs. This means you may have the choice of filling all the seats with passengers if you carry a reduced fuel load, or of having a long cruising range with full fuel tanks and less payload. Since very few airplanes can handle a full cabin and full fuel tanks, you must balance your needs within the capabilities of your airplane and your flying skills.

Payload Versus Useful Load

The Saturn 5 moon rocket was an extreme example of the difference between useful load and payload. The payload was the Apollo Command Module, the Service Module, and the Lunar Excursion Module. These components weighed about 109,000 pounds, depending on the mission. The weight of the fuel (and oxidizer) added about 5,785,500 pounds, for a useful load of 5,894,500 pounds. The empty weight of the boosters added another 528,500 pounds, for a total weight of 6,423,000 pounds at liftoff.

Many aircraft have different maximum weight limits for different stages of flight. The POH may list a **maximum ramp weight**, which is the maximum allowed for ground operations, such as taxiing. It's usually just a little more than the **maximum takeoff weight**. The difference allows for the weight of fuel used in engine start, taxiing to the runway, and runup checks. Although it does not amount to much in a relatively fuel-efficient light airplane, it may be several thousand pounds for a large transport. An aircraft's **maximum landing weight** is based on the amount of stress the landing gear can handle. The loads imposed by landing are much greater than the loads of the typical takeoff, so the maximum landing weight is lower to keep the gear from being damaged in the event of a hard touchdown or a landing on a rough runway. Maximum gross weight is a general term used in some POH's to describe the airplane's maximum weight limitation set by the manufacturer. [Figure 8-25]

Empty Weight: 60,000 pounds.

Cameras and Sensors

Payload: 4,720 pounds.

Fuel: 75,000 pounds.

Maximum Takeoff Weight: 145,000 pounds.

Maximum Aircraft Weight: 170,000 pounds.

Maximum Landing Weight: 68,000 pounds.

Figure 8-25. Inflight refueling makes it possible for the Lockheed SR-71's maximum weight in flight to exceed the maximum takeoff weight by 25,000 pounds. The maximum landing weight indicates that the airplane lands with little fuel remaining in the tanks.

Photos courtesy of NASA

The fuel available during flight is called **usable fuel**, and you will need to account for its weight in your weight and balance calculations. Gasoline weighs 6 pounds per gallon. This makes it very easy to calculate fuel weight by multiplying the number of gallons by 6 to get the weight in pounds. Oil weighs more — 7 1/2 pounds per gallon. Since oil is usually measured in quarts, each quart weighs 1 7/8 pounds.

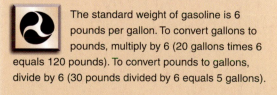
The standard weight of gasoline is 6 pounds per gallon. To convert gallons to pounds, multiply by 6 (20 gallons times 6 equals 120 pounds). To convert pounds to gallons, divide by 6 (30 pounds divided by 6 equals 5 gallons).

PRINCIPLES OF WEIGHT AND BALANCE

Children on a seesaw illustrate the basic ideas involved in balance theory. The seesaw is balanced when children who weigh the same amount sit an equal distance from the fulcrum. [Figure 8-26] Since children of different sizes often play together, they have to compensate by shifting their weight to make the seesaw balance. Although unaware of it, what they are doing is moving the center of gravity so it is directly over the fulcrum. While the principles of weight and balance are straightforward, applying them is not exactly child's play. With a small amount of work you can apply these principles to loading your airplane safely.

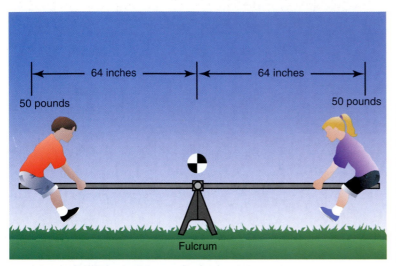

Figure 8-26. To balance the seesaw, the center of gravity must be over the fulcrum.

ARM AND MOMENT

The name for a distance from the datum is **arm**. On airplanes, the distances are generally measured in inches, and by tradition, distances aft of the datum are positive numbers and forward of the datum are negative. Fuselage station (abbreviated F.S. or sta.) is another term for the arm.

Landing Gear Configuration and Center of Gravity

The center of gravity is ahead of the main wheels in airplanes with tricycle landing gear. Airplanes with tailwheels (conventional gear) have their CG behind the main wheels.

This Piper design was created with conventional gear as the Pacer in 1950. When tricycle gear was offered as an option in 1952, it became the Tri-Pacer. [Figure A] The owner of this Tri-Pacer has converted his airplane to the tailwheel configuration by installing new landing gear legs that move the main wheels ahead of the CG. [Figure B]

Courtesy of Brian Thomas

A weight on the end of an arm creates a **moment**. Moment is a measurement of the tendency of the weight to cause rotation at the fulcrum. While an arm is simply a length, a moment is the length multiplied by a weight. When the weight in pounds and the arm in inches are multiplied together, the resulting moment is expressed in pound-inches. [Figure 8-27]

Figure 8-27. Moment is an arm mutiplied by the weight. In this example the datum is the left end of the seesaw, and any actual rotation would occur at the fulcrum.

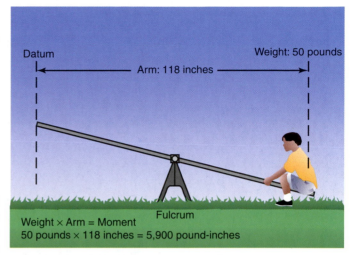

Datum

Weight: 50 pounds

Arm: 118 inches

Fulcrum

Weight × Arm = Moment
50 pounds × 118 inches = 5,900 pound-inches

CALCULATING THE POSITION OF THE CG

The position of the CG of the airplane usually is expressed in inches from the datum. Since a measurement from the datum is an arm, the term CG arm also is used to describe the location of the CG. To find the center of gravity of an object or a group of objects, the moments of all the parts are added, and this total is divided by the total weight of the parts. Figure 8-28 shows how to do this using the seesaw example.

Figure 8-28. Using the left end of the seesaw as the datum, the position of the CG is calculated using the children's weights and the weight of the seesaw itself.

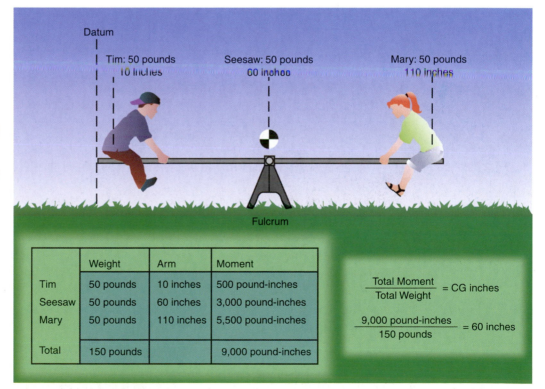

Datum

Tim: 50 pounds
10 inches

Seesaw: 50 pounds
60 inches

Mary: 50 pounds
110 inches

Fulcrum

	Weight	Arm	Moment
Tim	50 pounds	10 inches	500 pound-inches
Seesaw	50 pounds	60 inches	3,000 pound-inches
Mary	50 pounds	110 inches	5,500 pound-inches
Total	150 pounds		9,000 pound-inches

$$\frac{\text{Total Moment}}{\text{Total Weight}} = \text{CG inches}$$

$$\frac{9,000 \text{ pound-inches}}{150 \text{ pounds}} = 60 \text{ inches}$$

When looking at figure 8-28, you could probably guess that the CG was over the fulcrum, since the seesaw was in balance. Now, try to calculate the CG location using two new children with different weights. [Figure 8-29]

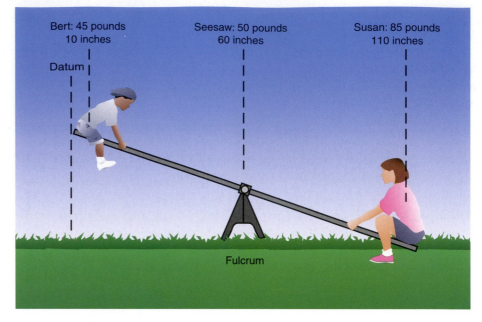

Figure 8-29. Where is the CG? You should get a total moment of 12,800 and a total weight of 180 pounds, for an answer of 71.1 inches.

You can use the same technique to find the CG of an airplane. Substitute the weight and moment of the airplane for the weight and moment of the seesaw. Combine it with the weight and moment of the pilot to obtain the new CG location, as shown in figure 8-30.

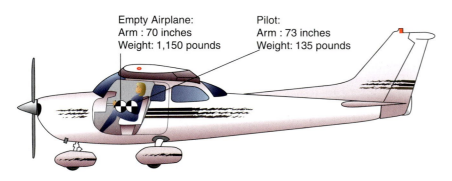

Figure 8-30. Multiply the pilot's weight by the distance from the datum to get her moment. The weight and moment of the airplane are found in its weight and balance documents.

	Weight		Arm		Moment	
Empty Airplane	1,150 pounds	X	70 inches	=	80,500	pound - inches
Pilot	135 pounds	X	73 inches	=	9,855	pound - inches
Total	1,285 pounds				90,355	pound - inches

$$\frac{\text{Total Moment}}{\text{Total Weight}} = \text{CG Arm} \qquad \frac{90,355 \text{ pound-inches}}{1,285 \text{ pounds}} = 70.3 \text{ inches}$$

To find the CG location, divide the total moment by the total weight.

SHIFTING WEIGHT TO MOVE THE CG

Returning to the example of the children on the seesaw from figure 8-29, to rearrange the children so that the seesaw balances, you should move the CG to the fulcrum. To do this, move the larger child, Susan, toward the datum so that her weight acts through a shorter arm, reducing her moment. [Figure 8-31] Of course, all of this can be described mathematically, as you will learn later.

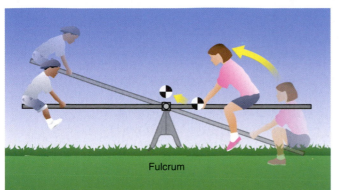

Fulcrum

Figure 8-31. Shortening the arm reduces the moment. As Susan moves toward the datum, her moment is reduced, which moves the CG toward the fulcrum until the seesaw is balanced.

DETERMINING TOTAL WEIGHT AND CENTER OF GRAVITY

In the seesaw examples, you used what is called the computation method. It demonstrates the principles of weight and balance most thoroughly. Using the computation method for airplanes requires multiplying and adding up large numbers, and there are plenty of opportunities to make mistakes, even if you use your calculator. To simplify the process, many manufacturers provide tables and/or graphs in the POH. You should be able to use all three methods (computation, table, or graph), since weight and balance information in your POH may be in any of the different formats.

Fortunately, there is only one way to calculate total weight. All you have to do is add the weight of your passengers, baggage, cargo, fuel, and yourself to the empty weight of the airplane. If you are working from a licensed empty weight, you would also include oil. You should try to be as accurate as possible and use the actual weight of each person and item of baggage, rather than trying to estimate.

COMPUTATION METHOD

Normally, the first step in any weight and balance computation is to see if the weight of what you want to load is within the maximum weight limits. Begin with the weight of the empty airplane and make a list of all the people and items you intend to load, noting the actual weight of each and including the weight of fuel. You may choose to add the weight of usable fuel at first and then subtract fuel to reduce the total weight to the maximum permitted, or you might calculate the total amount of fuel needed for the flight (with reserves) and add its weight to your list of passengers and baggage. You can use a printed weight and balance worksheet, or use the simple format shown here. [Figure 8-32]

Figure 8-32. Information regarding the empty weight and CG location is found on the airplane's weight and balance form. This airplane has a maximum takeoff weight of 2,500 pounds, so the total weight of the listed items is below the maximum.

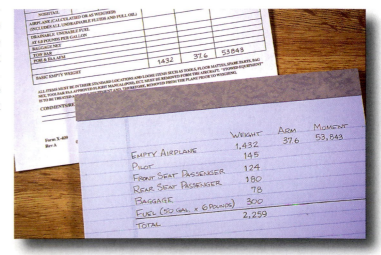

	WEIGHT	ARM	MOMENT
EMPTY AIRPLANE	1,432	37.6	53,843
PILOT	145		
FRONT SEAT PASSENGER	124		
REAR SEAT PASSENGER	180		
BAGGAGE	78		
FUEL (50 GAL. × 6 POUNDS)	300		
TOTAL	2,259		

If the total weight is greater than the maximum weight limit, you will have to leave something behind; either payload or fuel or some of each. Once you have the total weight within the limits, calculate the location of the center of gravity. You will need to fill out the remaining two columns on your original list. One column is for the arm (in inches) of each item. Remember, the arm is just the distance from the datum, and the manufacturer usually provides a diagram to help you to find it. If the chart gives a fore and aft position for adjustable seats, you can adjust the arm dimensions for people whose seats will be further forward or aft than average. For instance, if you always fly with the seat one inch back from the full-forward position, you would use 35 inches as your own arm in the example shown, since it is one inch behind the forward position of 34 inches. If your front seat passenger runs the seat all the way aft for an in-flight nap, you would use 46 inches for her arm.

In the last column, enter the moment for each item, obtained by multiplying each weight by the corresponding arm (weight × arm = moment). Adding up the moment column gives the total moment in pound-inches. Divide the total moment by the total weight to get the arm of the overall center of gravity in inches aft of the datum. Then check to see that the center of gravity falls between the forward and aft CG limits. [Figure 8-33]

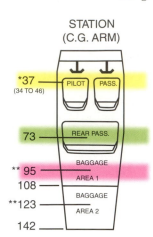

STATION
(C.G. ARM)

LOADING ARRANGEMENTS

*Pilot or passenger center of gravity on adjustable seats positioned for average occupant. Numbers in parentheses indicate forward and aft limits of occupant center of gravity range.

**Arm measured to the center of the areas shown.

NOTE: The rear cabin wall (approximate station 108) or aft baggage wall (Approximate station 142) can be used as convenient interior reference points for determining the location of baggage area fuselage stations.

Usable fuel CG arm is 46 inches.
Maximum baggage in Area 1 is 120 pounds.
Maximum baggage in Area 2 is 50 pounds.

Arm for pilot and front seat passenger is 37 inches.

Arm for rear passenger is 73 inches.

Arm for baggage is 95 inches.

Arm for fuel is 46 inches.

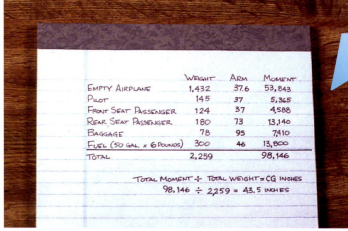

	WEIGHT	ARM	MOMENT
EMPTY AIRPLANE	1,432	37.6	53,843
PILOT	145	37	5,365
FRONT SEAT PASSENGER	124	37	4,588
REAR SEAT PASSENGER	180	73	13,140
BAGGAGE	78	95	7,410
FUEL (50 GAL. x 6 POUNDS)	300	46	13,800
TOTAL	2,259		98,146

TOTAL MOMENT ÷ TOTAL WEIGHT = CG INCHES
98,146 ÷ 2259 = 43.5 INCHES

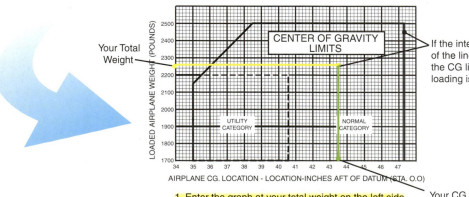

CENTER OF GRAVITY LIMITS

Your Total Weight

If the intersection of the lines is within the CG limits, the loading is acceptable.

LOADED AIRPLANE WEIGHT (POUNDS)

UTILITY CATEGORY

NORMAL CATEGORY

AIRPLANE CG. LOCATION - LOCATION-INCHES AFT OF DATUM (STA. O.O)

Your CG Location

1. Enter the graph at your total weight on the left side.

2. Draw a line from the bottom at your calculated CG.

3. The intersection of the lines is within the CG limits, so the loading is acceptable.

Figure 8-33. Use the diagram from the POH to find the arm for each item. When you have calculated the loaded CG, use the CG limits graph from the POH to see if the loading is acceptable.

TABLE METHOD

The table method uses a series of tables provided by the manufacturer to eliminate the multiplication and division, but not the addition. A **moment table** is provided for each of the most common payload areas, such as front seats, rear seats, usable fuel, and baggage area. The manufacturer has taken various weights and multiplied them by the arm for that location to obtain the numbers in the table. To find the center of gravity, start with your list of weights as before. Then look up the weight for each item in the appropriate table and read the moment given next to it. Write the moment for each item on your worksheet list and total it. Then, find the total weight on the **moment limits table** and read across to see if your number falls between the limits given for that weight. [Figure 8-34] If not, you will need to rearrange the load. The table method uses rounded weights and approximate arms, so it is not as precise as the computation method, but this method eliminates some of the chances for arithmetic errors. Notice that the table does not state the CG range in inches from the datum. Instead, it gives moment limits for a whole range of total weights. This eliminates the computation method's final step of dividing the moment by the total weight.

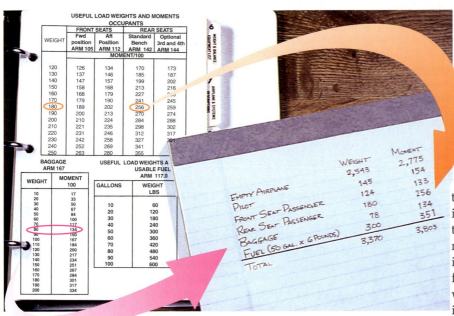

Figure 8-34. The airplane builder supplies tables with the moment already multiplied for you. Read the moment next to the weight for each item in the useful load. If the total moment falls between the moment limits in the table for that weight, the airplane will be loaded safely.

If the total moment falls between the fore and aft moment limits given in the table for that total weight, then the aircraft is within CG limits.

You may have noticed that the moments you were using in examples of the computation method were much larger than the moments provided in the tables in figure 8-34. When the manufacturer multiplies these rounded weights by the average arms, the last digits are inevitably zeros. To make the numbers more manageable, they drop these zeros from the table, in effect dividing the moments by 100 or 1,000. There will always be a note on the table to indicate this reduction factor. The reduction factor can be ignored when using the moment limits table, because the moments listed are reduced by the same factor. Remember to correct for the reduction factor by adding the appropriate number of zeros to the moment if you calculate the CG location by dividing total moment by total weight. It also is important to keep track of reduction factors when using electronic flight computers to solve weight and balance problems.

GRAPH METHOD

This method is similar to the table method, except that the values from the tables have been combined and plotted on a graph for you. This allows you to use values between the increments published in a table, so you can use actual weights instead of rounded values. Only two graphs are necessary for this method. The **loading graph** is used to find the moment for the loads you intend to put into the airplane, and the **center of gravity moment envelope** tells you if your proposed loading is within the weight and balance limits. [Figures 8-35 and 8-36] As with the table method, the graphs usually employ a reduction factor of 100 or 1,000.

① Find the weight for the pilot and front seat passenger.

② Read across to the diagonal line, then go to the bottom and read the moment.

③ Record the moment on your worksheet.

④ Repeat the process for rear seat passengers, baggage, and fuel.

Figure 8-35. Use the graph to find moments for each item in the load. After adding them, check the total moment against the total weight on the CG moment envelope graph.

 Find the total weight and total moment lines on the graph.

 If the intersection of the lines is within the envelope, the loading is acceptable.

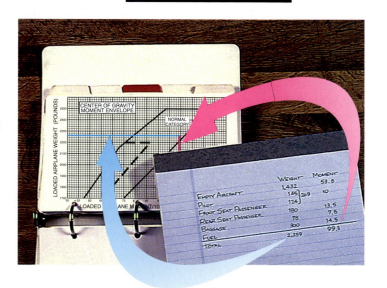

GROSS WEIGHT MOMENT LIMITS

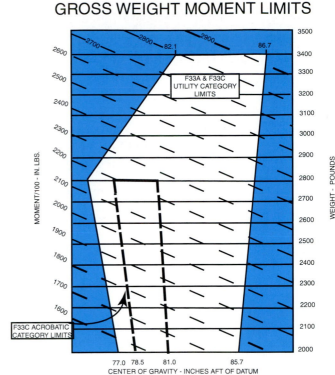

Figure 8-36. Some POHs use a different style for the graph. Gross weight is just another term for total weight.

WEIGHT-SHIFT FORMULA

Sometimes during weight and balance computations, you will find that the CG falls outside acceptable limits. You could rearrange the weights of passengers and baggage and calculate the CG location over and over, but there is an easier way. The following formula helps you to compute exactly what is necessary to bring the CG within limits.

$$\frac{\text{Weight Moved}}{\text{Weight of Airplane}} = \frac{\text{Distance CG Moves}}{\text{Distance Between Arms}}$$

To use the formula, you supply three of the variables and solve for the fourth. [Figure 8-37]

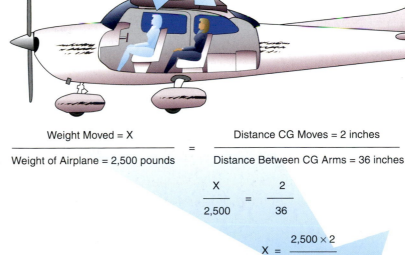

Figure 8-37 Suppose you need to change the load in an airplane to move the CG two inches. The total weight of the airplane is 2,500 pounds, and the difference between the arms for the front and rear seats is 36 inches. Solving the formula with these variables tells you how many pounds must be moved from one seat to the other to bring the CG within limits.

$$\frac{\text{Weight Moved} = X}{\text{Weight of Airplane} = 2,500 \text{ pounds}} = \frac{\text{Distance CG Moves} = 2 \text{ inches}}{\text{Distance Between CG Arms} = 36 \text{ inches}}$$

$$\frac{X}{2,500} = \frac{2}{36}$$

$$X = \frac{2,500 \times 2}{36}$$

$$X = 138.8 \text{ pounds}$$

You also can solve for the distance a specific weight would need to move. On the other hand, you can solve for how much the CG will change if you move a given weight a specified distance. [Figures 8-38 and 8-39]

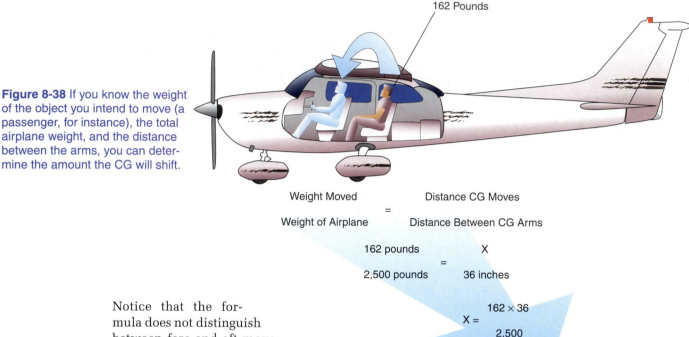

Figure 8-38 If you know the weight of the object you intend to move (a passenger, for instance), the total airplane weight, and the distance between the arms, you can determine the amount the CG will shift.

162 Pounds

$$\frac{\text{Weight Moved}}{\text{Weight of Airplane}} = \frac{\text{Distance CG Moves}}{\text{Distance Between CG Arms}}$$

$$\frac{162 \text{ pounds}}{2,500 \text{ pounds}} = \frac{X}{36 \text{ inches}}$$

$$X = \frac{162 \times 36}{2,500}$$

$$X = 2.3 \text{ inches}$$

Notice that the formula does not distinguish between fore and aft movement, so you have to keep track of the direction. You can always verify your answer with a final weight and balance check.

Figure 8-39. Suppose you know what you want to move and how far you need to shift the CG. You can use the formula to determine how far to move that item to acheive the desired CG change. In this example, the total airplane weight is still 2,500 pounds.

156 Pounds

$$\frac{\text{Weight Moved}}{\text{Total Airplane Weight}} = \frac{\text{Distance CG Moves}}{\text{Distance Between CG Arms}}$$

$$\frac{156 \text{ pounds}}{2,500 \text{ pounds}} = \frac{1.5 \text{ inches}}{X}$$

$$\frac{2,500 \times 1.5}{156} = X$$

$$X = 24 \text{ inches}$$

The weight shift formula can be used to calculate the amount of **weight** that must be moved a specific distance or to determine the **distance** a specific weight would need to move to bring the CG within approved limits. The formula is:

$$\frac{\text{Weight Moved}}{\text{Aircraft Weight}} = \frac{\text{Distance CG Moves}}{\text{Distance Between Arm Locations}}$$

SHIFTING CG AS A MEANS OF AIRCRAFT CONTROL?

Before the Wright brothers flew, German aviation pioneer Otto Lilienthal designed and flew a series of successful gliders. The gliders had no flight controls and no movable control surfaces. The pilot controlled them by swinging his legs and body to shift the center of gravity.

Professor R.H. Wood of Johns Hopkins University was a friend of Lilienthal, and had this to say after watching him fly:

What impressed me most was the tremendous amount of athletic work necessary to balance the machine. He was never still a moment, swinging his legs from side to side, and on landing he was all out of breath, though I doubt if he was in the air thirty seconds. It seemed to require as much exercise as a 100 yard dash.

One of your responsibilities as pilot in command is to assess your own physical condition and fitness to fly. You may not have to be as athletic as Herr Lilienthal to control your aircraft, but at the very least you should be rested, alert, and healthy.

"I Had All These Goats"

Merle K. Smith, an Alaskan bush pilot (who later became president of Cordova Airlines) recalls some CG problems:

In the old days we used to have what is now called unusual cargo. We called it good paying freight then.

There was a homesteader who decided that he needed fresh milk, so he sent to Seattle and ordered some goats. I loaded these goats into one of the old planes and started up there. Well, I had forgotten that goats like rope, and I had tied these goats to various places in the airplane with ropes so that they wouldn't get loose and annoy me or endanger the flight.

In about twenty minutes they had all the ropes chewed through. So then I had all these goats. They'd all frolic together. There must have been eight hundred pounds of goats; and they'd all get in the back of the airplane and I couldn't hold the nose down. They would all come up and chew on me a little bit, and chew my shirt, and I'd slap them away. But I decided not to do that any more, because the first time I did that, they all went to the back of the airplane. It got to be kind of a serious situation. By the time we got to where I could land these goats they had most of the fabric eaten off the inside of the airplane, and my shirt; and the seat I was sitting on was pretty well stripped of upholstery. But these little things happened. If you came out all right, as in this instance — well, it was funny.

As quoted in *The American Heritage History of Flight*

EFFECTS OF OPERATING AT HIGH TOTAL WEIGHTS

When you learned about the four forces, you found that lift must equal weight in level flight. If more weight is added, the wing needs to generate more lift. Changing the position of the CG also affects the total lift the wing must produce, even when the airplane's weight remains constant, since the wing must also counteract the tail-down force. You know that lift can be increased somewhat with additional speed or a higher angle of attack, but there is an upper limit to how much weight any wing can carry. You also know that the effective weight varies when you maneuver the airplane in flight. Remember how the load factor increases in turns, or in the pullout from a dive? If the wing is near its maximum load-carrying capacity, and the load factor is increased by a turn, a sudden pull-up, or turbulence, the structure of the wing could be damaged or fail. Engineers create an airplane with specific load-factor capabilities in mind. The landing gear is designed to support a certain amount of weight and absorb reasonable landing loads, and wings are designed to lift the airplane and its contents and still allow for load factors imposed by gusts, turbulence and maneuvers. Even though airplanes are built with a considerable margin of safety, the pilot is responsible for seeing that load factors remain within safe limits.

The specific problems of operating at or near the maximum weight limit are generally related to the wing having to fly faster or at a higher angle of attack to generate the additional lift required. When operating near the maximum weight limit, the takeoff roll is longer, since the airplane accelerates more slowly and also needs to reach a higher speed to generate enough lift for takeoff. Both angle and rate of climb are reduced from that achieved at lower weights. In cruise, range is reduced and speed is lower at any given power setting, since more energy is being used to generate lift and overcome the resulting induced drag. Since the wing is already flying at a higher angle of attack just to maintain level flight, it is that much closer to its stalling angle, and stalls at a higher speed than when lightly loaded. As you would expect, the brakes have to work harder to slow down a heavy plane. This, combined with the higher touchdown speeds, results in longer landing distances. Most of the performance numbers in the POH are found by testing the airplane at maximum weight, but the person who flies an overloaded airplane has just decided to be a test pilot, and is flying the airplane outside of the envelope, in areas that may not have been explored in flight testing.

FLIGHT AT VARIOUS CG POSITIONS

As you learned from the discussion of longitudinal stability, most airplanes are designed to fly with the CG slightly forward of the center of pressure. This gives the airplane a small nose-down moment. This tendency to nose down is counteracted by the tail exerting a down force. It acts as a sort of upside-down wing generating a small amount of lift in a downward direction. Arranging the forces this way makes the airplane more stable. If the nose is pitched up, the angle of attack of the tail is reduced, so it generates less down force, allowing the nose to drop. On the other hand, if the nose is pitched down, the tail creates more down force, raising the nose. This stabilizing effect increases as the CG is moved farther forward. A certain amount of stability is helpful, especially in turbulence or when flying by reference to instruments, but too much actually makes the aircraft harder to control, since elevator control input is resisted by the stability of the airplane. With the airplane nose-heavy, the stall speed also is higher. The forward CG requires a greater tail down-force, and this force is equivalent to adding weight. Since the wing must fly at a higher angle of attack to generate the lift to counteract the greater tail-down force, it is closer to its stalling angle of attack for any given speed.

With the CG at or behind the center of pressure, a conventional airplane is unstable in pitch. Since there is no automatic restoring force, when a small bump or control input starts the nose up, the nose continues to pitch up more and more unless the pilot acts. This can happen very quickly, and it is possible the force required to push the nose back down could exceed the aerodynamic capability of the elevators or stabilator. Although the control forces actually become lighter as the CG moves aft, the pilot's workload can be much higher. An unstable airplane requires constant attention and continuous control input even in calm air, and it is all too easy to overcontrol. Overcontrolling can result in dangerously high flight load factors, structural damage, and the breakup of the airframe. An aft CG makes it much easier to enter an accidental stall or spin, and the tail-heavy condition may cause the spin to be flat, characterized by a nearly level pitch attitude, rapid rotation rate, and high sink rate. Recovery may be impossible. [Figure 8-40]

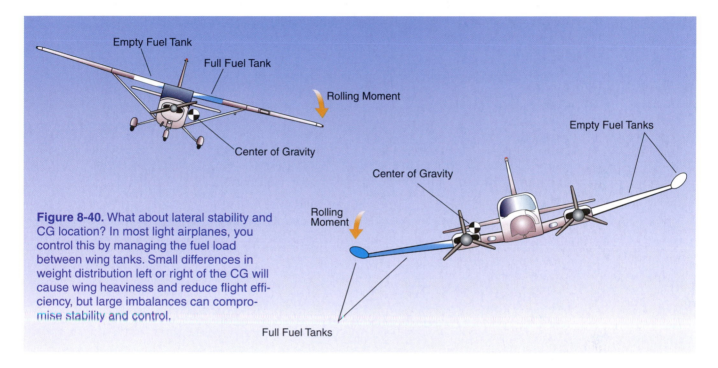

Figure 8-40. What about lateral stability and CG location? In most light airplanes, you control this by managing the fuel load between wing tanks. Small differences in weight distribution left or right of the CG will cause wing heaviness and reduce flight efficiency, but large imbalances can compromise stability and control.

Racers On the Edge

Flying the airplane with the CG forward enhances stability, since the tail-down force increases the tendency of the airplane to return to level flight if disturbed. However, it reduces fuel economy and speed slightly. On the other hand, cross-country racers try to fly with their CG at its aft limit, very close to the center of pressure of the wing. Because the wing is lifting only the weight of the airplane (and not the additional "weight" of tail down-force), the wing can be flown at a lower angle of attack, with less induced drag, giving a little more speed and better fuel efficiency. The difference is not great, but in a race, every little improvement helps. Monocoupes like these have been raced since the 1930's.

SUMMARY CHECKLIST

✓ Both the amount and the distribution of weight affect aircraft performance.

✓ The reference datum is the location from which all horizontal distances are measured for weight and balance purposes.

✓ An arm is a distance from the datum. Measurements aft of the datum are generally positive numbers, while those forward of the datum are negative numbers. A moment is a weight multiplied by an arm.

✓ To compute the location of the CG, add the moments for each item of useful load to the moment of the empty airplane and divide the total moment by the total weight.

✓ Ramp weight is the term used to describe the airplane loaded for flight prior to engine start. Subtracting the fuel burned during engine start, runup, and taxi, yields the takeoff weight. Landing weight is the takeoff weight minus the fuel burned enroute.

✓ To determine an airplane's useful load, either prior to engine start or at takeoff, you must subtract the basic empty weight from ramp weight or takeoff weight respectively. The useful load includes the weight of the flight crew and usable fuel, as well as any passengers, baggage, and cargo. Payload is the term used for the weight of only the passengers, baggage, and cargo.

✓ The maximum weight may be divided into categories such as maximum ramp weight, maximum takeoff weight, and maximum landing weight.

✓ When performing calculations, the empty weight, moment, and center of gravity information is obtained from the individual aircraft's weight and balance records.

✓ The pilot's operating handbook provides tables and/or graphs to help find the moment of occupants, baggage and fuel.

✓ An overloaded airplane will have diminished performance. It will have a longer takeoff roll, lower angle and rate of climb, higher stall speed, reduced range and cruise speed, and a longer landing roll than a properly loaded airplane.

✓ Moving the CG forward increases stability, due to the increased tail-down force required for trimmed flight. The airplane will also stall at a higher speed, due to the increased wing loading.

✓ If the CG is located ahead of the established CG range, the elevator may not have sufficient force to raise the nose for landing.

✓ If an airplane is flown with the CG aft of the CG range, it will be less stable in pitch. It will be difficult to control, and if a stall or spin is entered, it may be impossible to recover.

✓ Even when an airplane is loaded within CG limits, its handling characteristics will vary with the location of the CG.

KEY TERMS

Center of Gravity (CG)   Unusable Fuel

CG Limits   Licensed Empty Weight

Reference Datum   Ramp Weight

Basic Empty Weight   Takeoff Weight

Landing Weight   Arm

Useful Load   Moment

Payload   Moment Table

Maximum Ramp Weight   Moment Limits Table

Maximum Takeoff Weight   Loading Graph

Maximum Landing Weight   Center of Gravity Moment Envelope

Usable fuel

QUESTIONS

1. What is the term for the reference plane from which all horizontal measurements are made for weight and balance calculations?

2. How is unusable fuel defined?

3. What constitutes the difference between basic empty weight and licensed empty weight?

   A. The weight of usable oil
   B. The weight of unusable oil
   C. The weight of unusable fuel

4. If your weight check shows that the airplane will exceed the maximum ramp weight specified in the POH, which of the following actions would be appropriate?

   A. Take off at that weight, but not taxi.
   B. Rearrange the load to bring it within CG limits.
   C. Remove passengers, cargo, or fuel until the weight limit is reached.

5. What is the weight of 42 gallons of aviation gasoline?

   A. 242 pounds
   B. 248 pounds
   C. 252 pounds

6. The moment for a rear-seat passenger is 14,800. If this passenger sits in a front seat, will her moment be higher or lower?

7. True/False. Moment is expressed in inches.

8. You are planning a trip with three friends. You and your front seat passenger weigh a total of 366 pounds. The rear seat passengers each weigh 173 pounds. The suitcases weigh 150 pounds. Assume that 120 pounds of the baggage will be in Area A, with the remainder in Area B. Using the accompanying graph, find their total moment.

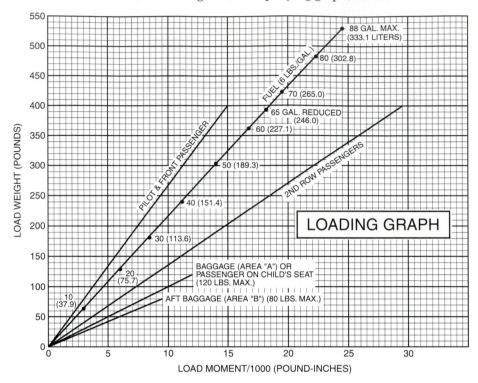

9. The airplane described in Question 8 has an empty weight of 1,850 pounds, and the empty moment is 64,900 inch-pounds. If it has a maximum weight of 3,100 pounds, how much usable fuel can be loaded and still remain within weight and CG limits? (Use the accompanying moment envelope.)

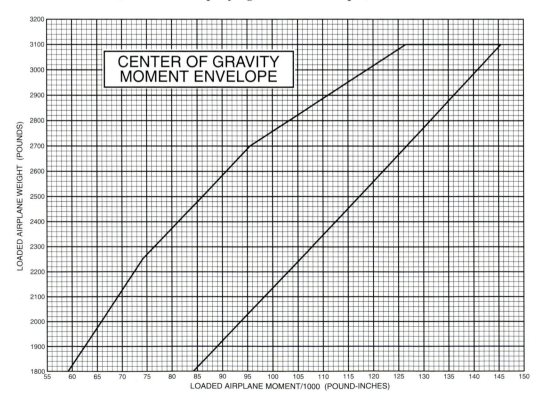

10. The center of gravity of the fully loaded airplane in Question 9 will be how many inches from the datum?

11. While preparing for a flight in another airplane, you discover that the proposed loading places the CG one inch behind the rear CG limit. The total weight is 2,655 pounds. Use the weight-shift formula to determine how much weight needs to be shifted from the baggage area (arm=140) to the back seat (arm=114) to bring the CG within limits.

12. If flight had been attempted without changing the loading described in Question 11, what flight characteristics could be expected?

    A. Tail-heaviness, requiring additional forward trim
    B. Light control forces, longitudinal (pitch) instability, and a higher cruise speed for the power setting
    C. All of the above

13. Compared to a lightly loaded airplane, what flight characteristics could be expected from a heavily loaded airplane?

    A. It will stall at a higher speed, cruise at a lower speed, and have less range.
    B. It will land at a lower speed, cruise at a higher speed, and stall at a higher angle of attack.
    C. It will have a higher cruise speed and range, a reduced rate of climb, and stall at the same speed.

14. If the center of gravity is too far forward, what flight characteristics would you expect?

    A. The airplane would be less stable, and easy to overcontrol.
    B. The airplane would be more stable, and stall at a higher speed.
    C. The airplane would be less stable, and stall at a higher angle of attack.

SECTION C
FLIGHT COMPUTERS

When you plan a long trip in your car, you probably make some rough estimates about how far you can drive in a day, where you intend to stop for meals, and where you will spend the night. With service stations every few miles, you may not worry about how far you can travel between fuel stops. The only times the wind becomes a concern are when blowing snow or dust makes driving difficult. By necessity, flight planning is more demanding and requires a certain degree of precision. The consequences of sloppy planning are seen in news reports of airplanes that make forced landings after running out of fuel and airliners that mistakenly land at the wrong airports. Flight computers were created to help pilots manage a variety of calculations. As with any new tool, becoming proficient with your flight computer will take some practice, but the time you invest in learning to use it will pay off in quick, easy, and accurate computations.

MECHANICAL FLIGHT COMPUTERS

Flight planning and enroute navigation require solutions to several different types of mathematical problems. The mechanical flight computer evolved to make these common calculations easier. At first glance it may look complicated, but each element has its purpose, and with a little practice it becomes familiar and useful. The computer has two sides: the **computer side**, with several scales and small cutout windows, and the **wind side**, with a large transparent window and a sliding grid. The computer side is used for solving ratio-type problems such as time-speed-distance, fuel consumption, and various conversions. The wind side takes most of the guesswork out of otherwise difficult wind-drift calculations.

USING THE COMPUTER SIDE

To get acquainted with the computer side, start by turning the inner disc until the pointer (called the **speed index** or **60 index**) points to 60 on the outer scale. Notice that the two adjacent scales match all the way around. The non-rotating outer scale is called the **A scale**, and the outermost rotating scale is the **B scale**. The A and B scales are identical. The scales are logarithmic, so the numbers are closer together as you go clockwise. The space between 80 and 81, for instance, is much less than the distance between 18 and 19. This difference in spacing lets you do multiplication and division by setting and reading the two scales. You may also notice that the number of increments **between** numbers varies. For instance, there are nine marks between 13 and 14, only four between 18 and 19, and none at all between 80 and 81. This is done because a full set of lines would become too hard to read as the numbers get closer together. To avoid mistakes, keep these differences in mind when you set up problems. [Figure 8-41]

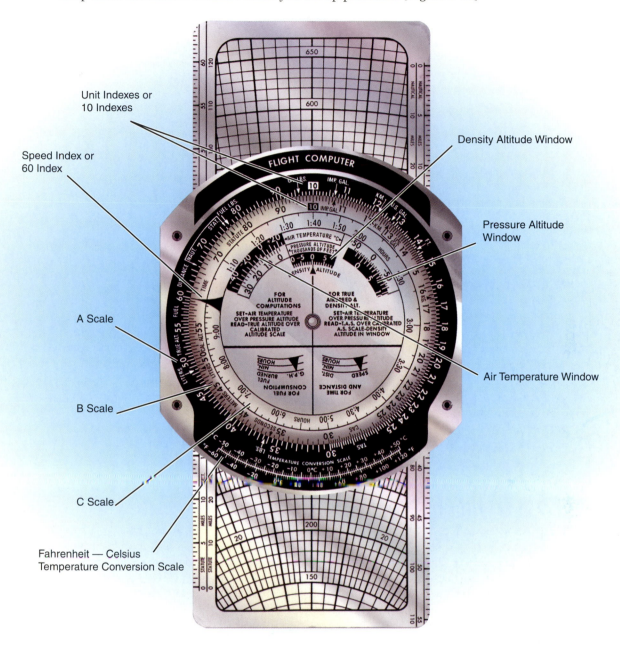

Unit Indexes or 10 Indexes

Speed Index or 60 Index

Density Altitude Window

Pressure Altitude Window

A Scale

Air Temperature Window

B Scale

C Scale

Fahrenheit — Celsius Temperature Conversion Scale

Figure 8-41. The computer side uses logarithmic scales to set up ratio-type mathematical problems, such as multiplication and division.

Both the A and B scales start at 10 and go up to 99. There are no numbers between zero and 9, and the next mark after 99 is 10. If you read the 10 as 100, you can go around the scale again — then 11 becomes 110, 12 becomes 120, and so on. When you get all the way around and pass 10 again, it represents 1,000. This characteristic makes the scale infinite. The trick works in both directions, so that if you start at 10 and go counter-clockwise, 90 becomes 9, 80 becomes 8, all the way back to 11 becoming 1.1, 10 becoming 1.0, and 90 becoming 0.9. There is no limit to the range of the numbers your computer can handle, but you have to keep track of the decimal place yourself. It's not as hard as it sounds. If you are solving for groundspeed and get an answer of 15.6, you know that the answer is not 1,560 knots or 15.6 knots, so 156 knots remains as the only reasonable choice.

There is a box around the 10 on each scale, called the **10 index** or **unit index** You can use it to do conventional multiplication and division problems. [Figures 8-42 and 8-43]

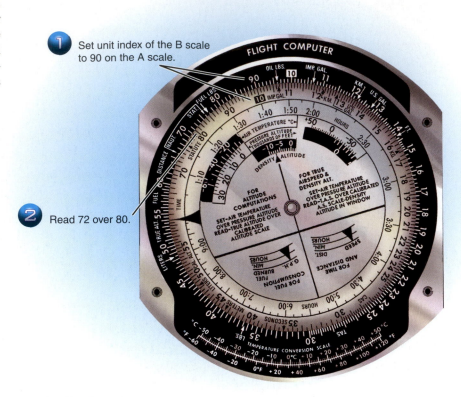

1 Set unit index of the B scale to 90 on the A scale.

2 Read 72 over 80.

Figure 8-42. To become familiar with operating the computer and to convince yourself that it works, multiply 9 × 8. Set the unit index on the inner scale (B scale) under 90 on the A scale. Now look above the 80 on the B scale. It points to 72 on the A scale. Sure enough, 9 × 8 = 72. Without changing the computer, you can multiply any number by 9. The B scale 90 is under 81 on the A scale, 60 is under 54, and 15 is under 135.

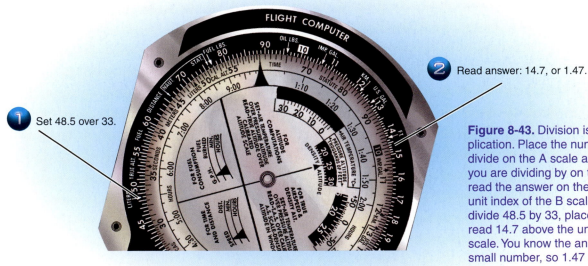

1 Set 48.5 over 33.

2 Read answer: 14.7, or 1.47.

Figure 8-43. Division is as easy as multiplication. Place the number you want to divide on the A scale above the number you are dividing by on the B scale and read the answer on the A scale above the unit index of the B scale. For example, to divide 48.5 by 33, place 48.5 over 33, and read 14.7 above the unit index of the B scale. You know the answer will be a fairly small number, so 1.47 must be correct.

The next scale inward from B is called the **C scale,** or **hours scale**. The big arrow at 60, called the speed index, is the unit index for the time scale. Since there are 60 minutes in an hour, you can either read minutes on the B scale, or hours plus minutes on the C scale. Thus, any combination of hours and minutes you find on the C scale accompanies the corresponding total number of minutes on the B scale. A handy rule of thumb for common calculations is that the speed index always points to a rate: knots, gallons per hour, etc.

AIRPLANES BEGIN TO GET AHEAD OF THEIR PILOTS

As aircraft became faster and more capable in the 1920s and 30s, the need for pilots to make in-flight calculations about fuel consumption, wind drift, and estimated time of arrival created a need for a simple, fast, and accurate computer. The problems of flying a marginally stable airplane in bad weather while trying to concentrate on handwritten math equations would tax the capabilities of the sharpest flyers. These were the days before autopilots and pressurization, and closed cockpits were just starting to gain acceptance. Long distance flights and new speed records between cities made headlines almost daily as engineers created more reliable and higher performance aircraft. Long range aircraft were employed to explore routes for the growing airlines, often flying to the very limits of their performance envelopes. Some companies provided an additional crew member to perform navigation calculations, while others tried to simplify the task so that the pilot could manage the math and fly the airplane at the same time. After all, an airline could sell another seat to a paying passenger if they could eliminate the need for a navigator.

Pilots soon discovered that they could reduce their workload in the air by planning and making as many calculations as possible on the ground before takeoff. The flight computer simplified many of the tasks that had to be handled in flight. Preparing for high workload situations during periods of lower workload is one of the central concepts in effective workload management.

Waterproof! Shock-Resistant! No Batteries!

In the days before pocket calculators, anyone who needed to make fast, accurate computations used a slide rule. As late as the 1970s these were a primary means of making quick calculations, from high school classrooms to the engineering departments of advanced aerospace companies. A circular slide rule (with the

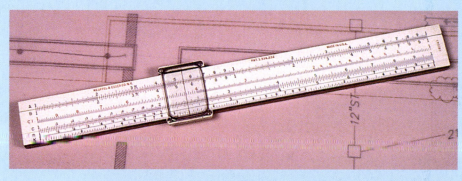

ends of the scales joined to read continuously in powers of ten) became a very handy device in the high-performance airplanes of the 1930s. It was easy to use, and could be operated with one hand.

Back in 1936, a Naval Reserve Lieutenant named Phillip Dalton had the idea of adapting the plotting board he had invented for aircraft carriers for use in airplanes. When this device was combined with a circular slide rule, it became a compact and versatile flight computer. Hundreds of thousands were made for the military as the E-6B. The mechanical flight computers of today are identical to the E-6B in most respects, right down to the big ring that was used to hang the computer on a hook in large airplanes or from a lanyard around the pilot's neck in single-seaters.

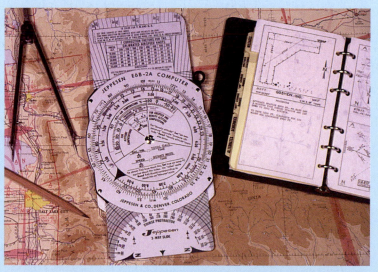

TIME, SPEED, AND DISTANCE

Time, speed, and distance (TSD) relationships are probably the most frequent problems you will solve with your computer. If you know two of these variables, you can quickly find the third. For TSD problems, the A scale is for distance, the B scale represents time in minutes, and the speed index always points to the rate of speed. [Figure 8-44]

4 To find out how many nautical miles you would cover in 45 minutes, find 45 on the B Scale. The answer is 84 nautical miles. You have just made three different calculations without even changing the setting!

2 Read the groundspeed, in this case 112 knots.

3 If the next checkpoint is 16 nautical miles away, you will be there in 8.6 minutes.

5 The C scale comes into play for figuring longer time periods. If you need to know how many miles you could fly in 3 1/2 hours, go to the 3:30 mark on the C scale and read 39, or 390 nautical miles, off the A scale.

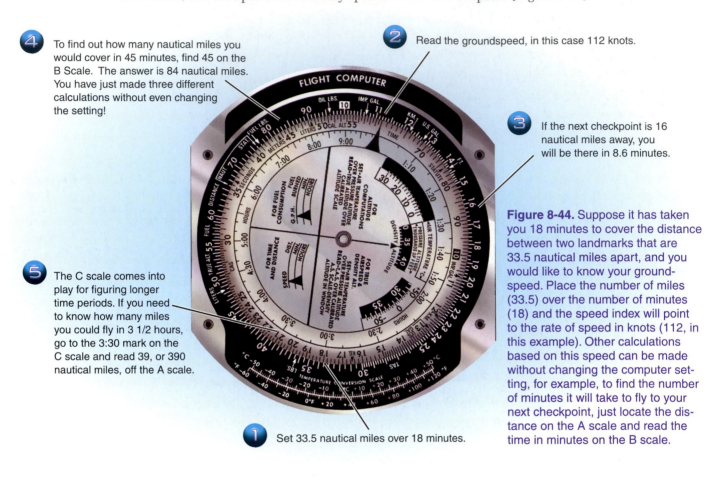

Figure 8-44. Suppose it has taken you 18 minutes to cover the distance between two landmarks that are 33.5 nautical miles apart, and you would like to know your groundspeed. Place the number of miles (33.5) over the number of minutes (18) and the speed index will point to the rate of speed in knots (112, in this example). Other calculations based on this speed can be made without changing the computer setting, for example, to find the number of minutes it will take to fly to your next checkpoint, just locate the distance on the A scale and read the time in minutes on the B scale.

1 Set 33.5 nautical miles over 18 minutes.

FUEL CONSUMPTION

Fuel consumption problems are similar to time, speed, and distance problems. The difference is that the speed index will indicate gallons per hour, and the A scale is used to represent gallons of fuel consumed instead of distance traveled.

FUEL REQUIRED

In planning a cross-country trip, you will need to determine how much fuel is necessary to complete the flight. The POH provides the rate of fuel consumption (fuel flow) at various cruise power settings. With this information and an accurate flight time, you can use the computer to solve for the amount of fuel needed. [Figure 8-45] Remember to add fuel needed for startup, taxi, takeoff, climb, and required reserves to determine the total fuel required for the flight. Naturally, if the fuel required is greater than the usable fuel available, you must plan a fuel stop.

ENDURANCE

Endurance is the amount of time you can remain aloft, based on a known fuel quantity and consumption rate. Since fuel consumption is not constant for the entire flight, think of endurance as an approximation, not an absolute value. This calculation is identical to the previous example, except that once the rate of consumption is set, the number of gallons available determines the endurance time. [Figure 8-46]

① Set 8.5 gallons per hour.

② Read fuel required, 18.4 gallons, for 2 hours 10 minutes at cruise.

Figure 8-45. Suppose you want to determine how much fuel you will need, based on a fuel consumption rate of 8.5 gallons per hour and a flight time of 2 hours, 10 minutes. The arrow points to the rate, gallons per hour in this case, so set the speed index to 85. Then, find the mark for 2:10 on the C scale, one increment above the 2:00 hour mark, and read the number of gallons from the A scale. It looks like 18.4 gallons will be needed for the cruise phase of the trip.

① Set 12.6 gallons per hour.

② Find 48 gallons on the A scale.

③ Read endurance of approximately 230 minutes or 3 hours 50 minutes.

Figure 8-46. To find the endurance of an airplane that uses 12.6 gallons per hour, and has 48 gallons of usable fuel, set the speed index to 12.6, find 48 on the A scale, and read the endurance off the B scale for minutes (230) or the C scale for hours (3:50).

ACTUAL CONSUMPTION RATE

After completing a flight, you might want to determine the actual fuel consumption rate based on the total amount of fuel used. You could then compare the result against the original fuel consumption rate and take it into consideration for future flight planning. You would set the number of gallons consumed on the A scale above the time on the B or C scale, then read the actual consumption rate over the speed index. [Figure 8-47]

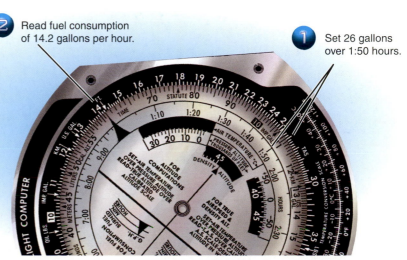

② Read fuel consumption of 14.2 gallons per hour.

① Set 26 gallons over 1:50 hours.

Figure 8-47. If you used 26 gallons in 1 hour and 50 minutes, you would set 26 on the A scale over 1:50 on the C scale, and read 14.2 gallons per hour at the speed index.

AIRSPEED AND DENSITY ALTITUDE CALCULATIONS

The airspeed indicator is a sensitive and precise instrument, but as air density decreases, indicated airspeed will be lower than true airspeed by about 2% per 1,000 feet of altitude. You can find the difference more accurately using the small scales toward the center of the computer. There are two different sets of scales and windows for air temperature and pressure altitude, one pair on each side of the small window labeled Density Altitude. For the true airspeed (TAS) calculation, use the scales to the right of the Density Altitude window. To calculate density altitude, use the same scales and set the pressure altitude opposite the outside air temperature. Read the density altitude in the center window. [Figure 8-48]

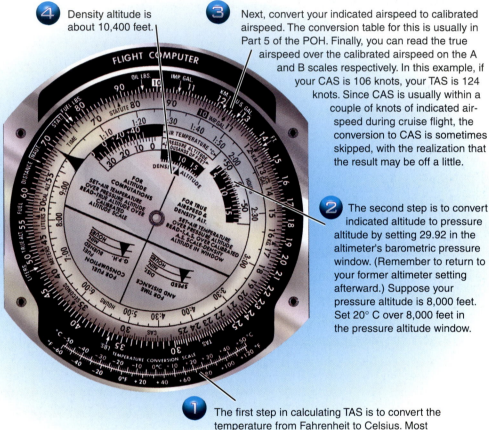

4 Density altitude is about 10,400 feet.

3 Next, convert your indicated airspeed to calibrated airspeed. The conversion table for this is usually in Part 5 of the POH. Finally, you can read the true airspeed over the calibrated airspeed on the A and B scales respectively. In this example, if your CAS is 106 knots, your TAS is 124 knots. Since CAS is usually within a couple of knots of indicated airspeed during cruise flight, the conversion to CAS is sometimes skipped, with the realization that the result may be off a little.

Figure 8-48. Say you are flying along at 7,500 feet MSL and the airplane's outside air temperature gauge indicates 68° F. True airspeed and density altitude can be calculated using pressure altitude and calibrated airspeed (CAS). As with the other computer solutions, if you know all but one of the variables, you can solve for the one remaining, so if you know your pressure altitude, the outside air temperature, and true airspeed, you can determine calibrated airspeed.

2 The second step is to convert indicated altitude to pressure altitude by setting 29.92 in the altimeter's barometric pressure window. (Remember to return to your former altimeter setting afterward.) Suppose your pressure altitude is 8,000 feet. Set 20° C over 8,000 feet in the pressure altitude window.

1 The first step in calculating TAS is to convert the temperature from Fahrenheit to Celsius. Most computers have this conversion scale printed on them. This shows 68°F to be 20°C.

WIND PROBLEMS

When an airplane moves through air that is also moving, it will affect the airplane's speed and its path over the ground. Since the air is almost always moving, you must routinely compensate for the effects of wind. The wind side of the calculator allows you to visualize these problems and solve them graphically. A little background may help you to understand the wind problem. [Figures 8-49 and 8-50]

Figure 8-49. Suppose you want to pilot a boat to a dock straight across the river. The boat moves in relation to the water, but the water is also moving.

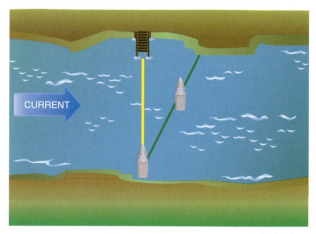

If you try to go straight across the river, your boat will reach the shore somewhere downstream of the dock, because the water itself is moving downstream with the current.

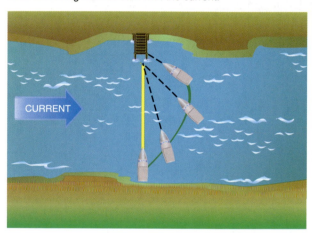

If you always keep the boat pointed directly at the dock, your path will be a curve.

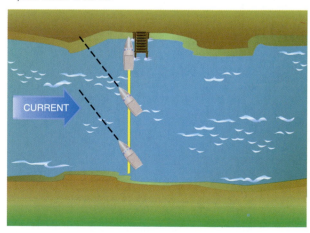

To go straight to the dock, you must compensate for the current by by pointing the boat upstream at an angle as you cross. But how would you know how much to angle the boat before starting out? This is the basic problem you solve on the wind side of the computer.

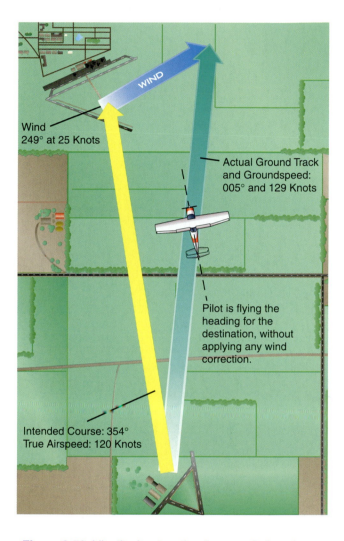

Wind
249° at 25 Knots

Actual Ground Track and Groundspeed: 005° and 129 Knots

Pilot is flying the heading for the destination, without applying any wind correction.

Intended Course: 354°
True Airspeed: 120 Knots

Figure 8-50. Like the boat on the river, an airplane in flight moves through a medium which is itself moving. If you just point the airplane in the direction you want to go, you are not likely to arrive at your destination. The relationship between these different movements can be described with arrows drawn to scale to represent the speeds and directions involved. Adding the vector representing the aircraft's airspeed to the one for wind speed gives a resultant vector that shows the speed and direction of the airplane as the wind will affect it.

COMPENSATING FOR WIND

When the wind is aligned with the direction of flight, it acts only to increase or decrease the groundspeed. [Figure 8-51] Headwinds reduce your groundspeed, and tailwinds add to your groundspeed. When the wind is not directly along your intended course, which is most of the time, it will tend to push the airplane off course. This error is called drift. To prevent drift and stay on course, you need to compensate by pointing the nose of the airplane a few degrees into the wind. Even though the airplane is in coordinated flight and staying on course, there is a difference between its heading and its course. This difference is the wind correction angle (WCA). [Figure 8-52] To put it another way, your course, corrected for wind, equals your heading.

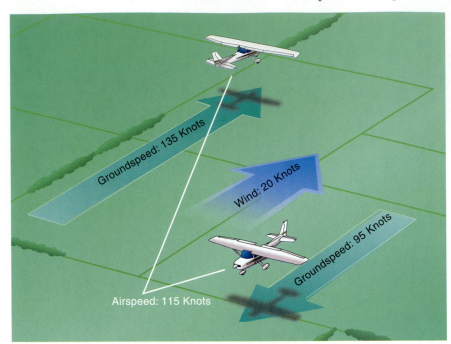

Groundspeed: 135 Knots

Wind: 20 Knots

Groundspeed: 95 Knots

Airspeed: 115 Knots

Figure 8-51. Even though both airplanes have the same airspeed, their groundspeeds differ by 40 knots.

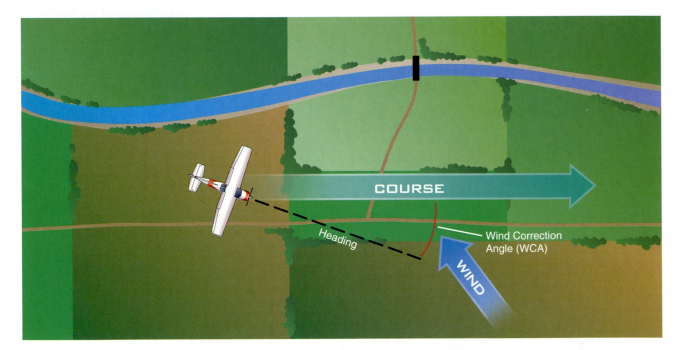

COURSE

Heading

Wind Correction Angle (WCA)

WIND

Figure 8-52. Course is the intended flight path, or direction of travel, over the surface of the earth with respect to north. Heading is the direction in which the airplane is pointing relative to north. In a no-wind situation, or with a direct headwind or tailwind, course and heading are the same. Wind correction angle (WCA) is the difference between the heading of an airplane and the desired course. It is the adjustment you apply to a heading to remain on course.

Vectors also are used to break down the effect of the wind into two components. One component acts in the direction of flight, either increasing or decreasing the groundspeed. This part of the wind is called the **headwind** or **tailwind component**. The other component acts perpendicular to the direction of flight. Called the **crosswind component**, it causes the airplane to drift off course. [Figure 8-53]

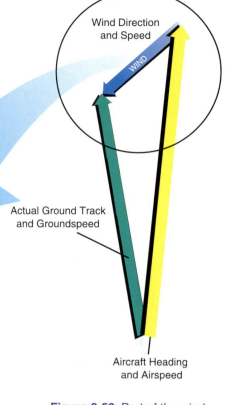

Wind Direction and Speed

WIND

Actual Ground Track and Groundspeed

Aircraft Heading and Airspeed

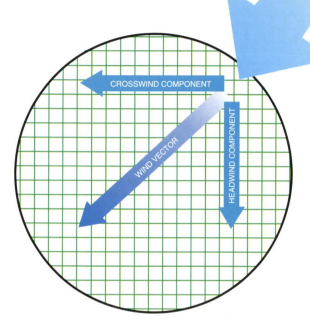

CROSSWIND COMPONENT

WIND VECTOR

HEADWIND COMPONENT

Figure 8-53. Part of the wind affects groundspeed, while the other part affects direction.

Compressibility

When an airplane moves through the air at relatively low speeds, air behaves as an incompressible fluid. The air molecules move out of the way as the airplane passes. As speed increases, the molecules are unable to move aside quickly enough, and air pressure begins to build up in front of the airplane. This effect is called compressibility, since the air begins behaving as a compressible gas.

Compressibility affects the accuracy of the airspeed indicator since the increased pressure at the pitot tube results in a higher airspeed indication. Air friction at high speeds also heats the outside air temperature probe, giving higher readings. These effects are negligible at speeds below 200 knots and pressure altitudes below 20,000 feet, but can increase the indicated airspeed by as much as 19% at 530 knots and 50,000 feet. Many mechanical flight computers have a chart for applying conversion factors for compressibility at various altitudes and speeds.

COMPRESSIBILITY CORRECTION

PRESSURE ALTITUDE	F CORRECTION FACTORS FOR **TAS** CALIBRATED AIRSPEED IN KNOTS							
	200	250	300	350	400	450	500	550
10,000 FT.	1.00	1.00	.99	.99	.98	.98	.97	.97
20,000 FT.	.99	.98	.97	.97	.96	.95	.94	.93
30,000 FT.	.97	.96	.95	.94	.92	.91	.90	.89
40,000 FT.	.96	.94	.92	.90	.88	.87	.87	.86
50,000 FT.	.93	.90	.87	.86	.84	.84	.84	.84

USE CALIBRATED AIRSPEED AND PRESS. ALT. TO OBTAIN **F** FACTOR. MULTIPLY **F** FACTOR BY **TAS** TO OBTAIN THE **TAS** CORRECTED FOR COMPRESSIBILITY

The wind side of the computer separates the wind components for you. Using the **azimuth plate**, **true index**, and a **wind dot**, you can determine how the wind will affect your airplane in flight. [Figure 8-54]

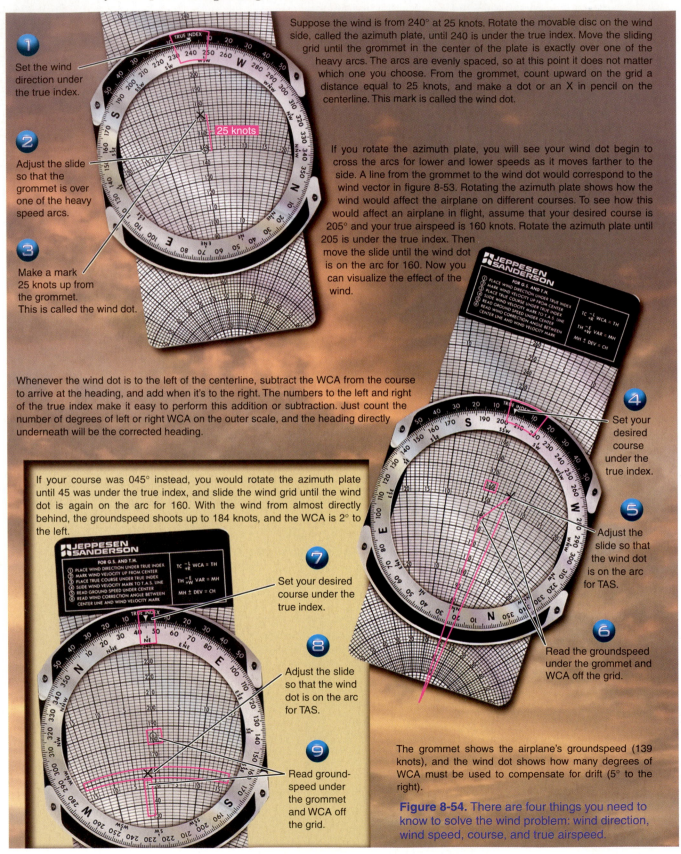

1 Set the wind direction under the true index.

2 Adjust the slide so that the grommet is over one of the heavy speed arcs.

3 Make a mark 25 knots up from the grommet. This is called the wind dot.

Suppose the wind is from 240° at 25 knots. Rotate the movable disc on the wind side, called the azimuth plate, until 240 is under the true index. Move the sliding grid until the grommet in the center of the plate is exactly over one of the heavy arcs. The arcs are evenly spaced, so at this point it does not matter which one you choose. From the grommet, count upward on the grid a distance equal to 25 knots, and make a dot or an X in pencil on the centerline. This mark is called the wind dot.

If you rotate the azimuth plate, you will see your wind dot begin to cross the arcs for lower and lower speeds as it moves farther to the side. A line from the grommet to the wind dot would correspond to the wind vector in figure 8-53. Rotating the azimuth plate shows how the wind would affect the airplane on different courses. To see how this would affect an airplane in flight, assume that your desired course is 205° and your true airspeed is 160 knots. Rotate the azimuth plate until 205 is under the true index. Then move the slide until the wind dot is on the arc for 160. Now you can visualize the effect of the wind.

Whenever the wind dot is to the left of the centerline, subtract the WCA from the course to arrive at the heading, and add when it's to the right. The numbers to the left and right of the true index make it easy to perform this addition or subtraction. Just count the number of degrees of left or right WCA on the outer scale, and the heading directly underneath will be the corrected heading.

4 Set your desired course under the true index.

5 Adjust the slide so that the wind dot is on the arc for TAS.

6 Read the groundspeed under the grommet and WCA off the grid.

If your course was 045° instead, you would rotate the azimuth plate until 45 was under the true index, and slide the wind grid until the wind dot is again on the arc for 160. With the wind from almost directly behind, the groundspeed shoots up to 184 knots, and the WCA is 2° to the left.

7 Set your desired course under the true index.

8 Adjust the slide so that the wind dot is on the arc for TAS.

9 Read groundspeed under the grommet and WCA off the grid.

The grommet shows the airplane's groundspeed (139 knots), and the wind dot shows how many degrees of WCA must be used to compensate for drift (5° to the right).

Figure 8-54. There are four things you need to know to solve the wind problem: wind direction, wind speed, course, and true airspeed.

ACTUAL WINDS ALOFT

During cross-country flights, you will learn that actual winds are seldom the same as forecast. As a result, you can usually expect your actual groundspeed to vary somewhat from your preflight estimate. If your groundspeed is slower than planned, you will use more fuel than predicted, so your reserve will be reduced. The additional time needed to complete the flight will translate directly into additional fuel consumed.

Solving for actual winds aloft is essentially the reverse of predicting groundspeed from forecast winds aloft. In this case, you will start with your groundspeed and wind correction angle, and use them to find wind direction and speed. [Figure 8-55]

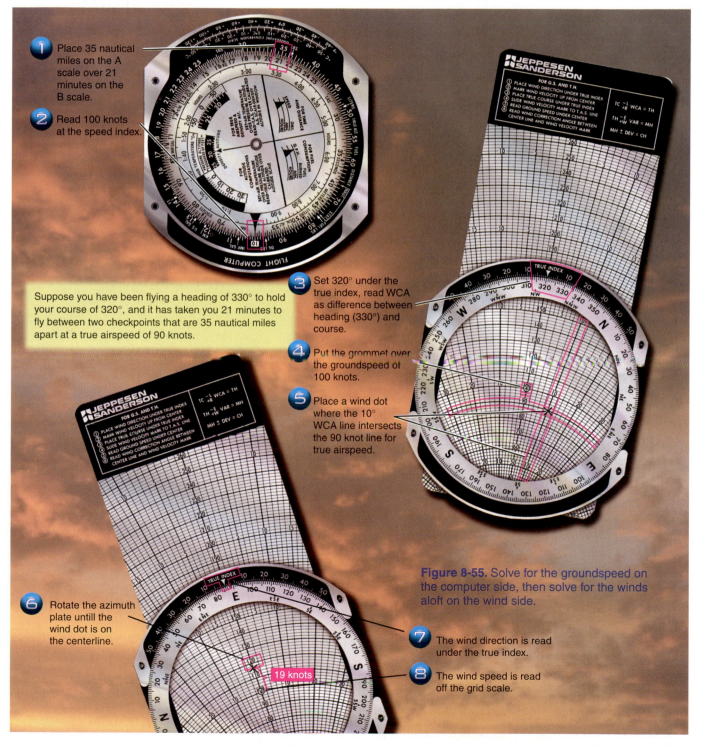

1. Place 35 nautical miles on the A scale over 21 minutes on the B scale.

2. Read 100 knots at the speed index.

Suppose you have been flying a heading of 330° to hold your course of 320°, and it has taken you 21 minutes to fly between two checkpoints that are 35 nautical miles apart at a true airspeed of 90 knots.

3. Set 320° under the true index, read WCA as difference between heading (330°) and course.

4. Put the grommet over the groundspeed of 100 knots.

5. Place a wind dot where the 10° WCA line intersects the 90 knot line for true airspeed.

6. Rotate the azimuth plate untill the wind dot is on the centerline.

Figure 8-55. Solve for the groundspeed on the computer side, then solve for the winds aloft on the wind side.

7. The wind direction is read under the true index.

8. The wind speed is read off the grid scale.

19 knots

MOST FAVORABLE WINDS

One of the factors you should consider in selecting a cruising altitude is the effect of wind on groundspeed. Because wind direction and speed usually change with altitude, it's difficult to tell which altitude will result in the best groundspeed. The flight computer offers a fairly simple method of determining which altitude offers the most favorable winds for a given course. [Figure 8-56] Of course, you will have to balance the influence of winds against other factors, such as safe terrain clearance, climb times, and VFR cruising altitude rules.

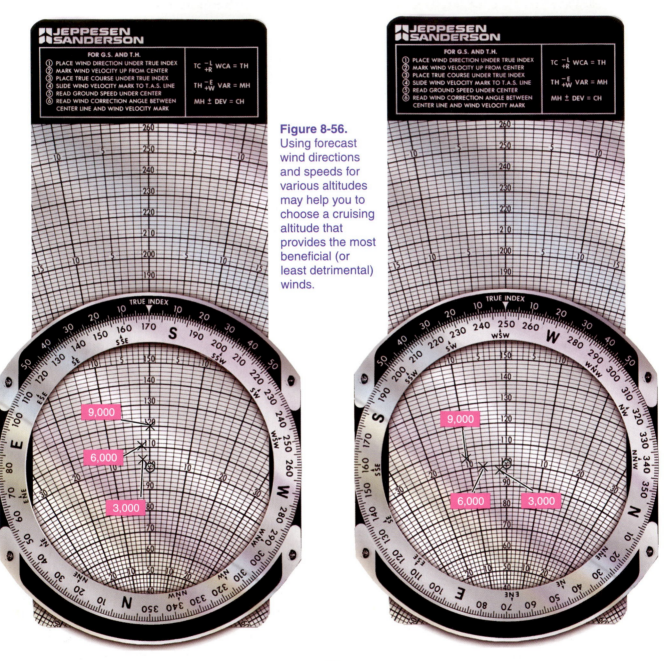

Figure 8-56. Using forecast wind directions and speeds for various altitudes may help you to choose a cruising altitude that provides the most beneficial (or least detrimental) winds.

 The first step is to plot the forecast winds for each altitude.
Wind at 3,000 feet MSL: 130° at 5 knots
Wind at 6,000 feet MSL: 150° at 12 knots
Wind at 9,000 feet MSL: 170° at 20 knots

 Then rotate the azimuth plate until your course is directly under the true index. By comparing the grommet to each wind dot, you can select the most favorable wind. Wind dots below the grommet represent tailwinds, while those above the grommet indicate headwinds.
On a course of 250°, the winds at 3,000 feet MSL provide a 2 knot tailwind.
The winds at 6,000 feet MSL have almost no effect on groundspeed.
The winds at 9,000 feet MSL produce a 6 knot headwind.

CONVERSIONS

Flight computers incorporate many different conversion scales. In fact, you have already used one of these — the temperature conversion scale located on the bottom of the computer side. Other conversion scales are located directly on the A and B scales.

STATUTE TO NAUTICAL

It is important to use the same size miles throughout your calculations. Nautical miles are 15% longer than statute miles, so mixing them with statute miles (or statute mile-based units such as miles per hour) results in significant errors. Many aircraft have airspeed indicators marked in statute miles per hour (mph), and their POHs have data such as power settings, fuel consumption, cruising speeds, and range based on statute units. As long as you are aware of the differences and use the same units consistently, you can use whichever system is more convenient. [Figure 8-57]

OTHER CONVERSIONS

Most flight computers allow you to directly convert aviation gasoline quantities between gallons and pounds. [Figure 8-58] Your computer will also manage conversions between statute miles and kilometers, U.S. gallons and Imperial gallons, U.S. gallons and liters, feet and meters, pounds and kilograms, and various other units. Since the procedures vary, read the computer's instruction manual for detailed directions.

1 To convert between statute and nautical miles, use the NAUT./STAT. arrows.

2 To convert 116 nautical miles to statue miles, put the NAUT. arrow over 116 and read the statute equivalent (133 s.m.) under the STAT. arrow.

3 To convert 133 statute miles per hour to knots, set the STAT. arrow over 133 and read 116 knots under the NAUT. arrow.

Figure 8-57. It is easy to convert between statute and nautical miles. When the nautical arrow points to any value on the B scale, the equivalent statute value is under the statute arrow.

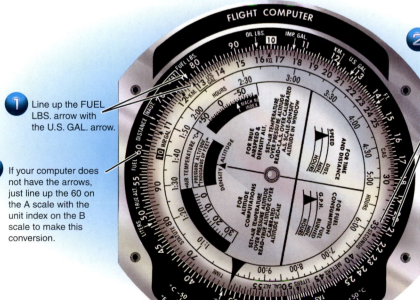

1 Line up the FUEL LBS. arrow with the U.S. GAL. arrow.

2 Find the fuel weight over the fuel gallons at any point around the computer. For example, 35 gallons weigh 210 pounds.

3 If your computer does not have the arrows, just line up the 60 on the A scale with the unit index on the B scale to make this conversion.

Figure 8-58. To convert between gallons and pounds of aviation gasoline, align the FUEL LBS. arrow with the U.S. GAL. arrow. Then, you can read pounds on the A scale opposite gallons on the B scale. Even if your computer does not have these arrows, you can do the same thing by placing the 10 index of the B scale under 60 on the A scale.

MULTI-PART PROBLEMS

Sometimes you may have to solve a series of related problems to obtain a particular solution. To find the fuel required for a proposed flight, for example, you would first find the true airspeed, then use the result to solve for the groundspeed and time enroute and, finally, determine the fuel required. Since a mistake in any step can lead to increased errors in subsequent steps, the key to successful multi-part problem solving is to work patiently and understand what information is needed for each step. [Figure 8-59]

 To find an estimated time enroute (ETE), first calculate groundspeed, then compute the time to cover the remaining distance. To compute an estimated time of arrival (ETA), add the estimated time enroute to the time over the last checkpoint. See figure 8-59.

ELECTRONIC FLIGHT COMPUTERS

In recent years, a variety of handheld electronic flight computers have become available. In addition to the functions of a mechanical flight computer, some can perform weight and balance calculations, or figure time-to-climb and rate-of-climb. Most include a timer or stopwatch function. While features and functions vary, most are similar enough in operation to permit a general description of their use. For these examples we will use the Jeppesen TechStar Pro, which is typical of many electronic flight computers. Although the TechStar Pro also functions as a personal organizer, this discussion is only concerned with its aviation functions. Be sure to read the instructions or operating manual for your particular computer, and become completely familiar with how it is used.

The electronic computer uses the same parameters to solve problems as the mechanical flight computer. Thus, if you want to solve for density altitude, you need to input pressure altitude and temperature, and if you want to find a wind correction angle, you need to start with the wind direction and speed, course, and true airspeed. Since the problems and their underlying principles are the same, you must still pay close attention to the details, such as converting temperatures from Fahrenheit to Celsius, and using either statute or nautical miles throughout. The solutions you get from any computer, electronic or mechanical, are only as good as the information you put into it.

Given:

Pressure Altitude... 7,500 ft
Temperature... 15°C (True)
Calibrated Airspeed.. 105 kts
Wind Direction... 035° at 12 kts
Course... 270°
Distance... 256 n.m.
Time Over the Most Recent Checkpoint.................... 11:24 a.m.

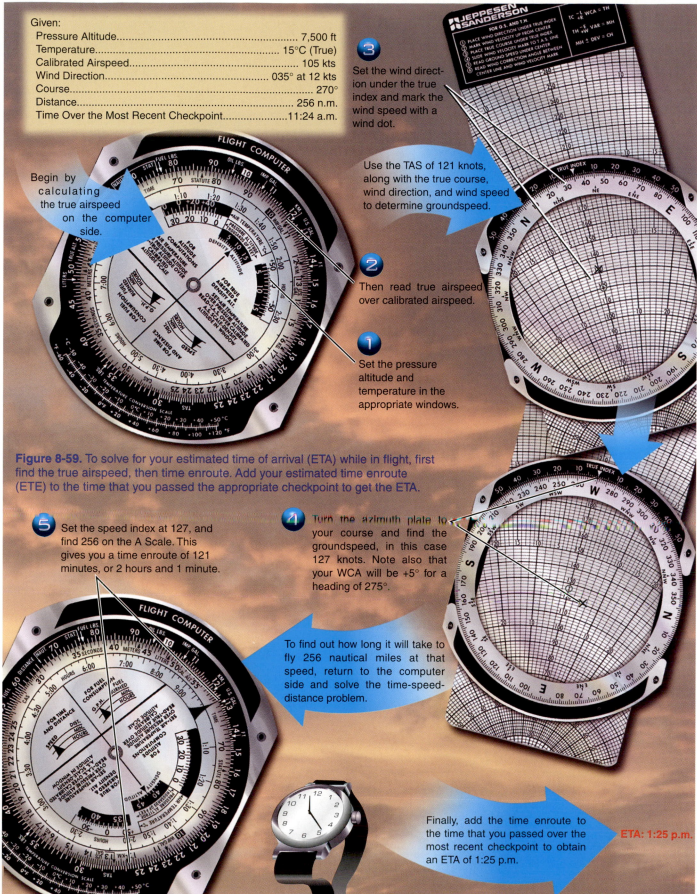

Begin by calculating the true airspeed on the computer side.

3 Set the wind direction under the true index and mark the wind speed with a wind dot.

Use the TAS of 121 knots, along with the true course, wind direction, and wind speed to determine groundspeed.

2 Then read true airspeed over calibrated airspeed.

1 Set the pressure altitude and temperature in the appropriate windows.

Figure 8-59. To solve for your estimated time of arrival (ETA) while in flight, first find the true airspeed, then time enroute. Add your estimated time enroute (ETE) to the time that you passed the appropriate checkpoint to get the ETA.

5 Set the speed index at 127, and find 256 on the A Scale. This gives you a time enroute of 121 minutes, or 2 hours and 1 minute.

4 Turn the azimuth plate to your course and find the groundspeed, in this case 127 knots. Note also that your WCA will be +5° for a heading of 275°.

To find out how long it will take to fly 256 nautical miles at that speed, return to the computer side and solve the time-speed-distance problem.

Finally, add the time enroute to the time that you passed over the most recent checkpoint to obtain an ETA of 1:25 p.m.

ETA: 1:25 p.m.

MODES AND BASIC OPERATION

After turning on the flight computer, the next step is to select the kind of problem you intend to solve. The TechStar Pro has seven categories of problems from which to choose. These **electronic computer modes** group similar types of problems together, such as time-speed-distance problems, altitude problems, or wind problems. [Figure 8-60] Pushing one

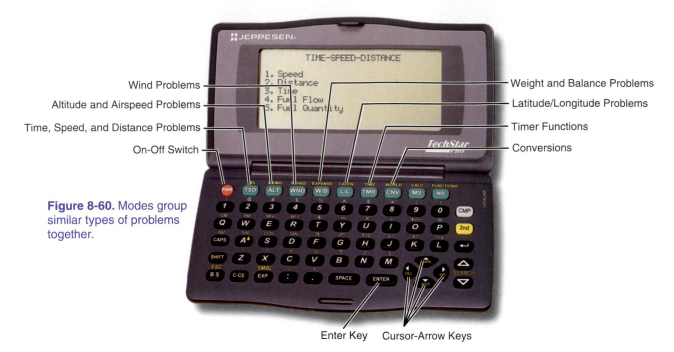

Wind Problems

Altitude and Airspeed Problems

Time, Speed, and Distance Problems

On-Off Switch

Weight and Balance Problems

Latitude/Longitude Problems

Timer Functions

Conversions

Enter Key   Cursor-Arrow Keys

Figure 8-60. Modes group similar types of problems together.

of the mode buttons displays a menu of values for which to solve. [Figure 8-61] To choose the unknown value you wish to determine from the menu, you can either press the number, or move the cursor to the item with the arrow keys and press ENTER. Once a specific unknown value is chosen, the computer will present a list of the parameters used to solve such problems, prompting you to enter the information required. Press ENTER after using the number keys to put in each required value. Once the computer has enough information to solve the problem, it will calculate and display the answer. Some computers may require you to use a separate COMPUTE key to complete the calculation.

ALTITUDE-AIRSPEED
1. Pressure Altitude
2. Calibrated Airspeed
3. True Airspeed
4. Density Altitude
5. Mach Number
6. Standard Temperature
7. True Altitude

WIND
1. Wind Direction and Wind Speed
2. Heading
3. Groundspeed
4. Crosswind Component

TIME-SPEED-DISTANCE
1. Speed
2. Distance
3. Time
4. Fuel Flow
5. Fuel Quantity

WEIGHT-BALANCE
1. Weight-Moment-CG
2. Shift CG
3. Percent MAC

Figure 8-61. Picking a mode displays a menu of values for which you could solve.

SAMPLE PROBLEMS

To help you become familiar with electronic flight computer operation, some typical problems will be solved using the TechStar Pro. If you are using a different type of computer, the exact keystrokes and information presentation may be different. [Figures 8-62 and 8-63]

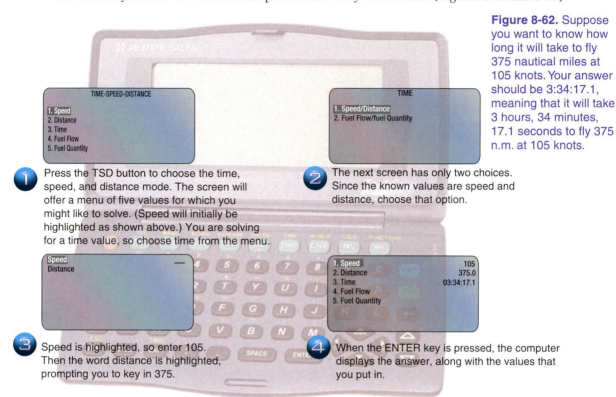

Figure 8-62. Suppose you want to know how long it will take to fly 375 nautical miles at 105 knots. Your answer should be 3:34:17.1, meaning that it will take 3 hours, 34 minutes, 17.1 seconds to fly 375 n.m. at 105 knots.

1 Press the TSD button to choose the time, speed, and distance mode. The screen will offer a menu of five values for which you might like to solve. (Speed will initially be highlighted as shown above.) You are solving for a time value, so choose time from the menu.

2 The next screen has only two choices. Since the known values are speed and distance, choose that option.

3 Speed is highlighted, so enter 105. Then the word distance is highlighted, prompting you to key in 375.

4 When the ENTER key is pressed, the computer displays the answer, along with the values that you put in.

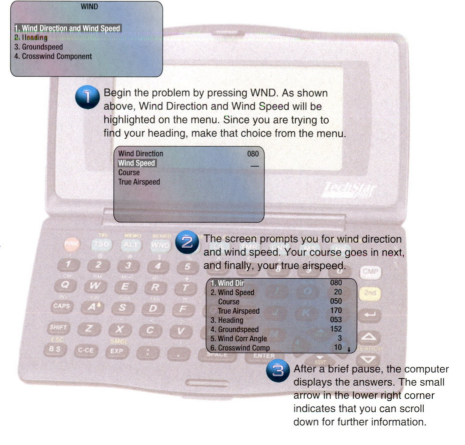

Figure 8-63. To solve for a wind correction angle and ground-speed, assume the forecast wind is 080° at 20 knots, and you are planning to fly a course of 050°. Use a true airspeed of 170 knots. The computer gives your wind correction angle (+3°), true heading (053°), and groundspeed (152 knots), as well as the crosswind component (10 knots).

1 Begin the problem by pressing WND. As shown above, Wind Direction and Wind Speed will be highlighted on the menu. Since you are trying to find your heading, make that choice from the menu.

2 The screen prompts you for wind direction and wind speed. Your course goes in next, and finally, your true airspeed.

3 After a brief pause, the computer displays the answers. The small arrow in the lower right corner indicates that you can scroll down for further information.

SUMMARY CHECKLIST

✓ On a mechanical flight computer, the A scale and B scale are identical.

✓ Multiplication and division are done using the unit index or 10 index.

✓ The speed index or 60 index is the unit index for the C scale, which is used for hours. Hours on the C scale correspond to minutes on the B scale.

✓ Time, speed, and distance problems are solved on the computer side. Fuel consumption, density altitude, true airspeed, and conversion problems also are done on the computer side.

✓ The wind vector can be separated into two components, a headwind or tailwind component, and a crosswind component.

✓ Course is the term for the intended path over the ground. Heading is the direction in which the nose of the airplane is pointed. An aircraft flying with a crosswind component will drift off course if the heading is the same as the course. By applying a wind correction angle, you can compensate for drift and remain on course.

✓ Wind correction angles are determined on the wind side of the computer. The effect of predicted winds aloft can be determined prior to takeoff, and actual winds aloft can be calculated using heading and ground reference information gathered in flight.

✓ Electronic flight computers duplicate many of the functions of mechanical flight computers, and some offer additional features such as timers or weight and balance functions.

KEY TERMS

Computer Side	Hours Scale
Wind Side	Wind Correction Angle (WCA)
Speed Index	Headwind Component
60 Index	Tailwind Component
A Scale	Crosswind Component
B Scale	Azimuth Plate
Unit Index	True Index
10 Index	Wind Dot
C Scale	Electronic Computer Modes

QUESTIONS

Solve the following problems with either an electronic or a mechanical flight computer.

1. If you cover 61 nautical miles in 41.5 minutes, what is your groundspeed?

2. After landing from a 362 nautical mile flight, you find that it takes 32.5 gallons to refill the fuel tanks. If the tanks were full when you took off, and your groundspeed was 138 knots, what was the average fuel consumption rate for the flight?

3. At a pressure altitude of 6,900 feet and an outside temperature of 7° C, your airspeed indicator shows 96 knots. What is your approximate true airspeed? Why is this number approximate?

4. Your POH provides a fuel consumption figure of 8.7 gallons per hour for your planned power setting and altitude. How much fuel would be used in 2 hours, 30 minutes?

5. How many nautical miles are in 148 statute miles?

6. With a true airspeed of 88 knots and winds from 240° at 16 knots, what heading would be required to maintain a course of 137°? What groundspeed would you expect?

7. What is the estimated time enroute for a flight of 194 nautical miles on a course of 084°. Your true airspeed is 129 knots, and pressure altitude is 5,200 feet. The wind is from 233° at 18 knots, and outside air temperature is 10° C.

8. Estimate the time enroute for a flight of 280 statute miles on a course of 022°. Your calibrated airspeed is 96 miles per hour, and pressure altitude is 9,000 feet. The wind is from 320° at 22 knots, and outside air temperature is 77° F.

9. Suppose you have been holding a heading of 140° to maintain a course of 133° between 2 checkpoints 128 nautical miles apart. It took 37 minutes to cover that distance at a true airspeed of 198 knots. What is the wind direction and speed?

10. What heading should you fly to hold a course of 355° if your true airspeed is 116 knots and the winds are from 050° at 15 knots? What groundspeed would you expect?

CHAPTER 9

NAVIGATION

Part IV, Chapter 9 — Navigation

SECTION A
PILOTAGE AND DEAD RECKONING

Your introduction to navigation initially takes you back to the methods used by the earliest cross-country pilots, as they learned to find their way from town to town by following roads and looking for landmarks from the air. This method was adequate for flights over distinctive terrain, but as pilots began to consider more challenging flights, over water or featureless deserts for instance, they borrowed the well-proven techniques used for centuries by ocean navigators. Pilotage and dead reckoning are still the most common methods of light plane navigation. Although presented separately, these two methods normally are used together, each acting as a cross-check of the other.

Three basic tasks of navigation are to create a course, fly the airplane so as to stay on the course, and make position checks to confirm that you are remaining on course. Finding your way to safety if you get lost also is an important element. Two terms used in connection with finding your position in flight are line of position and fix. A line of position is the simple concept that the airplane is located somewhere along a specific line. A **line of position (LOP)** does not establish the exact position of the airplane, but rather a line of possible positions, one of which is the airplane's actual position. The intersection of two different lines of position is a **fix,** which establishes your position at a definite location. If you are calling to report a fire in your neighborhood, and you tell the fire department it is on Elm Street, you have established a line of position. It does not identify the position of the fire, but it creates a string of possible locations (all the addresses on Elm Street) while eliminating other possible locations (Maple Street, Locust Street, Spruce Street, etc.). If you report the fire as being at Elm and Main, then you have created a fix, and the firefighters can go to a definite location. These terms are important in radio navigation as well as in pilotage and dead reckoning.

PILOTAGE

Before World War I, aviators seldom carried maps, relying on their familiarity with landmarks such as rivers or railroads. Since then, excellent aeronautical charts have been developed that make visual navigation practical in most areas of the country, whether the pilot is familiar with the local landmarks or not. Navigating by visual landmarks is called **pilotage**. Most pilots delight in looking at the ground as they fly, so pilotage can be a very interesting and enjoyable way to navigate. Your sectional charts provide a much more accurate and detailed representation of the landscape than the automobile road maps often used by early pilots. You must deal with a few complications that would have mystified the old-time aviators, such as special-use airspace and Mode C veils, but the basics remain the same for pilotage today: a good map, and a good view of the ground.

Preflight planning for pilotage begins with obtaining the correct charts. The high level of detail and the relatively large scale make sectional charts the best choice for visual navigation. Make sure that the charts you use are current. Although large permanent

Winning Races Against Faster Airplanes

French pilot Jean Conneau was a pioneer of aerial navigation, and one of the first to use maps in flight. In 1911 he overcame the problem of the map blowing away by mounting it on a pair of rollers that let him read it like a scroll as the flight progressed. He won air races against faster airplanes by using his map to fly straight lines between cities instead of following roads, an almost revolutionary concept at the time.

features such as mountains do not change much between chart editions, new towers are erected, ponds form or dry up, and airports open or close. You can get a good idea of which sectionals you will need for a trip by checking the chart coverage diagram on the front panel of any sectional chart.

COURSE CONSIDERATIONS

Once you have the appropriate chart or charts, arrange them so that you can view the entire route from departure to destination. For long routes, this might mean spreading the charts out on a large table, or on the living room floor. To line up adjacent charts precisely, match the latitude and longitude lines near the edges of each chart. If it happens that your departure and destination airports are on opposite sides of the same chart, follow the instructions printed on the margin of the chart to plot your course. [Figure 9-1]

Figure 9-1. Instructions on the chart provide a step-by-step procedure for plotting a route that crosses from one side of a chart to the other.

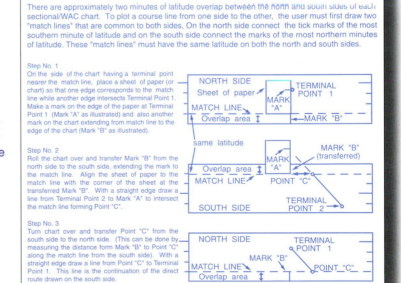

Look over the general route and decide whether there are areas you would like to avoid, such as special-use airspace, high mountains, or a large expanse of open water. [Figure 9-2] In areas where prominent landmarks are sparse, pilotage can be difficult, so you might choose to move your course a few miles to one side or the other to include some unmistakable landmarks. In many cases you will simply choose the direct route between

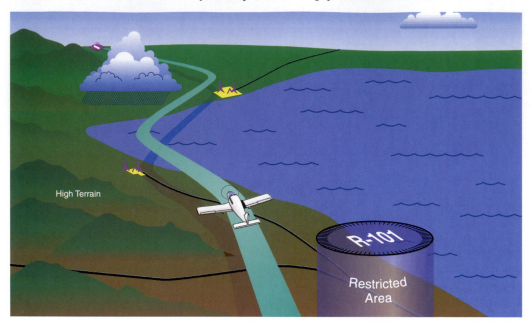

Figure 9-2. You may want to modify your course to avoid certain areas.

your departure and destination airports. Using a straightedge, draw a pencil line from one airport symbol to the other. This tentative course line will help you to refine your course still further, if necessary.

Use a plotter or ruler to measure the length of your course in nautical miles, taking care to use the correct scale for the chart. Using information from the POH and winds aloft forecasts, estimate the amount of fuel required for the trip, including takeoff, climb, and reserves. Be generous, since winds may shift direction and speed. If the amount of fuel required makes you think a fuel stop may be necessary, adjust your course to land at an airport with fuel service. It is worthwhile to telephone the fixed-base operators (FBOs) at your proposed fuel stops to verify that fuel of the proper grade will be available when you arrive, and that there will be someone to unlock the pumps and accept your payment. Information on FBOs at specific airports is found in a number of commercial publications.

CHECKPOINTS

Once you have finalized your course, you can begin selecting **checkpoints**. The best checkpoints are those that cannot be confused with anything else, for example, a lake with a distinctive shape, or a major highway crossing a river. Depending on the altitude you choose, you may be able to positively identify landmarks several miles either side of your course. These reference points can provide valuable cues to help you recognize and correct for drift.

Checkpoints are useful only if they can be positively identified from the air, so you should avoid choosing features that could become ambiguous in flight. For example, many small towns look alike from the air, and in many areas of the country they occur at regular intervals along railroads, a legacy of the era when steam locomotives needed periodic stops to take on water. You could be in a situation of knowing you are over one

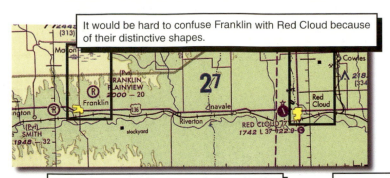

It would be hard to confuse Franklin with Red Cloud because of their distinctive shapes.

Figure 9-3. Small towns can be hard to identify, but small cities can usually be recognized by their distinctive shapes.

Isabel and Nashville have similar triangles formed by the railroad and the roads north and west of town. Nashville could be identified in flight by the towers north and south of town, as well as the jog in the road where it crosses the railroad east of town.

Clear Lake and Slapout could be easily confused from the air, because of the similar road patterns. Both have towers south of the town, but the towers are on opposite sides of the road.

of these railroad towns, but not which one, unless there are other landmarks to distinguish the town from the others up and down the line. On the other hand, small cities have excellent landmark value, since the yellow pattern on the chart attempts to show the actual shape of the city from the air. [Figure 9-3]

Although major roads are usually good checkpoints, secondary roads can be deceiving. Since only the most prominent secondary roads are portrayed on the chart, you may see many other similar roads in flight. When you think about using a road for a checkpoint, look for features that will be easy to distinguish from the air, such as unique bends or the relative location of railroads, streams, powerlines, etc. Keep in mind that new roads and highways are continuously under construction and may not even appear on a current chart. [Figure 9-4]

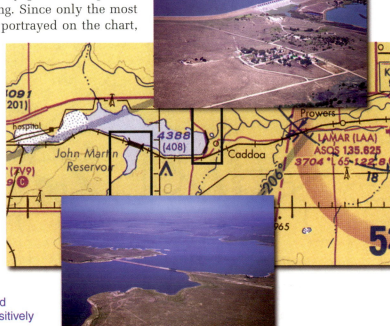

Figure 9-4. The reservoir, railroad bridge, and bends in the road positively identify Caddoa.

Do Your Navigation Methods Hold Water?

Water towers in small towns often have the town name painted on them. This can sometimes be an aid to pilotage, but you must descend to a low altitude to read the name, if it is there at all.

There once was a tradition that if a pilot circled the water tower (or the town) before landing at the airport, the local constable would come out and give him or her a ride into town. This tradition dates back to the time of the barnstormers.

Rivers usually make excellent landmarks, especially when they have distinctive bends or curves. Although the chart depicts most rivers very accurately, be alert for possible seasonal variations. During a flood stage, the appearance from the air may be quite different from the chart pattern. During a drought, on the other hand, the watercourse shown on a sectional may actually be a dried-up river bed. Lakes usually are good references, but in many parts of the country, hundreds of small lakes exist within close proximity, and identifying a particular one can be extremely difficult. In other areas, ponds depicted on the chart may have dried up without a trace. As with small towns and secondary roads, be sure to use other nearby landmarks to confirm identification of small or nondescript features.

The number of checkpoints needed for a particular flight is up to you, and depends on your confidence level, the presence or absence of other visual course cues such as fence lines, your altitude, and your use of dead reckoning or radio navigation. Try to plan a couple of prominent checkpoints shortly after takeoff, to help you get established on the correct course. The first checkpoint should be close enough to be easy to locate after takeoff, but far enough that you are clear of the airport traffic pattern before turning your attention to navigation. Once you have decided on your checkpoints, circle them on the chart so you can locate them easily without obscuring any details. Pencil lines can be difficult to find when you are dividing your attention between flying and reading the map, so go over your course lines and checkpoint circles with a pen or highlighter. Choose a color that does not blend in with the colors of chart features. You may also want to place tick marks along your course at 10 or 20 mile intervals, to help estimate distances along the route or to help monitor your progress.

 Section Lines and Subdivisions

Surveyors divide land into townships and sections for legal and real estate purposes. A township consists of 36 sections or subdivisions, each of which is one square mile in area. Farmers often plant their fields in sections, half sections, quarter sections, etc., and roads are usually laid out along the lines that divide sections. In many parts of the country, these section lines are very conspicuous from the air, and can be used as aids in both pilotage and dead reckoning. By comparing the angle at which your airplane crosses section lines with the course line on your map, section lines can be used as a sort of compass, since the lines run accurately north-south or east-west. If you happen to be flying parallel to the section lines, you can find groundspeed by timing yourself from one section line to the next. A section is one statute mile on each side, so a time of 30 seconds would indicate a groundspeed of 120 statute miles per hour, or about 104 knots.

FLYING THE COURSE

In flight, your objective is to make your path over the ground match the course line drawn on your chart. The easiest way to remain on course is to stay continuously aware of your position. Fold the chart so that only one or two panels are showing. Many pilots hold the chart so that the course line on their chart is aligned with the direction of flight. Consequently, the landmarks on the ground appear in the same relative positions as their respective chart symbols. Mark each checkpoint as you pass it, and if you see that you have drifted to one side of your course, mark your actual position rather than the intended checkpoint. Correct for drift by adjusting your heading. [Figure 9-5] Even if you are only off course by a small amount, make a correction to your heading, otherwise you will be off even farther at the next checkpoint, possibly far enough to miss the checkpoint entirely. Between checkpoints you can draw visual lines of position from landmarks that are to one side or the other of your course to find intermediate position fixes. For example, if you find that you are a few miles directly south of a certain town, and you are also passing over a railroad track that runs straight to another town to the southeast, you have established a fix from two lines of position.

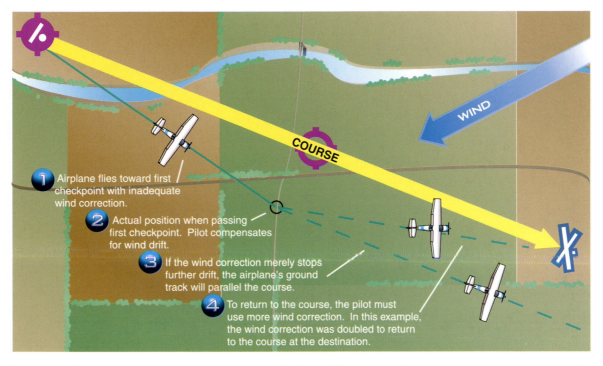

① Airplane flies toward first checkpoint with inadequate wind correction.

② Actual position when passing first checkpoint. Pilot compensates for wind drift.

③ If the wind correction merely stops further drift, the airplane's ground track will parallel the course.

④ To return to the course, the pilot must use more wind correction. In this example, the wind correction was doubled to return to the course at the destination.

Figure 9-5. If your correction is exactly right, you will still be off course by the same amount at the next checkpoint.

When flying by pilotage, match as much as possible of what you see on the ground to the features on your chart even when you are between checkpoints. Whenever you can, confirm each checkpoint by comparing it against a combination of several ground features. Remember, aeronautical charts do not show every detail of the earth's surface, and even those that are shown may have changed since the chart was updated.

DEAD RECKONING

The methods used by the navigators who explored the oceans in the 15th and 16th centuries sometimes are regarded as primitive from our modern perspective. In fact, these professionals achieved amazing accuracy without many of the things we consider indispensable, such as decent maps or reliable timepieces. With little more than a compass and an understanding of mathematics, they were able to navigate in spite of storms, changing winds, and variable ocean currents across thousands of miles of open sea and make reasonably accurate landfalls. Their methods are the basis of the modern navigation technique called **dead reckoning**. Based on calculations of time, speed,

Dead?

How did such a grim term come to be used for a method of navigation? Some sources say that the term comes from a contraction of the word "deduced" to "ded," because a navigator uses this technique to deduce position — which seems a little dubious. Others claim that it was coined by early pilots to bring home the fact that your reckoning had better be accurate, or you would soon be dead. In fact, the term was in use long before the beginning of human flight in the seafaring world, like so many other aviation terms and practices. It probably comes from the old use of the word "dead" to mean exact or absolute, as in dead center, dead level, dead on, dead right, and so forth. No matter what the derivation, the term has stuck.

With the advent of satellite-based navigation, easy-to-use computerized displays, inertial navigation, and extensive networks of electronic navigation aids, you might wonder if it is worthwhile to learn techniques that would be familiar to Fernando Magellan or Sir Francis Drake. Just as children need to learn arithmetic and mathematics in order to make the best use of computers, dead reckoning is the basis of most other forms of navigation. Dead reckoning is alive and well, and will remain important for many years to come.

distance, and direction, dead reckoning made possible the historic flights of Charles Lindbergh, Amelia Earhart, and other pioneering pilots. You may never fly over an ocean or a trackless desert, but even in perfect visibility over an ordinary landscape, dead reckoning is a valuable complement to pilotage.

COURSE

In pure pilotage, your course line and landmarks point the direction for you to fly. Since the idea of dead reckoning is to find your way without visual landmarks, the compass provides the necessary directional information. The course direction is measured with a **navigation plotter**. The plotter is a transparent plastic instrument that combines a straightedge for drawing a course line, a protractor for measuring the direction of flight, and distance scales for sectional, WAC, and VFR terminal area charts in both nautical and statute miles.

Draw your course on the chart as you would for a pilotage flight, including measuring the distance, calculating the fuel required, and planning any fuel stops. Then, use the plotter to measure your **true course** at the meridian nearest the center of the course. [Figure 9-6] Since the meridians converge toward the poles in the map projection used for sectional charts, the

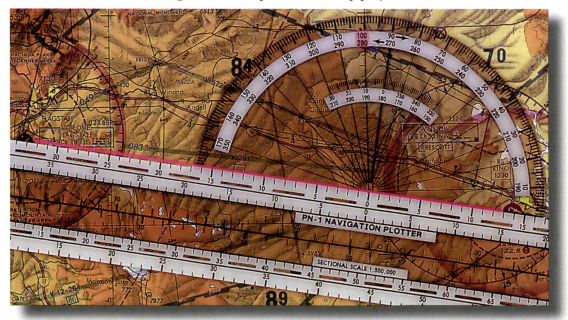

Figure 9-6. The true course from Flagstaff to Winslow is 100°, and the true course from Winslow to Flagstaff is 280°.

meridians toward the ends of the course would give slightly different true course readings. Measuring near the center of the course will put you on a nearly perfect great circle route between your departure and destination airports.

If your course line is more north-south, it may not cross any meridians. In this case, place the plotter along your course where it crosses a latitude parallel, and read the true course from the smaller auxiliary scale on the plotter. [Figure 9-7] The outer scale is for northbound courses, the inner for southbound.

FLIGHT PLANNING

The flight planning required for dead reckoning is a little more involved than for pilotage. Doing as much as possible on the ground before takeoff eases the workload in the air, giving you more time to enjoy the flying and leaving you better able to handle any problems that may arise. When navigating by pilotage, most of the navigation information you need can be found or recorded on your chart. The additional information used in dead reckoning is more easily handled by using a separate **navigation log**. This form is a convenient way to organize your preflight navigation planning, as well as to keep track of progress during the flight.

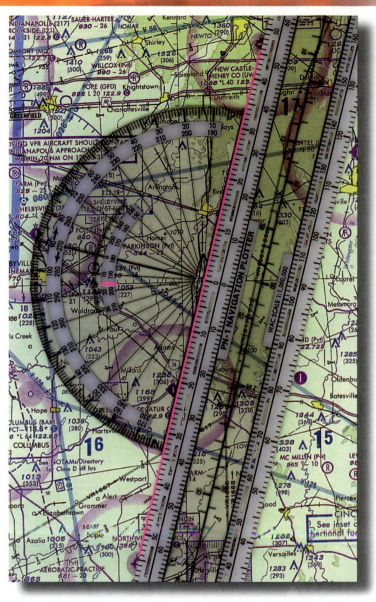

Figure 9-7. The true course from New Castle to North Vernon is 195°, and the true course from North Vernon to New Castle is 015°.

As you recall from pilotage, there are times when a direct route to your destination is impractical. In these situations, you would plan your flight to include additional legs. A **leg** may be any segment of a cross-country flight, such as the distance between checkpoints, intermediate stops, or course changes. After plotting your true course, list your significant checkpoints on the navigation log, along with the distance for each leg and the distance remaining. Find the true airspeed and fuel consumption in the POH and record it on the log.

Next, determine the effects of wind on your airplane using the techniques from Chapter 8. Applying a wind correction angle to your true course gives the **true heading**. If your trip is not direct, you will need to solve a wind problem for each separate leg. Record your true heading in the appropriate box for each leg of your flight.

Use the information in the POH to determine the time, speed, and distance to climb to your cruising altitude. Once you have determined your estimated groundspeed, use it to make a careful estimate of fuel requirements, and decide if you need to plan a fuel stop. Knowing the distance between checkpoints, along with your anticipated groundspeed, you can calculate the estimated time enroute (ETE) for each leg. The first part of your flight should take the lower speed of the climb into consideration as you calculate the ETE and fuel needs.

Finally, take a few minutes to jot down the radio frequencies you will need. In flight, it can be much easier to find one on the navigation log than to search for it on the chart. [Figure 9-8] While airborne, mark each checkpoint as you pass it, and make note of the time on your log. You may also want to write the time next to each checkpoint on the

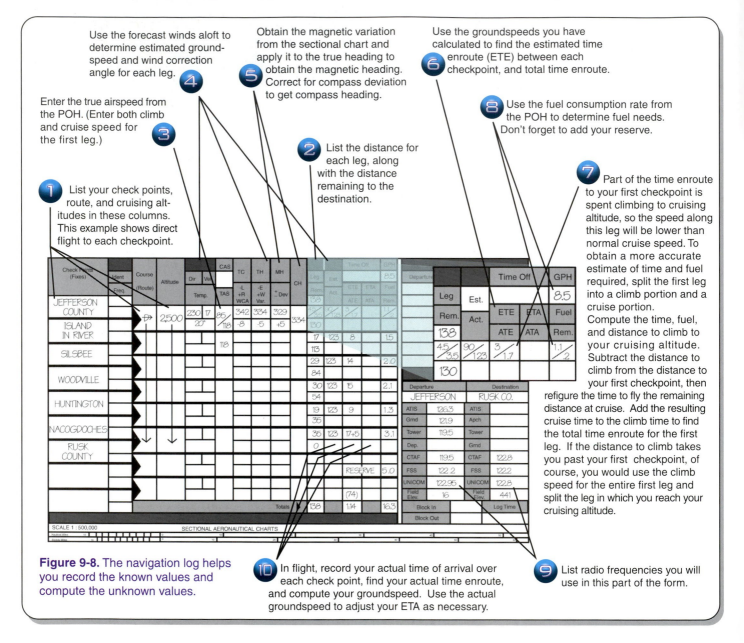

4 Use the forecast winds aloft to determine estimated ground-speed and wind correction angle for each leg.

5 Obtain the magnetic variation from the sectional chart and apply it to the true heading to obtain the magnetic heading. Correct for compass deviation to get compass heading.

6 Use the groundspeeds you have calculated to find the estimated time enroute (ETE) between each checkpoint, and total time enroute.

3 Enter the true airspeed from the POH. (Enter both climb and cruise speed for the first leg.)

8 Use the fuel consumption rate from the POH to determine fuel needs. Don't forget to add your reserve.

2 List the distance for each leg, along with the distance remaining to the destination.

7 Part of the time enroute to your first checkpoint is spent climbing to cruising altitude, so the speed along this leg will be lower than normal cruise speed. To obtain a more accurate estimate of time and fuel required, split the first leg into a climb portion and a cruise portion. Compute the time, fuel, and distance to climb to your cruising altitude. Subtract the distance to climb from the distance to your first checkpoint, then refigure the time to fly the remaining distance at cruise. Add the resulting cruise time to the climb time to find the total time enroute for the first leg. If the distance to climb takes you past your first checkpoint, of course, you would use the climb speed for the entire first leg and split the leg in which you reach your cruising altitude.

1 List your check points, route, and cruising altitudes in these columns. This example shows direct flight to each checkpoint.

Figure 9-8. The navigation log helps you record the known values and compute the unknown values.

10 In flight, record your actual time of arrival over each check point, find your actual time enroute, and compute your groundspeed. Use the actual groundspeed to adjust your ETA as necessary.

9 List radio frequencies you will use in this part of the form.

aeronautical chart, too. Record your actual time enroute (ATE) and compare it to your estimated time to keep track of your flight's progress. To calculate your groundspeed, use the elapsed time between two checkpoints to solve a time-speed-distance problem with your flight computer. If the actual winds aloft are substantially different than forecast, you can use your computer to recalculate your estimated time enroute and the fuel needed to reach your destination.

TRUE AND MAGNETIC VALUES

The magnetic compass in an airplane senses magnetic north, which can differ from true north by as much as 20° in the contiguous United States. In dead reckoning you normally fly by magnetic reference, so you will need to correct for the difference between true and magnetic direction, which is called variation. Local magnetic variation is shown on aeronautical charts by a dashed magenta **isogonic line**. [Figure 9-9] Correcting your true course for variation is simply a matter of adding or subtracting the value shown on the isogonic line. If the variation is east of true north, it is subtracted from the true course, and west variation is added to the true course, to obtain **magnetic course**. **East is least and west is best** is a memory aid that has helped generations of pilots to remember whether to add or subtract magnetic variation.

Figure 9-9. This isogonic line shows a magnetic variation of 8° east, therefore it is subtracted from the true course to obtain the magnetic course.

 Magnetic course is true course corrected for local magnetic variation.

The magnetic fields of items within the airplane can affect the accuracy of the magnetic compass, too. These errors are shown on the compass deviation card near the compass. Since deviation is only recorded for certain headings, you may have to interpolate to obtain the deviation for your course. Record the deviation for your course in the proper column on the navigation log, and add or subtract as appropriate to obtain your **compass heading**.

Some pilots choose to correct their true course for wind before correcting for variation, and others correct for variation before wind. The order in which the operations are done has no effect on the outcome, but different terms are used to describe some of the intermediate sums, and the wind direction must

 Magnetic heading is magnetic course corrected for the effects of wind.

be changed from true to magnetic if the variation is applied first. In all cases, you begin with the true course and end with the compass heading. A course is always the line drawn on the chart. The true course is measured from true north, and if the correction for variation is applied at this point, the result is expressed as magnetic course. A heading is always a direction measured relative to the longitudinal axis of the airplane, or in other words, the direction in which the airplane is pointed. True course corrected for wind gives a true heading, while magnetic course corrected for wind gives a magnetic heading. The compass heading is always found by correcting the magnetic heading for compass deviation. [Figure 9-10]

 Compass heading is magnetic heading corrected for compass deviation.

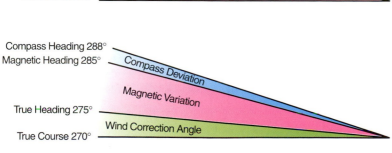

Compass Heading 288°
Magnetic Heading 285°
Magnetic Course 280°
Compass Deviation
Wind Correction Angle
Magnetic Variation
True Course 270°

Compass Heading 288°
Magnetic Heading 285°
Compass Deviation
Magnetic Variation
True Heading 275°
Wind Correction Angle
True Course 270°

Figure 9-10. Whether you compensate for variation or winds first, the same result is obtained. Although this example shows each value as positive, often one or more of the values is negative, in which case it is subtracted.

VFR CRUISING ALTITUDES

There are many factors to consider when selecting your cruising altitude for a cross-country flight. The first consideration should be your height above the terrain and obstructions. Your sectional shows terrain heights along your route as well as tall obstructions such as towers. In addition to the height of the terrain, you should also evaluate the topography in the area. A flight over high mountains with potentially strong downdrafts and nothing but rugged rock below would prompt a much higher cruising altitude than flat terrain with plenty of emergency landing sites within easy gliding distance. The effect of winds on your groundspeed and the performance of your aircraft are other factors that should be considered. In general, higher altitudes will provide better visibility of checkpoints, better radio range and reception, and more options in the event of an emergency.

Whenever you are in level cruising flight more than 3,000 feet above the surface, you must comply with the **VFR cruising altitude** rule. VFR aircraft on magnetic courses from 0° to 179° are required to fly at odd thousand-foot altitudes plus 500 feet, such as 3,500 feet MSL, 5,500 feet MSL, 7,500 feet MSL, etc., up to the flight levels. If you fly a magnetic course from 180° to 359°, your choices for VFR cruising altitudes are even thousands plus 500 feet, such as 4,500 feet MSL, 6,500 feet MSL, or 8,500 feet MSL. If you are maneuvering, turning, or changing altitude the rule does not apply. [Figure 9-11]

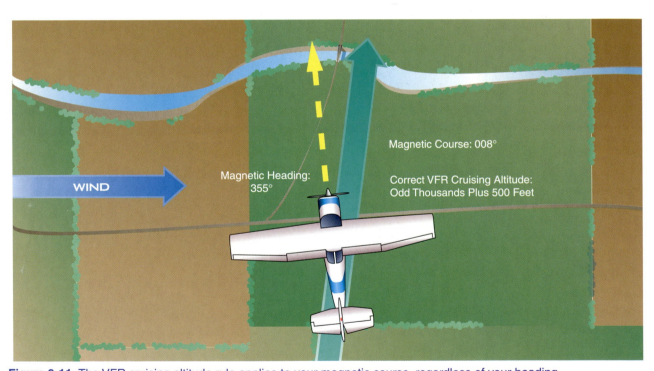

Magnetic Course: 008°

Correct VFR Cruising Altitude:
Odd Thousands Plus 500 Feet

Magnetic Heading:
355°

WIND

Figure 9-11. The VFR cruising altitude rule applies to your magnetic course, regardless of your heading.

The idea behind this rule is that eastbound and westbound VFR aircraft will theoretically be separated by a thousand feet, helping to reduce the possibility of head-on traffic conflicts. In practice, it is extremely important that you maintain your visual traffic scan at all times, since other aircraft can converge on you from any direction, in full compliance with the rule. For example, suppose you are flying south on a heading of 179° at a proper altitude of 5,500 feet MSL. You can expect VFR aircraft cruising at your altitude to converge on you from any direction to the left of the airplane,

 On magnetic courses from 0° to 179° above 3,000 feet AGL, VFR cruising altitudes are odd thousands plus 500 feet. On magnetic courses from 180° to 359° above 3,000 feet AGL, VFR cruising altitudes are even thousands plus 500 feet.

from directly behind you to nearly head-on. On courses that are more nearly east or west, be alert for aircraft coming from beside or behind you, where they can be more difficult to see. This is especially important when flying slower aircraft that may be overtaken by faster aircraft. Of course, aircraft changing altitudes can come from any direction, and since the rule only applies to cruising flight, any aircraft that is practicing maneuvers or turning need not comply. Finally, ATC may assign any altitude to IFR aircraft in controlled airspace. [Figure 9-12]

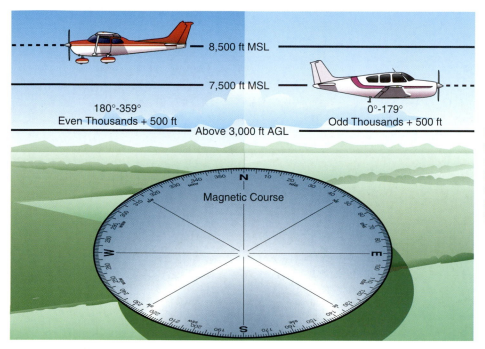

Figure 9-12. The VFR cruising altitude rule does not guarantee traffic separation. You must comply with it when you are cruising above 3,000 feet AGL.

FUEL REQUIREMENTS

FARs require that day VFR flights carry enough fuel to fly to the first point of intended landing at normal cruise speed, and to fly after that for an additional 30 minutes. (Night VFR flights must carry a 45 minute reserve.) These **fuel reserve** requirements should be considered a

Day VFR flights must carry enough fuel to fly to the first point of intended landing, and to fly after that for an additional 30 minutes. A reserve of 45 minutes is required for night VFR flights.

reasonable minimum, and if loading and performance considerations permit, you should consider carrying larger reserves. An unforecast headwind or a course deviation around an area of poor weather can quickly consume fuel reserves.

FLIGHT PLAN

As you have seen, thorough and detailed flight planning is fundamental to safe, organized, and enjoyable flight. The guidelines and techniques you have been learning are meant to bring all your flights to a safe conclusion at your destination, but your planning should also include some provision for starting a search if you fail to arrive. One good way of handling this precaution is to use the VFR flight plan service provided through flight service stations.

The VFR **flight plan** is simply a request that the FSS initiate a search for you if they have not heard from you by a certain time. It is not used by ATC to route traffic, nor does it provide any benefit to you in the air. Its sole purpose is to furnish some basic information to searchers if you do not arrive at your destination. When you file a flight plan with an FSS, a record is made that includes your destination, route of flight, arrival time, and the number of people aboard the airplane. Once airborne, you activate your flight plan by radio so the FSS can keep track of your airplane's estimated arrival time. If you do not close or extend your flight plan within 30 minutes after your stated ETA, the FSS will begin a preliminary search by telephone, then notify search and rescue organizations such as the Civil Air Patrol. [Figure 9-13] The FAA does not require pilots of VFR aircraft to file flight plans, however, if you file and activate a flight plan, you must close it after arriving at your destination. If you decide not to go to your original destination, or if you will be at least 15 minutes later than you had planned, inform the nearest FSS accordingly.

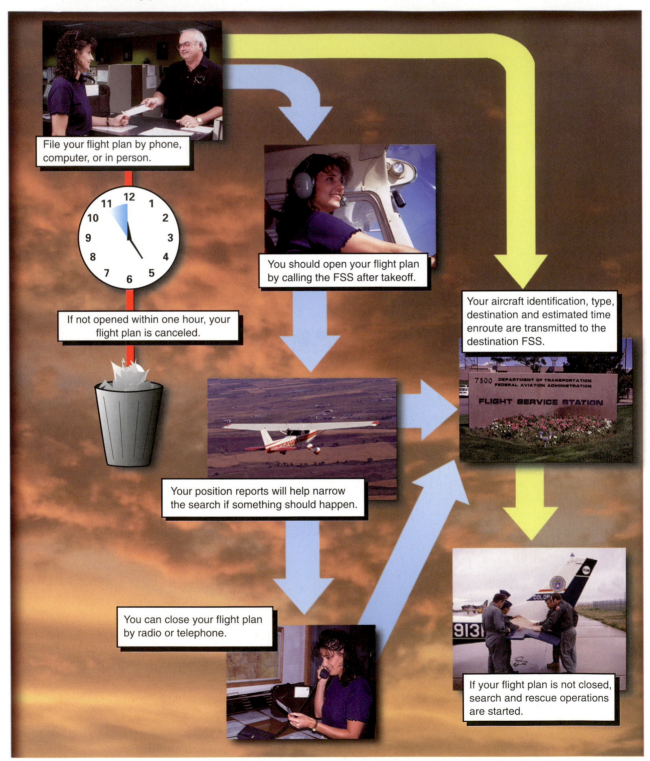

File your flight plan by phone, computer, or in person.

If not opened within one hour, your flight plan is canceled.

You should open your flight plan by calling the FSS after takeoff.

Your aircraft identification, type, destination and estimated time enroute are transmitted to the destination FSS.

Your position reports will help narrow the search if something should happen.

You can close your flight plan by radio or telephone.

If your flight plan is not closed, search and rescue operations are started.

Figure 9-13. Filing and activating a VFR flight plan ensures that search and rescue operations will be launched if your flight is overdue.

After you open your flight plan, you should give occasional position reports to FSSs along the way. This way, if you do not arrive at your destination, the FSS has an idea of your aircraft's last known position, which can reduce the size of the search area considerably. [Figure 9-14]

 TYPE OF FLIGHT PLAN
Mark VFR in this block, since you will be flying under visual flight rules. Only instrument-rated pilots can file IFR flight plans. Use DVFR when your flight will transit an Air Defense Identification Zone (ADIZ). You can find more information on DVFR flight plans in the *Aeronautical Information Manual.*

 AIRCRAFT IDENTIFICATION
Use the full identification number of your aircraft.

 AIRCRAFT TYPE AND SPECIAL EQUIPMENT
Enter the designator for your aircraft, followed by a slash and the code letter for the special equipment. You can find the equipment code letters in the *Aeronautical Information Manual* and at the bottom of the Jeppesen Sanderson flight plan form.

 TRUE AIRSPEED
Give this figure in knots, based on the estimated TAS at your intended cruising altitude.

 DEPARTURE POINT
Enter the airport identifier code or the name, if you don't know the identifier. Identifier codes are listed in the *Airport/Facility Directory.*

 DEPARTURE TIME
This is your proposed departure time stated in Coordinated Universal Time (UTC), or Zulu time. The use of Zulu time eliminates confusion when you cross time zone boundaries during a flight.

 CRUISING ALTITUDE
Enter only the inital VFR cruising altitude.

 ROUTE OF FLIGHT
Define your proposed route using identifiable points of reference, particulary those which will mark a change in direction. This will assist search and rescue in retracing your route. These points may be navaids, airways, or prominent geographic features. Use the term **direct** to describe a straight-line course between two points, and the Victor airway number if you will be flying on an airway.

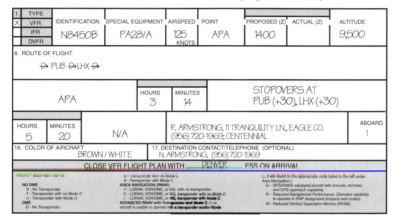

 DESTINATION
Enter your destination airport identifier code or the name, if the identifier code is unknown. Include the city and state, if the airport name alone might be confused with another.

 ESTIMATED TIME ENROUTE
Enter your total estimated time from take-off to landing in hours and minutes, based on the latest forecast winds. If you plan a stop of less than an hour along your route, be sure to include that time also. If you expect a stop to last more than an hour, it's best to file separate flight plans for each part of the trip.

 REMARKS
Use this block to enter remarks pertinent to ATC or to clarify other flight plan information. This information could include a stopover at an intermediate airport to pick up a passenger or to refuel. You can also use this block to request customs service at an airport of entry.

 FUEL ON BOARD
Enter the total usable fuel on board the aircraft in hours and minutes.

 ALTERNATE AIRPORT(S)
If you desire, specify an alternate airport.

 PILOT'S NAME, ADDRESS, TELEPHONE NUMBER, AND AIRCRAFT HOME BASE
Provide a telephone number where someone will answer who is knowledgeable about your flight. For aircraft home base, include the name of the FBO (if appropriate), as well as the airport name.

 NUMBER OF PERSONS ABOARD
Enter the total number of persons on board, including yourself and any other crew members.

 COLOR OF AIRCRAFT
List the major color or colors of your airplane.

 DESTINATION CONTACT/TELEPHONE (OPTIONAL)
Provide a telephone number where you can be reached at the destination should you fail to report or cancel your flight plan within one-half hour after your ETA. Record the name of the FSS that serves your destination airport.

Figure 9-14. It takes very little time or effort to file a flight plan since most of the information you need can be extracted from your navigation log.

The initial cruising altitude should be entered on the flight plan, even if an altitude change is anticipated later in the flight.

The fuel on board is the total amount of usable fuel in hours and minutes.

If you plan to fly over a large body of water, a swamp, or mountains, check the AIM to see if the area is part of the Hazardous Area Reporting Service provided through selected FSSs. When you participate in this service, you make frequent position reports to an FSS, and if contact is lost for more than fifteen minutes, search and rescue is alerted. The areas where this service is available are mainly in the northeastern area of the country (including the Great Lakes), and in the swamplands of Florida. Refer to the AIM for specific information on each location where the service is available.

If no stopover of more than one hour is expected, the name of the destination airport should be entered on the flight plan.

Activate your flight plan once you are airborne by calling the FSS and informing them of your actual time of departure. If your flight plan has not been activated, it will be kept on file by the FSS for one hour after your proposed departure time, after which you must refile. When you know your departure will be delayed beyond one hour, you should advise the FSS by phone. If you will be making a stop on your flight, to refuel for instance, the FAA recommends that you file a separate flight plan for each leg if the stop is expected to be more than one hour.

After the flight plan is activated, the FSS sends a flight notification message to the FSS nearest your destination containing only your aircraft identification, type, destination, and ETA. Normally, you close the flight plan when you arrive at your destination, either by radio or by telephone after landing. You may also close the flight plan with a flight service station other than the one serving your destination, however, you should inform the departure FSS of this decision when the flight plan is filed. In situations where an FSS is not available, you may

VFR flight plans must be closed with the nearest FSS or other FAA facility upon landing.

request any ATC facility to relay your cancellation to an FSS. Remember that VFR flight plans are never opened or closed automatically by control towers or FSSs. If your ETA changes significantly, you are responsible for extending your flight plan through any flight service station within radio range. If you decide to land at an airport other than your filed destination, inform the FSS of your original destination when you close. Each year several thousand searches are begun for pilots who fail to close their flight plans, often putting search and rescue personnel into danger during unnecessary searches. It is extremely important that you close your flight plan.

LOST PROCEDURES

Recognizing that you have become lost is not as easy as, for example, recognizing that the engine has quit. If a checkpoint does not appear on time, it is easy to wait a little longer to see if it will show up, then wait a little longer still. It is tempting to believe that the two-lane road below is really the superhighway shown on the sectional, or that the town on the north side of the road is the same one shown south of the road on the sectional, even though it does not have the powerline and radio tower depicted on the chart. If you get lost, don't panic. The five Cs are some common sense guidelines that have evolved to help you take positive action to establish your location: climb, communicate, confess, comply, and conserve.

Climbing to a higher altitude will usually let you see more of the ground, increasing your chances of spotting an identifiable landmark. It improves the reception range of your radios, so you might be able to pick up VOR or NDB signals, and it extends the range of your transmitter, which will help with communications or a DF steer.

Communicate with any available facility. Use the frequencies shown on your chart, including the RCO frequencies at VOR stations. If your situation becomes threatening, use the emergency frequency, 121.5 MHz. Confess your situation to any ATC facility, and comply with their suggestions. Conserve your fuel by reducing power and airspeed to the values for maximum endurance or range, whichever is most appropriate to your situation.

COMMUNICATED, CONFESSED, BUT DIDN'T COMPLY
From the files of the NTSB...

Aircraft: Cessna 150

Crew: One — uninjured

Narrative: The pilot made a forced landing in rugged tree covered terrain following a loss of power due to fuel exhaustion while on a cross-country flight. The pilot became lost near Livingston, TN, and contacted the Crossville and London FSS for assistance. The aircraft was located 5 miles west of the Livingston VOR, however, the pilot did not follow the headings issued for a DF steer to the airport. The forced landing was made approximately 10 miles north of the Livingston airport. Inspection of the aircraft revealed no fuel present in the carburetor or fuel lines. The two wing fuel tanks contained a total of 3.5 gallons of fuel. The aircraft has a fuel capacity of 26 gallons of which 3.5 gallons are unusable fuel.

On becoming lost, this pilot communicated with flight service and confessed the situation, but when a vector to the airport was given, elected not to comply. The crash site is within a few miles of the position initially provided by the FSS, but the synopsis does not indicate whether the pilot ran out of fuel just after being given the DF steer, or wandered unproductively until the engine quit. In either case, there is a good chance that communicating and confessing just eight minutes sooner, or complying with the help provided by the FSS, might have allowed this flight to end on the airport instead of in the woods.

In addition to the basic five Cs, you could add some others. Check the heading indicator against the magnetic compass and, before you reset it, note the direction of the error. This can help you determine whether you are to the left or right of your intended course. For instance, if the compass indicates 10° more than the heading indicator, you may be to the right of your intended course. Compare what you see outside to what is on your chart, looking especially for any large, clear landmarks.

SUMMARY CHECKLIST

✓ Pilotage is flying by reference to landmarks.

✓ Sectional charts provide the largest scale and most detailed representation of visual landmarks for most cross-country flights.

✓ The best checkpoints are those that cannot be mistaken for any other nearby features.

✓ Select checkpoints that present a number of features to create a unique combination or a distinctive pattern.

✓ Highlighting your course line on the chart will make it easier to follow.

✓ Maintaining a constant awareness of your position will reduce your chance of becoming lost.

✓ Pure dead reckoning is navigating by time, speed, distance, and direction calculations, without reference to visual landmarks.

✓ A navigation plotter combines a protractor, straightedge, and distance scales for various charts.

✓ Navigation logs help keep track of headings, times, distances, and fuel consumption during dead reckoning flights.

✓ The true course must be corrected for magnetic variation, wind drift, and compass deviation to arrive at the compass heading.

✓ The VFR cruising altitude rule dictates cruising altitudes above 3,000 feet AGL.

✓ Required VFR fuel reserves are 30 minutes for daytime flights and 45 minutes for night flights.

✓ A VFR flight plan is a request that a search be started if your flight does not arrive at your stated destination.

✓ If you become lost, climb, communicate, confess, comply, and conserve.

KEY TERMS

Line of Position (LOP)	Leg
Fix	True Heading
Pilotage	Isogonic Line
Checkpoints	Magnetic Course
Dead Reckoning	Compass Heading
Navigation Plotter	VFR Cruising Altitudes
True Course	Fuel Reserve
Navigation Log	Flight Plan

QUESTIONS

1. What is a line of position?

   A. A specific visual checkpoint, such as a road intersection, a bridge over a stream, or a racetrack
   B. A range of possible positions along a specific line, one of which is the actual position of the aircraft
   C. A dead reckoning course that has been corrected for wind drift as well as the effects of magnetic fields

2. What are the advantages of pilotage over dead reckoning?

3. True/False. The primary advantage of dead reckoning over pilotage is that it provides accurate navigation over areas that have few, if any, visual checkpoints.

4. True/False. Dead reckoning uses calculations of time, speed, distance and direction to navigate without reference to visual landmarks.

5. True/False. Magnetic variation is the difference between true north and magnetic north.

6. What information is usually entered on a navigation log?

   A. The boundaries of restricted airspace, engine power settings, and the names and locations of alternate airports along the course
   B. Information on the heights of obstructions along the route, and the lengths of the runways at the departure and destination airports
   C. Distance between checkpoints, cruising altitudes, true airspeed, wind correction angles, corrections for magnetic variation and compass deviation, estimated and actual groundspeed, fuel consumption rates, and estimated and actual times between checkpoints

7. Select the true statement regarding the magnetic compass.

   A. Magnetic fields within the airplane create magnetic variation.
   B. Because of variation, the magnetic compass never points to true north.
   C. The compass heading is the source used to set the gyroscopic heading indicator.

8. Name at least three factors that you would consider when choosing a cruising altitude.

9. What altitude would be required by the VFR cruising altitude rule for an airplane on a magnetic course of 240°?

   A. 2,500 feet MSL
   B. 3,500 feet MSL
   C. 4,500 feet MSL

10. With which FAA facilities should you close your VFR flight plan?

11. What should you do if you find that you will reach your destination 18 minutes after the ETA on your VFR flight plan?

12. True/False. When a VFR flight plan is opened, only the aircraft identification, type, destination, and ETA are transmitted to the destination FSS.

SECTION B
VOR NAVIGATION

During aviation's early years, it became evident that a system to assist the pilot in navigation would be necessary if the airplane was going to be useful as a transportation tool. Over the years, navigation systems evolved from bonfires to light beacons to radio navigation aids. Today, the **very high frequency omnidirectional range (VOR)** is the most commonly used radio navigation system in the U.S., with more than 1,000 stations in service. Even as other navigation systems become popular, VORs will continue to function as an important part of the airspace system for the foreseeable future.

GROUND EQUIPMENT

VORs operate in the very high frequency (VHF) range, on frequencies of 108.00 MHz through 117.95 MHz. VHF frequencies offer relatively interference-free navigation, but unlike lower frequency radio waves, which can skip within the atmosphere or travel over the ground for great distances, VOR reception is strictly line of sight. This limits usable signal range at low altitudes or over mountainous terrain. [Figure 9-15] When obstacles reduce VOR reception range below standard values published in the AIM, the affected route and the usable range appears in the *Airport/Facility Directory* (A/FD) under the individual VOR listings.

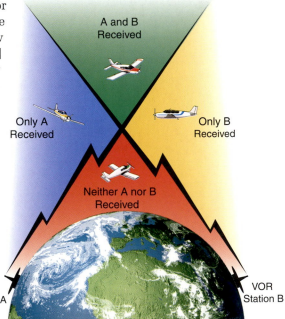

Figure 9-15. Because VOR reception is strictly line of sight, range is limited by the curvature of the earth.

◈	VHF OMNI RANGE (VOR)
◈	VORTAC
◈	VOR-DME

Figure 9-16. Sectional charts depict VORs, VORTACs, and VOR/DMEs with different symbols.

Basic VOR systems only provide course guidance, while **VOR/DME** and **VORTAC** facilities also provide distance information to aircraft equipped with distance measuring equipment (DME). [Figure 9-16] A VORTAC is a collocated VOR and military navigational aid called a TACAN. Civil aviation uses the portion of the TACAN system which provides distance information.

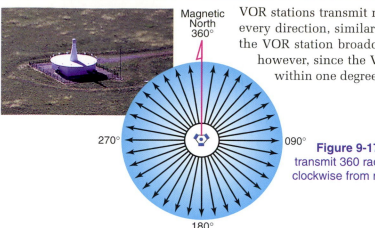

VOR stations transmit radio beams, or **radials**, outward in every direction, similar to spokes on a wheel. Technically, the VOR station broadcasts an infinite number of radials; however, since the VOR is considered to be accurate to within one degree, 360 radials are used. [Figure 9-17]

Figure 9-17. VOR stations, such as the one pictured, transmit 360 radials in one-degree increments, numbered clockwise from magnetic north.

VORs and their associated radials are depicted on sectional charts with circles, graduated in degrees, called **compass roses**. Many VOR stations are connected by specific radials, which form routes called Victor airways. [Figure 9-18]

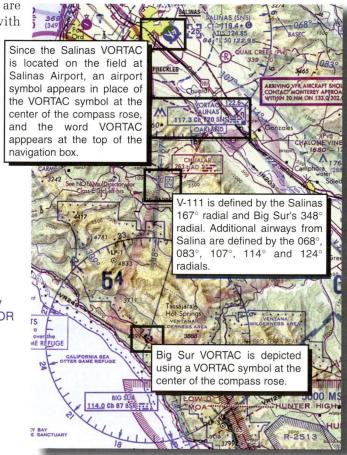

Since the Salinas VORTAC is located on the field at Salinas Airport, an airport symbol appears in place of the VORTAC symbol at the center of the compass rose, and the word VORTAC apppears at the top of the navigation box.

V-111 is defined by the Salinas 167° radial and Big Sur's 348° radial. Additional airways from Salina are defined by the 068°, 083°, 107°, 114° and 124° radials.

Figure 9-18. You can navigate across the country by flying published magnetic courses from one VOR to the next.

Big Sur VORTAC is depicted using a VORTAC symbol at the center of the compass rose.

VOR ground stations are divided into 3 classes according to their normal reception and altitude range. A **terminal VOR (TVOR)** is normally located on an airport and is designed to be used within 25 n.m. and below 12,000 feet AGL. You can use a **low altitude VOR (LVOR)** reliably up to 40 n.m. from the station at altitudes between 1,000 and 18,000 feet AGL. At altitudes above 18,000 feet AGL you may experience interference from other LVORs sharing the same frequency. A **high altitude VOR (HVOR)** offers a reception range of 40 n.m. up to 14,500 feet, and 100 n.m. between 14,500 feet and 18,000 feet. The HVOR's maximum range of 130 n.m. is available between 18,000 feet and FL450. Between FL450 and FL600, the reception range decreases to 100 n.m. You can find the class designation of a VOR facility in the A/FD.

Timing is Everything

VOR receivers determine azimuth (direction) from the station by comparing the timing, or phase, of two signals from that station. Imagine two light signals coming from the same geographic position. The first light is a white flashing reference signal visible in every direction. The second light is a narrow green beam (a variable signal) which rotates continuously at a specific rate. At any point, you see the rotating beam only at the instant it sweeps past your position. Now assume the white omnidirectional reference light flashes when the rotating (variable) green beam passes through magnetic north. Also assume the green beam rotates at one degree per second, making a full revolution every 360 seconds. With this arrangement, you can determine your radial from the light sources by measuring the time between your observations of white and green lights. For example, if you start a stopwatch when you see the white omnidirectional signal flash, and you see the green rotating signal 60 seconds later, you are located on the 60 degree radial from the station.

The VOR system uses the same principle, transmitting two navigation signal components. One of these signals, the reference signal, is a constant pulse at all points around the VOR. The other signal is electronically rotated at 1,800 r.p.m. The VOR receiver measures the phase difference between these two signals and calculates its direction from the station.

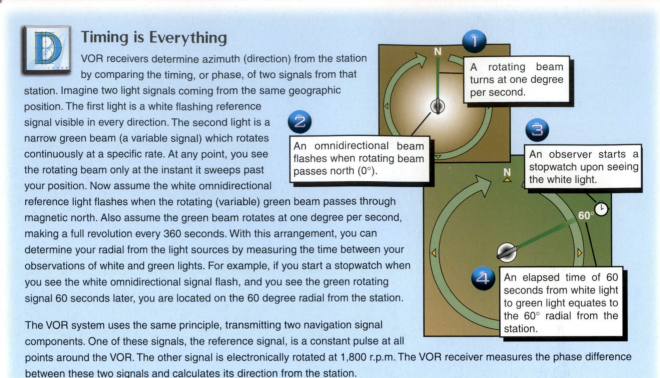

1 A rotating beam turns at one degree per second.

2 An omnidirectional beam flashes when rotating beam passes north (0°).

3 An observer starts a stopwatch upon seeing the white light.

4 An elapsed time of 60 seconds from white light to green light equates to the 60° radial from the station.

AIRBORNE EQUIPMENT

VOR airborne equipment consists of an antenna, receiver, and indicator. The VOR indicator consists of the course deviation indicator (CDI), the TO-FROM indicator, and the omnibearing selector (OBS), or course selector. [Figure 9-19]

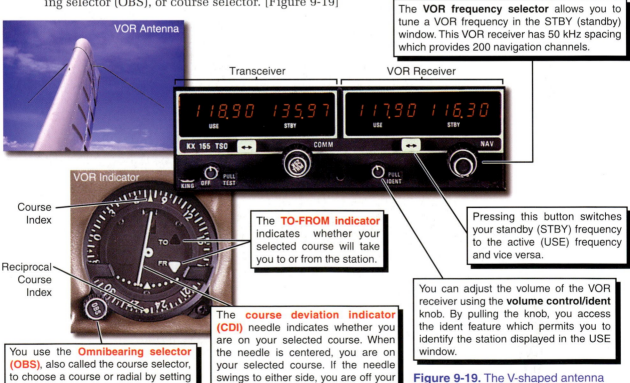

The **VOR frequency selector** allows you to tune a VOR frequency in the STBY (standby) window. This VOR receiver has 50 kHz spacing which provides 200 navigation channels.

VOR Antenna

Transceiver   VOR Receiver

Course Index

Reciprocal Course Index

The **TO-FROM indicator** indicates whether your selected course will take you to or from the station.

Pressing this button switches your standby (STBY) frequency to the active (USE) frequency and vice versa.

You can adjust the volume of the VOR receiver using the **volume control/ident** knob. By pulling the knob, you access the ident feature which permits you to identify the station displayed in the USE window.

The **course deviation indicator (CDI)** needle indicates whether you are on your selected course. When the needle is centered, you are on your selected course. If the needle swings to either side, you are off your selected course.

You use the **Omnibearing selector (OBS)**, also called the course selector, to choose a course or radial by setting it next to the course index.

Figure 9-19. The V-shaped antenna receives the VOR signal. The receiver interprets the signal and sends the resulting course information to the VOR indicator. Although most VOR equipment is similar in appearance and operation, you should consult your POH or radio manual to learn more about your aircraft's particular system.

NAVIGATION PROCEDURES

VOR is a relatively easy navigation system to use once you understand the basic navigation procedures. These operations include tuning and identifying a station, interpreting VOR indications, tracking, intercepting a course, and cross checking your position.

IDENTIFYING A STATION

Before using a VOR for navigation, you must tune your VOR receiver and identify the station to ensure you have chosen the right frequency and that the station is working properly. On many receivers you can monitor the station identifier by selecting the ident feature and turning up the volume. If you do not hear the VOR's Morse code identifier or voice identification, you cannot assume a reliable navigation signal. When a station is shut down for maintenance, it may transmit a T-E-S-T signal (— · ··· —); at other times there is no identifier at all.

INTERPRETING VOR INDICATIONS

Once you tune a VOR frequency, the VOR receiver automatically determines your magnetic direction, or radial, from the ground station. While some VOR receivers may display a digital readout of your radial, many units installed in light aircraft do not directly indicate your radial from the station. To determine your position relative to the station, turn the omnibearing selector (OBS) knob until the course deviation indicator (CDI) needle centers with a FROM indication and read the resulting radial next to the index mark on the top of the VOR indicator. The course to a station is the reciprocal of, or 180° from, the radial. If you set the OBS to center the needle with a TO indication, you can turn to the heading displayed on the VOR indicator and fly on course directly to the station, assuming there is no crosswind. [Figure 9-20]

To determine your present direction from a VOR station, tune in the station and turn the OBS knob until the CDI needle centers with a FROM indication.

Figure 9-20. You can quickly determine your radial from or course to a VOR station by twisting the OBS knob to center the CDI.

To determine the course from your present position to a VOR station, tune in the station and turn the OBS knob until the CDI needle centers with a TO indication.

When the CDI needle is centered with a TO indication, the radial you are on is the reciprocal of the course set by the OBS. To determine which course takes you to a VOR from a specific location on a sectional chart, plot the course and note where it intersects the VOR compass rose.

When you are off course, the CDI is designed to point toward your desired course. The scale underneath the needle shows how far you are off course, with each dot on the scale representing a course deviation of two degrees. For example, if your CDI is deflected two dots to the left of center, your desired course is four degrees to your left. [Figure 9-21]

The CDI indicates whether the aircraft is left or right of the station on the selected course. See figure 9-21.

This CDI indicates you are on the selected course.

This CDI indicates you are 4 degrees right of your selected course.

Figure 9-21. To determine your position relative to a VOR, it may help to visualize your airplane at the bottom of the VOR indicator.

REVERSE SENSING

A VOR airborne system does not perceive your aircraft's heading; it only senses your direction from the station and gives the same instrument indications regardless of which way the nose of the aircraft is pointing. If you mistakenly set your VOR indicator to the reciprocal of your desired course, your CDI will be deflected away from the course. In this **reverse sensing** situation, the normal procedure of correcting toward the needle will actually take you farther off course. For correct sensing, you must set the VOR indicator so it generally agrees with your intended course. [Figure 9-22]

The standard VOR indicator displays course information independent of aircraft heading. See figure 9-22.

If the VOR indicator is set to 090° in aircraft A and B, the CDI will deflect to the left with a FROM indication in both cockpits, even though the aircraft are headed in opposite directions.

090° Radial From ⟶

⟵ 270° Course To

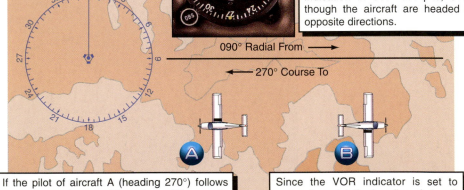

Figure 9-22. To avoid reverse sensing, always set the VOR indicator to approximately agree with your intended course.

If the pilot of aircraft A (heading 270°) follows normal procedures and turns toward the needle (left) to regain course, the aircraft will actually be flying away from the intended course.

Since the VOR indicator is set to generally match the heading of aircraft B (090°) a left turn (toward the needle) will result on the proper correction.

OFF INDICATIONS

As you reach a VOR station and fly over it, the TO indication disappears and is replaced briefly by any one of a variety of indications, depending on your equipment. The indications you may encounter include an OFF flag, a NAV indication, a red and white barber pole, or simply the absence of a TO or FROM indication. As you leave the station behind, the OFF flag (or similar indication) is replaced by a FROM indication, signaling that you are traveling away from the station. The area over the station in which the TO-FROM indicator changes is called the **cone of confusion**, or no-signal area. Due to its shape, flight through the cone of confusion can vary from a few seconds at low altitude up to several minutes at high altitude. You may also notice an OFF flag (or similar indication) when the aircraft is abeam the station on the selected course. [Figure 9-23]

When the VOR indicator displays an OFF flag (or similar indication), the aircraft is either directly over the station or 90° to either side of the course set in your VOR indicator. An OFF flag (or similar indication) also can mean that the tuned VOR station's signal is unreliable.

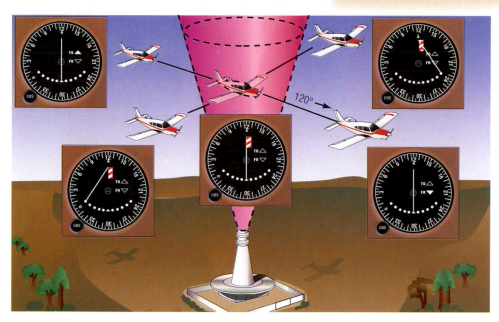

Figure 9-23. This TO-FROM indicator displays a red and white barber pole indicator when flying in the cone of confusion and when the aircraft is directly abeam the station on the selected course of 120°. If the same indication appears at any other time than when passing through the cone of confusion or when abeam the station, it means your VOR is not receiving a reliable navigation signal.

TRACKING

The most common VOR navigation you will perform is flying from one station to another, using a process called **tracking.** When tracking, you maintain the selected course by keeping the CDI centered. To stay on course in a crosswind, you use a technique called **bracketing**, which involves making a series of corrections to regain and maintain your desired course. [Figure 9-24]

Guiding Lights

In the days before radio navigation aids, many pilots relied on a series of beacon lights to guide them to their destination. The system consisted of lights installed at approximately 10-mile intervals along routes between major cities.

To navigate along the routes, a pilot would maintain course by flying from light to light in a sequence defined by the Morse code signal flashed by individual beacons. For example, the first beacon on an airway would flash the Morse code signal for the letter W; the second would flash the letter U; the third, V; and so on through the remaining seven letters (H, R, K, D, B, G, and M). The sequence would repeat every 10 lights until the end of the airway. To help them remember the code, many pilots would learn the mnemonic, **W**hen **U**ndertaking **V**ery **H**ard **R**outes **K**eep **D**irections **B**y **G**ood **M**ethods.

In 1946, the United States' beacon light system used 2,112 airway beacons to define 124 air routes. Of course, the system only was effective at night and in fair weather. These limitations fueled the search for alternative pathfinding methods and eventually led to the development of navigation aids based on radio signals.

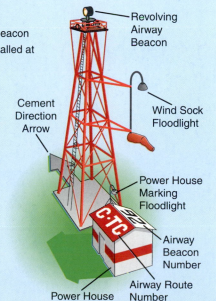

Revolving Airway Beacon

Wind Sock Floodlight

Cement Direction Arrow

Power House Marking Floodlight

Airway Beacon Number

Airway Route Number

Power House

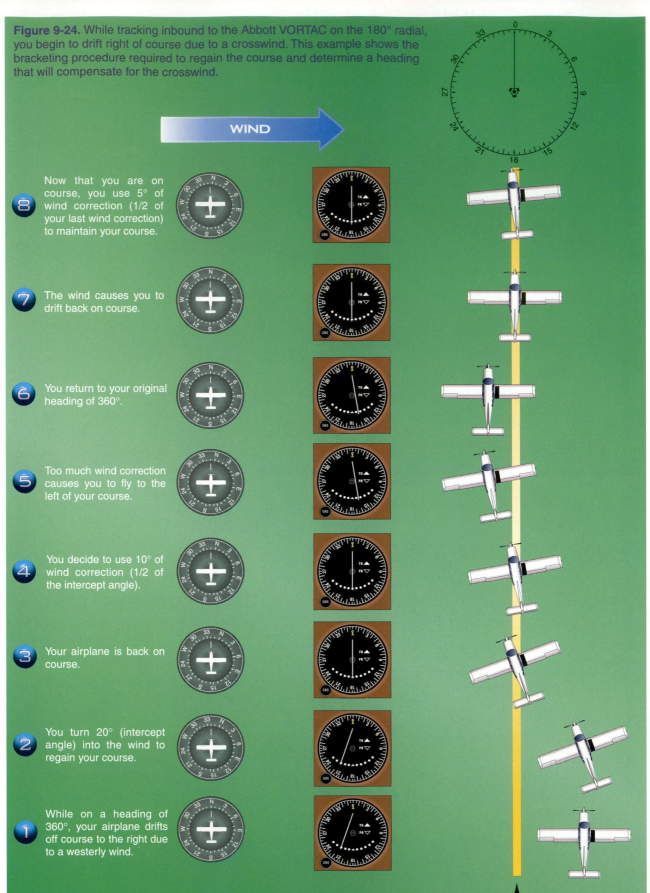

Figure 9-24. While tracking inbound to the Abbott VORTAC on the 180° radial, you begin to drift right of course due to a crosswind. This example shows the bracketing procedure required to regain the course and determine a heading that will compensate for the crosswind.

WIND

8. Now that you are on course, you use 5° of wind correction (1/2 of your last wind correction) to maintain your course.

7. The wind causes you to drift back on course.

6. You return to your original heading of 360°.

5. Too much wind correction causes you to fly to the left of your course.

4. You decide to use 10° of wind correction (1/2 of the intercept angle).

3. Your airplane is back on course.

2. You turn 20° (intercept angle) into the wind to regain your course.

1. While on a heading of 360°, your airplane drifts off course to the right due to a westerly wind.

INTERCEPTING A COURSE

In some situations, you may need to track to the station on a different course instead of flying direct from your present position. In these instances, you must fly from the radial you are currently tracking and intercept another radial inbound. [Figure 9-25]

When the CDI begins to center, you turn right and track inbound to the station.

You set up an intercept angle by turning left to a heading of 045°. Once established on your intercept course, you turn the OBS to set the new inbound course, 090°, in the VOR indicator.

45° Intercept Angle

090°
270°

070°
250°

While tracking inbound on the 250° radial, you see cumulus clouds ahead and decide to approach the station on the 270° radial.

Figure 9-25. This example uses a 45° intercept angle. The intercept angle you use in a particular situation may range from about 20° when you are close to the station, up to approximately 90° when the station is located a considerable distance away.

CROSS CHECKING YOUR POSITION

When you determine your radial from a station, you only establish that your location is on a line of position (LOP) extending away from the station. You can determine your exact position by cross checking with a second VOR station. To do this, determine your location from the second station and draw a line of position on that radial from the second VOR. Your position is where the two LOPs intersect. Determining your position this way is sometimes called **triangulation** since your position plus the locations of the two navaids make up three points of a triangle. [Figure 9-26]

Figure 9-26. You can determine your position by finding the intersection of lines of position from two VORs. For the most accurate results, you should select radials that are nearly perpendicular to each other.

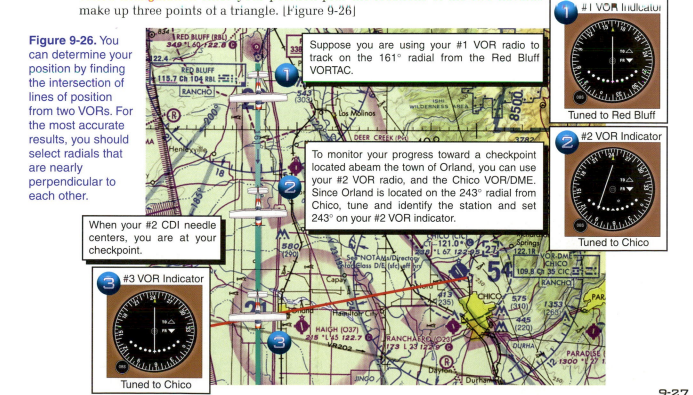

#1 VOR Indicator

Suppose you are using your #1 VOR radio to track on the 161° radial from the Red Bluff VORTAC.

Tuned to Red Bluff

#2 VOR Indicator

To monitor your progress toward a checkpoint located abeam the town of Orland, you can use your #2 VOR radio, and the Chico VOR/DME. Since Orland is located on the 243° radial from Chico, tune and identify the station and set 243° on your #2 VOR indicator.

Tuned to Chico

When your #2 CDI needle centers, you are at your checkpoint.

#3 VOR Indicator

Tuned to Chico

You can determine your position on a chart by plotting the intersection of LOPs from two or more VORs. An example is shown in figure 9-26.

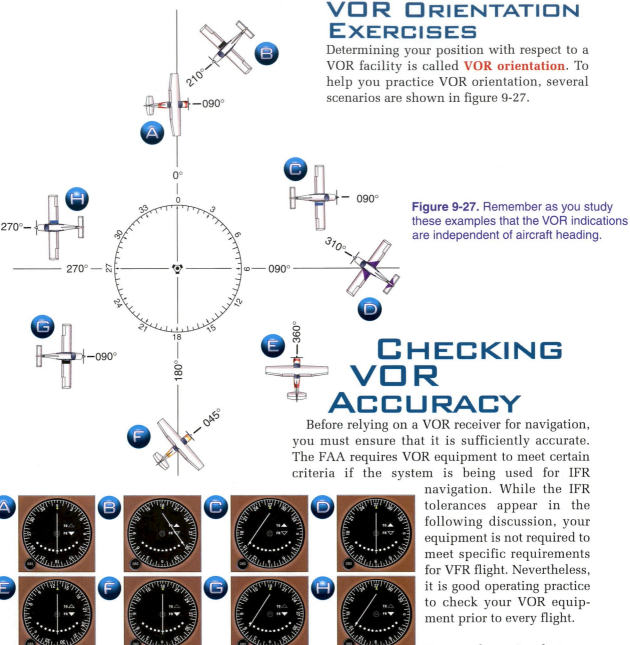

VOR ORIENTATION EXERCISES

Determining your position with respect to a VOR facility is called **VOR orientation**. To help you practice VOR orientation, several scenarios are shown in figure 9-27.

Figure 9-27. Remember as you study these examples that the VOR indications are independent of aircraft heading.

CHECKING VOR ACCURACY

Before relying on a VOR receiver for navigation, you must ensure that it is sufficiently accurate. The FAA requires VOR equipment to meet certain criteria if the system is being used for IFR navigation. While the IFR tolerances appear in the following discussion, your equipment is not required to meet specific requirements for VFR flight. Nevertheless, it is good operating practice to check your VOR equipment prior to every flight.

You can determine the accuracy of a VOR using ground or airborne **VOR checkpoints**. On the ground, you can taxi your aircraft to a specific point on the airport designated in the VOR Receiver Check section of the A/FD. After centering the CDI, compare your VOR course indication to the published radial for that checkpoint. The maximum permissible error for IFR navigation is ± 4°. Airborne checkpoints, also listed in the A/FD, are usually located over easily identifiable terrain or prominent features on the ground. With an airborne checkpoint, the maximum permissible course error is ± 6°. Another way to perform an airborne check is by using a VOR radial that defines the centerline of an airway.

Figure 9-28. In this example, your VOR indicator should display 164° (± 6°) FROM the North Bend VORTAC as you overfly the east edge of the town of Coquille.

To conduct the check, use your sectional chart to locate a prominent terrain feature under the centerline of an airway, preferably 20 miles or more from the facility. Maneuver your aircraft directly over the point, twist the OBS to center the CDI needle and note what course is set on the VOR indicator. The permissible difference between the published radial and the indicated course is ± 6°. [Figure 9-28]

You also can conduct a VOR check by comparing the indications of two VOR systems which are independent of each other (except for the antenna). If your aircraft is equipped with two VOR radios, set both to the same VOR facility and note the indicated readings on each. When you check one against the other, the difference should not exceed 4°.

VOR test facilities (VOTs) enable you to make precise VOR accuracy checks regardless of your position in relation to the facility. This is possible because VOTs broadcast a signal for only one radial — 360°. First, obtain the frequency from the A/FD, tune your VOR receiver, and identify the VOT signal; you should hear a series of dots or a continuous tone. Next, set a course of either 0° or 180° on the VOR indicator. If you set 0°, the CDI should center with a FROM indication. If you set 180°, the CDI should center with a TO indication. If the CDI does not center, you can determine the magnitude of the error by rotating the OBS until the needle moves to the center position. The new course should be ±4° of your test course (0° or 180°).

 A PERFECT PLACE FOR A MIDAIR COLLISION
From the files of the NTSB...

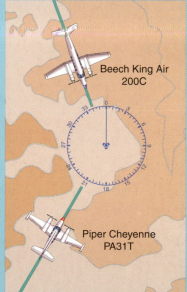

Aircraft: Piper Cheyenne, Beechcraft King Air
Crew and Passengers: 7
Narrative: A Piper PA-31T, N9162Y, and a Beech 200C, N390AC, were involved in a midair collision while both were cruising at 17,500 ft in unlimited visibility. The Piper was tracking inbound on the 210 deg [degree] radial of the Richmond VOR. The Beech was tracking inbound on the 340 deg [degree] radial of the Wilmington VOR. Both acft [aircraft] were substantially damaged, but both aircrew were able to continue flying and land safely.

The plt [pilot] of the Piper said that he saw a tan flash just before the collision. The pilot of the Beech did not see the Piper. The cockpit view of the PA-31 pilot was somewhat restricted by the left, windshield side post. Likewise, the Beech plt's [pilot's] view was somewhat restricted by the windshield center post and the windshield wiper arm. The acft [aircraft] converged on one another with a closure speed of about 420 kts and in the same general directions that the plt's [pilots'] views were obstructed.

If you think of each radial transmitted by a VOR as a highway, every VOR station is analogous to a 360-way road intersection — without a stop sign. A significant percentage of midair collisions and near-misses occur near VORs, even on days with unlimited visibility. In fact, in a recent year, more than 45% of all reported near-misses took place over a VOR. Not only can there be a concentration of aircraft in the vicinity of a VOR, but a pilot's workload generally increases with course changes, radio frequency and VOR indicator adjustments, time checks, and other cockpit duties. As you fly near VOR stations, you should concentrate on managing your workload efficiently, allowing yourself plenty of time to be on the lookout for aircraft on the other 359 highways in your portion of the sky.

HORIZONTAL SITUATION INDICATOR

A **horizontal situation indicator (HSI)** is an improved VOR indicator which you will find on many high-performance airplanes. The HSI combines a heading indicator and VOR indicator in a single display, providing you with an easy-to-interpret navigation picture. [Figure 9-29]

The **course indicating arrow** visually shows the orientation of the selected course relative to your current heading. Because of this, left and right indications on the course deviation bar are always properly oriented.

The **heading select bug** is used with an autopilot to automatically turn the aircraft to a newly selected heading.

The airplane's heading is displayed under the **heading index**, also called a lubber line.

The HSI contains a rotating **compass card** which indicates the aircraft's current magnetic heading. In situations where a standard VOR indicator gives you reverse sensing, the HSI compass card turns to provide normal sensing.

The **course deviation bar** performs the same function as the CDI on a basic VOR indicator, depicting how far you are off course. When you are on course, the course deviation bar is aligned with the course arrow and the reciprocal course pointer.

The **course set knob** controls the position of the course indicating arrow.

Each dot on the **course deviation scale** represents 2° for VOR navigation.

The **symbolic aircraft** shows your position in relation to the selected course as though you are above the aircraft looking down.

The **heading set knob** is used to position the heading select bug.

The **TO-FROM indicator** on an HSI points to the head of the course arrow when the selected course is inbound to the navigation facility. When the selected course is outbound from the navaid, the TO-FROM indicator points away from the course arrowhead.

Figure 9-29. This HSI shows the aircraft on a 070° heading, which is a 30° intercept angle for the 040° course from the station.

DISTANCE MEASURING EQUIPMENT

VOR/DME and VORTAC facilities give you distance information in addition to course guidance. If your aircraft is equipped with **distance measuring equipment (DME)**, you typically can obtain a readout of the distance in nautical miles to the associated VOR/DME or VORTAC site as well as groundspeed and time enroute to the station. To obtain a distance from the station, your aircraft's DME transceiver first transmits an interrogation signal to the station. The ground station then transmits a reply back to the aircraft. The aircraft's equipment measures the round trip time of this signal exchange, computes the distance in nautical miles, and displays it digitally in the cockpit. Depending on altitude and line-of-sight restrictions, you can receive a reliable signal up to 199 n.m. from the station. [Figure 9-30]

Transceiver

Antenna

Figure 9-30. The airborne DME equipment consists of a transceiver and shark's fin antenna.

DME IDENTIFICATION

Although you tune the DME using a VOR frequency, you should remember that the DME is a separate facility, even though it is collocated with a VOR. Each VOR frequency is tied to a specific DME channel under an arrangement called frequency pairing. When you tune and listen to the VOR, you should hear the VOR identifier repeated 3 or 4 times, followed by the DME identifier. A single-coded identification transmitted approximately every 30 seconds signals that the DME is functioning.

DME CAUTIONS

DME can be a very useful navigation aid, however, before using DME, you should understand its limitations. For example, since DME measures groundspeed by comparing the time lapse between a series of pulses, flight in any direction other than directly to or away from the station will result in an unreliable reading.

While DME normally is accurate to within 1/2 mile or 3% of the actual distance, whichever is greater, you should be aware that DME measures slant range, not horizontal distance to a station. **Slant range distance** is the result of two components — horizontal and vertical distance. The difference between the slant range distance and the horizontal distance is not significant if the aircraft is at least 1 mile from the station for every 1,000 feet of altitude. The error is greatest when the aircraft is directly above the station, where the DME simply indicates the aircraft's altitude in nautical miles. [Figure 9-31]

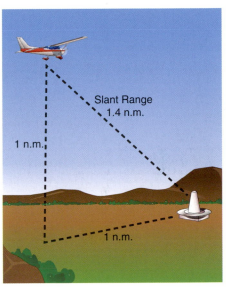

Figure 9-31. If you are flying at an altitude of 1 n.m. at a horizontal distance of 1 n.m. from the station, your DME will indicate a distance of 1.4 n.m.

SUMMARY CHECKLIST

✓ VORs only provide course guidance while VOR/DMEs and VORTACs also provide distance information.

✓ There are three classes of VORs with different coverage areas — terminal, low altitude, and high altitude.

✓ VOR radials and courses derived from radials are oriented to magnetic north and are depicted on most aeronautical charts using compass roses.

✓ Before using a VOR for navigation, always identify the station using the Morse code or voice identifier.

✓ To determine your location after tuning and identifying a VOR station, turn the course selector or OBS knob until the CDI needle centers with a FROM indication and read the radial next to course index. To determine your course to a VOR station, turn the course selector or OBS knob until the CDI needle centers with a TO indication, and read the magnetic course on the course index.

✓ The indications of a VOR receiver are not directly affected by aircraft heading. To avoid reverse sensing, always set the VOR indicator to generally agree with your intended course.

✓ Tracking involves flying a desired course to or from a station using a sufficient wind correction, if necessary.

✓ Bracketing is the process of determining and applying a wind correction which keeps you on course with the CDI needle centered.

✓ You can determine your position by cross checking between two VORs.

✓ You can check VOR receiver accuracy using ground and airborne checkpoints, or by using a VOT.

✓ An HSI is a VOR indicator combined with a heading indicator.

✓ DME automatically displays your slant range distance to a suitably equipped VOR ground station. Slant range error is greatest when your aircraft is directly over the transmitting station.

KEY TERMS

Very High Frequency Omnidirectional Range (VOR)

VOR/DME

VORTAC

Terminal VOR (TVOR)

Low Altitude VOR (LVOR)

High Altitude VOR (HVOR)

Radial

Compass Rose

Omnibearing Selector (OBS)

Course Deviation Indicator (CDI)

TO-FROM Indicator

Reverse Sensing

Cone of Confusion

Tracking

Bracketing

Triangulation

VOR Orientation

VOR Checkpoint

VOR Test Facilities (VOT)

Horizontal Situation Indicator (HSI)

Distance Measuring Equipment (DME)

Slant Range Distance

QUESTIONS

1. What is an advantage of the VHF frequencies used for VOR navigation?

   A. You can receive AM radio broadcasts over your VOR on these frequencies.
   B. VHF frequencies are not limited by mountains or the curvature of the earth.
   C. VHF radio waves are less susceptible to interference than low frequency radio waves.

2. What navigation capability does a VORTAC provide?

3. Identify the components of the VOR indicator shown in the accompanying figure.

4. Why is it important to set your VOR indicator to generally agree with your intended course?

5. If the CDI is deflected three dots to the right and your VOR indicator and heading indicator are in general agreement, where is your desired course?

   A. 6° left
   B. 3° right
   C. 6° right

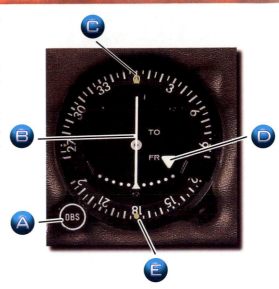

Refer to the following figure to answer questions 6 through 8.

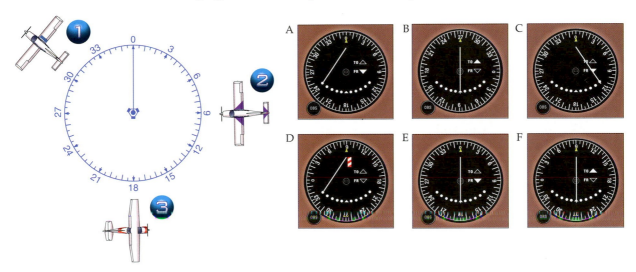

6. Which VOR indication would you expect for aircraft 1?

7. Which VOR indication would you expect for aircraft 2?

8. Which VOR indication would you expect for aircraft 3?

9. True/False. The indications on an HSI change with aircraft heading.

10. Approximately, what will a DME display indicate when you are directly over the station at 12,000 feet AGL?

SECTION C
ADF NAVIGATION

Navigation using nondirectional radio beacons (NDBs) is the oldest form of electronic navigation still in regular use. In the early days of aviation, the process of navigating between these beacons, called radio direction finding, required positioning the airplane's antenna to receive and interpret bearing information. The system was later improved so that the airborne receiver tracked a previously tuned station automatically. Although the use of NDBs diminished with the development of VOR systems in the 1940s, **automatic direction finder (ADF)** equipment still provides you with a useful navigation tool.

GROUND EQUIPMENT

Nondirectional radio beacons (NDBs) transmit low/medium frequency (L/MF) signals in the range of 190 kHz to 535 kHz. Since NDB signals are not limited to line of sight, the ADF system provides reliable navigation at lower altitudes than VOR equipment. In addition to NDBs, your airborne ADF equipment also can receive AM commercial broadcast stations, some of which appear on aeronautical charts. [Figure 9-32]

Figure 9-32. Selected NDBs and AM commercial broadcast stations are shown on aeronautical charts. Broadcast stations, such as KGRV, use the medium frequencies from 535 kHz to 1605 kHz and are normally marked with obstruction symbols. Commercial broadcast stations should be used only as supplementary VFR navaids.

AIRBORNE EQUIPMENT

ADF equipment in the aircraft permits L/MF signals to be received through the antenna, relayed to the ADF receiver where they are processed, and then sent to the ADF bearing indicator. Although most automatic direction finders are similar in appearance and operation, you should familiarize yourself with the make and model installed in your airplane by consulting the POH or other publication provided by the radio manufacturer.

ADF ANTENNAS

An ADF requires two antennas. The **directional antenna** is a flat device about the size of your hand, containing loops of wire that receive radio signals more efficiently in one direction than in others. You will normally find this antenna mounted on the bottom of the aircraft. The nondirectional **sense antenna** receives signals with equal efficiency in all directions. On many older aircraft, the sense antenna is a line which extends from the

top of the cabin to top of the tail. By analyzing the signals from both the directional antenna and the sense antenna, the ADF receiver determines the direction to the transmitting station. [Figure 9-33]

Figure 9-33. On this aircraft, the directional antenna and the sense antenna are combined in a single unit.

Hoops and Footballs

The heart of the direction finding concept is the loop antenna. [Figure A] By rotating a loop-shaped antenna and noting how the strength of the signal changed, pilots during the 1930s could determine the direction toward a radio transmitter. This gave a line of position to the station, which could be used either to fly to the station (homing), or to help establish position fixes along a route. To make the loop antenna assembly more streamlined and reduce static from particles in the slipstream, the loop antenna was often enclosed in a teardrop-shaped housing on the top or bottom of the fuselage. [Figure B]

ADF RECEIVER

The ADF receiver has an on/off/volume control, selectors for entering the station frequency, and several function or mode selectors. [Figure 9-34] Normally, you tune and identify a station with the ANT mode, since it provides maximum sensitivity to radio signals. After you enter the charted NDB or broadcast station frequency into the receiver, you should positively identify the station by listening to the Morse code identifier. You may also use the ANT mode to monitor voice transmissions such as weather broadcasts. The needle of the ADF bearing indicator does not function in this mode.

This function exchanges the standby frequency for the in-use frequency.

You can adjust the volume of the Morse code identification with the on/off/volume control.

This knob is used to select the appropriate L/MF frequency.

This selector allows you to choose the ANT mode to identify a station, or the ADF mode for navigation.

These controls allow you to operate the stopwatch function of this ADF model.

You select the BFO mode to tune and identify CW signals.

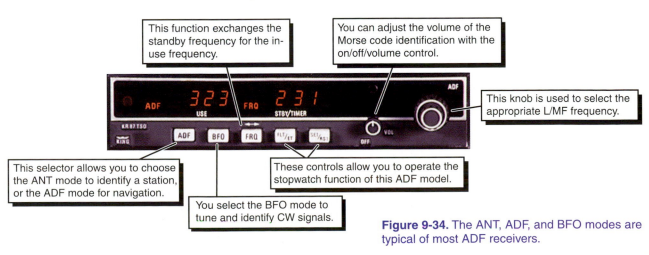

Figure 9-34. The ANT, ADF, and BFO modes are typical of most ADF receivers.

To send navigation information to the ADF indicator once you have tuned and identified the station, place the switch in the ADF mode. The needle on the bearing indicator will start to move as it searches for the station's relative position. Once a strong signal from the station is found, the needle will stop searching and steady itself. If you are in doubt about the quality of your ADF navigation signal, switch to the ANT mode and back to ADF and watch for the needle to return to a solid indication. Some receivers offer a test mode for this purpose.

The BFO (beat frequency oscillator) mode is used for tuning and identifying CW (continuous wave) signals, which are unmodulated compared to normal NDB signals. Within the contiguous United States, the BFO system usually is not required for station identification.

ADF BEARING INDICATORS

A **bearing** is the horizontal direction from one point to another. It can be measured clockwise in degrees from any reference point. A bearing indicator gives you the horizontal direction, or angle, between your aircraft and the L/MF station. Generally, there are three types of bearing indicators — the fixed-card, the movable-card, and the radio magnetic indicator (RMI). On a **fixed-card bearing indicator**, the number zero always appears at the top, and the numbers around the 360° azimuth card correspond to a station's bearing relative to the nose of the airplane. [Figure 9-35] You can rotate the azimuth card of a **movable-card bearing indicator**, so that the aircraft heading is under the top index. A **radio magnetic indicator (RMI)** is similar to the movable-card indicator except that it automatically adjusts itself to the present aircraft heading. More information about the movable-card and radio magnetic indicators is provided later in this section.

Figure 9-35. The fixed-card ADF bearing indicator is permanently positioned with the zero at the top.

The fixed-card bearing indicator measures **relative bearing** — the angular difference between the airplane's longitudinal axis and a straight line drawn from the airplane to the station. This value is measured clockwise from the airplane's nose. [Figure 9-36]

The needle on a fixed-card ADF points to the relative bearing. See figure 9-36.

Figure 9-36. The relative bearing is the angle between the nose of the aircraft and the station.

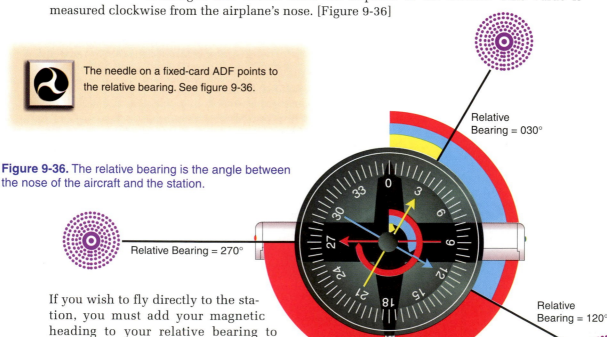

Relative Bearing = 030°

Relative Bearing = 270°

Relative Bearing = 120°

If you wish to fly directly to the station, you must add your magnetic heading to your relative bearing to determine your **magnetic bearing** to the station (magnetic heading (MH) + relative bearing (RB) = magnetic bearing (MB) to the

The ADF needle indicates the station is 060° to the right of the aircraft's nose.

N

Magnetic Bearing 030°

Magnetic Heading 330°

Relative Bearing 060°

MH (330°) + RB (060°) = MB (030°)

Turning 60° to the right puts the aircraft on a heading of 030° direct to the station (with no wind).

N

Magnetic Bearing 030°

Relative Bearing 0°

Magnetic Heading 030°

MH (030°) + RB (0°) = MB (030°)

Figure 9-37. The magnetic bearing will take you directly to the station.

station). If the total is more than 360°, you will need to subtract 360° to find the magnetic bearing to the station. [Figure 9-37]

Magnetic heading (MH) + relative bearing (RB) = magnetic bearing (MB) to the station. See figure 9-37.

Figure 9-38. The curved line is your flight path when homing to the station in a right crosswind. With no wind, your flight path would follow a straight line.

WIND

NAVIGATION PROCEDURES

While many of the fundamental operations involved in ADF navigation are similar to the procedures you use when navigating with a VOR, there also are some important differences. The following discussion covers the indications and procedures unique to ADF navigation. For consistency, a fixed-card bearing indicator is used in the examples.

HOMING

A procedure during which you always keep the nose of the aircraft pointing directly to the station is called **homing** to the station. To fly to an NDB using the homing procedure simply turn to position the head of the ADF needle on the aircraft's nose (0° on a fixed-card indicator). In a no-wind situation, a constant magnetic heading will keep the ADF needle positioned at 0° on the fixed card indicator as you fly inbound to the station. However, in a crosswind situation, the wind will cause your aircraft to drift off course, and you must adjust the magnetic heading to keep the nose of the aircraft pointing toward the station. [Figure 9-38]

"WHAT PUT US NORTH?"

The year was 1937. Amelia Earhart and her navigator, Fred Noonan, were on one of the longest legs of their around-the-world attempt — crossing the South Atlantic from Fortaleza, Brazil to Dakar, Senegal. As Amelia sighted the African coast in the distance, Fred, who was seated at the navigator's station behind the auxiliary fuel tanks, passed Amelia a note containing the latest course correction based upon his calculations:

3:36 Change to 36 degrees.
Estimate 79 miles to
Dakar from 3:36 p.m.

While Fred was an experienced navigator, Amelia chose to disregard his instructions. For some reason, she believed that they could not have drifted as far off course as Fred's navigation indicated. In fact, Amelia scribbled under Fred's note: *What put us north?*

Possibly assuming that Fred's inability to obtain a sextant shot due to the overcast skies had caused his calculations to be in error, Amelia followed her intuition and turned north upon reaching the coast instead of south, as Fred had instructed. After flying for another 50 miles, the two found themselves at Saint-Louis, Senegal, many miles north of their intended destination. If Amelia had turned south when she reached the coast, they would have arrived at Dakar within a half hour of 3:36 p.m. The occurrence, which Amelia later admitted was her error, fortunately only resulted in a short delay; the next day the pair flew south to Dakar to continue their journey.

Is there ever a time when your instincts should override the indications you are receiving from a normally reliable source? The answer is a qualified yes. Your instincts can help you determine that there is a problem, however, you should rely on less subjective resources to help you decide if, in fact, there is an error and, if so, what options you have available. For instance, if you begin to doubt the accuracy of a navaid, you should make every attempt to corroborate your feeling with a cross-check from another navaid or other resources such as a sectional chart or ATC facility. Not only is it your responsibility as pilot in command, but it also can save you several miles of travel in the wrong direction.

TRACKING

Normally, the best way to fly to or from a station is in a straight line, which requires tracking if any crosswind is present. The tracking procedure for an ADF is similar to VOR tracking; it involves turning a few degrees into the wind to compensate for its effect on your path over the ground. You determine the exact wind correction angle through bracketing, and hold the required heading to track the desired bearing to the station. [Figure 9-39]

 Once you are established on an inbound course with the proper wind correction, the head of the ADF needle indicates the wind correction angle and points in the opposite direction as the correction. See figure 9-39.

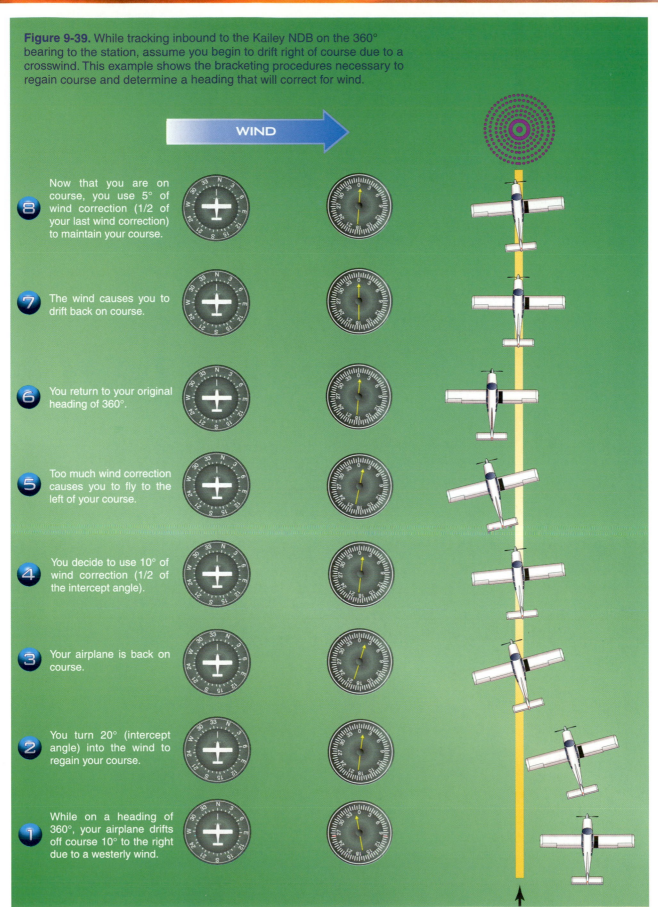

Figure 9-39. While tracking inbound to the Kailey NDB on the 360° bearing to the station, assume you begin to drift right of course due to a crosswind. This example shows the bracketing procedures necessary to regain course and determine a heading that will correct for wind.

WIND

8 Now that you are on course, you use 5° of wind correction (1/2 of your last wind correction) to maintain your course.

7 The wind causes you to drift back on course.

6 You return to your original heading of 360°.

5 Too much wind correction causes you to fly to the left of your course.

4 You decide to use 10° of wind correction (1/2 of the intercept angle).

3 Your airplane is back on course.

2 You turn 20° (intercept angle) into the wind to regain your course.

1 While on a heading of 360°, your airplane drifts off course 10° to the right due to a westerly wind.

When you are on course and tracking to the station, the wind correction angle (WCA) should equal the number of degrees the ADF needle points left or right of the aircraft's nose. For example, if your WCA is 10° left, the station is 10° to the right, and the ADF needle indicates 010°. As you pass over the station, the needle tends to fluctuate. Do not chase the needle, since indications may be erroneous close to the station. When the needle stabilizes at or near

the 180° position, you have passed the station. If you do not pass directly over the facility, station passage occurs when the needle is steady and points to either wingtip position. While tracking outbound, the wind correction angle should be exactly equal to the number of degrees the station is located to the left or right of the aircraft's tail. Remember, the tail of the aircraft is the 180° position on the fixed-card indicator. [Figure 9-40]

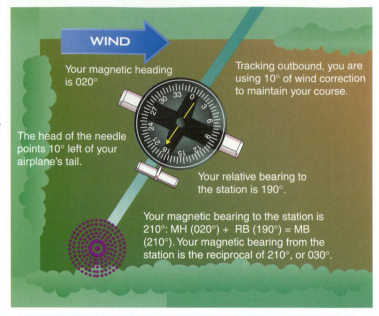

Figure 9-40. In this example, you are tracking outbound from the Steiner NDB on the 030° bearing and experience a crosswind from the west.

WIND

Your magnetic heading is 020°

The head of the needle points 10° left of your airplane's tail.

Tracking outbound, you are using 10° of wind correction to maintain your course.

Your relative bearing to the station is 190°.

Your magnetic bearing to the station is 210°: MH (020°) + RB (190°) = MB (210°). Your magnetic bearing from the station is the reciprocal of 210°, or 030°.

Home, Home on the Range

When airplanes first began to use radio for navigation, there were no specific radio navigation aids. Pilots used a direction-sensing antenna to determine lines of position from existing commercial broadcast stations. Before long, specialized aviation radio beacons were developed that made use of the long-distance characteristics of lower radio frequencies.

The old airway system consisted of a clever arrangement of multiple transmitters which allowed four courses, called ranges, to be transmitted from one radio facility. To intercept and follow these ranges, the pilot listened to the signals on a headset or speaker. As shown, the station broadcast the Morse code letter A (• —) in two quadrants and the letter N (— •) in the other quadrants. The areas where the signals overlapped formed the four legs of the range. The dots and dashes were sequenced so that when a pilot was receiving the A and the N with equal strength, there would be a steady tone in the headset. If the airplane drifted off the range into one quadrant or the other, one letter would be stronger, and depending on which letter was heard, the pilot knew which way to turn to get back on the beam. Ranges were the basis of the national airway system between the 1930s and 1950s, and were gradually replaced by VHF facilities in the 1950s and 1960s.

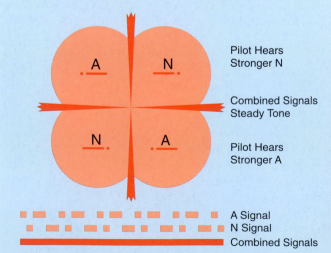

Pilot Hears Stronger N

Combined Signals Steady Tone

Pilot Hears Stronger A

A Signal
N Signal
Combined Signals

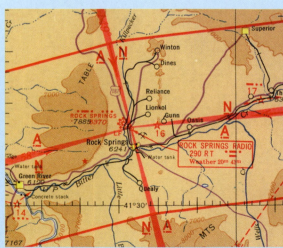

INTERCEPTING A COURSE

Intercepting a specific course to track to or from an NDB is accomplished by a method similar to that used in VOR navigation. Use the ADF formula to help you with this procedure. [Figure 9-41]

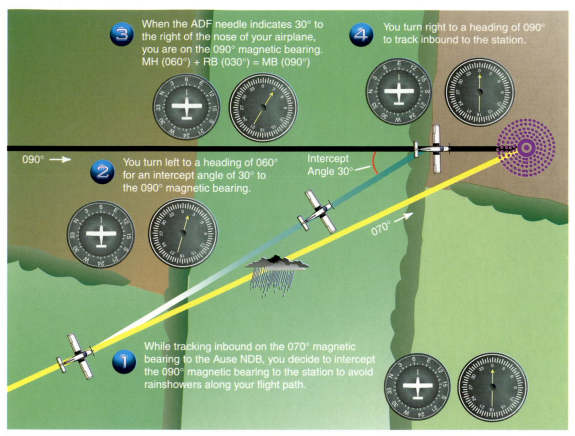

Figure 9-41. You are located southwest of Ause NDB on the 070° bearing and want to track inbound to the station on the 090° bearing. Although this example depicts the use of a 30° intercept angle, the angle which you use in a particular situation may range from 20° to 90° depending on your distance from the station.

ADF ORIENTATION

To locate your position on a chart using the ADF you need to add 180° to or subtract 180° from the magnetic bearing to determine the reciprocal bearing, which is the bearing from the station. For example, if your magnetic bearing to the station is 090°, the reciprocal bearing is 270° (090° + 180° = 270°). If your magnetic bearing is 210°, the reciprocal is 030° (210° − 180° = 030°).

You will have to plot your azimuth with reference to grid lines since a chart depiction of an NDB does not have a compass rose. Grid lines are referenced to true north so you need to convert your magnetic bearing to a true bearing. When you convert magnetic values to true values, you add easterly variation and subtract westerly variation. Plot your position on the chart by placing the edge of your plotter on the NDB and rotating it until the compass rose intersects a line of longitude at the same angle as your true bearing. By drawing the corresponding line, you have narrowed your position down to some point on that line. To find your exact location, you can use a second navaid, as discussed in the VOR section, or use identifiable landmarks and terrain beneath you. You may also use an NDB or radio station to the side of your route to fix your position. You can determine when you are abeam a station simply by watching for the needle to point to the 090° or 270° position.

MOVABLE-CARD INDICATOR

When you set your magnetic heading value under the top index of a movable-card indicator, the head of the ADF needle will directly indicate magnetic bearing to a station. In addition, the number under the tail of the needle indicates magnetic bearing from the station. The movable card reduces your workload since it does not require you to use the ADF formula to find the magnetic bearing. [Figure 9-42]

Magnetic Heading + Relative Bearing = Magnetic Bearing to Station
060°   030°   090°

When the magnetic heading is set on a movable-card ADF indicator, the head of the needle points to the magnetic bearing to the station and the tail of the needle points to the magnetic bearing from the station. To determine relative bearing, turn the knob so 0° is at the top, or subtract the magnetic heading from the magnetic bearing to the station. See figure 9-42.

Figure 9-42. The heading of 060° is set at the top of this movable-card ADF. The needle points to 090°, which is the magnetic bearing to the station.

RADIO MAGNETIC INDICATOR

The radio magnetic indicator (RMI) combines a heading indicator with two bearing needles. The RMI usually has a single-bar and a double-bar needle superimposed over a rotating compass card which is referenced to magnetic north. Although the single-bar needle normally points to a VOR and the double-bar needle points to a L/MF station, on many RMIs each needle can be set to either a VOR or an L/MF facility. You can think of the RMI as a movable-card ADF on which the card automatically adjusts itself to the present heading and the head of the needle points to your magnetic bearing to the station. [Figure 9-43]

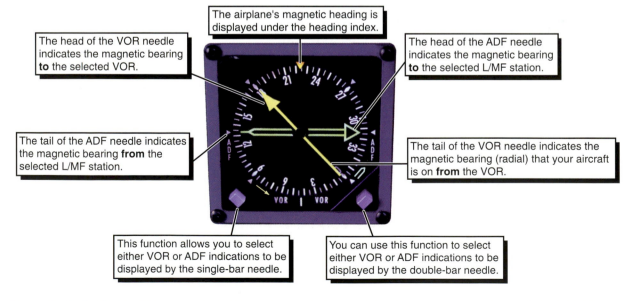

The airplane's magnetic heading is displayed under the heading index.

The head of the VOR needle indicates the magnetic bearing **to** the selected VOR.

The head of the ADF needle indicates the magnetic bearing **to** the selected L/MF station.

The tail of the ADF needle indicates the magnetic bearing **from** the selected L/MF station.

The tail of the VOR needle indicates the magnetic bearing (radial) that your aircraft is on **from** the VOR.

This function allows you to select either VOR or ADF indications to be displayed by the single-bar needle.

You can use this function to select either VOR or ADF indications to be displayed by the double-bar needle.

Figure 9-43. An RMI facilitates cross-checking between two navaids because you can see the radials or bearings from those facilities on the same instrument at the same time. Since the RMI incorporates a VOR pointer, you should perform a VOR receiver check prior to using the instrument in flight.

ADF LIMITATIONS

The ADF effectively supplements VOR and other navigation systems, however, you need to be aware of some of its limitations. Reception range for L/MF facilities can vary greatly, depending on transmitter power, atmospheric conditions, and time of day. Since the ADF indicator does not have an OFF flag, it is possible to inadvertently refer to the signal after it is no longer reliable. One way to make sure you have a usable signal is to leave the identifier turned up to an audible level whenever you use the ADF for navigation.

An accurate setting on the heading indicator is essential for accurate ADF tracking. If the heading indicator precesses 10°, then all your courses and intercepts will be off by that amount. Although this may not be significant when tracking close to the station, it can turn into large distances off course when you are a number of miles away from the station.

At times, NDB signals can be refracted by the ionosphere and return to earth 30 to 60 miles or more from the station, leading to ADF needle fluctuations. The phenomenon is called **night effect** and is most pronounced during the period just before and just after sunrise or sunset. To minimize the effect, you can average the fluctuations, fly at a higher altitude, or select a station transmitting on frequencies lower than 350 kHz, since night effect has little impact on this portion of the frequency range.

When in close proximity to an electrical storm, **thunderstorm effect** can cause the ADF needle to point to the source of the lightning flashes rather than the tuned NDB. **Precipitation static**, which is caused by a buildup of static electricity on an aircraft flying in rain, snow, or clouds, can interfere with ADF indications and cause the ADF needle to wander. **Terrain effect** can occur when mountains reflect the radio waves and cause erroneous bearing indications and, **shoreline effect** can degrade the accuracy of your ADF. [Figure 9-44]

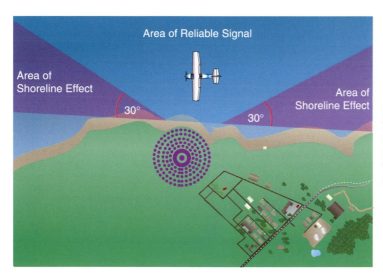

Figure 9-44. Shorelines can refract low frequency radio waves when they cross at small angles. You can minimize this phenomenon by using stations where the signals cross the shoreline at angles greater than 30°.

Airplane Tails

Perhaps you have wondered about the small plastic tails which hang from the trailing edges of wingtips and tail surfaces of many aircraft. As the airplane moves through the air, friction with rain, snow, ice crystals, dust particles, and the air itself can cause a buildup of static electricity. This charge can not only affect radio reception and navigation instruments, but it also may cause eerie displays of St. Elmo's Fire, which can look like miniature lightning bolts dancing from wingtips, antennas, and propellers. The devices on the trailing edges are static dischargers (also called static wicks or charge dissipaters). They allow the static charge to leak away gradually, preventing large accumulations and sudden discharges.

SUMMARY CHECKLIST

✓ An ADF receives low and medium frequency transmitting stations, including NDBs (190-535 kHz) and AM broadcast stations (535-1605 kHz).

✓ An ADF utilizes a directional antenna and a sense antenna, which are often combined into a single antenna mounted on the bottom of the fuselage.

✓ The head of the ADF indicator needle points to the station relative to the nose of the airplane.

✓ A fixed-card ADF indicator always displays 0° at the top of the azimuth card and the needle points to the relative bearing to the station.

✓ When you set your magnetic heading value under the top index of a movable-card indicator, the head of the ADF needle directly indicates magnetic bearing to the station.

✓ Magnetic heading plus relative bearing equals magnetic bearing to the station. (MH + RB = MB)

✓ To fly to an NDB using the homing procedure simply turn toward the ADF needle, then keep the head of the ADF needle on the aircraft's nose (0° on a fixed card indicator).

✓ A radio magnetic indicator (RMI) combines a heading indicator with two bearing needles which normally provide VOR and ADF indications.

✓ The low and medium frequency radio waves used by ADF can be adversely affected by a number of factors including the ionosphere, mountains, and shorelines.

KEY TERMS

Automatic Direction Finder (ADF)   Sense Antenna

Nondirectional Radio Beacon (NDB)   Bearing

Directional Antenna   Fixed-Card Bearing Indicator

Movable-Card Bearing Indicator   Night Effect

Radio Magnetic Indicator (RMI)   Thunderstorm Effect

Relative Bearing   Precipitation Static

Magnetic Bearing   Terrain Effect

Homing   Shoreline Effect

QUESTIONS

1. ADF equipment is capable of receiving signals from what type(s) of facility?

   A. Any FM radio station
   B. NDBs and AM commercial broadcast stations
   C. Specially equipped VOR or VORTAC stations

Use the fixed-card ADF indicators to answer questions 2 through 4.

2. What is your relative bearing to the station depicted on ADF indicator A? If your aircraft is on a heading of 050°, what is your magnetic bearing to the station?

3. What is your relative bearing to the station depicted on ADF indicator B? If your aircraft is on a heading of 120°, what is your magnetic bearing to the station?

4. What is your relative bearing to the station depicted on ADF indicator C? If your aircraft is on a heading of 135°, what is your magnetic bearing to the station?

Use the movable-card ADF indicators to answer questions 5 through 7.

5. What is your relative bearing to the station depicted on ADF indicator A? What is your magnetic bearing to the station?

6. What is the relative bearing to the station depicted on ADF indicator B? What is your magnetic bearing from the station?

7. What is the relative bearing to the station depicted on ADF indicator C? What is your magnetic bearing to the station?

8. If you are navigating with ADF indicator C and are on course tracking a bearing, what is your aircraft's direction of flight relative to the station, and the wind correction used?

    A. Tracking to the station with a 15° correction for a left crosswind
    B. Tracking to the station with a 15° correction for a right crosswind
    C. Tracking from the station with a 15° correction for a left crosswind

9. True/False./The ADF receiver gives you a clear warning when the station signal is unreliable.

10. Describe some of the limitations of ADF equipment.

SECTION D
Advanced Navigation

During World War II, the success of a bombing mission rested largely with an aircraft instrument called the Norden bombsight. Among other capabilities, the device was a sophisticated navigation computer which took much of the guesswork out of the grim task at hand. On a typical mission, the bombardier would input altitude, airspeed, and other variables into the system; then set the crosshairs of the telescopic sight on the target. After collecting data on the airplane's groundspeed and wind drift, the computer would calculate the correct dropping angle, and, in connection with an autopilot, keep the aircraft on the proper course to maintain the necessary line of sight to the target. The efficiency and accuracy of the instrument was so crucial to the success of the U.S. Army Air Forces' daylight bombing strategy that the associated technology was one of the most closely guarded secrets of the time.

Today, most advanced navigation systems are not super-secret devices limited to high-tech military aircraft. In fact, the pace of technological advancements has made it possible for manufacturers to design tremendously accurate and versatile navigation radios at a relatively low cost, making them available for use in almost any aircraft.

TYPES OF EQUIPMENT

Most advanced navigation equipment is designed to allow you to fly any desired course within the coverage of a station's navigation signals or within the limits of a self-contained system. This type of navigation, known as **area navigation (RNAV)**, is the basic method used by a variety of equipment including VORTAC-based area navigation systems, long range navigation systems, inertial navigation systems, and global positioning systems.

The following discussion is designed only to provide you with an overview of advanced aviation navigation systems. You should always refer to the respective operating handbook for further information on the capabilities, limitations, and authorized operations of the navigation equipment you plan to use in flight.

VORTAC-BASED AREA NAVIGATION

While the term, RNAV, technically encompasses most area navigation equipment for flight plan equipment code purposes, RNAV is commonly used to refer to VORTAC-based area navigation systems. In this context, RNAV permits more lateral freedom in navigating because it allows you to fly to a predetermined point without overflying VOR/DME or VORTAC facilities. This is accomplished with an RNAV computer which allows you to create electronic phantom stations, or waypoints, at any location within the reception range of the VORTAC or VOR/DME station. After you enter the desired

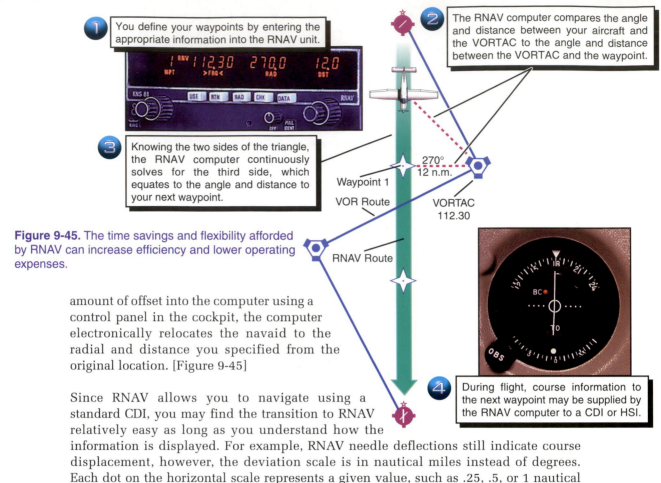

① You define your waypoints by entering the appropriate information into the RNAV unit.

② The RNAV computer compares the angle and distance between your aircraft and the VORTAC to the angle and distance between the VORTAC and the waypoint.

③ Knowing the two sides of the triangle, the RNAV computer continuously solves for the third side, which equates to the angle and distance to your next waypoint.

270°
12 n.m.

Waypoint 1

VOR Route

VORTAC
112.30

RNAV Route

④ During flight, course information to the next waypoint may be supplied by the RNAV computer to a CDI or HSI.

Figure 9-45. The time savings and flexibility afforded by RNAV can increase efficiency and lower operating expenses.

amount of offset into the computer using a control panel in the cockpit, the computer electronically relocates the navaid to the radial and distance you specified from the original location. [Figure 9-45]

Since RNAV allows you to navigate using a standard CDI, you may find the transition to RNAV relatively easy as long as you understand how the information is displayed. For example, RNAV needle deflections still indicate course displacement, however, the deviation scale is in nautical miles instead of degrees. Each dot on the horizontal scale represents a given value, such as .25, .5, or 1 nautical mile, depending on the particular RNAV unit.

Less is More

How do you reconcile a seemingly endless capability to provide information with the physical space limitations of the cockpit? Can an instrument panel with remarkably less clutter offer considerably more information to the pilot? With more navigation aids available than ever before, how can you take advantage of all they offer, allow yourself maximum flexibility, and still avoid information overload? One manufacturer, Collins Avionics (a division of Rockwell International Corp.) has answered those questions with its Pro Line 21 system, a derivative of which will be fielded with the launch of Raytheon Aircraft's new business jet, the Premier I. In the four 10 x 8 inch liquid crystal display configuration shown in the accompanying photo, Collins' Pro Line 21 avionics suite can provide the same functionality as the six screens installed in the typical Boeing 747-400.

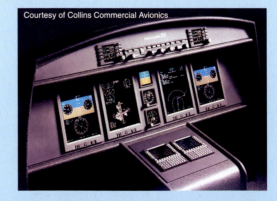
Courtesy of Collins Commercial Avionics

Increasingly, new cockpit displays are not only designed to consolidate information previously spread among multiple CRTs and electro-mechanical instruments, but also present the data in a clear and more usable format. In addition, the architecture of new navigation systems accommodates the future of airborne navigation while maintaining a capability to interface with traditional radio navaids. For example, while Collins' Pro Line 21 is designed to use GPS as its primary source of navigation information, it can quickly shift from space-based pathfinding to traditional ground-based navaids such as VORs and NDBs. And, the transition can take place on the same screen, creating a minimal amount of disruption while increasing pilot efficiency.

LONG RANGE NAVIGATION

Long range navigation (LORAN) is a continuous, all-weather, position determining system maintained by the U.S. Coast Guard for land, sea, and airborne applications. The current LORAN-C system was developed for the Department of Defense (DOD) to provide a radio navigation capability with much greater range and accuracy than its predecessor, LORAN-A. Early LORAN-A models, which were developed during World War II, were used for maritime navigation and were so heavy and cumbersome they were impractical for light aircraft. However, today's LORAN-C equipment takes advantage of the technological advances in microprocessors and circuit miniaturization to make the units small and lightweight enough to be suitable for aviation.

LORAN OPERATION

The LORAN system consists of ground-based low frequency (90-110 kHz) transmitting stations arranged in groups called chains. The principle behind LORAN operation is based on the measurement of time differences between the synchronized signals received from each transmitting station in a chain. One transmitting station in a chain is designated the master while all others are called secondaries. The master station transmits a group of coded pulses first; then, each secondary station transmits at a specific time interval after the master pulse. By measuring the **time difference (TD)** between the reception of a master station's signal and that of a secondary station, the LORAN computer determines your location along a string of possibilities, called a line of position (LOP). For the LORAN receiver to pinpoint your location, a second LOP is determined using another secondary station. The intersection of the two LOPs marks your position, which is then displayed by your LORAN receiver. [Figure 9-46]

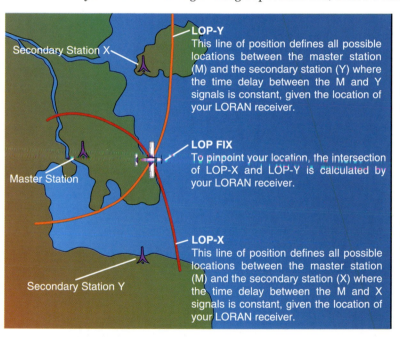

LOP-Y
This line of position defines all possible locations between the master station (M) and the secondary station (Y) where the time delay between the M and Y signals is constant, given the location of your LORAN receiver.

LOP FIX
To pinpoint your location, the intersection of LOP-X and LOP-Y is calculated by your LORAN receiver.

LOP-X
This line of position defines all possible locations between the master station (M) and the secondary station (X) where the time delay between the M and X signals is constant, given the location of your LORAN receiver.

Secondary Station X

Master Station

Secondary Station Y

Figure 9-46. Using a master station and two secondary stations, your LORAN receiver can calculate two lines of position. Your location can then be fixed at the intersection of the two LOPs.

For a flight, you can enter the coordinates of your destination, as well as other waypoints. Once the receiver has determined its location, it will calculate the course and distance to the point you specified, and continually update this information as you progress along your flight path. Most receivers also calculate your groundspeed, as well as distance and time remaining to the destination. In general, you can expect LORAN-C equipment to determine your position to within 0.3 n.m. or better. However, the exact accuracy largely depends on the geometry between the chain transmitters and the receiver.

LORAN RECEIVERS

There are many types of LORAN receivers on the market with different capabilities and operating requirements. Depending on the receiver's software program and/or database, it can provide you with navigation information such as wind direction and velocity, fuel consumption, nearest airports, radio frequencies, phone numbers, and audible warnings before you enter special use airspace. Generally, the more sophisticated a receiver is, the more capability it has, and the more extensive its database. [Figure 9-47]

Figure 9-47. Many types of LORAN receivers are in use today.

Although LORAN is a popular navigation system, it does have some drawbacks which limit many receivers to VFR operations. Since LORAN uses a low frequency AM radio signal, electrical disturbances such as lightning and static electricity can cause interference. Another major limitation of LORAN deals with characteristics of the radio signals themselves. Even though they are very accurate (especially over water), LORAN signals have a tendency to travel over land at different speeds. Surface type, foliage, seasonal changes, and weather can affect the speed of the radio waves and, consequently, their accuracy.

LORAN's FUTURE

While LORAN has been the navaid of choice for many people desiring a low-cost, long range navigation system, little to no growth is anticipated in the use of LORAN in the short-term. In fact, the explosive growth in the use of global positioning system navigation devices may have spelled the end of LORAN. Current plans call for LORAN-C to remain part of the radio navigation system only for the next few years. Continued support of LORAN-C over the long-term is likely only if it is determined that LORAN-C provides a service which cannot be met by another system.

INERTIAL NAVIGATION

An **inertial navigation system (INS)** is a totally self-contained system which supplies aircraft position and navigation information based on inertial forces measured by gyroscopic stabilized instruments called accelerometers. Once you set the initial position, the INS computer uses the data it receives from the accelerometers to calculate attitude, velocity, and heading information. The resulting data is then transmitted to a cockpit display and, in some cases, may be used to provide guidance or steering information for the autopilot and flight instruments. While it can be extremely accurate, the inherent size, weight, and relatively high cost of INS typically restricts its use to airline, military, and high performance business aircraft.

GLOBAL POSITIONING SYSTEM

The **global positioning system (GPS)** is a space-based radio positioning, navigation, and time-transfer system developed and maintained by the DOD. GPS, which gained full operational capability on July 17, 1995, has increased in popularity at an unprecedented rate primarily due to its ability to provide highly accurate position, velocity, and time information on a global basis at a relatively low cost. The system provides this service 24 hours a day to an unlimited number of properly equipped users.

GPS OPERATION

The global positioning system consists of three segments — space, control, and user. The space segment consists of 24 NAVSTAR satellites, 3 of which are spares, in circular orbits 10,900 n.m. above the earth. The satellites are positioned so that a minimum of 5 satellites are always in view to users anywhere in the world. The satellites continually broadcast navigation signals which are used by GPS receivers to calculate extremely accurate position information.

Five monitor stations, three uplink ground antennas, and a master control station located at Falcon Air Force Base in Colorado Springs, Colorado, make up the control segment. The stations track all GPS satellites and calculate precise orbit locations. From this information, the master control station issues updated navigation messages for each satellite, thereby maintaining the most accurate signal information possible.

The user segment, which includes antennas, receivers, and processors, uses the position and time signals broadcast from the GPS constellation to calculate precise position, speed, and time for pilots, mariners, and land-based operators. Similar in principle to LORAN, the GPS receiver establishes a position at the point of intersecting LOPs. By matching timing from the unique coded pseudo-random signal broadcast from each satellite in view, the GPS unit measures the time delay for each signal to reach the receiver to determine ranges. Measurements collected simultaneously from three satellites can produce a two-dimensional position. To determine a three-dimensional fix, signals from a minimum of four satellites must be received. [Figure 9-48]

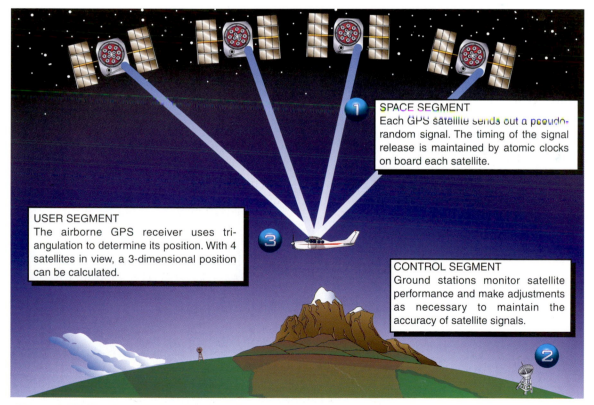

Figure 9-48. Precise global positioning information is made possible by the coordinated interaction of the satellite constellation, ground monitoring stations, and an airborne GPS receiver.

Once a GPS receiver calculates its own position, it can then determine and display the distance, bearing, and estimated time enroute to the next waypoint. Although

LOOK MOM, NO HANDS!

Born in law offices and hospitals where huge amounts of information must be transcribed in short periods of time, voice recognition systems are finding their way into modern aircraft. Currently in use in some military aircraft, voice activated systems are used to initiate computer performance of time-consuming and labor-intensive tasks, thereby decreasing pilot workload and increasing aviation safety. How far away is this technology from the general aviation cockpit? Not as far as you may think.

The avionics manufacturer, Honeywell, Inc., is currently developing a Voice Command System for use with its new Primus Epic integrated avionics system. The human-centered cockpit design will use a customized aviation vocabulary data base to interface with the pilot. Using the system, a pilot would be able to accomplish a variety of tasks which previously would have required hands-on, head-down time. Specific applications include:

• Tuning Radios — *"Tune COM 2, 118.1."*

• Accessing a Navigation Database — *"Display nearest airports."*

• Checklist Control — *"Flaps set and checked."*

• Modifying a Flight Plan — *"Enter holding at TERRO Intersection."*

Courtesy of Honeywell, Inc.

the GPS unit uses latitude and longitude coordinates to identify a position, it may display waypoint names, fix names, and database identifiers in lieu of latitude and longitude coordinates.

GPS ACCURACY

While GPS is an extremely accurate system, small errors are caused by a number of factors. Inherent errors, which are relatively small, include atmospheric interference, satellite position anomalies, and timing inaccuracies. A man-made error, called **selective availability (SA)** is considerably larger. SA is introduced by the DOD to degrade the accuracy of GPS for national security reasons. Nonetheless, the sum of all GPS errors still allows the DOD to guarantee that GPS will be accurate to within 100 meters of true horizontal position 95% of the time and within 300 meters of true horizontal position 99% of the time for most civil users. [Figure 9-49]

Figure 9-49. Even taking into account natural and man-made errors present in the satellite signals, GPS is generally more accurate than any other enroute navigation system.

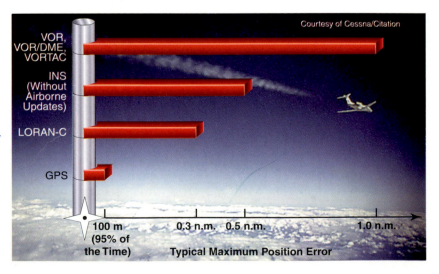

GPS RECEIVERS

There are several types of GPS receivers on the market today, ranging from low-cost handheld units to more expensive, and more capable panel-mounted units. The type of display usually varies with cost. For example, lower-priced units generally use a liquid crystal display (LCD) while high-end receivers may employ a light-emitting diode (LED) or even a cathode ray tube (CRT) display. The more expensive displays typically have less tendency to wash out in bright sunlight, are viewable from acute angles, and overall are more pleasing to the eye.

Like LORAN, the information available depends on the receiver capabilities and the database which is loaded into the unit. Since most data does not fit onto one screen, information is usually divided into categories, or modes, each of which may contain several pages of information. Typically, the manufacturer tries to put related information on a single page with supplemental data on subsequent pages. While the physical interface between you and the receiver usually cannot be altered, you can sometimes customize the content and organization of the display. [Figure 9-50]

Figure 9-50. GPS receivers come in many shapes and sizes with a variety of features and capabilities.

GPS is used for VFR and IFR navigation, and for designated instrument approaches. Typically, handheld GPS receivers are limited to use under VFR conditions. Some panel-mounted units also are restricted to VFR flight and must be placarded as such in the aircraft. An IFR GPS receiver also should be placarded if it is not authorized for GPS instrument approach operations. To determine the type and degree of authorized operations for a particular GPS receiver, you should refer to the supplements section of your aircraft's POH/AFM.

SUMMARY CHECKLIST

✓ Area navigation equipment is designed to allow you to fly any desired course within the coverage of a navaid's signals or within the limits of a self-contained system.

✓ VORTAC-based area navigation systems allow you to create waypoints at any location within the reception range of the VORTAC or VOR/DME station.

✓ The long range navigation (LORAN) computer determines your location by measuring the time difference between the reception of a master station's signal and that of two secondary stations. The intersection of the two associated LOPs mark your position.

✓ An inertial navigation system (INS) computer uses initial data and information it receives from accelerometers to calculate aircraft attitude, velocity, and heading.

✓ The global positioning system consists of space, control, and user segments.

✓ Signals collected by a GPS receiver from three satellites can produce a two-dimensional position. When a fourth satellite is added, a three-dimensional fix can be determined.

✓ Even with the effects of selective availability, GPS can accurately calculate your true horizontal position to within 100 meters 95% of the time and within 300 meters 99% of the time.

KEY TERMS

Area Navigation (RNAV)   Inertial Navigation System (INS)

Long Range Navigation (LORAN)   Global Positioning System (GPS)

Time Difference (TD)   Selective Availability (SA)

QUESTIONS

1. When using a VORTAC-based RNAV system, how does the course displacement display differ from that associated with traditional VOR navigation?

2. How does a LORAN-C receiver determine your position?

3. True/False. LORAN signals are unaffected by lightning.

4. Select the true statement(s) regarding INS.

   A. INS is a self-contained system.
   B. A typical INS unit derives its information from gyro-stabilized accelerometers.
   C. It is unusual to find an INS installed in a light general aviation training aircraft.

5. What are the three main GPS segments?

6. How many NAVSTAR satellites must be in view for a GPS receiver to calculate a three-dimensional position?

7. What is the maximum amount of position error which most civil users can expect from a GPS receiver 95% of the time?

8. True/False. A LORAN-C calculated position is typically more accurate than a VORTAC fix.

PART V
INTEGRATING
PILOT KNOWLEDGE
AND SKILLS

It is possible to fly without motors, but not without knowledge and skill. This I conceive to be fortunate, for man, by reason of his greater intellect, can more reasonably hope to equal birds in knowledge, than to equal nature in the perfection of her machinery.

— Wilbur Wright

PART V

Without knowledge and skill, the art of flying can never truly be mastered. You must apply the knowledge you have gained while exploring this manual with the skills you have acquired in the cockpit. Part V is designed to help you complete the journey toward your private pilot certificate by integrating the various elements you have already learned. Chapter 10, *Applying Human Factors Principles*, helps you to improve your judgment as pilot in command by increasing your knowledge of human factors concepts, such as aviation physiology and aeronautical decision making. *Flying Cross-Country* presents a flight scenario which provides a unique opportunity to examine pilot decision making.

CHAPTER 10

APPLYING HUMAN FACTORS PRINCIPLES

Part V, Chapter 10 — Applying Human Factors Principles

SECTION A
AVIATION PHYSIOLOGY

The bird is designed for flight. Its skeleton and feathers are strong but extremely light. The bird's system of balance correctly responds to the acceleration forces experienced in flight. An extraordinarily efficient respiratory system includes lightweight air sacs which allow fresh air to continually pass through the bird's lungs. Surface sensors provide the bird with a knowledge of the state of the air flow over its wings so the bird instinctively knows its airspeed, angle of attack and attitude in yaw, pitch, and roll. [Figure 10-1] Humans are terrestrial creatures, designed for earthbound endeavors. To fly, we have had to build efficient aerodynamic structures and invent instruments to tell us visually what the bird knows instinctively. Although we function best when we are on the ground, we have a remarkable ability to adapt to our surroundings. In flight, our bodies must adjust for significant changes in barometric pressure, considerable variation in temperature, and movement at high speed in three dimensions. Aviation would not be possible if we could not compensate for the physiological demands placed upon us by flight. However, there are limitations to the adjustments that the human body can make.

Figure 10-1. The wing span of the bald eagle typically reaches seven feet. Although eagles have about 7,000 feathers, together they weigh only approximately one pound and the entire eagle skeleton weighs little more than a half-pound. Eagles can see six to eight times better than humans and can spot a rabbit from as far as a mile away.

VISION IN FLIGHT

The eye works in much the same way as a camera. Both the eye and a camera have an aperture, lens, method of focusing, and a surface for registering images. [Figure 10-2] Vision is the result of light striking the retina after it enters through the cornea and passes

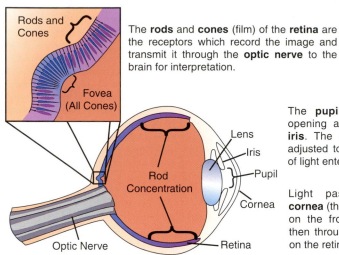

The **rods** and **cones** (film) of the **retina** are the receptors which record the image and transmit it through the **optic nerve** to the brain for interpretation.

Figure 10-2. A camera is able to focus on near and far objects by changing the distance between the lens and the film. You can see objects clearly at various distances because the shape of your eye's lens is changed automatically by small muscles.

The **pupil** (aperture) is the opening at the center of the **iris**. The size of the pupil is adjusted to control the amount of light entering the eye.

Light passes through the **cornea** (the transparent window on the front of the eye) and then through the **lens** to focus on the retina.

through the lens. The **retina** contains many photosensitive cells called cones and rods, which are connected to the optic nerve. The pattern of light that strikes the cones and rods is transmitted as electrical impulses by the optic nerve to the brain where these signals are interpreted as an image. The area where the optic nerve is formed on the retina contains no cones or rods, creating a blind spot in vision. Normally, each eye compensates for the other's blind spot. [Figure 10-3]

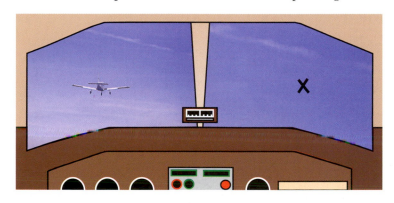

Figure 10-3. This illustration provides a dramatic example of the eye's blind spot. Cover your right eye and hold this page at arm's length. Focus your left eye on the X in the right side of the windshield and notice what happens to the aircraft as you slowly bring the page closer to your eye.

Cones are concentrated in the center of the retina in a slight depression known as the fovea. The cones gradually diminish and are replaced by rods as the distance from the fovea increases. Cones function well in bright light and are sensitive to colors. Compared to the rod cells, which group together to serve a single neuron, each cone cell has a direct neuron connection which allows you to detect fine detail. The cones, however, do not function well in darkness, which explains why you cannot see color and detail as vividly at night as you can during the day.

NIGHT VISION

The **rods**, which are concentrated outside the foveal area, react to low light but not to colors. It is estimated that, after adapting to darkness, the rods are 10,000 times more sensitive to light than the cones, which make them the primary receptors for night vision. Since the rods are not located directly behind the pupil, they also are responsible for much of your peripheral vision.

The concentration of cones in the fovea can make a night blind spot at the center of your vision. To see an object clearly at night, you must expose the rods to the image. This is accomplished by looking 5° to 10° off center of the object. For example, if you look directly at a dim light in a darkened room, the image can disappear. If you look slightly

off center of the light, it becomes clearer and brighter. When scanning for traffic at night, use off-center viewing to focus objects on the rods rather than on the foveal blind spot. [Figure 10-4]

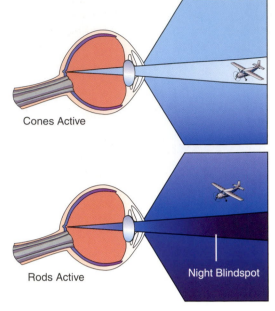

Cones Active

Rods Active

Night Blindspot

Figure 10-4. When you look directly at an object, the image is focused mainly on the fovea. At night, your ability to see an object in the center of the visual field is reduced as the cones lose much of their visual acuity and the rods become more receptive. You also lose much of your depth perception and your judgment of size.

 During night flight, the most effective method of looking for other aircraft is to scan small sectors slowly and to use off-center viewing.

In addition, if you stare at an object at night for more than 2 to 3 seconds, the retina becomes accustomed to the light intensity and the image begins to fade. Continuous scanning and changing the position of your eyes can keep the object clearly visible by exposing new areas of the retina to the image.

DARK ADAPTATION

Rods are able to detect images in the dark because they create a chemical called rhodopsin, also referred to as **visual purple**. As visual purple is formed, the rods can take

Hatbands and the Visual Field

When you look at an object to your right, both of your eyes are viewing what is called the right visual field, which is processed by your brain's left hemisphere. The information viewed in the left visual field is processed in the right hemisphere. In addition, in approximately 90% of humans, the centers for speech are located in the left hemisphere of the brain. Studies performed by Roger Sperry and coworkers at the California Institute of Technology, provide unique insight into how our brain processes visual information in each hemisphere.

In a series of experiments, observations were made of patients in whom the corpus callosum, the main bundle of neural fibers connecting the left and right hemispheres of the brain, had been severed for the treatment of epilepsy. In a typical experiment, the patient is presented with the word *hatband* flashed on a screen. *Hat* is placed in the left visual field and *band* in the right visual field. The patient reports that he saw the word *band*, but when asked what kind of band he saw, the patient cannot answer correctly. In terms of his ability to communicate verbally, he does not know that the right hemisphere has received a visual impression of the word *hat*. When the patient is asked to write what he saw (with his left hand placed inside a box), he writes the word *hat*. He knows that he has written something, but without seeing the paper, there is no way for the information to reach the left hemisphere which controls verbal ability.

HAT

HAT / BAND

Speech   Left Hand

"BAND"

BAND   HAT

up to 30 minutes to fully adapt to the dark. If you have ever walked from bright sunlight into a dark movie theater, you have experienced this adaptation period. When exposed to bright light, visual purple undergoes a chemical change causing the rods to lose their high sensitivity to light.

To keep your eyes adapted to the dark, avoid any bright light sources such as headlights, landing lights, strobe lights, or flashlights for 30 minutes before a night flight. The rods are least affected by the wavelength of red light so red cockpit lighting has been used in the past to help preserve night vision. However, since red light refracts less than other colors of white light, objects are no longer in focus using only red light, and it is more difficult to transition from near to distant vision. In addition, red light masks any red colored instrument markings or map symbols. It is recommended that you use red light only when trying to enhance the adaptation process. Low-level white light illuminating the instruments and within the cockpit should be used in flight. [Figure 10-5]

Figure 10-5. It is important that the intensity of the light can be controlled so as your eyes adapt to the low light, the brightness can be reduced. Checking the cockpit lighting is an important part of the preflight inspection.

Your diet and general physical health have an impact on how well you can see in the dark. For example, deficiencies in vitamin A affect the eye's ability to produce visual purple. Other factors, such as carbon monoxide poisoning, smoking, alcohol, certain drugs, and a lack of oxygen can greatly decrease your night vision.

To adapt the eyes for night flying, avoid bright white lights at least 30 minutes before your flight.

AIRCRAFT LIGHTING

According to FAR Part 91, all aircraft operated during the night hours must meet specific lighting and equipment requirements. The regulations also provide a definition of nighttime, describe night currency requirements, and specify minimum fuel reserves for night flights.

The approved aircraft position lights for night operations are a green light on the right wingtip, a red light on the left wingtip, and a white light on the tail. In addition, flashing aviation red or white anticollision lights are required for night flight. These flashing lights can be in a number of locations on the aircraft, but are most commonly found on the wingtips or tail. [Figure 10-6]

Interpreting the position lights of other aircraft can help you determine their direction of movement. For example, if you see a red position light to the right of a green light, the aircraft is flying toward you. A steady red and flashing red light indicate the aircraft is crossing to your left and a steady white light combined with a flashing red light identify an aircraft flying away from you. See figure 10-6.

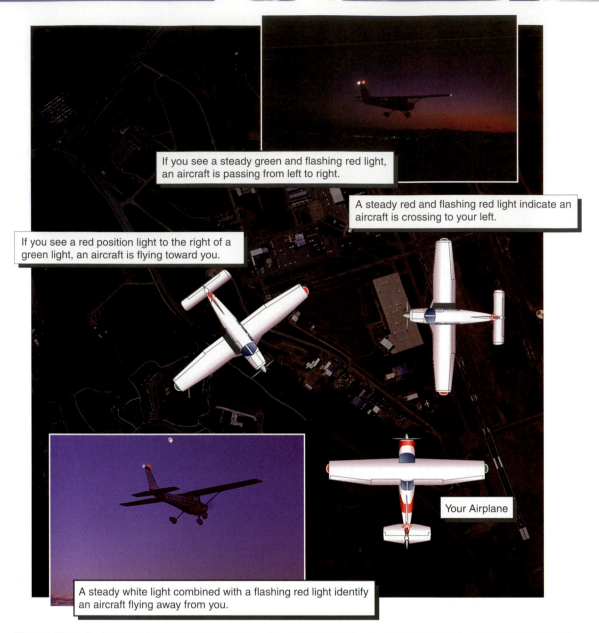

If you see a steady green and flashing red light, an aircraft is passing from left to right.

A steady red and flashing red light indicate an aircraft is crossing to your left.

If you see a red position light to the right of a green light, an aircraft is flying toward you.

A steady white light combined with a flashing red light identify an aircraft flying away from you.

Your Airplane

Figure 10-6. By interpreting the position lights of another aircraft, you can determine whether that aircraft is flying away from you or is on a collision course.

VISUAL ILLUSIONS

Every pilot can experience visual illusions, although they normally go undetected unless an accident or incident occurs. An illusion typically occurs when you do not have the necessary cues for proper interpretation. Understanding the various types of visual illusions and how they occur, as well as preventive measures when appropriate, will help you increase flight safety.

AUTOKINESIS

If you stare at a single point of light against a dark background, such as a ground light or bright star, for more than a few seconds, the light may appear to move. This false perception of movement is called **autokinesis**. To prevent this illusion, you should focus your eyes on objects at varying distances and not fixate on one target, as well as maintain a normal visual scan.

FALSE HORIZONS

Another illusion, that of a **false horizon**, occurs when the natural horizon is obscured or not readily apparent. For example, when flying over a sloping cloud deck, you may try to align the aircraft with the cloud formation. At night, ground lights, stars, and reflections on the windscreen can lead to confusion regarding the position of the horizon. Attempting to align your aircraft with a false horizon can lead to a dangerous flight attitude. [Figure 10-7]

Figure 10-7. At night, the horizon may be hard to determine due to dark terrain and misleading light configurations on the ground. A cloud deck also can create a false horizon.

LANDING ILLUSIONS

Landing illusions can be caused by a wide variety of factors including runway width, sloping runways and terrain, and weather conditions which reduce visibility. [Figure 10-8] For example, it is not uncommon to find public airports that have runways with a grade, or slope, of 3% or more. On a 6,000-foot runway, a 3% grade equals a 180-foot elevation difference between the approach and departure ends. Many private airports have even steeper runway grades. [Figure 10-9] At night, the potential for experiencing a visual illusion during landing increases due to the fact that you have fewer visual cues to rely on. Your landing approaches at night should be made the same as during the daytime to reduce the effects of landing illusions.

Elements that create any type of visual obstruction, such as rain or haze, can cause you to fly a low approach.

Over water, at night, or over featureless terrain, such as snow-covered ground, there is a natural tendency to fly a lower-than-normal approach.

Penetration of fog can create the illusion of pitching up which can cause you to steepen your approach.

Figure 10-8. A variety of runway, atmospheric, and terrain conditions can produce visual illusions.

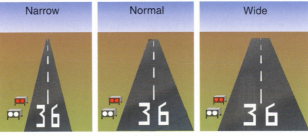

Due to the illusion of greater height, you may fly a lower approach than normal to a narrow runway. A wide runway can have the opposite effect and produce higher-than-normal approaches.

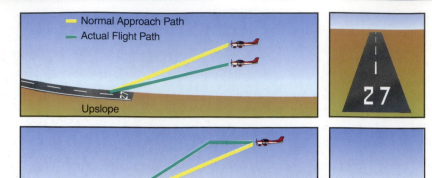

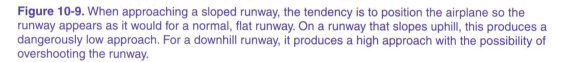

These runway views illustrate how normal 3° approaches might look for upslope and downslope runways.

Figure 10-9. When approaching a sloped runway, the tendency is to position the airplane so the runway appears as it would for a normal, flat runway. On a runway that slopes uphill, this produces a dangerously low approach. For a downhill runway, it produces a high approach with the possibility of overshooting the runway.

If you are aware of the contributing factors that lead to visual illusions you will be able to identify them long before they become problems. For advance warning of conditions that could cause visual illusions, obtain a thorough weather briefing, examine the applicable aeronautical chart, and consult the

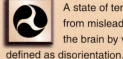

Your landing approaches at night should be made the same as during the daytime to reduce the effects of landing illusions.

Airport/Facility Directory listing for your destination airport. When available, take advantage of a visual glideslope indicator to verify your landing approach angle. In addition, look for other clues, such as steep or featureless surrounding terrain. If you suspect an illusion, fly a normal traffic pattern and avoid long, straight-in approaches.

FLICKER VERTIGO

A light flickering at a frequency of 4 to 20 flashes per second can produce **flicker vertigo** and although rare, it can lead to convulsions, nausea, or unconsciousness. Flicker vertigo can occur when you are looking through a slow-moving propeller toward the sun or when the sun is behind you, reflecting off the propeller. The best way to prevent flicker vertigo is to avoid looking at a light source through a propeller for any length of time. Making frequent but minor changes in propeller r.p.m. also can decrease your susceptibility to flicker vertigo.

DISORIENTATION

Sensory organs in various parts of your body provide your brain with information about your position in relation to your environment. During flight, you may encounter a variety of conditions which cause the brain to receive conflicting messages from your senses. **Disorientation** is an incorrect mental image of your position, attitude, or movement in relation to what is actually happening to your aircraft. This state of temporary confusion can be caused by misleading information being sent to the brain by your body's various sensory organs. Awareness of your body's position is a result of input from three primary sources: vision, the vestibular system located in your inner ear, and your kinesthetic sense.

Kinesthetic sense is the term used to describe an awareness of position obtained from the nerves in your skin, joints, and muscles. Using this sense is sometimes called "flying by the seat of your pants," and this is literally what you are doing. Kinesthetic sense is unreliable, however, because the brain cannot tell the difference between input caused by gravity and that of maneuvering G-loads.

A state of temporary confusion resulting from misleading information being sent to the brain by various sensory organs is defined as disorientation.

In good weather and daylight, you obtain your orientation primarily through your vision. At night or in marginal weather conditions there are fewer visual cues, and you rely upon the vestibular and kinesthetic senses to supplement your vision. Since these senses can provide false cues about your orientation, the probability of disorientation occurring at night and especially in IFR weather is quite high. Under these conditions, properly scanning and interpreting your flight instruments is extremely important. [Figure 10-10]

Figure 10-10. Unless you are an instrument-rated pilot, you are prohibited from acting as pilot in command in IFR conditions. However, you will receive training in flight by reference to instruments to help you orient yourself at night and in low visibility, as well as in the event that you inadvertently enter IFR conditions.

Fatigue, anxiety, heavy pilot workloads, and the intake of alcohol or other drugs increase your susceptibility to disorientation and visual illusions. These factors increase response times, inhibit decision-making abilities, and cause a breakdown in scanning techniques and night vision. Reducing your workload with the use of a simple autopilot and improving your cockpit management skills help prevent pilot overload and the possibility of disorientation.

 Relying on the instruments and believing their indications, regardless of how your body feels, are the keys to maintaining orientation during flight at night or in marginal weather conditions.

Lightheadedness, dizziness, the feeling of instability, and the sensation of spinning are often described by pilots and aircraft passengers as vertigo. Although the symptoms may be similar, vertigo usually is caused by a physical disorder, such as a tumor or an infection of the ear or central nervous system. Experiencing these sensations during flight normally is a result of spatial or vestibular disorientation. Although the term spatial disorientation often is used to describe vestibular disorientation, the two terms have different meanings.

SPATIAL DISORIENTATION

When other sensory input is contradictory or confusing, the brain relies primarily upon sight to determine orientation. Your peripheral vision is very strong in relaying body position to your brain. In darkness or limited visibility, when few outside visual references are available, you need to rely heavily on your **visual sense** to interpret the flight instruments for accurate information. **Spatial disorientation** can occur when there is a conflict between the information relayed by your central vision scanning the instruments, and your peripheral vision which has virtually no references with which to establish orientation (as in IFR conditions). The movement of rain or snow seen out the window by your peripheral vision also may lead to a misinterpretation of your own movement and position in space. This is similar to the illusion of motion that you experience when a train next to yours begins pulling away from the terminal. Your peripheral vision can misinterpret this visual cue and lead you to believe that your stationary train car is in motion.

The power of peripheral vision for orientation can be easily demonstrated. Stand on one foot, look straight ahead and focus on a small distant object. Close one eye and wait until your balance stabilizes. Hold your fist a few inches in front of your open eye to block your central vision. You still should feel relatively stable. Now take your fist away and hold a tube, such as the inner tube of a paper towel roll, against your face around your open eye, obstructing your peripheral vision. Since the brain no longer has peripheral vision to orient itself in space, you should feel a balance instability.

VESTIBULAR DISORIENTATION

Located in your inner ear, the **vestibular system** consists of the vestibule and the semicircular canals. The utricle and saccule organs within the vestibule are responsible for the perception of gravity and linear acceleration, which is movement forward and back, side to side, and up and down. A gelatinous substance within the utricle and saccule is coated with a layer of tiny grains of limestone called otoliths. Movement of the vestibule causes the otoliths to shift, which in turn causes hair cells to send out nerve impulses to the brain for interpretation.

The three **semicircular canals**, which are oriented in three planes perpendicular to each other, sense angular acceleration such as roll, pitch, and yaw. Each canal is filled with fluid and contains a gelatinous structure called the cupula. When you maneuver the airplane or move your head, the canal also moves but the fluid lags behind causing the cupula to lean away from the turn. Movement of the cupula results in deflection of hair cells which project into it. This in turn stimulates the vestibular nerve. This nerve transmits impulses to the brain which interprets the signals as motion around an axis. [Figure 10-11]

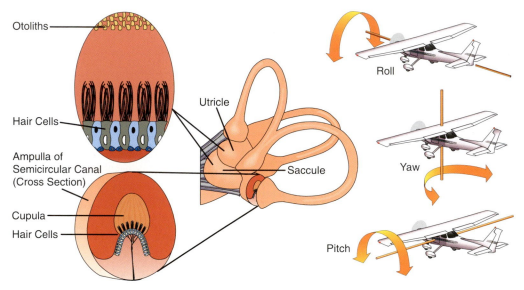

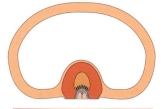

Figure 10-11. The semicircular canals, which lie in three planes, sense the motions of roll, pitch, and yaw. The vestibular nerve transmits impulses from the utricle, saccule, and semicircular canals to the brain to interpret motion.

You can experience a variety of illusions as your brain interprets vestibular signals as specific motions. When subjected to the different forces of flight, the vestibular system can send misleading signals to the brain resulting in **vestibular disorientation**. [Figure 10-12]

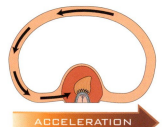
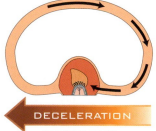

NO ACCELERATION

NO TURN
If no acceleration is taking place, the cupula is stationary and the hair cells are not deflected. No sensation of a turn is felt.

ACCELERATION

INITIATING A CLOCKWISE TURN
A clockwise turn deflects the hair cells in the direction opposite of the acceleration. You experience an accurate sensation of the turn direction.

NO ACCELERATION

PROLONGED CONSTANT-RATE TURN
During a prolonged constant rate turn, you may not sense any motion since the fluid in the canals eventually reaches equilibrium and the hair cells are no longer deflected.

DECELERATION

DECREASE IN RATE OF TURN
If you decrease the rate of turn, the deflection of the hair cells may produce a false sensation of a turn in the opposite direction. In this example, you experience the sensation of a counterclockwise turn.

Figure 10-12. During a prolonged, constant-rate turn, you may not sense any motion since the fluid in the semicircular canals eventually reaches equilibrium and the hair cells are no longer deflected.

ILLUSIONS LEADING TO DISORIENTATION

The majority of the illusions which lead to vestibular disorientation occur when visibility is restricted, either by darkness or by weather. It takes many hours of training and experience before a pilot is competent to fly an aircraft solely by reference to instruments. Each year, many fatalities result from noninstrument-rated pilots continuing flight into deteriorating weather conditions. [Figure 10-13]

 Actual Flight Path   ⬜ Perceived Flight Path

CORIOLIS ILLUSION
During a constant-rate turn, if you tilt your head down to change a fuel tank or pick up a pencil, the rapid head movement puts the fluid in motion in more than one semicircular canal. This creates an overwhelming sensation of rotating, turning, or accelerating along an entirely different plane. An attempt to stop the sensation by maneuvering the airplane may put it into a dangerous attitude. To avoid this illusion, do not move your head too fast in limited visibility or darkness.

GRAVEYARD SPIRAL
A loss of altitude in a prolonged constant rate turn may be interpreted as a wings-level descent, which can lead you to increase elevator back pressure and tighten the turn, increasing your altitude loss. A recovery to wings-level flight may produce the illusion that the airplane is in a turn in the opposite direction, resulting in a reentry of the spiral. This feeling must be fought until the fluid in your semicircular canals quits moving again.

LEANS
The leans occur when an abrupt recovery or a rapid correction is made to a bank. If you make such a recovery, your semicircular canals sense a roll in the opposite direction. This may cause you to reenter the original attitude. When you return the aircraft to a wings-level condition, you will tend to lean in the direction of the incorrect bank until the semicircular canal fluids return to normal. Maintaining a level attitude for a minute or two generally will stop the leans.

SOMATOGRAVIC ILLUSION
A rapid acceleration can produce the illusion that you are in a nose-high attitude, even though you are still in straight-and-level flight. This may prompt you to lower the nose and enter a dive. A deceleration, such as rapidly retarding the throttle, produces the opposite effect. You may think you are in a dive and raise the nose. If you raise the nose too far, a stall may be produced.

INVERSION ILLUSION
An abrupt change from a climb to straight-and-level flight can create the feeling that you are tumbling backward. The effect may cause you to lower the nose abruptly, which may intensify the illusion.

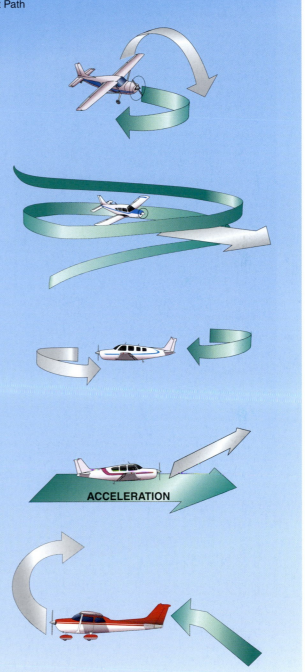

ACCELERATION

Figure 10-13. The coriolis illusion is considered to be one of the most deadly.

You are more susceptible to disorientation if you use body signals to interpret flight attitudes.

Disorienting Experiments

A thread attached to the inside of a glass of water can demonstrate how the semicircular canals sense motion. If you rotate the glass counter-clockwise, the water's inertia prevents the fluid from moving as rapidly as the glass, and the thread leans away from the rotation of the glass. If you continue to turn the glass at a constant rate, the water eventually catches up with the glass, and the thread hangs straight down. When this occurs in a semicircular canal and the hairs no longer lean to one side, the sensory system believes the body is again at rest. If the rotating glass is briefly decelerated, the water's inertia keeps it moving at the original speed and again there is a discrepancy between the speed of the glass and the speed of the fluid. The thread will now lean to the left in the direction of rotation. [Figure A]

A

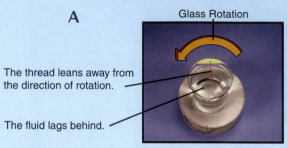

Glass Rotation

The thread leans away from the direction of rotation.

The fluid lags behind.

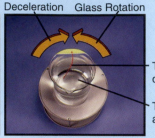

Deceleration   Glass Rotation

The thread leans in the direction of rotation.

The fluid continues to rotate as the glass decelerates.

In another experiment, you can experience the effects of vestibular disorientation. You will need a blindfold, a swivel chair, and some friends. With the blindfold on, tilt your head to one side. Then, have someone spin the chair at a constant rate for 30 to 60 seconds. The chair should then be brought to a gradual stop. When the chair has stopped, you will be told to raise your head. This action should produce the illusion of spinning or rotating. The simulation of disorientation can be so realistic that you should have someone close by to catch you if you fall out of the chair. [Figure B]

MOTION SICKNESS

Since vestibular disorientation can produce severe and intense feelings of instability, it often is the cause of motion sickness. Even experienced pilots can experience motion sickness under flight conditions which disrupt the vestibular system. However, passengers are more susceptible to motion sickness, since they often focus their attention inside the aircraft. Airsickness comes in many forms. Common symptoms of airsickness are general discomfort, paleness, nausea, dizziness, sweating, and vomiting.

Although specific remedies for airsickness can vary among people, there are some actions that generally seem to help. You can suggest that your passengers put their heads back and attempt to relax. With the head reclined, passengers are better able to tolerate the up-and-down motion common to flying in turbulent air. Since anxiety and stress can contribute to motion sickness, keep uneasy or nervous passengers informed on how the flight is progressing, and explain unusual noises such as flap or landing gear retraction and power changes. Opening the fresh-air vents and allowing cool, fresh air into the cabin also can improve the comfort level of your passengers.

Another suggestion which can reduce the possibility of airsickness is that passengers focus on objects outside the airplane. Have passengers follow along and pick out various landmarks on an aeronautical chart or road map. Avoid warm, turbulent air and suggest that your passengers use earplugs. Medications like Dramamine also can prevent airsickness in passengers. In addition, keep in mind that most passengers are not used to steep banks or quick maneuvers.

RESPIRATION

Respiration is the exchange of gases between an organism and its environment. The function of respiration in the human body is to get oxygen into the body and deliver it to the cells and to take carbon dioxide from the cells and remove it from the body. This process is composed of two primary activities – external respiration and internal respiration. [Figure 10-14]

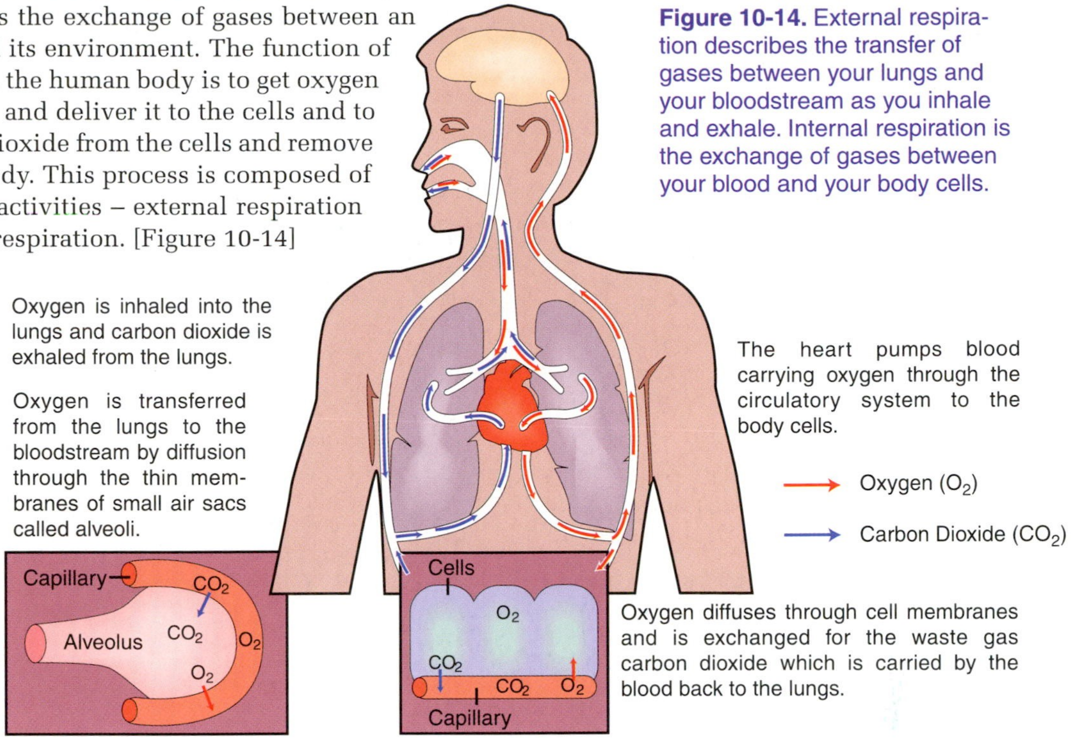

Figure 10-14. External respiration describes the transfer of gases between your lungs and your bloodstream as you inhale and exhale. Internal respiration is the exchange of gases between your blood and your body cells.

Oxygen is inhaled into the lungs and carbon dioxide is exhaled from the lungs.

Oxygen is transferred from the lungs to the bloodstream by diffusion through the thin membranes of small air sacs called alveoli.

The heart pumps blood carrying oxygen through the circulatory system to the body cells.

→ Oxygen (O_2)

→ Carbon Dioxide (CO_2)

Capillary — CO_2

Alveolus CO_2 O_2

O_2

Cells

O_2

CO_2

CO_2 O_2

Capillary

Oxygen diffuses through cell membranes and is exchanged for the waste gas carbon dioxide which is carried by the blood back to the lungs.

Approximately 95% of the oxygen transported in your body is attached to a substance called hemoglobin contained in your red blood cells, while the remaining oxygen is dissolved in the blood plasma. Oxygen and carbon dioxide are transferred through membranes from one part of the body to another by diffusion. This process is described by a physical law which states that a gas of high pressure exerts a force toward a region of lower pressure and, if there is a permeable membrane separating these regions of unequal pressure, the gas of higher pressure will diffuse through the membrane into the region of low pressure.

Each breath you inhale is composed of a mixture of gases. Life-sustaining oxygen makes up only about 21% of each breath, while 78% is nitrogen and 1% is other gases, such as carbon dioxide and argon. Each gas in the atmosphere has its own pressure at any given temperature within a given volume. A principle known as Dalton's Law states that the total pressure of a gas mixture is the sum of the pressure of each gas in the mixture. The pressure exerted by each gas in the mixture is called the partial pressure of that gas.

HYPOXIA

Hypoxia occurs when the tissues in the body do not receive enough oxygen. The symptoms of hypoxia vary with the individual. [Figure 10-15] Hypoxia can be caused by several factors including an insufficient supply of oxygen, inadequate transportation of oxygen, or the inability of the body tissues to use oxygen. The forms of hypoxia are divided into four major groups based on their causes; hypoxic hypoxia, hypemic hypoxia, stagnant hypoxia, and histotoxic hypoxia.

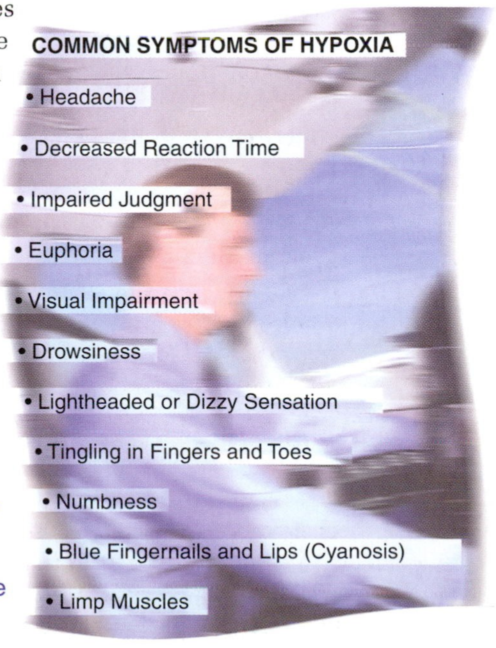

COMMON SYMPTOMS OF HYPOXIA

• Headache

• Decreased Reaction Time

• Impaired Judgment

• Euphoria

• Visual Impairment

• Drowsiness

• Lightheaded or Dizzy Sensation

• Tingling in Fingers and Toes

• Numbness

• Blue Fingernails and Lips (Cyanosis)

• Limp Muscles

Figure 10-15. Hypoxia can cause tunnel vision, slow thinking, and even diminish your sense of pain.

Hypoxia is a state of oxygen deficiency in the body.

Up to 25,000 Feet Without Ever Leaving the Ground

A flight in an altitude chamber can give you the chance to experience unpressurized flight, gas expansion, rapid decompression, hypoxia, and the use of oxygen equipment in a controlled and safe environment. An altitude chamber employs a vacuum pump to remove gas/pressure from the chamber to simulate the corresponding pressure of a particular altitude. Figure A shows the interior of the Carter P. Luna Physiology Training Center at Peterson Air Force Base in Colorado Springs, Colorado. [Figure A]

Official U.S. Air Force Photo

The first altitude chamber flight for training purposes took place in 1874 when Dr. Paul Bert of France, the first practicing flight surgeon, used a diving bell and a steam-driven vacuum pump to demonstrate the hazards of high altitude balloon flights. The FAA began altitude chamber flights for civilian pilots and crewmembers in 1962 and provides this opportunity through aviation physiology training conducted at the FAA Civil Aeromedical Institute (CAMI) and at many military facilities across the United States. A typical altitude chamber profile used by CAMI is shown in figure B.

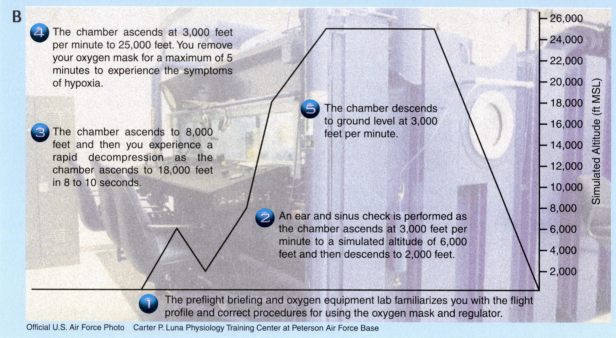

B

4. The chamber ascends at 3,000 feet per minute to 25,000 feet. You remove your oxygen mask for a maximum of 5 minutes to experience the symptoms of hypoxia.

5. The chamber descends to ground level at 3,000 feet per minute.

3. The chamber ascends to 8,000 feet and then you experience a rapid decompression as the chamber ascends to 18,000 feet in 8 to 10 seconds.

2. An ear and sinus check is performed as the chamber ascends at 3,000 feet per minute to a simulated altitude of 6,000 feet and then descends to 2,000 feet.

1. The preflight briefing and oxygen equipment lab familiarizes you with the flight profile and correct procedures for using the oxygen mask and regulator.

Official U.S. Air Force Photo   Carter P. Luna Physiology Training Center at Peterson Air Force Base

HYPOXIC HYPOXIA

Although the percentage of oxygen in the atmosphere is constant, its partial pressure decreases proportionately as atmospheric pressure decreases. As you ascend during flight, the percentage of each gas in the atmosphere remains the same but there are fewer molecules available at the pressure required for them to pass between the membranes in your respiratory system. This decrease of oxygen molecules at sufficient pressure can lead to **hypoxic hypoxia**.

Hypoxic hypoxia is considered to be the most lethal factor of all physiological causes of accidents. It can occur very suddenly at high altitudes during rapid decompression, or it can occur slowly at lower altitudes when you are exposed to insufficient oxygen over an extended period of time. The **time of useful consciousness** is the maximum time you have to make a rational, life-saving decision and carry it out following a lack of oxygen at a given altitude. You may also hear this time referred to as effective performance time. If you go beyond this time, you may not be able to place an oxygen mask over your face, even if you try. [Figure 10-16]

Altitude	Time of Useful Consciousness
45,000 feet MSL	9 to 15 seconds
40,000 feet MSL	15 to 20 seconds
35,000 feet MSL	30 to 60 seconds
30,000 feet MSL	1 to 2 minutes
28,000 feet MSL	2 1/2 to 3 minutes
25,000 feet MSL	3 to 5 minutes
22,000 feet MSL	5 to 10 minutes
20,000 feet MSL	30 minutes or more

Figure 10-16. Recovery from hypoxia usually occurs rapidly after a person has been given oxygen. However, if you have suffered severe hypoxia, your mental and physical performance may be reduced for several hours.

HYPEMIC HYPOXIA

When your blood is not able to carry a sufficient amount of oxygen to the cells in your body, a condition called **hypemic hypoxia** occurs. This type of hypoxia is a result of a deficiency in the blood, rather than a lack of inhaled oxygen and can be caused by a variety of factors. For example, if you have anemia, or a reduced number of healthy functioning blood cells for any reason (disease, blood loss, deformed blood cells, etc.), your blood has a decreased capacity for carrying oxygen. In addition, any factor which interferes or displaces oxygen that is attached to the blood's hemoglobin can cause hypemic hypoxia.

CARBON MONOXIDE

The most common form of hypemic hypoxia is **carbon monoxide poisoning**. Since it attaches itself to the hemoglobin about 200 times more easily than does oxygen, carbon monoxide (CO) prevents the hemoglobin from carrying oxygen to the cells. It can take up to 48 hours for the body to dispose of carbon monoxide. If the poisoning is severe enough, it can result in death.

Large accumulations of CO in the body can result in symptoms such as a loss of muscular power.

Carbon monoxide poisoning can result from a faulty aircraft heater. If you begin to experience any of the symptoms of hypoxia, such as a lightheaded sensation or loss of muscular power, and suspect carbon monoxide poisoning, you should turn off the heater immediately, open the fresh air vents or windows, and use supplemental oxygen if it is available.

Approximately 2.5% of the volume of cigarette smoke is carbon monoxide. A blood saturation of 4% carbon monoxide may result from inhaling the smoke of 3 cigarettes at sea level. This causes a reduction in visual acuity and dark adaptation similar to the mild hypoxia encountered at 8,000 feet MSL. Smoking at 10,000 feet MSL produces effects equivalent to those experienced at 14,000 feet MSL without smoking. Heavy smokers can have carbon monoxide blood saturation as high as 8%.

BLOOD DONATION

Hypemic hypoxia also can be caused by the loss of blood that occurs during a blood donation. Your blood can take several weeks to return to normal following a donation. Although the effects of the blood loss are slight at ground level, there are risks when flying during this time.

STAGNANT HYPOXIA

Stagnant hypoxia is an oxygen deficiency in the body due to the poor circulation of the blood. Several different situations can lead to stagnant hypoxia such as shock, the heart failing to pump blood effectively, or a constricted artery. During flight, stagnant hypoxia can be the result of pulling excessive positive Gs. Cold temperatures also can reduce circulation and decrease the blood supplied to extremities.

HISTOTOXIC HYPOXIA

The inability of the cells to effectively use oxygen is defined as **histotoxic hypoxia**. The oxygen may be inhaled and reach the cell in adequate amounts, but the cell is unable to accept the oxygen once it is there. This impairment of cellular respiration can be caused by alcohol and other drugs such as narcotics and poisons. Research has shown that drinking one ounce of alcohol can equate to about an additional 2,000 feet of physiological altitude. [Figure 10-17]

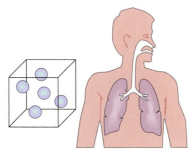

Hypoxic Hypoxia – Inadequate Supply of Oxygen

Hypemic Hypoxia – Inability of the Blood to Carry Oxygen

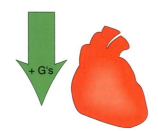

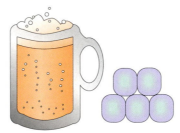

Stagnant Hypoxia – Inadequate Circulation of Oxygen

Histotoxic Hypoxia – Inability of the Cells to Effectively Use Oxygen

Figure 10-17. A combination of different types of hypoxia affecting your body may cause you to experience symptoms at much lower altitudes than expected.

PREVENTION OF HYPOXIA

You should not assume that if you learn the early symptoms of hypoxia that you will be able to take corrective action whenever they occur. Since judgment and rationality can be impaired when you are suffering from hypoxia, prevention is the best approach. Your susceptibility to hypoxia is related to many factors, many of which you can control. You can increase your tolerance to hypoxia by maintaining good physical condition, eating a nutritious diet, and by avoiding alcohol and smoking. If you live at a high altitude and have become acclimated, you normally have an increased tolerance to the conditions that would lead to hypoxia compared to a person living at a lower altitude.

Your body requires more oxygen during increased physical activity. For example, you can expect a higher risk of becoming hypoxic during a flight when you are flying the aircraft manually in turbulent conditions compared to a smooth flight on autopilot. Temperature extremes in the cockpit can make your body more susceptible to hypoxia. As your body copes with high heat and humidity or shivers when cold, you are using energy which is comparable to increased activity. The quicker you ascend, the less effective your individual tolerance and you may be less aware of approaching hypoxia. In addition, you can prevent hypoxic hypoxia by flying at low altitudes where hypoxia is not a factor or by using supplemental oxygen.

SUPPLEMENTAL OXYGEN

If you are planning a flight with a cruise altitude over 12,500 feet MSL, you should consult FAR Part 91 for the requirements regarding **supplemental oxygen**. Generally there are three types of oxygen regulators and masks; continuous flow, demand, and pressure demand. The continuous flow regulators provide a flow of 100% oxygen at a rate controlled by turning a valve. A demand regulator provides oxygen only when the user inhales. Pressure demand systems provide a positive pressure application of oxygen to the mask piece and are of great benefit at extreme altitudes such as 40,000 feet MSL or higher. Aircraft oxygen systems should always be filled with aviator's breathing oxygen. Medical oxygen contains too much moisture, which can collect in the valves and lines of the system and freeze, stopping the flow of oxygen. [Figure 10-18]

 Between cabin pressure altitudes of 12,500 feet MSL and 14,000 feet MSL, the flight crew is required to use supplemental oxygen after 30 minutes. Above 14,000 feet MSL, the crew is required to use supplemental oxygen for the entire duration of the flight and above 15,000 feet MSL, each aircraft occupant must be provided with it. See figure 10-18.

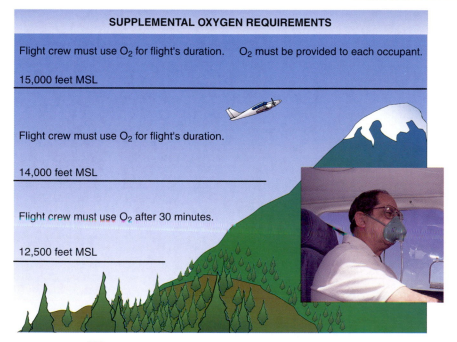

SUPPLEMENTAL OXYGEN REQUIREMENTS

Flight crew must use O$_2$ for flight's duration.   O$_2$ must be provided to each occupant.

15,000 feet MSL

Flight crew must use O$_2$ for flight's duration.

14,000 feet MSL

Flight crew must use O$_2$ after 30 minutes.

12,500 feet MSL

Figure 10-18. As a general rule, consider using supplemental oxygen when you fly above 10,000 feet MSL during the day or above 5,000 feet MSL at night.

PRESSURIZATION

Aircraft cabin **pressurization** is the maintenance of a cabin altitude lower than the actual flight altitude by a system which compresses air. Although pressurized aircraft reduce the physiological problems experienced at higher altitudes, the possibility of sudden loss of pressurization exists. **Decompression** occurs when the aircraft's pressurization system is unable to maintain its designed pressure schedule due to a malfunction in the pressurization system or structural damage to the aircraft. The primary danger of decompression is hypoxia. For example, if your aircraft decompresses above 30,000 feet MSL, you will become unconscious in a very short time unless you use supplemental oxygen equipment.

HYPERVENTILATION

The amount of carbon dioxide in your blood stimulates your respiratory system to stabilize your breathing rate at about 12 to 16 breaths per minute in a physically relaxed state. If you become physically active, your body cells use more oxygen and more carbon dioxide is produced. The respiratory system responds to this by increasing the depth and rate of your breathing to remove the excessive carbon dioxide.

Hyperventilation occurs when you are experiencing emotional stress, fright, or pain, and your breathing rate and depth increase although the carbon dioxide is already at a reduced level in the blood. The result is an excessive loss of carbon dioxide from your body which can lead to unconsciousness due to the respiratory system's overriding mechanism to regain control of breathing. After becoming unconscious, your breathing rate will be exceedingly low until enough carbon dioxide is produced to stimulate the respiratory center. [Figure 10-19]

Figure 10-19. Since many of the symptoms of hyperventilation are similar to those of hypoxia, it is important to correctly diagnose and treat the proper condition. If you are using supplemental oxygen, check the equipment and flow rate to ensure you are not suffering from hypoxia.

 Hyperventilation is rapid or deep breathing which can be caused by emotional tension, anxiety, or fear. Hyperventilation can occur while breathing supplemental oxygen.

The treatment for hyperventilation involves restoring the proper carbon dioxide level in the body. Breathing normally is both the best prevention and the best cure for hyperventilation. In addition to slowing the breathing rate, you also can breathe into a paper bag or talk aloud to overcome hyperventilation. Recovery is usually rapid once the breathing rate is returned to normal.

 You should be able to overcome the symptoms, or avoid the occurrence of hyperventilation by slowing the breathing rate, breathing into a bag, or talking aloud.

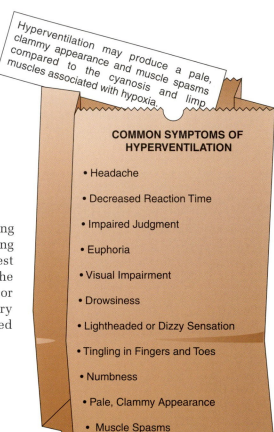

Hyperventilation may produce a pale, clammy appearance and muscle spasms compared to the cyanosis and limp muscles associated with hypoxia.

COMMON SYMPTOMS OF HYPERVENTILATION

• Headache

• Decreased Reaction Time

• Impaired Judgment

• Euphoria

• Visual Impairment

• Drowsiness

• Lightheaded or Dizzy Sensation

• Tingling in Fingers and Toes

• Numbness

• Pale, Clammy Appearance

• Muscle Spasms

SUMMARY CHECKLIST

✓ Cones function well in bright light, are sensitive to colors, and allow you to see fine detail. Cones are concentrated in the center of the retina in a slight depression known as the fovea.

✓ The rods are your primary receptors for night vision and also are responsible for much of your peripheral vision.

✓ While scanning for traffic at night, you should use off-center viewing to focus objects on the rods rather than on the foveal blind spot.

✓ As visual purple is formed, the rods can take up to 30 minutes to fully adapt to the dark.

✓ At night, interpreting the position lights of other aircraft can help you determine their direction of movement.

✓ Autokinesis is the false perception of movement after staring at a single point of light against a dark background for more than a few seconds.

✓ The false horizon illusion occurs when the natural horizon is obscured or not readily apparent.

✓ Landing illusions can be caused by a wide variety of factors including runway width, sloping runways and terrain, and weather conditions which reduce visibility.

✓ Disorientation is an incorrect mental image of your position, attitude, or movement in relation to what is actually happening to your aircraft.

✓ Kinesthetic sense is the term used to describe an awareness of position obtained from the nerves in your skin, joints, and muscles.

✓ Spatial disorientation occurs when there is a conflict between the information relayed by your central vision and your peripheral vision.

✓ The utricle and saccule organs within the vestibule are responsible for the perception of gravity and linear acceleration.

✓ The three semicircular canals, which are oriented in three planes perpendicular to each other, sense angular acceleration such as roll, pitch, and yaw.

✓ When subjected to the different forces of flight, the vestibular system can send misleading signals to the brain resulting in vestibular disorientation.

✓ Hypoxic hypoxia is due to a lack of available oxygen molecules at sufficient pressure for the body to use.

✓ Hypemic hypoxia occurs when your blood is not able to carry a sufficient amount of oxygen to the cells in your body.

✓ Since it attaches itself to the hemoglobin about 200 times more easily than does oxygen, carbon monoxide (CO) prevents hemoglobin from carrying oxygen to the body's cells.

✓ Stagnant hypoxia is an oxygen deficiency in the body due to inadequate circulation of the blood.

✓ The inability of the cells to effectively use oxygen is defined as histotoxic hypoxia.

✓ FAR Part 91 lists supplemental oxygen requirements for flights at cabin pressure altitudes above 12,500 feet MSL.

✓ Hyperventilation occurs when rapid or deep breathing removes too much carbon dioxide from the blood. It usually results from emotional stress, fright, or pain.

KEY TERMS

Retina	Landing Illusions
Cones	Flicker Vertigo
Rods	Disorientation
Visual Purple	Kinesthetic Sense
Autokinesis	Visual Sense
False Horizon	Spatial Disorientation

Vestibular System

Semicircular Canals

Vestibular Disorientation

Respiration

Hypoxia

Hypoxic Hypoxia

Time of Useful Consciousness

Hypemic Hypoxia

Carbon Monoxide Poisoning

Stagnant Hypoxia

Histotoxic Hypoxia

Supplemental Oxygen

Pressurization

Decompression

Hyperventilation

QUESTIONS

1. Explain the difference between the cone and rod cells of the retina.

2. While flying at night, you observe a steady red and flashing red light ahead of your aircraft. Based on this light configuration, what is the other aircraft's direction of movement?

   A. Flying toward you
   B. Crossing from right to left
   C. Crossing from left to right

3. What is the term for the visual illusion of movement which occurs when you stare at a fixed light against a dark background for more than a few seconds?

4. True/False. When landing on a runway which slopes uphill, the tendency is to fly an approach which is too low.

5. Name the three primary sensory sources which provide you with an awareness of your body's position in space.

6. Explain why your vestibular system does not sense any motion during a prolonged constant-rate turn.

7. What is the term used to describe the illusion of rotating in a different plane after moving the head during a constant-rate turn?

   A. Coriolis illusion
   B. Graveyard spiral
   C. Somatogravic illusion

Match the types of hypoxia to the appropriate descriptions.

8. The inability of the cells to effec-   A. Hypemic Hypoxia
    tively use oxygen

9. The inability of the blood to carry   B. Histotoxic Hypoxia
    sufficient oxygen to the cells due to
    anemia or carbon monoxide poisoning

10. A decrease of available oxygen
    molecules at sufficient pressure due   C. Stagnant Hypoxia
    to altitude

11. Oxygen deficiency due to inadequate
    circulation of the blood   D. Hypoxic Hypoxia

12. Select the true statement regarding FAR Part 91 supplemental oxygen
    requirements.

    A. Supplemental oxygen must be used by all aircraft occupants above cabin
        pressure altitudes of 14,000 feet MSL.
    B. The flight crew is required to use supplemental oxygen for the entire duration
        of the flight above cabin pressure altitudes of 14,000 feet MSL.
    C. The flight crew and aircraft occupants are required to use supplemental
        oxygen after 30 minutes of flight duration above cabin pressure altitudes of
        12,500 feet MSL.

13. How would you treat a passenger who is suffering from hyperventilation?

SECTION B
AERONAUTICAL DECISION MAKING

APPLYING THE DECISION-MAKING PROCESS

The person who merely watches the flight of a bird gathers the impression that the bird has nothing to think of but the flapping of its wings. As a matter of fact this is a very small part of its mental labor. To even mention all the things the bird must keep in mind in order to fly securely through air would take a considerable part of the evening.
— Wilbur Wright

The pilot, like the bird, must keep a great many things in mind to safely fly an aircraft. As pilot in command, you are faced with a continuous stream of decisions during each flight. Consider the following examples. What would you do in these situations?

- You are scheduled to fly to an important business meeting in another city. The weather briefing that you obtain an hour before your proposed departure time indicates that marginal VFR weather is forecast along your entire route.

- Shortly after takeoff on a cross-country flight, the low voltage light illuminates on your instrument panel.

- A friend asks you to take him up for a flight in the local area. The only rental aircraft available the day of the proposed flight is an airplane in which you have very little experience.

- You are on a pleasure flight with another pilot who is at the airplane controls. The pilot's reckless attitude and unfamiliarity with the airplane cause you to feel uncomfortable.

- During your aircraft preflight, you check your flight bag only to discover that you do not have your fuel tester with you.

- After receiving an in-flight weather report which indicates clear conditions along your route, you notice building thunderstorms ahead in the direction of your flight.

Although you cannot practice and prepare specifically for every situation which may occur during a flight, you can be prepared to make effective decisions regarding these situations. In Chapter 1, you were introduced to aeronautical decision making and some of the elements which affect this process. The Human Element Insets throughout this manual exposed you to examples of decision making and provided additional insight into the many factors which influence pilot judgment. As you read this section, you may want to review the human factors concepts in Chapter 1 and the Human Element Insets.

During each flight, you are required to make decisions regarding events which involve interactions between yourself as pilot in command, the aircraft, the environment, and the operation. The **decision-making process** involves an evaluation of each of these **risk elements** to achieve an accurate perception of the flight situation. [Figure 10-20]

Pilot — Evaluate your fitness to fly including your competency in the airplane, currency, and flight experience.

You are healthy, and well rested. You have been flying frequently and are experienced in the airplane.

Aircraft — The airplane's performance, limitations, equipment, and airworthiness must be determined.

Your airplane is in good condition and has received all the required inspections. However, it has a normally aspirated engine and its climb performance on a hot day at a high altitude needs to be considered.

Environment — Factors, such as weather, airport conditions, and the availability of air traffic control services, must be examined.

Although clear weather is forecast, hot temperatures and strong winds are expected over the mountains along your route.

Operation — The purpose of the flight is a factor which influences your decision on undertaking or continuing the flight.

You are leaving on a Friday to attend a friend's wedding the next day.

Situation — To maintain situational awareness, you need to have an accurate perception of how the pilot, aircraft, environment, and operation combine to affect the flight.

After considering each factor, you determine that the risk of flying over the mountains in the high winds and hot temperatures outweighs your desire to undertake the flight as planned. You may consider alternatives, such as plotting a course which allows you to circumnavigate the mountainous terrain, delaying the trip until the next morning when the temperatures are cooler and the winds are more favorable, or canceling the trip and driving to the wedding.

Figure 10-20. One of the most important decisions that you will make as pilot in command is the go/no-go decision. Evaluating each of these risk elements can help you decide whether a flight should be conducted or continued.

Typically during a flight, you have time to examine any changes which occur, gather information, and assess risk before reaching a decision. [Figure 10-21] However, some situations, such as an engine failure, require you to respond immediately using

The acronym DECIDE is used by the FAA to describe the basic steps in the decision-making process.

Detect the fact that a change has occurred.
Estimate the need to counter or react to the change.
Choose a desirable outcome for the success of the flight.
Identify actions which could successfully control the change.
Do the necessary action to adapt to the change.
Evaluate the effect of the action.

1 Recognize a change.

While on a cross-country flight, you discover that your time enroute between two checkpoints is significantly longer than the time you had originally calculated.

ETE	ETA	Fuel
ATE	ATA	Rem.
4+5	9:19	.7+.7
11	9:21	38.6
13	9:32	1.8
16	9:37	36.8
15	9:47	2.1
18	9:55	34.7
20	10:07	2.8
		31.9

2 Define the problem.

Based on your insight, your cross-country flying experience, and your knowledge of weather systems, you consider the possibility that you have an increased headwind.

You verify that your original calculations are correct and consider factors which may have lengthened the time between checkpoints, such as a climb or diversion off course. To determine if there is a change in the winds aloft forecast and to check recent pilot reports, you contact flight watch.

After weighing each information source, you conclude that your headwind has increased. To determine the severity of the problem, you calculate your new groundspeed, and reassess fuel requirements.

3 Choose a course of action.

After considering the expected outcome of each possible action and assessing the risks involved, you decide to refuel at an airport prior to your original destination.

4 Implement your decision.

You plot the course change and calculate a new estimated time of arrival, as well as contact the nearest FSS to amend your flight plan and check the weather conditions at your new destination.

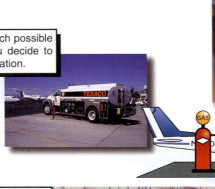

5 Ensure that your decision is producing the desired result.

To evaluate your decision and determine if additional steps need to be taken, you monitor your groundspeed, aircraft performance, and the weather conditions as the flight continues.

Figure 10-21. The decision-making process normally consists of several steps before you choose a course of action.

established procedures, with little time for detailed analysis. Traditionally, pilots have been well trained to react to emergencies, but are not as prepared to make decisions which require a more reflective response. Often times the consequences of a minor issue can be as serious as a major difficulty. Problems can accumulate due to an initial poor decision, or focusing on a minor occurrence may distract from the real problem. [Figure 10-22]

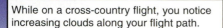

While on a cross-country flight, you notice increasing clouds along your flight path.

After trying to contact flight service and several airports in the vicinity, you discover that your radio is inoperative.

An uncontrolled airport which has maintenance services is within 15 nautical miles of your position.

You are concerned that if you land at the uncontrolled airport, you may be stranded overnight if poor weather moves in or if the radio cannot be repaired immediately.

You decide to continue the flight to your original destination, a tower-controlled airport, and plan to perform the lost communication procedure upon arrival.

As you get closer to your destination, the weather deteriorates to marginal VFR conditions and you become disoriented. Without an operable transceiver, you have no ability to request assistance from the control tower or from a nearby radar facility.

Figure 10-22. A decision to continue a flight as planned after a radio failure may not seem particularly hazardous. However, unexpected weather at your destination airport can turn a minor equipment problem into an emergency situation.

Although you may reach a decision and implement a course of action, the decision-making process is not complete. It is important to think ahead and determine how your decision could affect other phases of the flight. As the flight progresses, you need to continue to examine the outcome of your decision to ensure that it is producing the desired result.

ACCIDENTS AND INCIDENTS

An aircraft **accident** is an occurrence in which any person on board suffers death or serious injury, or in which the aircraft receives substantial damage. An **incident** is an occurrence other than an accident which affects the safety of operations. The **National Transportation Safety Board (NTSB)** is an independent Federal agency responsible for investigating every U.S. civil aviation accident and issuing safety recommendations aimed at preventing future

To pick up her brother for a weekend visit, Kathy rented an airplane in which she had little flying experience.

The night before the trip, Kathy attended a concert and arrived home after midnight.

After a stressful day at the office, Kathy arrived at the airport later than she had anticipated that evening.

Kathy used a performance chart in the airplane's POH to determine fuel burn, but did not note the reduced power setting on which the figure was based.

POWER APPROX. FUEL FLOW
75%   12 GPH
65%   10.8 GPH
55%   9.2 GPH

Already behind schedule, Kathy did not have the aircraft fuel tanks filled. Based on her fuel calculations and the aircraft fuel gauge indications, she concluded that she had plenty of fuel for the flight.

To reach her destination quicker, Kathy used full power and not the reduced power setting on which she had based her fuel calculations.

Upon reaching her destination, Kathy was unable to refuel the airplane since the FBO had closed for the night. Kathy disregarded the low fuel quantity gauge readings and convinced herself that she had enough fuel for the return flight.

Although she felt uneasy during the return flight as the fuel gauge needles bounced on empty, Kathy passed by several airports in an effort to get home quickly.

Not wanting to alert the controller to her fuel situation, Kathy followed ATC instructions to extend her downwind leg in the traffic pattern to follow an aircraft on an instrument approach.

Kathy's airplane ran out of fuel on final approach, two nautical miles short of the runway. While the aircraft sustained substantial damage, fortunately Kathy and her brother suffered only minor injuries.

accidents. In addition, the NTSB maintains the government's database on civil aviation accidents and conducts research regarding safety issues of national significance. More than 100,000 aviation accidents have been investigated by the NTSB since its inception in 1967. Examining NTSB accident and incident reports can help increase your awareness of how factors such as attitude, workload, situational awareness, fatigue, and stress can affect a pilot's decision-making ability. You also can learn how to recognize the many events which lead to a hazardous situation.

You can access accident and incident reports in the *NTSB Reporter* which is published monthly and on the NTSB world wide web site: **www.ntsb.gov**. A variety of other safety publications furnish accident synopses, including *Aviation Safety*, a twice monthly journal, and the AOPA Flight Safety Foundation's *Accident Prevention*.

POOR JUDGMENT CHAIN

Although in many accidents and incidents it may appear as if there is a single cause, there are typically numerous contributing factors which have occurred in a sequence. The **poor judgment chain**, sometimes referred to as the error chain, is a term used to describe this concept of contributing factors in a human factors-related accident. Breaking one link in the chain normally is all that is necessary to change the outcome of the sequence of events. [Figure 10-23]

Figure 10-23. At any point during this chain of events, the pilot could have made a different decision which may have prevented this accident.

ASSESSING RISK

NTSB, and other accident research can provide information which allows you to assess risk more effectively. For example, studies indicate the types of flight activities which are most likely to result in accidents. [Figure 10-24] In addition, by reviewing statistics, you can determine the phase of flight where accidents are most likely to occur and where your risk is the greatest. [Figure 10-25].

The majority of weather-related accidents occur after attempted VFR flight into IFR conditions and involve aircraft striking objects or terrain at cruise or higher airspeed, or crashing out of control.

Maneuvering flight is one of the largest single producers of fatal accidents. Many of these accidents are attributed to maneuvering during low, slow flight, often during buzzing or unauthorized aerobatics.

Figure 10-24. Weather, maneuvering flight, approaches, and takeoff/initial climb are the causes of the majority of fatal general aviation accidents.

Fatal accidents which occur during approach often happen at night or in IFR conditions.

Takeoff/initial climb accidents are usually caused by loss of control or stalls during, or shortly after, takeoff. This often is the result of a lack of awareness of the effects of density altitude on aircraft performance or other improper takeoff planning.

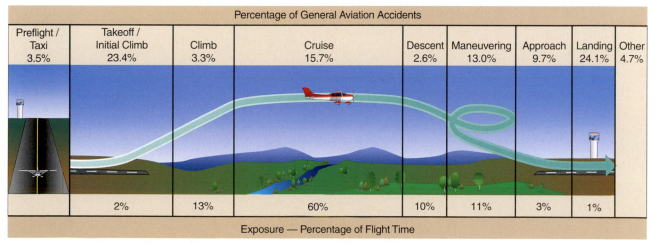

Percentage of General Aviation Accidents

Preflight / Taxi	Takeoff / Initial Climb	Climb	Cruise	Descent	Maneuvering	Approach	Landing	Other
3.5%	23.4%	3.3%	15.7%	2.6%	13.0%	9.7%	24.1%	4.7%
	2%	13%	60%	10%	11%	3%	1%	

Exposure — Percentage of Flight Time

Figure 10-25. The majority of accidents occur when approaching or departing airports. The workload is the greatest at these times, which increases the chance of error.

PILOT-IN-COMMAND RESPONSIBILITY

FAR 91.3 states the following:

(a) The pilot in command of an aircraft is directly responsible for, and is the final authority as to, the operation of that aircraft.

(b) In an in-flight emergency requiring immediate action, the pilot in command may deviate from any rule of this part to the extent required to meet that emergency.

As the pilot in command of an aircraft you assume a great responsibility. You have the skills and knowledge necessary to operate an aircraft, however, learning procedures and passing exams does not guarantee that you have the good judgment required to be a safe pilot. Judgment is not innate; it is learned, primarily through experience. Your life experiences can have a positive or negative effect on your ability to exercise good judgment in flight situations. Since judgment often is learned from making mistakes, in aviation it can be safer to learn from the experiences of others, such as your instructor, other pilots, and by reviewing flight safety publications. Although you may normally possess excellent judgment, your ability to make effective decisions during flight can be impaired by many factors. These factors, referred to as **stressors**, can increase your risk of error in the cockpit. [Figure 10-26]

Figure 10-26. Factors which increase your stress level during flight situations can be placed in three categories; physical, physiological, and psychological.

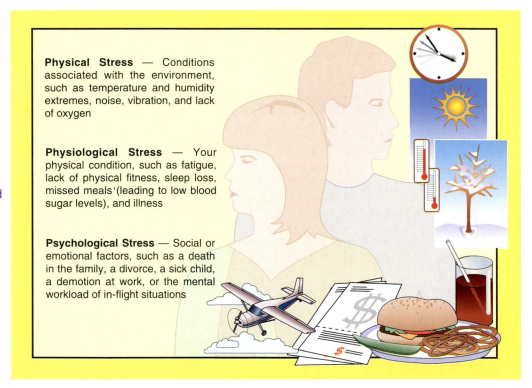

Physical Stress — Conditions associated with the environment, such as temperature and humidity extremes, noise, vibration, and lack of oxygen

Physiological Stress — Your physical condition, such as fatigue, lack of physical fitness, sleep loss, missed meals (leading to low blood sugar levels), and illness

Psychological Stress — Social or emotional factors, such as a death in the family, a divorce, a sick child, a demotion at work, or the mental workload of in-flight situations

SELF ASSESSMENT

Exercising good judgment must begin prior to taking the controls of your aircraft. Often, pilots thoroughly check their aircraft to determine if they are airworthy, yet do not evaluate their own fitness for flight. Just as you use a checklist when preflighting your aircraft, you can refer to a **personal checklist** to help you determine if you are prepared for a particular flight. For example, you can develop a checklist which specifies a maximum amount of time that may pass between flights without refresher training or review of the regulations and POH. Based on your experience and comfort level, determine your own weather minimums, which may be higher than those listed in the

Illness - Do I have any symptoms?

Medication - Have I been taking prescription or over-the-counter drugs?

Stress - Am I under psychological pressure from the job? Worried about financial matters, health problems, or family discord?

Alcohol - Have I been drinking within 8 hours? Within 24 hours?

Fatigue - Am I tired and not adequately rested?

Eating - Am I adequately nourished?

FARs, and set limitations for yourself regarding the maximum amount of crosswind that you are comfortable with. After you have reviewed your personal limitations, you can use the **I'm Safe Checklist** to further evaluate your fitness for flight. [Figure 10-27]

Figure 10-27. Check yourself as carefully as you check your aircraft before flight. If in doubt, do not fly.

HAZARDOUS ATTITUDES

You were introduced to **hazardous attitudes** in Chapter 1 and may have recognized some of these attitudes as you read about situations in the Human Element Insets. Most pilots will exhibit a hazardous attitude at some time. Being aware of, and alert to, hazardous attitudes in your own thinking is an important first step in preventing these thoughts from affecting your

The Fatigue Factor

The night before Charles Lindbergh's transatlantic flight, the weather forecast changed late in the evening and Lindbergh had to make arrangements late at night for a dawn departure. It was close to midnight before Lindbergh returned to his hotel room. Although he was hoping to get at least 2 1/2 hours of sleep, Lindbergh was disturbed by a friend whom he had posted as a guard outside his door. At 1:40 a.m., without having slept at all, Lindbergh departed for the airport.

Lindbergh was fighting exhaustion only 4 hours into the flight and, after 8 hours, his lack of sleep had become hazardous.

My eyes feel dry and hard as stones. The lids pull down with pounds of weight against their muscles. Keeping them open is like holding arms outstretched without support. I try letting one eyelid close at a time while I prop the other open with my will. But the effort's too much. Sleep is winning. My whole body argues that nothing, nothing life can attain, is quite so desirable as sleep. My mind is losing resolution and control.

After more than 22 hours into the flight, Lindbergh was falling asleep with his eyes open and he began to hallucinate.

These phantoms speak with human voices — friendly, vapor-like shapes, without substance, able to vanish or appear at will, to pass in and out through the walls of the fuselage as though no walls were there. . .

Although Lindbergh's story has a successful outcome, it graphically illustrates how deeply fatigue can affect a pilot's performance and judgment. If you had been in Lindbergh's place, would you have been so successful? How many pilots have been in a similar situation and have not survived to recount the incident?

decision making. If you recognize a hazardous attitude in your thought process, you can use a mental antidote which directs your thoughts to counteract the attitude. [Figure 10-28]

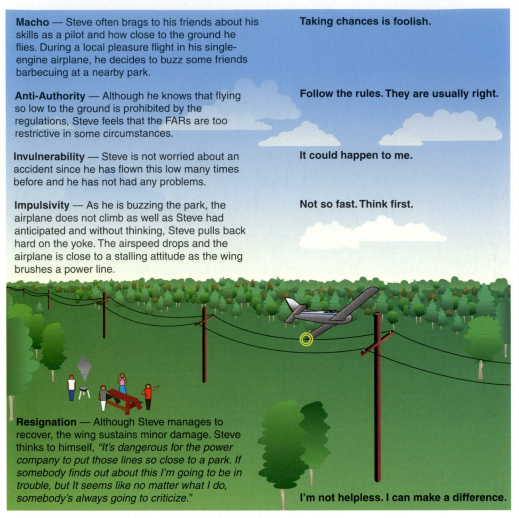

Macho — Steve often brags to his friends about his skills as a pilot and how close to the ground he flies. During a local pleasure flight in his single-engine airplane, he decides to buzz some friends barbecuing at a nearby park.

Taking chances is foolish.

Anti-Authority — Although he knows that flying so low to the ground is prohibited by the regulations, Steve feels that the FARs are too restrictive in some circumstances.

Follow the rules. They are usually right.

Invulnerability — Steve is not worried about an accident since he has flown this low many times before and he has not had any problems.

It could happen to me.

Impulsivity — As he is buzzing the park, the airplane does not climb as well as Steve had anticipated and without thinking, Steve pulls back hard on the yoke. The airspeed drops and the airplane is close to a stalling attitude as the wing brushes a power line.

Not so fast. Think first.

Figure 10-28. This scenario provides examples of each hazardous attitude and the antidote which can be used to counteract the hazardous thought. To prevent a hazardous attitude from impairing decision making, it is important to recognize the attitude, correctly label the thought, and then say its antidote to yourself.

Resignation — Although Steve manages to recover, the wing sustains minor damage. Steve thinks to himself, *"It's dangerous for the power company to put those lines so close to a park. If somebody finds out about this I'm going to be in trouble, but It seems like no matter what I do, somebody's always going to criticize."*

I'm not helpless. I can make a difference.

INTERPERSONAL RELATIONSHIPS

As pilot in command, it is important to form a productive relationship with each person on board the aircraft. For example, you are responsible for the safety and comfort of your passengers. Encourage passengers to speak up if at any time during the flight they experience discomfort or anxiety. Take time to explain how to operate the doors, seats, and seatbelts. If oxygen is required on the flight, describe how the oxygen masks are to be used.

Whether it is a training or pleasure flight, often there may be two pilots in the cockpit and it is essential to establish open communication in this situation. Prior to the flight, discuss how responsibilities will be divided and what each of you expect from the other. If it is not clear as to who will be performing specific tasks, an item may be overlooked. Another pilot's skills and knowledge can be a great resource, especially in a high workload or emergency situation. The interpersonal skills which you develop now also can be an asset if you advance to larger airplanes requiring multi-person crews. Often, pilots beginning their first job in a crew environment have had little or no training in the elements of cockpit teamwork.

COMMUNICATION

Perhaps no other essential activity in aircraft operations is as vulnerable to failure through human error and performance limitations as spoken communication. — Capt. William P. Monan, working for NASA's Aviation Safety Reporting System (ASRS)

Communication often incorporates words (language), inflection (tone, pitch, rate, volume, and emphasis), and body language (nonverbal). When you communicate with your instructor, another pilot, or a passenger you need to be alert for nonverbal cues which can help you interpret the message. For example, although passengers may indicate to you that they feel fine, their facial expressions may suggest anxiety regarding the flight. [Figure 10-29]

Figure 10-29. In a distress or urgency situation, your ability to effectively communicate becomes crucial. However, even during a routine flight, you are required to communicate frequently with numerous individuals such as FSS specialists, FBO line service personnel, aviation maintenance technicians, passengers, and ATC.

Pilot-controller communication presents unique challenges. No matter how simple and automatic the exchange of information between pilot and controller may seem, studies have shown that there is rarely a single flight leg flown where a communication error does not occur. Elements which lead to communication breakdown between pilots and controllers include confusion stemming from similar call signs, alpha-numeric errors, poor radio procedures, and readback problems. Other errors are caused when the pilot expects to hear a certain transmission and follows old habit patterns, only to learn later that ATC had requested something different. To help prevent a breakdown in communication, use correct radio procedures, read back clearances, and when in doubt, verify instructions with ATC. Be alert for similar call signs and use your call sign to acknowledge transmissions, not a double click of the mike or *"roger."*

EFFECTIVE LISTENING

Listening is the earliest communication skill acquired, and although the most frequently used, it is normally the least mastered. Failure to listen effectively can destroy the communication process. Active listening involves more than physically hearing the message. You must interpret and evaluate the message and then respond. **Feedback** confirmation ensures that an accurate exchange of information has taken place. If the receiver does not provide feedback, then it is the responsibility of the sender to ask for it.

Feedback normally takes the form of clarification, paraphrase, or summarization. Clarifying responses often begin with simple statements or open-ended questions. For example, *"Would you please clarify that?"* or *"I don't understand what you mean."* Paraphrasing is restating the speaker's statement in the listener's own words. This way the listener and the speaker can check the accuracy of what has been heard. Normally, a paraphrasing response begins with a phrase such as this, *"As I understand you . . ."* or *"In other words . . ."* Finally, summarizing responses concisely cover the main ideas expressed by the speaker and are especially appropriate for lengthy conversations. You may begin a summarizing response like this, *"Everything we have discussed so far. . ."*

During pilot-controller communication, the pilot often repeats the controller's instructions. This is called the readback. The act of a controller actively listening to the readback of an ATC clearance has been termed, the hearback. This important step in the communication process provides final confirmation that instructions have been received and understood. Do not assume controller silence after a readback is verification of your transmission. Ask the controller for a verbal confirmation.

BARRIERS TO EFFECTIVE COMMUNICATION

"Cessna 76195, fly heading 180, climb and maintain 8,500, squawk 4364, departure frequency will be 123.7, contact ground control 121.9 when ready to taxi."

The preceding statement would have little meaning to someone who is unfamiliar with the terminology used during flight operations. Effective communication requires a common core of experience between the communicator and the receiver. When you first begin flight training, the instructions you receive from air traffic controllers and even requests from your instructor may seem confusing. After learning the terminology and correct procedures for conveying information in the aviation environment, a common core of experience is established and your ability to communicate with your instructor, controllers, FSS specialists, and maintenance personnel is enhanced.

Misuse of terminology can lead to miscommunication. Consider the following example. An instructor informs his student that he *"has the aircraft"* referring to an earlier traffic advisory issued by ATC. The student believes that the instructor is taking the airplane controls and removes his hands from the yoke. Neither pilot is aware that no one is flying the airplane. Using the proper terminology is essential to conveying the correct information. Relating your position in the traffic pattern on the CTAF frequency, requesting a special VFR clearance, and declaring a state of distress or urgency are just a few of the situations where misuse of terminology could compromise safety.

A pilot leaves a note to the avionics technician to "check the radios." This is an example of an overuse of abstractions, another barrier to effective communication. Abstract words do not generate a specific mental image in the mind of the receiver. It is important to use concrete and specific words as much as possible to convey your message. For example, a more effective note may read, "I was advised by the tower controller that the number one radio was weak and unreadable, although I could receive just fine. When I transmitted on the number two radio using the same mike, I was told that I could be heard loud and clear." Figure [10-30]

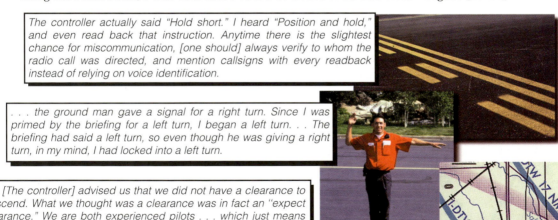

> The controller actually said *"Hold short."* I heard *"Position and hold,"* and even read back that instruction. Anytime there is the slightest chance for miscommunication, [one should] always verify to whom the radio call was directed, and mention callsigns with every readback instead of relying on voice identification.

> . . . the ground man gave a signal for a right turn. Since I was primed by the briefing for a left turn, I began a left turn. . . The briefing had said a left turn, so even though he was giving a right turn, in my mind, I had locked into a left turn.

> . . . [The controller] advised us that we did not have a clearance to descend. What we thought was a clearance was in fact an "expect clearance." We are both experienced pilots . . . which just means that experience is no substitute for a direct question to Center when you are in doubt about a clearance.

> About 7 miles west of [the Class B airspace], I called [approach control], and stated our position and intentions. Controller responded with a squawk number and ident, which was complied with. Approximately one minute later [now inside the Class B boundary], the controller came back with, "I guess a clearance means nothing, but you are cleared into the [Class B airspace]." I felt that once contact was made, the controller knew our intentions and a squawk and ident were given, that a clearance was imminent.

Figure 10-30. The examples shown here are excerpts from Aviation Safety Reporting System (ASRS) reports. More than 70% of ASRS incident reports include a problem with the exchange of information between humans. You can review ASRS reports in the publication, *Callback,* and by contacting the ASRS world wide web site at **www-afo.arc. nasa.gov/ASRS/ASRS.html**.

Miscommunication Mishap

Many accidents and incidents are the result of a lack of effective communication. For example, a Boeing 727-200 inadvertently landed with its gear retracted after the following series of miscommunications.

The First Officer, who was seated in the Captain's seat, gave an order for *"gear down"*. The Captain, who was in the right seat and flying the aircraft, assumed the First Officer was stating that the gear **was** down.

The before landing checklist was interrupted by radio communication and never completed.

The Ground Proximity Warning System (GPWS) installed on the aircraft alerted the crew to *"pull up"*, due to the aircraft's proximity to the ground with the gear retracted. However, the Flight Engineer believed that the GPWS warning was caused by flaps not in the landing position. The Flight Engineer disengaged the GPWS system by pulling the circuit breaker and the warning was silenced.

When it was observed that the 727 was on final approach with the gear retracted, the tower controller radioed, *"go around"* but used the wrong aircraft call sign.

RESOURCE USE

On a cross-country flight you become disoriented. The landmarks around you do not match any that you see on your sectional chart and fuel is running low. What resources do you have to assist you in this situation? In addition to learning how to recognize available resources, you must also be able to evaluate whether you have the time to use a particular resource and the impact that its use will have upon the safety of flight. For example, the assistance of ATC may be very useful if you are lost, however, in an emergency situation when you need to take action quickly, you may not have the time available to contact ATC immediately.

INTERNAL RESOURCES

Internal resources can be found in the cockpit during flight. Since some of your most valuable internal resources are your own ingenuity, knowledge, and skills, you can expand your cockpit resources immensely by improving your capabilities. You can do this through additional training after you obtain your private pilot certificate, and by frequently reviewing flight information publications, such as the FARs and the AIM.

A thorough understanding of the equipment and systems in your aircraft is necessary to fully utilize all of your resources. Knowing the location of every switch and its function is particularly important if you fly several different aircraft. An autopilot, on-board oxygen or pressurization system, and advanced navigation equipment, such as GPS or LORAN can be valuable resources provided that you understand how to operate them correctly. If you do not fully understand how to use the equipment in your aircraft, or if you rely on it so much that you become complacent, additional equipment can become a detriment to safe flight rather than an asset.

Checklists are excellent cockpit resources for verifying that the aircraft instruments and systems are checked, set, and operating properly, as well as ensuring that the proper procedures are performed if there is a system malfunction or in-flight emergency. In addition, the POH, which is required to be carried on board the aircraft, is essential for accurate flight planning and for resolving in-flight equipment malfunctions. Other valuable cockpit resources include current aeronautical charts and publications, such as the *Airport/Facility Directory*, or *JeppGuide*.

While another pilot on board the aircraft is clearly an excellent resource, passengers as resources are often overlooked. Passengers can help look for traffic and may be able to provide information in an irregular situation, especially if they fly frequently. For example, a strange sound or smell may alert a passenger to a potential problem.

EXTERNAL RESOURCES

Possibly your greatest **external resource** during flight is air traffic control, including flight service specialists. ATC can help decrease your workload by providing traffic advisories, radar vectors, and assistance in an emergency situation. Through ATC you also may be able to access maintenance personnel or other assistance needed in an emergency, such as the airplane manufacturer. Flight service stations can provide updates on weather, answer questions about airport conditions, and may offer direction finding assistance. In addition to requesting weather information from flight service, automated weather stations such as ASOS and AWOS may provide weather and airport conditions in flight. [Figure 10-31]

Figure 10-31. Recognizing both the internal and external resources available to you is the first step in effective resource use.

WORKLOAD MANAGEMENT

A pilot forgets to extend the landing gear and lands with the airplane's gear still retracted. While searching for information on a chart, a pilot misses several ATC traffic advisories. An aircraft's flaps are configured improperly for takeoff causing an accident soon after departure from the runway. A pilot inadvertently enters Class B airspace without a clearance. In each of these cases, operations which affect the safety of flight were not performed. The objective of effective workload management is to ensure that essential tasks are accomplished, and as pilot in command, you must learn how to manage workload and sequence tasks to achieve this goal.

PLANNING AND PREPARATION

To effectively manage your workload in the cockpit, you need to anticipate when your workload will be high and plan and prepare for this time during periods of low workload. For example, your workload normally is highest in the vicinity of an airport during departures and approaches. Prior to takeoff, tune each navigation radio and set the selectors for the proper courses based upon the initial departure routing. The tower frequency should be set in one communication radio, and either the departure, or the flight service station frequency in the other.

Keeping the radios set up well in advance of when they will be required helps eliminate a hurried search for a frequency on a chart. Before you arrive at your destination, review your chart, set radio frequencies, and visualize how you will fly the approach to a particular runway. As you approach an airport, monitor the ATIS, if available, and the tower frequency to get a good idea of what airport and traffic conditions to expect. Perform necessary checklists well in advance so that you have time to focus on traffic and ATC instructions. These procedures are especially important prior to entering a high density traffic area, such as Class B airspace. [Figure 10-32]

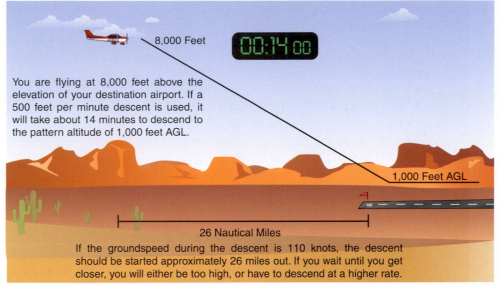

Figure 10-32. Planning your descent to pattern altitude will help alleviate workload as you approach an airport.

PRIORITIZING

As you manage workload, you must prioritize items. For example, if you need to perform a go-around, adding power, gaining airspeed, and properly configuring the airplane are priorities. Informing the tower of your balked landing should be accomplished only after these tasks are completed. Priorities change as the situation changes. If you determine that your fuel quantity is lower than expected on a cross-country flight, your priority can shift from making a scheduled arrival time at your destination, to locating a nearby airport to refuel. In an emergency situation, your first priority is to fly the airplane and maintain a safe airspeed.

WORK OVERLOAD

The first effect of high workload is that you will begin to work faster. As the workload increases and you cannot devote your attention to many tasks at one time, you may begin to focus on one item. When you become task saturated, you are not aware of inputs from various sources so decisions may be made on incomplete information, and the possibility of error increases. [Figure 10-33]

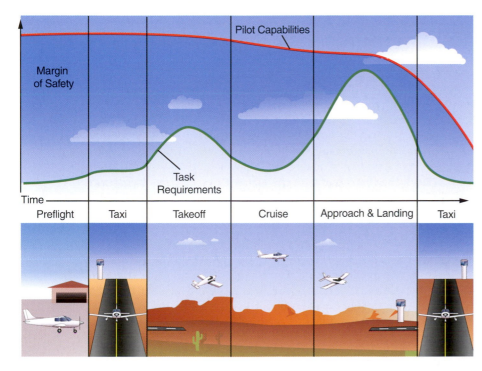

Figure 10-33. Accidents often occur when flying task requirements exceed pilot capabilities. The difference between these two factors is called the margin of safety. Note that in this idealized example, the margin of safety is minimal during the approach and landing. At this point, an emergency or distraction could overtax pilot capabilities, causing an accident.

You need to recognize work overload, stop, think, and slow down. An aircraft autopilot can be used to decrease your physical workload. If there is another pilot on board, you can delegate specific tasks and you also can enlist the assistance of ATC. For example, if you must divert to an alternate and you are under radar contact, you may request radar vectors from ATC.

SITUATIONAL AWARENESS

Maintaining situational awareness involves an understanding of all of the human factors concepts. For example, an accurate perception of the operational conditions of the flight, including the airplane systems, autopilot, and passengers can be obtained through workload management and communication skills. Effective use of resources will assist you in monitoring the environmental conditions of the flight, such as your relationship to terrain, traffic, weather, and airspace. Your ability to assess the future impact of these operational and environmental conditions is essential to exercising good judgment and decision-making skills. [Figure 10-34]

Figure 10-34. Situational awareness is an accurate perception of the operational and environmental factors which affect the aircraft, pilot, and passengers during a specific period of time.

OBSTACLES TO MAINTAINING SITUATIONAL AWARENESS

Fatigue, stress, and work overload can cause you to fixate on a single perceived important item rather than maintaining an overall awareness of your flight situation. A contributing factor in many accidents is a distraction which diverts the pilot's attention from monitoring the instruments or scanning outside the aircraft. Many cockpit distractions begin as a minor problem, such as a gauge which is not reading correctly, but result in accidents as the pilot diverts attention to the perceived problem and neglects to properly control the aircraft.

Complacency presents another obstacle to maintaining situational awareness. When activities become routine, you may have a tendency to relax and not put as much effort into your performance. Like fatigue, complacency reduces your effectiveness in the cockpit. However, complacency is harder to recognize than fatigue, since you perceive everything to be progressing smoothly. Cockpit automation can lead to complacency if you assume that the autopilot is doing its job, and do not cross-check the instruments or the aircraft's position as frequently. If the autopilot fails, you may not be mentally prepared to fly the airplane manually.

THE APPLICATION OF AERONAUTICAL DECISION MAKING

The following accident accounts provide examples of how human factors can greatly influence aeronautical decision making and the outcome of a flight. Although, these examples are both air carrier accidents, they provide excellent insight into many of the concepts explored in human factors training.

THE ACCIDENT THAT SHOULD NEVER HAVE HAPPENED

As Flight 401, a Lockheed L-1011, was on approach into Miami, the landing gear handle was placed in the down position. However, the green cockpit light which indicates that the gear is extended did not illuminate. The crew advised the air traffic controller that they would have to circle because of the light problem.

After climbing to 2,000 feet MSL and following a clearance to proceed west of the airport, the Captain instructed the First Officer to engage the autopilot. The crew focused their attention on the mechanical problem and the Captain instructed the Second Officer to go below and check the nose gear alignment. During this time, the yoke was inadvertently pushed, which disengaged the autopilot and the aircraft began descending at 250 feet per minute. The crew did not notice the altitude deviation warning and had lost awareness of the aircraft's position. Although the Second Officer reported that he could not see the nose gear alignment pins, neither crewmember nor a maintenance specialist on board, mentioned the special lights available to illuminate the pins.

A Miami controller noticed an altitude readout of 900 feet and indirectly questioned the status of the flight, *"How are things comin' along out there?"* Flight 401 replied that they would *"like to turn around and come, come back in."* As they started the turn, the First Officer said, *"We're still at 2,000 right?"* and the Captain exclaimed, *"Hey, what's happening here?"* Seven seconds later, the airplane crashed into the Everglades. Ninety-nine persons were killed.

The NTSB determined the probable cause of this accident was the failure of the flight crew to monitor the flight instruments during the final four minutes of flight and to detect an unexpected descent soon enough to prevent impact with the ground. Preoccupation with a malfunction of the nose gear position indicating system distracted the crew's attention from the instruments and allowed the descent to go unnoticed.

This was one of the primary accidents which motivated airlines to implement human factors training, or crew resource management (CRM). Examination of this accident reveals that the crew lost situational awareness through the distraction of a minor mechanical problem. Poor workload management and pilot-in-command responsibility were shown by the Captain who designated duties to crewmembers without ensuring that somebody was flying the airplane. Complacency was a factor since it was assumed that the autopilot was controlling the airplane. Information was not effectively exchanged between crewmembers and pilot-controller communication was deficient since the controller did not directly question the 1,100-foot altitude deviation. Poor use of resources, including a lack of knowledge of the airplane and the over involvement of too many crewmembers may have contributed to the confusion in problem definition.

HUMAN FACTORS TRAINING IN ACTION

On July 19, 1989, United Flight 232, a McDonnell Douglas DC-10, suffered a catastrophic engine failure while cruising at FL370. The destruction of the number two engine's fan rotor caused the loss of all three of the DC-10's redundant hydraulic flight control systems. The aircraft was rendered almost uncontrollable. Since the possibility of a catastrophic failure of all three hydraulic systems was considered by designers to be nearly impossible, there was no procedure in place for this occurrence.

Against all odds, Captain Alfred C. Haynes and his crew, with the help of a DC-10 instructor pilot who was aboard as a passenger, were able to guide the crippled aircraft to Sioux City, Iowa. Approximately 45 minutes after the hydraulic failure, the aircraft crash-landed at the Sioux City Municipal Airport. Of the 285 passengers and 11 crewmembers aboard, 174 passengers and 10 crewmembers survived. The ability of the crew to maintain any control of the airplane and land with survivors when faced with such daunting obstacles was acknowledged by the aviation industry as a feat requiring extraordinary piloting and crew coordination abilities. The degree of success of Flight 232 resulted from the effective application of many human factors-related skills. The NTSB stated that *"the UAL flight crew performance was highly commendable and greatly exceeded reasonable expectations."*

The first priority in an emergency situation is to fly the airplane. The number one and number three engines were still operating so the crew figured out a way to maintain some control of the airplane by adding thrust on one side and reducing thrust on the other to force the airplane in a skid to turn. As pilot in command, Captain Haynes was able to maintain situational awareness and delegate tasks to effectively manage the workload. He was open to input from the crew and assistance from a variety of resources.

Excellent communication took place between the crewmembers so each knew what his responsibility was. The First Officer was responsible for communicating with the San Francisco area maintenance facility which brought in a team of experts for assistance. A team of five controllers in the Sioux City Gateway Airport control tower, which was collocated with approach control, worked together to coordinate the aircraft's arrival. Although the heavy workload limited communication between the cockpit and cabin crew, the flight attendants were able to deduce the extent of the emergency just by observing non-verbal cues from the crew as to the intensity of the situation in the cockpit.

I am firmly convinced that CRM played a very important part in our landing at Sioux City with any chance of survival. I also believe that its principles apply no matter how many crew members are in the cockpit. Those who fly single-pilot aircraft sometimes ask, "How does CRM affect me if I fly by myself?" Well, CRM does not just imply the use of other sources only in the cockpit — it is an "everybody resource." To these pilots I say there are all sorts of resources available to them. Ask an astronaut if he thinks he got to the moon by himself. I don't think so — he had a great deal of help. — Captain Alfred C. Haynes

Human Factors in Space — Mission to Mars

Managing human factors issues during long stays in space is a unique challenge for scientists. Studies of the crews aboard Skylab, launched in 1973, and most recently aboard the Russian space station Mir, have shown that in addition to the physiological effects of living in space, there are many psychological factors to consider. [Figure A]

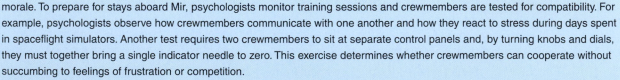
Courtesy of NASA

Crewmembers aboard Mir have expressed feelings of isolation and loneliness, and can become lethargic and depressed after as little as 2 months in space if steps are not taken to boost morale. To prepare for stays aboard Mir, psychologists monitor training sessions and crewmembers are tested for compatibility. For example, psychologists observe how crewmembers communicate with one another and how they react to stress during days spent in spaceflight simulators. Another test requires two crewmembers to sit at separate control panels and, by turning knobs and dials, they must together bring a single indicator needle to zero. This exercise determines whether crewmembers can cooperate without succumbing to feelings of frustration or competition.

The Russian space program has shown that stays in space of more than 400 days are possible, but what about a longer stay, with more risks, even further away from the home planet? Scientists are preparing for the technological and human challenges posed by a 600 to 1,000-day mission to Mars. It is not fully understood what effect a trip to Mars would have on a crew. Researchers must develop methods to help crewmembers cope with the severe isolation and boredom, which may result from living millions of miles away from home in a confined area with only electronic methods of contact with earth. In addition, the crewmembers must have the ability to manage the stress of performing risky and demanding jobs in this unique environment.

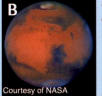
Courtesy of NASA

In the spirit of the aviation pioneers who overcame daunting obstacles to turn the dream of flight into reality, men and women will boldly face the many challenges which lay ahead to become the first humans to set foot on the surface of another planet. [Figure B]

SUMMARY CHECKLIST

✓ The decision-making process involves an evaluation of the pilot in command, the aircraft, the environment, and the operation to achieve an accurate perception of the flight situation.

✓ As a flight progresses, you need to continue to examine the outcome of your decisions made earlier to ensure they are producing the desired results.

✓ The National Transportation Safety Board (NTSB) is an independent Federal agency responsible for investigating every U.S. civil aviation accident and issuing safety recommendations aimed at preventing future accidents.

✓ The poor judgment chain is a term used to describe the concept of contributing factors in a human factors-related accident.

✓ NTSB accident and incident reports and other aviation safety research can provide information which allows you to assess risk more effectively.

✓ Your ability to make effective decisions during flight can be impaired by physical, physiological, and psychological stressors.

✓ To prevent a hazardous attitude from impairing effective decision making, it is important to recognize the attitude, correctly label the thought, and then say its antidote to yourself.

✓ Failure to listen effectively can destroy the communication process. Feedback confirmation ensures that an accurate exchange of information has taken place.

✓ Barriers to effective communication can include a lack of a common core of experience between the communicator and receiver, misuse of terminology, and an overuse of abstractions.

✓ Accidents often occur when flying task requirements exceed pilot capabilities. The difference between these two factors is called the margin of safety.

✓ Fatigue, stress, work overload, distractions, and complacency can all contribute to a loss of situational awareness.

KEY TERMS

Decision-Making Process	Stressors
Risk Elements	Personal Checklist
Accident	I'm Safe Checklist
Incident	Hazardous Attitudes
National Transportation Safety Board (NTSB)	Feedback
	Internal Resources
Poor Judgment Chain	External Resources

QUESTIONS

1. What are the four risk elements which must be considered during aeronautical decision making?

2. What is the role of the National Transportation Safety Board regarding aviation accidents?

3. True/False. Continued VFR flight into IFR weather conditions is not a factor in aviation accidents.

4. During which phases of flight do most general aviation accidents occur?

   A. Climb and cruise
   B. Maneuvering and descent
   C. Takeoff/initial climb and landing

5. What are the tools that you can use to evaluate your fitness to fly?

Match the thought regarding the following situation to the appropriate hazardous attitude.

You land at an unfamiliar airport and ask the receptionist at the FBO counter to *"fill it up"* and then continue to the pilot's lounge to make a phone call. Returning, you pay the bill and take off without checking the aircraft, the fuel caps, or the fuel.

6. You feel that it is a silly requirement to preflight an aircraft which you have just flown.

   A. Invulnerability

7. You just want to get underway quickly.

   B. Impulsivity

8. You have skipped preflights before and you have never had a problem.

   C. Anti-Authority

9. You feel that a pilot with your skill level can handle anything during the flight that may have been overlooked on the ground.

   D. Resignation

10. Since you pay for their services, you feel it is the responsibility of the FBO personnel to ensure the airplane was fueled correctly.

    E. Macho

11. Explain the barriers to effective communication and the elements which can cause a breakdown in pilot-controller communication.

12. If you have an in-flight aircraft equipment malfunction and need to divert to an alternate airport, what resources could you use to assist you?

13. True/False. Situational awareness is an accurate perception of the operational and environmental factors which affect the aircraft, pilot, and passengers during a specific period of time.

14. What are some of the obstacles to maintaining situational awareness.

    A. Complacency, fatigue, and prioritizing
    B. Complacency, distractions, and fatigue
    C. Distractions, checklist use, and feedback

CHAPTER 11

FLYING CROSS-COUNTRY

SECTION A
THE FLIGHT PLANNING PROCESS

With less than 60 hours of flight experience, Calbraith Perry Rodgers climbed into a canvas-covered biplane on September 11, 1911, and departed from Sheepshead Bay, Brooklyn on what would become the first transcontinental flight. Cal Rodgers' trip was sponsored by the Armour Company, which paid Cal $5.00 for every mile he flew with the company's soft drink name painted on the wing of his Wright EX, the *Vin Fiz*. In addition to the compensation he received from the Armour Company, Cal hoped to collect William Randolf Hearst's $50,000 prize for completing the first coast-to-coast trip in 30 days or less. Unfortunately for Cal, things deteriorated quickly. On the second morning of his journey, Cal flew into a tree on takeoff, severely damaging his aircraft. Following a costly three-day layover for repairs, Cal pressed westward using railroad tracks as a primary method of navigation, but even Cal's pilotage failed him — a wrong track took him to Pennsylvania instead of his intended destination in Elmira, New York. Back on course, but hardly on schedule, Cal continued to fly toward the west coast at an average speed of 52 miles per hour until the 30 day time limit ran out on him in Oklahoma, dashing his hopes of cashing in on Hearst's reward. Undaunted, and with the continued backing of the Armour Company, Cal doggedly forged ahead and ultimately achieved success. On November 5, he landed in Pasadena, California after 82 hours of flight time and 69 stops, many of them unplanned. The journey's hardships, which included 19 crashes, took its toll on both plane and pilot. So many airplane parts were replaced during the excursion that only the rudder and two wing struts remained from the original *Vin Fiz*. Cal himself did not fare much better — he completed his adventure with a broken leg and a nasty gash across his forehead.

While technological advancements can be given a large portion of the credit, thorough preflight planning and sound pilot decision making has played a major, if somewhat uncelebrated role, in making cross-country travel significantly more routine than in Cal Rodgers' day. Whether you are traveling across the continent, or simply across the county, the route to an enjoyable and safe flight begins with the **flight planning process**. This pattern of preflight activities requires that you put into practice all the knowledge and skills you have acquired throughout your training. As you gain experience, you may refine and customize your planning procedures, however, the general process should remain similar to that shown in figure 11-1.

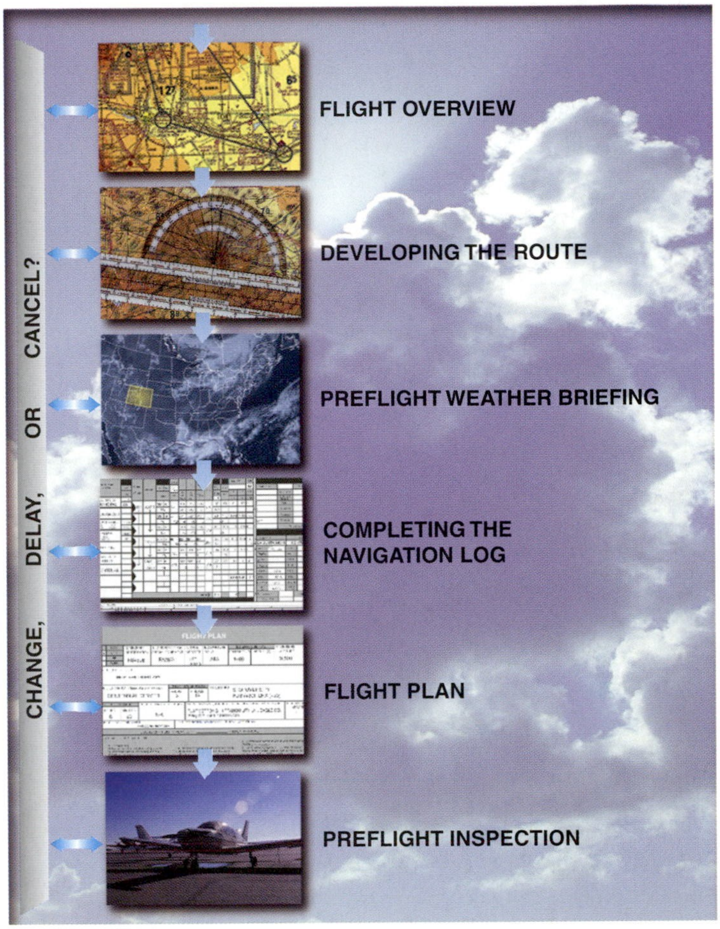

Figure 11-1. An efficient flight planning process involves several steps. You can decide to change, delay, or cancel a portion, or all, of your flight at any point in the process.

CHANGE, DELAY, OR CANCEL?

FLIGHT OVERVIEW

DEVELOPING THE ROUTE

PREFLIGHT WEATHER BRIEFING

COMPLETING THE NAVIGATION LOG

FLIGHT PLAN

PREFLIGHT INSPECTION

In the following scenario, Ryan, a student pilot, plans and flies a solo cross-country in the area south and east of his home airport located in Arapahoe County, Colorado. This section relates Ryan's preflight process from the initial phases through his preflight inspection. Section B, *The Flight*, follows Ryan's adventure from takeoff through final landing and postflight.

FLIGHT OVERVIEW

Thursday, 1736 MDT After a discussion with his flight instructor, Megan, Ryan plans to depart from Centennial Airport (APA) on a round-robin flight with stops at Pueblo Memorial Airport (PUB) and La Junta Municipal Airport (LHX). Each leg of the flight will emphasize a particular method of navigation — VOR, pilotage, or dead reckoning.

Thursday, 1748 MDT A call to the local TIBS facility reveals that the weather for the next several days is expected to remain good, with the typical summer afternoon isolated thunderstorms across the region. With this in mind, Ryan tentatively plans a Saturday morning departure.

Thursday, 1800 MDT As Megan departs for another flight, she suggests that Ryan further check the suitability of the route by referring to the World Aeronautical Chart (WAC) covering southern Colorado. After locating the chart, Ryan connects the three airports with straight course lines and examines the overall route. While there are several types of airspace and terrain in the vicinity of his proposed route, the flight initially seems feasible. [Figure 11-2]

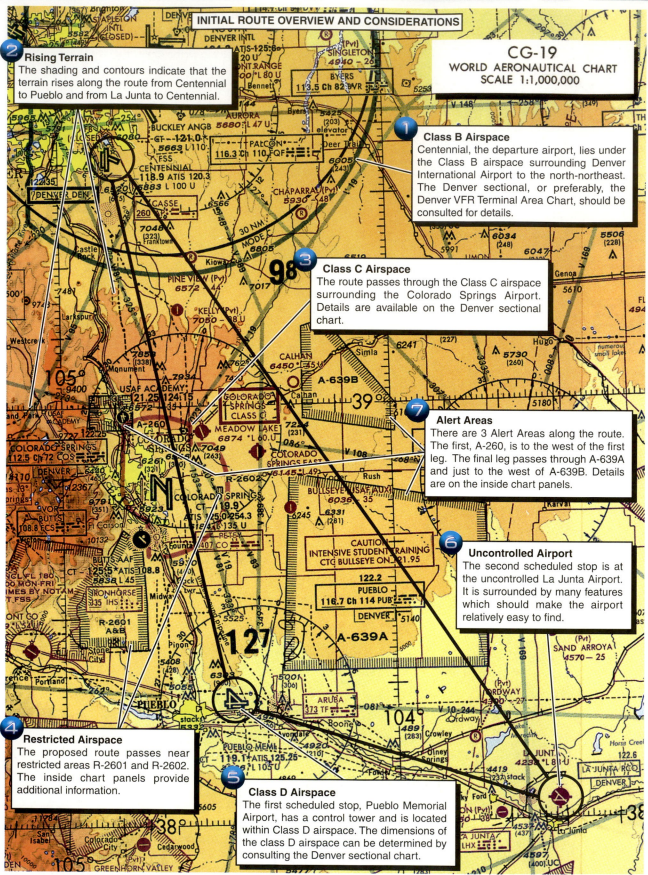

INITIAL ROUTE OVERVIEW AND CONSIDERATIONS

CG-19
WORLD AERONAUTICAL CHART
SCALE 1:1,000,000

2 Rising Terrain
The shading and contours indicate that the terrain rises along the route from Centennial to Pueblo and from La Junta to Centennial.

1 Class B Airspace
Centennial, the departure airport, lies under the Class B airspace surrounding Denver International Airport to the north-northeast. The Denver sectional, or preferably, the Denver VFR Terminal Area Chart, should be consulted for details.

3 Class C Airspace
The route passes through the Class C airspace surrounding the Colorado Springs Airport. Details are available on the Denver sectional chart.

7 Alert Areas
There are 3 Alert Areas along the route. The first, A-260, is to the west of the first leg. The final leg passes through A-639A and just to the west of A-639B. Details are on the inside chart panels.

6 Uncontrolled Airport
The second scheduled stop is at the uncontrolled La Junta Airport. It is surrounded by many features which should make the airport relatively easy to find.

4 Restricted Airspace
The proposed route passes near restricted areas R-2601 and R-2602. The inside chart panels provide additional information.

5 Class D Airspace
The first scheduled stop, Pueblo Memorial Airport, has a control tower and is located within Class D airspace. The dimensions of the class D airspace can be determined by consulting the Denver sectional chart.

Figure 11-2. Although sectional and VFR Terminal Area charts should be used for detailed planning, a WAC chart can be helpful in providing an overview of the type of airspace, terrain, and navaids along a proposed route.

DEVELOPING THE ROUTE

Friday, 0916 MDT Following an early morning flight, Ryan discusses his review of the WAC chart with Megan. She concurs with Ryan's assessment of the route and suggests that he continue his planning using more detailed charts.

Referring to a sectional chart front panel, Ryan quickly determines that he needs Denver and Wichita sectionals. In addition, Ryan decides to pick up a Denver VFR Terminal Area chart since his home airport lies under Denver Class B airspace. After gathering his charts, Ryan assembles other materials and reference sources necessary for refining his cross-country route such as a plotter, flight computer, navigation logs, flight plan, NOTAMs, and the Southwest *Airport/Facility Directory* (A/FD).

Friday, 0931 MDT With his planning materials in hand, Ryan returns home ready to begin a detailed analysis of his route. As he selects his checkpoints, he pays close attention to factors such as terrain and special use airspace. During this process, Ryan also notes easily identifiable intermediate checkpoints which will help him maintain orientation and keep track of his progress during his flight. As he plots his course, he also considers his options in the event he needs to divert due to adverse weather, aircraft emergency, or some other unexpected circumstance. In doing so, he notes the airfields along his route, especially those with services available, and checks for navaids which he could use in the event of a diversion.

After checking the terrain and obstruction heights, Ryan selects a preliminary altitude for each leg of his flight, considering FAR requirements and VFR cruising altitudes. Of course, the actual altitude he flies will be determined by the winds aloft and cloud cover on the day of the flight.

As he plans each leg, Ryan checks pertinent flight publications for expanded and updated information. He refers to the A/FD for airport information such as available services, traffic pattern and runway information, as well as any pertinent special notices. [Figure 11-3] He also consults the A/FD for data on communications facilities, radio aids to navigation, parachute jumping areas, and any changes to his VFR charts. After analyzing the available data, Ryan settles on the route shown in figure 11-4.

Figure 11-3. Ryan uses the *Airport/Facility Directory* to familiarize himself with the Pueblo and La Junta airports.

```
PUEBLO MEM    (PUB)   5 E   UTC-7(-6DT)   N38°17.35' W104°29.79'                    DENVER
4726   B   S4   FUEL 100LL, JET A   ARFF Index B                                    H-2D, L-6E
RWY 08L-26R: H10496X150 (ASPH-PFC)   S-75, D-170, DT-260   MIRL                      IAP
   RWY 08L: SSALR.        RWY 26R: REIL. VASI(V2L)—GA 3.0° TCH 25'. 0.3% up.
RWY 17-35: H8308X150 (ASPH-PFC)   S-93, D-110, DT-170   MIRL
   RWY 17: REIL. 1.0% down.      RWY 35: VASI(V2L)—GA 3.0° TCH 36'. 1.0% up.
RWY 08R-26L: H4073X75 (ASPH)   S-20
   RWY 08R: Rgt tfc.       RWY 26L: Gnd.
AIRPORT REMARKS: Attended 1300-0500Z‡. For fuel after hours call 719-948-4560/2447. Rwy 08R-26L avbl to acft
   under 12,500 pounds during dalgt hours. Sequencing for VFR acft is avbl. When twr closed ACTIVATE HIRL Rwy
   08L-26R, MIRL Rwy 17-35, ALS Rwy 08L, VASI Rwy 35, REIL Rwy 26R and Rwy 17-CTAF. NOTE: See Land and
   Hold Short Operations Section.
WEATHER DATA SOURCES: ASOS (719) 948-4206.
COMMUNICATIONS: CTAF 119.1   ATIS 125.25 (1300-0500Z‡)   UNICOM 122.95
   DENVER FSS (DEN) TF 1-800-WX-BRIEF. NOTAM FILE PUB.
   RCO 122.2 (DENVER FSS)
Ⓡ APP/DEP CON 120.1 (N/S) (1300-0500Z‡)
Ⓡ DENVER CENTER APP/DEP CON 128.375 (0500-1300Z‡)
   TOWER 119.1 (1300-0500Z‡)   GND CON 121.9
AIRSPACE: CLASS D svc effective 1300-0500Z‡ other times CLASS E.
RADIO AIDS TO NAVIGATION: NOTAM FILE PUB.
   (H) VORTACW 116.7   PUB   Chan 114   N38°17.66' W104°25.77'   251° 3.2 NM to fld. 4760/13E.
   MERTZ NDB (LOM) 302   PU   N38°17.04' W104°38.82'   076° 7.1 NM to fld.
   ARUBA NDB (MHW/LOM) 373   TF   N38°17.45' W104°21.30'   '258° 6.7 NM to fld.
   ILS 108.3   I-TFR   Rwy 26R.   LOM ARUBA NDB.
   ILS 109.5   I-PUB   Rwy 08L.   LOM MERTZ NDB. Unmonitored when twr closed.
   ASR (1300-0500Z‡)

LA JUNTA MUNI    (LHX)   3 N   UTC-7(-6DT)   N38°03.08' W103°30.64'                 WICHITA
4238   B   FUEL 100LL, JET A                                                        H-2D, L-6F
RWY 12-30: H8277X150 (ASPH)   S-50, D-65, DT-100                                     IAP
   RWY 30: 0.4% up.
RWY 08-26: H6852X100 (ASPH-RFSC)   S-50, D-70, DT-120   MIRL   1.9% up W
   RWY 08: REIL. VASI(V4L)—GA 3.0° TCH 45'. Road.   RWY 26: REIL. VASI(V2L)—GA 3.0° TCH 26'.
AIRPORT REMARKS: Attended continuously. Antelope on and invof arpt. Rwy 12-30 200' on each end of rwy is conc.
   center 50' is seal coated entire length. Rwy 08-26 MIRL operates dusk to dawn, for changes in ints call arpt
   manager 719-384-8407. ACTIVATE VASI Rwy 08 and Rwy 26 and REIL Rwy 26-CTAF.
WEATHER DATA SOURCES: ASOS 135.525 (719) 384-5961.
COMMUNICATIONS: CTAF/UNICOM 123.0
   DENVER FSS (DEN) TF 1-800-WX-BRIEF. NOTAM FILE LHX.
   RCO 122.6 (DENVER FSS)
   DENVER CENTER APP/DEP CON 133.4
RADIO AIDS TO NAVIGATION: NOTAM FILE LAA.
   LAMAR (H) VORTAC 116.9   LAA   Chan 116   N38°11.83' W102°41.26'   246° 39.9 NM to fld. 3950/12E.
   NDB (MHW) 239   LHX   N38°02.89' W103°37.27'   078° 5.2 NM to fld. NOTAM FILE LHX.
```

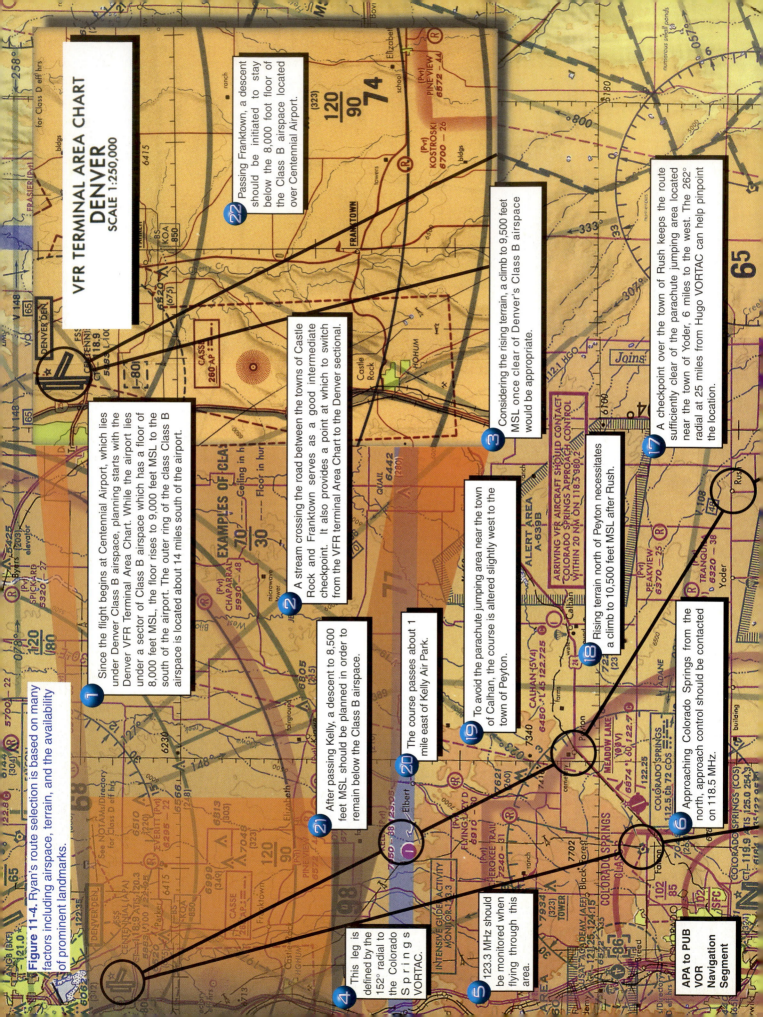

Figure 11-4. Ryan's route selection is based on many factors including airspace, terrain, and the availability of prominent landmarks.

VFR TERMINAL AREA CHART
DENVER
SCALE 1:250,000

22 Passing Franktown, a descent should be initiated to stay below the 8,000 foot floor of the Class B airspace located over Centennial Airport.

1 Since the flight begins at Centennial Airport, which lies under Denver Class B airspace, planning starts with the Denver VFR Terminal Area Chart. While the airport lies under a sector of Class B airspace which has a floor of 8,000 feet MSL, the floor rises to 9,000 feet MSL to the south of the airport. The outer ring of the class Class B airspace is located about 14 miles south of the airport.

2 A stream crossing the road between the towns of Castle Rock and Franktown serves as a good intermediate checkpoint. It also provides a point at which to switch from the VFR terminal Area Chart to the Denver sectional.

3 Considering the rising terrain, a climb to 9,500 feet MSL once clear of Denver's Class B airspace would be appropriate.

17 A checkpoint over the town of Rush keeps the route sufficiently clear of the parachute jumping area located near the town of Yoder, 6 miles to the west. The 262° radial at 25 miles from Hugo VORTAC can help pinpoint the location.

18 Rising terrain north of Peyton necessitates a climb to 10,500 feet MSL after Rush.

19 To avoid the parachute jumping area near the town of Calhan, the course is altered slightly west to the town of Peyton.

20 The course passes about 1 mile east of Kelly Air Park.

21 After passing Kelly, a descent to 8,500 feet MSL should be planned in order to remain below the Class B airspace.

6 Approaching Colorado Springs from the north, approach control should be contacted on 118.5 MHz.

4 This leg is defined by the 152° radial to the Colorado Springs VORTAC.

5 123.3 MHz should be monitored when flying through this area.

APA to PUB
VOR
Navigation
Segment

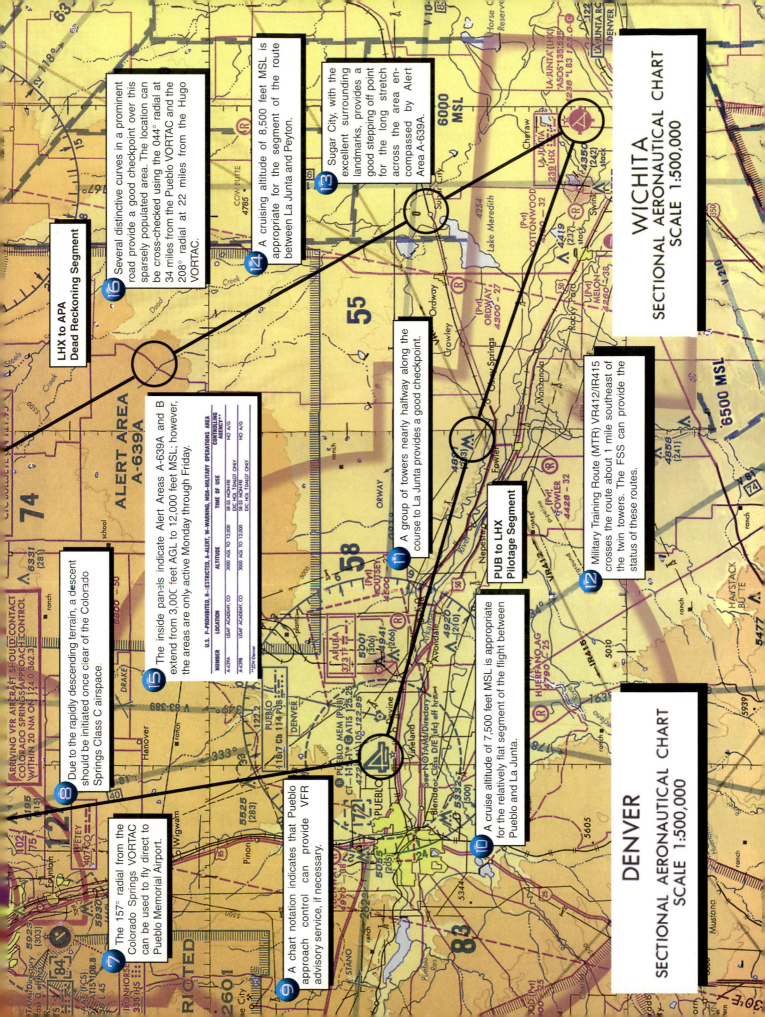

WICHITA
SECTIONAL AERONAUTICAL CHART
SCALE 1:500,000

DENVER
SECTIONAL AERONAUTICAL CHART
SCALE 1:500,000

LHX to APA
Dead Reckoning Segment

16 Several distinctive curves in a prominent road provide a good checkpoint over this sparsely populated area. The location can be cross-checked using the 044° radial at 34 miles from the Pueblo VORTAC and the 208° radial at 22 miles from the Hugo VORTAC.

14 A cruising altitude of 8,500 feet MSL is appropriate for the segment of the route between La Junta and Peyton.

13 Sugar City, with the excellent surrounding landmarks, provides a good stepping off point for the long stretch across the area encompassed by Alert Area A-639A.

ALERT AREA
A-639A

15 The inside panels indicate Alert Areas A-639A and B extend from 3,000 feet AGL to 12,000 feet MSL; however, the areas are only active Monday through Friday.

U.S. P–PROHIBITED, R—RESTRICTED, A–ALERT, W–WARNING, MOA–MILITARY OPERATIONS AREA			
NUMBER	LOCATION	ALTITUDE	TIME OF USE	CONTROLLING AGENCY**
A-639A	USAF ACADEMY, CO	3000 AGL TO 12,000	SR-SS MON-FRI	NO A/G
			EXC. HOL 1DAILY ONLY	
A-639B	USAF ACADEMY, CO	3000 AGL TO 12,000	SR-SS MON-FRI	NO A/G
			EXC. HOL 1DAILY ONLY	

8 Due to the rapidly descending terrain, a descent should be initiated once clear of the Colorado Springs Class C airspace.

ARRIVING VFR AIRCRAFT SHOULD CONTACT COLORADO SPRINGS APPROACH CONTROL WITHIN 20 NM ON 124.0 362.3

11 A group of towers nearly halfway along the course to La Junta provides a good checkpoint.

PUB to LHX
Pilotage Segment

12 Military Training Route (MTR) VR412/IR415 crosses the route about 1 mile southeast of the twin towers. The FSS can provide the status of these routes.

7 The 157° radial from the Colorado Springs VORTAC can be used to fly direct to Pueblo Memorial Airport.

9 A chart notation indicates that Pueblo approach control can provide VFR advisory service, if necessary.

10 A cruise altitude of 7,500 feet MSL is appropriate for the relatively flat segment of the flight between Pueblo and La Junta.

Friday, 0955 MDT Following his route selection, Ryan begins to fill out his navigation logs. Although he cannot complete many of the sections until he receives his weather briefing, he still fills in checkpoint, preliminary altitude, true course, distance, and radio frequency data as well as airplane related information such as fuel flow for the cruise portion of the flight. Since this flight contains multiple segments, Ryan decides to use a separate log for each segment. [Figure 11-5]

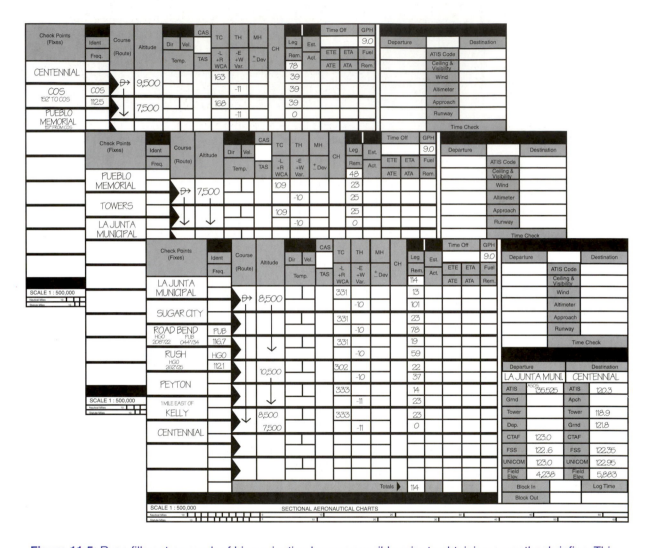

Figure 11-5. Ryan fills out as much of his navigation logs as possible prior to obtaining a weather briefing. This allows him to calculate an approximate time enroute which the briefer can use to provide the most appropriate forecast for Ryan's flight.

Friday, 1024 MDT Thinking ahead to tomorrow morning's weather briefing, Ryan uses his partially completed navigation logs to calculate an approximate no-wind time enroute. He uses the standard cruise speed of the airplane he anticipates taking on his flight, Piper Archer 8450B. At 120 knots, Ryan estimates that the total flight time for the 240 n.m. trip will be about 2 hours. Allowing approximately one-half hour for each stop, he calculates that he should arrive back at Centennial Airport approximately 3 hours after his departure.

Friday, 1116 MDT Since it has been nearly 18 hours since he last obtained a weather forecast for Saturday, Ryan logs on to the Internet and accesses the National Weather Service (NWS) homepage. After reviewing several reports and forecasts, he downloads a significant weather prog chart and the latest satellite photo. [Figure 11-6]

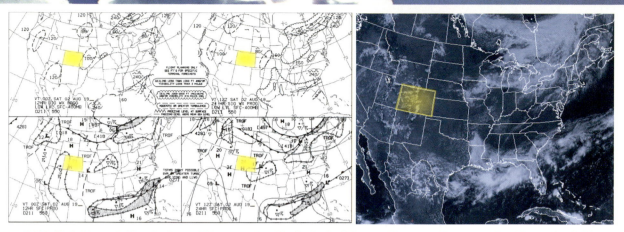

Figure 11-6. Both the satellite photo and the prog chart indicate that the weather over the area should remain stable over the next few days. At this point, Ryan concludes that conditions remain favorable for his planned cross-country on Saturday.

Friday, 1145 MDT Considering the TIBS recording, which called for afternoon convective activity, Ryan decides he should plan on completing his flight before noon on Saturday. Using his no-wind flight time calculations, he tentatively plans on a 0800 MDT (1400Z) departure from Centennial Airport. Picking up the phone, Ryan calls his flight instructor and informs her of his plans. Megan concurs that an 0800 departure is appropriate given the forecast for afternoon thunderstorms. During the conversation, Megan and Ryan agree to meet at 0700 the next day to review the latest weather and Ryan's completed navigation logs.

PREFLIGHT WEATHER BRIEFING

Saturday, 0630 MDT In the interest of procuring the most up-to-date information, Ryan waits until an hour and a half before his departure to obtain a preflight weather briefing. Prior to calling the FSS to request a standard briefing, Ryan makes sure that he has his route data and a blank weather log handy. After identifying himself as a student pilot flying VFR, Ryan provides the briefer with the type and registration number of his airplane, his approximate cruising altitude, and estimated time of departure. An excerpt from Ryan's briefing is shown in figure 11-7.

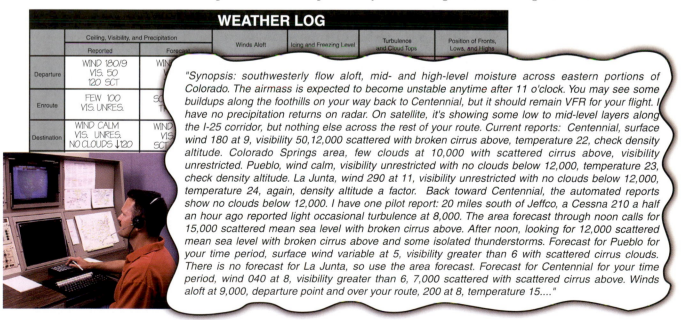

WEATHER LOG

	Ceiling, Visibility, and Precipitation		Winds Aloft	Icing and Freezing Level	Turbulence and Cloud Tops	Position of Fronts, Lows, and Highs
	Reported	Forecast				
Departure	WIND 180/9 VIS. 50 120 SCT	WIN				
Enroute	FEW 100 VIS. UNRES.	S				
Destination	WIND CALM VIS. UNRES. NO CLOUDS ↓120	WIND VIS SCT				

"Synopsis: southwesterly flow aloft, mid- and high-level moisture across eastern portions of Colorado. The airmass is expected to become unstable anytime after 11 o'clock. You may see some buildups along the foothills on your way back to Centennial, but it should remain VFR for your flight. I have no precipitation returns on radar. On satellite, it's showing some low to mid-level layers along the I-25 corridor, but nothing else across the rest of your route. Current reports: Centennial, surface wind 180 at 9, visibility 50, 12,000 scattered with broken cirrus above, temperature 22, check density altitude. Colorado Springs area, few clouds at 10,000 with scattered cirrus above, visibility unrestricted. Pueblo, wind calm, visibility unrestricted with no clouds below 12,000, temperature 23, check density altitude. La Junta, wind 290 at 11, visibility unrestricted with no clouds below 12,000, temperature 24, again, density altitude a factor. Back toward Centennial, the automated reports show no clouds below 12,000. I have one pilot report: 20 miles south of Jeffco, a Cessna 210 a half an hour ago reported light occasional turbulence at 8,000. The area forecast through noon calls for 15,000 scattered mean sea level with broken cirrus above. After noon, looking for 12,000 scattered mean sea level with broken cirrus above and some isolated thunderstorms. Forecast for Pueblo for your time period, surface wind variable at 5, visibility greater than 6 with scattered cirrus clouds. There is no forecast for La Junta, so use the area forecast. Forecast for Centennial for your time period, wind 040 at 8, visibility greater than 6, 7,000 scattered with scattered cirrus above. Winds aloft at 9,000, departure point and over your route, 200 at 8, temperature 15...."

Figure 11-7. This excerpt from Ryan's preflight weather briefing indicates that current conditions along the route are generally good with scattered clouds at 12,000 feet and visibilities 20 miles or greater. The forecast shows no adverse weather except for some thundershower activity in the afternoon. Winds over the route at 9,000 feet are expected to be from 200° at 8 knots. Ryan summarizes and records the briefer's comments on his weather log for future reference.

During the briefing, the FSS specialist informs Ryan that the Runway 8 Right/26 Left at Pueblo Memorial is closed. Otherwise, no other NOTAMs affect his route of flight. An inquiry about special use airspace in the vicinity of the route reveals that the MTRs in southeastern Colorado will not be active today, however, the La Veta Low MOA, located 20 n.m. southwest of Pueblo and well clear of Ryan's planned course, will be in use until 2200Z. Following a quick review of his notes, Ryan thanks the briefer, and hangs up with the intention of calling back later to file his flight plan.

COMPLETING THE NAVIGATION LOG

Saturday, 0638 MDT With the information provided by the briefer, Ryan determines that, although the winds at 9,000 feet are not entirely favorable, a higher cruising altitude could place him in the vicinity of the scattered clouds reported at 12,000 feet. Settling on an initial cruising altitude of 9,500, Ryan finishes the navigation log by computing wind correction angles, magnetic headings, the time, fuel and distance to climb, cruise performance figures, groundspeed, estimated time enroute, estimated time of arrival, and the total fuel requirements. He also calculates takeoff distance, and landing roll for the enroute and destination airports. [Figure 11-8] After determining his fuel requirements, Ryan performs a weight and balance calculation on Piper 8450B. Without passengers, and little baggage, the airplane is well within its weight and CG limits.

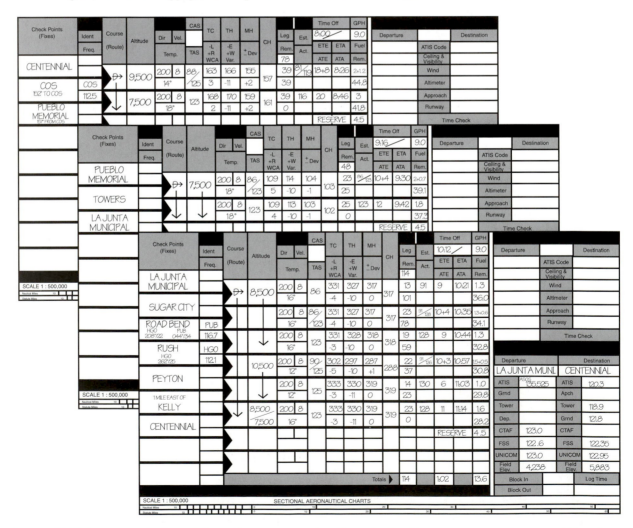

Figure 11-8. Ryan uses the latest information to ensure that his navigation logs are as accurate as possible prior to takeoff.

FLIGHT PLAN

Saturday, 0706 MDT Upon completion of his navigation logs, Ryan reviews the results with Megan. Neither Ryan nor his flight instructor find anything which would cause him to change, delay, or cancel his flight. Nonetheless, she cautions him to be particularly wary of any cumulus clouds building along his route. After assuring her that he will pay close attention to changes in the weather, Ryan proceeds to fill out his flight plan. [Figure 11-9]

FLIGHT PLAN

1. TYPE	2. AIRCRAFT IDENTIFICATION	3. AIRCRAFT TYPE/ SPECIAL EQUIPMENT	4. TRUE AIRSPEED	5. DEPARTURE POINT	6. DEPARTURE TIME		7. CRUISING ALTITUDE
X VFR IFR DVFR	N8450B	PA28/A	125 KNOTS	APA	PROPOSED (Z) 1400	ACTUAL (Z)	9,500

8. ROUTE OF FLIGHT
D→ PUB D→LHX D→

9. DESTINATION (Name of airport and city)	10 EST. TIME ENROUTE		11.REMARKS
APA	HOURS 3	MINUTES 14	STOPOVERS AT PUB (+30), LHX (+30)

12. FUEL ON BOARD		13. ALTERNATE AIRPORT (S)	14. PILOT'S NAME, ADDRESS. TEL. NO. & AIRCRAFT HOME BASE	15. NUMBER ABOARD
HOURS 5	MINUTES 20	N/A	R. ARMSTRONG, 11 TRANQUILITY LN., EAGLE CO. (956) 720-1969; CENTENNIAL	1

16. COLOR OF AIRCRAFT	17. DESTINATION CONTACT/TELEPHONE (OPTIONAL)
BROWN / WHITE	N. ARMSTRONG, (956) 720-1969

CLOSE VFR FLIGHT PLAN WITH ___DENVER___ FSS ON ARRIVAL

AIRCRAFT EQUIPMENT SUFFIXES		
NO DME X - No transponder T - Transponder with no Mode C U - Transponder with Mode C **DME** D - No transponder B - Transponder with no Mode C	A - Transponder with Mode C **AREA NAVIGATION (RNAV)** Y - LORAN, VOR/DME, or INS with no transponder C - LORAN, VOR/DME, or INS, transponder with no Mode C I - LORAN, VOR/DME, or INS, transponder with Mode C **ADVANCED RNAV with Transponder and Mode C (If an aircraft is unable to operate with a transponder and/or**	Mode C, it will revert to the appropriate code listed to the left under Area Navigation.) G - GPS/GNSS equipped aircraft with enroute, terminal, and GPS approach capability. R - Required Navigational Performance. (Denotes capability to operate in RNP designated airspace and routes) W - Reduced Vertical Separation Minima (RVSM)

Figure 11-9. Most of the information used to complete Ryan's flight plan is taken from his navigation logs.

Saturday, 0713 MDT Although there are several ways to file his flight plan, Ryan does so by reading it over the phone to an FSS specialist. This strategy provides an opportunity to check for any significant changes in the weather since his preflight briefing. After the briefer confirms that the weather is progressing as forecast, Ryan hangs up and makes a note to activate his flight plan on departure.

PREFLIGHT INSPECTION

Saturday, 0719 MDT Prior to collecting his supplies and walking to the airplane, Ryan performs a personal preflight using the I'm Safe Checklist. Determining that he is fit to fly, Ryan proceeds to check the aircraft logbooks to ensure that the plane has been maintained in accordance with the FARs. The owner or operator is primarily responsible for maintaining the aircraft in an airworthy condition. Since a satisfactory review indicates that the **airworthiness certificate** for the airplane is still valid, he continues to the airplane to complete his preflight inspection.

An airworthiness certificate is not valid unless the aircraft is maintained according to FARs.

The owner or operator is promarily responsible for maintaining an aircraft in an airworthy condition.

During the preflight inspection the pilot in command is responsibe for determining that the aircraft is safe for flight.

Saturday, 0725 MDT As pilot in command, Ryan is responsible for determining that the aircraft is safe for flight. During the preflight inspection, Ryan checks the aircraft components in a logical sequence using the appropriate checklist. He closely examines the fuel samples to check for contamination and

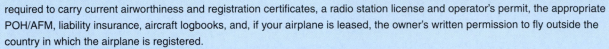

Crossing the Border

Can you envision flying along the Canadian Rockies? Have you always wanted to cruise over the Baja? Do you have an irresistible desire to island hop in the Caribbean? At one time or another, you may find the lure of international travel too great to ignore. While expanding your horizons beyond the U.S. border is not necessarily difficult, a thorough knowledge of customs and flight plan requirements is essential. Some commonly asked questions and the respective answers are shown below.

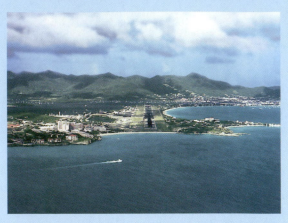

What are the pilot requirements to fly internationally?
Although the requirements may vary from country to country, generally you need to hold at least a private pilot certificate. Upon landing, you should be prepared to present customs officials with your pilot certificate, current medical certificate, proof of citizenship, and pilot logbook.

What are the airplane requirements to fly internationally?
In most cases, the aircraft you fly over the border must be equipped with a two-way radio and Mode-C transponder. You also are usually required to carry current airworthiness and registration certificates, a radio station license and operator's permit, the appropriate POH/AFM, liability insurance, aircraft logbooks, and, if your airplane is leased, the owner's written permission to fly outside the country in which the airplane is registered.

What type of flight plan do I have to file?
If you are flying VFR, you should check the Defense Visual Flight Rules (DVFR) block of the FAA flight plan. Also, you should include a request for customs services in the remarks section of your flight plan. In addition, if you are entering the United States, you should include the estimated time of ADIZ penetration on your flight plan.

Can I land at any airport in a foreign country? How about when I return to the United States?
On your initial flight to another country, you normally are required to land at a designated Airport of Entry (AOE). These airports generally have a customs facility at which you can be processed through immigration. Similarly, when you enter the United States, you typically must land at an airport which offers customs services.

Where can I find additional information about flying internationally?
Several sources are available which offer further insight into the specific requirements for flights across the border. For detailed customs information regarding U.S. entry procedures, you can refer to the pamphlet, *Customs Guide for Private Flyers*, which is available from the U.S. Customs Service. Since procedures for entry into foreign countries vary considerably, you should contact the individual country for details.

For general flight procedure information, you should refer to FAR Part 99. You can obtain expanded information for popular destinations such as the Bahamas by consulting any of the numerous commercially produced books, videos, and flight planning kits.

verifies that the airplane has been serviced with the correct grade and amount of fuel for the flight. Ryan is careful to complete the aircraft preflight inspection for the first flight of the day by using a through and systematic means recommended by the manufacturer.

 An aircraft preflight inspection for the first flight of the day, should be accomplished by a through and systematic means recommended by the manufacturer.

Saturday, 0730 MDT When checking the oil quantity, Ryan notices that it is one quart low. After adding the needed oil, Ryan stows an extra quart on board in case he needs to add oil at an intermediate stop. As he continues his inspection, he checks for damage or obstructions caused by animals, birds, or insects.

Saturday, 0738 MDT As Ryan moves to the front of the aircraft, he checks the nosewheel and notices that the nose gear strut seems to be underinflated. The checklist indicates that the normal extension should be 3-1/4 inches, but Ryan estimates that it's 2 inches at the most. He makes note of the discrepancy and finishes his preflight inspection with otherwise satisfactory results.

 Always perform a walkaround inspection prior to every flight. During your preflight, you should use a written checklist to ensure that all necessary items are checked in a logical sequence.

Saturday, 0743 MDT Ryan heads to the maintenance hanger, finds the mechanic on duty, and informs him of the problem. Although the mechanic suspects that the strut probably just needs to be serviced, he indicates that he will check the strut thoroughly and let Ryan know if it needs more extensive maintenance. If it only needs servicing, the mechanic estimates that the airplane should be ready to go in about 20 minutes.

Saturday, 0745 MDT Ryan walks next door to the flight school and finds his instructor. After discussing the situation, Ryan and Megan agree that a delay of less than an hour is acceptable. Anything longer, however, would require a reevaluation of the situation, since an excessive delay could place Ryan at a greater risk of encountering thunderstorm activity during his cross-country flight.

Saturday, 0800 MDT Arriving back at his airplane, Ryan meets the mechanic just as he finishes servicing the nose strut. The mechanic confirms that the strut is now serviced to acceptable limits and does not appear to be leaking. After a satisfactory reinspection of the nosewheel and strut, Ryan removes the chocks and walks around the right wing to the cockpit.

Saturday, 0807 MDT Settling into the pilot's seat, Ryan organizes his materials to ensure the utmost in efficiency. He double checks to make sure all his documents, charts, and equipment appropriate for the flight are aboard and readily accessible. Finally, he adjusts his seat to a comfortable position in preparation for the adventure which lies ahead.

SUMMARY CHECKLIST

✓ You can decide to change, delay, or cancel a portion or all of your flight at any point during the flight planning process.

✓ For detailed planning, you should use sectional and VFR Terminal Area charts.

✓ You should calculate an approximate no-wind time enroute in order to provide the weather briefer with estimated times of arrival at airports along your route.

✓ As part of your preflight activities, you should always conduct a personal evaluation of your fitness to fly.

✓ Unless the aircraft is maintained according to FARs, an aircraft's airworthiness certificate is not valid.

✓ Prior to every flight, you should perform a walkaround inspection using a written checklist to ensure that all necessary items are checked in a logical sequence.

KEY TERMS

Flight Planning Process

Airworthiness Certificate

QUESTIONS

Refer to figure 11-3 to answer questions 1 through 4.

1. How long is Runway 17 at Pueblo Memorial Airport?

2. What is the slope of Runway 17 at Pueblo Memorial Airport?

3. What type of fuel is available at La Junta Municipal Airport?

4. What hazard may be present on or in the vicinity of La Junta Municipal Airport?

Refer to figure 11-4 to answer questions 5 through 9.

5. What frequency should you use to activate your flight plan after departure from Centennial Airport?

6. What is the lowest cruising altitude you could fly eastbound over Colorado Springs Airport to avoid the Class C airspace?

7. What is the height of the Class D airspace surrounding Butts Army Airfield (8 n.m. south-southwest of Colorado Springs)?

8. What is the significance of the notation, 6000 MSL, shown approximately 10 n.m. north of La Junta Municipal Airport?

9. If you had to divert to Meadow Lake Airport (3 n.m. east of the Colorado Springs VORTAC), what frequency would you use to obtain an airport advisory? How long is the runway at Meadow Lake?

10. In which reference source can you find information regarding parachute jumping areas?

11. Given the planned fuel flow of 9.0 g.p.h. and assuming a groundspeed of 120 knots, how far could Ryan fly on the 4.5 gallon fuel reserve?

12. True/False. An airworthiness certificate is always valid unless it is revoked by the aircraft manufacturer.

SECTION B
THE FLIGHT

Courtesy of NASA

I feel that we are on the brink of an area of expansion of knowledge about ourselves and our surroundings that is beyond description or comprehension at this time....Our efforts today and what we've done so far are but small building blocks on a very huge pyramid to come.... Knowledge begets knowledge. The more I see, the more impressed I am not with how much we know but with how tremendous the areas are that are as yet unexplored.

— U. S. Marine Corps Lt. Col. John H. Glenn, Jr., addressing a joint session of Congress six days after orbiting the earth three times in a Mercury space capsule, the *Friendship 7*

While *Friendship 7's* extraordinary journey would have been impossible without countless hours of preflight preparations, it was the flight which made headlines. And it was John Glenn, the pilot, who was largely responsible for transforming the dream into reality. Like a bird, it is in flight where the pilot truly flourishes. Whether in space, or closer to home, the skill and judgment of the pilot ultimately determines the success of every flight.

In this section, you will follow Ryan as he flies the cross-country described in Section A, *The Flight Planning Process*. To help you keep track of his position in relation to the checkpoints and other landmarks, the charts, figures, and photographs are oriented with the direction of flight. As you will see, not everything on Ryan's flight goes according to plan, yet in the end, Ryan knows himself, his airplane, and the world of aviation a little better.

APA TO PUB

① **Saturday, 0818 MDT** Ryan starts the Archer's engine following the appropriate checklist procedures. After a check of the engine instruments, which confirms that the powerplant is running smoothly and within limits, Ryan brings the avionics to life by turning on the radio master switch. Then, working from his charts and navigation log, Ryan methodically sets his radio frequencies. [Figure 11-10]

② **0825 MDT** Setting his audio control panel switches to the proper position, Ryan listens and records the ATIS broadcast. When setting his altimeter to 30.20, Ryan cross-checks the displayed altitude with the field elevation. Next, Ryan switches his #1 radio to tower frequency and sets the Colorado Springs Approach frequency, 118.5, as the standby.

③ **0827 MDT** After switching his audio control panel, Ryan calls for, and receives, taxi instructions. Ryan releases his brakes, checks the area around his airplane clear, then adds power to begin taxiing. As the airplane begins to roll, he reduces the power and tests the brakes for proper operation. Readjusting the power, he turns out of the parking spot, assumes a safe taxi speed, and sets the flight controls to the appropriate position considering the relative wind direction. During his taxi, Ryan checks for proper operation of instruments such as the magnetic compass, directional gyro, and turn coordinator.

④ **0833 MDT** Approaching the north end of the taxiway, Ryan selects a suitable spot in the runup area and positions the nose of his airplane into the wind, as shown by the nearby wind sock. Following a satisfactory runup check, Ryan double checks that the materials needed for the trip are readily available.

⑤ **0836 MDT** Assured that everything is in order, Ryan taxis to the hold short line for Runway 17 Left and calls the tower using his #1 com radio. After receiving clearance, he notes the time, turns his transponder to ALT, flips on his landing light, and increases power to taxi onto the runway. Adding power to maximum, the aircraft rolls down the runway; at approximately 55 knots, Ryan increases back pressure and the airplane becomes airborne. Adjusting the nose attitude to maintain a normal climb speed, Ryan begins his climbout. At about 500 feet above the runway, he turns to 157°, the first heading listed on his navigation log.

⑥ **0838 MDT** As he reaches 6,500 feet, Ryan spots the town of Castle Rock in the distance and estimates that he is slightly right of course, probably due to the heading he held immediately after takeoff. He clears the area to his left and turns to intercept his plotted course.

⑦ **0840 MDT** After referring to his nav log for his departure time, Ryan switches his #2 com radio frequencies and calls FSS to activate his flight plan. Passing through 7,300 feet, Ryan spots the road leading west out of Franktown. Visually following the road westward, he identifies the second stream and estimates that he will be crossing over the road and stream intersection shortly. Confirming that he is on course, he turns off his landing light, then switches from the VFR terminal area chart to his sectional chart. Since he is clear of Centennial's Class D airspace, he switches his #1 com radio to monitor Colorado Springs Approach and his #2 com radio to 123.3 to keep track of any glider activity. With the two standby com frequencies open, he sets 120.1 (Pueblo Approach) in his #1 radio and 125.25 (Pueblo ATIS) in his #2 radio. With his attention directed to his instrument panel, Ryan notices his #2 CDI centering, putting him on the 332° radial from the Colorado Springs VOR-TAC, right on course.

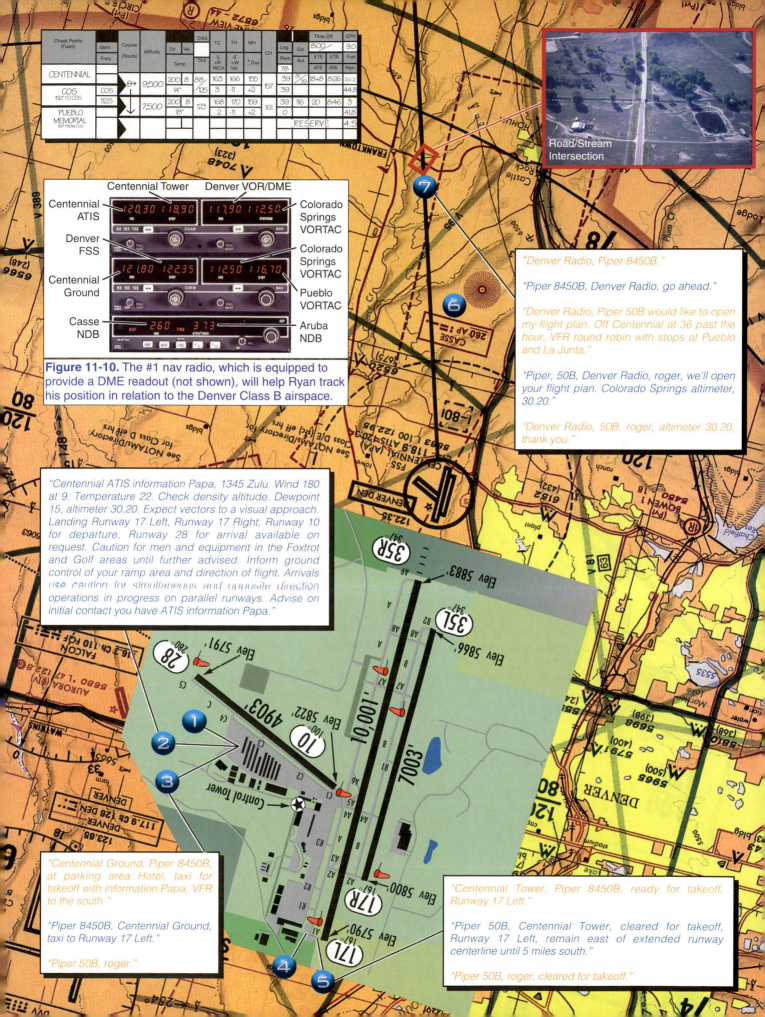

Check Points (Fixes)	Ident Freq.	Course (Route)	Altitude	Dir. Vel.		CAS TAS	TC	TH	MH	CH	Leg Rem. Act.	Est.	ETE ATE	ETA ATA	GPH Fuel Rem.
				Temp.									Time Off 8:00		9.0
CENTENNIAL		⊕↑	9,500	200 8 14°	88 /125	163	166	155	157	78 39	39 81/ 119	18+8	8:26	2+12 44.8
COS 152 TO COS 112.5	COS	↓	7,500	200 8 18°	123 2	168	170	159	161	39	116	20	8:46	3 41.8
PUEBLO MEMORIAL 157 FROM COS		▶									RESERVE			4.5

Figure 11-10. The #1 nav radio, which is equipped to provide a DME readout (not shown), will help Ryan track his position in relation to the Denver Class B airspace.

Labels on radio stack: Centennial Tower, Denver VOR/DME, Centennial ATIS, Colorado Springs VORTAC, Denver FSS, Colorado Springs VORTAC, Centennial Ground, Pueblo VORTAC, Casse NDB, Aruba NDB

Road/Stream Intersection

"Denver Radio, Piper 8450B."

"Piper 8450B, Denver Radio, go ahead."

"Denver Radio, Piper 50B would like to open my flight plan. Off Centennial at 36 past the hour, VFR round robin with stops at Pueblo and La Junta."

"Piper, 50B, Denver Radio, roger, we'll open your flight plan. Colorado Springs altimeter, 30.20."

"Denver Radio, 50B, roger, altimeter 30.20; thank you."

"Centennial ATIS information Papa, 1345 Zulu. Wind 180 at 9. Temperature 22. Check density altitude. Dewpoint 15, altimeter 30.20. Expect vectors to a visual approach. Landing Runway 17 Left, Runway 17 Right, Runway 10 for departure, Runway 28 for arrival available on request. Caution for men and equipment in the Foxtrot and Golf areas until further advised. Inform ground control of your ramp area and direction of flight. Arrivals use caution for simultaneous and opposite direction operations in progress on parallel runways. Advise on initial contact you have ATIS information Papa."

"Centennial Ground, Piper 8450B, at parking area Hotel, taxi for takeoff with information Papa, VFR to the south."

"Piper 8450B, Centennial Ground, taxi to Runway 17 Left."

"Piper 50B, roger."

"Centennial Tower, Piper 8450B, ready for takeoff, Runway 17 Left."

"Piper 50B, Centennial Tower, cleared for takeoff, Runway 17 Left, remain east of extended runway centerline until 5 miles south."

"Piper 50B, roger, cleared for takeoff."

8 **0847 MDT** As he tracks to the station, Ryan glances at the DME readout in time to see it change to read 30.3 n.m. from the Denver VOR. Realizing that he has flown out from under the furthest reaches of the Denver Class B airspace, Ryan decides to switch the frequency in his #1 nav to the Colorado Springs VORTAC. Seconds after dialing in 112.5, the DME displays the distance to COS as 21.8 n.m. After identifying the station, he sets the associated CDI to his inbound course and watches the needle center. As a backup, he leaves his #2 nav radio set on COS.

9 **0854 MDT** Ryan lowers the nose of his aircraft and retrims for cruise flight as he reaches 9,500 feet. Scanning to the east, he notices a paved airstrip about 4 to 5 miles off the left side. Looking at his sectional, he identifies the north/south runway as Kelly Air Park, which helps confirm that his VOR tracking is keeping him on course. As his speed increases, he adjusts the power to maintain his planned airspeed. By this time, the DME shows that he is 16.5 miles from the Colorado Springs VORTAC. Given that the station is located about 8 miles north of the airport, Ryan figures that he should contact approach control when he is about 12 miles from VORTAC. He estimates that he will be at that point in about 2 minutes at his calculated groundspeed.

10 **0856 MDT** About 20 minutes after takeoff, as he expected, Ryan approaches 20 miles from the Colorado Springs Airport. After checking that his audio panel switches are in the correct position, he contacts Colorado Springs Approach.

11 **0857 MDT** Ryan sets the code in his transponder and soon receives a response from approach control. As he turns toward 170°, Ryan continues to scan outside the cockpit and spots 3 radio towers — 2 close together, and a lone tower on a higher ridge. He correctly identifies the lone tower as the VFR checkpoint depicted about 7 miles northwest of the Colorado Springs VORTAC.

12 **0900 MDT** Continuing on a heading of 170°, Ryan realizes that he will not pass directly over the VORTAC. Watching his DME, he notes the mileage readout beginning to increase after a continual decrease since picking up the signal soon after takeoff. Checking the CDI, he notices that the TO/FROM flag is now showing a FROM indication. Understanding that he has passed abeam the station, he dials his planned outbound radial, 157°, into both VOR indicators. Although the needles do not center, he will have them set to resume course when released by approach control.

13 **0904 MDT** Ryan passes almost directly over the top of the Colorado Springs Airport still flying on a heading of 170°. The radio chatter continues as the approach controllers work to sequence traffic on visual approaches to the airport as well as coordinate transient aircraft such as Ryan's. A few miles ahead, Ryan begins to pick out Interstate 25 heading southeasterly. Checking his chart, he determines that he will be clear of the Class C airspace about the time his flight path crosses the highway.

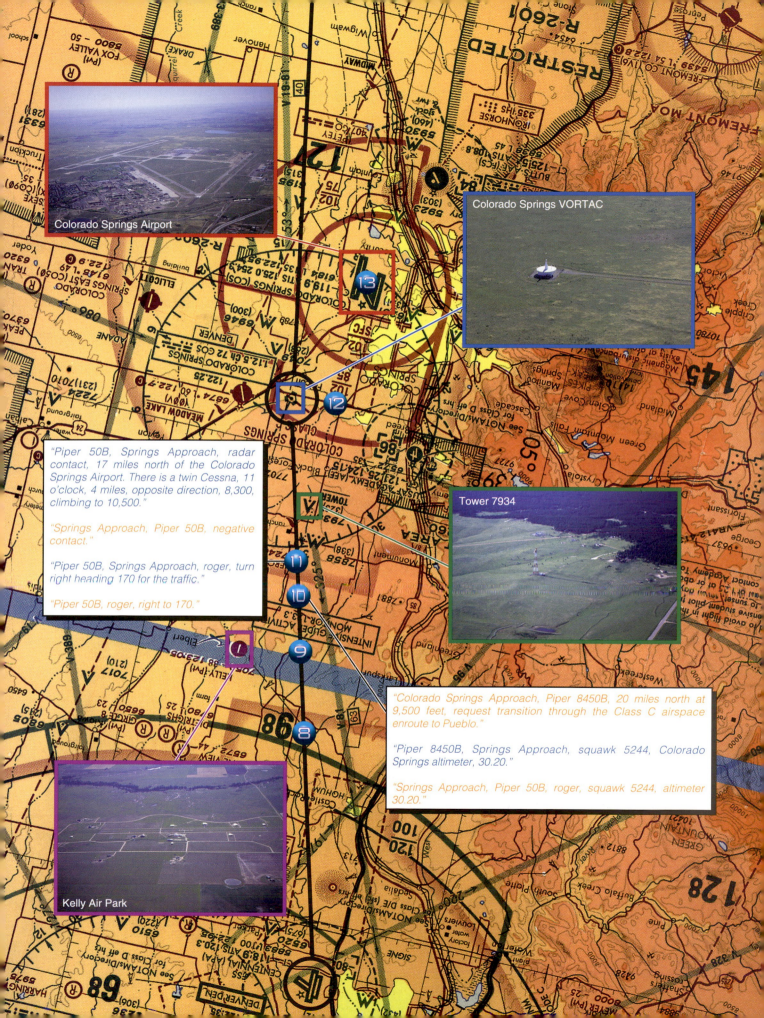

Colorado Springs Airport

Colorado Springs VORTAC

Tower 7934

Kelly Air Park

"Piper 50B, Springs Approach, radar contact, 17 miles north of the Colorado Springs Airport. There is a twin Cessna, 11 o'clock, 4 miles, opposite direction, 8,300, climbing to 10,500."

"Springs Approach, Piper 50B, negative contact."

"Piper 50B, Springs Approach, roger, turn right heading 170 for the traffic."

"Piper 50B, roger, right to 170."

"Colorado Springs Approach, Piper 8450B, 20 miles north at 9,500 feet, request transition through the Class C airspace enroute to Pueblo."

"Piper 8450B, Springs Approach, squawk 5244, Colorado Springs altimeter, 30.20."

"Springs Approach, Piper 50B, roger, squawk 5244, altimeter 30.20."

14 **0905 MDT** Thinking ahead to his arrival in Pueblo, Ryan switches to the standby frequency set in his #2 com radio, Pueblo ATIS. Although somewhat weak, the broadcast is easily readable. Listening to the broadcast completely through twice, Ryan verifies that he correctly recorded the pertinent data. Putting down his pencil, he tunes 119.1, Pueblo Tower, as the primary frequency into his #2 com radio.

15 **0908 MDT** As he passes over I-25, Ryan's DME reads 18.7 miles from the Colorado Springs VORTAC. With Colorado Springs behind him, Ryan decides to switch his #1 nav radio to 116.7, the Pueblo VORTAC. Although the station is not located at the field, Ryan figures that the distance to the VORTAC should be only 2 or 3 miles further than that to the airport. In addition, since he is no longer on his planned route, DME from Pueblo may prove more useful than distance from Colorado Springs.

16 **0909 MDT** To help pinpoint his current position, Ryan twists the OBS for his #1 nav radio and watches the CDI center to indicate that he is on the 313° radial from the Pueblo VORTAC. Immediately thereafter, Colorado Springs Approach hands him off to Pueblo Approach.

17 **0910 MDT** Switching to the standby frequency in his #1 com radio, Ryan contacts Pueblo Approach. In response to the request from approach control, Ryan reaches over and sets 4344 in his transponder then pushes the ident button. While waiting for approach control to call back, Ryan sets the standby frequency in his #1 com radio to Pueblo Ground, 121.9.

18 **0913 MDT** Pueblo approach issues Ryan arrival instructions as he continues to fly on a southerly heading. Quickly, he turns on his landing light and retards the throttle to begin a descent out of 9,500 feet for the Pueblo traffic pattern altitude of 5,700 feet. Next, Ryan determines that attempting to regain his plotted course would take him well out of his way. With I-25 now to his left, he roughly estimates that a turn to 130° will take him toward the airport. A quick plot refines the course to 133°, to which he turns during his descent.

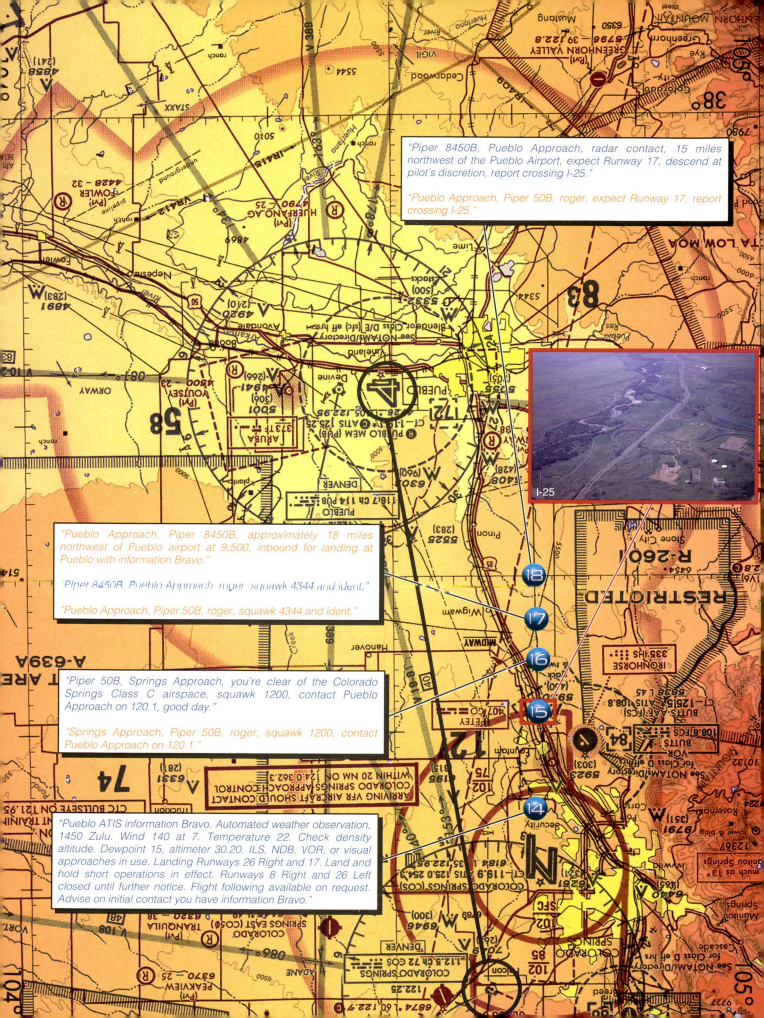

"Piper 8450B, Pueblo Approach, radar contact, 15 miles northwest of the Pueblo Airport, expect Runway 17, descend at pilot's discretion, report crossing I-25."

"Pueblo Approach, Piper 50B, roger, expect Runway 17, report crossing I-25."

I-25

"Pueblo Approach, Piper 8450B, approximately 18 miles northwest of Pueblo airport at 9,500, inbound for landing at Pueblo with information Bravo."

"Piper 8450B, Pueblo Approach, roger, squawk 4344 and ident."

"Pueblo Approach, Piper 50B, roger, squawk 4344 and ident."

"Piper 50B, Springs Approach, you're clear of the Colorado Springs Class C airspace, squawk 1200, contact Pueblo Approach on 120.1, good day."

"Springs Approach, Piper 50B, roger, squawk 1200, contact Pueblo Approach on 120.1."

"Pueblo ATIS information Bravo. Automated weather observation, 1450 Zulu. Wind 140 at 7. Temperature 22. Check density altitude. Dewpoint 15, altimeter 30.20. ILS, NDB, VOR, or visual approaches in use. Landing Runways 26 Right and 17. Land and hold short operations in effect. Runways 8 Right and 26 Left closed until further notice. Flight following available on request. Advise on initial contact you have information Bravo."

19 **0916 MDT** Looking down, Ryan sees a four-lane highway crossing his flight path. Heading southeasterly with his DME showing 11.1 miles from the VORTAC, he confirms he is over I-25 and calls Pueblo Approach.

20 **0917 MDT** Glancing at his #2 com radio, Ryan confirms that Pueblo Tower is set as the primary frequency. After adjusting the switches on his audio control panel, Ryan calls the tower. Descending through 7,500 feet, Ryan checks his chart to help him locate the airport. Looking east of the city, he locates the airport off the nose of his airplane. Scanning outside the cockpit, he spots a two lane road running northeast out of the city, and further in the distance, what appears to be the approach end of Runway 17. Realizing that he still has quite a bit of altitude to lose, Ryan confirms that his carburetor heat is on, and reduces power to increase his rate of descent.

21 **0919 MDT** Estimating that he is about 2 1/2 miles from the airport, Ryan turns to set up for a base leg to Runway 17. Continuing his descent, Ryan calls the tower.

Reaching base leg, Ryan performs his landing checklist. After ensuring that his airspeed is below V_{FE}, he lowers 25° of flaps and retrims the airplane.

22 **0921 MDT** Checking for traffic on final approach and finding it clear, Ryan initiates a descending right turn to intercept the extended runway centerline. Upon rolling out, Ryan checks his approach airspeed, makes a slight pitch adjustment and retrims to maintain his rate of descent. Confirming the runway number and checking the wind sock, Ryan concentrates on the last few hundred feet of his approach. About 10 seconds after crossing the runway numbers, he flares, floats briefly, then settles onto the runway.

23 **0924 MDT** As he applies the brakes during his rollout, Ryan hears the tower issue additional instructions. A fleeting sense of uneasiness washes over him as he realizes that he has no idea where the Bravo taxiway is located. The feeling quickly passes however, when he spots the yellow taxiway sign just ahead on his left.

24 **0925 MDT** After coming to a stop on the taxiway, Ryan turns off his landing light and completes his post-landing checklist. Then, he switches his #1 radio to ground control, positions his audio control panel switches, and calls for taxi clearance. As he taxis to the FBO, Ryan reflects on his flight so far. He feels good about handling the vectors from Colorado Springs Approach and the unexpected handoff to Pueblo Approach, all of which resulted in the requirement for some quick in-flight adjustments. However, he had initially misjudged his needed descent rate after passing Colorado Springs, and he had completely forgotten to study the Pueblo airport diagram so he would be familiar with the taxiway location. Even though everything did not go as planned, all things considered, he is feeling fairly good about his flight as he parks his airplane on the flight line in front of the FBO.

After completing his shutdown checklist, Ryan collects his flight planning materials, performs a postflight walkaround, and proceeds inside. Informing the FBO personnel that no service is required and that he will be leaving in about 30 minutes, he walks to the flight planning room and calls the FSS for an update on the weather.

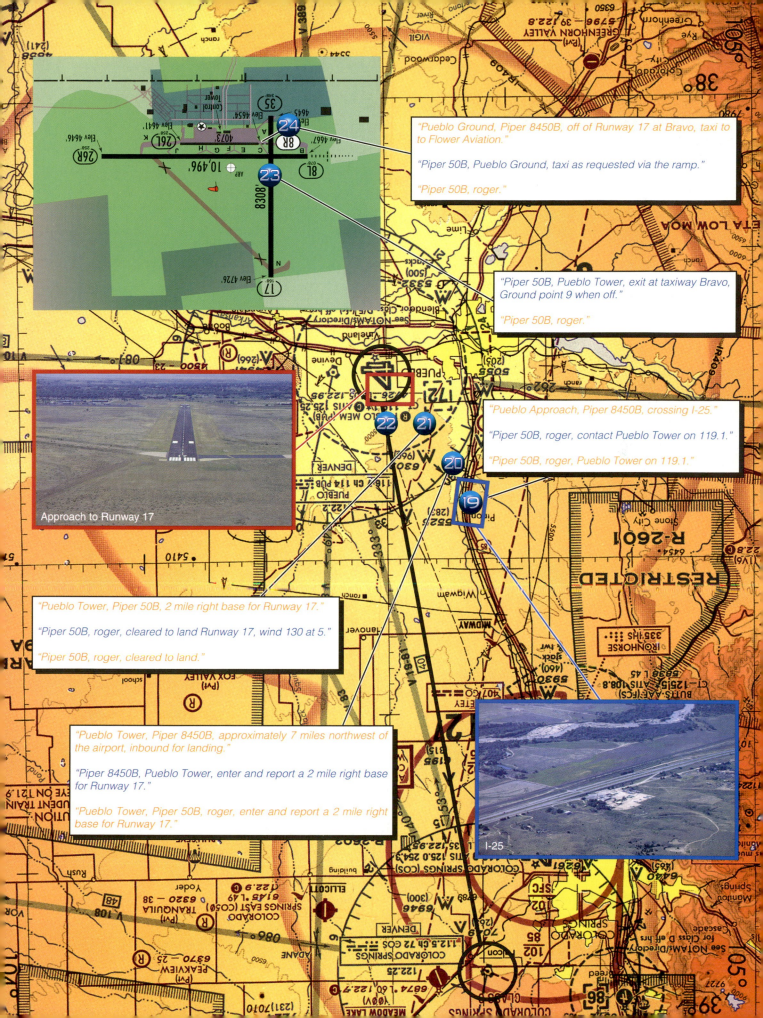

"Pueblo Ground, Piper 8450B, off of Runway 17 at Bravo, taxi to Flower Aviation."

"Piper 50B, Pueblo Ground, taxi as requested via the ramp."

"Piper 50B, roger."

"Piper 50B, Pueblo Tower, exit at taxiway Bravo, Ground point 9 when off."

"Piper 50B, roger."

"Pueblo Approach, Piper 8450B, crossing I-25."

"Piper 50B, roger, contact Pueblo Tower on 119.1."

"Piper 50B, roger, Pueblo Tower on 119.1."

Approach to Runway 17

"Pueblo Tower, Piper 50B, 2 mile right base for Runway 17."

"Piper 50B, roger, cleared to land Runway 17, wind 130 at 5."

"Piper 50B, roger, cleared to land."

"Pueblo Tower, Piper 8450B, approximately 7 miles northwest of the airport, inbound for landing."

"Piper 8450B, Pueblo Tower, enter and report a 2 mile right base for Runway 17."

"Pueblo Tower, Piper 50B, roger, enter and report a 2 mile right base for Runway 17."

I-25

PUB TO LHX

0935 MDT The FSS specialist indicates that the weather remains as forecast along Ryan's route from Pueblo to La Junta. While the prediction still calls for afternoon thunderstorms, the briefer was not picking up any returns on his radar except over the mountains to the west. Sitting down with a snack and drink, Ryan reviews his planning for the next portion of his cross-country, taking into consideration the lessons he learned from the first segment. For one thing, he decides to calculate a descent point for his landing at La Junta. Assuming a 500 f.p.m. rate of descent, he figures it should take a little over 4 minutes to descend from the planned cruise altitude of 7,500 feet to a standard pattern altitude at La Junta Municipal Airport. At a ground speed of 123 knots, that equates to a distance of over 8 n.m. Therefore, Ryan calculates that he should begin his descent about 10 miles from La Junta to ensure that he reaches pattern altitude well outside the traffic pattern. Checking his chart, he finds a road west of Lake Meredith, running south across his route which provides a good point from which to initiate his radio call and descent. Ryan makes a note on his nav log and finishes reviewing the information for the remainder of his route. Satisfied that he is ready, Ryan gathers his materials and returns to his airplane.

0948 MDT After placing his equipment in the airplane, Ryan performs a thorough preflight inspection which he completes with satisfactory results. Ensuring that all the chocks are removed, Ryan moves to the cockpit, organizes his materials, fastens his seat belt, and pulls out his prestart and start checklists. With the engine running smoothly, Ryan flips on his radio master switch. As the avionics come to life, he consults his navigation log to set the frequencies. [Figure 11-11]

Adjusting the volume on his #1 com radio, Ryan listens to the Pueblo ATIS broadcast. With the airport information recorded on his navigation log, Ryan switches frequencies in his #1 radio and changes the alternate frequency to 122.2, Denver FSS.

Following one last check of his cockpit, Ryan changes to his #2 radio and calls ground control for taxi clearance. Although he landed on Runway 17, the reported wind direction and speed makes Runway 8 Left appropriate for departure. In fact, the easterly orientation of the runway will place Ryan closer to his planned course.

0959 MDT Arriving in the runup area, Ryan completes his ground and before takeoff checks, remembering to switch to the fuller tank in accordance with the fuel management procedures contained in the Archer's POH. Taxiing forward to the hold short line, he switches his #2 radio to departure control and dials the La Junta ASOS (135.525) in as the standby frequency.

1000 MDT Changing to his #1 com radio, Ryan calls the tower. He looks left to check the approach path clear, then taxis onto the runway. As he does so, he notes the time, turns his transponder to ALT, and checks his landing light on. Looking down the runway, Ryan adds power and the aircraft begins to accelerate. Feeding in right rudder to counteract the torque effect, Ryan maintains the nose on centerline. Reaching rotation speed, he eases back on the yoke and the airplane becomes airborne for the second time of the morning.

1001 MDT With the aircraft trimmed for normal climb, Ryan switches to his #2 radio and calls departure control. Determining that the reported traffic is no factor, Ryan looks to the right to see a highway and railroad track running eastward. Since this corresponds to the road which touches his course line about 5 miles from the airport, Ryan turns to intercept his route.

Radio panel (Figure 11-11):

- Pueblo ATIS — Pueblo Tower: 125.50 119.10
- Pueblo VORTAC — Hugo VORTAC: 116.70 112.10
- Pueblo Departure — Pueblo Ground: 121.90 120.10
- Hugo VORTAC — Colorado Springs VORTAC: 112.10 112.50
- Aruba NDB — La Junta NDB: 3.73 2.39

Figure 11-11. Ryan sets the radio frequencies so that they will be available in the order he expects to use them.

Navigation log table:

Check Points (Fixes)	Ident / Freq	Course (Route)	Altitude	CAS	Dir. / Vel. / Temp.	TC	TH	MH	Dev.	CH	Leg Rem / Est / Act	Time Off 9:16	GPH 9.0
PUEBLO MEMORIAL		→→	7,500	86 / 123	200 / 8 / 18°	109	114	104	-1	103	48 / 23 /	ETE 10+4 ETA 9:30	Fuel 2+0.7 39.1
TOWERS		↓	↓		5 / -10						25		
LA JUNTA MUNICIPAL				123	200 / 8 / 18°	109	113	103	-1	102	25 / 0	ETE 12 ETA 9:42	Fuel 1.8 37.3
					4 / -10							RESERVE	4.5

Photo caption: Road/Railroad Tracks

"Pueblo Ground, Piper 8450B, at Flower Aviation, taxi for takeoff, VFR to La Junta, with information Delta, request traffic advisories on departure."

"Piper 8450B, Pueblo Ground, taxi to Runway 8 Left via taxiway Bravo, squawk 4421."

"Pueblo Ground, 50B, roger, squawk 4421."

"Pueblo ATIS information Delta, Automated weather observation, 1545 Zulu. Wind 110 at 5. Temperature 23. Check density altitude. Dewpoint 14, altimeter 30.20. ILS, NDB, VOR, or visual approaches in use. Landing Runways 8 Left and 17. Land and hold short operations in effect. Runways 8 Right and 26 Left closed until further notice. Flight following available on request. Advise on initial contact you have information Delta."

"Pueblo Departure, Piper 8450B, off of Pueblo climbing through 5,000 for 7,500, heading 080."

"Piper 8450B, Pueblo Departure, radar contact, resume own navigation to La Junta, traffic 3 o'clock, 2 miles, climbing through 7,300, headed northbound."

"Piper 8450B, roger, traffic in sight."

"Pueblo Tower, Piper 8450B, holding short of Runway 8 Left for takeoff."

"Piper 50B, Pueblo Tower, after takeoff, fly runway heading and contact departure control on 120.1. Cleared for takeoff, Runway 8 Left, wind calm."

"Piper 50B, roger, cleared for takeoff."

6 **1003 MDT** Quickly picking up his course, Ryan turns to his planned heading of 103°. As he rolls out of his turn, he notices his altitude climbing through 6,000 feet. Checking his chart, Ryan selects a road bend just past the town of Boone as an intermediate checkpoint to verify his ground track.

7 **1004 MDT** As he scans outside the cockpit for the landmark, departure calls. In response, Ryan immediately reaches over and resets his transponder to the VFR squawk. He also takes this opportunity to readjust his com radios in preparation for the remainder of his flight. In case he needs to talk to FSS, he switches the #1 radio to the standby frequency. Then, for future use, he dials in the La Junta UNICOM, 123.0 as the second frequency in his #1 radio. Moving La Junta ASOS to the primary position in the #2 com radio allows Ryan to pick up the latest weather as soon as he comes within range. Finally, he reaches over and turns off his landing light.

8 **1007 MDT** Ryan notices what appears to be the town of Boone at approximately 11 o'clock, less than a mile away. Looking further ahead, he makes out the highway and railroad tracks crossing his route to the southeast. Running more easterly is the river as depicted on his sectional.

9 **1010 MDT** Reaching 7,500 feet, Ryan lowers the nose of the Archer and retrims for level flight as the airplane accelerates to cruise speed. Continuing eastward, Ryan notices a power line which seems to be converging on his course from the left. Following the wires toward the nose of the airplane aids him in locating the twin towers.

10 **1013 MDT** Flying past the towers, Ryan adjusts his heading slightly to the right and takes note of the time and fuel quantity. Referring to his nav log, he determines that he arrived at his checkpoint about a minute earlier than expected. He attributes this small increase in groundspeed to a greater than anticipated tailwind component. As Ryan scans ahead of his airplane, he notes the northeasterly turn of the highway and railroad which have been paralleling his course. Checking his chart, he estimates that he will cross the road as planned, just southwest of Olney Springs.

11 **1014 MDT** As he crosses the highway, Ryan looks to the right and spots the Arkansas river, and beyond that, another major highway, both of which run southeasterly toward the town of La Junta. About the same time, he begins to pick up the computer generated voice from the La Junta Municipal Airport ASOS. From the observation, Ryan keys on two important facts. First, the wind speed and direction, if similar to the winds at his cruising altitude, would confirm his suspicion that his groundspeed variance is due to a change in the predicted winds. Second, the remark concerning density altitude reminds him of the increased ground roll he should expect upon landing at La Junta.

12 **1016 MDT** Having just crossed a road running north-south, Ryan begins to look for the second road which he had previously designated as a landmark at which to contact La Junta UNICOM and begin his descent from 7,500 feet. A glance to approximately 10 o'clock reveals Lake Meredith 4 to 5 miles away. Returning his scan to the front of his airplane, Ryan soon picks out the road about 2 to 3 miles ahead crossing perpendicular to his flight path. Given his increased groundspeed, Ryan decides to begin his descent before he reaches the road. Using the appropriate procedures, Ryan reduces power, retrims to maintain his cruise speed, and turns on his landing light.

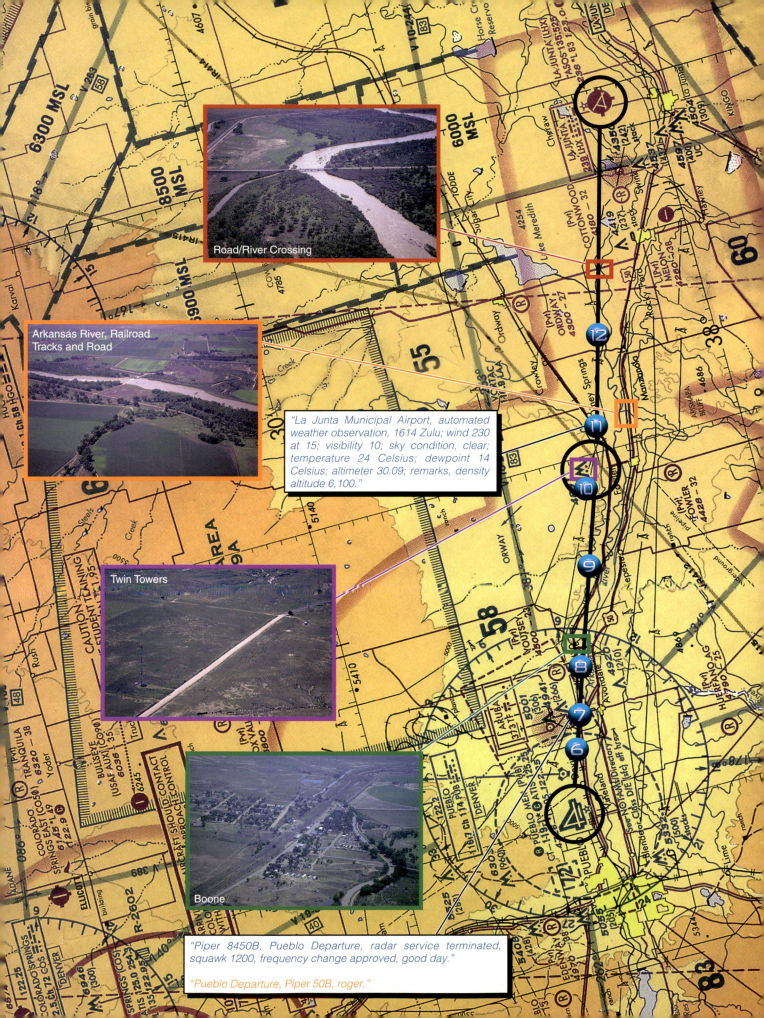

Road/River Crossing

Arkansas River, Railroad Tracks and Road

Twin Towers

Boone

"La Junta Municipal Airport, automated weather observation, 1614 Zulu; wind 230 at 15; visibility 10; sky condition, clear; temperature 24 Celsius; dewpoint 14 Celsius; altimeter 30.09; remarks, density altitude 6,100."

"Piper 8450B, Pueblo Departure, radar service terminated, squawk 1200, frequency change approved, good day."

"Pueblo Departure, Piper 50B, roger."

13 **1018 MDT** Once established in the descent, Ryan switches his #1 com radio frequency, checks his audio control panel switches in the proper position, and makes his initial call to La Junta UNICOM. Although he does not have the airport in sight yet, Ryan begins to think about the orientation of Runway 26 and the pattern direction. Checking his chart, he decides to maintain his current course until he reaches the lake located near the La Junta NDB. From there, he plans to turn to a southeasterly heading not only to stay clear of the aircraft in the pattern, but also to put himself in a position from which to safely enter the downwind at a 45° angle.

14 **1021 MDT** As Ryan approaches the lake, he switches his ADF to La Junta and watches the needle swing toward his right wing, verifying his position. Although the only aircraft he has heard over the UNICOM is a Cessna, realizing that there is no requirement to make radio calls at uncontrolled airports such as La Junta, he aggressively scans for traffic, particularly any that may be departing from Runway 26. With the airport in sight, Ryan initiates a turn to the southeast.

15 **1022 MDT** After rolling out of his turn, Ryan notices his altimeter passing through 5,300 feet, quickly approaching pattern altitude. Readjusting his power and retriming, Ryan levels off at pattern altitude and begins maneuvering to set up for his pattern entry.

16 **1024 MDT** Scanning outside, Ryan spots the Cessna beginning a turn to base. At the same time, he hears the Cessna announce its turn. With the position of the Cessna verified, Ryan looks for any other traffic while flying on a heading of 035° about a mile outside of his planned downwind entry point.

17 **1025 MDT** As he approaches abeam the midpoint of Runway 26, Ryan takes one last look over his left shoulder to ensure the airspace is clear. Turning back around, he keys his mike and makes a call entering downwind. Rolling out parallel to the runway, Ryan notices that the wind sock located off his left wing is indicating that the wind has shifted to about 20° off the runway heading to the north.

18 **1026 MDT** As he completes his landing checklist, Ryan glances at the runway to check his position in preparation for his turn to base. Upon reaching 45° from his desired touchdown point, Ryan begins his turn to base, announcing his position at the same time.

19 **1027 MDT** During his descent on base leg, Ryan looks to the runway and notices the Cessna beginning a climbout after its touch-and-go. Beginning his turn to final, Ryan broadcasts his intentions. After rolling out on final, Ryan determines that, not only is he slightly left of centerline, but he is also below glidepath. To compensate, he turns more to the right and adds power. As he reaches the extended centerline, Ryan readjusts his heading but lowers his right wing to compensate for the crosswind. With some minor power and attitude adjustments, Ryan crosses the runway threshold at approximately 50 feet AGL. Maintaining his wing low position, he touches down smoothly on the right main, then lowers the left main, followed by the nosewheel. Slowing the aircraft, Ryan exits the runway at the mid-field taxiway, turns off his landing light, and completes his post-landing checklist.

20 **1030 MDT** As he taxis to the ramp, Ryan makes a his final radio call. Taxiing straight ahead, Ryan parks his airplane in front of the FBO and performs the items contained in the checklist for shutting down the avionics and engine. After recording his landing time, gathering his materials, and inserting the control lock, Ryan opens the cabin door and is greeted with a hot breeze. As he places chocks under the aircraft's wheels, he carefully conducts a postflight inspection. During his walk across the ramp to the FBO, several large clouds on the northwestern horizon catch Ryan's eye. Although they look to be quite distant, he hurries inside to call Flight Service and get an update on the weather.

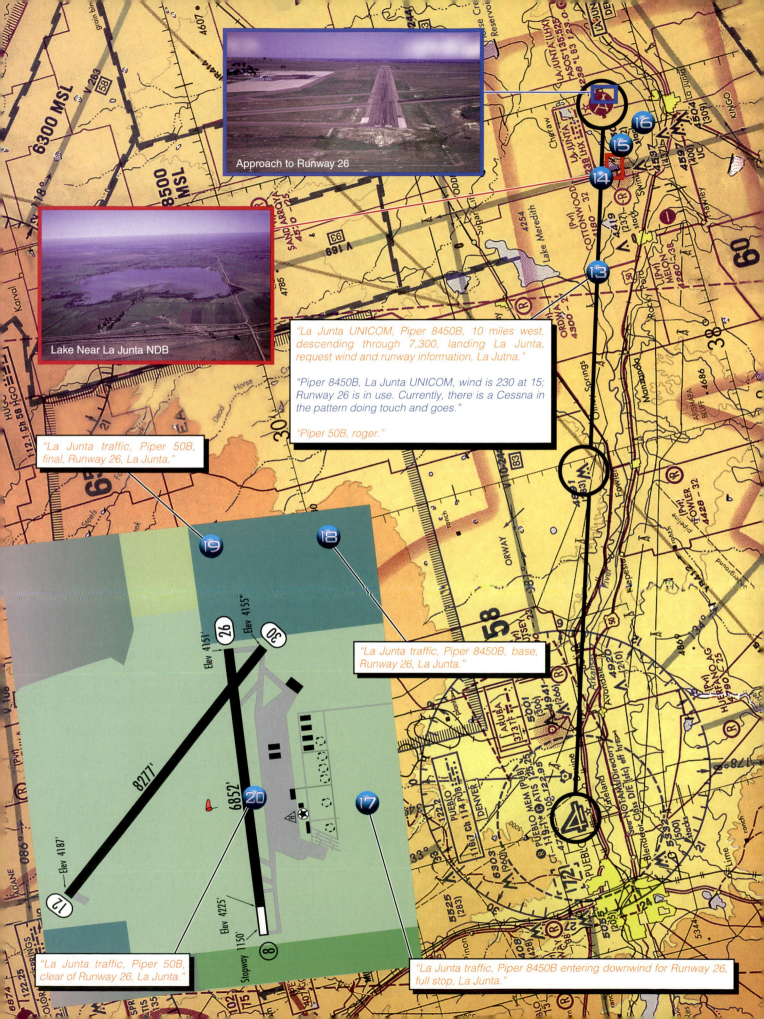

Approach to Runway 26

Lake Near La Junta NDB

"La Junta UNICOM, Piper 8450B, 10 miles west, descending through 7,300, landing La Junta, request wind and runway information, La Jutna."

"Piper 8450B, La Junta UNICOM, wind is 230 at 15; Runway 26 is in use. Currently, there is a Cessna in the pattern doing touch and goes."

"Piper 50B, roger."

"La Junta traffic, Piper 50B, final, Runway 26, La Junta."

"La Junta traffic, Piper 8450B, base, Runway 26, La Junta."

"La Junta traffic, Piper 50B, clear of Runway 26, La Junta."

"La Junta traffic, Piper 8450B entering downwind for Runway 26, full stop, La Junta."

LHX TO APA

① **1035 MDT** In the FBO flight planning room, Ryan picks up the telephone and dials 1-800-WX-BRIEF. After a short delay, he is connected to a briefer who informs Ryan that current reports indicate the weather is progressing as forecast along his route. Although she doesn't see any large areas of precipitation on radar, the briefer emphasizes that thunderstorms can build quickly, and that Ryan should contact Flight Watch for updates while enroute. Feeling more assured, Ryan thanks the specialist, hangs up, and proceeds to review the last segment of his flight and prepare for his trip home. Since the winds aloft forecast had not been updated, Ryan decides not to adjust his calculated groundspeeds. Rather, he plans on adjusting his times and headings as necessary after his first checkpoint. Otherwise, the flight as planned seems to remain feasible. Still, the thought of the clouds building to the northwest prompts Ryan to analyze his route and explore his options in the event he needs to divert due to bad weather. Several airfields to the west and south of his route are options, while the Limon airport, located about 35 miles northeast of Rush, provides another alternative.

Going over the previous segment of the flight in his mind, Ryan recalls some things which went well and some things which could have been done better. In particular, he decides that preplanning his descent worked out nicely and saved him some last-minute adjustments entering the traffic pattern where he was otherwise very busy. His approach to landing, however, was not the best. While he had the foresight to check the wind sock and notice the change in wind direction, he hadn't remembered and applied what Megan had taught him about flying a landing pattern in an undershooting crosswind. On the positive side, he thought he made the proper adjustments on final and actually had executed a nice crosswind landing.

② **1050 MDT** As he walks out to his airplane, Ryan gets the impression that the wind is stronger than before, yet the sky still looks clear near the airport and, as he looks toward the northwest, he notices little change in the cloud formations since he landed. After conducting a thorough preflight inspection, Ryan straps into the pilot's seat and prepares his materials for his flight. Satisfied that everything is in order, Ryan starts the engine in accordance with the checklist. As he has on every flight, he pulls out his chart and nav log to help him set his com and nav radios so that the frequencies will be available in logical sequence. [Figure 11-12]

Checking his audio control panel switches and adjusting the volume on his #2 com radio, Ryan listens to the latest ASOS broadcast. After turning the volume down on his radio, Ryan checks his POH and finds the maximum demonstrated crosswind component listed as 17 knots. He determines that, at the peak gust of 22 knots, he would exceed the limits of the airplane if he used Runway 26 for takeoff. Not only would using Runway 30 alleviate this possibility, it also would more directly align him with his planned course. Prior to taxiing toward the east side of the airport, Ryan adjusts his audio control panel and broadcasts his intentions on UNICOM.

③ **1055 MDT** During his runup, Ryan hears a Mooney call entering downwind for landing on Runway 30. When he looks up, he is unable to spot the airplane and decides to wait for it to land. Ryan takes advantage of the delay to switch his #2 radio to FSS (122.2) and dial in a standby FSS frequency, 122.35. As Ryan pulls to the hold short line of Runway 30 in preparation for takeoff, he hears the Mooney call turning final. Looking out the right window, he spots the aircraft rolling wings level about a mile from the approach end of the runway. Before long, he watches the airplane pass in front of him and execute a smooth landing about 500 feet down the runway. Glancing at his airport diagram, Ryan realizes that the Mooney will have to taxi back on the runway to reach the ramp area, so he decides to hold his position until the airplane is clear.

④ **1102 MDT** The Mooney turns right onto Runway 26 and continues taxiing to the ramp. With the airplane well clear of Runway 30, and no other aircraft in the area, Ryan writes down the time, turns his transponder to ALT, flips on his landing light, and broadcasts his intentions. In position on Runway 30, Ryan completes one last check inside and outside his airplane and pushes the throttle forward to begin his takeoff.

⑤ **1103 MDT** On climbout, Ryan trims to maintain the proper attitude and turns to 317° enroute to his first checkpoint, Sugar City. Looking to the left of the airplane's nose, he begins to discern the outline of Lake Meredith approximately 10 miles away. Since he figures that the winds aloft may have shifted, as they did near the surface, Ryan plans on using the northeast tip of the lake to help him navigate his first leg to Sugar City.

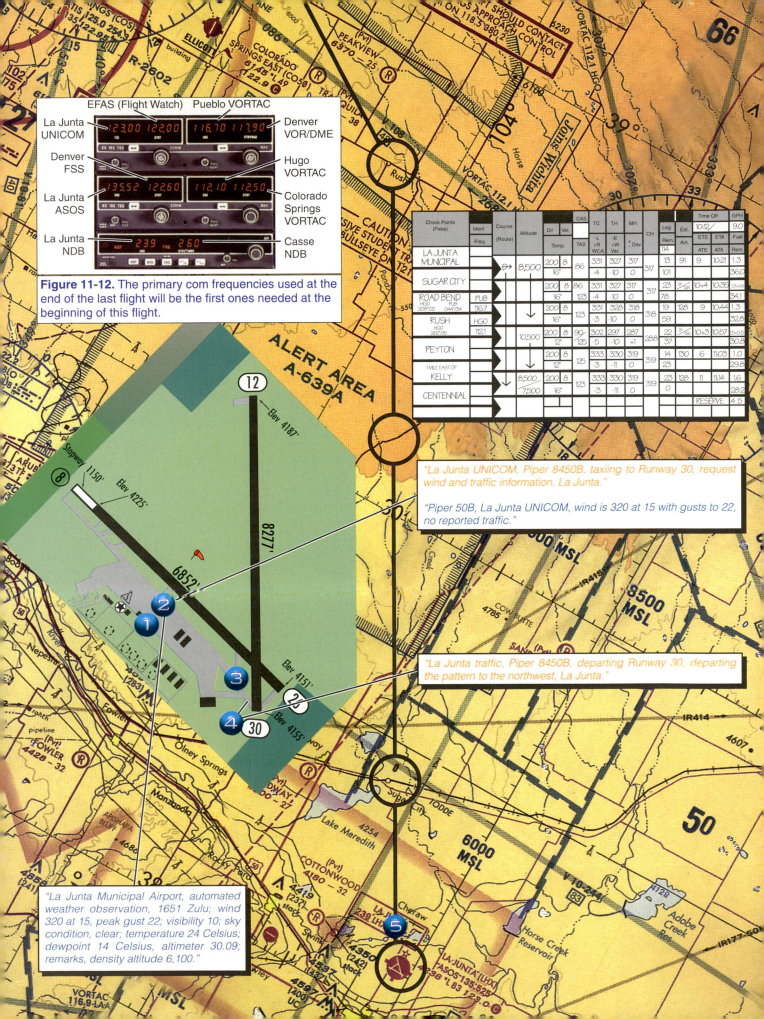

Figure 11-12. The primary com frequencies used at the end of the last flight will be the first ones needed at the beginning of this flight.

EFAS (Flight Watch) — 123.00 122.00
Pueblo VORTAC — 116.70 117.90
La Junta UNICOM
Denver VOR/DME
Denver FSS — 135.52 122.60
Hugo VORTAC — 112.10 112.50
La Junta ASOS
Colorado Springs VORTAC
La Junta NDB — 23.9 260
Casse NDB

Check Points (Fixes)	Ident Freq.	Course (Route)	Altitude	CAS		TC -L +R WCA	TH -E +W Var.	MH ± Dev	CH	Leg Rem. Act.	Est.	Time Off		GPH
				Dir Vel								ETE ETA		
				Temp.	TAS							ATE ATA		Fuel Rem.
LA JUNTA MUNICIPAL		⟶	8,500	200 8	86	331 327 317		317	13 91	9	10:12		9.0
				16°		-4 -10 0			101				36.0
SUGAR CITY				200 8	86	331 327 317		317	13	3½	10+4 10:35	13+06	
				16°	123	-4 -10 0			78				34.1
ROAD BEND	PUB 116.7 208?/22 044?/?34	↓		200 8	123	331 328 318		318	19 128	9	10:44	1.3	
				16°		-3 -10 0			59				32.8
RUSH	HGO 112.1 282?/25		10,500	200 8	90	302 297 287		288	22	3½	10+3 10:57	15+05	
				12°	125	-5 -10 +1			37				30.8
PEYTON		↓		200 8	125	333 330 319		319	14 130	6	11:03	1.0	
				12°		-3 -11 0			23				29.8
1 MILE EAST OF KELLY		↓	8,500 7,500	200 8	123	333 330 319		319	23 128	11	11:14	1.6	
				16°		-3 -11 0							28.2
CENTENNIAL											RESERVE		4.5

12 — Elev 4187'

8 — Stopway 1150' — Elev 4225'

8277'

6852'

ALERT AREA A-639A

① ② ③ ④

21 — Elev 4151'

30 — Elev 4155'

"La Junta UNICOM, Piper 8450B, taxiing to Runway 30, request wind and traffic information, La Junta."

"Piper 50B, La Junta UNICOM, wind is 320 at 15 with gusts to 22, no reported traffic."

"La Junta traffic, Piper 8450B, departing Runway 30, departing the pattern to the northwest, La Junta."

"La Junta Municipal Airport, automated weather observation, 1651 Zulu; wind 320 at 15, peak gust 22; visibility 10; sky condition, clear; temperature 24 Celsius; dewpoint 14 Celsius, altimeter 30.09; remarks, density altitude 6,100."

⑤

6 **1113 MDT** With Lake Meredith passing off his left side, Ryan quickly approaches the town of Sugar City. After confirming his position with the road, railroad, and lake north of town, he jots down his time of arrival over Sugar City. Next, he turns off his landing light and switches his audio control panel to the #2 radio to monitor FSS. Passing through 6,700 feet, Ryan continues his climb and, given that very little course adjustment was needed enroute to Sugar City, maintains his planned course of 317°. Referring to his navigation log, Ryan determines that it took him 2 minutes longer than planned to fly the 13 miles to his first checkpoint. Reaching in his flight bag, Ryan removes his flight computer, and calculates a groundspeed of 71 knots. Comparing this to his true airspeed, he concludes that the wind speed must be approximately 15 knots. Applying the headwind to the next leg of his flight, Ryan estimates that it should take an additional 2 minutes to reach the road bend located near the center of Alert Area A-639A.

7 **1121 MDT** As he levels off at a cruising altitude of 8,500 feet, Ryan notices a road off his right side which he assumes is the road which runs south toward Lake Meredith. In about another 7 minutes, he estimates that he should come across his next checkpoint. Retarding his throttle to maintain cruise speed, Ryan retrims and begins another scan for traffic. Looking to the northwest does not reveal any traffic, however, the fair weather clouds which he remembers from the ramp at La Junta now look much larger and more threatening. Although they still seem 40 to 50 miles away, they unfortunately seem to be stretching along the foothills from near Pueblo northward toward Denver. Deciding that it is time to obtain a weather update, Ryan switches frequencies in his #1 com radio and attempts to call Flight Watch. Waiting several seconds without a response, he tries to raise Flight Watch again. Another minute passes without a response and he transmits for a third time. Still not making contact, he thinks about the procedures Megan taught him about lost communications. First, he checks to ensure that the proper frequency, 122.0, is dialed in his radio. Next, he tries the volume control on the radio and finds that it is turned up. Then, he checks the switch positions of his audio control panel and discovers that they are positioned incorrectly. Upon resetting the switches, the radio comes to life with chatter.

8 **1126 MDT** After a rather lengthy discussion with the Flight Watch specialist, Ryan develops a picture of the weather facing him. According to Flight Watch, a fast-moving line of thunderstorms currently located in the area between 20 miles south of Pueblo and 5 miles north of Denver is tracking southeast at 20 miles per hour. The latest weather report from Centennial indicates that a thundershower with moderate rain was present in the airport vicinity. From this information, Ryan concludes that it will be difficult, if not dangerous, to get to his destination by flying his planned route. After consulting his chart, Ryan wonders if it might be possible to fly around the weather and approach Centennial from the west. However, when considering this option, several problems come to mind. First, while Flight Watch defined the area of precipitation, Ryan is still not quite sure how far south or north the clouds extend, making it difficult to calculate a time enroute. This also brings up the question of fuel — Ryan figures that he currently has about 2 1/2 hours of fuel on board, not counting his reserve. Venturing off for an undetermined distance with a finite amount of fuel does not make him very comfortable. Plus, if he did make it around the storms to the west, he would have to fly over extremely rough terrain in less than ideal conditions. Without the proper training, Ryan can see where an unplanned foray into the mountains could make matters even worse. Finally, even if he managed to overcome all the obstacles, there is no guarantee that Centennial's weather will have improved by the time he gets there.

9 **1133 MDT** Eliminating a circumvention of the weather as an option, Ryan concludes that he has 2 alternatives left — he can continue to remain airborne and wait for a break in the clouds, or he can find a place to land and reevaluate the situation. Remembering Megan's sage advice, "It's better to be on the ground wishing you were in the air than in the air wishing you were on the ground," Ryan decides to find a suitable alternate airport. Since the airfields to the west seem to be out of the question, he checks his chart and locates Limon Municipal Airport, north of his course. As he prepares to plot a course to Limon, he realizes that, with all the distractions, he has lost track of his current position. Checking the time, he finds that he should have reached his last checkpoint about 2 minutes ago. Quickly figuring the time to his next checkpoint, Ryan calculates that he should reach the town of Rush in about 5 minutes. To confirm, Ryan adjusts his VOR indicator associated with the Hugo VORTAC. Although the needle centers at 046° TO the station, he notices that the OFF flag is intermittently flashing. With the reliability of the signal in question, Ryan tries the Pueblo VORTAC. The CDI centers at 032° FROM the station and the DME reads 31.0. Plotting the results on his sectional, Ryan determines that he has, indeed, passed the road bend and is about halfway to Rush. Looking ahead, Ryan decides that he can easily fly to his next checkpoint without encountering any of the weather ahead. Proceeding ahead to Rush also will allow him time to plot a course direct to Limon. Before he does, however, he decides to call FSS to obtain the current reported weather at Limon and amend his flight plan.

1136 MDT After informing Ryan that the weather at Limon was reported as clear with winds of 320° at 8 and an altimeter of 30.18, the FSS specialist gladly amends Ryan's flight plan. Drawing a line on his chart, Ryan finds that Limon is located 33 miles from Rush on a magnetic course of 027°. Using his flight computer and his estimated winds aloft, he calculates that he will need to fly from Rush on a heading of 021° for 17 minutes enroute to Limon.

1138 MDT As Ryan makes another scan for traffic, he spots 2 roads, about a mile apart, running east-west across his path. Several buildings at an intersection along the northern-most road are located where Ryan expects the town of Rush to be located. Since there is a crossroads in the center of town instead of a T-intersection as depicted on the chart, Ryan is not confident that he has actually located the town. Although the street pattern does not exactly match the chart depiction, Ryan recalls Meagan's warning that the sectional may not always show everything that is visible from the cockpit. Instead of continuing on a blind search, Ryan decides to cross-check his location using the VOR. Dialing the Colorado Springs VORTAC into his #1 nav radio yields a radial and DME which correspond to the location of Rush. Convinced that he is, indeed, over the town of Rush, he turns to 027° toward Limon.

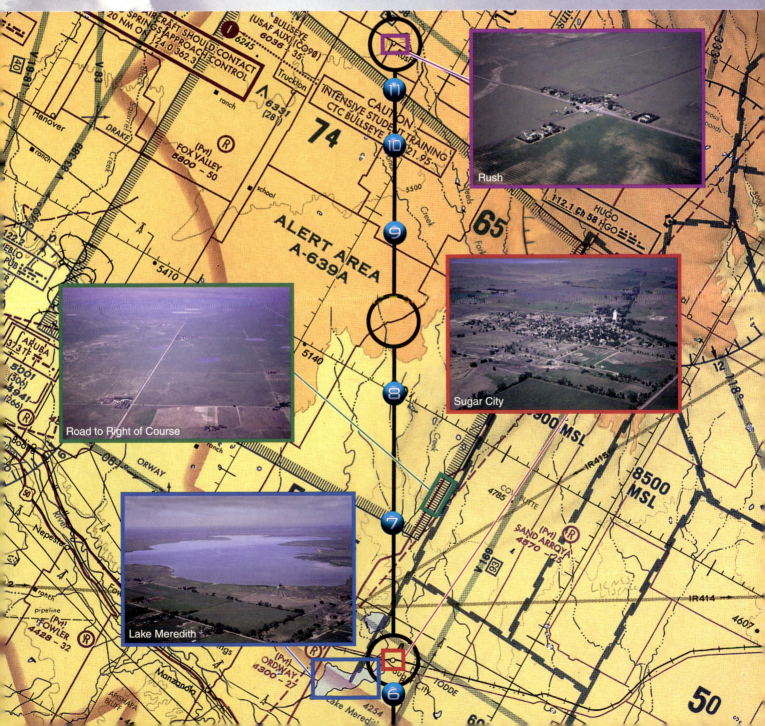

Rush

Sugar City

Road to Right of Course

Lake Meredith

12 **1140 MDT** As he rolls wings level, Ryan begins a descent to 7,500 feet. To help keep track of his progress, he selects a road bend in the vicinity of three small ponds as an intermediate checkpoint. A quick measurement and calculation results in a time enroute to the checkpoint of 8 minutes.

13 **1147 MDT** Looking out the right side of his airplane, Ryan spots the ponds and bend in the road. Confident that he is on course, Ryan begins to prepare for his arrival at Limon by setting his #1 com radio to 122.9. Although he expects to land on Runway 34, since the field is unattended he plans on overflying the field at 1,500 feet AGL to check the wind direction.

14 **1153 MDT** Scanning outside, Ryan begins to make out the town of Limon and the interstate highway located north of town and south of the airport. The lakes north of town help confirm his position and aid in locating the airport. Estimating that he is approximately 10 miles from the airport, Ryan turns on his landing light, begins a descent to 1,500 feet AGL, and broadcasts his intentions on CTAF.

15 **1156 MDT** During the last few minutes Ryan heard several calls on 122.9, however all the broadcasts were from aircraft operating at airports other than Limon. With no indication of traffic in the area, and with the airport in sight, Ryan maneuvers to overfly the airport. Easily locating the segmented circle and wind sock to the west of the runway, Ryan notes that the wind appears to be favoring Runway 34, necessitating a left turn to set up for a left downwind entry. Extending away from the airport, Ryan descends to pattern altitude and turns to 115° which will set him up on a 45° intercept to downwind.

16 **1159 MDT** Approaching his pattern entry point, Ryan scans for other traffic, makes his entry call, and double checks the wind sock to confirm the wind direction. Flying downwind, Ryan finds that he is drifting slightly closer to the runway even though he is maintaining a heading of 160°. After turning to regain the proper distance from the runway, Ryan decides to use a slight crab into the apparent crosswind.

17 **1201 MDT** With his landing checklist complete, Ryan checks his position in relation to the runway. On about a 45° bearing from his intended point of landing, Ryan begins a turn to base and transmits his intentions. As he rolls out on base leg, Ryan reduces power to compensate for the crosswind which is pushing his airplane toward the extended centerline more quickly than normal. Cross-checking the wind sock, he estimates a crosswind about 30° west of the runway heading at about 10 knots.

18 **1202 MDT** Ryan begins his turn to final accompanied by his self-announce transmission. Remembering his experience at La Junta, Ryan maintains a few degrees left wing down to compensate for the wind. With a few minor adjustments, he arrives over the runway aligned with the centerline and executes a smooth landing.

19 **1203 MDT** On rollout, Ryan applies the brakes, slows to a safe speed, and turns onto a taxiway just past midfield. After making his final radio call, he turns off his landing light and completes the post-landing checklist.

20 **1205 MDT** A few minutes later, Ryan arrives at the ramp parking area and shuts down his engine. After completing the checklists and gathering his materials, Ryan exits the cockpit. With chocks in place, Ryan walks to the only building on the airport and finds a telephone. First placing a call to the FSS, he closes his flight plan and asks for an update on the weather. According to the specialist, the thunderstorm activity is moving toward the southeast with clear skies behind. If things continue to progress as they have, VFR flight from Limon to Centennial should be possible in about 2 hours. After finishing with Flight Service, Ryan calls his flight school and promptly gets in touch with his instructor. Ryan fills Megan in on his flight and the forecast he just received from Flight Service. Megan expresses her confidence in Ryan's ability and praises his good judgment in landing at Limon. Nonetheless, she is wary of letting him continue given the current weather conditions. After some discussion, Megan and Ryan agree that he should plan a flight from Limon to Centennial, obtain a thorough weather brief, and call back prior to filing a flight plan and departing.

"Limon traffic, Piper 50B, clear Runway 34, Limon."

LIMON MUNI (LIC) 1 NE UTC−7(−6DT) N39°16.37′ W103°39.98′   WICHITA
  5365 B S2 **FUEL** 100LL   L−6F
  RWY 16−34: H4700X60 (CONC) S−12.5 MIRL
    RWY 16: PAPI(P2L)—GA 3.0° TCH 36′.   **RWY 34:** PAPI(P2L)—GA 3.0° TCH 40′. Trees.
  AIRPORT REMARKS: Unattended. For fuel svc call Limon Police Dept at 719−775−2346/9211. Deer on and invof arpt.
    Uncontrolled vehicle access to fld. Twy marked with blue reflectors. ACTIVATE MIRL Rwy 16−34 and PAPI Rwy 16
    and Rwy 34—CTAF.
  WEATHER DATA SOURCES: ASOS (719) 775−0515
  COMMUNICATIONS: CTAF 122.9
    DENVER FSS (DEN) **TF** 1−800−WX−BRIEF. NOTAM FILE LIC.
  RADIO AIDS TO NAVIGATION: NOTAM FILE DEN.
    HUGO (H) **VORTACW** 112.1   HGO   Chan 58   N38°48.90′ W103°37.56′   344° 27.5 NM to fld. 5233/12E.

"Limon traffic, Piper 50B, final, Runway 34, Limon."

"Limon traffic, Piper 50B, base, Runway 34, Limon."

"Limon traffic, Piper 50B, entering downwind Runway 34, full stop, Limon."

"Limon traffic, Piper 8450B, 10 miles southwest, descending through 7,400, landing Limon."

Approach to Runway 34

Limon

Road Bend and Ponds

LIC TO APA

① 1220 MDT Sitting down to start his flight plan in the relative solitude of the Limon airport, Ryan has his first chance to reflect on the his flight from La Junta. Initially, he is annoyed by his lapses while attempting to call Flight Watch and missing his checkpoint. On the other hand, he feels good about his decision making, in-flight route adjustments, and his handling of the crosswind during the approach and landing at Limon. All in all, he believes that he handled the situation well and benefited from what he learned on the first two segments of his cross-country. While he is confident that, if the weather improves, he will successfully complete his journey, he knows he cannot do anything without a good plan. With that in mind, he turns his attention to the task at hand.

1258 MDT Ryan develops a route back to Centennial by applying the same procedures he used to create his initial plan. In support of his plan, he completes a navigation log and a flight plan. Based upon the winds he calculated during the latest portion of his flight, Ryan estimates that it will take him 37 minutes to cover the 58 miles from Limon to Centennial.

1406 MDT Walking out onto the ramp, Ryan notices that the dark clouds have moved south. Estimating that the line of thunderstorms are clear of the route between Limon and Centennial, Ryan heads toward the telephone to call FSS for a weather brief. The briefing confirms that the thunderstorm activity has moved out of the Denver area to the south, making a VFR flight from Limon to Centennial feasible. The latest weather report from Centennial shows that the wind is calm and the visibility is 20 miles with scattered high clouds. The forecast calls for continued fair weather with a reduced chance of thunderstorms for the remainder of the day. After hanging up and reviewing his notes, Ryan places a call to Megan. Once in touch with his instructor, he relays the latest weather as well the results of his flight planning. Megan confirms that the weather at Centennial has improved dramatically and that there are no indications of severe weather on the horizon. Upon further discussion, Megan and Ryan agree that he should depart for Centennial as soon as he is ready.

1418 MDT Collecting his planning materials, Ryan walks back out to his airplane to begin his fourth preflight inspection of the day. Again finding everything satisfactory, Ryan removes the chocks, climbs in the cockpit, and latches the door. Methodically running through the appropriate checklists, Ryan starts the airplane's engine. After a check of the engine instruments, Ryan proceeds to set his radios. [Figure 11-13]

② 1424 MDT Ready to taxi, Ryan makes the appropriate call and taxis toward Runway 34. Stopping short of the runway, Ryan performs a runup, then looks for traffic on approach.

③ 1428 MDT With the pattern clear, Ryan transmits his intentions and takes the runway while turning his transponder to ALT and his landing light on. Double checking the wind sock, which is now showing calm winds, Ryan advances the throttle. The airplane begins to move down the runway and becomes airborne with about 2,000 feet of runway remaining.

④ 1430 MDT Ryan checks for traffic toward the northwest as he trims the aircraft for the proper climb attitude. The lakes west of the airport provide good landmarks for him to pick up his course. Flying on a heading of 281°, Ryan looks ahead to see the bend in the interstate highway. As he flies toward the highway, Ryan calls Flight Service and activates his flight plan.

⑤ 1443 MDT Reaching 8,500 feet Ryan lowers the nose, retrims for cruise flight, and turns off his landing light. Continuing on course, Ryan spots a road converging from the right side of his airplane. Checking further ahead, he detects a tower in the distance which could be the microwave tower depicted on his sectional. For greater detail around this checkpoint as well as the remainder of his flight, Ryan switches to the Denver VFR Terminal Area Chart.

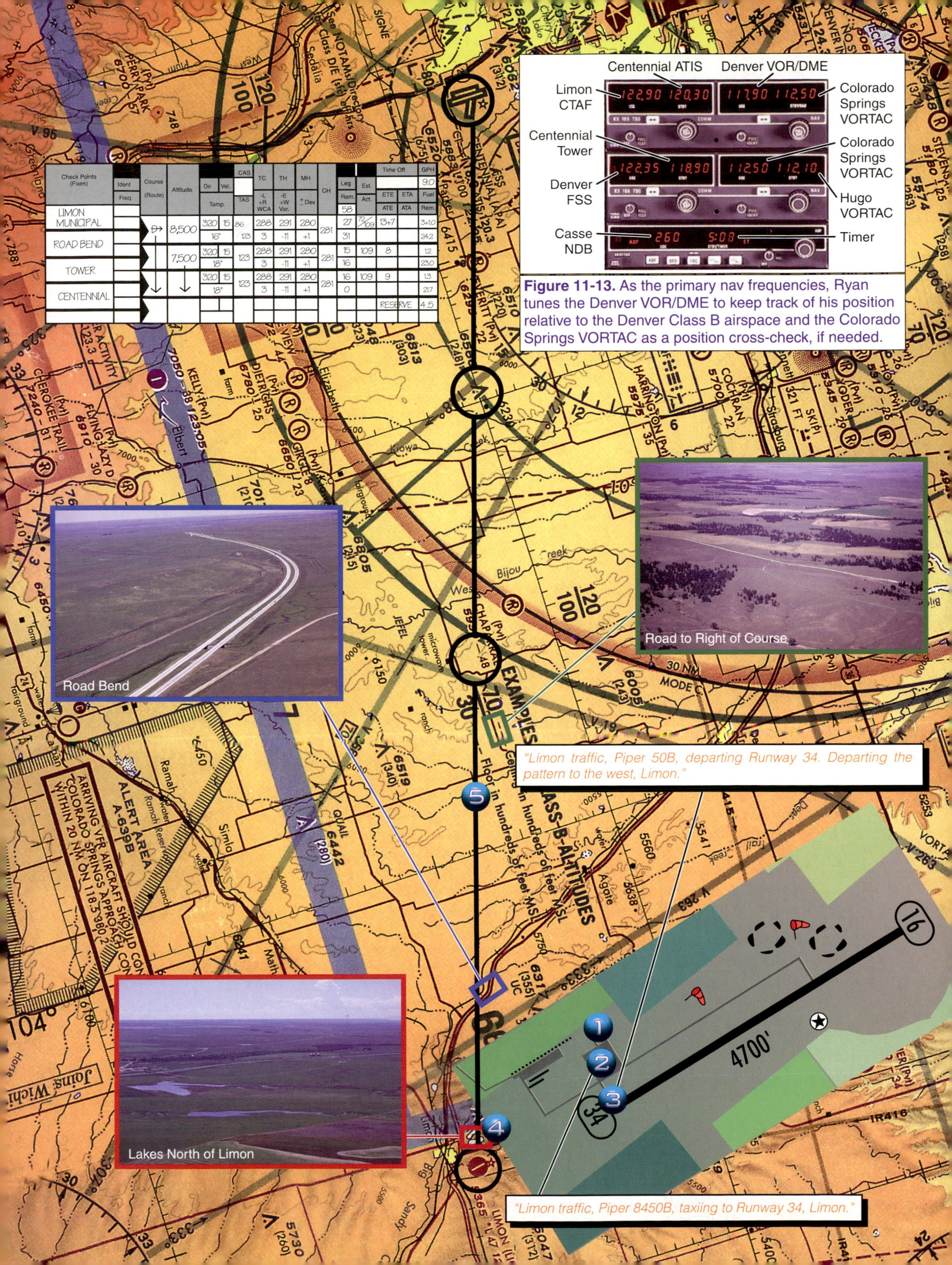
Centennial ATIS
Denver VOR/DME
Limon CTAF
Colorado Springs VORTAC
Centennial Tower
Colorado Springs VORTAC
Denver FSS
Hugo VORTAC
Casse NDB
Timer
Road Bend
Road to Right of Course
Lakes North of Limon
"Limon traffic, Piper 50B, departing Runway 34. Departing the pattern to the west, Limon."
"Limon traffic, Piper 8450B, taxiing to Runway 34, Limon."
4700'

Check Points (Fixes)	Ident / Freq.	Course (Route)	Altitude	Dir / Temp.	Vel.	CAS / TAS	TC / -L +R WCA	TH / -E +W Var.	MH / ± Dev	CH	Leg / Rem.	Est. / Act.	Time Off / ETE / ATE	ETA / ATA	GPH / Fuel / Rem.
											58				9.0
LIMON MUNICIPAL		D→	8,500	320 / 16°	15	86 / 123	288 / 3	291 / -11	280 / +1	281	27 / 31	72/109	13+7		3+1.0 / 24.2
ROAD BEND		↓	7,500	320 / 18°	15	123	288 / 3	291 / -11	280 / +1	281	15 / 16	109	8		1.2 / 23.0
TOWER		↓	↓	320 / 18°	15	123	288 / 3	291 / -11	280 / +1	281	16 / 0	109	9		1.3 / 21.7
CENTENNIAL													RESERVE		4.5

Figure 11-13. As the primary nav frequencies, Ryan tunes the Denver VOR/DME to keep track of his position relative to the Denver Class B airspace and the Colorado Springs VORTAC as a position cross-check, if needed.

6 **1447 MDT** Approaching the microwave tower, Ryan looks down and matches the bends in the road with his chart. Confirming his position, Ryan notes that he has arrived at the checkpoint earlier than expected. The increase in groundspeed coupled with his ability to maintain course with little to no corrections leads Ryan to believe that the wind at altitude, like that at Limon, is essentially calm.

As he consults his nav log, Ryan determines that he should begin a descent to prepare for his arrival at Centennial and to keep him below Denver Class B airspace. Recalculating his estimated times of arrival reveals that he should reach his next checkpoint in about 7 minutes. At that point, he will need to be below 8,000 feet to stay clear of the Class B airspace.

7 **1449 MDT** Just as he levels off at 7,500 feet, Ryan notices that he is passing over a stream running in a north-south direction. Again referring to his chart, he determines that he is crossing West Bijou Creek, right on schedule.

8 **1454 MDT** Passing over the tower which defines his last checkpoint prior to Centennial, Ryan prepares for his arrival. Ensuring that his audio control switches are in the correct position, he tunes in the ATIS broadcast.

9 **1458 MDT** As another microwave tower passes off the right side of his airplane, Ryan spots Everitt, a private grass airstrip. Calculating that he is about 9 miles from Centennial, he checks his radios and switches and makes his initial call to tower. From his experience flying out of Centennial, Ryan determines that he is about 6 miles from Parker Road. Turning on his landing light and beginning a descent from 7,500 feet, Ryan catches sight of the airport in the distance.

10 **1501 MDT** Level at pattern altitude, and approaching Parker Road, Ryan runs through his landing checklist then makes the call requested by the tower controller. As he begins his descent, Ryan spots the VASI lights near the approach end of Runway 28 and determines that he is on glidepath. Flying a smooth approach, he touches down on the runway for the final landing of the day.

11 **1503 MDT** As Ryan slows on the runway, the tower controller provides him with instructions. He turns off at the Charlie 2 taxiway, turns off his landing light, and completes the post-landing checklist.

12 **1504 MDT** After dialing in the ground frequency, 121.8, Ryan calls for taxi. With clearance, he adds power and taxis toward his parking area.

13 **1506 MDT** Coming to a stop in front of the parking spot, Ryan conducts his shutdown checklist. After everything is secured, he climbs out of the cockpit, attaches the tow bar to the nosewheel and pushes his airplane into the spot. Following a thorough postflight inspection, he ensures that the airplane is tied down, gathers his materials, and heads into the flight school.

14 **1515 MDT** Proceeding directly to the telephone, Ryan calls Flight Service and closes his flight plan. After hanging up, he walks over to the flight school's counter to complete the required paperwork. While filling out his logbook, Megan greets him and offers her congratulations on completing the flight. She asks him about his experiences and compliments him on his decision making. With only five syllabus flights remaining, Megan assures him that he is progressing well and should be ready for his private pilot check flight in less than a week.

15 **1530 MDT** After scheduling his next flight, Ryan walks to the parking lot and gets into his car. During the drive home, he has an opportunity to reflect on his flight as a whole. While he made some mistakes, he feels he made the proper corrections, and just as importantly, he applied what he learned to avoid repeating the same mistakes. Overall, he is happy with his performance and is more confident in his ability to handle unforeseen circumstances. Finally, he realizes that what he accomplished today exemplifies why he got into aviation in the first place — challenge, excitement, and lots of fun.

The completion of this manual does not signify an ending, but a beginning to a journey in aviation filled with possibilities. As a private pilot, you will be able to experience the science, freedom, beauty, and adventure that the world of aviation has to offer. Your future is now.

The time has come, at last, for action. — Charles Lindbergh, *The Spirit of St. Louis*

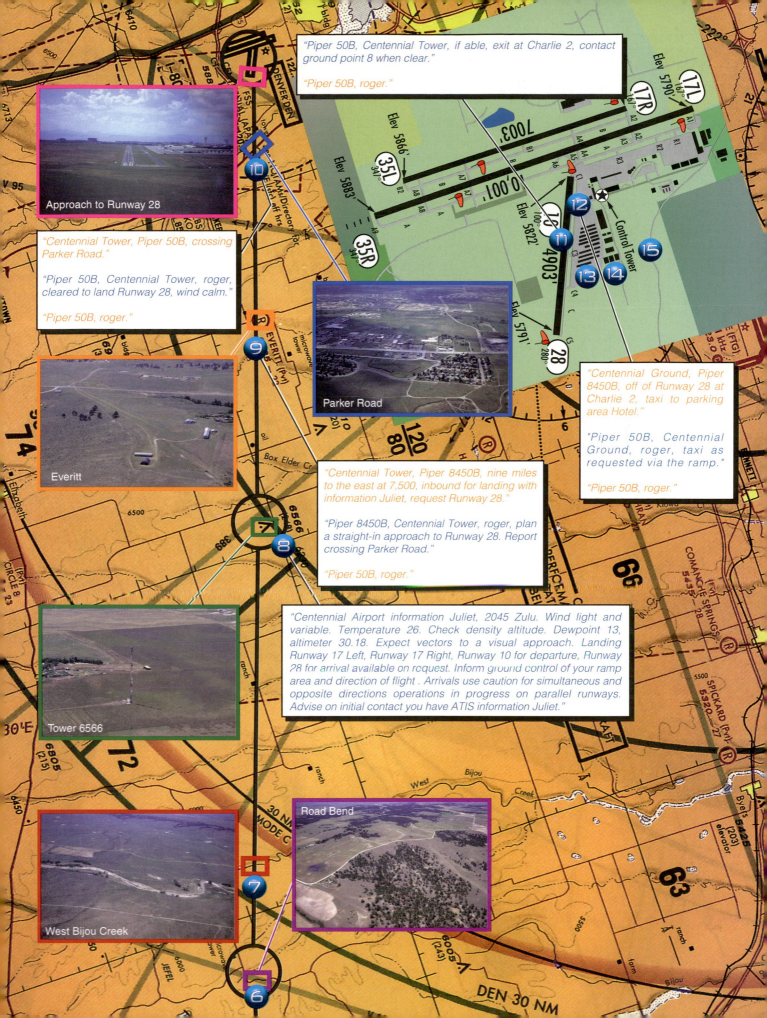

"Piper 50B, Centennial Tower, if able, exit at Charlie 2, contact ground point 8 when clear."

"Piper 50B, roger."

Approach to Runway 28

"Centennial Tower, Piper 50B, crossing Parker Road."

"Piper 50B, Centennial Tower, roger, cleared to land Runway 28, wind calm."

"Piper 50B, roger."

Parker Road

Everitt

"Centennial Ground, Piper 8450B, off of Runway 28 at Charlie 2, taxi to parking area Hotel."

"Piper 50B, Centennial Ground, roger, taxi as requested via the ramp."

"Piper 50B, roger."

"Centennial Tower, Piper 8450B, nine miles to the east at 7,500, inbound for landing with information Juliet, request Runway 28."

"Piper 8450B, Centennial Tower, roger, plan a straight-in approach to Runway 28. Report crossing Parker Road."

"Piper 50B, roger."

"Centennial Airport information Juliet, 2045 Zulu. Wind light and variable. Temperature 26. Check density altitude. Dewpoint 13, altimeter 30.18. Expect vectors to a visual approach. Landing Runway 17 Left, Runway 17 Right, Runway 10 for departure, Runway 28 for arrival available on request. Inform ground control of your ramp area and direction of flight . Arrivals use caution for simultaneous and opposite directions operations in progress on parallel runways. Advise on initial contact you have ATIS information Juliet."

Tower 6566

Road Bend

West Bijou Creek

QUESTIONS

1. What is the UNICOM frequency at Centennial Airport (see page 11-17)?

2. What NDBs are available for navigation in the vicinity of the Colorado Springs Airport (see page 11-21)?

3. What is the elevation of the approach end of Runway 17 at Pueblo Memorial Airport (see page 11-23)?

4. What is the nearest emergency alternate airfield to the twin towers located 23 miles east of Pueblo? What is the length of the runway (see page 11-27)?

5. What type of operations can be conducted on the stopway located at the departure end of La Junta's Runway 26 (see page 11-29)?

6. What is the maximum elevation figure in the vicinity of Limon Municipal Airport (see page 11-35)?

7. Is fuel available at Limon Municipal Airport? If so, how can it be obtained (see page 11-35)?

8. What is the base of the Class B airspace over Everitt Airfield (located 9 miles east of Centennial; see page 11-39)?

9. Plan a cross-country flight in your local flying area which meets the following minimum requirements: 150 n.m. in length; full-stop landings at 3 points; one segment consisting of 50 n.m. between takeoff and landing locations.

APPENDIX A
ANSWERS

NOTE: THERE ARE NO QUESTIONS FOR CHAPTER 1 — DISCOVERING AVIATION.

CHAPTER 2
SECTION A

1. A. Fuselage
   B. Wings
   C. Powerplant
   D. Empennage
   E. Landing Gear

2. The monocoque design uses the skin to support almost all imposed loads while the semi-monocoque system uses a substructure riveted to the airplane's skin to maintain the shape of the airframe and increase its strength.

3. Up

4. False

5. Trim devices aerodynamically help move a control surface, or maintain the surface in a desired position.

6. Conventional landing gear

7. Accessories mounted on, or connected to the engine generate electrical power, provide a vacuum source for some flight instruments, and, in most single-engine airplanes, provide a source of heat for the pilot and passengers.

8. B

9. A

10. C

SECTION B

1. A. Power
   B. Intake
   C. Exhaust
   D. Compression

2. Lean the mixture

3. Your first indication of carburetor icing in an airplane with a fixed-pitch propeller will be a decrease in engine r.p.m.

4. There can be a sharp temperature drop in a float-type carburetor due to fuel vaporization and decreasing air pressure in the venturi. If water vapor in the air condenses when the carburetor temperature is at or below freezing, ice may form. Since engines equipped with a fuel injection system eliminate the carburetor, they are relatively free from the formation of induction icing.

5. Detonation. Since detonation can occur when the engine overheats, if you suspect detonation while in flight you should attempt to lower the cylinder temperature. Methods include retarding the throttle,

enriching the fuel mixture, and/or lowering the nose to increase airspeed and the cooling airflow around the engine.

6. You should not use a fuel grade lower than specified because it can cause cylinder head and engine temperatures to exceed normal operating limits. You may substitute the next higher grade, but only if it is approved by the manufacturer.

7. The engine oil system performs many functions including lubricating the engine's moving parts, cooling the engine by reducing friction and removing some of the heat from the cylinders, providing a seal between the cylinder walls and pistons, and carrying away contaminants which are removed as the oil passes through a filter.

8. Low

9. True

10. No

SECTION C

1. Standard atmospheric pressure and temperature at sea level equals 29.92 in. Hg. and 15°C, respectively.

2. The airspeed indicator is the only instrument which uses pitot pressure.

3. A. V_{S0}
   B. V_{S1}
   C. V_{FE}
   D. V_{NO}
   E. V_{NE}

4. Maneuvering speed (V_A)

5. C

6. D

7. B

8. A

9. No. If you fly from an area of high pressure to an area of low pressure without resetting your altimeter, the altimeter will sense the decrease in pressure as an increase in altitude. The altitude indicated on the altimeter will be higher than the true altitude of the airplane.

10. At altitudes above the point where the static ports became clogged, the airspeed indicator will indicate slower than actual because the trapped static pressure is higher than normal for that altitude. At altitudes lower than the point where the static ports became clogged, the airspeed will indicate faster than actual since the trapped static pressure is lower than normal for that altitude.

11. Pitch

12. False

CHAPTER 3
SECTION A

1. B

2. A. Upwash
   B. Leading edge
   C. Trailing edge
   D. Downwash
   E. Flight path
   F. Relative wind
   G. Camber
   H. Chord line
   I. Angle of attack

3. According to Bernoulli's principle, the increase in speed of air on the top of an airfoil produces a drop in pressure and this lowered pressure is a component of total lift. In addition, a downward-backward flow of air is generated from the top surface of the wing. Newton's third law of motion explains how the action of downwash and the airstream striking the lower surface of the wing results in a reaction of positive lift.

4. False

5. A. Aspect Ratio = 7
   B. Aspect Ratio = 7
   C. Aspect Ratio = 3.4

6. You can control lift by changing airspeed, changing angle of attack, or by employing high-lift devices such as trailing edge flaps.

7. Increase

8. It is preferable for the wing root to stall first. If the wingtips stall before the root, the disrupted airflow near the wingtip can reduce aileron effectiveness to such an extent that it may be impossible to control the airplane about its longitudinal axis.

9. Parasite drag normally is divided into three types; form drag, interference drag, and skin friction drag. Streamlining decreases form drag, and design features, such as wheel fairings and retractable landing gear, can reduce both form and interference drag. Skin friction drag can be minimized by eliminating protruding rivet heads, and employing a glossy flat finish to airplane surfaces.

10. Induced drag is caused by the downwash created by wingtip vortices formed when the wing is generating lift. As the air pressure differential between the upper and lower surfaces of the wing becomes greater with an increase in angle of attack, stronger vortices form and induced drag is increased. Since the wing is usually at a low angle of attack at high speeds, and a high angle at low speeds, a relationship between induced drag and speed can be determined. Induced drag is inversely proportional to the square of the speed.

11. One wingspan

SECTION B

1. A. Lateral
   B. Pitch
   C. Vertical
   D. Yaw
   E. Roll
   F. Longitudinal

2. B

3. A

4. C

5. Forward

6. On many training aircraft, an increase in thrust increases the pitching moment and nose heaviness due to the placement of the thrustline of the aircraft. This helps counteract the longitudinally destabilizing effect of increased downwash that results from an increase in power and extension of high lift devices.

7. Upwash passing around the fuselage just ahead of the wing tends to roll a high wing aircraft toward the upright position, contributing to lateral stability. In a low wing airplane, the downwash around the fuselage tends to be laterally destabilizing since it tends to increase the roll. The amount of dihedral is adjusted to compensate for the effects of fuselage upwash and downwash resulting in a greater requirement for dihedral in a low wing airplane than in a high wing configuration.

8. Decreases

9. Spiral instability

10. True

11. • Decrease the angle of attack.
    • Smoothly apply maximum power.
    • Once the airplane recovers, adjust the power as necessary while maintaining coordinated flight.

12. • Throttle to idle.
    • Neutralize the ailerons.
    • Determine the direction of rotation.
    • Apply full opposite rudder.
    • Briskly apply elevator (or stabilator) to neutral or slightly forward of neutral.
    • As rotation stops, neutralize the rudders.
    • Gradually apply aft elevator (or stabilator) to return to level flight.

SECTION C

1. Thrust

2. Low airspeed, high power settings, and high angles of attack.

3. Left turning tendencies can be corrected for, in part, through the employment an offset vertical stabilizer and/or a rudder trim tab.

4. Yes. Variations in weight do not affect the glide ratio of an airplane, but the heavier aircraft will sink faster, and reach the ground sooner. To travel the same distance as the lighter aircraft, a higher airspeed will need to be maintained by the heavier airplane. This higher airspeed, which corresponds to the best glide airspeed at that weight, increases ground speed and allows the

heavier aircraft to cover the same horizontal distance even though its rate of descent is higher.

5. When an airplane is banked, lift is comprised of two components. The airplane turns because the horizontal component of lift creates a force directed inward toward the center of rotation.

6. Decrease airspeed

7. 59 knots

8. 66 knots

9. 110 knots

10. False

CHAPTER 4
SECTION A

1. The most effective way to scan during daylight is through a series of short, regularly spaced eye movements, focusing for at least one second in 10° sectors. This method, which brings successive areas of the sky into the central visual field, is compatible with how the eyes function. Although two normal healthy eyes have a visual field of approximately 200°, the area in which the eye can focus sharply and perceive detail is a relatively narrow cone (usually only about 10° wide) directly in the center of the field of vision. Beyond this area, visual acuity decreases sharply in all directions.

2. False

3. B

4. A

5. B

6. A

7. C

8. A

9. B

10. C

11. A three step process is recommended when exchanging flight controls. The pilot passing the controls should announce, *"You have the flight controls."* The pilot passing the controls should continue to fly until the pilot taking the controls acknowledges the exchange by saying, *"I have the flight controls."* A visual check is recommended to ensure that the other pilot actually has the controls. The pilot passing should then state, *"You have the flight controls."*

SECTION B

1. Runway numbers correspond to a magnetic north reference. The runway's magnetic direction is rounded off to the nearest 10°, with the last zero omitted. Any runway that is between the headings of 010° and 090° is designated with a single-digit runway number. The number at the end of the runway corresponds to the direction that you are heading when taking off or landing on that runway. For example, a runway labeled 9 on one end is labeled 27 on the opposite end.

2. B

3. Usually, a displaced threshold indicates that there are obstructions such as trees, powerlines, or buildings off

the end of the runway. This might prohibit a normal descent and landing on the initial portion of the pavement. Although the pavement leading up to a displaced threshold may not be used for landing, it may be available for taxiing, the landing rollout, and takeoffs.

4. A closed runway is designated by a yellow X.

5. A

6. C

7. B

8. A

9. True

10. B

11. A

12. C

13. C

14. E

15. F

16. B

17. To activate three-step pilot-controlled lighting, the mike must be keyed seven times on the specified frequency to turn all the lights on at maximum intensity. The mike is keyed five times for medium-intensity, and three times for the lowest intensity lighting. The mike must be keyed the required number of times within a period of five seconds.

SECTION C

1. 40°9′N — 122°15′W

2. 4,000 feet MSL. The contour line indicates that the elevation of the Conboy Lake National Wildlife Refuge is 2,000 feet MSL. To fly 2,000 feet above the surface over this special conservation area, you should fly at least 4,000 feet MSL.

3. D

4. C

5. A

6. E

7. B

8. False

9. 120.1 MHz

10. 544 feet MSL

11. True

12. Pounds Airport has services and fuel available during normal business hours.

13. The airport has a rotating beacon which normally operates from sunset to sunrise.

14. No

15. Fort Worth FSS

16. B

SECTION D

1. 1 statute mile, clear of clouds

2. C

3. 3 statute miles visibility; 500 feet below, 1,000 feet above, and 2,000 feet horizontally from clouds

4. Salina Airport

5. Floor — 2,200 feet MSL; ceiling — 5,000 feet MSL

6. False

7. 3 statute miles visibility; clear of clouds

8. 18,000 feet MSL

9. 250 knots

10. It would be necessary to request a special VFR clearance if you wished to operate within the area of Class B, C, D, or E airspace which extends to the surface around the airport, when the ground visibility is less than 3 statute miles and the cloud ceiling is less than 1,000 feet AGL. A special VFR clearance may allow you to enter, leave, or operate within most Class D and Class E surface areas and some Class B and Class C surface areas if the flight visibility is at least 1 statute mile and you can remain clear of clouds. At least 1 statute mile ground visibility is required for takeoff and landing, however if ground visibility is not reported, you must have at least 1 statute mile flight visibility. Special VFR is not permitted between sunset and sunrise unless you have a current instrument rating and the aircraft is equipped for instrument flight.

11. A, D, and E

CHAPTER 5
SECTION A

1. The limitations of primary radar include the bending of radar pulses (anomalous propagation) and the blocking of radar returns by precipitation or heavy clouds. Two of the most significant drawbacks to the primary radar system are its inability to easily identify an individual aircraft return and to display an aircraft's altitude.

2. Decoder, interrogator, transponder

3. C

4. D

5. B

6. A

7. False

8. B

9. B

10. B

11. ATC issues a safety alert when an aircraft is in unsafe proximity to terrain, obstructions, or other aircraft.

12. C

13. Automatic terminal information service (ATIS)

14. VHF transmitter and receiver

SECTION B

1. B

2. *"Cessna six four niner Sierra Papa"*

3. 2100Z

4. 1700Z

5. The three methods are communication with a UNICOM operator, contacting an FSS on the field, or making a self-announce broadcast.

6. 10 miles

7. False

8. B

9. Set your transponder code to 7600. Remain outside or above the Class D airspace until you have determined the direction and flow of traffic. Then, join the airport traffic pattern and maintain visual contact with the tower to receive light signals. In the daytime, acknowledge light signals by rocking your wings, and at night, by blinking your landing or navigation lights. A steady green signal indicates that you are cleared to land.

10. A

11. C

12. B

13. The FARs require that the ELT battery must be replaced, or recharged if the battery is rechargeable, after one-half of the battery's useful life or if the transmitter has been used for more than one cumulative hour.

SECTION C

1. Three nautical miles east

2. 2,778 feet MSL

3. Runway 12L/30R is 8,000 feet long and 150 feet wide.

4. C

5. C

6. False

7. 2015Z

8. Columbus FSS

9. NOTAM file LBF

10. B

11. NOTAM(D) information is disseminated for all navigational facilities which are part of the U.S. airspace system, all public use airports, seaplane bases, and heliports listed in the A/FD. NOTAM(L)s are distributed locally and contain information such as taxiway closures, personnel and equipment near or crossing runways, and airport rotating beacon and lighting aid outages. FDC NOTAMs, issued by the National Flight Data Center, contain regulatory information such as temporary flight restrictions or amendments to instrument approach procedures and other current aeronautical charts.

12. *Advisory Circular Checklist* (AC-00-2)

CHAPTER 6
SECTION A

1. A. Troposphere

   B. Stratosphere

   C. Mesosphere

   D. Thermosphere

2. The troposphere

3. As air is heated, it expands and becomes less dense than the surrounding air. As air cools, its molecules become packed more closely together, making it

denser and heavier than warm air. As a result, the cool, heavy air tends to sink and replace warmer, rising air.

4. Unequal heating of the earth's surface

5. False

6. The amount of deflection an object experiences due to Coriolis force is a function of distance traveled, position on the earth's surface (latitude), and speed of the object.

7. In the upper atmosphere, pressure gradient force and Coriolis force cause wind to flow roughly parallel to the isobars. However, within approximately 2,000 feet of the ground, friction caused by the earth's surface slows the movement of air. This reduces the effect of Coriolis force and causes the pressure gradient force to divert the wind toward the lower pressure area.

8. D

9. A

10. B

11. C

SECTION B

1. 2°C (3.5°F) per 1,000 feet

2. When air rises into an area of lower pressure, it expands to a larger volume. As the molecules of air expand, the temperature of the air lowers. As a result, when a parcel of air rises, pressure decreases, volume increases, and temperature decreases. When air descends, pressure increases, volume decreases, and temperature increases.

3. Evaporation and sublimation

4. 2,000 feet AGL

5. A. Cirrus

   B. Altocumulus

   C. Stratus

   D. Towering Cumulus

6. False

7. For precipitation to occur, water or ice particles must grow in size until they can no longer be supported by the atmosphere.

8. Rain generally falls at a relatively steady rate and stops gradually. On the other hand, rain showers generally begin, change intensity, and stop suddenly.

9. A stable airmass generally exhibits widespread stratiform clouds, restricted visibility, smooth air, and steady rain or drizzle.

10. B

11. C

12. A

SECTION C

1. Thunderstorm formation requires unstable conditions, a lifting force, and high moisture levels.

2. As the vertical motions slow near the top of the storm, winds tend to spread the cloud horizontally, forming the anvil shape. Since the anvil's shape is formed by upper-level winds, it points in the approximate direction of the storm's movement.

3. If you encounter turbulence during flight, slow the airplane to maneuvering speed or less, maintain a level

flight attitude, and accept variations in altitude. If you expect turbulent or gusty conditions during an approach to a landing, you should consider flying a power-on approach at an airspeed slightly above the normal approach speed.

4. False

5. The most dangerous condition for landing is a light, quartering tailwind since it can move the upwind vortex of a landing aircraft over the runway and forward into the touchdown zone.

6. C

7. Mountain wave turbulence

8. In humid climates where the bases of convective clouds tend to be low, microbursts are associated with a visible rainshaft. In drier climates, the higher thunderstorm cloud bases result in the evaporation of the rainshaft. The only visible indications under these conditions may be virga at the cloud base and a dust ring on the ground.

9. B

10. C

11. A

12. A

CHAPTER 7
SECTION A

1. False

2. Short periods of time

3. Numerical weather prediction uses mathematical equations which relate atmospheric conditions with other variables. The system of equations represents the physical laws which govern the behavior of the atmosphere. The computer applies the model to the current atmospheric conditions to forecast minutes in the future. The process is repeated many times to create a prediction for the next day or two.

4. A

5. Large storms and major heat waves

SECTION B

1. Prevailing visibility is the greatest distance an observer can see and identify objects through at least half of the horizon. RVR is based on what a pilot in a moving aircraft should see when looking down the runway.

2. B

3. At the time of the observation, clouds with bases at 800 feet AGL covered 5/8 to 7/8 of the sky.

4. Routine observation...William P. Hobby Airport...on the 22nd day of the month at 1835Z...wind 170° at 9 knots...prevailing visibility 2 statute miles...thunderstorm with light rain...scattered clouds at 400 feet AGL...broken clouds at 900 feet AGL...overcast skies at 1,500 feet AGL...temperature 21°C, dewpoint 20°C...altimeter 30.04 in. Hg....remarks...thunderstorm began 12 minutes past the hour...sea level pressure 1017.0 mb (hPa)...temperature 20.6°C, dewpoint 19.6°C.

5. True

6. B

7. A gradual change in the weather will take place between 0300Z and 0500Z.

8. Routine forecast...Pittsburgh International Airport...on the 9th day of the month at 1730Z...valid for 24 hours from 1800Z on the 9th to 1800Z on the 10th...wind from 220° at 20 knots...visibility 3 statute miles...light rain showers...broken clouds at 2,000 feet AGL. From 2030Z...wind 300° at 15 knots, with gusts to 25 knots...3 statute miles visibility...rain showers...sky overcast at 1,500 feet AGL...temporary conditions between 2000Z and 2200Z...visibility 1/2 statute mile...thunderstorm and rain...sky overcast with bases of cumulonimbus clouds at 800 feet AGL. From 0100Z...wind 270° at 8 knots...visibility 5 statute miles...light rain showers, broken clouds at 2,000 feet AGL...overcast skies at 4,000 feet AGL. A 40% probability...between 0400Z and 0700Z...wind 270° at 8 knots...visibility 1 statute mile...light rain. From 1000Z...wind 220° at 10 knots, visibility 5 statute miles, light rain showers, sky overcast at 2,000 feet AGL. Becoming...between 1300Z and 1500Z...wind 200° and 10 knots...visibility greater than 6 statute miles...no significant weather.

9. You should expect ceilings from 1,000 to 3,000 feet AGL and visibility 3 to 5 statute miles.

10. You can expect a groundspeed of 155 knots and an outside air temperature of –2°C.

11. B

12. False

SECTION C

1. A square station model indicates an automated observation site.

2. IFR conditions with ceilings less than 1,000 feet and/or visibility less than 3 miles

3. 0200Z

4. 50,000 feet MSL

5. Southwest at 4 knots

6. The visible satellite weather picture generally is used to determine the presence of clouds as well as the cloud shape and texture. An infrared photo, on the other hand, depicts the heat radiation emitted by various cloud tops and the earth's surface. For this reason, the infrared picture can be used to determine cloud height. Usually, cold temperatures show up as light gray or white, with high clouds appearing the whitest.

7. C

8. Moderate turbulence from the surface to 10,000 feet MSL

9. The severe weather outlook chart

10. 170° at 20 knots; 3°C

SECTION D

1. When you request a briefing, identify yourself as a pilot flying VFR and provide the briefer with your aircraft number or your name, aircraft type, departure air- port, route of flight, destination, flight altitude(s), estimated time of departure (ETD), and estimated time enroute (ETE).

2. A standard preflight briefing is the most complete weather briefing, and assumes you have no basic familiarity with the overall weather picture. An abbreviated briefing is appropriate for situations when you need only one or two specific items or would like to update weather information from a previous briefing or other weather sources. You should request an outlook briefing when your proposed departure time is six or more hours away. An outlook briefing will provide you with forecast information appropriate to your proposed flight, and can help you make an initial judgment about the feasibility of your flight.

3. False

4. B

5. Sectional charts and the *Airport/Facility Directory* (A/FD)

6. C

7. 122.0 MHz

8. The automated surface observation system (ASOS)

CHAPTER 8
SECTION A

1. In the Performance section of your airplane's POH

2. As density altitude increases, engine horsepower decreases for normally aspirated engines since the actual amount of air to support combustion has decreased. In addition, both the wing and the propeller lose efficiency in the thinner air.

3. True

4. Headwind: 17 knots; crosswind: 10 knots.

5. B

6. Ground roll: 1,665 feet; total distance to clear a 50-foot obstacle: 3,300 feet.

7. False

8. Time, fuel, and distance

9. B

10. 495 nautical miles with reserves; 555 nautical miles without reserves.

11. False

SECTION B

1. Datum or reference datum

2. Fuel which cannot be drained or safely used in flight

3. A

4. C

5. C

6. Lower

7. False

8. 55,000 inch-pounds

9. 64.67 gallons

10. 44.65 inches

11. 102 pounds

12. C

13. A

14. B

SECTION C

1. 88 knots

2. 12.4 gallons per hour

3. 107 knots; Indicated rather than calibrated airspeed was used.

4. 21.8 gallons

5. 129 nautical miles

6. 147°; 90 knots

7. 81 minutes

8. 2 hours, 46 minutes

9. 248° at 27 knots

10. 001°; 107 knots

CHAPTER 9

SECTION A

1. B

2. Positions are found by direct observation of visual landmarks, off-course drift can be detected in between checkpoints, and the results of course corrections or changes in winds can usually be observed directly. It is the simplest form of navigation, requires no equipment other than a chart and a pencil, and is immune from mechanical failures or breakdowns.

3. True

4. True

5. True

6. C

7. C

8. Terrain and obstruction clearance, climb time and aircraft performance, effects of headwinds or tailwinds, radio reception range, and the VFR cruising altitude rule.

9. C

10. Flight service stations

11. Extend your ETA by calling any FSS within radio range.

12. True

SECTION B

1. C

2. Course guidance and distance information

3. A. Omnibearing selector (OBS) or course selector

   B. Course deviation indicator (CDI)

   C. Course index

   D. TO/FROM indicator

   E. Reciprocal course index.

4. To avoid reverse sensing

5. C

6. C

7. B

8. D

9. True

10. 2 nautical miles

SECTION C

1. B

2. RB = 0°, MB = 050°

3. RB = 045°, MB = 165°

4. RB = 135°, MB = 270°

5. RB = 120°, MB = 180°

6. RB = 230°, MB = 140°

7. RB = 345°, MB = 225°

8. B

9. False

10. Reception range for L/MF facilities can vary greatly, depending on transmitter power, atmospheric conditions, and time of day. Since the ADF indicator does not have an OFF flag, it is possible to inadvertently refer to the signal after it is no longer reliable. If the heading indicator precesses or is not set correctly, your courses will be off by as many degrees as the heading indicator is in error. Night effect may cause NDB signals to be refracted by the ionosphere and return to earth 30 to 60 miles or more from the station which leads to needle fluctuations on the ADF indicator.

   When in close proximity to an electrical storm, thunderstorm effect can cause the ADF needle to point to the source of the lightning flashes rather than the tuned NDB. Precipitation static can interfere with ADF indications and cause the bearing indicator to wander. Terrain effect can occur when mountains reflect the radio waves and cause erroneous bearing indications. In addition, shorelines can refract low frequency radio waves when they cross at small angles causing fluctuations in bearing indications.

SECTION D

1. The deviation scale is in nautical miles instead of degrees.

2. The LORAN receiver measures the time difference between the reception of a master station's signal and that of a secondary station to determine a line of position (LOP). Using another secondary station, the LORAN receiver calculates a second LOP and fixes your position at the intersection of the two LOPs.

3. False

4. A, B, and C

5. Space, control, and user

6. Four

7. 100 meters

8. True

CHAPTER 10

SECTION A

1. Cones are concentrated in the center of the retina in a slight depression known as the fovea. The cones are sensitive to bright light and colors. The cones also allow you to see fine detail, but they do not function well in darkness. The rods, which are concentrated outside the foveal area, react to low light and are responsible for most of your night and peripheral vision. The rods do not perceive color or detail well.

2. B

3. Autokinesis

4. True

5. Awareness of your body's position is a result of input from three primary sources: vision, the vestibular system, and your kinesthetic sense.

6. During a prolonged constant-rate turn, your vestibular system may not sense any motion since the fluid in the semicircular canals eventually reaches equilibrium and the hair cells are no longer deflected.

7. A

8. B

9. A

10. D

11. C

12. B

13. Suggest that the passenger slow his or her breathing rate, breathe into a paper bag, or talk aloud.

SECTION B

1. Pilot in command, aircraft, environment, and operation

2. The National Transportation Safety Board (NTSB) is an independent Federal agency responsible for investigating every U.S. civil aviation accident and issuing safety recommendations aimed at preventing future accidents. In addition, the NTSB maintains the government's database on civil aviation accidents and conducts research regarding safety issues of national significance. Examining NTSB accident and incident reports can increase your awareness of the factors which affect a pilot's decision-making ability and help you learn to recognize the chain of events which lead to an accident.

3. False

4. C

5. You can refer to a personal checklist which specifies limitations such as a maximum amount of time that may pass between flights without refresher training or review of the regulations and POH, your own weather minimums, which may be higher than those listed in the FARs, and the maximum amount of crosswind that you are comfortable with. After you have reviewed your personal limitations, you can use the I'm Safe Checklist to further evaluate your fitness for flight.

6. C

7. B

8. A

9. E

10. D

11. Barriers to effective communication include a lack of a common core of experience between the communicator and receiver, misuse of terminology, and an overuse of abstractions. Elements which lead to communication breakdown between pilots and controllers include confusion stemming from similar call signs, alpha-numeric errors, poor radio procedures, and readback problems. Other errors are caused when the pilot expects to hear a certain transmission and follows old habit patterns, only to learn later that ATC had requested something different.

12. The aircraft POH; aeronautical charts; flight computer and plotter; the *Airport/Facility Directory* or similar airport information source; ATC assistance, including FSS specialists; another pilot or passenger on board; navigation equipment such as VOR, ADF, GPS, LORAN; an autopilot; and your own ingenuity, knowledge, and skills

13. True

14. B

CHAPTER 11

SECTION A

1. 8,308 feet

2. 1.0% down

3. 100LL and Jet A

4. Antelope

5. 122.35 MHz

6. 11,500 feet MSL

7. 8,400 feet MSL

8. The notation indicates that the floor of Class E airspace in the area is at 6,000 feet MSL.

9. 122.7 MHz; 6,000 feet

10. The *Airport/Facility Directory*

11. 60 n.m.

12. False

SECTION B

1. 122.95 MHz

2. Petey (407 kHz) and Ironhorse (335 kHz)

3. 4,726 feet

4. Fowler; 3,200 feet

5. The stopway can be used an by an aircraft to decelerate and come to a stop only; it cannot be used for landing, takeoff, or taxiing.

6. 6,600 feet MSL

7. Yes. Fuel can be obtained by calling the Limon Police Department.

8. 8,000 feet MSL

APPENDIX B
ABBREVIATIONS

A/FD — *Airport/Facility Directory*

AC — advisory circular

AC — alternating current

AC — convective outlook (weather)

ADF — automatic direction finder

ADIZ — air defense identification zone

ADM — aeronautical decision making

AFM — airplane flight manual

AFSS — automated flight service station

AGL — above ground level

AIM — *Aeronautical Information Manual*

AIRMET — airman's meteorological information

ALS — approach light system

ARSR — air route surveillance radar

ARTCC — air route traffic control center

ARTS — automated radar terminal system

ASOS — automated surface observation system

ASR — airport surveillance radar

ATA — actual time of arrival

ATC — air traffic control

ATCRBS — ATC radar beacon system

ATD — actual time of departure

ATE — actual time enroute

ATIS — automatic terminal information service

ATP — airline transport pilot

AWOS — automated weather observing system

AWW — alert severe weather watch

BFO — beat frequency oscillator

BHP — brake horsepower

CAP — Civil Air Patrol

CAS — calibrated airspeed

CAT — clear air turbulence

CDI — course deviation indicator

CFI — certificated flight instructor

CG — center of gravity

CFR — Code of Federal Regulations

C$_L$ — coefficient of lift

CO — carbon monoxide

CO$_2$ — carbon dioxide

CTAF — common traffic advisory frequency

CRM — crew resource management

CW — continuous wave

CWA — center weather advisory

DA — density altitude

DC — direct current

DF — direction finder

DG — directional gyro

DME — distance measuring equipment

DUATS — direct user access terminal system

DVFR — defense visual flight rules

EFAS — enroute flight advisory service

ELT — emergency locator transmitter

ETA — estimated time of arrival

ETD — estimated time of departure

ETE — estimated time enroute

f.p.m. — feet per minute

FA — aviation area forecast

FAA — Federal Aviation Administration

FARs — Federal Aviation Regulations

FBO — fixed base operator

FCC — Federal Communications Commission

FD — winds and temperatures aloft forecast

FDC — Flight Data Center

FL — flight level

FM — frequency modulation

FSDO — Flight Standards District Office

FSS — flight service station

g.p.h. — gallons per hour

GPS — global positioning system

GS — groundspeed

HF — high frequency

HIRLs — high intensity runway lights

HIWAS — hazardous in-flight weather advisory service

hPa — hectoPascal

HSI — horizontal situation indicator

HVOR — high altitude VOR

Hz — hertz

IAS — indicated airspeed

ICAO — International Civil Aviation Organization

IFR — instrument flight rules

ILS — instrument landing system

IMC — instrument meteorological conditions

in. Hg. — inches of mercury

INS — inertial navigation system

IOAT — indicated outside air temperature

IR — IFR military training route

ISA — International Standard Atmosphere

kHz — kilohertz

KIAS — knots indicated airspeed

KTAS — knots true airspeed

L/MF — low/medium frequency

LAA — local airport advisory

LAHSO — land and hold short operations

LAT — latitude

LF — low frequency

LIRLs — low intensity runway lights

LLWAS — low level wind shear alert system

LONG — longitude

LOP — line of position

LORAN — long range navigation

LVOR — low altitude VOR

MB — magnetic bearing

mb — millibar

MEF — maximum elevation figure

METAR — aviation routine weather report

MH — magnetic heading

MHz — megahertz

MIRLs — medium intensity runway lights

MOA — military operations area

MSAW — minimum safe altitude warning

MSL — mean sea level

MTR — military training route

MULTICOM — frequency used at airports without a tower, FSS, or UNICOM

MVFR — marginal VFR

n.m. — nautical miles

NAVAID — navigational aid

NDB — nondirectional radio beacon

NOAA — National Oceanic and Atmospheric Administration

NOS — National Ocean Service

NOTAM — notice to airmen

NPRM — notice of proposed rule making

NSA — national security area

NTAP — *Notices to Airmen Publication*

NTSB — National Transportation Safety Board

NWS — National Weather Service

OAT — outside air temperature

OBS — omnibearing selector

p.s.i. — pounds per square inch

PA — pressure altitude

PAPI — precision approach path indicator

PCL — pilot controlled lighting

PIC — pilot in command

PIM — pilot information manual

PIREP — pilot weather report

PLASI — pulsating approach slope indicator

POH — pilot's operating handbook

PTS — practical test standards

r.p.m. — revolutions per minute

RAREP — radar weather report

RB — relative bearing

RCO — remote communications outlet

REIL — runway end identifier lights

RMI — radio magnetic indicator

RNAV — area navigation

RVR — runway visual range

s.m. — statute mile

SAR — search and rescue

SCATANA — Security Control of Air Traffic and Air Navigation Aids

SD — radar weather report

SIGMET — significant meteorological information

SPECI — non-routine (special) aviation weather report

SVFR — special VFR

TACAN — tactical air navigation

TAF — terminal aerodrome forecast

TAS — true airspeed

TC — true course

TDWR — terminal Doppler weather radar

TEL-TWEB — telephone access to TWEB

TH — true heaing

TIBS — telephone information briefing service

TRACON — terminal radar approach control facilities

TRSA — terminal radar service area

TVOR — terminal VOR

TWEB — transcribed weather broadcast

UHF — ultra high frequency

UNICOM — aeronautical advisory station

UTC — coordinated universal time (Zulu time)

UWS — urgent weather SIGMET

VAFTAD — volcanic ash transport and dispersion chart

VASI — visual approach slope indicator

VFR — visual flight rules

VHF — very high frequency

VHF/DF — VHF direction finder

VMC — visual meteorological conditions

VOR — VHF omnidirectional receiver

VOR/DME — collocated VOR and DME

VORTAC — collocated VOR and TACAN

VOT — VOR test facility

VR — VFR military training route

VSI — vertical speed indicator

WA — AIRMET

WAC — world aeronautical chart

WCA — wind correction angle

WH — hurricane advisory

WS — SIGMET

WST — convective SIGMET

WW — severe weather watch bulletin

APPENDIX C
GLOSSARY

ABSOLUTE ALTITUDE — Actual height above the surface of the earth, either land or water.

ABSOLUTE CEILING — The altitude where a particular airplane's climb rate reaches zero.

ADIABATIC COOLING — A process of cooling the air through expansion. For example, as air moves up a slope it expands with the reduction of atmospheric pressure and cools as it expands.

ADIABATIC HEATING — A process of heating dry air through compression. For example, as air moves down a slope it is compressed, which results in an increase in temperature.

ADVECTION FOG — Fog resulting from the movement of warm, humid air over a cold surface.

AGONIC LINE — Line along which the variation between true and magnetic values is zero.

AIR DENSITY — The density of the air in terms of mass per unit volume. Dense air has more molecules per unit volume than less dense air. The density of air decreases with altitude above the surface of the earth and with increasing temperature.

AIR ROUTE TRAFFIC CONTROL CENTER (ARTCC) — A facility established to provide air traffic control service to aircraft operating on IFR flight plans within controlled airspace, principally during the enroute phase of flight.

AIR TRAFFIC CONTROL (ATC) — A service provided by the FAA to promote the safe, orderly, and expeditious flow of air traffic.

AIRMASS — An extensive body of air having fairly uniform properties of temperature and moisture.

AIRMET — In-flight weather advisory concerning moderate icing, moderate turbulence, sustained winds of 30 knots or more at the surface, and widespread areas of ceilings less than 1,000 feet and/or visibility less than 3 miles.

AIRPORT ADVISORY AREA — The area within 10 statute miles of an airport where a flight service station is located, but where there is no control tower in operation.

AIRPORT SURVEILLANCE RADAR (ASR) — Approach and departure control radar used to detect and display an aircraft's position in the terminal area.

ALERT AREA — Special use airspace which may contain a high volume of pilot training activities or an unusual type of aerial activity.

ALTIMETER — A flight instrument that indicates altitude by sensing pressure changes.

ALTIMETER SETTING — The barometric pressure setting used to adjust a pressure altimeter for variations in existing atmospheric pressure and temperature.

ALTITUDE — Height expressed in units of distance above a reference plane, usually above mean sea level or above ground level.

ANGLE OF ATTACK — The angle between the airfoil's chord line and the relative wind.

ANGLE OF INCIDENCE — The angle between the chord line of the wing and the longitudinal axis of the airplane.

ARM — The distance from the reference datum at which a weight may be located. Used in weight and balance calculations to determine moment.

ASPECT RATIO — Span of a wing divided by its average chord.

AUTOMATED SURFACE OBSERVATION SYSTEM (ASOS) — Weather reporting system which provides surface observations every minute via digitized voice broadcasts and printed reports.

AUTOMATED WEATHER OBSERVING SYSTEM (AWOS) — Automated weather reporting system consisting of various sensors, a processor, a computer-generated voice subsystem, and a transmitter to broadcast weather data.

AUTOMATIC DIRECTION FINDER (ADF) — An aircraft radio navigation system which senses and indicates the direction to an L/MF nondirectional radio beacon (NDB) or commercial broadcast station.

AUTOMATIC TERMINAL INFORMATION SERVICE (ATIS) — The continuous broadcast of recorded noncontrol information in selected terminal areas. Its purpose is to improve controller effectiveness and to relieve frequency congestion by automating the repetitive transmission of essential but routine information.

BASIC RADAR SERVICE — A radar service for VFR aircraft which includes safety alerts, traffic advisories, and limited radar vectoring, as well as aircraft sequencing at some terminal locations.

BEARING — The horizontal direction to or from any point, usually measured clockwise from true north (true bearing), magnetic north (magnetic bearing), or some other reference point, through 360°.

BEST ANGLE-OF-CLIMB AIRSPEED (V_X) — The airspeed which produces the greatest gain in altitude for horizontal distance traveled.

BEST RATE OF CLIMB AIRSPEED (V_Y) — The airspeed which produces the maximum gain in altitude per unit of time.

BLAST PAD — An area associated with a runway where propeller blast can dissipate without creating a hazard to others. It cannot be used for landing, takeoffs, or taxiing.

BRACKETING — A navigation technique which uses a series of turns into a crosswind to regain and maintain the desired course.

CALIBRATED AIRSPEED (CAS) — Indicated airspeed of an aircraft, corrected for installation and instrument errors.

CALIBRATED ALTITUDE — Indicated altitude corrected to compensate for instrument error

CAMBER — The curve of an airfoil section from the leading edge to the trailing edge.

CATEGORY — (1) As used with respect to the certification, ratings, privileges, and limitations of airmen, means a broad classification of aircraft (airplane, rotorcraft, glider, lighter-than-air, and powered lift). (2) As used with respect to the certification of aircraft, means a grouping of aircraft by intended use or operating limitations (transport, normal, utility, acrobatic, limited, restricted, experimental, and provisional).

CEILING — The height above the earth's surface of the lowest layer of clouds which is reported as broken or overcast or the vertical visibility into an obscuration.

CENTER OF GRAVITY (CG) — The theoretical point where the entire weight of the airplane is considered to be concentrated.

CENTER OF PRESSURE — A point along the wing chord line where lift is considered to be concentrated.

CENTRIFUGAL FORCE — An apparent force, that opposes centripetal force, resulting from the effect of inertia during a turn.

CENTRIPETAL FORCE — A center-seeking force directed inward toward the center of rotation created by the horizontal component of lift in turning flight.

CHORD — An imaginary straight line between the leading and trailing edges of an airfoil section.

CLASS — (1) As used with respect to the certification, ratings, privileges, and limitations of airmen, means a classification of aircraft within a category having similar operating characteristics (single-engine land, multi-engine land, single-engine sea, multi-engine sea, gyroplane, helicopter, airship, and free balloon). (2) As used with respect to certification of aircraft means a broad grouping of aircraft having similar characteristics of propulsion, flight, or landing (airplane, rotorcraft, glider, balloon, landplane, and seaplane).

CLASS A AIRSPACE — Controlled airspace covering the 48 contiguous United States and Alaska, within 12 nautical miles of the coasts, from 18,000 feet MSL up to and including FL600, but not including airspace less than 1,500 feet AGL.

CLASS B AIRSPACE — Controlled airspace designated around certain major airports, extending from the surface or higher to specified altitudes where ATC provides radar separation for all IFR and VFR aircraft. For operations in Class B airspace, all aircraft must receive an ATC clearance to enter, and are subject to the rules and pilot/equipment requirements listed in FAR Part 91.

CLASS C AIRSPACE — Controlled airspace surrounding designated airports where ATC provides radar vectoring and sequencing for all IFR and VFR aircraft. Participation is mandatory, and all aircraft must establish and maintain radio contact with ATC, and are subject to the rules and pilot/equipment requirements listed in FAR Part 91.

CLASS D AIRSPACE — Controlled airspace around at least one primary airport which has an operating control tower. Aircraft operators are subject to the rules and equipment requirements specified in FAR Part 91.

CLASS E AIRSPACE — Controlled airspace which covers the 48 contiguous United States and Alaska, within 12 nautical miles of the coasts, from 14,500 feet MSL up to but not including 18,000 feet MSL but not including airspace less than 1,500 feet AGL. Class E airspace also includes Federal airways, with a floor of 1,200 feet AGL or higher, as well as the airspace from 700 feet or more above the surface designated in conjunction with an airport which has an approved instrument approach procedure.

CLASS G AIRSPACE — Airspace that has not been designated as Class A, B, C, D, or E, and within which air traffic control is not exercised.

CLEAR AIR TURBULENCE (CAT) — While CAT is often encountered near the jet stream in clear air, it also may be present at lower altitudes and in non-convective clouds.

CLEARING TURNS — Turns consisting of at least a 180° change in direction, allowing a visual check of the airspace around the airplane to avoid conflicts while maneuvering.

COLD FRONT — The boundary between two airmasses where cold air is replacing warm air.

COMMON TRAFFIC ADVISORY FREQUENCY (CTAF) — A frequency designed for the purpose of carrying out airport advisory practices while operating to or from an uncontrolled airport. The CTAF may be a UNICOM, MULTICOM, FSS, or tower frequency and it is identified in appropriate aeronautical publications.

COMPASS HEADING — Aircraft heading read from the compass. Compass heading is derived by applying correction factors for variation, deviation, and wind to true course.

CONDENSATION — A change of state of water from a gas (water vapor) to a liquid.

CONDENSATION NUCLEI — Small particles of solid matter in the air on which water vapor condenses.

CONE OF CONFUSION — The cone-shaped area above a VOR station in which there is no signal and the TO/FROM flag momentarily flickers to OFF (or a similar indication).

CONES — The cells concentrated in the center of the retina which provide color vision and sense fine detail.

CONTROLLED AIRPORT — An airport which has an operating control tower, sometimes called a tower airport.

CONTROLLED AIRSPACE — Airspace designated as Class A, B, C, D, or E, within which some or all aircraft may be subject to air traffic control.

CONVECTION — A circulation process caused by unequal air density which results from heating inequities.

CONVECTIVE SIGMET — A weather advisory concerning convective weather significant to the safety of all aircraft. Convective SIGMETs are issued for tornadoes, lines of thunderstorms, thunderstorms over a wide area, embedded thunderstorms, wind gusts to 50 knots or greater and/or hail 3/4 inch in diameter or greater.

CONVENTIONAL LANDING GEAR — Two main wheels located on either side of the fuselage and a third wheel, the tail wheel, positioned at the rear of the airplane.

COORDINATED UNIVERSAL TIME (UTC) — A method of expressing time which places the entire world on one time standard. UTC also is referred to as Zulu time.

CORIOLIS FORCE — A deflective force that is created by the difference in rotational velocity between the equator and the poles of the earth. It deflects air to the right in the northern hemisphere and to the left in the southern hemisphere.

COURSE — The intended or desired direction of flight in the horizontal plane measured in degrees from true or magnetic north.

CROSSWIND — A wind which is not parallel to a runway or the path of an aircraft.

CROSSWIND COMPONENT — A wind component which is at a right angle to the runway or the flight path of an aircraft.

DEAD RECKONING — A type of navigation based on the calculations of time, speed, distance, and direction.

DENSITY ALTITUDE — Pressure altitude corrected for nonstandard temperature.

DEPOSITION — The direct transformation of a gas to a solid state, where the liquid state is bypassed.

DEPRESSANTS —Drugs which reduce the body's functioning usually by lowering blood pressure, reducing mental processing, and slowing motor and reaction responses.

DETONATION — An uncontrolled, explosive ignition of the fuel/air mixture within the cylinder's combustion chamber.

DEVIATION — A compass error caused by magnetic disturbances from electrical and metal components in the airplane. The correction for this error is displayed on a compass correction card placed near the magnetic compass in the airplane.

DEWPOINT — The temperature at which air reaches a state where it can hold no more water.

DIHEDRAL — The upward angle of an airplane's wings with respect to the horizontal. Dihedral contributes to the lateral stability of an airplane.

DIRECTIONAL STABILITY — Stability about the vertical axis.

DISPLACED THRESHOLD — When the landing area begins at a point on the runway other than the designated beginning of the runway.

DISTANCE MEASURING EQUIPMENT (DME) — Equipment (airborne and ground) to measure, in nautical miles, the slant range distance of an aircraft from the navigation aid.

DRAG — A backward, or retarding, force which opposes thrust and limits the speed of the airplane.

EMERGENCY LOCATOR TRANSMITTER (ELT) — A battery-operated radio transmitter attached to the aircraft structure which transmits on 121.5 MHz and 243.0 MHz. It aids in locating downed aircraft.

EMPENNAGE — The section of the airplane which consists of the vertical stabilizer, the horizontal stabilizer, and the associated control surfaces.

EMPTY FIELD MYOPIA — The normal tendency of the eye to focus at only 10 to 30 feet when looking into a field devoid of objects, contrasting colors, or patterns.

EVAPORATION — The transformation of a liquid to a gaseous state, such as the change of water to water vapor.

FLIGHT SERVICE STATION (FSS) — An air traffic service facility that provides a variety of services to pilots, including weather briefings, opening and closing flight plans, and search and rescue operations.

FREEZING LEVEL — A level in the atmosphere at which the temperature is 32°F (0°C).

FRONT — The boundary between two different airmasses.

FUSELAGE — The cabin or cockpit, is located in the fuselage. It may also provide room for cargo and attachment points for other major airplane components.

GLOBAL POSITIONING SYSTEM (GPS) — A satellite-based radio positioning, navigation, and time-transfer system.

GREAT CIRCLE — The largest circle which can be drawn on the earth's surface. A great circle's plane must pass through the center of the earth dividing it into two equal parts.

GROUND EFFECT — A usually beneficial influence on aircraft performance which occurs while you are flying close to the ground. It results from a reduction in upwash, downwash, and wingtip vortices which provide a corresponding decrease in induced drag.

GROUNDSPEED (GS) — Speed of the aircraft in relation to the ground.

HAZARDOUS IN-FLIGHT WEATHER ADVISORY SERVICE (HIWAS) — Continuous recordings of hazardous weather information broadcast over selected VORs.

HEADING — The direction in which the longitudinal axis of the airplane points with respect to true or magnetic north. Heading is equal to course plus or minus any wind correction angle.

HEADWIND COMPONENT — That part of the wind which acts directly on the front of the aircraft and decreases its groundspeed.

HECTOPASCAL (hPa) — The metric equivalent of a millibar (1 hPa = 1 mb).

HIGH PERFORMANCE AIRPLANE — An airplane having more than 200 horsepower, or retractable landing gear, flaps, and controllable-pitch propeller.

HOMING — A method of navigating to an NDB by holding a zero relative bearing.

HUMIDITY — Water vapor content in the air.

HYPERVENTILATION — The excessive ventilation of the lungs caused by very rapid and deep breathing which results in an excessive loss of carbon dioxide from the body.

HYPOXIA — The effects on the human body of an insufficient supply of oxygen.

INDICATED AIRSPEED (IAS) — The speed of an aircraft as shown on the airspeed indicator.

INDICATED ALTITUDE — The altitude shown by an altimeter set to the current altimeter setting.

INDUCED DRAG — That part of total drag which is created by the production of lift. Induced drag increases with a decrease in airspeed.

INSTRUMENT FLIGHT RULES (IFR) — Rules that govern the procedure for conducting flight in weather conditions below VFR weather minimums. The term IFR also is used to define weather conditions and the type of flight plan under which an aircraft is operating.

INTERNATIONAL STANDARD ATMOSPHERE (ISA) — Standard atmospheric conditions consisting of a temperature of 59°F (15°C), and a barometric pressure of 29.92 in. Hg. (1013.2 mb) at sea level. ISA values can be calculated for various altitudes using standard lapse rates.

INVERSION — An increase in temperature with altitude.

ISOBAR — A line which connects points of equal barometric pressure.

ISOGONIC LINES — Lines on charts that connect points of equal magnetic variation.

JEPPESEN INFORMATION SERVICES — A subscription service for pilots which provides revisions for several flight information publications including the *Jeppesen AIM, Jeppesen FARs for Pilots,* the *Jeppesen Airport Directory, JeppGuide,* and the *GPS/LORAN Coordinate Directory.*

JET STREAM — A narrow band of winds with speeds of 100 to 200 m.p.h. occurring between approximately 32,000 and 49,000 feet.

KATABATIC WIND — Any downslope wind usually stronger than a mountain breeze. A katabatic wind can be either warm or cold.

LAND BREEZE — A coastal breeze blowing from land to sea caused by temperature difference when the sea surface is warmer than the adjacent land. The land breeze usually occurs at night and alternates with a sea breeze which blows in the opposite direction by day.

LAPSE RATE — The rate of decrease of an atmospheric variable with altitude.

LATERAL STABILITY — Stability about the longitudinal axis.

LATITUDE — Measurement north or south of the equator in degrees, minutes, and seconds. Lines of latitude are also called parallels.

LIFT — An upward force created by the effect of airflow as it passes over and under the wing.

LOAD FACTOR — The ratio of the load supported by the airplane's wings to the actual weight of the aircraft and its contents.

LOCAL AIRPORT ADVISORY (LAA) — Advisory service provided to pilots by an FSS at airports without an operating control tower. Information includes known traffic and weather conditions.

LONG RANGE NAVIGATION (LORAN) — A navigational system by which lines of position are determined by measuring the difference in the time of reception of synchronized pulse signals from fixed transmitters.

LONGITUDE — Measurement east or west of the Prime Meridian in degrees, minutes, and seconds. Lines of longitude are also called meridians. The Prime Meridian is 0° longitude and runs through Greenwich, England.

LONGITUDINAL STABILITY — Stability about the lateral axis. A desirable characteristic of an airplane whereby it tends to return to its trimmed angle of attack after displacement.

MAGNETIC BEARING — The magnetic course you would fly to go direct to an NDB station.

MAGNETIC COURSE — True course corrected for magnetic variation.

MAGNETO — A self-contained, engine-driven unit that supplies electrical current to the spark plugs which is completely independent of the airplane's electrical system. Normally there are two magnetos per engine.

MANEUVERING SPEED (V_A) — The maximum speed at which you can use full, abrupt control movement without overstressing the airframe.

MAYDAY — International radio distress signal. When repeated three times, it indicates imminent and grave danger and that immediate assistance is requested.

MEAN SEA LEVEL (MSL) — The average height of the surface of the sea for all stages of tide.

MESOSPHERE — A layer of the atmosphere above the stratosphere .

MICROBURST — A strong downdraft which normally occurs over horizontal distances of 1 n.m. or less and vertical distances of less than 1,000 feet. In spite of its small horizontal scale, an intense microburst could induce wind speeds greater than 100 knots and downdrafts as strong as 6,000 feet per minute.

MILITARY OPERATIONS AREA (MOA) — Special use airspace of defined vertical and lateral limits established to help VFR traffic identify locations where military activities are conducted.

MILITARY TRAINING ROUTE (MTR) — Route depicted on an aeronautical chart for the conduct of military flight training at speeds above 250 knots.

MILLIBAR (mb) — A unit of atmospheric pressure equal to a force of 1,000 dynes per square centimeter.

MOMENT — A measurement of the tendency of a weight to cause rotation at the fulcrum.

MOUNTAIN BREEZE — A downslope wind flow at night, caused by the cooling of the air at higher elevations.

MULTICOM — A frequency (122.9 MHz) for pilots to use as a common traffic advisory frequency to self announce their position and intentions at airports that don't have a tower, an FSS or a UNICOM.

NOTICE TO AIRMEN (NOTAM) — A notice containing time-critical information which is either of a temporary nature or is not known far enough in advance to permit publication on aeronautical charts or other operational publications.

OBSTRUCTION LIGHT — A light, or one of a group of lights, usually red or white, mounted on a surface structure or natural terrain to warn pilots of the presence of a flight hazard.

OCCLUDED FRONT — A frontal occlusion occurs when a fast-moving cold front catches up to a slow-moving warm front. The difference in temperature within each frontal system is a major factor in determining whether a cold or warm front occlusion occurs.

OROGRAPHIC — Associated with or induced by the presence of rising terrain, such as orographic lifting.

PARASITE DRAG — That part of total drag created by the form or shape of airplane parts. Parasite drag increases with an increase in airspeed.

PILOT CONTROLLED LIGHTING (PCL) — Runway lighting systems which are controlled by keying the aircraft's microphone on a specific frequency.

PILOT IN COMMAND (PIC) — The pilot responsible for the operation and safety of an aircraft.

PILOT WEATHER REPORT (PIREP) — A report, generated by pilots, concerning meteorological phenomena encountered in flight.

PILOTAGE — Navigation by visual landmarks.

PRECESSION — The tilting or turning of a gyroscope in response to external forces causing slow drifting and erroneous indications in gyroscopic instruments.

PREIGNITION — Occurs when the fuel/air mixture is ignited in advance of the normal timed ignition and is usually caused by a residual hotspot in the cylinder.

PRESSURE ALTITUDE — Height above the standard pressure level of 29.92 in. Hg. Obtained by setting 29.92 in the barometric pressure window and reading the altimeter.

PREVAILING VISIBILITY — The greatest horizontal visibility throughout at least half the horizon.

PROGRESSIVE TAXI — Precise taxi instructions issued to a pilot unfamiliar with an airport, usually issued in stages as the aircraft proceeds along the route.

PROHIBITED AREA — Airspace of defined dimensions identified by an area on the surface of the earth within which the flight of aircraft is prohibited.

RADAR ADVISORY — Information or advice provided to pilots based on radar observations.

RADAR CONTACT — Term used by ATC to advise a pilot that the aircraft is identified on radar.

RADAR VECTOR — A heading issued by a radar controller to the pilot of an aircraft to provide navigational guidance.

RADIAL — A navigational signal generated by a VOR or VORTAC, measured as a magnetic bearing from the station.

REFERENCE DATUM — An imaginary vertical plane from which all horizontal distances are measured for balance purposes.

RELATIVE BEARING — Angular difference between the airplane's longitudinal axis and a straight line drawn from the airplane to the station. It is measured clockwise from the airplane's nose.

RELATIVE HUMIDITY — The actual amount of moisture in the air compared to the total that could be present at that temperature.

RESTRICTED AREA — Designated special use airspace within which aircraft flight, while not prohibited, is subject to restrictions.

RETINA — The photosensitive portion of the eye which is connected to the optic nerve and contains cells called rods and cones.

RETRACTABLE GEAR — A pilot controllable landing gear system, whereby the gear can be stowed alongside or inside the structure of the airplane during flight.

RIGIDITY IN SPACE — The principle that a wheel with a heavily weighted rim spun rapidly will remain in a fixed position in the plane in which it is spinning.

RODS — The cells concentrated outside of the foveal area which are sensitive to low light and not to color.

RUNWAY GRADIENT — The amount of change in elevation over the length of the runway.

RUNWAY VISUAL RANGE — An instrumentally derived value representing the horizontal distance a pilot in a moving aircraft should see down the runway.

SAFETY ALERT — An alert issued by an ATC radar facility when an aircraft under its control is in unsafe proximity to terrain, obstruction, or other aircraft.

SATURATED AIR — Air containing the maximum amount of water vapor it can hold at a given temperature (100% relative humidity).

SEA BREEZE — A coastal breeze blowing from sea to land, caused when the temperature difference when the land surface is warmer than the sea surface. The sea breeze usually occurs during the day and alternates with the land breeze which blows in the opposite direction at night.

SECTIONAL CHART — Most commonly used chart for VFR flight. Each chart covers 6° to 8° of longitude and approximately 4° of latitude and is given the name of a primary city within its coverage. The scale of a sectional chart is 1:500,000.

SEGMENTED CIRCLE — A set of visual indicators which provide traffic pattern information at airports without operating control towers.

SERVICE CEILING — The maximum height above mean sea level, under normal conditions, at which a given airplane is able to maintain a rate of climb of 100 feet per minute.

SIGMET — An in-flight advisory which is considered significant to all aircraft. SIGMET criteria include severe icing, severe and extreme turbulence, duststorms, sandstorms, volcanic eruptions, and volcanic ash lowering visibility to less than three miles.

SKID — A flight condition in which the rate of turn is too great for the angle of bank.

SLIP — A flight condition in which the rate of turn is too slow for the angle of bank.

SPATIAL DISORIENTATION — A feeling of balance instability caused by a conflict between the information relayed by your central vision, and your peripheral vision.

SPECIAL USE AIRSPACE — Defined airspace areas where aircraft operations may be limited. Examples include: alert area, controlled firing area, military operations area, prohibited area, restricted area, and warning area.

SPECIAL VFR CLEARANCE — An ATC clearance which allows you to operate within the lateral boundaries of the surface areas of Class B, C, D, or E airspace when the ceiling is less than 1,000 feet AGL and/or visibility is below 3 statute miles. While operating under special VFR, you must maintain 1 statute mile visibility and remain clear of clouds.

SPIN — An aggravated stall which results in the airplane descending in a helical, or corkscrew path.

SQUALL LINE — A continuous line of non-frontal thunderstorms.

STALL — A rapid decrease in lift caused by the separation of airflow from the wing's surface brought on by exceeding the critical angle of attack.

STANDARD LAPSE RATE — For 1,000 feet of altitude in the lower atmosphere (below 36,000 feet), the standard pressure lapse rate is 1.00 in. Hg., and the standard temperature lapse rate is 2°C (3.5°F).

STATIONARY FRONT — A boundary between two airmasses which are relatively balanced.

STIMULANTS — Drugs which excite the central nervous system and produce an increase in alertness and activity.

STOPWAY — An area beyond the take-off runway which is designed to support an airplane during an aborted takeoff without causing structural damage to the airplane. It cannot be used for takeoff, landing or taxiing.

STRATOSPHERE — The first layer above the tropopause extending to a height of approximately 160,000 feet, with a composition much like the troposphere.

SUBLIMATION — Process by which a solid is changed to a gas without going through the liquid state.

SUPERCOOLED WATER DROPLETS — Water droplets that have been cooled below the freezing point, but are still in a liquid state.

TAILWIND — Any wind more than 90° from the magnetic heading of the runway.

TAILWIND COMPONENT — That part of the wind which acts directly on the rear of the aircraft and increases its groundspeed.

TELEPHONE INFORMATION BRIEFING SERVICE (TIBS) — Telephone recording of area and/or route meteorological briefings, airspace procedures, and special aviation-oriented announcements.

TERMINAL RADAR SERVICE AREA (TRSA) — Airspace surrounding designated airports in which ATC provides radar vectoring, sequencing, and separation for all IFR aircraft and participating VFR aircraft.

TERMINAL VFR RADAR SERVICE — A national program which extends the terminal radar services for IFR aircraft to VFR aircraft.

TETRAHEDRON — Device used as a landing direction indicator, usually at nontower airports. The small end points into the wind, or in the general direction of landing.

THERMOSPHERE — The area of the atmosphere above the mesosphere.

THRESHOLD — The beginning of the landing area of the runway.

THRUST — A forward force which propels the airplane through the air.

TOTAL DRAG — The sum of parasite and induced drag.

TRACK — The actual flight path of an aircraft over the ground. Also called ground track.

TRACKING — Flying a desired course to or from a station using a sufficient wind correction, if necessary.

TRAFFIC ADVISORIES — Advisories issued to alert a pilot to other known or observed air traffic which may be in such proximity to their position or intended route of flight as to warrant their attention.

TRAFFIC PATTERN — The traffic flow that is prescribed for aircraft landing and taking off from an airport. The usual components are the departure, crosswind, downwind, and base legs; and the final approach.

TRANSCRIBED WEATHER BROADCAST (TWEB) — A continuous recording of weather and aeronautical information broadcast over selected NDB or VOR stations.

TRANSPONDER — An electronic device aboard the airplane that enhances an aircraft's identity on an ATC radar screen.

TRICYCLE GEAR — Two main wheels located on either side of the fuselage and a third wheel, the nosewheel, positioned on the nose of the airplane.

TROPOPAUSE — An area at an average altitude of 36,000 feet which acts as a lid to confine most of the water vapor, and the associated weather, to the troposphere.

TROPOSPHERE — The layer of the atmosphere extending from the surface to an average altitude of about 36,000 feet.

TRUE AIRSPEED (TAS) — The speed at which an aircraft is moving relative to the surrounding air.

TRUE ALTITUDE — The actual height of an object above mean sea level.

TRUE COURSE (TC) — The intended or desired direction of flight as measured on a chart clockwise from true north.

TRUE HEADING (TH) — The direction the longitudinal axis of the airplane points with respect to true north. True heading is equal to true course plus or minus any wind correction angle.

UNCONTROLLED AIRPORT — A nontower airport where control of VFR traffic is not exercised.

UNCONTROLLED AIRSPACE — Airspace designated as Class G airspace within which air traffic control is not exercised.

UNICOM — A nongovernment communications facility which may provide airport information at certain airports.

USABLE FUEL — The amount of fuel available during flight.

USEFUL LOAD — The difference between the basic empty weight of the airplane and the maximum weight allowed by the manufacturer's specification.

VALLEY BREEZE — An upslope wind flow caused by the heating of the mountain slope which warms the adjacent air.

VAPOR LOCK — A condition in which it may be difficult, or impossible, to restart the engine. Vapor lock may occur as a result of running a fuel tank completely dry allowing air to enter the fuel system. On fuel injected engines the fuel may become so hot it vaporizes in the fuel line, not allowing the fuel to reach the cylinders.

VARIATION — The angular difference between true north and magnetic north; indicated on charts by isogonic lines.

VFR CRUISING ALTITUDE — When flying above 3,000 feet AGL on magnetic headings from 0° to 179° you must fly at odd thousand-foot altitudes plus 500 feet and on headings from 180° to 359° you are required to fly at even thousands plus 500 feet up to the flight levels.

VICTOR AIRWAY — An airway system based on the use of VOR facilities.

VISUAL FLIGHT RULES (VFR) — Rules which specify minimum cloud clearance and visibility requirements for flight. The term VFR also is used to define weather conditions and the type of flight plan under which an aircraft is operating.

VISUAL PURPLE — Another term for rhodopsin, the chemical created by the rods that provides a perception of dim light.

VOR — Ground-based navigational system consisting of very high frequency omnidirectional range (VOR) stations which provide course guidance.

WARM FRONT — The boundary between two airmasses where warm air is replacing cold air.

WARNING AREA — Airspace of defined dimensions, extending from three nautical miles outward from the coast of the United States, which contains activity that may be hazardous to nonparticipating aircraft.

WEIGHT — A downward force caused by gravity. Weight opposes lift.

WIND CORRECTION ANGLE (WCA) — The angular difference between the heading of the airplane and the course.

WIND SHEAR — A sudden, drastic shift in wind speed, direction, or both that may occur in the vertical or horizontal plane.

WINGTIP VORTICES — Spirals of air created by an airfoil when generating lift. Vortices from medium to heavy aircraft may be extremely hazardous to small aircraft.

WORLD AERONAUTICAL CHART (WAC) — Similar to a sectional chart, but with a scale of 1:1,000,000 provides less detail and is best suited for flight planning.

ZULU TIME — A term used in aviation for coordinated universal time (UTC) which places the entire world on one time standard.

CHAPTER 2
ANSWER SHEET

SECTION A

1. A. _____   B. _____   C. _____

   D. _____   E. _____

2. _____

   _____

   _____

   _____

   _____

3. _____

4. _____

5. _____

   _____

6. _____

7. _____

   _____

   _____

   _____

   _____

   _____

8. _____

9. _____

10. _____

SECTION B

1. A. _____   B. _____

   C. _____   D. _____

2. _____

3. _____

   _____

4. _____

   _____

   _____

   _____

   _____

   _____

5. _____

   _____

   _____

   _____

   _____

6. _____
_____
_____
_____
_____

7. _____
_____
_____
_____
_____
_____
_____

8. _____

9. _____

10. _____

SECTION C

1. _____
_____
_____

2. _____

3. A. _____   B. _____   C. _____

   D. _____   E. _____

4. _____

5. _____

6. _____

7. _____

8. _____

9. _____
_____
_____
_____
_____

10. _____
_____
_____
_____
_____
_____
_____

11. _____

12. _____

CHAPTER 3
ANSWER SHEET

SECTION A

1. _____

2. A. _____ B. _____ C. _____

   D. _____ E. _____ F. _____

   G. _____ H. _____ I. _____

3. _____

   _____

   _____

   _____

4. _____

5. A. _____

   B. _____

   C. _____

6. _____

   _____

7. _____

8. _____

   _____

   _____

   _____

9. _____

   _____

   _____

   _____

10. _____

    _____

    _____

    _____

    _____

11. _____

SECTION B

1. A. _____ B. _____ C. _____

   D. _____ E. _____ F. _____

2. _____

3. _____

4. _____

5. _____

6. _____

_____

_____

_____

7. _____

_____

_____

_____

_____

_____

8. _____

9. _____

10. _____

11. _____

_____

_____

12. _____

_____

_____

_____

_____

_____

_____

_____

SECTION C

1. _____

2. _____

3. _____

_____

4. _____

_____

_____

5. _____

_____

6. _____

7. _____

8. _____

9. _____

10. _____

CHAPTER 4
ANSWER SHEET

SECTION A

1. _____
   _____
   _____
   _____

2. _____
3. _____
4. _____
5. _____
6. _____
7. _____
8. _____
9. _____
10. _____
11. _____
    _____
    _____
    _____

SECTION B

1. _____
   _____
   _____
   _____

2. _____
3. _____
   _____
   _____
   _____

4. _____
5. _____
6. _____
7. _____
8. _____
9. _____
10. _____
11. _____
12. _____
13. _____
14. _____

15. _____

16. _____

17. _____

_____

_____

SECTION C

1. _____

2. _____

_____

3. _____

4. _____

5. _____

6. _____

7. _____

8. _____

9. _____

10. _____

11. _____

12. _____

13. _____

14. _____

15. _____

16. _____

SECTION D

1. _____

2. _____

3. _____

4. _____

5. _____

6. _____

7. _____

8. _____

9. _____

10. _____

_____

_____

_____

_____

_____

_____

_____

_____

11. _____

CHAPTER 5
ANSWER SHEET

SECTION A

1. _____
_____
_____
_____
_____

2. _____

3. _____

4. _____

5. _____

6. _____

7. _____

8. _____

9. _____

10. _____

11. _____

12. _____

13. _____

14. _____

SECTION B

1. _____

2. _____

3. _____

4. _____

5. _____
_____
_____
_____

6. _____

7. _____

8. _____

9. _____
_____
_____
_____
_____

10. _____

11. _____

12. _____

13. _____

_____

_____

_____

SECTION C

1. _____

2. _____

3. _____

4. _____

5. _____

6. _____

7. _____

8. _____

9. _____

10. _____

11. _____

_____

_____

_____

_____

_____

_____

_____

_____

_____

_____

12. _____

Name: _____

CHAPTER 6
ANSWER SHEET

SECTION A

1. A. _____   B. _____

   C. _____   D. _____

2. _____

3. _____
_____
_____
_____

4. _____

5. _____

6. _____
_____
_____
_____
_____

7. _____
_____
_____
_____
_____
_____
_____

8. _____

9. _____

10. _____

11. _____

SECTION B

1. _____

2. _____
_____
_____
_____

3. _____

4. _____

5. A. _____   B. _____

   C. _____   D. _____

6. _____

7. _____
_____
_____

8. _____

_____

_____

9. _____

_____

_____

10. _____

11. _____

12. _____

SECTION C

1. _____

_____

_____

2. _____

_____

_____

_____

_____

3. _____

_____

_____

_____

_____

4. _____

5. _____

_____

_____

_____

6. _____

7. _____

8. _____

_____

_____

_____

_____

9. _____

10. _____

11. _____

12. _____

Name: _____

CHAPTER 7
ANSWER SHEET

SECTION A

1. _____
2. _____
3. _____
   _____
   _____
   _____
   _____
   _____
4. _____
5. _____

SECTION B

1. _____
   _____
   _____
   _____
2. _____
3. _____
4. _____
   _____
   _____
   _____
   _____
   _____
   _____
5. _____
6. _____
7. _____
8. _____
   _____
   _____
   _____
   _____
   _____
   _____
   _____
   _____
9. _____
10. _____
11. _____
12. _____

SECTION C

1. _____

2. _____

3. _____

4. _____

5. _____

6. _____

_____

_____

_____

_____

7. _____

8. _____

9. _____

10. _____

SECTION D

1. _____

_____

_____

_____

2. _____

_____

_____

_____

_____

_____

3. _____

4. _____

5. _____

6. _____

7. _____

8. _____

CHAPTER 8
ANSWER SHEET

SECTION A

1. _____
2. _____
   _____
   _____
   _____
   _____
3. _____
4. _____
5. _____
6. _____
7. _____
8. _____
9. _____
10. _____
11. _____

SECTION B

1. _____
2. _____
3. _____
4. _____
5. _____
6. _____
7. _____
8. _____
9. _____
10. _____
11. _____
12. _____
13. _____
14. _____

SECTION C

1. _____
2. _____
3. _____
4. _____
5. _____
6. _____

7. _____

8. _____

9. _____

10. _____

CHAPTER 9
Answer Sheet

SECTION A

1. _____
2. _____
   _____
   _____
   _____
3. _____
4. _____
5. _____
6. _____
7. _____
8. _____
   _____
   _____
9. _____
10. _____
11. _____
12. _____

SECTION B

1. _____
2. _____
3. A. _____ B. _____ C. _____
   D. _____ E. _____
4. _____
5. _____
6. _____
7. _____
8. _____
9. _____
10. _____

SECTION C

1. _____
2. _____
3. _____
4. _____
5. _____
6. _____

7. _____

8. _____

9. _____

10. _____

_____

_____

_____

_____

_____

_____

_____

_____

_____

_____

_____

_____

_____

_____

_____

_____

_____

_____

_____

SECTION D

1. _____

2. _____

_____

_____

_____

_____

3. _____

4. _____

5. _____

6. _____

7. _____

8. _____

CHAPTER 10
ANSWER SHEET

SECTION A

1. _____
   _____
   _____
   _____
   _____
   _____
   _____

2. _____

3. _____

4. _____

5. _____
   _____
   _____
   _____
   _____

6. _____
   _____
   _____
   _____

7. _____

8. _____

9. _____

10. _____

11. _____

12. _____

13. _____
    _____
    _____
    _____

SECTION B

1. _____

2. _____
   _____
   _____
   _____
   _____
   _____

3. _____

4. _____

5. _____
   _____
   _____
   _____
   _____
   _____

6. _____

7. _____

8. _____

9. _____

10. _____

11. _____
    _____
    _____
    _____
    _____
    _____

12. _____
    _____
    _____
    _____
    _____
    _____
    _____
    _____

13. _____

14. _____

Name: _____

CHAPTER 11
ANSWER SHEET

SECTION A

1. _____
2. _____
3. _____
4. _____
5. _____
6. _____
7. _____
8. _____

_____

9. _____
10. _____
11. _____
12. _____

SECTION B

1. _____
2. _____
3. _____
4. _____
5. _____

_____

_____

_____

6. _____
7. _____

_____

8. _____

The NOTAMs Section is designed to inform you of recent developments that could affect your training.

CHANGES TO
AERONAUTICAL CHARTS

Visual aeronautical charts, terminal area charts, VFR flyway planning charts, world aeronautical charts, and helicopter route charts are undergoing some changes designed to eliminate confusion and increase user friendliness. The changes include:

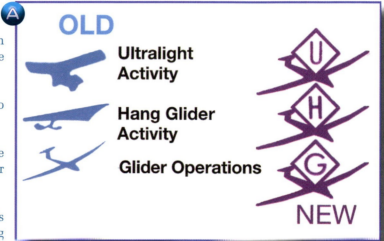

- Tints indicating water are being changed so that the user can distinguish between open water and inland water. The tints are changing to improve definition.

- Roads are being changed from magenta to black.

- New symbols are being used to indicate areas of hang gliding, ultralight, and glider operations. [Figure A]

- The parachute jumping area symbol is changing from blue to magenta and changing to brown on helicopter route charts.

- Boxed notes indicating approach control frequencies for Class B and C airspace are being changed to contain more concise wording, and the notes are being printed on a white background to make them more readable. [Figure B]

- The Mode C symbol and type is changing from blue to magenta and changing to brown on helicopter route charts.

- Terminal area charts and VFR flyway charts are being changed to include new IFR arrival/departure route symbols.

- The border used on sectional charts to show terminal area chart coverage and/or inset is changing to a white border with blue type. The corresponding note also is changing. [Figure C]

LAND AND HOLD SHORT OPERATIONS (LAHSO)

LAHSO is an air traffic control procedure that requires pilot participation to balance the needs for increased airport capacity and system efficiency, consistent with safety. This procedure can be done safely provided pilots and controllers are knowledgeable and understand their responsibilities.

PILOT RESPONSIBILITIES AND BASIC PROCEDURES

At controlled airports, air traffic may clear a pilot to land and hold short. Pilots may accept such a clearance provided that the pilot in command determines that the aircraft can safely land and stop within the available landing distance (ALD). ALD data are published in the special notices section of the *Airport/Facility Directory*. Controllers will also provide ALD data upon request. Student pilots or pilots not familiar with LAHSO should not participate in the program.

The pilot in command has the final authority to accept or decline any land and hold short clearance. The safety and operation of the aircraft remain the responsibility of the pilot. Pilots are expected to decline a LAHSO clearance if they determine it will compromise safety.

To conduct LAHSO, pilots should become familiar with all available information concerning LAHSO at their destination airport. Pilots should have, readily available, the published ALD and runway for all LAHSO runway combinations at each airport of intended landing. Additionally, knowledge about landing performance data permits the pilot to readily determine that the ALD for the assigned runway is sufficient for safe LAHSO. Pilots should determine if their destination airport has LAHSO. If so, their preflight planning should include an assessment of which LAHSO combinations would work for them given their aircraft's required landing distance. Good pilot decision making is knowing in advance whether one can accept a LAHSO clearance if offered.

Pilots also need to have a good understanding of LAHSO markings, signage, and in-pavement lighting when installed. Examples are included in this NOTAM and Chapter 4, Section B of this manual, as well as in the chapter titled Aeronautical Lighting and Other Airport Visual Aids in the *Aeronautical Information Manual* (AIM). LAHSO visual aids consist of a three-part system of yellow hold-short markings, red and white signage, and, in some cases, in-pavement lighting.

If, for any reason, such as difficulty in discerning the location of a LAHSO intersection, wind conditions, aircraft condition, etc., the pilot elects to request to land on the full length of the runway, to land on another runway, or to decline LAHSO, a pilot is expected to promptly inform air traffic, ideally even before the clearance is issued. **A LAHSO clearance, once accepted, must be adhered to, just as any other ATC clearance, unless an amended clearance is obtained**

LAND AND HOLD SHORT OF A DESIGNATED POINT ON A RUNWAY OTHER THAN AN INTERSECTING RUNWAY OR TAXIWAY

Departing Aircraft

This aircraft is cleared to land and hold short.

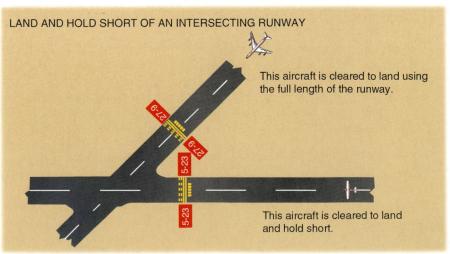

LAND AND HOLD SHORT OF AN INTERSECTING RUNWAY

This aircraft is cleared to land using the full length of the runway.

This aircraft is cleared to land and hold short.

or an emergency occurs. A LAHSO clearance does not preclude a rejected landing.

A pilot who accepts a LAHSO clearance should land and exit the runway at the first convenient taxiway (unless directed otherwise) before reaching the hold short point. Otherwise, the pilot must stop and hold at the hold short point. **If a rejected landing becomes necessary after accepting a LAHSO clearance, the pilot should maintain safe separation from other aircraft or vehicles, and should promptly notify the controller**.

Controllers need a full readback of all LAHSO clearances. Pilots should read

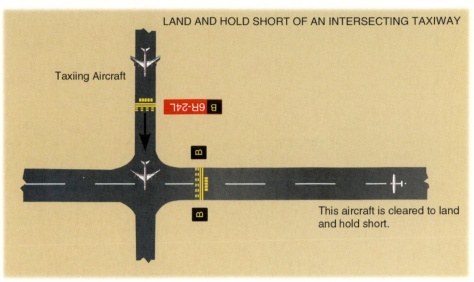

LAND AND HOLD SHORT OF AN INTERSECTING TAXIWAY

Taxiing Aircraft

This aircraft is cleared to land and hold short.

back their LAHSO clearance and include the words, *"Hold short of (runway / taxiway / or point)"* in their acknowledgement of all LAHSO clearances. To reduce frequency congestion, pilots are encouraged to read back the LAHSO clearance without prompting. Do not make the controller have to ask for a readback!

SITUATIONAL AWARENESS

Situational awareness is vital to the success of LAHSO. Situational awareness starts with having current airport information in the cockpit, readily accessible to the pilot. For example, an airport diagram assists pilots in identifying their location on the airport, thus reducing requests for progressive taxi instructions from controllers. Situational awareness includes effective pilot-controller radio communication. ATC expects pilots to specifically acknowledge and read back all LAHSO clearances.

> **EXAMPLES OF PILOT-CONTROLLER COMMUNICATION**
>
> **ATC:** *"Cessna 45321, cleared to land Runway 6 Right, hold short of Taxiway Bravo for crossing traffic (type aircraft)."*
>
> **Pilot:** *"Cessna 45321, wilco, cleared to land Runway 6 Right to hold short of Taxiway Bravo."*
>
> **ATC:** *"Cessna 45321, cross Runway 6 Right at Taxiway Bravo, landing aircraft will hold short."*
>
> **Pilot:** *"Cessna 45321, wilco, cross Runway 6 Right at Bravo, landing traffic (type aircraft) to hold."*

For those airplanes flown with two crewmembers, effective intra-cockpit communication between cockpit crewmembers is also critical. There have been several instances where the pilot working the radios accepted a LAHSO clearance but then simply forgot to tell the pilot flying the aircraft.

Situational awareness also includes a thorough understanding of the airport markings, signage, and lighting associated with LAHSO. As indicated in the accompanying illustrations, these visual aids assist the pilot in determining where to hold short. Pilots are cautioned that not all airports conducting LAHSO have installed any or all of the above markings, signage, or lighting.

Pilots should only receive a LAHSO clearance when there is a minimum ceiling of 1,000 feet and 3 statute miles visibility. The intent of having basic VFR weather conditions is to allow pilots to maintain visual contact with other aircraft and ground vehicle operations. Pilots should consider the effects of prevailing inflight visibility (such as landing into the sun) and how it may affect overall situational awareness. Additionally, surface vehicles and aircraft being taxied by maintenance personnel may also be participating in LAHSO, especially in those operations that involve crossing an active runway.

VFR WAYPOINTS DEBUT ON TERMINAL AREA CHARTS

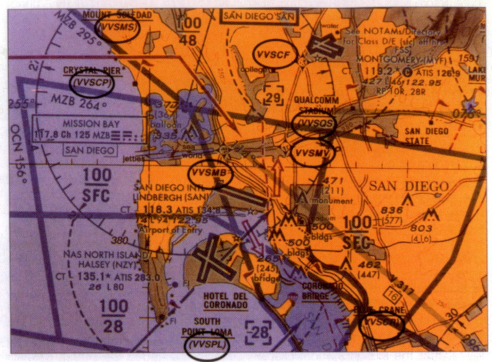

   To help GPS-equipped pilots navigate complex Class B and C airspace, new VFR waypoints are being tested on the San Diego and Los Angeles Terminal Area Charts. If all goes well, these waypoints will appear on all Terminal Area Charts within the next two years. The waypoints are indicated on the chart with a four-point star or a flagpole-and-pennant and are named in the database with five-letter identifiers beginning with "VV."

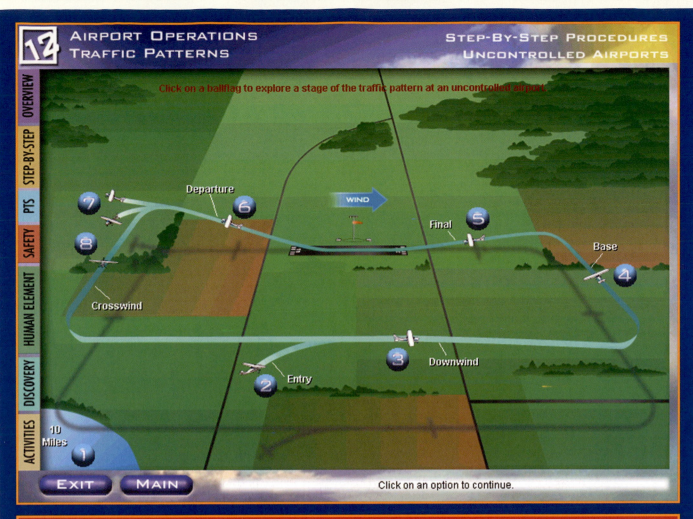

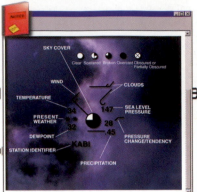

AVIATION WEATHER TEXT

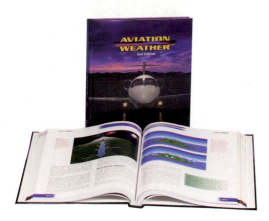

AVIATION WEATHER 2ND EDITION

The most comprehensive, award-winning aviation weather book just got better. New 480-page hard cover edition is extensively updated with the latest METAR, TAF, and Graphic Weather Products from AC00-45E, Aviation Weather Services. Full-color illustrations and photographs present detailed material in an uncomplicated way. International weather considerations are included as well as accident/incident information to add relevance to the weather data. Expanded coverage of icing, weather hazards, and flight planning. Review questions with answers at the end of the book. All new expanded appendices cover common conversions, weather reports, forecasts, and charts, as well as domestic and international METAR, TAF and graphic weather products. Completely revised Instructor's Guide available on CD-ROM (for flight school use only.)

AVIATION WEATHER TEXT
ITEM NUMBER JS319010 $54.95

FAR/AIM MANUAL AND CD ROM

FAR/AIM MANUAL

This manual is an excellent study or reference source. Complete pilot/controller glossary. Changes conveniently indicated. Includes FAR parts 1, 43, 61, 67, 71, 73, 91, 97, 119, 133, 141, 142, HMR 175 and NTSB 830. Uses special study lists to direct students to the appropriate FARs. Check student's understanding of FARs with exercise questions tailored for Private, Instrument, Commercial, and Helicopter.

FAR/AIM MANUAL ITEM NUMBER JS314125 $16.95

FAR/AIM CD-ROM

Contains the same features of the manual, plus FAR parts 125 and 135, but in a browseable CD-ROM format. Search by part, chapter, word, or phrase. Included with the revision service is the initial CD-ROM and two additional updates. System requirements: PC with 486 or faster processor, 2x CD-ROM drive, Windows 3.1 or Windows 95.

FAR/AIM CD-ROM ITEM NUMBER JS206350 $19.95
FAR/AIM REVISION SERVICE ITEM NUMBER JS206443 $60.95

AVIATION HISTORY

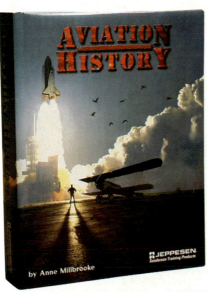

AVIATION HISTORY BOOK

Aviation History is an exciting new full-color book that gives both new and experienced pilots a unique perspective on international aviation history. Each of the ten chapters is packed with information, containing over 950 photographs and color graphics. Aviation History explores the question, "What was aviation?" from its birth in Annonay, France, in 1873, to the exhilirating accomplishments in space. Through personal profiles, you are able to meet the people who made significant contributions to aviation. You will explore historical evidence and see how historians use the artifacts of aviation to confirm what happened.

AVIATION HISTORY BOOK
ITEM NUMBER JS319008 $69.95

TechStar Pro and Datalink

Jeppesen's "Next Generation" Aviation Computer

Jeppesen's innovative TechStar Pro is the first handheld flight computer and personal organizer. Combining the latest technology and ease of use, TechStar Pro gives you a 7-function aviation computer and an 8-function personal organizer. All-in-one compact handheld unit. Students to Airline Transport Pilots, use it in the cockpit, home, office or classroom.

TechStar Pro
Item Number JS505000 $99.95

TechStar Pro Datalink Software and Cable

- Simple to use - Windows 3.1 or higher
- Backup data on your Techstar Pro
- Edit, add and delete records from your PC and then download the records
- Save time when inputting data

Datalink
Item Number JS505050 $12.95

Datalink sold separately.

JeppShades

IFR Flip-Up Training Glasses

- Replaces bulky, hard-to-use instrument training hoods
- Improved design allows better student/instructor interaction
- Cockpit proven design works conveniently under headsets
- Universal adjusting strap reduces pressure on ears and temple
- Velcro™ strap fits comfortably under headsets
- Flip-Up lens allows convenient IFR/VFR flight transition
- High quality polycarbonate lens is impact resistant

JeppShades Item Number JS404311 $24.95

Fuel Tester

The last fuel tester you'll ever need! Strong, clear butyrate plastic resists cracking, breaking and yellowing. Works with both pin and petcock actuators. Removable splash guard prevents fuel spillage and attaches to side for flat, slimline storage. Solid bronze rod actuator prevents breaking and pushing down. Measures 8.25″ x 3.25″ x 1″.

Fuel Tester
Item Number JS628855 $13.95

Jeppesen Flashlight Kit

Made of a space-age polycarbonate that is watertight and guaranteed against breakage. Its unique nonincendiary design is safe in hazardous explosive environments such as checking aircraft fuel levels at night. Easily switches from a clear lens to the new narrow band blue/green filter lens for protected night vision and outstanding chart legibility. Flight-ready with two AAA batteries included.

Jeppesen Flashlight Kit
Item Number JS404500 $18.95

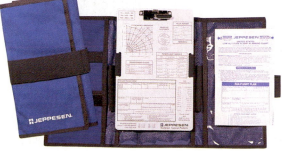

Three-Ring Trifold Kneeboard

- Great for holding approach charts • Valuable IFR flight information on clipboard (also available separately) • Includes three approach chart pockets • Features collapsible rings • Elastic, pen/pencil and penlight holder • Includes Free U.S. Low Flight Planning Chart!
- Measures 10" x 20" open

Kneeboard/Clipboard Item Number JS626010 $39.95
Clipboard Only Item Number JS626011 $15.95

Visit Your Jeppesen Dealer or Call 1-800-621-5377
Make sure to check out our web page at http://www.jeppesen.com
Prices subject to change.

INTRODUCING JEPPESEN FLIGHT BAGS

THE CAPTAIN FLIGHT BAG

The Jeppesen *Captain Flight Bag* is the most versatile bag available. The headset bags can be removed and attached together to form a dual headset bag. The removable Transceiver/GPS bag can be worn on your belt. The flexible design allows you to add or subtract components to match your flying needs. The roomy interior has a 4-way custom divider that can hold four Jeppesen binders. An exterior zippered pocket provides a convenient storage space to help pilots organize their supplies. Two large zippered storage pockets can hold glasses, charts, pilot operating handbooks and other miscellaneous accessories. Carry your supplies in comfort with a wide cushioned shoulder strap. 12″x22¹⁄₂″x8″

THE CAPTAIN FLIGHT BAG (BLACK OR BLUE)
ITEM NUMBER JS621214 (BLACK) $139.95
ITEM NUMBER JS621251 (BLUE) $139.95

THE NAVIGATOR FLIGHT BAG

The *Navigator Flight Bag* includes all of the features and benefits of the Captain Flight Bag, except the removable Transceiver/GPS bag and the two zippered exterior storage pockets. Instead, it includes two exterior pockets for easy access to sectional and world aeronautical charts. 12″x22¹⁄₂″x8″

THE NAVIGATOR FLIGHT BAG (BLACK OR BLUE)
ITEM NUMBER JS621213 (BLACK) $99.95
ITEM NUMBER JS621250 (BLUE) $99.95

THE PROTECTOR HEADSET BAGS

The *Protector Headset Bags* are constructed of fully padded 600 denier poly for extra protection. Each bag comes with its own snap-on handle grip for comfort. Large enough to fit the ANR headsets (12″x2³⁄₄″x8″). Offered in both a single and dual configuration. Designed to fit the Core Captain Flight Bag.

THE PROTECTOR HEADSET BAGS (BLACK)
SINGLE JS621220 $17.95
DUAL JS621219 $35.95

THE STUDENT PILOT FLIGHT BAG

The *Student Pilot Flight Bag* is designed for new student pilots. Numerous outside pockets will organize charts, flight computer, fuel tester, plotter, pens and pencils, flashlight and much more. Additional features include a wide removable shoulder strap for comfort and a reinforced bottom. 10″x5¹⁄₂″x17″

THE STUDENT PILOT FLIGHT BAG (BLACK)
ITEM NUMBER JS621212 $41.95

NEW! THE AVIATOR BAG

The *Aviator Bag* is constructed of fully padded vynlon for extra durability. Each bag includes one headset bag and one Transceiver/GPS bag. The interior has a 2-way divider that can be used to separate your pilot accessories.

THE AVIATOR BAG (BLACK)
ITEM NUMBER JS621252 $79.95

VISIT YOUR JEPPESEN DEALER OR CALL 1-800-621-5377
MAKE SURE TO CHECK OUT OUR WEB PAGE AT HTTP://WWW.JEPPESEN.COM
PRICES SUBJECT TO CHANGE.